Man on the Flying Trapeze

The Life and Times of W. C. Fields

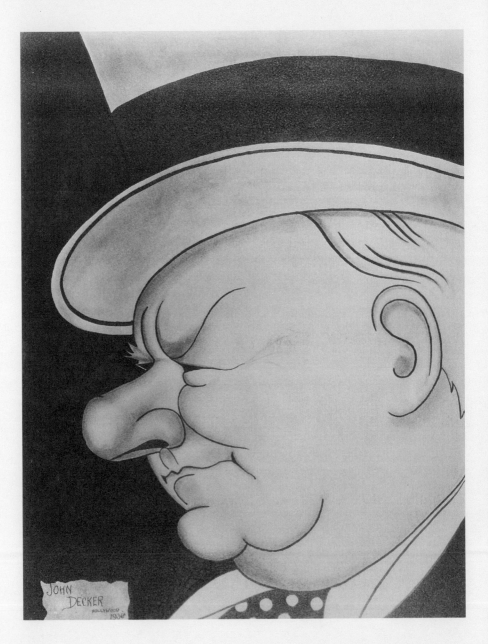

W. C. Fields as portrayed by the artist John Decker.

Man on the Flying Trapeze

The Life and Times of W. C. Fields

Simon Louvish

W. W. Norton & Company
New York   London

For information about permission to reproduce selections from this book, write to Permissions,
W. W. Norton & Company, Inc., 500 Fifth Avenue, New York, NY 10110.

**Selected works and photographs of W. C. Fields printed with permission of W. C. Fields
Productions, Inc., Los Angeles, California 90045, USA**

Illustrations courtesy of BFI Posters, Stills and Designs; W. C. Fields Productions; University of
Austin, Texas; The Museum of Modern Art Stills Archive; Joel Finler Collection; Will Fowler / Tim
Walker Collection

Library of Congress Cataloging-in-Publication Data
Louvish, Simon.
   Man on the flying trapeze : the life and times of W. C. Fields /
Simon Louvish. — 1st American ed.
     p.   cm.
   Includes bibliographical references and index.
   ISBN 0-393-04127-1
1. Fields, W. C., 1879–1946. 2. Comedians—United States—Biography. 3. Motion picture
actors and actresses—United States—Biography. I. Title.
PN2287.F45L68 1997
791.43'028'092—dc21
[B]
                          97-23731
                            CIP

W. W. Norton & Company, Inc., 500 Fifth Avenue, New York, N.Y. 10110
http://www.wwnorton.com

W. W. Norton & Company Ltd., 10 Coptic Street, London WC1A 1PU

Contents

List of Illustrations

W. C. Fields, comedian of the seventh edition of Earl Carroll's *Vanities*, now in its last week at the Forrest Theatre, strolled back stage from the last scene of the show. He entered his dressing-room, took off his coat, loosened his collar and sat down.

'I don't know a thing to say,' he remarked. 'I haven't thought up anything to say lately. If I said anything, it would probably not be true.

'I guess golf is about the safest topic. Once upon a time I talked on prohibition, but every time I start now, the thought of grand juries and inquests and other unpleasant things sends cold shivers all over me and I stop. Too many people say too many things in this world. I have to talk enough as it is when I am on the stage . . .'

The comedian told of his experience as a movie actor. He seemed displeased with the work and glad that he was back on the legitimate stage. And on the stage, in the many characters he portrays in his revue, he appears older than with his make-up off.

In his room, with very little audience, W. C. Fields appears as a youngish, sandy-haired, pleasant-faced fellow, serious at times and very willing to help – if he had only thought up a couple of good stories . . .

(from an unpublished draft by F. E. Crosman of a publicity piece
for Earl Carroll's *Vanities*, 1928)

Part I
It Baffles Science!

Prologue

The circus sign says:

WHIPSNADE'S CIRCUS GIGANTICUS
LARSON E. WHIPSNADE
PRESIDENT AND GENERAL MANAGER.

The Master of Ceremonies and General Manager himself strides out from behind a tent flap, pushing his way vigorously through the thin crowd of dilapidated fun-seekers, swinging a cane and wearing an immense Texan hat. The vigour of his pace belies his years and eminently corpulent figure. His bulbous nose leads him unerringly to the carriage platform, upon which two equally non-descript, emaciated hillbilly types with conical hats and long, obviously false beards are swaying in a moronic stupor. The master of ceremonies calls out to the crowd in a distinct nasal twang:

This way, ladies and gentlemen this way, step right up to this platform. The world's greatest novelty – the Punkwat twins! Elwood and Brentwood. Elwood is ten minutes older than Brentwood and has been in a hurry ever since. Ladies and gentlemen, Brentwood is the smallest giant in the world, whilst his brother, Elwood, is the largest midget in the world. THEY BAFFLE SCIENCE!

Cut, to a later sequence, in which Whipsnade, standing in for the ventriloquist, who is hovering above in the circus's balloon, attempts vainly to whip up applause by performing with the substitute dummy, while clad in a stovepipe hat and a frightful false moustache with attached buck teeth to try to cover his clumsy mouthings:
'Ladies and gentlemen, Whipsnade and his little friend Oliver . . .'
The audience remains sullen.
'Mr Whipsnade!'
'Yes, Oliver?'
'Can I ask you a conundrum?'

3

'Why certainly, Oliver, go right ahead. What is it?'

'Mr Whipsnade, why is a cat's tail like a long journey?'

'I don't know, Oliver, why is a cat's tail like a long journey?'

'Because it's fur to the end.'

'Because it's – heh heh heh – what do you think of that?'

The audience are still stony-faced, as Whipsnade tries desperately to shore up his act: 'Ladies and gentlemen! Drinking and singing simultaneously! It baffles science!' Commences a horribly tuneless rendition, while spilling a glass of water down his coat, of 'His heart was set on becoming a banker, and wearing a tall silk hat . . .' But the audience remains as cold as a dead fish, until a ballast sack, falling from the balloon above, conks the maestro on the head and lays him out flat.

But hold on a minute. Let us rewind the reel of this 1939 comedy from Universal Pictures, *You Can't Cheat an Honest Man*, and stop, at the old chestnut of the cat's tail, a joke, if it can be dignified by that term, which stretches back into the depths of time. And let us all be researchers, and make our way into the repository of old archives, into the Library of Congress in Washington, through the cavernous catalogue room and leading from there through echoing polished corridors to the underground tunnel which leads from the spanking new Madison Building to the nineteenth-century Jefferson Building, to the quiet and solemn room of the Rare Books Collection, where, undisturbed for ninety years, lies a blue carbon copy typescript of a forgotten musical play by George Hobart and entitled *The Ham Tree*, registered at the Library of Congress on 15 August 1905. The researcher opens it up to find, enfolded in a rather trite drawing-room drama with characters such as Mrs Nicklebacker, Lord Spotcash and his valet, Ponsonby, the preserved routines of an old minstrel act: The Georgia Minstrels, by James McIntyre and Thomas K. Heath, who had been presenting their show, virtually unchanged, upon the American stage since the year 1874. Performing in traditional black-face, with McIntyre as Alexander, the shambling country rube, and Heath as Henry (or Hennery), the city slicker, they enacted a familiar, age-old routine:

ALEXANDER: I don't like that theatre acting, I jest like that minstrel acting.

HENRY: What did you do with the minstrels?

ALEXANDER: I was the endman.

HENRY: What jokes did you tell?

ALEXANDER: Here is a fine joke I told but the audience didn't appreciate it.

HENRY: What was it, Alexander?

ALEXANDER: What is the best way to make a lean baby fat? Throw it out of the window and let it come down plump.

HENRY: That's pretty good, did you tell any more?

ALEXANDER: Why is a cat's tail like the end of the world? Because it is so fur to the end.

HENRY: Tell it to me again. (ALEXANDER *repeats*.)

ALEXANDER: Can you stand it again?

HENRY: Wait till I get over this spasm. (HENRY *grabs* ALEXANDER.) That is the reason they didn't laugh.

ALEXANDER: Why?

HENRY: Because it is so fur to the end . . .

The Ham Tree, apart from combining the incongruous ingredients of the minstrel show and drawing-room farce, also boasted another innovation. It was the first appearance, on the 'legitimate' American stage, of a young performer hitherto known for his irrepressible comedy juggling act, a twenty-five-year-old professional vaudevillian playing under the stage name of W. C., or William Claude Fields. He appears as Sherlock Baffles, a mysterious detective, who comes on stage and emits crazy lines:

(*Enter* SHERLOCK BAFFLES, *an eccentric character*.)

BAFFLES (*looking at pedometer*): I have walked 986 miles. I am Lieutenant Peary and I'm looking for the North Pole. (*Sees ice in pail; takes some of it off.*) Nope! It's too cold. I'll have to get another job. I think I'll be a detective. I must go and find somebody to detect. (*Runs off.*)

Looking for the roots of humour, the author becomes like Lewis Carroll's Alice, rushing to fall down the rabbit hole. Where do jokes come from? The question that has no answer. But one can look at the sources, the deep wells, from which the century's greatest comedians, Chaplin, Keaton, Lloyd, the Marx Brothers, or W. C. Fields, derived the material with which they convulsed the world. For these roots nourish the gags, the lines, the stories, the structures which created the golden age of comedy, and which feed any performance that has worth to this day. For so much of humour is in recognition, in our encounter with a truth that looms up before us in an unexpected, distorted form. The great comedians sought, in the main, only to entertain, not to philosophize, to make us laugh, not to make us think. But in their vulgar pursuit of the best gags, the best means to part us from our money and enrich them in their robust prancing upon stage or screen, they are connecting us to something lost, something perhaps deeply buried, a very basic awareness of the absurdity and the vitality of sheer existence. Something that transcends our many differences, our creeds and our apparent beliefs. Something rooted, even, in the casting out of the most ancient fears: the fear of failure, of shame, of humiliation and of death –

Because it is so fur to the end . . .

Chapter 1

'It's a Funny Old Life; Man's Lucky If He Gets Out of It Alive.'

At 11.30 a.m. on Thursday 2 January 1947, a clear, blue-skied California day, a motley crowd gathered at the Church of the Recessional at Forest Lawn Memorial Park in Pasadena. They included Jack Dempsey, former heavyweight champion of the world; movie directors Leo McCarey, Gregory La Cava, Eddie Sutherland and Eddie Cline; actors' agent Bill Grady; screenwriters Ben Hecht and Gene Fowler; and Fowler's son, Will, who was also covering the event for the *Los Angeles Examiner*. Beside them, along the flower-rimmed casket, was a trim and vivacious woman with flashing, mischievous eyes, sitting alongside her father, sister, and two nieces: her name was Carlotta Monti. At a discreet distance from her sat two persons who appeared out of place in this assembly of Hollywood luminaries: a rather dumpy, elderly woman in widow's black, and a sleek and quiet man who looked much like an attorney, which in fact he was. His name was W. Claude Fields Jr. and the lady was his mother, Harriet 'Hattie' Fields. Two other older persons sat together with them: the deceased man's brother, Walter, and his sister, Adel.

An electric organ played Bach's 'Jesu, Joy of Man's Desiring'. Then a single speaker stood up. His name was Edgar Bergen, and he had been the co-star of the Universal classic *You Can't Cheat An Honest Man*, together with his famous ventriloquist's dummy, the obnoxious Charlie McCarthy. But Bergen spoke this time through his own mouth. He said of the deceased:

> He requested his friends not to weep in mourning for him. Of the five hundred religions in the world he had his own, and he hoped that his friends would understand his requests. It seems wrong not to pray for a man who gave such happiness to the world. But this was the way he wanted it. Bill knew life, and knew that laughter was the way to live it. He knew that hap-

piness depended on disposition, not position. We simply say farewell.

Despite his request for no funeral service, W. C. Fields was blessed with three. When Bergen had stepped down, the casket was carried by the attendants into the Great Mausoleum of the Church, where a Catholic service was held, attended only by his widow, Hattie, his son Claude and brother and sister Walter and Adel. Although the deceased had specified in his will that he should be cremated, his widow objected on the grounds that this was not favoured by the Catholic Church. She had stated, through her attorney: 'While we favoured burial in the ground, he always opposed being buried in the earth and we are sure that he would be comfortable with what we have done.' If she heard a familiar cantankerous voice from above mumbling violent objections, she did not let on. The attendants dutifully placed the casket into a crypt and sealed it in behind a marble slab.

When the relatives had left, Carlotta Monti and her entourage were allowed to enter the Mausoleum. Will Fowler has described the scene:

[I walked up to] the niche where Uncle Claude was going to be filed for a few years until the family would finally allow his body to be cremated . . . There sat Uncle Claude's mistress Carlotta Monti on a folded wooden chair . . . her black dress veiled over her seat . . . In a way, Carlotta represented a modern *pieta*, now that she had finally lost her intimidating sugar daddy.

She had brought along a spiritualist Minister, one Mae Taylor, who conducted her own ceremony before the floral heart of white chrysanthemums and scarlet roses which Carlotta had sent ahead. Outside the crypt, while waiting for the widow and relations to come out, Carlotta had told Will Fowler that her watch had stopped when they went in. When the family had gone, her watch had started working again. She said she had already spoken to the dead man – whom she referred to by her private pet name of 'Woody' – through her counsellor, Miss Taylor. 'Woody' had told her to 'get a front seat at the three-ring circus.' Alas, she could only attend the second performance. But, she declared, she would continue to be in touch with 'Woody' well beyond the grave.

As Carlotta and her group were leaving, Will Fowler recorded the following incident:

A little man, stooped and unshaven, tugged timidly at an attendant's sleeve. His eyes were hollow, his cheeks sunken. A newspaper grew out of his coat pocket. He wore a spotted sweater under the coat. His collar and cuffs were wilted.

'Where is Mr Fields' crypt?' he asked softly. 'I knew him for 35 years, in vaudeville first. Duffy and Sweeney . . .' The attendant said he couldn't say where the crypt was. The little stooped man's eyes narrowed and seemed to flood with reminiscence. 'Well, I guess it was all right that I just came here anyway,' he said. He shuffled away and nobody took his picture.

Will Fowler's report – which was in fact drafted by his father, Gene – was on the front page of the next day's *Examiner*. The news heralded the start of the most protracted inheritance battle in Hollywood history, as the widow sought to overturn the dead man's will, amid a flurry of claimants, real and bogus. They included a blind woman, Edith Williams, who claimed the comedian had married her under a false name, in 1893 (a year when he was in fact thirteen years old!) when she was herself thirteen years of age and had escaped from a convent in a laundry basket to consummate her love. She claimed she had borne Fields, who had called himself 'Billy Williams', seven children before he abandoned her to an uncertain fate, and she produced thirty-five witnesses, mostly old vaudevillians, who offered to support her case. Her claim was eventually thrown out of court. More damaging was the appearance of an alleged illegitimate son, William Rexford Fields Morris, who claimed to be the offspring of an alliance between the actor and a Ziegfeld Follies chorus girl, Bessie Poole, back in 1917. This alliance had indeed been authentic. Letters supporting and refuting the twenty-nine-year-old Morris's case were brought forth, and he walked out of court, dazed, seven years later, with a mere $15,000 for his pains. The bulk of the estate, reckoned at $771,428, was the subject of a fierce legal war which Hattie Fields eventually won, a pyrrhic victory, in 1954, when she was seventy-five years old . . .

In his death, as in his life, W. C. Fields was surrounded by conflicting versions and variations of his life and times. In any attempt to tell his tale, the teller must beware of pitfalls and traps that lurk at every step. Most people seem to know W. C. Fields, an instantly recognisable figure, second only to Charlie Chaplin as a classic icon of the movies. Many people think they know his oft-told story: the climb from rags to riches – the boy who ran away from home and lived a Dickensian life in the streets of Philadelphia of the 1890s, only to pull himself up by his own bootstraps to become a vaudeville and Broadway star, and then the Greatest Movie Clown of his age. The curmudgeon who was in his life as on screen: the hater of children and dogs, who made a million laughs out of his own pain and his traumatic, miserable past.

The only problem with this familiar version is that it is completely untrue.

Telling the tale of W. C. Fields is like the unravelling of a detective story. It is not a Whodunnit, but a Who-is-it? For apart from being arguably the World's Greatest Clown, Fields was also the World's Greatest Liar. In investigating his life, the author is drawn into a maze of mirrors, with deceptive arrows pointing down dead ends and passages that curve in on themselves, leading back to the point of entry. Fields told so many lies about his own past, his early years, and his childhood, that he eventually fixed on the false version and encouraged it to be peddled as the truth. In this, as in many other matters, he was a true showman, a master ham, a vaudevillian from his toes to his fingertips. He was forever inventing and re-inventing himself, supplying the audience with the act it wanted, or the act he had trained it to demand. By definition, show people are show people: they put on masks and play to the public, which, if it wants reality, should look elsewhere.

But the story which W. C. Fields concealed, buried and covered up with acres of flamboyant flim-flam turns out, on investigation, to be even more flamboyant, even more entertaining, even more astounding than the lies which he so carefully and deliberately constructed. In the words of the master himself: IT BAFFLES SCIENCE!

The road to the uncovering of Fields, for it is indeed an act of archaeology, stretching back into the last two decades of the nineteenth century, leads through the musty files, boxes and manuscripts lying in scattered archives such as those of the Library of Congress, the Lincoln Center Library of the Performing Arts in New York, the Free Library of Philadelphia, the Academy of Motion Picture Arts and Sciences in Los Angeles and other collections, foremost among them: the personal scrapbooks and records of W. C. Fields himself, kept in secret storage by his estranged wife, Hattie, and now in the possession of their grandchildren. The false trails are so numerous and stubborn that a word must be said about sources.

Fields own tall tales and selective recollections were eventually codified in a biography, written in 1948 by Robert Lewis Taylor: *W. C. Fields – His Follies and His Fortunes*, which is still in print. Taylor wrote after Fields' death, without access to either the public or the private archives. His main source appears now to be a massive tranche of notes written by Gene Fowler, W. C. Fields' closest friend and confidant in the last ten years of his life. Gene Fowler, as we shall relate in due course, was a journalist, novelist, biographer and screenwriter of prodigious talents who was also, like all Fields' true friends, a prodigious imbiber of the amber nectar. Fields had authorized Gene Fowler to be his biographer, as Fowler had published, in 1943, an acclaimed biography of another confidant and fellow boozer, the great actor John Barrymore, entitled *Good Night, Sweet Prince*. As a result of that book, Fowler was besieged with offers to write other biographies, but wanted to return to novels. When the dynamic journalist Taylor turned up with his own proposal on Fields, Gene Fowler turned over all his notes. These, according to Gene's son, Will, Taylor put willy-nilly into his narrative, filling in the gaps with old items of Fieldsian wish-wash and even clips from movie publicity press-books, which are by definition hypes and puffs. Having dipped his mitt into this *mélange*, Taylor emerged with an entertaining tale, resonating, to those who know, with Gene Fowler's voice, but without Fowler's special touch.

Since then, two academic scholars have dug into the archaeological mound left by the Master Ham's carousing. A *Biobibliography*, and an *Annotated Guide*, by Wes Gehring and David T. Rocks respectively, have established a listing of sources to a serious Fieldsian study, including an invaluable fingering of the public archives in which Fieldsiana such as books, clippings, articles, and, most importantly, the essential 'vaudeville sketches' are to be found. Neither had access to the family vaults.

The most important challenge to Taylor's flawed account was mounted, in 1973, by Fields' own grandson, Ronald J. Fields, in his book, *W. C. Fields by Himself, His Intended Autobiography*, culled from the private scrapbooks and a mass of previously unknown letters, essays and sketches found in Hattie Fields' home in Los Angeles after her death in 1963. Ronald Fields' interpretation of this material has been disputed both by Rocks and Gehring, but the broad thrust of his revision cannot, I think, be refuted. At any rate, having been given access to the materials in question, I have allowed myself to reach my own conclusions.

Certain mysteries may never be cleared up. If a man wishes to reinvent his past, it is no easy task to overturn this, given the lack of any living witnesses to Fields' life up to the early 1920s. But there remain clues, scattered through the various tales, documents, and the comprehensive stage journals of record of the day, notably the *New York Dramatic Mirror* and London's *The Era*, that enable us to lift the veil and re-discover the lost and wondrous age of American vaudeville and the European music-hall which has long perished from the earth. The age of McIntyre and Heath's ancient minstrel show, the bawdy world of turn-of-the-century burlesque; of Sandow the Strong Man, and Busch's Plunging Elephants; of Captain Spaulding, the eater of molten lead, and the great Houdini Whom No Prison or Chains Could Hold; of the great Tramp Jugglers – Harrigan, Tom Hearn, and O. K. Sato, young Fields' mentors – and of the great variety theatres of the Edwardian era: the London Hippodrome with its spectacular reconstructions of volcanic eruptions, snowstorms and typhoons, the *Folies Bergère* with its looping cyclists, nude dancers and tigers. And, with it all, the hard nightly grind, the dismal hotel rooms and snowbound railway stations which were the jobbing actor's lot in life. We shall also reprise the weird and wonderful world of Florenz Ziegfeld, the golden era of Broadway razzle-dazzle, as well as the neglected period of Fields' silent film career, including a peek at what remains of his five missing movies. We shall follow the rise to stardom of the Fieldsian voice, that unique, grating drawl, as the comedian drew on all his old resources in the Hollywood factory, culminating in his battles with the motion-picture censors, whose war on Fields' subversive dialogue is, perhaps, the least known of the slings and arrows that our hero, armed with nought but brain and bottle, opposed with such ferocious glee.

It is the tale of a man who, famed for his film career, spent thirty years upon the stage before he abandoned it completely for the screen. It is an actor's tale, the story of a creative artist whose greatest creation was himself, a fully achieved, imaginary person, who completely subsumed his creator. It is the saga of a performance, which began when the horseless carriage was still an amazing invention, and ended in the age of the first jet aircraft, of mass communications, and of total war.

Chapter 2
In the Beginning – 'All Jumbled Up Togayther . . .'

The little man tugged timidly at the attendant's sleeve, his face, as Will Fowler described it, 'hollowed from seasons of disappointment . . . "I knew him for 35 years, in vaudeville first. Duffy and Sweeney . . . "' He shuffled away and nobody took his picture. And from that day to this nobody knew his name.

But we can trace him now. Duffy and Sweeney. They were, in the jargon of the stage, a 'nut act'. That is, an act in which the protagonists beat each other up on the stage. Sweeney would begin a pointless story while Duffy dozed in a chair. Duffy would wake, slap his partner in the face, and bow to the audience. Sweeney would smack Duffy on the jaw. Then they would fall on and off the chair. Duffy had begun his career as a child with his father and mother as Duffy, Sawtelle and Duffy, at the turn of the twentieth century. In the week of 4 November 1899 they were appearing at Tony Pastor's Vaudeville Theatre, and the critic of the *New York Dramatic Mirror* wrote:

> Master Duffy carries off the honours. He should be instructed to speak much more slowly and distinctly, as many of his best gags lose their effect on account of his quickness, which necessitates the repetition of the lines by his elders.

Master Duffy was then ten years old. On the same bill, the great Tony Pastor himself sang every evening, and a speciality was presented, 'A Trip to the Vaudevilles', written by another young man going places, George M. Cohan. On the same page of the *Mirror*, the critics noted that Irwin's Burlesquers appeared at Miner's Eighth Avenue Theatre, and 'introduced Carver and Pollard, Sisters Tredwyn, Bailey and Madison, Mlle. Marie, Thompson and Carter, and W. C. Fields. Business excellent.'

Later in his career, James Terence Duffy joined with an actress named Mercedes Lorenz, 'in odds and ends of rhyme and melody', but he was already becoming known for another factor of the actor's life through the ages – that is, the curse of strong drink. Duffy soon teamed up with another lover of the sauce, Frederick Sweeney, with whom he toured the various circuits. Duffy and Sweeney became as famous for their drinking prowess as for their act, so well known that even George Burns, in his own reminiscences seventy years later, recounted a typical tale of their exploits: Duffy and Sweeney are drinking steadily at a bar, until suddenly, without warning, Sweeney keels over on the floor. Duffy, without batting an eye, continued to swig his drink, commenting: 'I like a man who knows when to stop.'

Duffy came to a tragic end. In the spring of 1939, when, despite his alcoholism, he had been taken on for a radio show with NBC, his body was found in a doorway at the corner of 8th Avenue and 42nd Street in New York. Sweeney headed out west, to Albuquerque, New Mexico, and then to Hollywood, where he found work in tiny, unrecorded bit parts. It was thus Sweeney who turned up at the Forest Lawn Memorial Park Mausoleum on 2 January 1947, to miss the funeral of one of his greatest contemporaries on the vaudeville stage. He died in December 1954, at the age of sixty.

Frederick Sweeney was one of hundreds of foot soldiers of the army of actors who trod the boards of theatres throughout North America and, indeed, the world, and who would do anything, undergo any hardship, endure any humiliation and risk the failure, obscurity and oblivion that overtook so many. When previous writers wrote about W. C. Fields' anxieties, fears and paranoias, attention has always been paid to the supposed hardships of his early youth, his teenage years. But every actor, basking in the warmth of an ephemeral acclaim, the passing adulation of the public, knew how fleeting fame could be. They were aware of such items as the following in the *Dramatic Mirror* of 9 October 1909:

CIRCUS PERFORMER IN POORHOUSE

Diavolo, the original 'loop the loop' rider on a bicycle, who made a tremendous fortune with the Barnum and Bailey circus seven years ago, is reported to be in the workhouse at Milwaukee, Wis.. He is reported to have been arrested for vagrancy a week ago and to have been sentenced by a judge of the District Court.

No wonder W. C. Fields was said to have salted away money in seven hundred different bank accounts all over the world, although this, too, like so many other legends, turns out to be just another tall tale.

In looking at that vanished world of theatrical show business, before the advent of the motion picture, of radio, and finally of television – the technologies which changed show business for ever – we have first to define our terms. Names like 'vaudeville', 'variety', 'music hall', 'burlesque', 'revue', tend to be used promiscuously. Strange forgotten words, like 'olio', crop up, in different contexts, to confuse the reader. Other concepts, like 'medicine shows' and 'dime museums', cloud the air still further. The 'dime museum' was a euphemism for the freak show, pioneered in spectacular fashion by the 'Prince of Humbugs', Phineas T. Barnum, who began, as long ago as the 1830s, to exhibit an aged black woman named Joice Heth as the '160 year old nurse of George Washington' and a dried-up sewn-together mummy of a tunafish and a monkey as the 'Feejee Mermaid'. Show business was nothing if not eclectic from its earliest days in North America. The great Houdini himself began his career in a 'museum', as he related in his regular Vaudeville column, 'Houdini's Entertaining Chat', in the *New York Dramatic Mirror* – writing from Germany, on 8 November 1902 (he was reporting on freak shows in Munich):

> It reminded me of the time when I was travelling with the Welsh Brothers' Circus through Pennsylvania and had to be a freak myself. I was put in a small den and called 'Projea, the Wild Man of Mexico.' I remember once when Clint Newton threw me some raw meat to eat. He hit me in the eye, and I would not look at him for three weeks, as my eyes were closed. This caused me to become tame, and some one else had to play wild man of Mexico.

These kinds of circuses were probably the earliest form of entertainment in the American colonies. The diaries of Thomas Jefferson, in 1771, record:

> Paid for hearing the musical glasses – 3 shillings.
> Paid for seeing the alligator – 1 shilling, 3d.

And in 1786:

> Paid for seeing figure of King of Prussia – 12 francs.
> Paid for seeing a learned pig – 1 shilling.

Before photography, panoramas and wagon shows entertained the people with colourful views of western life and magic lantern shows. Before the building of the mighty railroads which tied America together, these shows travelled on the waterways, giving birth to the heyday of the showboats, which was to be reconstructed a century later in Florenz Ziegfeld's epic version of Edna Ferber's novel. The largest showboats could seat one thousand persons. The band would play into the night and the variety acts would perform under the stars as the great boats churned down the Mississippi. These were images which would return, on stage, and burn themselves too, into the imagination of the young William Claude, featuring in his 1935 film *Mississippi*, in which he would share the honours with another old-time nostalgist, Bing Crosby. Just as the circus would return again and again in his fictions, from *Sally of the Sawdust* in 1925, through the missing film *Two Flaming Youths* of 1927, *The Old Fashioned Way* of 1934 and up to Larson E. Whipsnade . . .

The prototype of the circus barker and entrepreneur was of course P. T. Barnum himself. The master of fakery and the king of show business, Barnum could fleece the American, and eventually the European public, like no man before or after. After coining it in with the 'Feejee Mermaid', which even he admitted was a fake, he exploited the young midget Charles Stratton as the marvellous 'General Tom Thumb', exhibiting him all over the country and presenting him in London to Queen Victoria, in Napoleonic garb.

Although 'Tom Thumb' did not do badly by Barnum – he married a fellow midget, Lavinia Warren, and retired with a fair stack of cash – there was no doubt who raked in the main share. Less fortunate than the midgets were the more traditional exhibits, like 'Zip' the 'What Is It?', a retarded cone-headed black man named William Henry Johnson, whom Barnum displayed as the 'missing link': 'Is it a lower order of MAN? Or a higher order of MONKEY?' One has to remember that Darwin's *Origin of Species* had only recently exploded upon the philosophical scene. Other coups of Barnum's included his American touring of the 'Swedish Nightingale', Jenny Lind, whom Barnum built up into a paragon of art and beauty, auctioning tickets for her shows to the highest bidders and thus adding to his already fabulous pile. Despite his later bankruptcy, the indefatigable Humbug bounced back, transporting London Zoo's famous elephant, Jumbo, to become a world-wide household name. Even when the poor pachyderm died its carcass was exhibited around the country to yet more box office cheer.

One of the best descriptions of the old style 'dime museum' can be found in Fred Allen's autobiography *Much Ado About Me*. Fred Allen (1894–1956) began, like Fields, as a comedy juggler, but went on to become a major radio star, though he turned away from motion pictures. He describes the famous Austin and Stone 'museum', on Boston's Scollay Square, which was run by the colourful Professor Hutching. At these establishments there was always a 'Professor', explaining the marvels within, a character taken over whole by Fields in his basic role as 'Eustace McGargle' in his first major stage hit, *Poppy*, in 1923. The Professor would introduce his attractions – Chang, the Chinese Giant; Miss Eva Eversole, the Armless Wonder; Miss Corbin, 'the four-legged girl born with four perfectly formed legs'; Riley, the man-fish, 'who eats, drinks, reads and smokes under water'; Jo-Jo, the Dog-Faced Boy, et al., in loud flowery tones. The Professor, who, Allen writes, 'was loath to use one word if eight or nine would do', would proclaim loftily: 'My constant aim is to elevate and instruct humanity.'

Across the road, the new Nickelodeon would charge five cents to see the moving pictures or bioscope, and ten cents extra to see the Big Girl Show, featuring 'dance routines completely devoid of skill or rhythm. If sex had been known in Boston at this time,' writes Allen, 'these girls would have set sex back two hundred years.' Other theatres presented the more full-blown burlesque: two acts consisting of varied sketches with a number of vaudeville or variety turns in between. This in-between category was known as the 'olio', which later, in the larger scale of vaudeville proper, came to describe the juggling and stand-up acts which were performed in front of the dropped curtain while the more complex routines were preparing behind it. The olio was the place in which new acts were often tried out and given their chance to blossom or die. It was better than coming on as the very first act, during which the audience was still coming in, banging and scraping their seats and shouting at each other across the hall.

Burlesque was rough and ready. At the Old Howard in Boston, Fred Allen relates, a burly policeman with a billy club kept order, appearing at the first row just before the show started to call out: 'Hats off! And no smoking! Keep your feet off the rails!' He would then smite the gallery rail with his billy, producing loud metallic vibrations which would smother the yelling of the patrons.

Burlesque, as ex-burlesque queen Ann Corio put it: 'was the breeding grounds for . . . great comics. It gave them a stage, an audience, and a chance to develop the acts, mannerism, pantomime, or whatever made them famous. Al Jolson sang his first song in a burlesque house. Joe E. Brown was part of an acrobatic team.' Others in the Hall of Fame of comedy who began in burlesque were Will Rogers, Bert Lahr, Ed Wynn, Buster Keaton, Eddie Cantor, Jimmy Durante, and, as we shall see, W. C. Fields. The whole point of the burlesque, despite all of these gentlemen, was to bring on the girls. Burlesque ladies were famed for all manner of gyrations and contortions which they performed on stage and were immortalised in cigarette cards, which doubled as pin ups. These 'Ballet Queens' were almost invariably of ample proportions, and some would put the alumni of modern body-building emporiums to shame. Contemporary photographs show them bursting out of their ornate if flimsy attire capped by hats of the most outrageous mode. As the years moved on the attire became flimsier, eventually giving way to what we know today as 'strip-tease'. Even in the 1890s, when very little was revealed to the panting male public, burlesque was a byword for immorality, potential or actual, to stern reformers and ranting ministers of the cloth. The best managers protected their female performers from both their male colleagues and the mob. The worst absconded with everyone's funds.

The writer and critic Bernard Sobel described a typical burlesque show, in his *Pictorial History of Burlesque*:

> The opening chorus goes something like this: 'College girls, college girls, we are the college girls.'
>
> Then the oversized prima donna appears with a letter in her hand and reads: 'I just received this letter from two millionaires, Mr Clancy and Mr Schwartz. Shall we show the gentlemen a good time?'
>
> 'You bet!' shouts the entire company.
>
> At this cue, the orchestra starts playing 'The Wearing of the Green' and the Irishman appears, saying, 'By golly, where's Schwartz?'
>
> Immediately the Dutch comedian rushes in, shouting, 'Is dis de place?'

If it wasn't, it's difficult to imagine what was. This was the well-spring of American comedy. In the intermission, the audience would adjourn to the next-door saloon or to the sidewalk to chat up the girls or send a discreet note backstage. Then, in the 'olio', the speciality acts would come on, the knife-throwers, contortionists, musical-glass players, acrobats, singers, ventriloquists, the jugglers, and the 'added attractions', which might include a monologue by a famous celebrity such as a retired boxer, or a strong man. The famous Sandow, who was discovered by a young Florenz Ziegfeld, began his career in such shows, exhibiting 'his extraordinary command over his entire muscular system by making his muscles dance'. The boxers Jim Jeffries and James J. Corbett appeared often on these stages.

The most electrifying phenomenon in old burlesque was undoubtedly the infamous 'hootchie-cootchie'. This dance was apparently introduced to America by a lady known as 'Little Egypt', whose real name seems to have been Fahreda Mahzar Spyropolos. She first presented her gyrations at the Chicago World's Fair in 1893, and stopped the show. Within a year there were hundreds of 'Little Egypts' wiggling their limbs throughout the United States. It appears to have been a kind of Balkan belly dance, but it set puritan American males into spasms. This special attraction would often herald the finale of a burlesque show, which would consist of a parade of all the girls, in patriotic star spangled banners, kicking their legs high above the perspiring clientele.

The burlesque shows spawned Weber and Fields, perhaps the most influential of the ethnic acts which proliferated in a country of churning immigrations. From humble beginnings in New York's Jewish Lower East Side, Joe Weber and Lew Fields became an inseparable double-act (until their separation in 1904) which practically wrote the rules of American musical comedy with shows produced at their own theatre, Weber & Fields' Music Hall. Beginning as a kid act playing make-believe Irish comedians, they performed a clog dance at various amateur nights before breaking through at Miner's Bowery Theatre. The act they then went on to perfect, as 'Mike and Meyer', became a hallowed teaching ground for many double-acts which formed later, and one can clearly see the origins of the Marx Brothers Groucho–Chico routines in their happy mangling of immigrant English:

MIKE: I am delightfulness to met you.

MEYER: Der disgust is all mine.

MIKE: I receivedid a letter from mein goil, but I don't know how to writteninin her back.

MEYER: . . . How can you answer her ven you don't know how to write?

MIKE: Dot make no nefer mind. She don't know how to read.

They would then go into heavy knockabout stuff, beating each other over the head, poking in the eye and kicking in the shins with an explosive cap in the toe of the boot. Joe Weber was short and fat and Lew Fields was tall and thin. Laurel and Hardy of course also come to mind. As they became more famous they began to pioneer the combination of stage play and musical numbers which would mutate into the American musical. But in their early days they also developed a successful pool act, with all kinds of comedy business around a pool table, the balls falling into the pockets in all manner of miraculous ways.

Weber and Fields performed their pool act in variety theatres all over the Eastern United States in the early 1890s. They certainly performed in Philadelphia, in the years when a young teenager called William Claude Dukenfield was playing hookie from school, carousing with his friends in the streets and sneaking in to see the shows, with or without payment . . .

Ethnic comedy was popular in all venues. The Black, the Irish, the 'Hebrew', were the mainstay of many standard acts. To broaden their appeal, Jewish acts like Weber and Fields became known as 'Dutch' acts, or 'German comedians'. (All the Germans became Dutch, much later, during the First World War.) Black acts in variety and vaudeville were rare, but present, memorably the great Bert Williams, who played with W. C. Fields in the Ziegfeld *Follies* from 1915, and Ernest Hogan, who performed at the turn of the century as 'the unbleached American'. They worked in a strange symbiosis with the white 'blackface' acts, which derived from the older minstrel shows. The convention required that even black actors like Williams (with George Walker, his collaborator) and Hogan appeared on stage blacked up with burnt cork. The songs they sang went under the general heading of 'coon songs', a term pejorative even then but adopted in preference to the despised 'nigger'. Ernest Hogan became famous for his own composition entitled: 'All coons look alike to me'. It made his fortune, spawning a whole genre of popular 'coon songs' which were sung by black and white performers alike.

Vaudeville was an entertainment for white America. When one looks at the period, and at the racial prejudices of so many white performers, one has to realize the full impact of racial separation. This was an era in which you would go to the funfair and throw three balls to 'Hit the Coon'. Songs like 'Old Zip Coon', and the original 'Jim Crow' song and dance, were among the oldest material in popular American entertainment, echoing and distorting the songs of legendary black performers like Picayune Butler and 'Old Corn Meal'. A white performer, Thomas 'Daddy' Rice, is credited with originating what became the 'minstrel show' with an 'Ethiopian Opera' at New York's Bowery Theatre in 1833. This blackface frolic became, amazingly, the most popular form of entertainment in America for almost fifty years, and even black African-American actors performed in their own minstrel troupes. The most famous of the white blackface teams which endured was that of McIntyre and Heath, which was to play, as we have seen, and shall return to later, such a pivotal and unexpected role in the burgeoning comedy art of William Claude Fields.

Minstrelsy, burlesque, variety, circus, showboats, fairgrounds, medicine shows. Painless dentists and vendors of quack nostrums haunted every sideshow and carnival. A typical exemplar might be Diamond Kit, who frequented Milwaukee Fairs in an outlandish coat whose buttons were set with rhinestones, and a circlet of shining stones set around his pillbox cap. Stuffing his patent painkiller in the victim's mouth, he would extract the tooth and cry triumphantly: 'Did I hurt you?' Then he would make his spiel. A fan of W. C. Fields will discern a number of clues in this prevalent character . . . Larger, tent medicine shows might include their own little acts, such as the 'Kickapoo Indian Ballplayers' in their 'Buffalo Dance', or 'Kickapoo Indians Hunting Buffalo for Tallow to Make Kickapoo Indian Salve', available at a generous discount to the public.

These were the ragged edges of what were to become the great 'Wild West' shows of the 1880s and 1890s, the most famous of which was Buffalo Bill Cody's extravaganza, which toured the world in the early 1900s, with such luminaries as sure-shot Annie Oakley and the Indian chief Sitting Bull himself. And of course, there was always the circus, with its strong men, clowns, dare-devil riders, acrobats and incredible diving horses . . .

The 'legitimate' theatre blurred readily with this carnivalesque bacchanal. Players in stock travelling companies crossed over into burlesque and variety. Frederick Sweeney, Jimmy Duffy's partner, was one of them. From the 1850s on, Harriet Beecher Stowe's anti-slavery melodrama, *Uncle Tom's Cabin*, became a mainstay of theatres around the country. Towns which had no theatres staged its dramatization in blacksmith's shops and in the open air, long before the Civil War. Soap operas like *East Lynne* and epics like *Michael Strogoff* were performed in town halls everywhere. Plays which were moral tracts were popular, none more so than the 'great moral drama' of *The Drunkard*, which was first presented in Boston in 1841 and was the first American play to run more than one hundred consecutive performances. *The Drunkard; or, The Fallen Saved* preached Temperance, Purity, and Love, and was destined to live forever as a segment in our hero's moving-picture presentation of *The Old Fashioned Way* in 1934 – perhaps the most blatant of Bill Fields' tributes to the vanished world of the nineteenth-century stage. In Fields' oeuvre, nothing was allowed to go to waste, as we shall, in the due fullness of time, find out . . .

The most spectacular blurring of 'legitimate' theatre and variety, however, was without doubt the work produced in New York, in the mid-1870s, by perhaps the greatest of all American popular stage enterprises, the theatre of Harrigan and Hart.

For fourteen years, from 1871 to 1885, Edward 'Ned' Harrigan and Tony Hart reigned supreme. Edward Harrigan, a New Yorker born and bred in the Irish community of the city's east riverfront, with no formal education, wrote thirty-five full length plays, which he produced and starred in himself. Tony Hart, born in Massachussets, was an actor who excelled at female impersonation, a category that was a fully accepted part of the variety stage, then as later. Performing first as 'the Nonpareils', they later acquired the Théâtre Comique, at Broadway and Lafayette Street, in 1876, as a stage for their own productions. Harrigan's plays were robust satires of life in the ethnic slums of New York: the Bowery gangs, the newsboys, the flower girls, the *habitués* of dives and dance halls, swaggering toughs and drunken sailors. There was a great deal of what Harrigan himself called 'knockdown and slapbang'. The writer E. J. Kahn, the duo's biographer, described a typical lithographic advertisement for a Harrigan and Hart play as showing 'a Chinese, holding a trombone, being flung out of a second-storey tenement-house window onto the head of an unsuspecting Negro strolling by below'. One critic wrote about one of Harrigan's plays, *Marty Malone*: 'As I tottered away, I felt as if Ali Baba and his forty thugs had clubbed me with Chicago sandbags, and all the wild mustangs in all the stables on Portland Street had run over me, and all the stable boys had caressed me with currycombs, and Wagner had been sung in a boiler factory.'

Their most famous creation was 'The Mulligan Guards', a crazy, mixed-up militia of braggarts, whose song became so famous it was paraphrased in Rudyard Kipling's *Kim* twenty-nine years later. Harrigan parodied the ethnic conflicts and battles of post-civil New York with savage accuracy and abandon. This was the heyday of Tammany Hall, when corrupt politicians and even more corrupt cops held sway over the seething, violent streets. One infamous Grand Sachem of Tammany was John Kelly, known as 'Honest John' because he was marginally less crooked than his predecessor, Boss Tweed. The Bowery B'hoys and the Dead Rabbits were the two leading gangs of the day, and one Murdering Mike McGloin charged two bucks for a simple beating and a hundred dollars per killing. In this milieu Harrigan gathered his plots in the streets, wandering about, looking for the seediest tramp clothing which he would often buy off the wearer to use authentically on the stage. He even tried casting gang members plucked off the street in his plays.

Blacks, Jews, Italians, Germans, Irish – all were lampooned with equal vigour. One chorus of Harrigan's *McSorley's Inflation*, produced in 1882, introduced what was to become a familiar comic-strip image, the tenement huddle of 'McNally's Row of Flats':

It's Ireland and Italy, Jerusalem and Germany,
Oh, Chinamen and nagers, and a paradise for rats,
All jumbled up togayther in the snow or rainy weather,
They represent the tenants in McNally's row of flats.

The targets of Harrigan and Hart's satirical shafts, rather than howling them off the stage, drowned them in plaudits and bouquets. They were compared to Gilbert and Sullivan, and Harrigan was hailed as an American Dickens. The politicians they scourged and leading figures like Mark Twain came to enjoy their shows. It was almost as if their stage was the actual melting pot of the metaphor of America's 'E pluribus unum' – the huddled masses become one. Springing forth from New York, they performed all over the eastern United States, and were by far the most influential theatrical force of their time.

In 1877 Harrigan wrote a sketch called *Old Lavender*, which he expanded to a full-length play a year later. It became his most famous work. Harrigan himself played Old Lavender, a cashier who was fired from his brother's bank for inadvertently cashing a bad check. As E. J. Kahn writes: 'He became a courtly, philosophical alcoholic (one of his lines, anticipating W. C. Fields, was, "I've been imposed upon by water"), and at the end saved his brother's tottering bank by means of some previously worthless mining-stock certificates that suddenly turned valuable.' The resemblance to Fields' own masterpiece, *The Bank Dick*, produced sixty years later, springs immediately to mind. And indeed the character of the genteel drunk, who sees the world going to pot around him, has echoes that reverberate down the decades.

In 1885, Hart dramatically split from Harrigan after a series of disasters which included the burning down of their Théâtre Comique on Broadway. Harrigan continued on his own, having outlived his era, and was still presenting sketches and versions of his old famous plays throughout the 1890s and until 1908. He toured the Keith and Proctor vaudeville circuit both in the United States and in Europe as 'a wanderer over the face of the earth playing in continuous shows'. Tony Hart had fallen ill with syphilis in 1887 and died in the insane asylum, in 1891, three months after his thirty-sixth birthday. Kahn says: 'He left an estate later apprised at eighty cents.' Harrigan died in 1911 at the age of sixty-seven. He had outlived his time and could not understand why the audiences had dwindled and the chorus of praise receded to a whisper. But his plays had become as familiar a part of the variety theatre's background as Neil Simon is to us today. Every vaudeville performer of the age, W. C. Fields included, was exposed to his spell.

Ned Harrigan's theatre straddled the gap between vulgar 'variety' and polite 'vaudeville'. 'Polite Vaudeville' was, in fact, the very term used to distinguish a new and indeed revolutionary trend in the presentation of popular mass entertainment. The progenitor of this new form is generally considered to be the extremely ambitious Tony Pastor. Born probably in 1837, Tony began his career as a child clown prodigy at P. T. Barnum's New York Museum. Circus performer and acrobat, he became the youngest ringmaster in America at the age of fourteen. During the Civil War, at the age of twenty-four, he opened his first theatre, at 444 Broadway, and starred there himself as a singer of patriotic Yankee songs. Like Harrigan, he took the subject matter of his songs from the streets of the city.

Pastor's dream was to make the variety theatre an acceptable venue for 'ladies and gents'. This was to be a new, 'cleaned-up' variety with comedy, song and dance acts, monologues and Tony himself singing old favourites such as 'The Strawberry Blonde' and 'Lula, the Beautiful Hebrew Girl'. Most importantly, there was to be no vulgarity, no 'blue' jokes, no suggestive stuff. In his patent leather boots, opera hat and twirlable handlebar moustache, he created a stock figure to characterise the new age. A devout Catholic, he followed his dream to the end, only to see it usurped and turned into gold by more ruthless operators than himself.

'Polite Vaudeville' had to be merchandised before it could sweep all else before it. The agents of this commercial explosion were Edward Franklin Albee and Benjamin Franklin Keith.

Both these worthies had unpromising starts. Albee was the type of circus barker known as an 'outside ticket' man. He stood outside the tents and shouted: 'Don't miss this greatest show . . . see the mammoth menagerie . . . the wild man, eating bumbergriff . . . get your tickets here . . . thank you, folks . . .' Keith was also in the circus, a 'grifter' who sold novelties on the lot. He sold 'blood testers', which purported to show if your haemoglobin was up to scratch: 'An infallible test . . . the famous Professor Spivins spent forty-two years in perfecting this instrument . . .' Later, Keith married a devout Catholic, Mary Catherine Branley, whose influence on the development of 'Polite Vaudeville' was to be crucial. Together with a partner, Colonel William Austin, Keith opened a 'museum' in Boston, whose opening attraction was one 'Baby Alice'. Billed as being so small she could fit in a milk bottle, 'Baby Alice' swiftly outgrew her berth, but Keith soldiered on, with a new partner, until young Albee, fed up with the circus, walked into his office and asked for a job.

The two grifters never looked back. In 1885 they opened their first theatre, the Bijou, in Boston, charging one dime admission, and a chair for an extra five cents. Mrs Keith established the iron ground rules. She put up notices, which were to become standard in practically every vaudeville theatre:

NOTICE TO PERFORMERS
You are hereby warned that your act must be free from all vulgarity and suggestiveness in words, action and costume . . . and all vulgar, double-meaning and profane words and songs must be cut out of your act before the first performance . . . Such words as Liar, Slob, Son-of-a-Gun, Devil, Sucker, Damn and all other words unfit for the ears of ladies and children,

also any references to questionable streets, resorts, localities, and bar-rooms, are prohibited under fine of instant discharge.

From Boston to Providence, and then to Philadelphia, Keith and Albee began building an empire. In 1893, they opened the Union Square Theatre on Fourteenth Street in New York. Their theatres became more and more opulent. No longer the honky tonk dives, they had ornate lobbies, with ushers dressed in Turkish costumes or military uniforms. The name of the new entertainment was now 'Vaudeville', a French sounding name which might have derived from the *vaux-de-Vire*, or popular songs practised in the valleys of Normandy. Perhaps Mrs Keith dreamed the name up. But it had the sound of 'class', of a departure from the rough and tumble of common variety.

The key to vaudeville's success was industrialisation: the creation of unified booking systems and continuous performances, which were being pioneered both by Keith and Albee and by another theatre owner, F. F. Proctor, in New York. Proctor vowed to make vaudeville a daily habit for families. His slogan was: 'After breakfast, go to Proctor's. After Proctor's, go to bed.' Matinees began at noon and the theatre stayed open till midnight. Headliners appeared twice a day and lesser acts might perform five times a day. Keith and Albee developed and streamlined this system.

During the 1880s, vaudeville theatres spread all over the United States. The New York *Clipper* was filled with advertisements calling for 'quality acts'. Roughly every two years, the number of variety companies touring the Eastern circuits doubled, from less than twenty in 1885 to sixty in 1890. By the turn of the century, there were estimated to be about fifteen thousand actors working in variety and vaudeville shows. Vaudeville was becoming *the* form of entertainment, at a time when another medium, the motion picture, was only crawling out of its cradle.

In May of 1887, the theatre managers met in Philadelphia to set up the Board of Managers of Vaudeville Theatres, standardizing their booking systems, with a central office in New York. This enabled vaudeville to be run as any other business, rationalizing unit costs like the railroads, or US Steel. A whole stratum of organized managers and middle men, talent spotters who travelled around to book acts, was the next logical step. The business of vaudeville meant higher salaries, particularly for top acts: Lillian Russell was paid $3,150 per week, and the bottom rung was around $75. The punters paid fifty cents for the best seats, one dollar for orchestra seats in the best New York houses, ten cents in most houses for the gallery. Keith's Orpheum circuit was operating on assets of around five million dollars, and had built its own theatres, at a cost of between $250,000 to $300,000.

It was a long road from the 'dime museum', the freak show in which Harry Houdini appeared as the Wild Man of Mexico for under fifty dollars a week. And it was in this period of sudden growth that a wayward teenage boy in Philadelphia fell in love with this dynamic, vivid new entertainment which could promise its own glittering version of the American Dream . . .

Chapter 3
'Philadelphia Will Do . . .'

Conflicts over the true facts of W. C. Fields' life being at the moment he was born. His original biographer, Taylor, even got this wrong, dating his birth at 9 April 1879, which would have made him an authentic bastard, as his parents were only married on 18 May of the same year. According to family lore, the Great Man was born on 29 January 1880, in a small hotel in Darby, Pennsylvania, just outside the Philadelphia city limits. The name of the Hotel, the family recalls, was the Arlington, though another name mentioned in dispatches is the Buttonwood. It stood at Main and Ninth Streets, though other locations have also been touted, such as Lehigh Avenue near 10th Street in Germantown, Philadelphia, and Rising Sun Village, junction of Rising Sun Avenue, Germantown Avenue and Old York Road. Latter-day fans in Philadelphia, notably journalist James Smart and researcher Milton Kenin, plumped for the hotel in Darby. According to a *Philadelphia Inquirer* report, it still stood in 1980, renamed the National, though some folks in the saloon denied all knowledge of the earthshaking events of one hundred years before: 'I never heard that story,' said the bartender, 'W. C. Fields born here – no, I never heard that one.'

'Sure, I heard that before,' said an oldtimer sipping a small draft beer. 'That was before my time, of course, but I heard that he was born here.'

He certainly did not linger long, retiring to the family home at 6320 Woodland Avenue (some say it was 6328) which was torn down in 1922 and replaced by the Benn Theatre.

Confusion over the birth date was due to the disappearance of any birth certificate, but a census taker who visited the Woodland Avenue home on 5 June 1880 recorded the existence of little Claude, 'four-twelfths of a year old'.

He was born William Claude Dukenfield. His youngest brother,

Leroy, who was born fifteen years later, recalled, in a 1969 interview, their mother as saying that in the hotel 'there was a coloured woman named Kitty, and when Big Nose was born she came up and put a gold spoon in his mouth, and said he was going to get someplace'. She then disappeared from history, probably in a puff of smoke.

Baby Claude's Pa was an English immigrant, James L. Dukenfield, who had arrived in the United States from Sheffield on 13 November

1 James Dukenfield, the Civil War veteran.

2 Kate Felton-Dukenfield, with W. C.'s son, Claude Jr. (photograph from 1907).

1854. James was then thirteen and accompanied by his father, John Dukenfield, a combmaker, and several uncles, some say as many as nineteen. James settled in Philadelphia and became so deeply attached to his newly adopted country that he fought in the Civil War for the Union. His brother, George, who enlisted too, was killed at Gettysburg. James was said to have lost two fingers of his right hand in the Battle of Lookout Mountain, in Tennessee, 1863. The Philadelphia City Directory listed him, in 1876, as a clerk.

Bill Fields told so many outrageous tales of his father that the historian might be forgiven for pausing at times to take a stiff snorter before carrying on. A typical tale was recounted to the press in November 1941. 'I'm glad my poor father isn't alive,' Fields said. 'After getting out of jail for picking pockets, he turned bartender, and spent the rest of his life drinking up the profits. The old gentleman would turn over in his grave, could he see the sad end of his only son . . .' And elsewhere, speaking to columnist Ed Sullivan:

> As someone more eloquent than I has said: 'It is a pity that youth is wasted on the very young.' Youth should be reserved for old codgers like me. I'd know how to use it. Kids just squander it. They have no judgment of distance, no change of pace. They want to go roller-skating or ride on a bike. Now you know that is silly, when there are so many worthwhile things to do. As a child I was a brat. A man once said to my father, in our parlour: 'I've never met such a repulsive child as your son. He will probably become a juggler.' At this, my father started sobbing and, as the man turned his back, Pa hit him a terrible blow. When the man fell, from Pa's cowardly blow, I hit him in the face. But although we got him down, truth would not be suppressed. I *did* become a juggler.

Kate Felton, Fields' mother, was a native Philadelphian from a large family with a German background. A photograph of her in middle age shows a startling resemblance to the features of her famous son in later years. She was clearly the humorous one of the family. Leroy remembered her as 'an old fashioned homebody. She would put on a wrapper and leave that on for a couple of days and never go out of the house. The only time I remember her getting dressed up is when Big Nose came in to town with the Ziegfeld Follies or something, and then she would go out to see him.'

Leroy also confirmed the general impression of James as a rather dour character:

Dad, for me, was a foreigner . . . he never seemed to take much interest. What I remember about him the most is that, before we would leave the house, he would take out his handkerchief and spit on it and wipe my face. He had a thoroughbred racehorse, besides his workhorse. He never raced it, but he had it. The first snow up at Valley Green Inn, the first sleigh that gets there gets a bottle of wine. He always tried to get that.

James Dukenfield and Kate Felton were married at the Memorial Methodist Episcopal Church, at 8th and Cumberland Streets, which called itself 'The Church of the Glad Hand'. James was a Roman Catholic and Kate a Methodist, although neither was a great church-goer. In the first six years of little Claude's life they changed addresses three times, moving to 2552 Germantown Avenue, then 2559 North 11th Street, and then to 929 Somerset Street. James managed the bar at the Arlington but Kate made him give up the job once Claude was born, so as not to be a bad example to their tot. This strategy was evidently a failure, as time would prove. But in the early days life was reasonably tranquil. Four more children were born, Walter, Adel and May during the 1880s, and Leroy in 1895.

James took a job as a commission merchant for fruit and vegetables, though he still dabbled in part-investments in taverns, according to Fields' only son, Claude, who wrote: '[He] would, when the opportunity presented itself, sing and even dance a bit for the edification of the customers. While it was reported that he had a pleasant voice, it was certainly not of operatic standard.' In the stories recounted by Taylor, off Gene Fowler's notes of Fields' own tales, Pa Dukenfield had a penchant for sentimental and religious songs, such as 'The Little Green Leaf in the Bible', 'Annie Laurie' and 'Oh, Genevieve', which Fields claimed he detested to his dying day. There is no doubt that Fields had a great fear of vocal music, and was particularly disturbed, in his later years, when Deanna Durbin, the child singing star, took up residence in a neighbouring property. He also fought a losing battle against his last mistress Carlotta Monti's burning ambition to exercise her larynx in a professional mode.

Whatever the choral status in the Dukenfield household was in reality, all sources confirm the continual ribbing by Ma Dukenfield of Pa's lingering English Midlands accent (though some dubbed it 'cockney' by mistake). She would sit on the porch and mumble cutting asides about the neighbours as they passed. 'She would say, "Hello Mr Nesselrode, how are you doing today?" "Oh, I feel a little bit under the weather."

31

"Oh, that's a shame." Then she'd mumble to her family: "Last night he was under the table . . . " ' related her great-grandson, Ronald Fields.

This was by no means a poor family. A great deal of misunderstanding bolstered by W. C. Fields' tall tales, has been caused by a misreading of the nature of Philadelphia, as a city, in those days. Philadelphia, cradle of the American Revolution, in whose State House the Declaration of Independence of the Thirteen United States was signed and its bell tolled to proclaim Liberty, was also the centre of American puritanism, the Quaker town par excellence. The Protestant and Germanic virtues of thrift and sobriety gave the city a particularly priggish air. One observer, Elizabeth Robbins Pennell, wrote that 'the Philadelphia law of laws obliged every Philadelphian to do as every other Philadelphian did'. A city so austere and prudish, that, as Fields said himself years later: 'Anyone found smiling after curfew was liable to get arrested. If a woman dropped her glove on the street she was liable to be arrested and hauled before a judge on a charge of strip-teasing.'

But this was only part of the story. Philadelphia may have had seven hundred churches by 1900, but it also had three hundred known houses of prostitution. Between the end of the Civil War in 1865 and the end of the century, Philadelphia was being transformed into an industrial giant. Iron and steel, coal and oil, made the State of Pennsylvania into America's foundry, and Philadelphia was a major port city, oversitting two major rivers, the Schuylkill and the Delaware. The Centennial Exposition of 1876 presented Philadelphia as the mistress of Technology – the Queen of the Engine. The Pennsylvania railroad was the largest rail enterprise in the country. Its main Broad Street Station was opened at the hub of the city, west of City Hall, in 1882, when William Claude Dukenfield was two years old. By 1894, when he was fourteen, 530 trains carrying 60,000 people were arriving and departing at Broad Street every day. Philadelphia produced ships, machine tools, locomotive turntables, pipes, elevators, sewing machines and bath tubs. Smaller plants turned out banjos, brooms, buttons, watch cases, cordage, parasols and umbrellas, paper boxes and cigar boxes, which were to play a seminal part in the juggling repertoire of one alienated Philadelphia youth . . .

Not surprisingly, the city grew both in space and population. It was, in sheer geographical area, the largest city in the United States, covering 129 square miles by 1904. In 1901 there were 1,293,000 inhabitants. Already by 1880 Philadelphia was foremost among American cities in its length of horse-car lines, 264 miles of track. Cable cars and electric trolleys, introduced in 1892, rapidly replaced the horses, which were phased out in 1897. But, due to its geographical spread, the city's boroughs developed differently from a compact entity like Manhattan. Philadelphia was mostly composed of separate neighbourhoods, which often had little in common with each other except their architecture, a plethora of row houses, many of them owner-occupied rather than rented. Many low income families who might have been packed in 'McNally's Row of Flats' in New York City lived, like the Dukenfields, a life of relative comfort, able to move from dwelling to dwelling without risk of economic disaster.

As in every other American city, immigrants were a vital factor in supplying the workforce of the industrial boom. But in 1880 foreign-born citizens comprised only 24 per cent of the citizenry. This was mainly the 'Old Immigration', English, German, and Irish. The next large group entering the city were Italians, followed, in the last decade of the century, by the Jews of Russia and Eastern Europe. Prominent also was the internal migration from the south, swelling the black population of the city in their segregated districts. But even in the black neighbourhoods the ubiquitous architecture of small houses prevented the worst tenement despair.

A characteristic of these Philadelphia houses was a garden, at the back, facing more open countryside, rather than on the street side. This 'back porch' was to play a role in our hero's work far beyond its humble start. The separation of neighbourhoods meant that life could be lived at a less hectic pace than the nature of the boom city might suggest. Thus, Leroy Dukenfield could relate to his interviewer, in 1969, that 'from our front step on Marshall Street we could see the trolleys on York Road. There were cornfields in between.' He was speaking of 3923 North Marshall Street, a later Dukenfield address. This fitted with the central idea of the city's founder, William Penn, of an English style *rus in urbe*, the countryside within the town. Close to the centre of the city there was Fairmount Park, the largest city park, it was said, in the world, stretching along twelve miles. This was the city's playground, with lots of shady nooks for picnics, boats lazily drifting up the Schuylkill and miles of carriage drives. Out to the northwest was Willow Grove Park, where Fields later remembered the ferris wheel and the great summer concerts by the bands of Gillmore and John Philip Sousa. Bicycle races were an 1890s craze, as well as baseball, which the city excelled at, supporting two major league clubs, the Athletics and the Phillies.

A vibrant, upbeat metropolis. Yet W. C. Fields has, perhaps more than any other single person, managed to portray his native city as the dullest backwater in the known universe. Witness his cry, as Cuthbert J. Twillie, charlatan and hustler, in his 1940 film with Mae West, *My Little Chickadee*, when he is about to be hanged by irate townspeople who have decided he is the marauding 'masked bandit'. In answer to the query: 'Have you any last words?' – 'Yes, I'd like to see Paris before I die' and, as the rope tugs – 'Philadelphia will do!'

A recurring legend has it that Fields is buried under a tombstone which says: 'I'd rather be in Philadelphia.' A typical canard. (His ashes, for his friends finally fulfilled his wish to have his remains cremated, lie in a reliquary with a gold plaque that says simply W. C. FIELDS – 1880–1946.) In reality he returned to Philadelphia often, both on tour when his act took him to the variety theatres of the city, or to visit his family. But it was certainly the case that Philadelphia did not, in the eyes of the impatient youth, offer him the kind of future he was beginning, at an early age, to crave.

As a small boy, Claude Dukenfield rode on the vegetable wagon his father used to take produce to the markets. Legend has him calling out with his father: 'Watermelons! Swee-eet Sugar Corn! Re-ed Tomayters!' or exotic names which his father wasn't carrying, such as 'Rutabagas!' This was said to have occasioned the first of many wallops on the back of his head from his father's knuckles. He would also make fun of his father's horse, White Swan, or mimic his Pa's non-American accent, possibly at his peril.

James Smart, the local chronicler of young Claude's life in Philadelphia, was unable to establish which school the boy attended for the three or four grades he did bother to show up. One candidate was William Adamson Public School on 4th Street south of Lehigh Avenue, the school closest to the family home at that time, at 10th and Somerset. Another venue might have been the Fairhill School at Somerset and Marshall, but this was not built until 1887. It was, in Smart's words: 'A typical "modern" schoolhouse of the day – a two-storey brick eight-room building with a brick-paved schoolyard and detached, unheated outhouses.'

Bill Fields appeared to have told no tales of these few years of his formal schooling, but he has left us a unique sketch, written many years later and performed in the 1928 production of Earl Carroll's *Vanities*. Since Fields replaced fact with fiction in his own reminiscences, I might be forgiven for quoting his only record of the boy Claude's experiences of education as provided by the State of Pennsylvania. The sketch, reposing in the box of W. C. Fields Vaudeville Sketches in the Washington Library of Congress, is a brief two-page typescript whose typed title was SCHOOL DAYS, but which Fields amended on either side in handwriting to MY SCHOOL DAYS ARE OVER:

SCENE: *Interior of schoolroom. Three children's desks and chairs strung out across stage right facing left. Platform with small table and high stool stage left. Just behind children's desks, blackboard about three feet by five feet. Cat, dog and probably childish figure of a man adorn blackboard.*

CHARACTERS:

TEACHER
PUPIL RICHARD BOLD
PUPIL GORDON DOOLEY
PUPIL BILL FIELDS

At opening children are seated. TEACHER *is on platform, rule in hand.*

TEACHER: Now children, to what kingdom does the peanut belong, animal, vegetable or mineral?

BOLD (*raising hand*): I know, teacher, animal.

TEACHER: No, you are thinking of the horse-chesnut. (*Drops rule, stoops to recover it with back to pupils.*)

(BOLD *laughs heartily.*)

TEACHER: Well, why do you laugh?

BOLD: I saw you[r] stocking garter.

TEACHER: Well I never. Leave the room. Go home and do not return to this school for a week. Do you understand, a week.

(BOLD *leaves room exit right, snickering.* TEACHER *leans over again with back to pupils and this times recovers rule.* DOOLEY *laughs unrestrainedly.*)

TEACHER: Well, what are you laughing at?

DOOLEY: I saw your bare leg.

TEACHER: Merciful heavens! What next – Gordon Dooley you leave this room and do not return for a month. Do you understand? Do not return for a month.

(DOOLEY *leaves room exit right grinning with hand over mouth.* TEACHER *mounts stool, placing her feet on rungs, arms akimbo and surveys room defiantly.* FIELDS *tries to suppress laugh by placing hand over mouth.*)

TEACHER (*yelling*): Well, what is the matter with you?

FIELDS (*starting to leave*): My school days are over.

This, incidentally, reveals the older Fields' penchant for a somewhat smutty humour, which was to get him into endless battles with the stern guardians of Hollywood censorship several years down the line. But, whatever the forbidden fruits young Fields may or may not have glimpsed in the schoolroom, he was certainly absent from the age of eleven or twelve. It is at this point that fact and fantasy begin to come into more serious conflict.

Most people who have read or heard about W. C. Fields are aware of the legend: how he left home after a violent argument with his father and never returned home for several years, living rough in the streets of Philadelphia with a gang of friends, living off his wits, mainly by stealing food from street vendors or money from Chinese laundries. The most authoritative of these accounts was that published – with Fields' full endorsement – by Alva Johnston in the *New Yorker*, in a three-part profile entitled *Legitimate Nonchalance*, in February 1935:

One afternoon, late in the administration of Benjamin Harrison, a tow-headed boy of eleven years stood on a chair just inside the kitchen door of his home on a poverty-stricken street in Philadelphia. He was waiting for his father. The white-haired lad, strong for his years, balanced over his head a heavy wooden box called a lug box. The old gentleman entered. The boy crowned him. The father fell to the floor. The son ran out of the house and never returned.

The crisis began, according to Johnston, when Pa Dukenfield stepped on a shovel, which sprang up to hit his shin, in one account, or nip him in the face, according to another. He took the shovel and hit his son on the head to warn him not to leave tools lying around. The boy waited his chance to even the score.

> The foundation for the comedian's career was laid in those days. In order to live, he had to cheat and steal. By cheating at cards and by robbing tills and fruitstands, he gained a quickness of hand which disposed him to take up juggling. Constant colds caused by exposure in childhood helped to give him his arresting voice, husky and rasping . . .

For four years, the legend goes, Fields was a big-city Huckleberry Finn, or, as Taylor colourfully put it: 'Philadelphia's most distinguished vagrant since Benjamin Franklin.' The first night he slept in a hole in the ground. Taylor even revealed the month of this momentous event – March, still the icy clutches of an east coast winter. A colleague known as 'Pot-head' Edwards (though we do not know to what circumstance he owed this appellation) passed by and was called to hoarsely from the bushes. Thus, like Oliver Twist, he found his youthful companions (though not his Fagin), who brought food and drink to his meagre hideaway. Within a week, the fugitive waif had found refuge with a group of youths who had a room over the shop of a blacksmith named Wheeler. They called themselves the Orlando Social Club, aping the real 'Social Clubs' which were common all over Philadelphia high and low society (the Penn Club, the Sketch Club, the Acorn, the Racquet Club, ad infinitum, not to speak of the Philosophical Society). These Dickensian ragamuffins terrorised the city, and Claude became the bane of shop owners and small businesses. 'The Philadelphia police,' wrote Taylor, 'came to regard him as a one-child crime wave. He was frequently seized and flung into jail, but always, he maintained, for something of which he was innocent. "They never got me for the right offence," he liked to say.' Alva Johnston had dated the Orlando Social Club later: 'At fifteen . . . he was appointed honorary member and unpaid janitor of the Orlando Social Club, which had headquarters over a wheelwright's shop. He made a bed by nailing burlap on the clubroom door and stuffing it with excelsior. Late at night he would take the door off its hinges and sleep on it, returning it to its place in the morning.'

One can see the honest and eager Johnston, leaning forward at Chasen's Restaurant in Los Angeles, taking down the reminiscences of the Great Man as he lolled back and drawled on in that inimitable voice, in between the ubiquitous Martinis. Gene Fowler, who must have heard these stories so often, set them out in his notes, but might well, had he penned the Great Man's biography himself, have applied some elementary verification. But it was not until the youngest grandson, Ronald, began talking to his Great-Aunt Adel in the later 1960s, that a different story emerged.

Some caution might have been applied much earlier, given the different and often incompatible versions of his story that Bill Fields himself related. To an interviewer for *Silver Screen*, in April 1935, he related that he had run away from home at the age of nine and claimed: 'I was fifteen when I had my first real meal; steak and fried potatoes. And I still get a thrill out of steak and fried potatoes!' You bet. But he was trying to illustrate his maxim that 'a comedian is best when he's hungry! . . . To know what laughs are made of, one must suffer. Every laugh is built on heartaches, sometimes tears.' Fields knew what these eager scribblers wanted.

As early as 1910, he was giving out the molasses, as exemplified in this unique account which turned up in the *Pittsburgh Post*:

. . . W. C. Fields, inimitable, eccentric juggler, confesses that he was born in the Quaker city. Now we know why Mr Fields exhibits so admirably the physical manifestations of what the French call 'ennui.' He ran away from home after making a declaration of war against pater familias at the age of 11. With a chum he jumped a freight train and remained on the 'blind baggage' until the railroad police gave them the high sign of '23' some place in the woolly West. He could sing a little bit and his chum could play the piano, so rather than go home and face the music the pair of them determined to scrape up a livelihood by making their own music. They appeared before various men's clubs throughout the West and passed the hat for recompense.

Coming East at Cleveland, Mr Fields' companion contracted galloping consumption and passed away. This left the young Philadelphian at 14 years of age on his uppers. Still he was too proud to go home, for he feared the paternal ire. He worked his way across East as far as Jersey and applied to the manager of a park for a trial performance at a single turn. In the meantime he had practised some at juggling and had become quite dexterous in the manipulation of tennis balls. After a great deal of persuasion and some pleading on the part of Fields, the manager, who was very measly, consented to give him a trial, provided he agreed to sort of 'grubstake' it for a week.

Fields hadn't any makeup and he had never done a single turn in his life, but he was game. He made a virtue of necessity, however, and concluded that the easiest wardrobe to procure would be that of a tramp. He held up a real 'hobo' on the streets, exchanged clothes with him, borrowed some makeup from some fellow performers at the park and introduced for the first time on any stage the idea that has since been so extensively copied – that of a tramp juggler . . .

Alas, the clipping does not contain the name of the writer who was taken in by such outrageous flim-flam. For it must be stated, quite firmly, that not only does the above account contain not one iota of the truth, but, in sum, all the stories of W. C. Fields running away from home to live as a hobo in the streets of Philadelphia during his teenage years are wholly, completely, bunk.

Common-sense can establish the few grains of truth in the myth. Clearly, young Claude, like old Claude, was becoming his own man, a pugnacious, argumentative and strong-willed character. It should surprise no one that he had rows with his father, or that his father, like almost all fathers of that day and age, clipped him over the earhole on numerous occasions, and probably for good reason. Another early tale recounts that the young Claude's experiments in juggling with his father's produce left part of the family business squashed and splattered on the floor. It is probably true that he ran away from home, more than once. The Orlando Social Club – or the Orland Social Club, as he referred to it in an off-hand tribute in the 1935 movie *Man On the Flying Trapeze* – was undoubtedly real. In an early scene of that movie, when the two burglars break in to the cellar of Fields' house, pouring two mugs of his stored applejack, they reminisce:

BURGLAR I (LEGS): What does this applejack remind you of?

BURGLAR 2 (WILLIE THE WEASEL): It reminds me of the old Orland Social Club . . . Remember how Saturday night we used to get plastered on applejack, and what we used to sing?

LEGS: 'On the banks of the Wabash, far away . . .'

[They sing]*Oh, the moonlight spreads the night upon the Wabash . . . Through the fields has come the breath of new mown hay . . . of new mown ha-ay . . .*

Indeed, in a letter published by Ronald Fields in 1973, Bill Fields writes on 23 June 1938 from Bel-Air, California, to a Mr Thos. A. Hunt of 5120 Arch Street, Philadelphia, who wrote to him following his successful radio broadcasts, mentioning some financial distress, and to whom Fields is sending a cheque for 'twenty-five smackers in case you can use it', continuing:

I have never forgotten the old days at the Orland Social Club, over Mr Wright's wheelwright shop (I think that was his name) up at the shady trees, when you had me elected janitor without dues; when I slept in the back room on an improvised bed made by removing one of the doors and using several bags of hay to pinch-hit for a box-springs mattress. Those were the happy days. Of all my friends – Eddie Tishner, Jack Sparks, Charlie Tishner, Dick Gamble, Martin Quinn, the Kanes, the McCaffreys, the Garrs, Eddie Roach, Feet Leibie, etc. – you are the most vivid in my memory.

I hope you are well and happy.

Sincerely, your old tramp friend,

Whitey

Those were happy days. The reader should be appraised, at this point, of one of the more startling discoveries of the real, rather than the mythical, William Claude Dukenfield-Fields – his apparently photographic memory. This, despite contradictory tales concerning his inability to memorise scripts, presumably those he thought were too dumb to memorise. In his personal letters, particularly his later ones, he displays powerful recall of names and events of decades before. Here then are the names of the authentic Orland Social Club, the rascal boys of Philadelphia – and no mention, alas, of 'Pot-head' Edwards. This introduces us to something we will find characteristic, if surprising, given the myth of the loner and misanthrope, of Fields' life from vegetable cart to Hollywood: the existence of a close-knit circle of friends, mostly male, with whom he spent much of his time, whom he loved and who loved him, and who were the only persons who, in their period, really knew the man, not the invention.

One need only apply a little broad common-sense to the legend to realize it cannot hold water. Philadelphia, as we have seen, was not the kind of wide open city as New York, with its wild, deadly juvenile street gangs. A well-policed and stern metropolis, it had its crime waves, brothels, saloons and taverns. But it does not make any sense to assume that a lower-middle class youth like Claude Dukenfield could live a life of consistent petty crime, punctuated by arrests and jail, without being assigned to the reformatory, or at least leaving a substantial dent in the family memory about his felonious past. Cuffs on the ear by burly Irish beat cops may well have occurred, but led no further.

The true tale appears to be this: having left school, young Claude's family, particularly his grandmother, who was his chief support when he had rows with his father, found him several jobs commensurate with his age and social position. His first job, according to James Smart, was assisting the owner of a neighbourhood cigar store. Smart quotes a Fields memory of his first boss, in one of his rare veracious moods: 'He only carried one brand of cigar. It sold for three cents. If a customer asked for a ten-cent cigar, he was handed one which sold for three cents. "The customer is always right," my boss would say, "so never allow him to be disappointed."'

His next job, according to all accounts, and verified by photographs of the cash boys of the shop, was at Strawbridge and Clothier's Department Store. This great store, founded by Quakers, was known for the amenities, like lunchrooms and loan associations, which it provided for its employees, though in the early 1890s it still drew the line at affording equal opportunities for blacks. As a cash boy, young Claude's job involved him carrying change from counter to counter, a responsibility which, he later claimed, vied too heavily with his larcenous proclivities at the time. 'I did everything possible to get myself discharged,' Smart quotes him. 'I walked through a skylight three times with the hope that it would make the owners irritated enough to discharge me. Instead, they mended the skylight and congratulated me upon my escape from death.'

The fourth time, Fields related, he walked through the skylight and fell on the general manager's head. The good Quakers still wished him to carry on provided he apologised to his inadvertent victim. He refused and was able to walk away from the job.

The records of Strawbridge and Clothier's do state that Claude W. Dukenfield quit, but also that soon after he left the job it was eliminated by automation. As Smart relates, the cash boys were replaced by pneumatic tubes. Next, Claude found employment as a scullery boy in a Chestnut Street oyster saloon. Oysters were, it appears, a craze on the eastern coast of the United States from the 1870s through the gay 1890s, as they were said to aid virility. The specific influence of these crustaceous morsels upon the young man's tender libido has never, to my knowledge, been studied, and I leave it as a fertile field for aspiring scholars.

Claude's break with his father, according to Smart, occurred around this time. But, according to family accounts, there is no evidence to suggest anything other than sporadic spats, with the boy running off to stay with his grandmother, or one of his uncles, for a few days, thereafter returning home to his mother. The later ice wagon and newspaper delivery jobs all appear part of this pattern.

The bottom line is that Claude W. Dukenfield lived with his parents – albeit in a state of tension – until the age of eighteen. But long before this, he had already alighted upon the recreation which would become an obsession, and then an escape route, and a career . . .

Chapter 4
'Jugglers In Their Dreams . . .'

3 The young man in his twenties, set to conquer the world.

The traditional account has it that young Claude Dukenfield sneaked into the variety theatre one day to watch an act called the Byrne Brothers juggle. This, too, is part of the myth. There was an act called the Byrne Brothers, who performed in Philadelphia at the Peoples' Theatre in October 1893, but they were not jugglers. Their act was a 'mechanical' music show entitled 'Eight Bells', with 'agile characterizations' and 'enjoyable added songs and dances'. Most probably Bill

Fields was recalling his very first outing to the theatre, aged thirteen. The juggling bug bit some two years later, as Fields recounted, in a typical report, in the press book of *Man on the Flying Trapeze, circa* 1935:

I was fifteen years old when the juggling urge first asserted itself. I was watching a vaudeville performance from the top of the gallery and the juggler came out to do his stuff. A glow came over me – a glow that still lingers in the famous Fields nose. I went out and started practicing and, believe it or not, it wasn't long after that I managed to get a job juggling on the stage . . .

Press books, of course, are notoriously unreliable sources of real information, since we now know some of the articles bylined 'W. C. Fields' were in fact written by Paramount's publicity department, mainly by Fields' favourite publicist, Teet Carle. In another publicity piece, for *The Big Broadcast of 1938*, Fields (allegedly) wrote:

I still carry scars on my legs from those early attempts at juggling. I'd balance a stick on my toe, toss it into the air, and try to catch it again on my toe. Hour by hour, the damn thing would bang against my shinbones. I'd work till the tears were streaming down my face. But I kept on practising, and bleeding, until I perfected the trick. I don't believe that Mozart, Liszt, Paderewski, or Kreisler ever worked any harder than I did.

In contradiction, Fields told another story entirely to the Sunday newspaper, *The Sun*, in Australia, in 1914: 'I was born with a fatal facility for juggling things. It was no trouble for me to juggle and to learn tricks.' Bill's son, Claude Junior, quoting this, related that one day, little William Claude was reclining under a Pennsylvania sickle tree, when a pear fell, and then another. He began juggling them skilfully, and 'from then on, any vegetable, fruit, ball or article that could withstand juggling was subjected to W. C.'s endeavours. While he was helping his father in his duties and business, he would indulge in juggling some of the fresh produce, much to the dismay and anger of his father.'

This Newtonesque account places the juggling bug much earlier in young Claude's development, possibly as early as age nine or ten. However it was, there is no doubt that anything close to a professional standard could only be reached by obsessive practise and willpower. 'I used any articles which lent themselves to juggling and made up my own routine,' Fields was quoted later, in another press release, for *Million Dollar Legs*, 1932. 'I evolved one trick with small cups on the ends of rods, catching small balls in the cups and continuing to juggle meanwhile. I made the rods from broom sticks and took the cups from the oil burners in my rooming house. I drilled holes in the latter and nailed them to the broom sticks. Without money to buy tights, I had to do a tramp act with my old, tattered clothes.'

The variety stage that was beckoning to the young reluctant fruit and veg heir was, as we have seen, undergoing a great transformation. Philadelphia was dotted with variety theatres old and new, the largest being Gilmore's Grand Central Theatre. There was Hashim's Grand Opera House, at Broad Street and Montgomery, or Enochs' Varieties, a converted church, at 7th Street, below Arch: Grand Family Matinees every Tuesday and Friday, at 2 o'clock, sharp. Night prices, in the gallery, 10 cents. Here, young Claude might have sat, gobbling candy, goggling at a full bill of robust novelties, including:

MISS MINNIE HALL,
IN HER UNAPPROACHABLE MALE IMPERSONATIONS.

THE GREAT KERNELLS – HARRY AND JOHN –
IN THEIR ORIGINAL IRISH SPECIALITY – THE O'HOOLAHANS.

BLANCHE DALEY'S FLAG SONG.

BURLEY AND MARR – IN THEIR CELEBRATED ETHIOPIAN
SPECIALTIES.

SERIO-COMIC SONG – MISS MILLIE LA FONT.

FANCY DANCE, ZINGARELLA – MISS LIZZIE WALKER.

THE EVENING'S ENTERTAINMENT WILL CONCLUDE WITH THE
THRILLING SENSATIONAL BORDER DRAMA ENTITLED

RED DICK!

RED DICK, THE TERROR OF THE PLAINS – MR JOSEPH HURLEY
BEAR TAIL, AN INDIAN CHIEF – MR J. M. BRADFORD
ROLAND HOWARD, A HALF BREED – MR LOU FRAZER
PETE, A LIVELY COON – MR WILLIAM MARR
MR MORGAN – MR P. WALLIS
CLARA WELLS, FLOWER OF THE BORDER – MISS MINNIE HALL
MRS MORGAN – MISS LINDA REVERE

Might such a finale have planted in a young boy's mind the seeds of a Western melodrama that might bloom into celluloid forty-five years later? We are as entitled as anyone else to speculate. But even were he only to concentrate on the jugglers, there would be an embarrassment of riches. Touring the circuits were Nello, Zimmer, Drawee, Radford and Winchester Comedy Jugglers, Doll and Burden Club Jugglers, Hale and Frances, Jugglers and Hoop Rollers. There was Charles T. Aldritch, already building a strong reputation, and O. K. Sato, Comedy Juggler, who performed in clown costume and sailor's cap. There was James Harrigan (not to be confused with 'Ned' Harrigan the playwright), billed as 'The First Tramp Juggler'. There was Sparrow, 'the Mad Juggler', whose act was famed as the sloppiest ever presented: he would throw melons or pumpkins in the air, miss them and catch them in the face. He would exhibit the same incompetence with goldfish bowls, eggs and turnips, performing in a linoleum dress suit and a rubber shirt front. At the end of his act the stage was littered with smashed fruit and vegetables and broken items, then he would walk away to great applause.

But the greatest of all jugglers, whom young Claude, according to the Fields family, dreamed to emulate, was the legendary Paul Cinquevalli, Prince of Jugglers, who did indeed perform around the east coast cities during 1895 and 1896. This great showman, who later toured the European circuits at the same time as William Claude Fields, was also a strong man, and a moustachioed dandy. The son of a Polish miller who had fallen from the circus high wire in his youth, Cinquevalli's act included juggling with plates, cannon balls, umbrellas, tables and chairs which he would toss up and catch to balance on his chin. His most difficult trick, he confessed to the correspondent of the *New York Dramatic Mirror* in 1896, was 'the one in which I balance two billiard balls on the end of a cue. It took me several months to perfect.' And cue the young Claude, goggling . . . The *North American Review* of January 1902 gushed:

Ask any boy you meet just what it is that makes Cinquevalli differ from other jugglers, even as Mark Twain's jumping frog outclassed all the frogs in Calaveras County. He'll explain the thing to you, and he'll add indignantly – if you make the comparison and he knows his Mark Twain – that Dan'l was a fraud who could win only when his rivals were heavily handicapped, but that Cinquevalli does the things other jugglers in their dreams think of doing.

To wish to compete with such effervescence was real ambition. But one could not think small in vaudeville. By the mid-1890s there were over four hundred acts jostling and cavorting about the proliferating stages. There were trapeze acts; sand jigs; egg dances (dancing between some twenty eggs placed strategically about the stage); Blatz the Human Fish, who ate a banana, read a newspaper, went to sleep and played a trombone under water; Hernandez, the guitar-playing contortionist, who could sink his head into his shoulders; Captain McCrosson, who appeared soon after the Civil War, in a Zouave uniform, twirling his rifle, bayonet point down, on the palm of his hand. There was the Cat Piano, whose live cats in wire cages seemed to miaow the 'Miserere' when their tails were pulled (in reality the performer did the miaowing). Polite Vaudeville was slowly divesting itself of these worthies, but some, like Captain Spaulding, who ate molten lead and lit gunpowder on his tongue, became standards well into the 1900s on both sides of the Atlantic. Billed as 'The Man Who Is Hotter Than Vesuvius', he must have lent his name, by creative osmosis, to the famous African explorer portrayed by Groucho Marx thirty years later, on stage and screen. And, already in 1894, there was Sandow, compered by young Florenz Ziegfeld, billed as 'Physically perfect. Acknowledged by Anatomists to be the strongest in the world.'

To a young stage-struck boy, it was the equivalent of a lad in the 1930s looking up at the dazzle of Jimmy Cagney, Edward G. Robinson, Clark Gable, Joan Crawford, Bette Davis. So if young Claude Dukenfield wanted to escape from hearth and home to show-biz fame, the variety theatre was the only road to glory.

Dreaming of Cinquevalli, and juggling his cups and turnips, young Claude still had to eke out a living. After the department store, the lore goes, came a job racking balls in a pool hall, which taught the boy a whole raft of new tricks, watching the hustlers and their moves, perhaps practising the Prince of Jugglers' billiard cue trick or the routines of Weber and Fields. He learned trick pool shots, and, also around this time, developed a trick with cigar boxes he picked out of cigar store dump bins. There was also the legendary period as a newsboy, developing his fear of vicious dogs. He later claimed that, even in Hollywood, dogs would snarl and bite at him, recognising the young tramp inside. An apocryphal sales trick is said to be his habit of hefting his pile of papers, crying out: 'Five men swindled! Five men swindled!' Then, when someone bought a copy, changing the call to 'Six men swindled! Six men swindled!'

After the newsround came another job arranged by his grandmother, as an assistant to the local iceman. The Philadelphia sleuths claim this worthy's name was Andy Donaldson, but Fields later claimed he was called 'Gomer Wheatley'. Fields' period on the ice wagon provided him another stock villain, and the irascible iceman is a character who pops up more than once in his later skits and movies. In one of his early sound shorts, *The Dentist*, 1932, his daughter even wants to marry the iceman, a matter of ultimate shame which can only be countered by the argument, 'We're going to get a fridgidaire.'

Young Claude's motivation for taking up a life in show business is subject, of course, to the usual controversy. The legend has it that the young boy was congenitally unprepared for any metier which would involve an early rising. His sister Adel told her great-nephew Ronald that Claude hated getting up in the morning. Fields himself encouraged this view, telling another interviewer, Helen Hanemann, in a 1926 issue of *Motion Picture*: 'It's been a case of pure laziness. I went on the stage as a kid of eleven – I'd run away from home, you see, and I never went back – so that I could sleep late in the mornings. Now I'm in the movies partly because I've changed and hate going to bed late.' Helen Hanemann called her article: 'HE HATED ALARM CLOCKS: And Proves That Old Saying About The Early Bird Is Not to Be Taken Too Seriously.'

Perhaps Claude was extrapolating from one of his later colleagues, Tom Hearn, who was billed as 'the lazy juggler'. There seems very little that was lazy about this young man who was determined to make good and definitely not follow in his father's footsteps. His first professional engagement as a juggler has been subject to the usual scholarly squabbles, but all accounts agree that young Claude was casting about in his mid-teens to earn some money at the bottom end of show business. In a later article about this early stage, he mentions a mentor, one Bill Daily, whom he describes as 'an expert shell manipulator'. Fields relates:

Those who knew him well referred to him as The Professor. His paraphernalia and luggage consisted of three half walnut shells and a small piece of rolled dough which he referred to as the 'little pea'. Mr Daily above all things shunned conventionalities and luxuries. So early one rather perky autumn about four or five o'clock, I accompanied him to Wayne Junction, a suburban stop on the outskirts of Philadelphia for New York bound trains. As the train stopped to take on milk the Professor and myself climbed surreptitiously up the steps of the blind baggage just behind the tender. Everything went well until we reached the bridge across the Delaware River . . . [missing segment] As we came upon the bridge, the fireman, the engineer, or the door slinger dropped the scoop into the trough and we took 'water on the fly'. The tank overflowed and the Professor and myself received an unexpected cold shower – or shall I say deluge.

One might pause here to take note that, while this account has a more authentic ring to it than Fields' usual wish-wash, this exact scene with a train occurs in his first silent feature-length film, *Sally of the Sawdust*, directed by D. W. Griffith in 1925, based on Dorothy Donnelly's stage play of 1923, *Poppy*, which was his breakthrough starring role in the theatre. I cannot tell whether this scene was written at Fields' own instigation (as much of his character in that play, 'The Professor', Eustace McGargle, was indeed conceived for him), or whether Fields, in hindsight, blurred his fiction, once again, with his life. We know there was a real Bill Daily (or Dailey), who might well have been the inspiration for the seminal 'Professor McGargle', due to his expertise with the shell scam, or, as it was called, 'The Old Army Game'. Dailey worked, in later years, for the Reading Railroad and Fields wrote him a number of letters many years after, recalling that grandmother Felton wanted to have him arrested, as she blamed him for losing young Claude his job on the ice wagon. 'I might still have that job,' Fields wrote, 'or a better one, or even have my own wagon and route by this time.' At any rate, Fields proceeds to describe the outcome of his early escapade in typically florid tones:

Soaked to the buff, the Professor and I disembarked just beyond the station. We ran for a while hoping the heat of our bodies would dry our clothes. We then collected breakfast from the front porches, consisting of bread, rolls, butter and milk, that the considerate milkman and baker had deposited for the residents. Still chilly and damp we headed for the fairgrounds. The gates were not open at the early hour so we climbed the fence and waited for the sun which grudgingly put in its appearance. Was it cold? Did I suffer? Did my one-dollar pair of pants shrink? My shirt and bedraggled tie did not enhance my appearance. My abhorrence and loathing for water fructificated in my receptive adolescent brain. In retrospect the sufferings of the Noah family, the Johnstown flood and other nefarious pranks water had played kaleidoscoped through my immature brain . . .

Fields was playing the 'shill', or bait, for the suckers, or 'gilpins', while Dailey stood on a box and called out: 'It's the old army game. One will get you two, two will get you four, four will get you eight. Find the little pea . . . A boy can play as well as a man . . .' The shill, trying the first time, walks off with some cash as the real suckers step up. But a 'gildersleeve', or policeman, 'arrived on the scene with the stealth of a Brahma bull . . . The Professor was placed in durance vile and I claim to this day that if it hadn't been for the water I would still be making an honest living as a shill or might have had my own shells and pea by this time and been in business for myself. I took an oath then never to drink water from that day on.'

On second thoughts, this gallant tale fits in too well with Fields' fond routines recounting his fear and loathing of the common H_2O. But it does appear that Bill Dailey did act as a manager to secure the young Claude some appearances around the city, or in outlying towns. James Smart of Philadelphia placed an early stunt, the 'great umbrella caper', in 1895, when Claude was fifteen. (As Smart places the later Batley Hall 'Benefit', which we can now trace to 1898, in 1897, and if Claude was indeed inspired by Cinquevalli around 1895, perhaps we can push the umbrella caper forward a year, to age sixteen.) Engaged to do his juggling act at a Methodist Church strawberry festival, on a rainy day, Claude and an assistant, a friend known as 'Troubles' (they probably all were) were turned away because the cigar boxes, Claude's favourite prop, were considered sinful, as smoking was not allowed in the church. Having convinced the stern authorities that these were just empty vessels, the performance proceeded, but payment was not forthcoming. Claude and Troubles therefore availed themselves of thirty-one umbrellas and sold them in a local pawn shop to buy steak dinners. Perhaps this was the 'first real meal' he told Silver Screen about many years later – the first proper recompense for his art.

Certainly the cigar-box trick appears to be the first proper 'act' that William Claude Dukenfield devised. It became a staple of his routine, first in burlesque, then on the vaudeville stage, on both sides of the Atlantic. The act was performed in New York; in Toronto; in San Francisco; in Sydney, Australia; in Cape Town, South Africa; in

London; Paris; Berlin; Milan; Brussels; Madrid. It turns up in fragment in Fields' silent films (*Sally of the Sawdust, Two Flaming Youths*), and in whole, preserved – in a later version – for ever, finally, in *The Old Fashioned Way*, in 1934. It was written about in articles and reviews, but its best description is inevitably Fields' own, which he published in a curious volume first printed in 1902, in London, called *The Magician's Handbook*, compiled by one 'Selbit', a stage wizard whose real name was Percy Thomas Tibbles. Fields contributed two short essays to this book, the other being 'A New Hat and Cigar Effect'. But here is 'The Great Cigar-Box Trick', reprinted for the first time since 1904. Ladies and gentlemen – IT BAFFLES SCIENCE!

THE GREAT CIGAR-BOX TRICK
BY WM. C. FIELDS, THE COMEDY JUGGLER.

Although this trick has been one of the greatest successes of my act, it is really surprising that very few people have caught on to it, and consequently there are not many performers introducing the same trick upon the stage. Why this is I do not know, especially when considering that the experiment possesses an advantage over many others, inasmuch as the performer nearly always brings the house down with appreciation for his almost miraculous dexterity, and afterwards secures a laugh so hearty as to nearly shake the foundations of the theatre when the audience see how they have been sold.

The effect appears somewhat as follows: labouring, or pretending to labour, under the burden of carrying five cigar boxes, the performer drags himself to the centre of the stage; when the weight appears too heavy the boxes are dropped to the floor, upon which they scatter in all directions. After gathering them together, the juggler packs the boxes all square and rests them on the table, while he advances to the front and makes a speech, announcing 'that after years and years of continual practice, and probably longer than that! – but perhaps the audience would rather see the trick? Oh, very well then – I'll show it to you.' So saying, the performer brings the boxes to the front, and after referring again to 'years of continual study and thought', tosses them into the air and catches the whole five balanced upon each other's end, making quite a tall pile as they steady down. Allowing the applause which is sure to greet the feat to reach its highest point, the juggler then turns round to bow his accomplishments; but while doing so, quite forgets to bestow any attention upon the balanced boxes, which consequently lose their equilibrium and tumble backwards. However, they do not fall to the floor, neither do they separate, and the smile of the audience as they see that the boxes are in some manner joined together, would take more pages to describe than I am entitled to occupy with my contribution to this book . . .

The secret of the trick, Fields related, was to pass a string through a dummy stack of boxes, and then, by sleight of hand, to substitute them for the loose stack:

. . . the left hand meanwhile being slipped into the loop and held as far away from the boxes as the length of cord will permit. At the proper moment the left hand approaches the boxes in order to give slack to the cord, and then the top four are tossed upwards, the fifth being held tightly, the left hand then sharply pulling the cord away, which naturally brings all the boxes tightly together on their ends, and holds them there.

The next method is the one I use myself, and is, to my mind, a much better and more artistic way of presenting the trick. If this method be adopted, a little extra preparation will have to be made. Each box will have to be drilled in both narrow ends except the top and bottom ones, which are only provided with a hole in one end. Across the undrilled side pieces of the first and fifth boxes a wooden bar is glued through which passes a very strong piece of elastic cord, penetrating in its journey each of the intermediate boxes. Now they are stacked together as described for the first method, and the preparation will be quite clear if reference is made to the explanatory drawing. Now the working of the effect will be readily understood. This stack of boxes is brought to the front, the bottom one gripped tightly and the rest thrown sharply in the air, the elastic recoiling bringing them together in the desired manner, the next illustration showing how the elastic works. Having explained everything that needs an explanation for the accomplishment of this taking trick, I trust that many jugglers will now be able to add it to their repertoire.

The above is the first extant writing of W. C. Fields. It contains several interesting clues to our quest for the 'true' nature of the man. First, one notes the elegance of the delivery, given that we are speaking here of a man with three or four years of formal education, though we can infer that some editing was done to standardise Fields' essays with the rest of the contributions to Selbit's handbook. It has been commonly assumed that Fields began his self-education on the road, as a showperson, particularly when he journeyed abroad and discovered that many of his fellow performers, particularly the English, were widely read and well-informed. But clearly a fair deal of self-education had already taken place.

At this stage, we can also see, the young juggler was, perhaps naively, generous in revealing his trade secrets to fellow performers. Later on, we know, Fields became, like almost all professional performers, obsessed with protecting his material. Comedians in particular stole shamelessly from each other – and Fields himself was not averse to this, as we shall see. But vaudevillians were plagued by rivals who pirated their jokes, moved to another town and delivered them as their own before the originator arrived, only to find a stony audience muttering darkly, or fondling rotten fruit.

The third conclusion to be drawn from this piece is that young Claude realized, early on, that whatever his natural skill as a juggler, he could not conquer the world by juggling alone. Try as he might, he was not Cinquevalli. He had to have his own angle. As he said, in 1935, to his interviewer, Maude Cheatham:

> The first thing I remember figuring out for myself was that I wanted to be a definite personality. I had heard a man say he liked a certain fellow because he always was the same dirty damn so and so. You know, like Larsen in Jack London's 'Sea Wolf'. He was detestable, yet you admired him because he remained true to type. Well, I thought that was a swell idea so I developed a philosophy of my own, *be your type!* I determined that whatever I was, I'd *be* that, I wouldn't teeter on the fence.

In a 1931 interview with Bernard Sobel for a book on the burlesque era, Fields dated this budding thought to his days with Irwin's Burlesquers – in 1899 – when he decided: 'I thought I'd try to develop personality. Then it wouldn't matter whether my tricks or my sketches were so good. So long as I have this personality, I can go along and continue. I wouldn't have to learn different tricks and work the muscles. I was lazy. I thought I would develop a style of comedy and hope that the audience would like it . . .'

The decision was of crucial importance. It was the principle which would transform the young juggler into someone else, a distinct, wholly invented individual, who was eventually to have a new name, a new past, a new history, and who would supplant his creator as powerfully as any Hyde would supplant his personal Jekyll.

The final revealing clue we can deduce from the Cigar-Box essay is that, from the start, Bill had a patter to go with the juggling. Later, as he honed his performances abroad to non-English speaking audiences, Fields developed his act as a pantomime. Nevertheless, there was a patter, never formally recorded, whenever he performed before a British or American audience, until, at a later stage, he came to bill himself officially as 'The Silent Humorist'. The only hint of its content comes in the memoirs of a British vaudevillian, W. Buchanan-Taylor, who knew Fields in the English music halls. He wrote: 'He always talked to his "properties". He would reprimand a particular ball which had not come to his hand accurately, whip his battered silk hat for not staying on his head . . . mutter weird and unintelligible expletives to his cigar when it missed his mouth . . .'

Indeed, we can picture the bold twenty-year-old, as he strode on to a stage, in his tramp make-up and ragged false beard, divesting himself of a moth-eaten fur coat and getting to the business at hand in his shirt sleeves. That twangy developing drawl, announcing, in the patter learned from so many hustlers, 'Professors', shell-game hucksters and 'museum' barkers –

'Ladies and gentlemen . . .'

We can only imagine . . . But if we turn the pages back, to 1898, we can at last discover the moment when conjecture ceases, and the juggler steps, like all good heroes, out of guesswork and into proper history.

Chapter 5
'Two Will Get You Four, Four Will Get You Eight . . .'– From Boy Juggler to Star Comedian

4 'Mr William C. Fields – Tramp Juggler; we think you will like him . . .'

From the month of January, 1898, William Claude Dukenfield began compiling a scrapbook of the professional life of his creation, W. C. Fields. The scrapbooks proliferated, growing fatter and fatter as the years went by, and Claude continued to paste in, with meticulous rigour, every news clipping, every playbill and programme, even steamship itineraries of his wanderings. In later years, he used a clippings agency to supply him with the voluminous movie reviews, probably stuck in the books by his long-term secretary, Magda Michael (alias Mickey Mouse). But in the early years, the thumb prints on the cuttings must be Claude Dukenfield's own. These scrapbooks, now zealously preserved by The Great Man's grandsons, are an invaluable record both of the man and the era. There are gaps, and several missing years, but where the record has been kept it provides a proven rebuttal of the wilder assumptions about the juggler's early days.

The first item, on the first page of the first scrapbook, is a small playbill from the 'Natatorium Hall – Broad Street above Columbia Avenue'. It is dated precisely: 'Thursday Evening, January 13, 1898.' Just above 'Miss Emma Otterback – Soprano Solo – Comic', is listed 'Wm. C. Felton – Comic Juggling.' Next to it, on the same page, is a second item:

Programme of the First Grand Concert and Hop
of Lady Meade Lodge, No. 88 Association.
Peabody Hall, Friday Evening,
Eighth and Eneu Sts, March 11th, 1898 . . .
Recitations – Sentimental Song –
The German Barber (Sketch), Messrs Schroder and Hecker,
Tramp Juggler – Mr Wm. C. Fields.

For those who still like to think that Claude Dukenfield ran away from Philadelphia at the age of eleven and never returned until he was an established performer, here is proof that the juggler's very first professional appearances were in local, Philadelphian Masonic halls. In the first instance, he has taken the name of his mother, Kate Felton. In the second, he has already adopted the stage name that will carry him on from that point. We do not know if his shell-game 'manager', Bill Dailey, was involved in these early shows, as legend has it. But on 29 April 1898, Claude was again performing. This time it was at the 'Third Grand Concert of Manhattan Athletic Club', to be held at the Batley Hall, 2748 Germantown Avenue, under the curious heading of 'H. Fields – Tramp

Juggler'. He was appearing together with: 'Kensington's Favourite – Wm. Higgins, the Lockwoods – in their funny act, J. Woolen – Champion Bag Puncher of America', and 'the Irish Comedians, Mountney and Neff'. A 'Characteristic Song' was to be sung by Miss Katie Kewick and 'Scientific Boxing Exhibitions' were to be given by 'Joe Siddons of Philadelphia versus Lew Remlein of Allentown'.

In an immediate follow-up, Claude arranged a familiar stage ploy, a 'benefit', at the Batley Hall, to raise money to enable him to pursue his career outside the confines of Philly. According to legend, Claude was billed at this engagement as 'Whitey, the Boy Wonder'. The programme in the scrapbook, however, lists 'Select Vaudeville Entertainment tendered to William C. Fields (Tramp Juggler)'. The date was Monday evening, 13 June 1898. Admission was 15 cents. Entertainment was given by one Geo. G. Meade, 'Circle No. 5, B.U.H. of F.' And so, in an ironic twist, young Claude was helped to leave Philadelphia by the Friendly Societies of the very city he was to lampoon all his life.

The Batley Hall Benefit raised, according to one Fields account, $98. Papa Dukenfield added $2 to the take so that he could buy a new suit of clothes. These included a pair of checkered pants, pointed-toed shoes, a straw hat and a 'three inch Piccadilly collar'. Clad in his well-gotten gains, William Claude Dukenfield departed, at last, on the grand tour of his life.

In Taylor's biography, an entire vista is spread forth of the young boy's early days on the road. 'He tramped to the booking offices, he starved, he froze, and he became so threadbare he was ashamed to ask for jobs.' At one point, we are told, he took a job with a circus, as a peg boy, working with the roustabouts wielding their mauls. His next assignment was to service the elephants, and dispose of their prodigious waste. He did not get on with the recalcitrant pachyderms, but the job enabled him to learn the lore of the sawdust, and brought him nearer and nearer to New York.

As usual, there is not a thread of evidence to support this jaunty tale. Weber and Fields did a stint with a circus, which nearly killed them, but W. C. Fields almost certainly did not. Within weeks, if not days, of his Batley Hall benefit, young Claude obtained his first professional booking, at Flynn and Grant's Park, also known as Plymouth Park, in Norristown, Pennsylvania. Fields himself often placed this gig much earlier, in keeping with his child prodigy tale. In an article he wrote in 1928, for *Theatre* Magazine, entitled *From Boy Juggler to Star Comedian*, he wrote that it was only a twenty-five cent trolley ride from Philadelphia. His salary was five dollars a week. Fields wrote:

> I got the five dollars, but I had to pay a dollar and a half commission to the booking-office, and it cost me four dollars to ride back and forth to the park. I was rooming in a club over a blacksmith's shop, and foolishly came into Philadelphia every night to sleep in my old haunt.

More likely he returned each night to Ma Dukenfield or to Grandma Felton. In a later article about the Plymouth Park booking he commented: 'Norristown is famed for its insane asylum.' This was Claude's stepping stone to his first proper job outside Pennsylvania, at Fortescue's Pavilion, in Atlantic City. In his talk with Bernard Sobel, for Sobel's history of burlesque, *Burleycue*, Fields also elaborated on this story: 'I came to Atlantic City,' Bill explains, 'by way of Morristown [*sic*] Pennsylvania. I was a kid then and had a little job in an amusement park. Bickel and Watson were on the same bill, and they were doing a German act.'

The programme in the scrapbook, however, clipped from the *Plymouth Park Gazette*, lists Price and Watson, 'Great Dutch Character Comedians and laugh producers', as well as Miss Flora Parker, 'America's youngest and most charming soubrette', Dick Leggett, 'Eccentric Character Comedian, Grotesque and Long Wooden Shoe Dancer', who presented something called 'The Growing Bog, like buckwheat cakes, he rises before your very eyes[!]' as well as an Afterpiece entitled 'Lunatic Asylum'. W. C. Fields is listed as 'The Wonderful Tramp Juggler, in Original, Intricate and Difficult Feats.' The date is 1 August 1898. The proprietor and Manager is listed as one J. Fortescue – clearly the link to Fields next engagement, in Atlantic City, New Jersey.

It is at this summer beach spot that another of W. C. Fields' enduring legends was born. Let us allow him to relate the tale in his own words to Bernard Sobel:

> I worked on the stage at this place which was a kind of restaurant. There was no admission. Patrons would buy a glass of beer for five cents and the sale helped pay our expenses. Business would get pretty bad after a while so it would be necessary for them to take me out and drown me. This was more simple than it sounds.

I would swim out to the ocean, and when I got out some distance, I'd holler 'Help', go under, come up for a moment, spitting a lot of water. Then two or three men, all plants, waiting on the shore, would swim out to me, battle around me while everyone would run up to see what the excitement was. 'Someone's drowning,' they'd all begin shouting, and start a ballyhoo. Then when the crowd was big enough the men would drag me in. I'd be spitting water here and there, and sometimes one of the bystanders would get a faceful . . . Next, they'd throw me across a table and begin working over me. But by this time the band would be playing, and the funny Irishman would walk out on the stage. So they'd all begin to look at him and forget about me. Finally I'd get up weakly and slouch away. Those still standing around would say, 'Oh, he'll be all right. He's all right. Lets take a look at the show now that we're here.'

This was a tale Fields repeated again and again, with greater and greater relish, claiming it as yet another of the original traumas which caused his lifelong aversion to water. But Fields himself slipped up, in a couple of places, letting the cat out of the bag about 'Fortescue's Pavilion' in the *Theatre* article of 1928:

The things we did were quite laughable as I look back on them. A favorite way to fill up the place was to work a fake rescue. One of the performers would go out in the surf, pretend to be caught in the undertow, and shout for help. We would all be ready, rush in the water and drag the rescued person into the pavilion. Naturally the crowd followed, and if it was a woman we rescued the crowd was particularly large. Once inside they bought drinks and we were supposed to be entertaining enough to keep them there.

In other words, it was not only Claude who pretended to drown, the girls in the show also took their turn, and the whole trick may not have been tried more than a couple of times anyhow. Thus are great mythologies born.

The summer of 1898 was, nevertheless, the crucial turning point in the Boy Juggler's career. The first official notice of the new artist's profession appeared in the *New York Clipper* on 1 October 1898, which announced that at the Gaeity Theatre in Albany, New York, James C. Fulton's burlesque show, the Monte Carlo Girls, appeared: 'The olio included the Fulton Bros., Wm. C. Fields, Eva Swinburne, W. T. Bryant.' The *Clipper* had reported, on 3 September, that the Monte Carlo Girls would open their season on 19 September, under the management of James C. Fulton.

The transformation of Dukenfield into Fields was, by now, complete. Bill Fields claimed later that he had tried simply to clip the 'Duken' off the 'Field', but that bookers kept sticking on the 's', so he gave up arguing. But the fact that 'Fields' was a familiar theatrical name clearly did him no great harm. Vaudeville had the illustrious Lew Fields (partner of Weber), Happy Fanny Fields, Joe Fields, comedian and impersonator, and Al G. Fields, the famous minstrel show actor. 'Fields', not Field, might well have been a calculated choice. Future events will show that such calculation, a hard-edged business sense, was to be characteristic of Fields throughout his working life. From Batley Hall onwards, William Claude attended very carefully to business. Nothing that happened to him was haphazard. This was not the impression he wished to give to the world, but it was, behind the mask, a firm principle from this point on.

Claude's change of name, according to family research, was only formalised legally by the Court of Common Pleas in Philadelphia on 13 May 1908. And so, despite the legends of total family estrangement, Fields remained only a stage pseudonym for the first ten years of the young juggler's career, while William Claude Dukenfield still lived on, behind the nom-de-theatre.

W. C. Fields related his passage to his first regular troupe to Bernard Sobel, in 1931. He had befriended at Plymouth Park a man called William Bryant, who was half of an act called Bryant and Richmond. It was Bryant who persuaded him to join him in a show called the 'Monte Carlo Girls':

> When the show was set we started off with just enough money to get to the first town. I did my juggling act and also played several parts. We showed at one night stands. The first week we didn't get any money, nor the second, nor the third. In fact, the whole time I was with this show we didn't get any salaries. But we were on the lookout for the money just the same. We used to stand watch in the hotel all night in front of the manager's door to find out if he was going to duck. We had a rumor – there were always such rumors – that he was going to skip with the twenty-five dollars or whatever it was, and go to New York and leave us flat. I can remember one night, it was my turn to stand guard. Being a kid, I was so sleepy that I thought if I could get one hour's sleep I wouldn't care if the whole world came to an end. For hours I sat in the dark narrow corridor of that old hotel staring at the manager's door under the faint little gas jet, and trying to keep awake.

Fields is constantly saying 'I was only a kid' in this interview, though he dates the events correctly, to 1898, when he was eighteen years old. Records on the Monte Carlo Girls are sparse. This was not a show that set the world on fire. Nevertheless, at the New Mountain Theatre in Altoona, Pennsylvania, in November 1898, the *Clipper* noted, 'they had originally booked for only three days, but attendance was such as warranted their remaining the rest of the week'.

The programmes in the Fields scrapbook reveal a show typical of that period of burlesque. Its full name, according to the bill of 29 September 1898, was 'THE MONTE CARLO GIRLS, in An Outing on Picnic Grounds at Camp Wikcoff. An operatic burletta in a scene introducing Military Maids, Naval cadets, with Mr William C. Fields – As a Tramp Juggler. We think you will like him.'

In keeping with the burlesque formula the evening's show concluded with the entire chorus of the Monte Carlo Girls 'in W. T. Bryant's burlesque, christened KI-KI – Burlesque on the famous 'Mme Fifi', with the ladies presenting characters with names such as Goodfell Diamondace, Miss Ducepot, Miss Queenheart, Miss Kingbeen, Miss Straightflash, Miss Holdout, Jane Crazy Patch, with Bryant himself as Mr Monte Carlo. The programme wraps with a flourish: 'Time – What do you care? Place – None the best. Scene – Warm and thermometer rising. Opinion – who wouldn't be a real fellow?'

Who, indeed? But this devil-may-care attitude did not help very much, because, some time that winter, in Kent, Ohio, the manager abandoned the company and returned to New York, neglecting to pay the troupe's hotel bills. A kindly ticket agent at the railway station, according to legend, gave Claude $10 for the fare back to New York, where he repaired to the nearest soup kitchen, for a pauper's Christmas dinner and a sagging bed. The violins wail, and the snow falls, dramatically. But Fields told this tale a little differently to Sobel, in a revealing scene of old Americana:

In those days – and this was 1898 – the railroads were sort of personal, human organizations. You could talk to them as you would to a friend.

Once when I was stranded I went up to the agent of the Baltimore and Ohio Railroad ticket office and said: 'I want to get back to New York. I have eight dollars.'

'Well,' replied the agent, 'the fare is about seventeen dollars or seventeen-twenty.'

'Sorry, I only have eight dollars. What can I do about it?'

'I don't know, but I can wire to the President of the road if you want me to.'

'I'd be much obliged.'

'All right. If he's willing we can have the ticket for tomorrow.'

The next day I went back anxiously. The agent was at the window. 'The President says it's O.K. We'll take the eight dollars.'

Young Claude travelled east towards his Yuletide calvary. But, true to form, a resurrection was at hand. On 28 January 1899, lo and behold, the *New York Dramatic Mirror* announced that at Miner's Bowery Theatre, 'the Monte Carlo girls have two burlesques and an olio presenting Hi Tom Ward, Fulton Brothers, Byron G. Harlan, Eva Swinburne, Cross & Holden, William C. Fields, Ramza and Arno, and Marie Rogers'.

William Claude had indeed arrived in the Big City. And Miner's Bowery Theatre was a New York institution. Standing at 165–167 Bowery, just north of Broome Street, it had been founded back in 1878 by Harry Miner, a local boy and ex-cop. Miner had perfected the type of programme that Tony Pastor had initiated: a series of specialty acts – the olio – followed by a melodramatic skit, or 'burlesque', played by the specialty actors in different costumes. Everybody doubled or tripled up. Miner's Bowery was Weber and Fields' home theatre, it was where their great acts had been born: Mike and Meyer's knockabout comedy, their first revues, their pool sketch. Other great vaudevillians who opened here included McIntyre and Heath, the Four Cohans, Gus Williams, Eddie Cantor. The show would last up to three hours and Harry Miner also had a saloon and poolroom in the building. Waiters would serve the patrons who raised a hand and passed a nickel down the row for a mug of foaming beer. Fred Stone, half of Montgomery and Stone 'Eccentric Blackface Comedians', recalled his own first New York appearance at this historic hall:

The audience was made up almost entirely of men and when the curtain rose one could hardly see for the smoke screen they sent up. Boys went around hawking popcorn, peanuts, cigars, chewing gum, and the latest song hits, while in the top gallery there was always a mob of kids, whistling, yelling to one another, raising a terrific uproar.

Just as the curtain was about to go up, a man hit the edge of the gallery railing twice with a big cane, and after that you could have heard a pin drop! Remembering that theater, it is staggering to think of the improvement that has come about in recent years. The chief wonder is that so many of the theatrical people of that day were as decent as they were . . .

It was at Miner's Bowery, incidentally, that the institution known as 'The Hook' was born, though this did not occur until 1903: Having pioneered 'amateur nights' where aspiring acts could be given a chance, Miner's manager took to using a crook-handled cane to yank a particularly painful ham off the stage. But in 1899 this indignity was only a gleam in the eye . . . On 4 February the *Dramatic Mirror* published its review:

> The Monte Carlo girls make their first local appearance this season under the management of James C. Fulton. The olio contained several pleasing numbers. The Fulton Brothers did a good trick house act. William C. Fields proved a fairly pleasing tramp juggler. Eva Swinburne warbled ditties that were broader than they were long. The brace of burlesques were of indifferent merit, being hardly up to the standard set by other companies.

This 'brace of burlesques', if one looks at the programmes, consisted of two sketches, one featuring Hi Tom Ward as Mr Monte Carlo and W. C. Fields as 'Dr Newpenny'; the other with Byron Harlan as 'Mr Whop Flop, a nice young man,' and W. C. Fields as 'Si Flappum, a regular playactor'. These were the very first spoken parts for young Claude on the stage, both alas, totally lost to posterity. The *Dramatic Mirror*'s review has to be counted a sour one, given that variety notices, in this period, were almost uniformly generous. It's clear that in the eyes of the *New York Dramatic Mirror*, not to put too fine a point on it, the Monte Carlo Girls stank. It was a journalistic Hook. Whatever the reconciliation between James Fulton and his company, there was no great future for a young man going places here.

Nevertheless, Fields remembered Fulton without rancour, when he wrote, in 1928, in *From Boy Juggler*: 'All that bothered Jim was that every time he interested an "angel" in the show to pay the bills, the angel got stuck on his wife. He said it seemed odd to him that with twenty other girls in the show every backer that came along couldn't find anyone else but Mrs Fulton to be smitten with.'

The angels might not, but young William Claude had. It was an inevitable feature of the small, huddled world of burlesque shows that pairing off should take place. Fields told writer Bernard Sobel that 'it was a regular thing for the managers of the companies to get up and make a speech before the troupe went on tour, a speech which included this stern prohibition: "We won't have any 'sketching' in this company. We won't stand for any 'doubling up.'"

'Yet,' Sobel wrote, 'the show wouldn't be running two weeks before girls and boys would pair off, according to their liking. The liking, however, was sometimes oddly assorted, a stagehand with the prima donna and a veteran comic with a teen-age chorus girl.' The managers would sometimes capitalize on this when times were bad, slashing the pair's salary in half, on the basis that 'Two can live as cheap as one.' The average salary for chorus girls, Sobel relates, was fifteen or sixteen dollars a week until the 1900s. This would be just about enough for bed and board, with a dollar or two to spare spending money. For this the girls had to rehearse, play, wash their own clothes and prepare their own food. It was a hard grind of work and often seedy hotels. One wonders what kind of stars were in these young girls' minds, as they bumped and ground towards glory? No wonder pairing up, with a male performer earning twenty-five or thirty dollars a week, became an alluring option, even in those Victorian days.

And so young Claude, at eighteen a rugged and handsome youth, despite his Big Nose (always a major feature) was inevitably smit by one of the young ladies of the chorus. There is every evidence to suggest that she was his first true love, and, in keeping with true romance, he married her. Her name was Harriet 'Hattie' Hughes.

As we might expect, the dawn of this alliance, which was to turn, in later years, into the marital war of the twentieth century, has been veiled in obfuscation. Half a century later, Harriet Fields, née Hughes, appeared before the Court of Superior Judge William McKay in Los Angeles, claiming her share in the estate left by her deceased husband. She told the court that she had met her late husband in 1898 at a girls' school reception in Brooklyn, and had then become his stage assistant. According to the *Los Angeles Times* of 5 May 1949, Harriet Hughes said her mother had taught her to sing and dance while she attended high school, and, while still in her teens, she entertained at clubs and church affairs after school.

Hattie was covering up vigorously. The programmes of the Monte Carlo Girls clearly record Hattie Hughes – also named in some programmes as 'Flossie Hughes', performing in the musical chorus the song 'Flora, You All Adore Her', as well as playing 'Miss Holdout' in the burlesque. As for the rest of her background, vagueness is the prevailing theme. The Fields family are unsure of her origin. Her mother, Elizabeth, or Lizzie Hughes, had also been an actress of some kind, long retired. There was a stepfather, whose first name is not known, as well as a sister, Kittie, also for some time in show business. Hattie, stubbornly reconstructing her past, sometimes claimed that her forefathers were 'Lees from Virginia', but Bill Fields himself used to riposte that she was more of a 'Levy from Brooklyn'. (We will find echoes of this in the great domestic scenes in *So's Your Old Man* and *You're Telling Me*, three decades later.) The family themselves are somewhat perplexed by this claim, which is given some credence by the fact that, while previous biographers have listed Hattie as a Catholic from birth, it appears that she converted to the faith as late as 1906, baptising little Claude, their only son, with her, an event which sheds some light on the Great Man's virulently anti-religious beliefs, which had not been so apparent before.

The case for the 'Levy from Brooklyn' theory is, however, weakened by the fact of Fields' own prejudices, which have to be understood in their context. Fields was a man of his time and his class. His primal politics appeared to be a gut patriotism probably inherited from his immigrant father's zeal in rushing to fight for his adopted country in the Civil War. In later years Fields was to display an irrational dislike for 'foreigners' which seeped, in a bowdlerized form, into his scripts and sketches. The repetitive 'What are you, Chinese peoples?' as well as veiled racial jokes about 'a Ubangi in the fuel supply' and 'Who's the head ingerooni around here?' were leaks from his unkinder demons. Grandson Ronald Fields has even, with admirable candour, included in his compilation of W. C.'s letters and essays two letters containing anti-Semitic jibes against President Roosevelt (whom Fields calls 'Franklin Disraeli Rosefeld' in one sour note in 1942). We shall deal with these hairy warts later. But if Fields indulged in anti-Semitism, it was the kind which did not prevent him from having long-standing friendships with such prominent show-business Jews as Eddie Cantor and Fanny Brice. Quite literally, 'some of his best friends were Jews'. It could not be otherwise, in a business, both on stage and screen, littered with more Jews than you could shake a stick at. Equally, his stereotype views on black people did not prevent him appearing on equal terms on stage with Bert Williams, Broadway's greatest black star and even complaining, as we shall see, about his colleague's shabby treatment offstage.

So Fields' private mumbling about Hattie's Jewish origin might have simply been another round in the war of words which erupted after their separation, a thirty-years war in which each side tried to depict the other as the devil-monster from hell. Hattie herself, having determined to bring up her son in devout opposition to her 'unchristian' spouse, was understandably determined to put deep water between herself and her burlesque past. The chorus of the Monte Carlo girls, kicking their heels and wiggling their behinds at an audience of crazed Bowery B'hoys shouting, spitting and making catcalls was not an image she wished to recall.

One thing is clear – this was a new life for young Claude. In August 1899 he wrote off to Hattie's mother, Lizzie, asking for her daughter's hand in marriage. Ronald Fields has published her answering letter, which suggests that, at this point, stepfather Hughes was not in the picture. Lizzie Hughes wrote, on 22 August:

> I am at a loss to extend permission to you for the hand of my daughter Hattie in marriage, having never met you. However under the circumstances, and believing you possessed of every noble quality of a man, and gentleman, I consent. She is a noble, and superb girl well worthy to be a wife, qualified with every amiable trait of character.
>
> Trusting your path through this life of struggle may be truly happy, and prosperous as husband to my dear child Hattie, you have my heartfelt good wishes, trusting we may meet on your return to the city.
>
> I have the pleasure to remain,
>
> Yours sincerely,
>
> Lizzie Hughes

Reading this letter carefully one might guess that her daughter's marriage, even to an impoverished vaudevillian, was a proposal Mrs Hughes received with some relief. In the event, Claude and Hattie were married on 8 April 1900, in San Francisco, when both were on tour for the Keith Circuit.

Before his marriage, Fields toured for eight months with Fred Irwin's Specialty Burlesquers. The Monte Carlo Girls had finally self-destructed in June 1899, failing to appear at the Lyceum, Washington, DC, after four months of peripatetic management. On 3 June the *Clipper* announced that 'Byron C. Harland (and others of the troupe) issued an attachment against their manager, James C. Fulton, and garnished all the money due the company.'

The Monte Carlo Girls had finally run out of steam. During July Claude obtained employment with a minstrel troupe – 'Murphy and Gibson's American Minstrels', playing the Steel Pier in Atlantic City. This might have been the only time in which W. C. Fields appeared in traditional blackface, but, alas, we have no pictures to prove or disprove this. But by 26 August Fields was appearing, in Cincinatti, Ohio, with Fred Irwin's Burlesquers.

Irwin's Burlesquers were a good solid presence on the variety stage. Fred Irwin was a far more canny manager than Fulton ever was, and a shrewd developer of talent. Fields told Sobel: 'He was the Ziegfeld of burlesque and an honorable man. Ran a show legitimately; was on the up and up. Old circus man; and circus people were always honest and real people in those days.'

Fields wrote later, in *From Boy Juggler*, of his constant wars with Irwin over his salary, which began, he said, at $35 a week. 'All I heard from Irwin was that he could never make any money paying me such a big salary. I kicked for a good spot on the bill, claiming I wanted a chance to earn the money. Some critic gave me a big boost. I heard, afterwards, that he never even saw the show.'

Money was not the only problem. The art itself had not yet been fully mastered. Fields told Bernard Sobel:

I tried to perfect my work, but the most awful feeling I ever had in my life began to develop in me at this time . . . Before every performance of the show I would do all the tricks I knew. Juggling is difficult and the first five, six or seven years, you don't know your tricks well enough to do them with your eyes shut. What would worry me, therefore, especially on opening night, was failure . . . Occasionally those days I'd miss a trick and so I began to worry: supposing I go out tonight and do twenty tricks of juggling and miss most of them. Suppose I miss every trick. It was torture. I prayed for the day I could get over this misery, the dread of missing – those fear complexes. Out on that stage I was frightened to death – desperate.

Nevertheless he soldiered on. Fields claimed about those days: 'I was singing, clowning, juggling and talking comedy.' Hmmm. The very idea of Fields singing on stage might be enough to curdle the blood. His attempts to warble, later on, in films like *Man on the Flying Trapeze* and *It's a Gift*, reveal him to be, to put it kindly, tone deaf.

Although, we will discover, he did yodel a few bars, during the Ziegfeld Follies . . . But Fields was trying out his new wings. For this engagement he had redefined himself, and was billed as –

THE TRAMP JUGGLER
W. C. FIELDS
DIFFERENT FROM ALL OTHERS

It is reasonable to assume that Hattie Fields first became his stage assistant during this time, though I have not seen a programme that proves this. It was a period which also produced the first properly printed and designed poster for the new aspiring star. It shows the tramp in a ragged overcoat and battered stovepipe hat, clutching a straight cane and a cigar in his right hand. The face is covered with a stubbly dark beard. Beside him stands an elegant table with his cigar-box props and juggling balls. At its feet lies an assortment of hats and a small loose carpet bag. The heading is IRWIN'S BURLESQUERS – DIRECTION FRED IRWIN. The footing: WM. C. FIELDS – DIFFERENT FROM THE REST.

Fields often claimed that he had adopted his tramp costume out of necessity because he couldn't afford a proper stage costume. In fact, the tramp figure, later to be universalised by Chaplin, was already familiar on the stage. Nat Wills, billed as 'The Happy Tramp', was to become a great rival. James Harrigan became so perturbed at having his line filched that he later billed himself as 'The First Tramp Juggler'. O. K. Sato, another tramp juggler and an early mentor of Fields, chided Bill with this in a letter written several years later, in November 1904, when both were on the European tour, in separate cities. Sato wrote to Fields:

And did You pass anything else excepting the back door at Miner's Bowery theatre, the night that Harrigan was waiting so patiently in front of house for You, so that He could aim a few little pouts in Your direction? And did you put only a pair of scissors and a hammer on Your clothes as a little precaution should He happen to catch a glance of You?

The young man was certainly aware of his prestigious competition . . .
On 28 October 1899, Irwin's Burlesquers opened in New York, at Miner's 8th Avenue Theatre, a twin of Miner's Bowery but slightly further uptown. Bill's fellow performers included Carver and Pollard 'in their Eccentric Peculiarities'; the Tredwyn Sisters; Bailey and

5 Poster of Fields in character.

Madison – 'Acrobatic Grotesque Eccentriques'; and Mlle. Marie in 'Artistic Poses with Electrical Effects'. The *Dramatic Mirror* of 4 November applauded the show, noting: 'Business excellent'. On 30 December they returned for a Christmas booking, to further acclaim.

This was W. C. Fields' first proper tour, and he played all over the eastern U.S.: Chicago, Cleveland, Albany, Baltimore, Cincinatti, Louisville Kentucky, Saint Louis Missouri, Washington, DC. In mid-December 1899, he played a week in Philadelphia, his first full professional engagement in his home town. We do not know if Ma and Pa attended to see their son in false beard and schmutters wowing the audience for a living, but we might be allowed to speculate upon a warm maternal tear.

In February 1900, Irwin's Burlesquers played a week in Indianapolis (February 10) followed by a week in Saint Louis (February 17). This authenticated schedule lends credence to another detailed and candid fragment from an unpublished piece written by Fields in 1930 as publicity for his short-lived appearance as Cap'n Andy in *Showboat*, produced by the St Louis Municipal Opera. This show played for two weeks in August 1930, and Fields contributed a rare reminiscence of St Louis in a piece entitled: *It's A Tough Spot* (the original is an uncorrected typescript) –

'It's a tough spot,' said my friend in Indianapolis. 'It's the toughest spot on the Empire Circuit. You'll never forget St Louis. And a hard-boiled audience? Boy, there's nothing like that Standard Theatre audience, except in Washington.'

That was my introduction to St Louis. I was a comedian in burlesque. And in those days you played 14 shows a week in burlesque and made a Saturday night jump to open with a Sunday matinee. And you didn't squander $1.50 in sleeper fare, either. If you were sick, maybe, you'd double up with someone else and each pay 75 cents to get an upper. Well, we gave two shows in Indianapolis Saturday. Sometime about noon Sunday we reached St Louis, and I had my first glimpse of 'the toughest spot on the Empire Circuit.'

I found the theater, the old Standard. And then a hotel – the Rillings hotel which stood just across the street, where the famous Barr Garage is now. It was a famous actor's boarding house. Five dollars a week would get you room and board.

Half dopey from lack of sleep I went across to the theater to get ready for the show. I found my dressing room. There was a stool in it. I sat down upon the stool, my head in my hands wondering if ever on earth I's [*sic*] get caught up with sleep.

A stage hand came in. 'Mind looking here a minute?' he said. I got up and he grabbed my stool and made off with it.

I followed. Upstairs. Demanding my stool. As he got to the top step he swung around and faced me – and brought the stool down upon my head. I caught up with sleep right then. Its the old Paglicci [*sic*] story. The show must go on. They brought me around in time to play that afternoon. But with what a headache.

When my friend in Indianapolis told me St Louis was 'a tough spot' he gave me some inside information. 'Why they've even got one of the James Boys as doorkeeper at the Standard Theater', he said. And he told the truth. All my life I had heard about the exploits of Jesse James. Well, here was his brother Frank – his comrade and companion in those exploits which had made him synonymous with terror. Well, I saw Frank James. He was gallery door-keeper at the Standard. A slight, quiet, retiring sort of man, who looked as though he had just recently come in from the country, and whose drooping moustache sort of suggested the small town sheriff of the period. Nothing big, nothing boisterous about him. And a kindly soul. Yet I have seen a cold steely glitter in his gray eyes.

I didn't try to fool with Frank James. Nor with anyone else in the old Standard. If a fellow wanted my stool he could have it. I made that a rule at the Standard. And I left town intact.

In those days I used to think I had 'arrived.' I was getting $18 a week. It had been a hard job working up to that. In the end I managed to get $35 a week. When I got it.

This unusually self-deprecating piece rings more true than many other Fieldisms. It also, interestingly, contradicts Bill's own assertion elsewhere that his starting salary was $35. Incidentally, this was another piece in which he related the 'drowning' act at Fortescue's as something involving other performers. At some points, Fields let down his guard, allowing truth to leaven the mythology. But not very often.

Fields might not have 'arrived', with Irwin's Burlesquers, but he was getting noticed. The main vaudeville circuits, now in full swing, had booking agents and talent scouts out scouring the various shows for new acts. Fields was already a tireless self-promoter, sending out hand-bills, quoting reviews, arranging for his posters. According to his own account, the most go-getting agent in the business, the original William Morris, came backstage one night to woo him into mainstream vaude-ville. But in the same Saint Louis essay quoted above, Fields described this next step a little differently:

I had done a lot of comedy in burlesque, so I fixed up a line of patter with my juggling act and then started out in vaudeville. It happened this way. Our burlesque show had gotten in to New York and was booked into a theater which that very week changed its policy. It changed from burlesque to vaudeville. Our manager took the acts out of our olio and booked them as vaudeville acts. I had my juggling and I mixed in some of the comedy from the show. William Morris, the booking agent saw me and booked me over the Orpheum Circuit. Then he got me engagements with Keiths and finally at Koster & Bials. I was going good – as a juggler.

In March 1900, one month after being conked on the noggin with a stool by Frank James' crony at the old Standard Theater, W. C. Fields left Irwin's Burlesquers to begin touring, with Hattie, as an independent act. He opened at the Orpheum on Market Street in San Francisco, California, claiming the positively princely salary of $125 a week.

The boy juggler was on his way.

Chapter 6
My Lady Vaudeville

W. C. Fields' timing was impeccable. He entered vaudeville at the dawn of its Golden Age. As Douglas Gilbert wrote in his vital *American Vaudeville* about this birthing moment of the twentieth century:

> Many of America's great fortunes were on the make or already made, and soon we were to hear the early Roosevelt's cry – 'malefactors of great wealth.' At the turn of the century the dandies of the nineties became the dudes of the 1900s – 'sports' in paddock overcoats, peg top trousers, wide-flanged buttoned shoes of horrendous yellows . . . Seasonal hats were a weighty derby or an enormous straw called a 'katy', which was battened against the wind by a silken cord affixed to the lapel of the coat; a fastening called a trolley . . .
>
> The period was a paradise for con men, quacks, and gold-brick peddlers. Many a sucker let go a dollar for that 'steel engraving of George Washington,' receiving by return mail a United States postage stamp . . . The growing pains of our people were fostered by an imperialism deriving from our victory over Spain and the acquisition of the Philippines. It was a great sprawling era . . . geyserish in effort, fullsome in tone, hilarious and jerky; and into this picture vaudeville fitted like the final piece of a jigsaw puzzle . . .

This was the period in which 'sixty-cent' Albee and 'grifter' Keith garnered dividends from their organisation of show business. It was in 1900 that Albee, Keith, F. F. Proctor and a number of other theatre owners founded the United Booking Office, fixing a commission of 5 per cent out of the 10 per cent acts had to pay their agents, and adding another 2.5 per cent for collecting the agent's five. Contracts allowed cancellation at the manager's discretion up to the third performance. In response to this a radical actor and monologuist, George Fuller Golden, organised a vaudevillians' union – the White Rats, inspired by the British organisation named the Water Rats – Rats being 'Star' spelled backwards. Seven vaudevillians formed the Union at the Parker House bar on Broadway on 1 June 1900. The initial attempt at strike action failed, but hundreds of vaudevillians signed up for the union. Although Fields played no active part in it at this time, his card was included in the advertising section of the Rats' official book, 'My Lady Vaudeville', published in 1909.

Vaudevillians were considered a breed apart from the actors on the 'legitimate' stage. They may have joined the White Rats to fight for their salaries, but their concerns were inwardly turned and obsessive. The inveterate survivor George Burns has given us some sage observations about the strange 'vaudebeeste':

> We were in love with show business, with the excitement of getting onstage. Nothing else mattered to us. The only politics any of us cared about was why the Orpheum Circuit had booked 'Flora D'Aliza's Educated Roosters' instead of 'Camilla's Pigeons'. The only thing any of us knew about sports was what boxing champion or Olympic medal winner was playing Hammerstein's. The only thing that really mattered to any of us was getting the next booking.

Fred Allen, in his autobiography *Much Ado About Me*, wrote:

> A vaudeville actor could relax and enjoy himself only in the company of another vaudeville actor. You could sit a vaudeville actor in front of a mirror and he would stay there contentedly for days on end . . . There was a time when the actor was *persona non grata* at the better inns, and this was especially true of vaudevillians, who were presumed to be irresponsible from the very fact that their profession was uncertain and their living precarious . . . Many hotel and rooming-house owners were complaining that some vaudeville people were stealing towels. This practice was so common that jokes were being told about it. One joke was about the vaudeville actor who died and left an estate of eight hundred hotel and Pullman towels . . .

Anyone could be in vaudeville provided that they had 'a minimum of talent or a maximum of nerve'. George Burns, who began in small-time vaudeville, wrote:

> When I started out there were more than 5,000 vaudeville theaters in the country. Every city had several theaters and most small towns had at least one . . . There were so many theaters on the vaudeville circuits that if a performer had fourteen good minutes he could work six years without changing a word or playing the same theater twice . . .

Anything could be the basis of an act. Mind reading, mental telepathy and hypnotism were popular. Posing acts pretended to be statues – maybe they did nothing, but they did it beautifully. One performer ate paper, wood, flowers, light bulbs and matches, while another man bit railroad spikes in half . . . There was even 'The Wrestling Cheese', a slab of cheese that could not be lifted off the stage, and a Chinese act that put chopsticks through their noses . . .

But, at the upper end of vaudeville, one could see the stars glitter and shine: there was Eva Tanguay, 'the Girl Who Made Vaudeville Famous', who broke B. F. Keith's puritanical house rules by singing 'I Want Someone to Go Wild With Me' and 'Its All Been Done But Not the Way I Do It', two decades before Mae West. She was soon to be receiving $3,000 a week. There was Nora Bayes, the 'Singing Comedienne', whose reputation was set to grow and grow. There were the great comedians Joe Cook, Joe Welch and Frank Tinney, who convulsed audiences by his tragic attempts to play the 'Miserere' on bagpipes. And there were the great international acts, imports from France and Great Britain, like Jenny Lind, Anna Held, Yvette Guilbert, the English coster singer Albert Chevalier, who sang 'Me Old Dutch', 'Knock 'em On the Old Kent Road' and 'Wot's the Good of Hanyfink? Why, Nuffink!' There was Marie Lloyd, and the legendary Lillie Langtry, and Sarah Bernhardt – already moonlighting in vaudeville. Great names, who have faded to shadows, like Vesta Victoria and Vesta Tilley, the fabulous male impersonator, performing in top hat and tails. These great showpeople, who were earning what must have seemed like millionaire's fees in those days, whetted the appetite of American vaudevillians for the next stage in their bid for success and stardom – the European tour.

Some American acts had already been pioneers in the late 1890s, of the Atlantic crossing. 'Happy' Fanny Fields, Mike Whalen, Harry Houdini, and O. K. Sato were trend setters. In May 1899, when young Claude Dukenfield was wrestling with the slings and arrows of the Monte Carlo Girls, O. K. Sato was wowing the crowds as a 'tramp juggler' at the *Folies Bergère* in Paris. At another Paris theatre in the same week, the Olympia, the legendary Little Tich was starring, together with the prince of European jugglers, Severus Schaeffer. The Olympia, says the contemporary review (in *The Era*), 'is invariably in possession of the most attractive female performers, and the seven cardinal sins are, so to say, presented by magnificent specimens'.

These were not enticements a self-respecting up-and-coming vaude-villian like W. C. Fields, despite his recent happy marriage, could afford to long ignore. In fact, his marriage seemed to set himself up as a familiar going concern. One billing, at the Orpheum, Kansas City, 26 November to 1 December 1900, had the act down as 'Mr & Mrs W. C. Fields', the only point, as far as I can discover, at which this form was used. But vaudeville families were a familiar phenomenon. Fred Allen wrote:

Vaudeville families endured for generations. The female of the species foaled on trains, in dressing rooms, in tank towns, and in the big cities. The show must go on. At the theater the baby slept in the top of the trunk in the dressing room. At the hotel a crib was improvised by removing a large bureau drawer and placing it on the bed or between two chairs . . . The smalltime vaudeville mother had the endurance of a doorknob. She did three or four shows a day as part of the act. She cared for her baby on the road and prepared its food. She did the family washing: there was always a clothesline hanging and dripping away in the dressing room and the boardinghouse, and the sinks were filled with diapers. As the family grew larger, the kids were packed like sardines into upper berths. (Midgets often traveled in clusters in upper berths; an actor in a lower berth once com-plained that he had been kept awake all night by a midget with insomnia who had been walking up and down in the upper berth.)

One remembers Duffy, Sawtelle and Duffy. Or perhaps the most famous of vaudeville families, Joe and Myra Keaton and their baby son, 'Buster', who first trod the boards in October 1900, in Wilmington, Delaware, at the age of five years. (Fields would perform on the same bill as the Keatons at the Tremont Theatre in Boston in October 1907.) No wonder then, that Fields the vaudevillian might have expected his wife, and later his baby son, to fit in with this age-old pattern. No wonder, either, that Hattie Hughes-Fields might, on reflection and after hard experience of life on the road, balk at such a bleak prospect. Poverty it might not have been. Hardship and uncer-tainty, guaranteed.

But these domestic problems lay in the future. Throughout the first year of his marriage, the first year of the twentieth century, Fields con-tinued to tour with the Keith Circuit, achieving the accolade, on 9 June, of opening at the prestigious Koster & Bial's in New York. 'Good sized audiences greeted a fair bill,' wrote the *Dramatic Mirror* on 16 June. 'William C. Fields, who was returned for a second week, repeated his success. He is a comedy juggler who has some original ideas.' This appearance also earned him his first mention abroad, in the 'American Vaudeville' column of the English stage journal *The Era*, which noted, on 30 June: 'W. C. Fields, tramp juggler.' In September he was playing the main Keith theater on 14th Street, at Union Square. Then followed Boston, Mass., the Chicago Opera House and the family billing in Kansas City.

Somewhere between Boston and Chicago a fateful decision was made. A tiny note in the 'Vaudeville Jottings' column of the *New York Dramatic Mirror* announced:

W. C. Fields, the eccentric juggler, will sail for Germany on the 'Deutschland' to open at the Winter Garden Berlin, January 1 1901.

Fields said simply, in *From Boy Juggler to Star Comedian*: 'I wanted to see the world, and booked for a tour of Europe.' As usual, this conceals more than it reveals. After only a single season on the mainstream vaudeville circuit, the young artist was striking out in a wholly new direction. Perhaps he had dreamed of it all along. Or perhaps he met his juggling mentors and predecessors, O. K. Sato, Cinquevalli and another close friend to be, Tom Hearn ('The Lazy Juggler'), who had already gone down this path. His already acute business sense would have told him that this was a hard, but fast path to glory. An actor could play the circuits for years and just tread water, but a foreign tour conferred status. The colourful stickers for London, Paris, Berlin, Brussels, Madrid and Milan, and the even more exotic Durban, Cape Town, Johannesburg, Sydney and Melbourne were badges of rank, medals for the vaudevillian's tramp uniform. (There was even reputedly a company which sold ready-made foreign stickers for landlubbers . . .)

Twenty, going on twenty-one-year-old Claude could not wait. The young man had the wanderlust, as well as the lust to succeed. Boarding the great Teutonic ocean liner with his new bride of eight months, he embarked on a new, enthralling adventure . . .

Part II
The Tramp Abroad

Chapter 7
'I Thought I Knew Him Directly I Saw Him . . .'

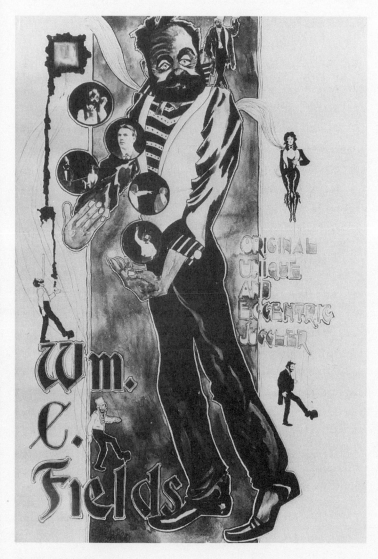

6 The Tramp Juggler.

A TRAMP JUGGLER
A NEW AND CLEVER 'TURN' AT THE PALACE THEATRE

I thought I knew him directly I saw him. This, said I, was his second visit to the Palace Theatre. Apparently he had made some alterations to his 'act', for certain features were new to me. But I felt confident about the personality – it did not seem possible to make any mistake about the figure – such a figure! Clothes – old, torn, loose and unclean; boots – big and bulging; hat – an artistic wreck. And the face! Hirsute and blotchy, with a ludicrous expression of countenance that was most diverting. Yes, I thought that must be my shabby old friend back again. And with this conviction firmly established in my mind I sat through and enjoyed the performance, none the less because my thoughts were reminiscent.

Subsequently came the awakening! Later, in the evening, stumbling across a friend of mine, I remarked about this turn, calling his attention to the fact that it was rather different in detail to that presented on a previous occasion. 'That cannot be,' said he, 'for this is the first time it has been seen in this country, and has been at the Palace only a week.' I am neither a pugnacious nor a self-assertive man, but I felt monstrously inclined to take up an attitude of firmness in this matter. I suspected that he was deliberately attempting to deceive me. Yet he was not, for correct he was. It was an entirely new turn, but so like a previous one in many respects that I excused myself for mistaking them. It was yet another of the apparently extensively patronised type of tramp which appears to be indigenous to American vaudeville entertainments. It is always the same: hairy and florid face, seedy attire, grotesque movements. Sometimes it is a juggler, at others a cyclist, anon a musician. Take Ritchie, Harragan and Fields – the last named the subject of this article – place them in a row, and lo! 'Tom, Dick and Harry!' As like as three peas.

In the 'business' of the latest of these bedraggled gentlemen there is much that is new, and the act, taken as a whole, is worthy of some sort of distinction in dress . . . Mr Fields, who is assisted in a measure by a young and attractive lady, does not crowd the stage with apparatus. In fact, there is little to be seen when the curtain goes up. Just a small table on which are a few cigar-boxes. The latter, however, supply an opportunity for some really remarkable tricks in dexterity which set at nought all laws of gravitation. Mr Fields takes six or eight of the boxes and holds them together horizontally between his hands; he then proceeds to detach them one at a time by hitting them sharply on the top, retaining the horizontal position till they have all been dislodged. He does it with such speed and precision that it appears as easy as amorously saluting your hand . . .

One of the tricks which Mr Fields performs is *not* clever, but is certainly very funny. And thereby hangs a tale . . . The juggler produces from his table a few cigar-boxes, reposing one on top of the other in the orthodox manner. He makes a great show of preparing for a *coup*, something to startle you; and does, in fact, perform what you believe to be a really remarkable feat of manipulation. Anyway, you applaud vigorously, and are sorry for it afterwards. I freely admit I did applaud and was sorry; annoyed, almost savage. I was within an ace of blushing, a thing I have not known myself to do for many years.

Well, with a sudden twist of the wrist the boxes are shot into the air and come to rest end on end. Then, when the applause is at its loudest the juggler allows the boxes to fall over, but not to the ground. They are fastened together *with string!* . . .

Until I saw Mr Fields I did not know that tennis balls could be made to perform such remarkable and such a variety of evolutions . . . They fly about all over his body, resting now and again in the most inconceivable places, with a maximum of movement to a minimum of effort . . . Another very good trick is with two tall hats, a black and a white, both more or less dilapidated. One the juggler places on his head and the other on his outstretched foot. Simultaneously he jerks the latter up on to his head, and drops the former on to his foot. Then he turns his attention to a hat, a cigar and a whisk brush. For this he utilises a large pocket at the back of his trousers, just below the waist. He tosses the articles about in a similar manner to the tennis balls, and finally gets the hat on to his head, the cigar into his mouth, and the brush into his back pocket.

Mr Fields is unconventional in many things, not the least striking of these being the way he ignites a match on the side of his face.

H. L. Adam, *Black and White Budget Magazine*,
London, 16 March 1901.

Our image of the comedian W. C. Fields is that of a rather shabby, middle-aged or even elderly man shambling through life's endless turmoils. It is no part of this book, or can be of any book, to explain *why* W. C. Fields, or any other great comic, is funny. Funny is in the eye of the beholder. But perhaps we respond to the ageing clown Fields because he has so obviously been a reluctant passenger on life's old rickety omnibus, the irascible grouch in all of us who can rasp at a petrol-pump attendant: 'Hurry up! You're going to lose my trade!' – or who tries to buy and tug home an ostrich to placate an angry wife. But we have to cast our minds back to the image of Bill Fields as a very funny *young* man, a youth of twenty convulsing an audience more with his comic moves than with his skill at juggling, which was a common, albeit astounding, talent of so many other performers of his time. The competition was so fierce. Everyone had to have an act which was 'The Greatest Novelty to be Put Before the Public'. What was it that made this young man's clowning so special?

The common, and in fact pat theory till now has been that, as Fields himself averred: 'To understand comedy, to know what laughs are made of, one must suffer. Every laugh is built on heartaches, some-times tears.' *A comedian is best when he's hungry.* Of course, all the great comics built on situations of absurd and extreme adversity to enable the hero to succeed, either by his own cunning or by happen-stance. Chaplin, Keaton, Lloyd, Langdon. 'Comedy is tragedy that is happening to someone else.' It has been assumed, therefore, that Fields' own life provided the extreme adversity from which his comedy flows. The only flaw in this is that, compared to so many others of his generation and profession, Bill Fields' life was not that tragic.

We have seen that his childhood and teens were not the Dickensian hell that myth and legend invented. His father was not the storybook tyrant, and Fields' family was, in the main, supportive of his stage ambi-tions, Papa James' initial hostility apart. His brother Walter even accom-panied him on one of his world tours, as we shall discover. His marriage to Hattie turned bad, after five years, no great unusual circumstance. His son was estranged from him by his wife. He wrote his wife vitriolic let-ters and she responded, casting blame and counter-blame, for over twenty years. But he continually sent her money, week by week, with few omissions, throughout his life. He was a disappointed husband and father, and he poured this disappointment into his later stage acts, his written sketches, and his films. Hattie was to become the shrewish wife, the harridan of *So's Your Old Man*, *It's a Gift*, *You're Telling Me*, *Man On the Flying Trapeze*, and *The Bank Dick*. In Freudian terms, he was classically sublimating his pain. It certainly did not prevent him from seeking solace elsewhere, as a string of girlfriends and mistresses, hith-erto ignored, can attest to. In fact, Hattie, in her court appearance to claim her share of her husband's inheritance, in 1949, said, under cross-examination, that the cause of her separation from her husband, around 1907, was 'another woman'. She did not name her. '"I knew about her for some time before I mentioned it," she said.'

So where does that unique brand of Fields comedy come from? Chaplin lived the Dickensian childhood that Bill Fields pretended to have endured. Eddie Cantor, his later partner in the Ziegfeld *Follies*, was a poor orphan in New York's Lower East Side. But Fields had to pander to the myth: from rags to riches. Out of the American Nightmare – the American Dream.

The truth may be far more elusive, and deeper. In an obituary tribute to W. C. Fields, the British writer J. B. Priestley wrote, in 1947:

I saw him long before he found his way to Hollywood, before 1914, when he was touring the halls in England with his juggling and trick billiard table act. He was very funny even then, and I seem to remember him balancing a number of cigar boxes and staring with horror at a peculiar box, in the middle of the pile, that wobbled strangely, as if some evil influence were at work. All his confidence, which you guessed from the first to be a desperate bluff, vanished at the sight of this one diabolical box, which began to threaten him with the nightmare of hostile and rebellious things.

And this, I fancy, was the secret of his huge and enchanting drollery – though, oddly enough, it seems to have been missed – that he moved, warily in spite of a hastily assumed air of nonchalant confidence, through a world in which even inanimate objects were hostile, rebellious, menacing, never to be trusted. He had to be able to *juggle* with things, to be infinitely more dexterous than you or I need be, to find it possible to handle them at all. They were not, you see, his things, these commonplace objects of ours. He did not belong to this world, but had arrived from some other and easier planet.

All the truly great clowns – and Fields was undoubtedly one of them – have the same transient look. They are not men of this world being funny. They are serious personages – perhaps musicians like Grock, ambassadors with attendants like the Fratellini, or hopeful inventor-promoters like Fields – who have, through some blunder on the part of a celestial Thomas Cook, landed from the other side of Arcturus on the wrong planet. They make the best of a bad business, but what is easy for us – merely picking up a bag of golf clubs or moving a chair – is horribly difficult for them. Things that give us no trouble offer them obstacles and traps, for nothing here is on their side.

As an analysis of the essence of the Fields persona – as well as Chaplin, Keaton, Lloyd et al., not to speak of the Martian Brothers

Marx – this makes real sense. The American critic Heywood Broun wrote, in 1931:

> Like the best of modern painters, Fields can afford to depart from the orthodox because he is heretical from choice and not through incapacity . . . Certainly, there is something admirable in the ability to emotionalize the task of tossing spheres in the air and catching them in rhythm . . . Mr. Fields at play among the planets suggests to me an Einsteinian quality.

Pardon the hyperbole . . . In being accused of being a 'Tartuffle', by an enraged upper-class host in *You Can't Cheat an Honest Man*, Fields responds: 'What kind of a Tartuffle? Are there two kinds, male or female?' The man from beyond Arcturus is always trying to make sense of his strange location. He is always reaching out towards new horizons.

At Christmas 1900, Mr and Mrs W. C. Fields arrived at the port of Hamburg, Germany. They did not have long to sightsee. By the 1st of January, Fields' act had to be ready for the stage at the Berlin Wintergarten, his first foreign appearance. He often said later that he was taken aback by the powerful bank of lights that shone down on him from the great ceilings of the European music halls. In Berlin, he looked up, as the juggler does, into the dazzle and almost missed his balls. But he was, to all accounts, a hit. A Berlin review, pasted in the 1901 Fields scrapbook, notes, in Gothic type: 'W. C. FIELDS WIR AUCH SCHON GUTE JONGLEURKUNSTLER.' Back home the *New York Dramatic Mirror* noted in its Vaudeville jottings on 1 February:

> W. C. Fields, the eccentric juggler, opened recently at the Wintergarden, Berlin, Germany, and made such a success that after the first performance the management tried to prolong his engagement, but could only extend it to two weeks, as he was booked at the Palace, London, for an indefinite engagement to open February 4. The Palace time was set back for two weeks, and he opens in London February 18. Mr Fields writes that Webb and Hassan opened January 1, and made a big hit. All the Americans in Europe are doing well.

This was indeed accurate, and Fields first trod the boards at the great Palace Theatre of Varieties in London's Shaftesbury Avenue on the night of 23 February 1901.

*

Fields' previous biographers have tended to treat his foreign tours as a movement from the centre, New York, to the provinces. How ignorant can you get? At the turn of the century, young Bill Fields' journey to Europe was in fact the opposite of what has been assumed: it was a journey from the periphery to the centre. Paris and London, in particular, were the hub of it all, the great world centres of music-hall, the Hollywoods of their day. New York, in comparison, was still developing. London and Paris had arrived.

This was *La Belle Époque*, the new era of modernity, the triumph of the machine age. The Eiffel Tower, its most potent symbol, had been completed in 1889. In 1895 the first great car race, from Paris to Bordeaux and back, had taken place. In the same year the Lumière brothers developed their camera, Marconi invented radio telegraphy, and Roentgen unveiled the X-ray. In Paris, at the end of 1900, the second World's Fair had just been dismantled. Beautiful palaces of tents and pavilions still lay in dwindling piles along the River Seine. The hoards of foreigners who came to marvel at the massed exhibits had departed, but left their money behind. Paris was rich, and her music halls were booming: the Hippodrome, the Casino de Paris, the Olympia, the Nouveau-Cirque and the *Folies Bergère*.

In London, many of the great variety houses were monuments of a previous generation, the fun-houses of Victorian glory: the Oxford, the Tivoli, the Alhambra, the London Pavilion. A brand new theatre, the London Hippodrome, had been opened on 15 January 1900. Its only rival, the Palace Theatre, had been opened in 1891 as the Royal English Opera House, but was renamed the Palace Theatre of Varieties in 1892.

In the 1900s, grand theatres were going up all over the country. One can cite the new Palace Theatre in Leicester, a provincial industrial town, with no distinguished artistic heritage to speak of, which was opened in June 1901. The stage journal, *The Era*, described it thus:

> The building, which has a holding capacity of 3,500, has been erected for
> . . . that Napoleon of managers, Mr Oswald Stoll . . . The centre is carried
> up with a lofty pediment, on which a wrought iron panelled grill proclaims
> the words 'Palace Theatre' in electric letters, the facade being flanked by
> octagonal minarets, surmounted by flambeux, the sides of the building
> being finished with an ornamental parapet . . . The principal entrance is
> through two pairs of polished walnut doors into a large vestibule, with a
> balcony round it, finished at a great height by a richly-designed Mauresque

dome . . . The walls are enriched with panels, and faced with embossed Oriental tiles brought specially from Spain. A wide marble staircase, divided by a marble column and brass rails branching off at each side of the main landing . . .

Three years later, W. C. Fields would be performing in this theatre, one of the many provincial halls he appeared in during his nine separate tours of Great Britain and Ireland.

The Leicester Palace was not untypical of theatres being built all over the Midlands and the North of England. One can imagine the opulence of the halls in the hub of variety, London. The king of English comedians, Dan Leno, once described the Imperial city as a 'large village on the Thames where the principal industries are the music-halls and the confidence trick'. The peculiar terminology of the English theatre attests to it's semi-divine status – divided into the upper galleries – 'the Gods' – and 'the Pits' or stalls. Music-hall had prospered in England since the early nineteenth century, deriving from the 'Pleasure Gardens' of the eighteenth, at the time when Thomas Jefferson was paying one shilling for seeing 'a learned pig'. The stars of the English music-hall, like Marie Lloyd and Albert Chevalier, galvanised the American variety halls throughout the 1890s. Vesta Tilley wowed them with her male impersonations. The most unlikely star of them all, the four foot tall Little Tich, born with five fingers and a thumb on each hand, paraded in huge pointed boots on the stage and wowed English and French audiences alike with his English-French patter and songs.

The essence of English music-hall was a gentle debunking of authority and a kind of seedy anarchy. The genteel tramp was a staple that suited artists as diverse as Dan Leno and George Robey. The strange Canadian-born singer-raconteur R.G. Knowles appeared in a battered frock-coat and top hat, with white trousers, singing melancholy songs and delivering his long monologues and 'lectures' in a husky, staccato voice. Like Fields, he travelled the world, and they were to share the stage more than once, in venues as far afield as the Coliseum in London, and the Tivoli in Cape Town, South Africa.

Many of these performers were extremely literate, well versed in the European classics. Fields, self-taught as he was, clearly felt like a country-cousin beside them. It was in this period, legend and common-sense coincide for once in agreeing, that he began hunkering down to his serious study of the great writers: Dickens, Hardy, Milton,

Shakespeare, Dumas, Victor Hugo. Mark Twain was already an old acquaintance. Taylor quotes a pretty story about Fields fetching up at a second-hand bookstore in England with a stage trunk and asking the bookseller to fill 'er up:

'Anything particular the gentleman desires?' asked the proprietor (according to Fields) . . . 'Gentleman favour any particular colour? . . . Volumes as will set well in a trunk – records of incoming and outgoing vessels, together with tonnage, since 1832 . . .'

'There seems to be some misapprehension,' said Fields, 'I want the best books you've got, the finest authors in English literature . . .'

Embroidery apart, the smart, self-educated music-hall artistes of Great Britain set Bill Fields a new benchmark. He could not afford to be left behind. Fields own tales about the early period in his life abound with accounts, as we have seen, of how tired, nervous and ill-prepared he often thought he was for his act. To be in the same playing-field as such artists as George Robey and Little Tich, who held their audiences in the palm of their hand, and, offstage, both dabbled in painting, photography and book-collecting, was to be keenly aware of his limits. It was this feeling of inferiority, I think, that lay at the roots of the vice which would endure all his life: the obsessive telling of tall tales, the mixture of self-deprecation and self-aggrandizement, the downright lies, the grotesque inventions. Like everything else in his life, his modest background, his eventually souring marriage, his sense of isolation and alien-ness from the common run of humanity, he turned this into an advantage: It became his material, the common clay from which Claude Dukenfield, the stubborn boy from Philadelphia, would create W. C. Fields, the monster ego, the clown of clowns, the Great Silly, as he dubbed himself at one tell-tale moment. And because he had, in the process, become a very different person from the ignoramus he thought he had once been, he had to conceal that fact, to hide the real Bill Fields behind the mask which was his stock in trade.

Typical of this concealment was his obsessive fear of being upstaged by other acts – a familiar vaudeville vice which Fields contracted in its most virulent form. This led him to suppress practically all the true facts concerning the fourteen years of his repeated foreign tours. The gist of the legend runs as follows:

As a young man of twenty-one, Fields toured the world, gaining spectacular success as The Greatest Comedy Juggler in the World. He travelled in Europe and Africa, Australia and Samoa, India and China. He performed before all the crowned heads of Europe. King Edward VII came down to his dressing-room once and invited him to play at Buckingham Palace. He played to audiences of all colours and creeds, performing for bearded Boers and native Waziris in turn. He met another rising American star, Will Rogers, in South Africa, when they appeared on the same bill. Everywhere he went he was a real tearaway, sampling the jails of many different countries. He was jailed in London for 'socking a bobby' and in Germany for throwing 'an overripe bockwurst' on a café floor. Everywhere he went he opened bank accounts under a plethora of bizarre names. In Spain he was a 'Senor Guillermo McKinley, a half-breed from Guatemala'. He was born full blown, so to speak, from his own invention.

So much for myth. And now for the facts.

Chapter 8
'Already a Great Favourite'

In 1904, I was with Col. Catnip's Cat and Dog Circus doing an act.
I followed the trained armadillos and my speciality was escaping from a
strait-jacket in two minutes flat ...

Fields for President, 1940

Manager . . . . Mr. CHARLES MORTON.
Assistant Manager and Treasurer - - - Mr. PHILIP YORKE.

5/3/1901

Programme ▪ ▪ ▪ ▪ ▪ **6d.**

1.	OVERTURE "Le Domino Noir"	*Auber.*	7.45
2.	LA SERENADA TRIO.		7.52
3.	BEATRICE WILLEY. Vocalist.		8.0
4.	PROVEANIES TROUPE OF CYCLISTS.		8.8
5.	LEONIE ROY. Comedienne.		8.21
6.	W. C. FIELDS. Juggler.		8.29
7.	FLOYE REDLEDGE. Comedienne.		8.42
8.	HENRI LEONI. Chanteur Français.		8.50
9.	"THE FOLLIES"		8.57

In a Selection from their "PIERROT ENTERTAINMENT."
Messrs. H. G. PÉLISSIER, N. A. BLUME and LEWIS SYDNEY, Misses EVELYN HUGHES,
DORIS LIND and IVY MOORE.

10.	J. M. CAMPBELL. Mimic		9.15
11.	HOWARD THURSTON. The King of Cards.		9.23
12.	LUCY NANON. Chanteuse Française.		9.38
13.	LE THERESE. The New Century Hypnotist.		9.48
14.	Orchestral Intermezzo—		10.3
	Selection from "Lohengrin"	*Wagner.*	
15.	CLOWN CABAN with his Menagerie.		10.15
16.	AQUAMARINOFF TROUPE of Russian Dancers and Singers.		10.30
17.	**THE AMERICAN BIOGRAPH.**		10.39

Invented by HERMAN CASLER, of New York.
LIST OF LATEST PICTURES.

7 Bill of the Palace Theatre of Varieties. Fields is Number 6.

At his first engagement in London, which lasted four weeks from 23 February 1901, the bill W. C. Fields appeared on was as follows:

1 OVERTURE 'LE DOMINO NOIR'
2 LA SERENADA TRIO
3 BEATRICE WILLEY, VOCALIST
4 PROVEANIES TROUPE OF CYCLISTS
5 LEONIE ROY, COMEDIENNE
6 W. C. FIELDS, JUGGLER
7 FLOYE REDLEDGE, COMEDIENNE
8 HENRI LEONI, CHANTEUR FRANÇAIS
9 'THE FOLLIES'
IN A SELECTION FROM THEIR 'PIERROT ENTERTAINMENT'
10 J. M. CAMPBELL, MIMIC
11 HOWARD THURSTON, THE KING OF CARDS
12 LUCY NANON, CHANTEUSE FRANÇAISE
13 LE THERESE, THE NEW CENTURY HYPNOTIST
14 ORCHESTRAL INTERMEZZO – SELECTION FROM
LOHENGRIN, WAGNER
15 CLOWN CABAN WITH HIS MENAGERIE
16 AQUAMARINOFF TROUPE OF RUSSIAN DANCERS
AND SINGERS
17 THE AMERICAN BIOGRAPH
INVENTED BY HERMAN CASLER OF NEW YORK.

LIST OF LATEST PICTURES:
FUNERAL OF THE QUEEN – (INCLUDES:)
THE CORTÈGE ON ITS WAY FROM OSBORNE TO TRINITY PIER.
ARRIVAL OF THE CORTÈGE AT TRINITY PIER.
THE 'ALBERTA' CONVEYING THE ROYAL BIER, AND
'VICTORIA AND ALBERT,'
WITH ROYAL MOURNERS ABOARD, PASSING THROUGH LINE OF
BATTLESHIPS.
THE PROCESSION PASSING MARBLE ARCH.

THE KING AND GERMAN EMPEROR PASSING THROUGH
HYDE PARK.
THE ROYAL PROCESSION ON ITS WAY TO PARLIAMENT.

BLOEMFONTEIN – UNFURLING THE FLAG.
WITH THE FLAG TO PRETORIA – THE UNION JACK BEING HOISTED AT
PRETORIA ON
ARRIVAL OF LORD ROBERTS, JUNE 5TH 1900 . . .
SIKHS GUARDING DONKEY TRAIN.
CHINESE HORSELESS CARRIAGES.
JOHN CHINAMAN AT HOME.
PICTURESQUE PANORAMIC SCENERY IN CANADA.

THE MUSIC COMPOSED BY ALFRED PLUMPTON.
GOD SAVE THE KING.

A close examination of the programme at the Palace Theatre reveals the precise times at which each of the acts came on, commencing at 7.45 p.m. The Comedy Juggler, Fields, is on from 8.29 to 8.42 – thirteen minutes. The longest act, the local troupe 'The Follies', are on from 8.57 to 9.15 – eighteen minutes.

A more recent celebrity, Andy Warhol, said that in the future every one would be famous for fifteen minutes. The English music-hall already beat him to it. This was not a wide-open window to fame. You had to leap on, capture the audience in your first few seconds, and hold them for your brief sojourn in the lights. Then it was on to the next act.

The reviewer from *The Era* was kind, but even more brief:

Another new turn at the Palace is W. C. Fields, a tramp juggler, whose quaint methods of performing familiar tricks are quite American. He is already a great favourite.

Most of the review dwells on the drolleries of the *Follies*, who were a standard variety turn. Their current act was a burlesque of various musical schools, from 'Eastern' music to Italian grand opera. Mr Alfred Plumpton's score provided a suitable funeral march for the Biograph's presentation of Queen Victoria's funeral, and doubtless, stirring tunes for the scenes from Pretoria and Bloemfontein. The Boer War was then in full swing, and in the veldt of South Africa, Boer guerrillas were harrying the British armed forces. Unlike a later war, these battles abroad did not interrupt the normal flow of life at home.

There was no need at all for foreigners to be affected by the war three thousand miles away. The young juggler, clutching his special feature from the *Black and White Budget* of 16 March, could see recognition flowing his way. He was clearly happy in England, and sent home to Philadelphia a promotional postcard illustrated by himself. The juggler stands, with his balls, his name imprinted behind him, while a demure female figure in frock-coat and black satin panties stands over the E of the 'Fields'. The full ornate inscription reads: 'W. C. Fields, Tivoli, Leeds. Original, Unique, Eccentric.' It is the first extant example of the juggler's artwork, his sideline of graphic cartoons of himself, which would become more common later on.

W. C. Fields in Leeds began a pattern of appearances which was to become a routine of his tours. He would play the capital city whenever possible and then branch out into the provinces. This would be most beneficial in Britain, where the provinces, as we have noted, were richly endowed with venues. In London, Fields was one among many. In Leeds, Bradford, Sheffield or Liverpool, he could headline. The Tivoli, Leeds, in March 1901, was the first engagement in which W. C. Fields, comedy juggler, heads the bill. His competition there – the acrobatic Garganis; Alethea, lady gymnast; Edmunda the ventriloquist; and the Kesslers, 'vocalists' – were minor enough for him to star. In Bradford, in April, at the People's Palace, he could shine again: 'Crowded auditoriums have been the rule here this week. W. C. Fields is a host in himself as a juggler, his tricks being vastly clever and his humour delightful.' Once again, we are given hints that the comic patter is still going strong.

In speaking or writing in later years about his foreign tours Fields allowed himself the maximum possible embellishment. Here was where his tall tales became taller, scraping the sky and punching holes in the clouds. Even in as sober a piece as *From Boy Juggler to Star Comedian*, in 1928, he would blithely state: 'I played the Malay Straits, down through India, Australia, to New Zealand and back, through Samoa and India, skirting the coast of Africa.' Who was going to check him out? Even in speaking of his European tours, he fantasized, exaggerated, lied and made up outrageous stories, mainly concerning his close personal acquaintance with Royalty, and Edward the Seventh in particular. Taylor's biography takes up two pages with a marvellously colourful description of Fields' engagement at Buckingham Palace, complete with Indian Maharajahs, whose dogs were quick to identify the usurping tramp and kept leaping up to knock down his cigar boxes, ruining his tricks. Taylor writes: 'The King greeted the juggler with effusion, although, Fields said later, a couple of nearby earls and a bishop were seen to shift their pocket watches . . .'

Alas, this droll event never took place. Fields performed under the British Royal aegis twice: once, obscurely, as a featured performer at Queen Alexandra's Christmas Dinner for Soldiers' Widows and Orphans in December 1902, and once, more publically, alongside Sarah Bernhardt, at the Coliseum in London, in 1913, a tale which shall be told in due course. But the only Palaces he saw were the chain of vaudeville theatres of that name.

Why did Fields tell so many lies? Apart from the joy of the chase? The answer, is, I believe, implicit in the wider context of variety, its hectic nature, its competitive edge.

W. C. Fields never mentioned acts which upstaged him, and therein lie several intriguing tales. In fact, Fields rarely mentioned any of the hundreds of other acts with which he appeared, or which were on tour with him. His personal letters provide clues for the particular fraternity of American comedy jugglers. But there were others about which he was completely tight lipped.

The most glaring omission is a famous name which appeared to shadow him everywhere. From his first appearance in Europe at the Wintergarten, Berlin, through London and his many provincial tours, one other American was always around to gall him, stealing his thunder, gaining the limelight. This irksome rival was Harry Houdini.

One cannot discuss the era without mentioning this phenomenon, the self-styled 'Handcuff King'. Where Fields aspired, Houdini triumphed. Where Fields desired, Houdini conquered. At the age of twenty-six he was The Big Success Story of the variety circuits. Where every act advertised itself as being The Greatest Novelty to be Put Before the Public, Houdini's act was it.

He had been born as Ehrich Weiss in Budapest in 1874, and brought to the United States as a small boy, with his five siblings. The boy had read the marvellous exploits of the French magician Robert-Houdin and adopted his name. He entered show business at the age of seventeen and began his career, as we have related before, in the seedy 'dime museums'. Marrying young, like Fields, he performed with his wife, Bess, who was at his side throughout his life. His secret was his in-depth knowledge of locks and their keys. His entire act was a spectacular subterfuge. Escaping from handcuffs, from a locked box, from inside safes, from strait-jackets, he developed a genius for publicity that was unsurpassed by any other showman. From his humble beginnings in vaudeville he realized, like Fields, that the European tour was a short cut to glory. Arriving in London in the spring of 1900 he leapt to public attention by means of his first great publicity stunt – slipping out of handcuffs at Scotland Yard. From London he proceeded to Berlin, where he played the Wintergarten for over a month in the winter preceding Bill Fields. Then he preceded him, once again, to London, performing for over six weeks at the Alhambra Theatre until 26 January 1901.

Although Fields never mentioned Houdini, both played the same English circuits, at different venues but at the same time. Both played in Germany, though Houdini was more at home there because he could speak the language. They were to appear together on the same bill only once, at the London Hippodrome, Easter of 1904. It is probably not surprising that Fields, teeth gnashing, shut this out, since it followed on the heels of one of Houdini's most famous stunts – getting out of a set of fiendish special handcuffs in front of an eager crowd of one hundred pressmen. Concealed in a small tent, he strained and perspired for over an hour, amid cries of 'Give it up!' and 'Go on Houdini!' until he emerged pale-faced and free. (In his provincial tours he often had himself locked in jails, to walk free after equally titanic struggles.)

Houdini's other secret, apart from his knowledge of locks, was banal – his wife, Bess, slipped him his tiny lockpicks or keys. With these, smartly palmed, Houdini astounded the world for twenty years. But wherever he went, the press followed in droves, finessed by his intense, 'superhuman' glare, by his compact physical agility and his daredevil courage.

But a significant aspect of Houdini's tours, for our story, is a fact that appears to have escaped his own biographers. For several years, from 1902, Houdini contributed an irregular column on European Vaudeville to the *New York Dramatic Mirror*. In searching for clues about Fields's foreign tours, I was astonished to find these pithy, humorous and very informative essays.

Here is Houdini writing, for example, about the British circuit, in November 1902, including detailed information on the mysteries of British transport, which bedevilled the travelling artiste much as they continue to bedevil the public today:

To play one provincial town in England means to play the whole of England, as the cities are all alike, with very rare exceptions. The English professional does nothing on Sunday but travel, and the 'town folks' generally go to the depot and watch the 'Pros,' as music-hall performers are called, pass through. The connections on the railroads are about as bad as you can find anywhere, especially on Sundays . . .

I have made a few inquiries regarding the different railroad fares, and have discovered a few extraordinary things that for eccentric tariffs would be hard to beat. For instance, by consulting a railroad guide one can find that by buying a ticket to a town actually beyond one's destination the fare is less than by taking a ticket direct to the place where one wants to go. If the traveler takes an ordinary third-class return ticket from Glasgow to York the fare is £1 11s. 10d. A week-end ticket (which is good for three days) to Harrogate (some distance further) via York, however, only costs eighteen shillings, the difference between the two thirteen shillings and ten pence.

Some things never change.

In particular, Houdini provided invaluable descriptions of the vaudeville circuit in Germany, which Fields was to return to in the autumn of 1902 and then again in subsequent years. On 18 August 1902, Houdini wrote from Dusseldorf, Germany:

At the Wintergarten, Berlin, W. C. Fields and Josie De Witt have scored hits. There are but twelve acts on the programme of this great establishment and only one comedy act. American performers should take notice that at present there is a perfect famine of comic actors in Germany, and any and all kinds of salaries await the comedian that is naturally funny and can make the people laugh. Also notice that green trousers, yellow vests and red coats are not considered very funny in this country, as the German comedians, with the exception of the comic singers, all have strange looking costumes that are supposed to be funny but fail to accomplish their mission. Comic singers, like Otto Reutter, come out in dress suits, sing six to twelve songs, and get 6,000 marks, and now that Reutter is ill the Wintergarten has actually been unable to find another comedian to take his place. When you consider that Reutter plays the Berlin Wintergarten about six months every season, it shows that comic acts are scarce and hard to be found at any price . . . With rare exceptions, all American comedy acts have met with success over here. The Juggling Johnsons with the Bratz Brothers are headliners at Mellini's Theatre, but the Johnsons easily are the hit of the programme . . . A novel act, by the way, is a man that does a slide for life, Japanese fashion, but instead of sliding on his feet slides on top of his head. He has a steel wig and this prevents him from cutting his skull open. This act is creating a sensation in Russia, and ought to be good for America.

The weird nature of some of the German acts is highlighted in some of Houdini's other reports. Earlier that summer, on 5 June, Houdini had reported that 'the police of Berlin have forbidden Pappuss, "the King of the Starvers" to appear'. Afficionados of Franz Kafka might remember the 'Hunger Artist', which many readers might have considered a fantasy of the Czech fabulist's mind. But this seemed to be grist to the mill of German vaudeville. On 28 July 1902, Houdini reported that –

In Posen the Howling Dervishes certainly have had a good chance to do all the howling they want, as their manager, after carefully counting up the receipts, also carefully managed to evade all watchers and carried the money away with him. The Howling Dervishes naturally are left without any means, and, to make them howl all the more, the manager also managed to abduct the 'permission to exhibit', without which no one is allowed to perform.

The perils of vaudeville appeared to be standard everywhere. But both Houdini and Fields were now famous enough to avoid this once-familiar fate. As Houdini continued to tour England and Germany in the summer of 1901, Fields concluded his mini-tour of the English provincial towns and proceeded to Paris.

In May 1901, Fields opened in Paris, at the *Folies Bergère*. This must have been one hell of a summer for the young man from Philadelphia. From the enchanted kingdom of the English music-hall he was catapulted into another, of legendary proportions. The *Folies Bergère* had been opened in 1869 and undergone a number of changes before becoming the unique home of international variety and revues. It vied for fame with the Casino de Paris, the *Folies-Marigny* and the Olympia, as well as Circus arenas like the Nouveau-Cirque, the Hippo-Palace, and the Medrano. Charles Chaplin, who played at the *Folies* in 1909, wrote in his autobiography:

No theatre, I thought, ever exuded such glamour, with its gilt and plush, its mirrors and large chandeliers. In the thick carpeted foyers and dress circle the world promenaded. Bejewelled Indian princes with pink turbans and French and Turkish officers with plumed helmets sipped cognac at liqueur bars. In the large outer foyer music played as ladies checked their wraps and fur coats, baring their white shoulders.

These were the famous *habitués* of the *promenoir*, a great circle at the back of the stalls from which spectators could see the stage. The ladies of the *promenoir* could obtain a two week pass which allowed them to enter the theatre unaccompanied by gentlemen. Chaplin also wrote about the interpreters, who would communicate between the ladies and their enthusiastic foreign clients. Attempting to pick up one gracious lady, the young Chaplin quickly discovered that he was to pay a substantial sum for a quick grope in the lady's apartment, rather than the cool night-long dream he had pined for.

The sumptuous foyer of the *Folies* leads to two magnificent staircases which swept up to the dress circle and swing doors that opened on to the *promenoir* and the stalls. The entertainments on the stage ran the gamut of every conceivable variety act: Ballets, 'eccentric' dances, sketches, acrobats, jugglers, tightrope walkers, magicians and animal acts. Elephants had appeared on this stage since the late 1870s. Freak shows abounded. Barnum himself had exhibited 'The Dogman and his Son', as well as other offerings from his strange stable. A Boxing Kangaroo enjoyed a brief vogue. Wild West acts, strong men and wrestling matches were perennial favourites. A grandiose series of wrestling bouts for the world championship were being played all over the Paris halls in the year preceding Fields' appearance, and were to continue later.

The *Folies* were the gold cuff-links on the dress suit of *La Belle Époque*. The great painters of the day, such as Manet and Toulouse-Lautrec, immortalized the theatre in such paintings as Manet's 'Bar at the *Folies Bergère*'. Several of the great beauties of the era danced on the stage, notorious courtesans like Liane de Pougy, Cleo de Merode and La Belle Otero. The writer Colette caused a major scandal when she appeared bare breasted, in 1907. In later years Mata Hari herself cavorted on the same stage.

When Fields appeared, tickling the margins of this high glamour, he was accompanied, of course, by Hattie at his side. In his first engagement, in May 1901, he shared his début with another American act, the trick cyclist Bud Snyder. Also appearing were Burns and Evans, 'eccentrics', and the De Toma troupe of acrobats. The following week they were joined by 'Katinka', with her 'weird and interesting Bohemian dances, accompanied by that talented Tsigane musician, Boldi'. Fields was described as 'a most skilful and eccentric Yankee juggler, from the Palace Theatre, Shaftesbury Avenue'.

It was a long hot summer, and we can only imagine Hattie and Bill's delight in the world capital of culture and art. Fields' personal letters begin to give us clues to his thoughts later on, when he is separated from and writing to Hattie. When they were together they kept themselves to themselves. One can imagine Hattie keeping a close eye on the temptations of the *promenoir.* On 1 June *The Era* was reporting from Paris that Fields, the comic juggler 'keeps adding to his already great reputation'.

There is no doubt that Fields was a hit in Paris. But this first foreign tour was all too brief for him (in the context of the long voyages of those days). He had to return to the United States in August to fulfil engagements on the Keith circuit. The ocean voyage, aboard the RMS *Majestic*, of the White Star Line, provides us with a little coda, in the shape of a programme for the on-board 'Concert In Aid of Seamen's Charities'. It records a Recitation by Mrs W. C. Field. Her husband, perhaps, was not up to performing gratis at this point. Or perhaps he was rolling in his bunk, contemplating the mundane juggling grind that was about to resume once again.

Chapter 9
The Volcano and the Cycling Baboons
(Twice Daily)

On 23 August 1901, the *New York Dramatic Mirror* reported:

> W. C. Fields, returned from Europe, dealt out his comic juggling act with marked success and made everyone happy by his quaint humor and his clever performance. His comely assistant is a valuable quantity in the fun-making . . .

A roll-call of his appearances reveals the juggler's routine, from city to city, hotel to hotel, between August 1901 and July 1902, as he plied the US circuits:

1901:
August
    23, Keith's, New York

September
    7, Keith's, Providence

October
    5, Shea's, Toronto
    19, Duquesne's, Pittsburgh
    26, Columbia, Cincinatti

November
    12, Olympic, Chicago
    16, Columbia, St Louis
    23, Opera House, Chicago
    30, Grand Opera House, Indianapolis

December
    7, Empire, Toledo
    14, Shea's, Buffalo

1902:
February
  15, Orpheum, Omaha

March
  15, Duquesne's, Pittsburgh
  29, Olympic, Chicago

April
  3, Haymarket, Chicago
  12, Columbia, St Louis
  26, Empire, Cleveland

May
  10, Orpheum, Brooklyn
  24, Keith's, Boston
  31, Keith's, New York

June
  14, Electric Park, Baltimore
  28, Shea's, Buffalo

July
  12, Brighton Beach, Long Island

How he must have pined for his second foreign tour! In summer, business traditionally fell in the US, with halls as yet unacquainted with air-conditioning. Those who could, decamped to cooler climes. While Sparrow, 'the Mad Juggler', and others sweated in New York, Bill and Hattie set off again for Germany, appearing at the Wintergarten in August, as noted by Houdini. They stayed in Germany until mid-September, and then moved on to the Orpheum, Vienna. In November they were playing the Théâtre Variété in Prague.

The variety stage in what was then the Austro-Hungarian Empire was less developed than the stage in Germany. In a somewhat disparaging report, the American vaudevillian, Claude C. Bartram (who often wrote in conjunction with Houdini) wrote in the *New York Dramatic Mirror* on 7 June 1902:

VAUDEVILLE IN AUSTRIA–HUNGRY BY CLAUDE C. BARTRAM
In this part of the world the principal thing lacking in a *variété* programme is variety . . . The first number is a serio-comic, then comes a little acrobatic or juggling act, and then begin the attractions which consist of every avail-

able kind of novelty act – which we will call, for want of a better name – dumb acts. These dumb acts seem all cut out of the same piece and after the same pattern, as though at some period, remote in the mists of the past, a genius had existed who loved his labor more than his profit and had made pattern of an act, and then had died, and that artists had been cutting their acts after this pattern ever since . . . Last before the pause comes a *komiker*. He never varies in appearance or repertoire. When you have seen one, you have seen his whole species. A dress suit, *chapeau claque* in hand, and a smooth-shaven face decorated by a bland smile, is his make up. He sings songs which he calls couplets, which are sundry words written to any music that happens to be at hand . . .

There are also pantomimes of the old Humpty-Dumpty order in which slapsticks, trick sceneries and dummies play the most important roles, which, after a Damen Ensemble, who sing and march in burlesque style, concludes this programme, remarkable only for its dearth of comedy . . .

(In Prague) the Théâtre Variété, is but a few minutes from the Vienna stadium. It is a large theatre furnished with tables, where meals and drinks are served, as is customary in all the varieties of Central Europe.

(In Vienna) the Orpheum plays both variété and operetta . . . The idea seems to have proved a good one, for (the) small theatre is always well patronized in spite of the fact that it is situated in a little street in one of the unfrequented parts of the city . . .

The 'Occasional Correspondent' of *The Era* was less laudatory about the Prague variety theatre, sniffing about the public consumption of 'sausage, sauerkraut and beer to the accompaniment of the German equivalent of comic songs or the patter of one of their somewhat dreary comedians'. The English correspondent also waxed wroth about the penchant of Teutonic porters and concierges to extract gratuities from artistes for the privilege of finding them an overpriced hotel or apartment, as well as the Viennese municipality's outrageous demand of an income tax from performers. Fields himself spoke of this obnoxious aspect of Austro-Hungarian mores once, in March 1913, to an interviewer for the US newspaper, *The Standard*:

I'll tell you of an experience I had in Bohemia. In that country the authorities collect taxes for almost anything under the sun. When I went to – lets take the name of the place for granted, but it may rhyme with 'plague' . . . One night, as I was entering my hotel about eleven o'clock, I was stopped by a policeman who carried a long pole and a lantern, and was informed that I would have to pay a tax of five cents for coming home at that hour. (It appears they tax everyone who remains out after nine o'clock.) I asked the policeman what would happen if I didn't come home at all. He said I wouldn't have to pay, in that case. And, ashamed as I am to tell it, I must admit that I strolled away and didn't come back to my rooms for two weeks – and then I left without paying half the taxes I owed the city. See what I have on my conscience.

There were other unusual hazards in the Empire, such as the performance at Kaschau, in Hungary, at which, according to *The Era*: 'An officer among the audience committed suicide by shooting himself through the head with a revolver. The report of the pistol caused a panic in the house, and several people were hurt in the rush for the doors. The officer was in love with the leading lady of the company, but his affection was not returned.' The next item on the same page also reports, ominously, that 'Fraulein Frisch, a German actress, has been fined £2 for using the word "Archduke" on the stage at Vienna, and thereby infringing a police regulation.'

It was in these conditions that Fields began, very wisely, to develop his juggling routine as a purely silent act. What could charm an audience in Buffalo or Leicester could certainly not work in Prague or Berlin, though a more sophisticated French audience might not mind. Fields tried apparently to learn some German phrases, but the risk of misunderstandings was, as noted above, fraught with peril. As one gathers from Houdini's note about the Howling Dervishes, every performer required a 'licence to perform' from the police, at least in Germany, which could be revoked at will.

This, by the way, disposes of another fond Fieldsian myth, that of his sojourns in various European jails. According to Taylor, he was jailed in London, Paris, Germany and Australia, but still believed Philadelphia jails were the best. In fact, disappointingly enough, Fields appeared to have been astonishingly well-behaved on his travels. The 'Music Hall Gossip' section of *The Era* chronicled the merest infractions by the most obscure vaudevillians, even devoting whole columns to the new exotic motoring offences, not to speak of serious brushes with the law. I have gone blind looking for Fields' British peccadillos. In vain.

From Paris he once wrote to his juggling colleague, O. K. Sato, about a confrontation with some French artistes ('Miss Bouliko et son excentrique') who were plagiarising the jugglers' material, but no police involvement is mentioned. Regarding Australia there has been a persistent legend of his beating up a man who insulted Hattie, with subsequent action by the antipodean gendarmes, but there is no trace of this event in any document.

Fields crossed the oceans to perform, to make a living, not to sow his wild oats. He was, contrary to all previous assumptions, a very serious young man, ambitious and attentive to business. And so, at the end of November 1902, having enlivened the somewhat cheerless stages of Vienna and Prague, he arrived in London to open at a completely new venue, the Hippodrome, in Leicester Square.

This was the true golden age of British music-hall. At the same time as Fields opened at the Hippodrome, the following acts were on other stages:

Dan Leno, at the London Pavilion.
Vesta Victoria, at the Tivoli, the Oxford and the Camberwell Palace.
Lillie Langtry, at the Middlesex Music Hall and at the New Grand,
   Clapham Junction.
Harry Tate, at the London Pavilion and Gatti's Palace of Varieties.
Fred Karno's Troupe of Famous Comedians, at the Middlesex Music
   Hall, in their Farcical Sketch 'The New Woman's Club'.

The reader may be puzzled at the multiple-appearances of the same acts at different halls. This was indeed one of the more fatiguing aspects of English music-hall life – performers rushing across town, playing in as many as four theatres on the same night. Fields mentioned this in one of his dispatches, allowing the inference that he followed the same routine. But it was far too hectic for his tastes, or, possibly, impossible for his booking agents to provide.

Another piquant item in this same week of 29 November 1902, is the 'New Edisonograph' presentation of 'A Fantastical Trip to the Moon' at Gatti's Palace of Varieties. This revolutionary little film by the Frenchman George Melies was to prefigure a whole world of filmed fiction. Harry Tate is another name we should note. His famous sketch, 'Motoring', had not yet been written, but it, too, will play a role in our story.

The Hippodrome, at this time, was London's newest music-hall. It had first opened its doors to the public on 15 January 1900. It was a state of the art auditorium, the absolute acme of theatrical design and construction. The floor of the vestibule was laid with Mosaic, its wall covered with Italian marble, its ceiling a beautifully decorated dome. The Grand Saloon was furnished as a ship's bar, its walls and ceiling covered with fumed oak. 'The counters, fittings, etc, are in keeping with the idea, even to the portholes, showing a view of the sea beyond . . . every detail is studied down to the attendants, whose costumes are semi-naval . . .' The stage was cantilevered, able to rise over a water tank with a circumference of 230 feet and a capacity of about 100,000 gallons. Its Hydraulic rams, cages and fountains could serve a variety of spectacularly staged events, a veritable 'Disneyland' fifty years ahead of its Californian rival. Over the years it was to stage the following stupendous happenings:

The Flood, with 'its almost appalling scene of wreck and devastation'.

The Earthquake, 'a vivid representation of a city square, in a few seconds converted into a mass of wreckage'.

The Typhoon, 'presenting a ship at sea with such accuracy of detail that many seafaring men expressed their delight and congratulations to the management'.

All this in the mundane urban surroundings of Cranbourne Street, two hundred yards from Piccadilly Circus! The Sands o' Dee, the Avalanche, The Redskins ('shooting the rapids from a height of nearly 70 ft') and Siberia were to add to this repertoire. But one of the first of these all-stops-out spectacles was the one enacted at Fields' Hippodrome première in November 1902. It was certainly an act calculated to upstage a juggler, and it was no wonder that Fields never mentioned it. Just as he never mentioned Herr Grais' performing baboons, who preceded him on the same bill. There can be few things more galling for an actor than to appear after bicycling and rope-walking monkeys, particularly as the records do not state whether, given the proclivities of these agile primates, the stage was swept between the acts.

The epic which headed the bill at the Hippodrome in November 1902 is best described in the words of the anonymous reviewer for *The Era*, in all the naive and racially dubious, if not downright nauseating, manner of that Imperial age:

The management of the Hippodrome introduced to their patrons a novelty on Monday, in the shape of a representation of the volcanic eruption of Mont Pelee and the destruction of the city of St. Pierre, which took place on May 10th last. Before the show, a gentleman gifted with enviable powers of eloquence and an excellent delivery, came forward and made a stirring appeal to the audience to welcome the native men, women and children – survivors of the population of the ill-fated town – who had been engaged to give samples of their artless methods of rejoicing, the entertainment opening by a dusky serenade . . . a love song for a lady love perched up aloft. Then came 'jollifications' by a number of 'niggers' of both sexes and various ages, dressed in the brilliant colours which harmonise so well with their rich complexions . . . Next came a wedding procession, the leader bearing a banner with the inscription 'Vive les nouveaux maries' – and very much alive both they and the nuptial party appeared to be. There was a great deal of running round with bunches of ribbons fixed to the tops of poles, and finally, after we had been acquainted with all the Martinique methods of innocent gaiety, the volcano, which was depicted on the drop scene let down as a background, burst into eruption; showers of glowing cinders descended on the devoted city; a general conflagration ensued; and amidst the frantic screams and gesticulations of the men and women the curtain descended on the interesting, effective, and well-arranged tableau.

This was the time of the Boer War and Kipling, the year of the death of Cecil Rhodes, who spoke of the 'lesser breeds without the law'. The Hippodrome was a typical arena of an Imperialism unable to distinguish between non-white man and animal, real and fake. We do not know if the actors on the stage of 'Martinique' were actual surviving islanders shipped over by the entrepreneurial H. E. Moss, or God knows who blacked up at bottom-of-the-barrel wages. Within a couple of years the Hippodrome would be famed for animal acts supplied from the bounteous wildlife of the Congo by the genocidal King Leopold of the Belgians, culminating, without shame, in the troupe of Congo pygmies whose click-language no one could understand but who gained the accolade, denied, alas, to our hero, of an appearance at the Buckingham Palace Royal Garden Party, where they gave 'a curious and interesting exhibition that attracted much attention from the Duke of Connaught'. But let us return to *The Era*, November 1902:

A great sensation at the Hippodrome is the feat of 'Cycling the Loop,' which is performed by a daring young baboon in the possession of Herr Grais. A loop of the usual shape is erected at the back of the stage, and the animal, being placed on the machine, rides down a slope, round the curves of the loop, and down to the stage at a rattling pace . . . Herr Grais' rope-walking baboon is as expert as ever, and his somersaults are done with wonderful activity and precision. A most amusing juggler is W. C. Fields, whose skill and drollery combined make him very popular indeed. The way in which he juggles with indiarubber balls is surprisingly smart, and the business which he introduces proves irresistible, chiefly owing to the natural and comical acting of this very funny artist. It is impossible not to laugh at Fields, and the most thoughtful and philosophic must be taken off their guard and made to smile by his unexpected acts.

In *The Tatler*, 10 December, another reviewer put it thus:

A HUMORIST JUGGLER

I am not such a violent pro-American that I cannot see anything good in England, but I must confess that the performances of American music-hall artists amuse me a great deal more than the antics of my own countrymen. For example, the American with his quickness, his enormous energy, and his coolness has practically driven from the field the English knockabout artist of the 'Two Macs' type. If you go to the Hippodrome you will see a remarkably clever comic juggler, W. C. Fields, performing all sorts of tricks with an apparent contempt for his own cleverness. Many of the tricks we have seen over a hundred times before, but this American's manner invests them all with a new interest; it is not exactly what he does but the tricky way he does it.

It's not what he does but the way that he does it. That is as good a take on Fields as any. Fields appearance at the Hippodrome, tucked away as it was among fifteen other acts, set a benchmark for his reputation as a fixture on the European circuit. This was his first taste, to be renewed later, of the curious tradition of the English Christmas Pantomime, as he juggled on the fringes of the Hippodrome's production of 'Dick Whittington', with the male lead played by Miss Ruth Lytton, and Miss Ray Cantor as Lieutenant Bowline, who sang 'a pussy-cat ditty with much smartness and expression'. Fields also logged his first appearance for Royalty, on 27 December, at Queen Alexandra's charity dinner for soldier's widows and orphans (presumably of the Boer War), which was held at the Alexandra Trust Buildings. The cream of the British music-hall were invited to appear, including Albert Chevalier, George Robey, Gus Elen, Vesta Tilley and Harry Lauder.

The young juggler had clearly been accepted among the front rank, but he was still restless, already making plans to extend his range still further.

After London, Fields fulfilled a couple of provincial bookings, headlining at Leeds and Birmingham in January of 1903. At Leeds, the reviewer noted 'his real clever work being sandwiched among various laughable antics'. Incidentally, we can note, for those who still insist on seeing that bygone age as more refined than our own, that, on the same bill, 'lady wrestlers are here led by Madame Appolins'. Also at this time, at the Leicester Palladium, 'Houdini . . . established a record both in attendance and money taken.' The unchained shadow was still haunting Fields.

By 7 February Fields was back in America, losing no time in performing at Keith's in Providence, Rhode Island; 14 February, Keith's Boston; 28 February, Keith's Union Square, New York. And on 7 March a homecoming to Philadelphia, where he appeared at Keith's old Orpheum on a major bill including Sandow the Strong Man (back in the US after a two-year tour abroad), Jennie Yeamans, Belle Hathaway's monkeys (there was no getting away from those incontinent beasts!), and Captain Spaulding, the fiery eater of molten lead. The *New York Dramatic Mirror* noted: 'It is the best offering of the season to the usual crowded houses.' One cannot doubt that, this time at least, the family came out to see the new star shine.

Fields had arrived. He had every reason to feel confident. He had travelled through the main countries of Europe. He had topped the bill in many provincial cities. He had played the top music-halls of London, Paris and Berlin, with his beloved wife at his side. He was twenty-three years old, and in the front rank, crowded as it was, of his profession. But he did not intend to stand still.

Without a pause, he returned to the grindstone: 21 March, Orpheum, Kansas City; 28 March, Orpheum, New Orleans; 4 April, Orpheum, San Francisco; 25 April, Orpheum, Los Angeles; but the juggler was travelling west for a purpose. No sooner had W. C. Fields arrived in Los Angeles than he set off again, further afield than ever . . .

Chapter 10
The Reigning Spirit of the Antipodes

In 1903 I circumnavigated the globe leaving New York and going west to San Francisco on to Honolulu, Pago Pago, New Zealand, Australia, Africa and back to Europe and returned to New York after three years. Everywhere I went alcohol was the reigning spirit. (Pardon me.) The aborigines, the natives, in every land in which I visited took two or three days and nights off to go on a bender every so often with some sort of native brew distilled from potatoes, maize, fruits, etc. ad lib . . .

William Claude Fields

Before Fields set out on his circumbobular journey, another revolutionary step had taken place, without fanfare, on the stage at Keith's Union Square theatre on New York's 14th Street, on 28 February 1903. The *New York Dramatic Mirror* takes up the tale:

> One of the big laughing hits of the bill was made by W. C. Fields, the eccentric juggler, who has been in Europe for several seasons. He has improved greatly in his work and has invented any number of foolish little tricks that are bound to bring laughs even from the most *blasé*. His facial expressions and gestures are funny in the extreme. A new trick with a billiard table brought the set to a brilliant finish, and Mr Fields was forced to make several bows. The billiard table trick will not be described here, lest it may be snapped up by the pirates, but it is what is known as a 'knockout'.

Confusion has, as usual, surrounded the date of the unveiling of this seminal Fieldsian artifact. The trick pool table became Fields' most recognisable and favourite prop, and it travelled the world with him, packed in its massive crate, over land and sea, mountain and plane, country and city, down the years and decades. It eventually wore out, and was replaced by a duplicate table for the Ziegfeld *Follies of 1915*, which in turn found use in several of the comedian's films, ending up in a glass case in The Magic Castle, in Los Angeles, where it is enshrined as a kind of battered Excalibur.

Like the trick cigar box, the trick pool table was a simply engineered illusion, in which a hidden crank would pull all fifteen balls, attached to invisible strings, simultaneously into different pockets, enabling the player to be seen to pot all the balls in one stroke. The table was also built with rounded cushions, so that the balls would bounce back at various angles, to land in the player's hip pocket or on his chin. Another little touch was a hole through which the player could drive the cue, 'by mistake', into the surface of the table. It was this trick that climaxed the long verbal routine of the pool sketch in the 1936 film, *Six of a Kind*. The trick balls were pastiched in Fields' first movie, the silent short, *Pool Sharks*, in 1915, but the effect there was achieved by trick photography.

This was not the only bulky item that Bill Fields took with him on his world tour. Apart from the usual accompaniment of his wife, Hattie, his brother, Walter, joined the act. Once again, the tale is blurred and uncertain. Ronald Fields reports that his Aunt Adel, Bill Fields' sister, claimed Walter to be the real funny man of the family. But like Gummo, the invisible fifth Marx Brother, Walter's qualities are lost in the realm of myth. According to Ronald Fields, he played the part of the juggler's stooge, first played by Hattie, and decades later to be fulfilled by long-suffering sidekicks like William Blanche (alias 'Shorty'), and Tammany Young in *Six of a Kind*.

The act continued, in 1903, to be billed as W. C. Fields alone. Fields was very protective of his solo billing and trade name. But both Walter and Hattie were at Bill's side on his Australian and South African tour.

From San Francisco to Honolulu and Pago Pago . . . Bill made much in later years of these tingling names, of the exotic nature of his travels. But we should not be fooled, yet again, by our ignorance of the nature of the world and of vaudeville at the turn of the century. We may live today in a global village, where no part of the world is more than twenty-four hours away, but the world then was crisscrossed with a busy network of shipping which connected the continents, slowly, but surely. Well back into the 1890s variety artists, particularly from the English music-hall, were crossing the oceans on a regular basis to entertain and earn cash at the furthest ends of what was then the unsunset British Empire.

Fields has left us no reliable descriptions of his antipodean tour, but another vaudevillian, once again our old stalwart Fred Allen, wrote a detailed account of his own Australian tour, albeit one decade later, in 1914. This was the year of Fields' second Australian tour, but conditions could hardly have been any easier in 1904. The ships to Australia were not the prestigious giant liners like the *Deutschland* or the *Majestic* which plied the Atlantic routes. Tiny staterooms were crammed below decks in conditions which would have made even the Marx Brothers hesitate to draw in more guests, let alone a posse of stewards. Allen reported being sick in his bunk all the way to Honolulu, where the 'natives' swam up in a noisy shoal and demanded that the passengers throw money into the water. In those days, wrote Allen, nobody in Hawaii knew what a tourist was: if you walked down the main street with clothes on, they knew you were off the boat, if not, you were a local. Six seasick days further on lay the island of Pago Pago. This was an American fueling station, and if Fields performed here, it was without doubt to an expatriate American workforce. One can take it for granted they were overjoyed at the diversion. Fields wrote later in one of his 1943 letters that the native Polynesians would rush at you and say, 'Give me money, I get girl $1.00.' This is borne out by Allen's similar tale of an old man who tempted the passengers into the green hills for 'flifty cents' and 'half-clown', to meet a bevy of village housewives. But time has drawn a veil over the outcome.

Australia herself lay twenty-one more days down the line. The Fields scrapbooks reveal that Bill stopped over in Auckland, New Zealand, but there is no record of his performing there. He had just enough time to visit the races, and a racing programme dated 3 June has the letters 'Dead Heat' scrawled in hand over the entries. Having failed, apparently, to make a killing on the horses, the Fields entourage continued aboard the SS *Sonoma* to their final destination.

Fields had been signed to appear in the chain of Tivoli Theatres, whose doyen, in 1904, was the colourful antipodean impresario, Harry Rickards. An ex-performer himself, he liked to be photographed in Napoleonic garb, with matching pose. He commuted regularly to England to sign up the best acts, and having previously snapped up Paul Cinquevalli and such luminaries as Marie Lloyd, his offer to Fields was not one that could be refused.

In a special feature about Rickards in *The Era* in 1909, the impresario was quoted as saying:

The Australian people will have nothing but the very best . . . no act or artist is too big for them. As it appears to all who take an interest in the subject that an era of undreamt of prosperity is dawning in Australia, the requirements of those who purvey for the public amusement will be of a character that will give rise to a steady stream of immigration, temporary or permanent, of the ablest entertainers the Mother Country can supply.

In 1903, in fact, Fields arrived in a new nation. The Commonwealth of Australia was officially formed on 1 January 1901, out of the constituent colonies of the vast continent. Australia was experiencing a vigorous industrial growth combined with its first Immigration Restriction Act, which aimed for a racially homogenous country. Women's suffrage was established in 1902, sixteen years ahead of the Mother Country. The political balance of power was held by the Labour Party, whose position on immigration was the most restrictive of all. The old dumping ground of England's prisoners was to be a Pacific power, and its new bourgeoisie craved entertainment.

The record shows that Fields opened in Melbourne, in mid-June, 1903, his début at Rickard's Opera House marked by the local column *Table Talk*:

> Mr. W. C. Fields makes his entry dressed in sleighing costume, fur coat and cap, with dark goggles, and carrying a driving whip. After divesting himself of these impedimenta, he gives an exhibition of juggling with hats, balls, sticks, boxes etc. Mr. Fields has already established himself as a favourite . . .

(The 'sleighing costume' was a very early precursor of the Alaskan prospector of the 1928 stage sketch, *The Stolen Bonds*, later to become *The Fatal Glass of Beer* for Mack Sennett in 1933.) The Australian magazine *Punch* added:

> He speaks not at all, he explains nothing, he is dressed in seedy black, and all his aparatus consists of three bouncing balls, a stick, a couple of hats, a cigarette and a dozen empty cigar boxes . . . He plays with the three balls in a most bewildering way. They seem to slip accidentally from his grasp whilst juggling, but only to bounce into play or to be stamped upon the hop once more into the unceasing 'juggle.'

Fresh from his triumph in Melbourne, Fields proceeded briefly to Adelaide, and then doubled back to open in Sydney on 21 July.

Sydney was, then as now, one of the great urban landscapes,

described by another travelling vaudevillian, Walter C. Kelly, as 'a place where land and sea blend into a harmony that is absolutely delightful . . . its industrial and commercial life is a pocket edition of our own whirling Metropolis, and yet the mellow stream of good fellowship flows through every thoroughfare'. Kelly wrote about the camaraderie between visiting artistes and the local vaudevillians, such as Fred Bluett, Tom Dawson, and Harry Rickards himself, presiding over his kingdom of fun from his mansion overlooking the harbour.

Fields performed, at the Tivoli, along with another international stalwart, Rudinoff, whose speciality was imitating bird calls and drawing 'smoke pictures' with a torch on a white enamel plate. (A typical offering would be a local subject: Moonlight in Sydney Harbour.) Bill remained at the Tivoli until the end of September, his longest single engagement, as a juggler, anywhere. The Sydney *Daily Telegraph* of 27 July introduced him thus: 'W. C. Fields, an "eccentric juggler" from America, made his first appearance, and was given an ovation. He makes up as a tramp, and his performance consists of many astonishingly clever juggling feats. The turn altogether is fresh, and in every way acceptable.' On 15 August the *Telegraph* announced that Fields 'will today introduce his original billiard table act'. Bill had perhaps held it back for more rehearsals until then.

In fact, Bill became, to all intents and purposes, an honorary citizen of this new, cohering society. He was at home enough to feature, perhaps for the first time, but not the last, in an advertisement, for 'Kinothol Pastilles', recommending 'to all who are annoyed with throat affections that ANTISEPTIC KINOTHOL PASTILLES give Greatest and Quickest relief'. IT CURES HOARSENESS!

The Tivoli proclaimed

W. C. FIELDS – THE ABSOLUTE GREATEST AND MOST VERSATILE
ECCENTRIC JUGGLER THAT HAS EVER APPEARED
THIS SIDE OF THE WORLD.

In a short time he supplanted Rudinoff as the audience favourite, and was the headliner for the rest of his stay. On 29 September *The Era*'s Australian correspondent wrote that, 'The comic juggler Mr W. C. Fields enlists the valuable aid of the orchestra, which plays appropriate music during the performance.' Clearly, Fields was having the time of his life in the antipodes, and his life with Hattie was probably at its happiest. Photographs in the family archive show W. C. on the beach with Hattie and other performers, and fooling about at the racetrack with a boomerang.

Fields left Sydney in October to return by rail to Melbourne, his embarkation reported in glowing terms by the *Music Hall and Theatre Review*:

> The send off given to Mr W. C. Fields, America's eccentric, on Friday evening, October 2nd, should make that gentleman very pleased with himself. The Redfern Railway Station was crowded with friends and well wishers to see him away, and when the time came for the train to start, 7.15, the handshaking, hurrahs, and waving of hats and handkerchiefs, as the train sped away, must have been, to say the least, very gratifying to Mr and Mrs Fields. Mr Fields is the greatest drawing card Mr Rickards has had for years.

On 19 October, the Fields' shared the bill at Melbourne's Opera House with 'a comedy sketch by moving pictures' depicting a Trip to the Moon – Uncle Melies again foreshadowing Uncle Claude. The Fields' remained at the Opera House to the end of the month, undeterred by a major outbreak of swine fever in the State, but had departed Melbourne by November, on the second leg of their Great World Tour.

It was about this time, biology suggests, that Claude Junior, W. C. Fields' son, was conceived. This might even have occurred on board ship, the *Commonwealth*, upon which the party embarked for South Africa. And so, unaware of the germinating seed both of hope and of future conflict, the Fields family embarked on the longest haul of all, thirty-three days tossing about the stormy Indian Ocean, towards their next port of call.

Fields has left us a colourful description, quoted by grandson Ronald, of his arrival with Walter at the port of Durban, and of being unloaded off the boat in great wicker baskets – although he omitted Hattie completely from his narrative. Zulu rickshaw boys, yelling 'Me Jim Fish!' raced them off the quayside to the Royal Marine Hotel, where they collapsed only to be eaten alive by mosquitoes which could 'break a child's leg with a kick'.

Taylor, Fields' erstwhile biographer, decided for some reason that Fields had arrived in South Africa during the Boer War, an error that could have been easily checked. In fact, the Boer War was over by May 1902, though the scars of the bitter conflict were evident. Fields wrote, on arrival in Johannesburg, according to Taylor, that 'the place is full of grim looking Boers with double-barreled guns and thickly bearded faces. They pass the lonely hours waiting for trouble by vying with each other to look the dirtiest.' But, it turns out, this description comes from a news cutting dating from Fields' second South African tour, in 1914. In *From Boy Juggler to Star Comedian*, Bill related another piquant anecdote:

> When I played the Orpheum Circuit for Martin Beck I got acquainted with a young humpbacked chap who sold candy and magazines on trains. Little did I know how he was going to help me in later years. When I reached South Africa I received a wire in Natal that the theatre in Johannesburg was burned, and not to come there. The Boer War was just over, and a traveler had to have a citizenship card to even purchase a railroad ticket. Here I was with a contract for Johannesburg and unable to reach the place. I was a dejected comedian sitting in a railroad station. A train pulled in, and the first person to jump off was the little candy butcher I had known on the Pacific Coast. He was a Boer. He had a card of citizenship which he loaned me and I got a ticket to Natal.

Fields can be so maddening in his tall tales! If he was a dejected comedian at a railway station, he was certainly not alone, since Hattie and Walter were with him. The tale of the candy butcher (or vendor) is sweet till we read that meeting a humpbacked person was considered good luck by superstitious vaudevillians. So we have to take the wicker baskets, too, on dubious trust. In the version quoted by Ronald Fields, W. C. tells how he and Walter feigned British accents to get permits to get to Johannesburg. He then relates how, en route to the consul, they saw a corral with mules, in which a young American was chewing gum and swinging a lariat. This turned out, Fields said, to be Will Rogers, later to shoot to fame and become Bill's colleague in the Ziegfeld *Follies*.

Here too, we hit a credibility bump. Fields' meeting with Will Rogers in South Africa became a staple of his story, but a recent definitive biography of Rogers, by Ben Yagoda, has established that the 'Cherokee Kid' had left South Africa for Australia in mid-August, 1903. Rogers had initially travelled to Argentina, but, having failed to find a job at a ranch there, sailed to South Africa, where he joined an act called Texas Jack's Wild West Show, at which he learned his life-long stunt of trick roping. Among other exploits with Texas Jack he blacked up and sang 'coon' songs, an experience about which he said later: 'My appearance amused the natives and Kaffirs greatly, as they had never seen the makeup of a colored performer before.'

Quite so. In a tribute to Rogers following his death in 1935, Fields wrote, more convincingly, that he had first met Will Rogers in Australia, and the chronology would allow them to meet in Melbourne, in November 1903. Rogers returned to America in March 1904, and was in Australia throughout Fields' stay in South Africa.

So far what W. C. Fields didn't do in South Africa. What he did was his act, first at the Standard Theatre in Johannesburg, then at the Tivoli in Cape Town, where he was billed as 'America's Greatest Burlesque Juggler'. Here too, audiences were very picky. South Africa was a rough country, a Wild South, with many hostile forces. The Boers, sullen in defeat, the black population, sidelined and unmanned. Here too, white socialist workers were agitating for a colour bar. (Racial separation was in fact less rigid at this time than under the later apartheid system.) The British-controlled government was legislating to introduce Chinese labour, amid much grumbling about the 'Asiatic danger'. White mine workers (who were mostly Boers) were constantly threatening strikes. No wonder the middle classes wanted jugglers. But a typical example of the prickly colonial psyche might be found in a letter written to *The Era* in London, by one signing himself 'Africander', in May 1904 (the following should be read aloud in a broad Soth-Efriken accent):

> Sir, – South Africa opens a new field for the showman, and by such I mean the legitimate showman, who caters for his public and endeavours, by a clean, attractive combination, to gain the confidence of his patrons, which always ensures success. Nothing succeeds like popularity and a strict attention to business. Many shows I have seen have failed through lack of energy, carelessness as to the many details necessary to make the public desirous of spending their money at the door, and the slovenly manner in which the arrangements are conducted to catch the eye of would-be-patrons . . . Merry-go-rounds are played out, while cinematographs are a thing of the past. To showmen who are desirous of trying their fortune in South Africa I say, bring out a good attractive show, comprising freak exhibitions and anything novel and catchy, and money can be made in this country . . .

Fields certainly seems to have passed muster. In mid-January he was invited to the residence of the British High Commissioner, Lord Alfred Milner, for a private performance at his residence, 'Sunnyside'. Fields has left us a reminiscence of this event in a piece entitled *Speaking of Benefits*, written in 1923 and reprinted in Donald Deschner's 1966 filmography:

> There was the time, when I was playing vaudeville in Johannesburg, South Africa. The Governor General – Lord Maulder, I think – sent around word that his children were having a party the next day at Governor's House and would I stage a few choice juggles for their benefit . . .
>
> For twenty minutes the next afternoon I stood in the pouring rain outside the Governor's house, loaded down with cigar boxes, golf clubs, and rubber balls, while a platoon of footmen debated whether I ought to be allowed to enter. Finally, I was told the Governor General was busy, but that I could go ahead and amuse his children.
>
> I amused them my very best for thirty minutes. I had a running refrain of 'Wot's 'E Do That For?' to help me along and the cunning little tykes were only too willing, whenever I dropped a prop in the mistaken notion that I was planting an effect, to pick it up and gum my trick for me. But even that half-hour came to an end.
>
> Three seconds before its end the Governor General himself appeared. And so I was privileged to do my bit all over again . . . When it was over, I was allowed to go out in the rain again and without a fine or anything . . .

At least he got off lighter than in Prague . . . Just to spoil the effect, I might quote from a contemporary report of this episode, which states that 'after tea about thirty ladies and gentlemen assembled to witness Mr. Fields' performance'. As Groucho Marx might have said: so who do you believe, me, or the evidence of your own eyes?

Late in February, Fields was joined on the Cape Town stage by an old acquaintance, R.G. Knowles, who sang 'Love, Marriage and Divorce' to great applause, but Fields and Hattie were probably not paying much attention, as they were preparing for their own act. The South African correspondent of *The Era* noted: 'W. C. Fields, in his remarkable juggling act, continues to be a hot favourite. He is so quaint and grotesque that the audience is convulsed whilst he is on stage.' Africander's contempt for the cinematograph notwithstanding, the Biograph concluded the programme.

Despite Taylor's tales, its clear that all these performances were for

Whites Only, whatever W. C. might have put on for his rickshaw drivers out of hours.

But it was here, in Cape Town, that Bill and Hattie discovered the earth-shaking fact of her pregnancy. And then a fateful decision was made.

We might recall that Fred Allen told us that the female vaudevillian gave birth wherever fate took her, 'on trains, in dressing rooms . . . the show must go on'. Fields might well have thought the rigours of South Africa were too heavy a risk to take at this point. Ronald Fields has passed on the family tale that W. C. was determined, if he had a son, that he should be born in America, otherwise he could not grow up to be President. Whatever the motive, Hattie was prevailed upon to return, accompanied by Walter, directly from South Africa to the United States.

This was a separation that was to have dire consequences, as the couple had been together constantly, in work and leisure, for almost four years. But Hattie did leave, and Bill Fields proceeded, alone, with the massive crate of the trick billiard table, from Cape Town to England, leaving the bearded Boers and the giant mosquitoes of Durban behind him, to arrive in London at the end of March 1904.

The Fields' departure was timely, because, in April, bubonic plague broke out in Johannesburg.

Chapter 11
A Brief Literary Interlude

Bill Fields' third return to London was a homecoming in many ways. It was a return to the city of his first real foreign triumph, to the city of so many fellow vaudevillians who lived and breathed the spirit of music-hall. It was a return to the Hippodrome, that vast arena of fantasies where he was truly in his element. And it was a return to the city of his beloved Dickens, the very font of his creative juices.

London in 1904 was no longer the dark Victorian swell of dingy streets and destitute alley dwellers, of Fagin and of Oliver Twist, Micawber and David Copperfield. London was a city which, like Paris, celebrated the new twentieth century in a vortex of renewal and growth. New grandiose music-halls were only one expression of a building boom which changed the face of the city between the late 1890s and 1914, connecting the once placid suburbs of London to the centre with spokes of mortar and bricks. The new Underground system burrowed beneath the city, drawing it even closer together at the same time as it enlarged its urban sprawl.

Fields, like his fellow performers, benefited from this new prosperity of what was to be called the Edwardian Age and celebrated with farcical images of vain young men in silly boating hats. But his own London remained, so characteristically, the vision of his favourite fiction. From an early age, the child Claude Dukenfield had viewed everything around him, in his own stolid Philadelphia, as larger than life, as more than real: the iceman Andy Donaldson who became Gomer Wheatley; the Orland 'Social Club'; his invented tyrannical father; his doyen and mentor, Bill Dailey, with his 'Old Army Game'; his sense, that so many gifted children have, of being a stranger in a strange land.

We might leap forward another decade and a half, and look at a Fields already formed: Fields the star of the Ziegfeld *Follies*, the most glittering of Broadway's shows in the era when to be a Broadway star was to have climbed the peak of the mountain. At this point he is at his most removed from the familiar Fields of myth: the misanthrope, the social misfit, the loner, whose only love is his solitary glass, preferably with an olive in it. We shall deal with this part of the myth later. But let us take a look at one of his closest colleagues at this time: his fellow comedian, Eddie Cantor. Cantor wrote two autobiographies, *My Life in Your Hands* and *Take My Life*. In the latter book, he writes about W. C. Fields, *circa* 1917:

> In his room at the hotel were three huge theatrical trunks. I'd noticed them and wondered, for Fields wasn't a dandy about dress. A few nights after we got to Boston he started talking to me about literature. Books were the keys to another world; you didn't know anything until you'd started to read. He went over to one of the big trunks and flipped back the lid. Not a thing in it but books! What he was looking for wasn't in that trunk, so he flipped the lid of the next one, fished out a copy of *Oliver Twist* and gave it to me. The next night when we got back after the show and had ordered up some food, he sat and questioned me about what I'd read. 'Just why did Nancy feel any loyalty to Bill Sykes?'
>
> Night school had started. After *Oliver Twist, Les Miserables*. We traveled together with the 1917 *Follies* and again with the *Follies of 1918* and I kept on reading: Dickens, Hugo, Dumas, Eliot, the works; and discussing them with Professor Fields. In the morning we'd have a session with the newspapers. It wasn't enough to read the story; what was behind it? The man had an amazing reading background. He was up on science, he was up on history; if he were alive today he'd murder them on the quiz programs. And he'd never had formal schooling.

This is an astonishing window into the unknown Fields. We are clearly dealing here with a diligent auto-didact. Cantor went on to relate how, before his trip to Australia, Fields filled up his trunk with books about Australia which he read on the long, tedious journey. One surviving volume from this batch is the comedian's own copy of Robert Louis Stevenson's 'Treasure Island' marked in the flyleaf with Field's own signature.

Fields son, W. Claude Fields Junior, wrote, in a 1969 'Tribute to W. C. Fields' mounted by the Gallery of Modern Art in New York, that 'it was from his wife that Fields acquired a lively interest in literature, from which he later improvised and burlesqued chapters, names, places and events'. This may well have played a part, but the boy Claude's intense curiosity was a lynchpin of his character long before he met Hattie. Contemptuous of all received wisdom, he had to find out for himself.

One can imagine how a boy to whom life appeared grotesque would have responded both to Dickens' characters and to the wayward boys of Mark Twain. We might recall Huckleberry Fields, as per the Pittsburgh Post, riding the rails west in the 'blind baggage' with his mythical companion, singing for his supper and passing the hat.

The scholar Wes Gehring has drawn attention to another Twain character, that of the huckstering Colonel Sellers in the 1873 novel *The Gilded Age* (Twain's first novel, co-authored by him with Charles Dudley Warner), which was later adapted for the stage. Gehring has pointed out the verbal slickness of Sellers, whose 'tongue was a magician's wand that turned dried apples into figs and water into wine as easily as it could change a hovel into a palace and present poverty into imminent future riches'. The resemblance is tempting, with Sellers spewing lines like: 'Why, my dear innocent boy, we would just sit on the front door steps and peddle banks like Lucifer matches!' Or: 'Never take an inferior liquor, gentlemen, not in the evening, in this climate.' But, whether Fields read this book or not, this kind of character would have had a more direct influence through his own fairground and burlesque experiences.

But there was another, older character, from Dicken's bustling London, who, we know in retrospect, impressed Claude as no other, and who was to form a crucial building block of the fictional Fields that was to evolve. Let us open the book where he makes his first entrance – young David Copperfield is narrating –

> The counting house clock was at half-past twelve, and there was general preparation for going to dinner, when Mr Quinion tapped at the counting house window, and beckoned me to go in. I went in, and found there a stoutish, middle aged person, in a brown surtout with black tights and shoes, with no more hair upon his head (which was a large one and very shining) than there is upon an egg, and with a very extensive face, which he turned full upon me. His clothes were shabby, but he had an imposing shirt-collar on. He carried a jaunty kind of stick, with a large pair of rusty tassels to it; and a quizzing-glass hung outside his coat – for ornament, I afterwards found, as he very seldom looked through it, and couldn't see anything when he did . . .
>
> 'This is Mr Micawber,' said Mr Quinion to me . . .
>
> I made him a bow.
>
> 'Under the impression,' said Mr Micawber, 'that your peregrinations in

this metropolis have not as yet been extensive, and that you might have some difficulty in penetrating the arcana of the Modern Babylon in the direction of the City Road, in short,' said Mr Micawber, in another burst of confidence, 'that you might lose yourself – I shall be happy to call this evening, and install you in the knowledge of the nearest way.'

I thanked him with all my heart, for it was friendly in him to offer to take that trouble.

'At what hour,' said Mr Micawber, 'shall I –'

'At about eight,' said Mr Quinion.

'At about eight,' said Mr Micawber. 'I beg to wish you good day, Mr Quinion. I will intrude no longer.'

So he put on his hat, and went out with his cane under his arm: very upright, and humming a tune when he was clear of the counting-house.

One need only add that rasping, mid-west drawl to hear the creative voice of Charles Bogle, Otis Criblecoblis, and Mahatma Kane Jeeves. But all this lies still far in the future. We do know, however, that Dickens' characters so fired Bill Fields' imagination that he decided to recast his life in their image. David Copperfield and Oliver Twist combined with Tom Sawyer and Huck Finn to create a mythical childhood. In the present, he might be Nicholas Nickleby, the young man determined to make good. In the future, Micawber loomed, with his irrepressible optimism despite the endless slings and arrows of life. Grafted together with all the other echoes of his show-business past, these would feed the character which would supplant Claude Dukenfield and reduce him to an elusive shadow . . .

Seeds, slowly germinating in the young juggler's mind. But he has as yet no thought to write his own material. He is still reading, reading, reading. His two early essays for 'Selbit', produced sometime in 1901, did not seem to lead to any further efforts. Extempore experiments in some of his letters of this period are balanced by comments on difficulty in adjusting to typewriting: 'Two sheets of paper, run through this typewriter, and me doing the dancing on the key board, is enough misery to inflict on any one person, even he be a comedy jug.' (Letter to O. K. Sato, 26 November 1904.) The seminal vaudeville sketches lay more than ten years in the future. The young man, in the early 1900s, was concentrating on his act, on the continuation of his epic world tour. Arriving in London from South Africa, he returned to the Hippodrome in Leicester Square, reporting for rehearsal for his opening there on 2 April 1904.

Chapter 12
Of Pachyderms, Paternity and Pantomime

Easter 1904, the dream billing of all time, at the Hippodrome

TWICE DAILY, AT 2 P.M. AND 8 P.M.
SANDOW, BUSCH'S PLUNGING ELEPHANTS,
HOUDINI, MARCELINE, SEGGOMER,
CHESTER'S STATUE DOG,
THE RAMONIERS, FROBEL AND RUGE,
THREE ROMAS, PICCHIANIS,
MORTON AND ELLIOTT, LEONARD GAUTIER,
W. C. FIELDS,
JACKSON FAMILY, JAS H. LEE,
THE TRAPNELLS, & C.

Oh, to be a spectator in the 'Gods'! You paid your two shillings and watched the Hippodrome pull all the stops out on its massive stage. The vaudeville clans had gathered in London. Houdini was making a special appearance, in the midst of his provincial tour. On 19 March he had surpassed himself by getting out of a fiendish set of manacles procured by the proprietor of a London newspaper from a 'celebrated locksmith in Birmingham'. They had taken five years to make, and were comprised of six sets of inner locks inside two outer locks. Houdini had sweated in his tent for over an hour and emerged triumphant, though what really transpired was not revealed until many years after his death (Houdini was stumped and had to beg the manager to allow him the key, to keep his reputation). At his Easter performance the Handcuff King reverted to a more mundane level, as the London *Morning Post* related: 'A youth with a black bag full of manacles and leg irons stepped into the arena and secured Mr. Houdini apparently as safely as could possibly be desired. But in less than ten minutes Mr. Houdini had handed the handcuffs and leg irons back to the youth and was trying his skill with others.' Kid's stuff. The strong man Sandow, too, was at the height of his popularity, having slipped the locks of Florenz Ziegfeld, who had moved on to greater things. Sandow's act consisted of a sober lecture about the methods of physical culture, during which he would introduce one of his pupils, 'a perfect picture of muscular development'. He would then sustain 'a number of men and women and a tremendous weight of dumbbells upon his chest'. The Spanish clown Marceline was to have a great influence over the as yet fifteen-year-old Charles Chaplin. Seggommer was a popular ventriloquist, and Madame Chester's Statue Dog held a series of poses before a set of black and white pictures. Acrobats and animal trainers filled out the bill, but the *coup de théâtre* was one of the Hippodrome's all-time spectacle greats:

Cue *The Era*, December 1903:

Everything that comes to the Hippodrome must 'plunge.' If Mr Moss had a gorilla or a mammoth in his company, it would have to plunge – or 'go.' The noble stud of elephants, not one of which weighs less than three tons, are to dive on Wednesday from an inclined plane running from the edge of the flooded arena to the upper part of the back wall. The top of this plane is reached by a succession of 'rakes,' up which the elephants will have to pass in single file. Mr Moss has had to instal and equip his stage with over seventy tons of steel girder work, in order that the elephants may pass from the stables to the landing, which is over 40 ft. high. Visitors uneasy about the elephants may rest assured that the 'cantilever system' will do all that can be required in the way of support; and those anxious for themselves need have no fear of spoiled clothing, as a special glass screen 20 ft. high has been constructed around the arena for the purpose of shielding them from the tremendous splash which will necessarily result.

W C. FIELDS

8 Hippodrome attractions, from *The Tatler*, drawn by S. H. Sime.

Busch's Plunging Elephants were part of what the programme of the Hippodrome called A Zoological and Aquatic Spectacle entitled THE GOLDEN PRINCESS AND THE ELEPHANT HUNTERS, with a human cast playing The Maharajah, His Mother-in-law, The Keeper of his Conscience, His Jester, The Golden Princess, The Silver Prince, The Duke of Brum, Physicians, Nautch Dancers, Suitors, Court functionaries, Heralds, Hunters, Cooks, etc. and so on.

Get on the stage and juggle after that! And yet *The Era* was once again effusive:

> Mr W. C. Fields . . . richly deserves the cordial reception he has had here. Fields is genuinely funny, and some of his tricks are truly astonishing. It is hard to say which we admire most, his remarkable skill or his irresistible drollery. With hats, with a cap and a stick, and with balls, he juggles with wonderful and almost bewildering accuracy; and ever and anon, a touch of comedy comes as a variation of the never-failing adroitness of the artist.

Strange acts and even stranger artists. This was the heyday of Dr Walford Bodie, who mesmerised the sick and crippled and cured them by means of electricity, conducting 25,000 volts through his own body to that of his patients. Testimonials to his success abounded. In August 1904, as a result of a challenge for £50, he entered the cages in the Zoo in Castle Street, Dundee, and mesmerised the hyenas and wolves (though he did not attempt, apparently, to electrocute them). An intrepid Scot, he was fond of quoting Rabbie Burns:

> But facts are chiels that winna ding,
> And dairna be disputed.

Another artiste, set to follow Fields at the Hippodrome, was Monsieur De Rougemont, 'an exponent of the art of turtle-riding', who contracted 'to ride a turtle in the arena of the Hippodrome when filled with water, to deliver a short lecture on his adventures in Australia while riding the turtle in the arena, and to use no cruelty to the turtle'. (The management of the Hippodrome accordingly challenged him, for £100 a week, to successfully ride a crocodile round the arena four times, offering to supply the crocodiles. History does not record if this challenge was taken.)

Another noteworthy novelty, introduced in April 1904, was the 'Biophotophone': 'The scientific alliance between the Cinematograph and the gramophone', invented by Herr Oscar Messler of Berlin and M. Gaumont of Paris. A demonstration film featured a scene from *Lohengrin*, 'in which every tone of the actress playing the part of Elsa synchronised so completely with her corresponding movement that it became exceedingly difficult for the spectators to keep the unreality of the performer in mind'. But this was, as yet, a false hope. Other, more traditional moving-picture shows offered 'The Lady Typist', 'The Parson's Cooking Lesson' and a Bioscopic production of the Charles Urban Company depicting 'The Russian Army in Siberia' at the start of the Russian-Japanese War.

Buoyed up by his month at the Hippodrome, Fields proceeded north, this time on a much lengthier tour of the British Isles than in previous years. He performed in Edinburgh, Glasgow, Bradford, Liverpool, Leeds, Hull, Sheffield, Manchester, Nottingham, Leicester and Cardiff, and on the Empire circuit within London, at Hackney, Holloway and Shepherds Bush. During this entire period a regular advertisement began appearing back home, in the *New York Dramatic Mirror*: 'W. C. FIELDS, TOURING THE WORLD', with a line detailing which venue in Europe he was playing. More and more, Fields was attending to business, making sure he did not vanish from view.

In Edinburgh, another Fieldsian mythlet was born, that of his self-cure from a diagnosed tuberculosis. This classic tale is told in Taylor's biography, but is summarised best in a short (and inaccurate) account by one Blythe Foote Finke (a posthumous Fields alias, from beyond the grave?), in a series called: 'Outstanding Personalities, No 48: W. C. Fields', *circa* 1972:

> On his European tour Fields fell ill in Edinburgh and was advised by a doctor to give up the tour and take a long rest. Instead, the actor went out and bought a bottle of whiskey, which he insisted cured him immediately. From that moment on he considered alcohol the best remedy for any ailment. Eventually it was to damage his liver and kidneys and cause his death.

Taylor relates how the doctor told Fields: 'You're a very sick man . . . You'll have to be hospitalized for a very long time and kept on a careful diet. If not you won't live six months.' Fields went out and bought his whiskey, consumed it in his room and then went and boarded a boat for Paris.

Well, er, no. In fact Fields went on to the Glasgow Empire and then carried on. In a later comment he verified the Edinburgh incident but said that he and his friends had indulged in a bottle of wine and gone driving out in a biting Scottish wind, which cured him of his ailment immediately. (The date of Fields' Edinburgh gig was June 5–10. It can be cold in Scotland any time of the year, but June is generally warm.) Nevertheless, some mythical moment had to be provided to begin the long saga of W. C. Fields and his Best Friend, Alcohol.

In this at least, the reader might be allowed a sigh of relief that myth and fact have some acquaintance. It would be amusing to say that Fields' drinking was also an invention and that he was in fact a teetotaller and life-long member of the Temperance League. The only person who suggested such a connection, though, was the blind claimant Edith Williams, who said her 'ex-husband', Fields-alias-Williams, had performed and sang in temperance halls. Alas, the poor lady was seriously challenged in more ways than one. Fields was, indeed, one of show business's most rumbustious boozers, a true Falstaff of the modern age. This cannot be taken away from the mythmakers. And yet here, too, there is controversy as to when this habit first began.

It has been generally accepted till now that Fields the juggler did not drink, and even shunned so mild a beverage as coffee, in order not to disturb the very intense concentration that the juggling act requires. In later years the tales of Fields' drinking were legion, and there can hardly be a Melanesian islander on the most remote atoll in the world who cannot relate at least one W. C. Fields drinking tale. Like everything, but with this above all, Fields made his material out of his troubles, real, invented or appropriated. Familiar declarations: 'I have a hangover, from 42 years of drinking about $185,000 of whisky.' Or a typical story related by Ed Sullivan in his Hollywood column in 1938:

After the Louis Massacre of Schmeling, Fields held forth long and earnestly on the conclusion to be drawn from Schmeling's explanation that the first blow to the kidney paralyzed him. 'It simply bears out what I've always contended,' said Fields, 'A kidney needs a good alcoholic lining to stand up under wear and tear. Shmeling was the victim of clean living. I dare say that if Louis or any other professional slasher dealt me such a blow that their hands would crumple from the impact. As a result of long and serious drinking, I've developed protective ripples of muscles over my kidneys. I will live to be 112 years old and perhaps a fortnight longer than that, and I deserve it, because I've gone out of my way to live the wrong way. Some of my best friends are bartenders, but most of them die young. They can dish it out, but they can't take it.'

Or: 'My best friend died of drinking too much. His was a case of internal drowning . . .' (1941)

And so on, ad infinitum. But we are still with Fields the younger. It is difficult to believe that, as a music-hall artiste, in the company of men and women who were renowned for their love of the saloon, pub and tavern, that the young man completely abstained. Probably he kept dry before a performance. But that he was a young man with healthy appetites was to be a problem sooner, rather than later, as we shall attempt to tease out.

We do not have many clues about the Fields married life offstage in this period. He would have been earning good money, between £30 and £50 per week. The equivalent in dollars would be up to $200. This in an age when the average salary of a clerk was not far above £5 per week. The record shows that Fields was performing almost continuously throughout his stay in Britain and Europe. He was still very far from the front rank who could command £500 a week, but he could afford to live well. He was performing for the best circuits, mainly the Moss Empires chain, though he played other halls as well, working through reputable agencies. (William Morris in New York, Somers & Warners in Tottenham Court Road, London, among others.) There was no need for him to put money by in multiple bank accounts, as legend insisted. On the contrary, that would have meant him having cash tied up in accounts he could not reach easily, something completely against the grain of so organised a young man.

He lived in hotels which were by all accounts as good as he could afford, and developed a taste for gourmet food which would be with him all his life. He had also, by this time, begun to indulge his greatest passion after his art – the acquisition of fast motor vehicles.

Ronald Fields has published the first extant account of Bill Fields' penchant for wheels, a report from the *Boston Globe* of his arrest for 'Fast Driving' down North Broad Street in 1902. He and a friend, one Charles Shrader, were apprehended by a police bicyclist and released on their own recognizance. They must have been doing at least 20 miles per hour. In later years, Fields wrote fondly to a correspondent who had sent him an old programme from the Palais d'Ete in Brussels about zapping around that city in 'an American Underslung car with 40 inch tires'. This was a fad that would just grow and grow.

Having sent Hattie ahead, to bring forth his child on hallowed American soil, they kept in touch by mail, as he breathlessly awaited the good news. Eventually it came, by telegram, as he was performing in Sheffield, on 28 July 1904. He wrote her an ecstatic letter, addressing her by the pet nickname, 'Bricket' –

Kitty's cable I recd. yesterday and was speechless for about two hours & then I was speechless as we all had a drink on the head of the kid a boy too & last night's show, I was next to the worst thing that ever went on the stage.

It is impossible Hat to tell you how glad I am to know all the worry is over. You are well and we have a little baby boy, ain't it great Hat? bring him over until I kick the stuffing out of him . . .

Soon as you are able write me a long letter explaining all. Tell me how it all happened, how you feel, if you are thin or fatter. Tell me all.

Am sending fifty for some fine clothes for to bring him over with, will send it next week.

Have just received a wire from Knowles will enclose same in this letter . . .

Will close now with lots of love & Kisses & quick recovery to health and strength.

Sod.

The joy of any happy father. Little Claude Junior was born into a family which was determined, at that point, to stay together. Nor were they alone in the world. Hattie still had her mother and the support of the large Dukenfield clan. Papa Dukenfield adored the new baby and Ronald Fields has a photograph of James Dukenfield holding little Claude aloft on the beach at Atlantic City like any proud grandfather. On their travels, the juggler and his mate were not alone either. They clearly had a wide network of vaudeville colleagues, as the Bill-Hattie letters reveal. R.G. Knowles had cabled his congratulations, and other messages were expected. Bill was also corresponding with his fraternal comedy jugglers, notably O. K. Sato, his predecessor and perhaps mentor on his European tour.

This exchange of letters with Sato, published by Ronald Fields, took place between October and November 1904, while Bill Fields was performing at the *Folies Bergère* in Paris. I have already referred to Fields' rambling tale, in his letter to Sato, of an altercation at the *Folies* with a rival performer over the pilfering of material. These somewhat cryptic letters are written in a jovial style that appears common among vaudevillians and provided Fields with experimental ground for developing his own particular tone –

(Fields to Sato):

I met (you) on Mittle Strasse and you spake saying – worketh not for less than 2500 german coins per month, and you spake again saying – spoileth not the salary. It was then that I knew that I had passed you, and you did not notice me laughing, and I told it to a friend it was so sad. He said isn't it a shame, for he is such a nice fellow, do you think it is a case where the straight jacket will be used, or only the padded cell? I said I hope neither, for he is so good to his folks, and the pavements were dry too.

The letter concludes: 'Give my regards to Little Fred' and signs off 'yours truly, William C. Fields, The Kensington Paradox', adding a coda: 'Tom Hearn told me something about a lamp trick he saw you do 12 years ago, the rubber lamp, what does he mean?'
Sato replies, from the Apollo Theatre Vienna, to 'Worst Case Fields – the human pimple', chiding him for using jokes out of 'Tit-Bits' and advising him to 'Keep a sharp lookout on that offspring of Yours, and don't let Him know you are His father until he gets stronger, or the poor lad may laugh himself to death.' Signing off 'Your sincere friend, O. K. Sato, the notsogoodasfields thegreat'.

The reference to Tom Hearn is interesting, for here is another of the fraternity of comedy jugglers: Tom (or T. Elder) Hearn worked the same circuits. He was billed as 'the Laziest Juggler on Earth', who 'gives a comicality to slackness . . . (and) keeps the house rocking with laughter from the time he tumbles out of bed until the curtains close down on him'. O. K. Sato himself was reviewed at the Palace, London as, 'a comic juggler of real inventiveness and humour. He is both skilful and original.' Little Fred, referred to by Fields, was, surprisingly to those acquainted with Fields' mythical phobias, a dog act, putting his frisky trained canines through their paces. The record shows Little Fred and Fields performed together many times, in the British Isles. So much for the anathema towards dogs. After the plunging elephants and the cycling baboons, I think they must have been a relief.

Sometime in October, Claude Jr., having been born in the US, and thus cleared to be President in due course, was brought over to Europe with Hattie. Before this, however, another family plan was put in action, a trip by Papa James Dukenfield to the land of his birth, which he had not visited since his youth. Fields took his father with him to Paris, but, according to family recollections, the British visit was not a success. Bill's sister Adel later told grandson Ronald that when James saw there was no place he could get a drink on New Year's Eve 'he had W. C. put him on the first boat home'. The record shows, however, that James spent a full two months in Europe. And it is scarcely credible that Papa Fields could obtain no booze on a New Year's Eve in Manchester, where Bill was performing at that point, unless it fell on a Sunday. Alas, in 1904 New Year's Eve was a Saturday.

Once again, memory and history blur. On 26 November, if we are to judge by Fields' letter to O. K. Sato of that date, from the Hotel de Geneve, Marseille (Bill was playing the Alcazar Theatre there, with Tom Hearn on the same bill, an unusual juggling double-header) both Mrs Fields and Claude Jr. are present with Bill. As Fields writes to Sato: 'The baby has just said ize wizzy. The wife told me he could say it but I doubted it.' Thus we can see that the entire Fields family was touring together for this halcyon period – Bill, Hattie, Papa James and baby Claude. Another nail in the coffin of the myth.

Of course we know that this idyllic picture was soon to fray and crumble. The grand bust up of W. C. Fields' marriage to Hattie is one of the toughest nuts of the legend to crack. It is difficult enough to figure out why two people we know decided to separate last week, let alone to open a window into a private trauma of two strangers in 1905. I am always amazed at biographies of long dead personages which blithely quote reams of dialogue of their subjects in private moments recorded by no one. Family memories fade, grinding axes echo, and the foolhardy fill the gaps with invention. Let us repair again to Blythe Foote Finke, just for kicks:

> Not long after the marriage he began to drink, graduating from ginger ale to beer to whiskey to Irish whiskey to bourbon to Martinis. And he made his first European tour. His marriage failed almost from the start. His wife found Fields impossible to live with. He did nothing to understand her love of religion and books. Before they parted, however, they had one son, Claude. The boy was never close to his father and grew up to be an active church worker . . . The couple never divorced because of her strict Catholic beliefs.

Indeed, Fields did tell his friends, decades later, and his mistresses, that his marriage had been a dud from the start. Carlotta Monti wrote that Fields, her 'Woody', had told her he was married once in San Francisco but 'the great earthquake and fire of 1907 destroyed the marriage certificate. There's no legal proof.' (The quake was of course in 1906.) We have seen that this version of the marriage was not true at all: Bill and Hattie travelled together for fully five years, separated only during her pregnancy. And yet this apparently happy alliance turned, some time later, into the marriage from hell. What happened?

The accepted version, which all, including myself, have subscribed to up to now, has been that Hattie, the new mother, finally longed for a different life, and wanted Bill to settle down and give up the road. He would not, could not, do this, and things went from bad to worse from this point.

Clearly something went sour in the marriage very soon after Claude Jr. was born. Having transported his wife and baby back over to England, Fields found them lodgings (at one point in Buchanan Street, Blackpool), and then continued his tour of Europe from March 1905. He was widening his scope, appearing at the Scala, Copenhagen, and then returning for a month in Berlin.

One can imagine the isolation of the young mother in a foreign country. But, the record shows, Fields was not completely ignoring his new-found obligations. He was factoring the need to stay as close as possible to his son and wife into his schedule both in the long and the short term.

In the long term, he was negotiating, as early as the autumn of 1904, for a complete break in his juggling routine, to take a part in a new musical play which was being planned by the blackface team of McIntyre and Heath. The Broadway producers Klaw and Erlanger had commissioned the play from veteran playwright George V. Hobart, under the title of *The Ham Tree*. In his letter to Hattie rejoicing at his son's birth, on 30 September, Fields adds that he has been asking for $275 a week for this show, but the producers are balking. Nevertheless, the show was set to open, in New York, in the summer of 1905. This would keep Fields in the United States for the run of the show, and, inevitably, closer to Hattie and baby Claude.

In the shorter term, Bill had also made arrangements which kept him closer to his family. Having played the Alcazar, in Marseilles, in November 1904, and the Eden Theatre, in Milan, Italy, in early December, the family returned to England for Christmas. Bill was going to take a break from touring his juggling act, to reprise an endeavour he had flirted with back in December 1902 – he contracted to appear, in a supporting role, in *Cinderella*, a Christmas Pantomime, at the Prince's Theatre, Manchester.

IT BAFFLES SCIENCE!

It is difficult, if not impossible, to convey to an American, or any non-English reader, the meaning and import of the English Pantomime. It is a mystery as impenetrable to the foreigner as the Japanese cha-o-nu ceremony is to the barbarian who merely dunks his bag of Tetley Tea. This series of musical revues based on traditional folk tales encompassing *Puss in Boots, Red Riding Hood, Aladdin, Babes in the Wood, Mother Goose*, among others, had become the form in which cross-dressing was most acceptable to the general public. The 'Pantomime Dame' is still a familiar staple, revived annually, to this day. The great music-hall comedian, Dan Leno, was the most famous of the Pantomime Dames, his 'Mother Goose' practically his signature upon the variety stage. Men dressed as women, women dressed as men, portrayed a world turned topsy-turvy, in which the harsh realities of life were transformed by the worlds of fantasy and fable.

W. C. Fields did not cross-dress in Manchester. He appeared as Freake, a palace attendant, in two separate scenes. The pantomime text, which is preserved in the British Museum's collection of 'Lord Chamberlain's Plays' – the copies that all playwrights were obliged to deposit for censorship – reveals that this was not a speaking part, perhaps because of Fields' American accent. But, intriguingly, it shows that Bill's juggling act was written into the printed text of the play. He first appears in a scene set in 'the Billiard Room of the Palace':

Enter Attendant, one of the Courtiers.

COURTIER: Freake! Freake! Where is that fellow?

(*Enter Freake.*) Get the room ready for play at once. I don't believe you've touched it this morning.

(*Exit Attendant.*) *JUGGLING SPECIALITY, and exit Freake.*

The Manchester *Cinderella* was essentially a vehicle for a famous English double act, the M'Naughtons, Fred and Tom, who played page and factotum to the Baroness and Baron De Boots – a kind of premature 'Rosencrantz and Guildenstern', ever commenting on the action. Freake appears again after the M'Naughtons, as Trim and Trott, play havoc with the guests' hats, until the attendant comes in –

TROTT: Oh well, you'll find everything properly looked after, and you needn't trouble to collect the money; we've done that. (*Exeunt Trim and Trott.*) *Freake picks up damaged hat; shakes fist after them. JUGGLING SPECIALITY, and exit Freake.*

Ergo: Fields performed his billiard act and juggled with hats, both scenes clearly inserted with him in mind by the pantomime's author, the veteran J. Hickory Wood, who had written some of Dan Leno's main pantomime roles. The production, by Oscar Barrett, was, according to *The Era*, 'distinguished by every splendid appurtenance of pantomime on the grand scale'. Of Fields' part, *The Era* noted: 'Mr W. C. Fields, the well-known eccentric juggler . . . does some wonderfully clever business in the style familiar to patrons of the halls. Mr. Fields' performance is, in fact, a memorable feature of the show.'

The Manchester *Cinderella* played from Christmas Eve 1904 well into February 1905: a hitherto unmentioned dry run for Fields' début upon the American stage. But before that he had that satchelful of engagements in Europe to fulfil: Copenhagen, Berlin, Leipzig, and a grand booking even further afield, that came to naught: on 6 May 1905, W. C. Fields' regular advert in the *New York Dramatic Mirror* displayed the following schedule –

W. C. FIELDS, TOURING THE WORLD – MOSCOW, RUSSIA,
MAY 1–30.

But, on 27 May, the *Mirror* reported:

FIELDS WILL NOT GO TO RUSSIA

W. C. Fields, the comedy juggler, has changed his mind about going to
Russia, on account of the unsettled fate of that country, and will continue
to amuse the people of the more peaceful European countries until it is time
for him to sail for America, in August, when he will come over to join
McIntyre and Heath in *The Ham Tree*.

The 'unsettled fate' referred to by the *Mirror* was, of course, the first,
premature, Russian Revolution which was crushed by the Tsar with
many dead in the streets of Saint Petersburg. In fact, Tsarist Russia was
on the periphery of the European vaudeville trail, and Houdini had
played there, in April 1903, so perhaps Fields felt he couldn't pass it
by.

Reading Houdini's blood-curdling account of his trip, one wonders
what Fields thought he would gain from Moscow – except the cachet
of having been there. Houdini related how, at the border, 'everybody
carrying books or newspapers had them taken away, with the exception of those that were on their persons. One passenger had a lot of
slippers wrapped in newspapers, and Mr Russian Searcher unwrapped
each one and took away the newspapers, with a knowing wink, as if he
had heard of "such things" before.' The trains were so crowded people
were hanging on the stairs and out the windows. But the Hermitage
Summer Garden and other theatres were doing business as usual, at
least then. Fields' change of mind thus precluded some of the more
interesting encounters of history, W. C. Fields and, say, Trotsky, if not
Lenin. Or Rasputin. Nevertheless, Fields' imaginary performance in
Moscow became another fond building block of his myth.

Instead of Moscow, however, Fields repaired to the safer precincts of
Hamburg, from which he dispatched the following note for his
Dramatic Mirror ad:

W. C. FIELDS, MONTH OF MAY HANSA THEATRE HAMBURG.
NEXT SEASON WITH MCINTYRE AND HEATH IN THE 'SCHINKEN
BAUM.'

Leaving Germany, Fields scored another first by opening at the Circo Parish, Madrid, from which he wrote a cryptic letter, from the Grand Hotel de Roma, to Hattie in Blackpool, urging her to be ready to 'git' and leave for America as soon as he arrived: 'I am going to do some neat foot work & side step these lawyers.' The only clue to whom these lawyers might be or what scrape Fields had got himself into with them might be in the aforementioned letter to Hattie of July 1904, in which he writes of receiving 'some very favourable replies from the Auto Co. I think I will get my money back O.K.' So perhaps Fields had sustained an early contretemps with an automobile here, certainly not the last. Be that as it may, the *New York Dramatic Mirror* at least positions us once again in the realm of verifiable facts, with:

JULY 22, VAUDEVILLE JOTTINGS:
W. C. Fields, the comedy juggler, arrived in New York last week on the 'Deutschland' from his tour of the world, and immediately began rehearsals with McIntyre and Heath in *The Ham Tree*, which will be produced in New York in August.

Home is the sailor, home from the sea, and the juggler home for the shills . . .

Chapter 13
American Ham; or, Mogo on the Gogogo

The curtain rises.

SCENE I: *Exterior. Full stage. The 'Traveler's rest', a country hotel in Marion, North Carolina, showing right with practical veranda on which are tables where the guests may dine. To the left the entrance to a bar is shown up stage. Harness, curry-combs, blankets, etc., hanging on wall of barn. Drop in back shows Southern country with a river in the foreground. Scene to be full of color and realistic. The New York Society Girls, together with a few young men are discovered at the tables on the porch, having a late breakfast. Waiters busy. Colored servants busy about the lawn. Others in background at various tasks.*

Nothing has dated so much in show business as the minstrel show. Those caricatures of blacks, with enlarged, white looped eyes, and that painted broad white smile. In the symbolism of the cinema it heralds, by sheer fluke or coincidence, the transition from old into new, as Al Jolson's blackface Jazz Singer croons 'Mammy' in the first commercially realized fully synchronised song. But blackface minstrelsy was, as we have found, an astonishingly resilient form of American entertainment, which endured for most of the nineteenth century.

Controversy has always surrounded the question of how much of minstrel forms were derived from observation of authentic African-American or slave culture. James McIntyre and Tom Heath, whose old routine, 'The Ham Tree', was the basis for the 1905 musical play of the same name, claimed, in later interviews, that their stories and dances were taken from genuine black sources. In discussing 'ragtime' in a 1913 item in *The Era*, McIntyre 'tells us that he picked up rag-time from the darkies in the days when he was making pilgrimages through Dixieland with a little wagon circus shortly after the Civil War. It was a sort of African chant he learned from the negroes. He was 12 or 14 years old at the time. All we can say to this confession is that Mac when we met him didn't look a day more than 45!'

But in truth McIntyre and Heath were inheritors of a tradition that had already crystallised by the early 1840s. Thomas 'Daddy' Rice, a white performer, claimed to have observed an old stiff-legged black man dance the original shuffling 'Jim Crow' routine in 1828 ('Weel about and turn about an do jus so – ebery time I weel about, I jump Jim Crow') and imitated it in his act. By the 1840s groups like the 'Ethiopian Serenaders' were playing at the White House, to amuse President John Tyler. The Buckley Serenaders, Christy's Minstrels in New York and Sanford Minstrels in Philadelphia ran for years to packed houses. This portrayal of blacks, in broad caricature, for whites, was given a further twist by the appearance of all-negro blackface groups, caricaturing the white caricatures of themselves. Two early New Orleans black singers, Picayune Butler and 'Old Corn Meal', who appeared on stage as a street vendor with his horse and cart, also had a wide influence on white minstrel groups as early as the 1830s.

Having performed with Lew Dockstader, another legendary minstrel troupe leader, who would later showcase Al Jolson, McIntyre and Heath played small-time houses all over the East Coast for years with a show they called 'The Georgia Minstrels', although they were not the only group with that name. The development of their sketch 'The Ham Tree' is dated at or around 1874. The sketch was played, again and again, with no appreciable changes, down to our year of 1905, when a trio of songwriters and playwrights, George Hobart, William Jerome and Jean Schwartz, expanded it into a three-act musical play. This expansion took the shape of adding, without much apparent reason, a totally incongruous 'English drawing room drama' around the original unaltered sketch. When we read the McIntyre and Heath routines in the 1905 *Ham Tree*, we are therefore looking at some of the oldest material in American popular humour.

Either Hobart, Jerome or Schwartz, probably Hobart, added the material of the eccentric Sherlock Baffles, which was clearly written with Fields in mind – one stage instruction reads: BAFFLES JUGGLING ROUTINE –

Enter Sherlock Baffles, an eccentric character –

BAFFLES (*looking at pedometer*): I have walked 986 miles. I am Lieutenant Peary and I'm looking for the North Pole. (*Sees ice in pail – takes some of it off*) Nope! Its too cold. I'll have to get another job. I think I'll be a detective. I must go and find somebody to detect! (*Runs off.*)

Enter MRS NICKLEBACKER *followed by* MR NICKLEBACKER.

MRS NICKLEBACKER (*speaking as she comes on*): Hurry Lawrence! do hurry!

LAWRENCE: Yes, yes, my dear! I am hurrying!

MRS NICKLEBACKER: Our private car must be attached to the next train for Washington. It leaves in forty minutes!

The absurd (if not downright silly) plot involves Mrs Nicklebacker's desire to present 'those famous representatives of the East Indian nobility, the Rajah of Fuzzywishwash and the Ranee of Giz', to New York society, at the same time as announcing the engagement of her daughter, Tessie, to the golf-playing Lord Spotcash of Blitheringham Towers. (Of course, Tessie would rather die.) The fly in the ointment of Mrs Nicklebacker's plans is her wayward son, Lawrence Nicklebacker, who insists on following 'that idiotic minstrel show' from town to town. Lawrence claims the show is curing his rheumatism:

LAWRENCE: I love 'em! Where can you find an old fashioned man who doesn't love an old fashioned minstrel show with the grinning black faces on the end and the solemn black faces in the middle! . . . And the parade! When the music of the silver cornet band strikes up and the minstrels in their gaudy coats and hats begin to march I can feel the blood leaping through my veins. I feel like a boy once more. There I am, bare-legged and bare-footed with one toe tied up in a bag standing on the corner of the old village street watching that parade with my soul in my eyes . . .

This image of the white boy idolising the black troupe is more characteristic of the development of the American jazz age than anyone might normally admit at the time. But to offset this we are soon introduced to some more daffy characters, namely Desdemona, a coloured maid, and Ponsonby, valet to Lord Spotcash, at his New York hotel. Here, once again, Sherlock Baffles the tramp detective enters, comparing Lord Spotcash to a photo taken from his pocket.

LORD SPOTCASH: I say, Ponsonby! There's that deuced tramp chap again. He stared at me so rudely at the depot and now he's staring rudely at me again! I say, tramp chap, who are you?

BAFFLES: Hssh! I am one of the original Florodora sextette!*

LORD SPOTCASH: Deuced singular how you have changed. I say, Ponsonby, is he spoofing us?

PONSONBY: It sounds suspicious, your lordship!

Enter ERNEST EVERHART [*manager of the Georgia Minstrels*].

LORD SPOTCASH: I say, tramp chap! You must not loiter in my immediate neighborhood – I won't have it!

BAFFLES *moves closer to* ERNEST, *at his elbow* –

BAFFLES: Never give up the ship!

ERNEST: Who the devil are you?

BAFFLES: Hssh! I am John W. Gates – bet a million! I'm a mystery! I'm here, there and everywhere – nobody knows who I am – and I know who everybody is. I'm covered with rubber shoes. I butt-in everywhere and nobody can put me out. I'm the best-natured man in the world but whenever I get mad you can hear the ambulance bell. I'm six and carry two, I am, and I'm on the trail!

ERNEST: Are you some sort of private detective?

BAFFLES: Don't ask me questions or I'll begin to brag about myself. I'm watching somebody!

ERNEST (*excitedly*): Oh say! Did you follow that English Lord here?

BAFFLES (*mysteriously*): Hssh!

ERNEST: Tell me, are you really shadowing Lord Spotcash, and what for?

BAFFLES: For practice. I'm studying to be a detective – and he looked like a good thing to start on! Hssh!

ERNEST: Gee whiz! You're just the very man I've been looking for. If you succeed in frightening Lord Spotcash back to England I'll give you a thousand dollars!

BAFFLES *falls flat on stage.*

ERNEST: What's the matter?

---

* These were a burlesque group of ladies whose hair hung down famously to their rumps.

BAFFLES (*looking up*): The pipe was strong and I haven't smoked for a year. (*Goes up.*)

ERNEST: I mean it. One thousand dollars in your hand the day Lord Spotcash sails for London. Trail him!

BAFFLES: Yes, trail him!

ERNEST: Never leave him!

BAFFLES: Never leave him!

ERNEST: Frighten him!

BAFFLES: Frighten him!

ERNEST: Scare him!

BAFFLES: Scare him!

ERNEST: You have the face and figure to do it!

Of course, even with the text, we have no way of fully gauging Fields' first speaking part on the American stage. He appeared in a kind of tweed coat with a 'fore-and-aft deerstalker' and a large stage moustache. Apart from his continuing cryptic remarks ('I am Thomson Lawson, of Boston – and I'm prospecting for Standard Oil!') he also, at some point, or several points, worked in his juggling act. There is no doubt that during the show's two seasons – it ran to the summer of 1907 – Fields ad libbed where the fancy took him. The contemporary reviews certainly gave him a warm welcome. The *New York Dramatic Mirror* of 9 September 1905 said: 'W. C. Fields surprised only those who were not familiar with his famous and highly clever Tramp Juggler act,' hinting once again that Fields speaking upon the stage was not as unheard of as has been previously assumed. Another journal, *Metropolitan* wrote:

> To their loved old Georgia Minstrels McIntyre and Heath have added a young chorus that will find no difficulty in being loved, a plot that modestly withdraws at any point where it might interfere with anything else and a last act that stretched the performance to the required two hours and a half. This combination they have christened 'The Ham Tree', though it might as well appropriately have been called 'The Doughnut Shoveller' or 'The Flock of Sausages.'

The plot wrangles over Baffles, Everhart and a factotum, Jimpsey, finally usher in the mainstay of the piece – McIntyre and Heath's age-old routine, with McIntyre as Alexander, the gullible rube, and Heath as Henry, the citified dandy who leads him on into the travelling minstrel life. As the *Metropolitan* described it: 'As of old, Alexander leaves his good job in a livery stable, with three good meals a day, for the alluring uncertainties of a artistic career on the minstrel stage, and, also as of old, the show disbands for want of patronage and he and his tempter have to walk home, a prey to hunger and carrying a large trunk and a bass drum.'

Looking at these old routines, one can conjure up the later borrowings of Laurel and Hardy, and the Marx Brothers, as well as many vaudeville double-acts that never made it to the storage of the screen. Fields, like all comedians, stole shamelessly – routines, individual jokes, ideas, bits of physical business, odd lines. But what he derived from *The Ham Tree* was, I think, a deeper thing than just material, the individual puns he was still using thirty-five years later in *You Can't Cheat an Honest Man* – 'Why is a cat's tail like the end of the world?' – but a whole world of melancholy and the theme of the showman's unrequited desire, as set out in Heath's discourse to McIntyre about the joys of travelling the minstrel road:

HENRY: My boy, you don't know what life is like till you travel. You must travel to learn the experience of the world. You get up in the morning, after a swell breakfast, put your satchel over your shoulder, walk to the depot, get in the cars, look out of the car windows and from the windows of these cars until you see the beautiful scenery, as if you are passing by. The rocks, the mountains, and the valleys and lambs gambolling on the green. Then you arrive at the town. You alight from the train. You get in a coupe.

ALEXANDER: What chicken coop?

HENRY: No coop. You arrive at your hotel, the footman opens the coupe door, the porter takes your luggage in the hotel. You register, you are assigned a room and bath.

ALEXANDER: Do I have to take a bath?

HENRY: Optional with yourself. Then the dinner bell rings. By the way, did you ever eat at a high class hotel?

ALEXANDER: No, I never did. I only eat in the kitchen, and the stable.

HENRY: Get ready, my boy, get ready. Dis troupe only stops at the finest.

One might leap forward thirty years, to the troupe of travelling players of the 'McGonigle Repertory Company' in Fields' 1934 film *The Old Fashioned Way* . . . The troupers rushing to their meagre dinner in the dining room of boarding house owner Mrs Wendelschaeffer . . . Later in *The Ham Tree*, we find the duo again, with their trademark trunk and bass drum, their material so deeply ingrained the playscript has dispensed with the names of the characters, and reverts to the performers:

MCINTYRE: How far have we walked now?

HEATH: Two hundred and sixty-eight miles! . . .

MCINTYRE (*puts down trunk*): Well, if I ever get back to that livery stable and get that job back it'll be the last time you ever get me travelling on the road with the Georgia Minstrels . . .

HEATH: How did you get along with that stout lady I sent you up to this morning?

MCINTYRE: Where do you mean – where those children was eatin' bread and molasses?

HEATH: The place I sent you up to get something to eat.

MCINTYRE: You sent me up – you send me up all the time. I'm getting the cadging story down so fine now every time I come to a house I cry before I get to it. I went up to that lady this morning with as much confidence as if she was my own mother, and looked her right in the eye and said: 'Lady, will you please give me something to eat? I'm travelling.' She says, 'Keep on travelling – keep on travelling.' And I walked in the next yard and I thought of that old minstrel joke. I set down on the steps and commenced to eat the grass in front of the steps, and that lady came out and looked at me with tears in her eyes and said, 'Man alive you must be hungry to sit there and eat that grass.' I says, 'Lady, I'm starving.' 'Well,' she says, 'that's too bad. Come round to the back of the house with me and I'll show you where the grass is longer.'

Surely we can recognise the contours of an authentic black slave joke when we hear it . . . Heath/Henry jumps up from his trunk, looking astonished at McIntyre/Alexander:

HEATH: Well, you're up against it. What was you doin' runnin' through the woods this mornin' after that man? I seen you and I thought you was goin' to kill him.

MCINTYRE: I seen him run and I run after him to see what he was runnin' after and when he got the other side of the fence what you reckon he put his hand on?

HEATH: A ham sandwich!

MCINTYRE: Let up once in a while. If you can't get it don't put it in my membrance all the time. How could a man find a ham sandwich in the woods?

HEATH: Drops off a ham tree! (*Business of* HEATH *taking off plug hat and working it with handkerchief.*)

MCINTYRE: Dropped off what? (*Looking hard at* HEATH.)

HEATH: Off a ham tree! (*Mac looks hard at him again.*) . . . Didn't you never see a ham tree?

MCINTYRE: The ham growing on the trees? . . . That's a new one on me; I always thought them hams grew on hogs.

HEATH: You have reference to pork – they're on the hog.

MCINTYRE: Yes, and we're on the hog. Is the covers on the ham from the trees like you buy them from the stores?

HEATH: Only when they are ripe. So now Alexander be careful. If we come across a ham tree don't touch a ham without it's got the cover on. If you do you'll get that disease called more-go on the go-go . . .

STOP!! The fan will leap up here, recognising a familiar late Fieldsism – 'that dread Everglades disease, mogo on the gogogo'. So now we know where it comes from . . . Robert C. Toll, chronicler of the American nineteenth-century Minstrel Show, has written about the tall tales characteristic of the genre. Like the heroes of the frontier, minstrel characters inhabited a world of make believe and exaggeration. They pulled steamboats out of the water with fishing poles, scratched out panthers' eyes with their toenails, or sailed down the Mississipi on the backs of alligators – just as Fields, as the steamboat Commodore in his own *Mississippi*, the Paramount film of 1935, would try to impress his passengers, a lady of a certain age, and a

Planter, with his own tall tales of derring do:

COMMODORE: My last encounter with the Redskins was over thirty-five years ago. I was a mere stripling.

PLANTER: Is that so?

COMMODORE: Yeah. I whipped out my revolver –

PLANTER: Revolvers weren't invented thirty-five years ago.

COMMODORE: Uh – uh – I know that, but the Indians didn't know it. It doesn't matter. I threw it away.

WOMAN: Oh, how exciting! Please don't interrupt.

COMMODORE: I'd just swum the rapids. Had my canoe under one arm and a Rocky Mountain goat under the other.

PLANTER: How could you swim without the use of your arms?

COMMODORE: Uh – uh – in those days, I had – uh – I had very strong legs – uh – uh – excuse me – very strong limbs.

WOMAN: You must have been full of fire in your youth!

COMMODORE: I had to carry fire insurance until I was over forty. (*Engine noises.*) As I arrived on the river bank, I was encountered by the entire tribe of the Shug Indians, the most ferocious – (*to* PLANTER) Have you ever been in the Shug country?

PLANTER: No, I haven't.

COMMODORE: Ah, that's fine. I unsheathed my bowie knife and cut a path through this wall of human flesh, dragging my canoe behind me. (*WOMAN gasps and faints.*)

COMMODORE: Oh, I'm sorry, perhaps I've gone too far.

PLANTER: But what happened to the goat?

COMMODORE: He was very good with mustard.

The braggart, the pioneer, the compulsive hustler, these were to become familiar elements, adding to the synthesis which was to be the Fields of fiction. The master showman drew on many sources, but we respond, perhaps, because, without necessarily knowing it, we feel his roots go deep and wide.

Fields' character in *The Ham Tree* was one-dimensional, having neither development nor direction. He plays a role in trying to fool Mrs Nicklebacker into believing Henry/Heath is the Rajah of Fuzzywishwash, so that she might look kindly on minstrel manager Everhart who has fallen in love with her daughter. In the end, Lord Spotcash sportingly gives up his claim, Alexander falls in love with the maid Desdemona, is cured of travelling and is ready to go back to North Carolina, Mrs Nicklebacker falls in with the deception so as not to disappoint her guests, and Sherlock Baffles announces: 'When it comes to helping people with time or money I'm a regular Russell Sage!' Thus inaugurating a familiar later attribute as the Falstaffian Cupid who re-unites the lovers.

GRAND FINALE, with full Chorus, and – CURTAIN . . .

But the show, of course, goes on . . .

Chapter 14
The Man Who Juggles

In the summer of 1907 Bill Fields resumed his juggling act and from 1908 until 1914 he continued to tour Europe annually, repeating his tour of South Africa and Australia in 1914. His world travels were only cut short by the irresistible force of the outbreak of what became known as the First World War.

9 W. C. Fields with Hattie Hughes-Fields in happier times.

But long before then Fields' marriage to Hattie had irretrievably broken down. It was already getting shaky during the second half of 1905. Fields' part in *The Ham Tree*, which might have been devised to keep him closer to home, in fact continued taking him on tour, through the Eastern and Midwest circuits. From Dayton, Ohio, Springfield, Illinois, Marion, Fort Wayne, Toledo, Bill kept writing Hattie and sending her money for Claude Junior, but his letters became increasingly petulant. From Cincinatti, Ohio, 18 December: 'Dear Wife, Your letter to hand. Wired you $100 so you won't have to walk the Streets with the boy. Had you answered when you should have you wouldn't have had to wait a minute for your money . . . I also want to know from time to time how the boy is. Now don't go fooling too much as you may regret it . . . Love to my boy, Your Husband.'

The reason for the marriage rift is not easy to pin down. If it were true that Hattie wished her husband to give up his career in show business, and become a stay-at-home Dad and Hubby, then indeed 'twas a grievous fault, and grievously hath Hattie suffered for it. But she, who met him on the road, and toured with him so long, surely could not have thought this possible. The theatre was truly in his blood, and his trips abroad already a deep addiction.

The family themselves, the five grandchildren of this Great Schism, have no clear view of its genesis. Their rather forbidding grandmother, in her last days, was not one to volunteer such information. One piece of family lore has it that Bill and Hattie had agreed that if their child to be was female, Hattie would decide on its upbringing, and if a male, Bill would prevail. Another view is that Bill fully expected to bring up a vaudeville family, but Hattie, from the start, had other plans. Whatever their private pacts, Bill's dreams were shattered, and his wrath burned exceeding.

Sometime in 1906, according to the family, Hattie formally converted to the Catholic Church, taking little Claude Jr. into baptism. From that point on, religion began to play an important part in her life, and her 'Christianising' of young Claude became another deep bone of contention between her and her estranged husband.

Nevertheless, and despite reams of angry, bitter and reproachful letters, there are pitfalls in the assumption of the unbridgeability of this gulf. Reading the letters carefully, a picture emerges of some kind of tacit deal. Each side struck blows, as estranged couples do, in defence of their own hard-fought positions, but always within defined rules.

Despite the verbal aggression, Bill Fields sent money to Hattie, practically every week, for almost thirty years. In return, he maintained a contact, tenuous but more lasting than might be assumed, with Claude Junior. And there was another quid pro quo.

In return for his financial support, Hattie accepted that Bill should go his own way, in terms of his personal and sexual life. For one clue to this, we can leap forward, again, to the inheritance war which followed Fields' death. As I have noted, Hattie told the Judge adjudicating her claim for Bill's estate, in 1947, at one point, that she had left him over a woman. This can neither be confirmed nor denied. Certainly Bill's later pattern of regular girlfriends and mistresses suggests that he could hardly have been a less lusty lover in his late twenties than he was in his mid-thirties and forties. There is nothing to suggest that he 'fooled around' while still with Hattie, but there are some clues that he might well have responded to her perceived treachery over Claude Jr. by finding solace elsewhere, pretty soon.

These are the shaky grounds of speculation, not the terra firma of fact, but there are intriguing clues. A letter to Bill's father, on 6 April 1906, states: 'Glad to hear all at home are well. Regarding a certain person, I don't care to know any more about her, and am positive Mother gave her all she gave Mother.' And yet the letters to Hattie both before and after this date are still part of a regular, even a polite contact. So the 'her' in this letter may not be Hattie at all, but – ? Another tiny clue might be a clipping from the *New York Dramatic Mirror* of 8 June 1907, announcing Fields' ambitious plans to tour the Orient with his own repertory company, which was to include one Carolyn Gordon, 'the American dancer, recently with McIntyre and Heath in The Ham Tree'. Carolyn Gordon played Tessie Nicklebacker, the giddy love interest in the play. Was she the primary Fields paramour?

Later on in Bill's life we will find a pattern: luscious young ladies of the Broadway chorus lines, from the Ziegfeld *Follies* to Earl Carroll's *Vanities*. Hattie named two of them, Mildred L. Blackburn and Fay Adler, in her 1947 suit for half a million dollars she claimed Fields had given away to his lady friends. A third name listed by Hattie, Grace George, has proved untraceable in the chorus lines. But there was a Grace George, born in 1879, whose first appearances on stage in the 1890s included a version of the same 'Mdlle. Fifi' that the Monte Carlo Girls had burlesqued. During Fields' run in *The Ham Tree* she was acting on the legit New York stage. She later starred in many Bernard

Shaw plays. (She died in 1961.) If she was a lover, this would have had to be hush hush, since she had been married since 1899 to William Brady, a major theatrical agent.

Was something like this the background to Hattie's sudden conversion? Whatever the obscured facts, there is no doubt that Hattie's new-found religiosity tied W. C. Fields to a bed of nails. Divorce became impossible. His overriding priority was to maintain his link to Claude. Thus, in an uneasy balance, these two tussled and squabbled, the spark of anger flaring, then dulling into embers, turning into a bitter sludge of ashes, down the years – until it came to be converted, phoenix-like, in the alchemy of scripts and screenplays, into creative gold.

In 1907 brother Walter replaced Hattie as Bill's on-stage assistant and stooge, wearing the footman's livery his on-stage assistants had been clad in at least since 1904. In May, the act resumed in Rochester, the week after in Philadelphia, and at the end of May, it opened at a new venue, the 'Jardin de Paris' roof garden over the Criterion Theatre in New York. The chief feature of the programme was 'Empire Living Statuary', twelve reproductions of famous paintings and sculptures embodied by New York lovelies in scanty attire or no attire at all, entitled 'Cupid's Spell', 'The Ducchess of Devonshire' and 'The Bath of Psyche'. Vaudeville acts were the supporting programme: 'The biggest individual hit was scored by W. C. Fields, the comedy juggler, who, having no talk in his act, had the advantage of some of his less fortunate brethren, who had to try to make their voices reach to the limits of the block long auditorium.'

This performance gave rise to another Fieldsian folderol, an apocryphal tale of how he brought his uncle, the Reverend W. C. Felton (The W. C. is a dead giveaway!) to view the 'Empire Pictures', but the good minister rushed off after the first few samples, muttering 'Suffering sciatica! I hope Brother Hoofnagle or any of the flock (don't) get to hear of my forgetting myself this way!' But Fields was still chaffing at the bit and raring to find new realms to conquer. The aforementioned item in the *Dramatic Mirror*, on 8 June, heralded an outstanding breakthrough:

W. C. FIELDS TO TOUR THE ORIENT
W. C. Fields, the comedy juggler, who added another to his long list of hits at the New York Roof last week, will start early in the spring of 1908 on a long tour of the Far East, heading a company playing a repertoire of musi-

cal comedies. A few days ago Fields received a letter from Mr Dow, who has had much experience in piloting companies in that portion of the world, informing him that the company had been booked over the following route: Honolulu, four weeks: Yokohama, two nights: Kobe, Japan, one night: Shanghai, eight weeks: Hong Kong, two weeks: Manila, ten weeks: Hong Kong, one week: Singapore and Straits Settlements, two weeks: Penang, two nights: Calcutta, ten weeks: some one, two and three night stands in India, and then Bombay, two weeks. Fields will be the star of the organisation . . .

Alas, this is the only surviving vestige of the enduring legend of Fields' adventures in the Far East. For as we approach the target date, on 30 May 1908, the *New York Dramatic Mirror* announces:

W. C. FIELDS DEPARTS

W. C. Fields, the eccentric juggling comedian, sailed for England May 20, and will open his European tour on June 1, at the Hippodrome, after which he will play other engagements covering the entire Summer and Fall. He will return early in November and will resume his American dates at the Colonial, this city, on November 9.

In between these dates lie verified engagements all around the United States and Canada, with nary a week to spare. In short, the Great Tour of the Orient never happened. Somewhere in between these two clippings the obscure Mr Dow vanished from the picture, and the well-laid plans fell apart. W. C. Fields never went to Japan, China or India, the Malay Straits or any of those places, despite the fact that credulous journalists wrote about him in later years that 'he has also performed before the Maharajahs of India and even astonished the Indian magicians with his art'.

This, to me, has been the saddest cut of all. There were, indeed, vaudeville circuits in all those far eastern places. Other performers had played them, notably R. G. Knowles, who had been everywhere, and used his recollections of the 'fine art' of the beggars of Colombo to enrich his globe-trotting monologue, 'Trifles That Trouble the Traveler'. So clearly Fields had to have been there too, but, alas, only in his dreams.

Instead the grind went on. The Grand Theatre, Birmingham; Shepherds Bush Empire, London; Coventry Empire; Glasgow; Leeds; Liverpool; Manchester. In August, the Hippodrome, London, *The Era* noting:

That delightful humorist, W. C. Fields, gives us many mirthful moments as an eccentric juggler, especially in his billiard playing with tennis balls . . . He discards the dirty make-up and ragged garments of the tramp, and for this relief much thanks.

Fields was well aware of the need to change his act, to try and avoid the fate of so many who misjudged their time, and became fads of the past. An item in *Variety*, in April, had announced, intriguingly, that Fields had been rehearsing a completely new routine to add to his act abroad, 'featuring a burlesque croquet shot in which the croquet ball is made to go through all the wickets in one shot, the trick being patterned after the pool shot now used in his act'. The item also claimed that 'Mr Fields will carry two or three people with the new act, one being Leo Donnelly, the Philadelphia newspaper man who recently broke into vaudeville with a monologue.' I can find no further mention of Donnelly, though it might be assumed that brother Walter went with Fields abroad no more.

In 1908, he was returning to familiar hunting grounds. Old stalwarts were also doing the rounds. Fred Karno's troupes, George Robey, Vesta Tilley, et al. Paul Cinquevalli was touring the same Moss Empires circuit, with his green and gold costume and a billiards act of his own – potting the balls into his coat pockets – one wonders where he got it from.

Indeed an item in the *Sunday Chronicle* of London reported on a juggler who 'was one of the many who have stolen the tricks, mannerisms, make-ups, attitudes and quaint conceits of W. C. Fields, the American . . .' The paper continued: 'It may be a compliment to Fields that he is probably the most copied man on the vaudeville stage, but it may be an unpleasant experience for him when he returns to this country . . . to find that the feats he spent years in evolving have been used by a dozen others at least . . .'

This purloining – or 'borrowing' – was not all one way. Another act, the Englishman Harry Tate's 'Motoring' sketch, was touring the Midlands at the same time as Fields. This was fast becoming a milestone act, and was later performed at the first Royal Command Performance, at the Palace Theatre, in July 1912 (Fields was in the United States for that summer). In the 'Motoring' act, Harry, a Friend, a Chauffeur, Harry's Wife, Son and Son's Friend, are trying to leave London for a holiday jaunt in a 'battered old car'. (How old a car could have been in 1908 is of course a matter of some interest.) But the various attempts to start the car and push off are frustrated by revolver shots fired behind the car, Tate's inability to get the engine started, the family's bickering and the chauffeur's incompetence, and interference from outside parties. At the end a policeman saunters up and cites them for 'furious driving', to which Tate ripostes: 'Furious driving? My dear fellow, we've been stuck here for the last half hour.' At an earlier point the family are all seated and ready to go, waving to the Friend on the sidewalk (the following text is from the 1912 version):

TATE: Right you are, I'll see you down there!

FRIEND: Yes, do . . .

TATE: Goodbye!

FRIEND: Goodbye!

SON: Goodbye!

FRIEND: Goodbye!

SON: Goodbye!

TATE (*looks round at son, annoyed*): Shut up you little fool. (*Biz with levers and steering wheel. Revolver shot.* TATE *gets out of car and walks round to the front of it.* TATE *to* CHAUFFEUR) Have you been taking any friends out in this car?

CHAUFFEUR: No, sir, oh no sir. No. No. No. No. No.

The resemblance to Field's oft-repeated sketch, 'The Family Ford', recast in several versions, will be recalled later on. It was eventually to be immortalised in Fields' 1934 masterpiece, *It's A Gift*, an astonishing example of cross-fertilisation across the gulf from the English music-hall to Hollywood.

Fields on his British tour might have already been experiencing a rather heavy *déjà-vu*, which he could not easily shake off. Returning to New York in November, he shared top billing with Nat Wills, the 'Happy Tramp'. Wills, still playing in tramp costume, was one of the highest paid acts in vaudeville, but his routine has not stood the test of time – 'Mr Wills' story . . . about the darkey and the little yaller dog that died, is one yell,' said the *New York Star*. Hmmm. But the *Star* was equally upbeat about Fields:

W. C. Fields, who recently returned from a successful tour of the English and Continental music halls, is again making vaudeville audiences laugh in this country. Mr Fields does all kinds of things with all kinds of articles. What he can't do with billiard balls and billiard cues; with hats and cigars and other articles is scarcely worth doing. He is the only man in the world today who plays billiards on an india-rubber table with india-rubber billiard balls (we hope that's right, though Mr Fields refuses to say whether it is or not); and the way he makes the balls carom around the table and land in his capacious hip pocket is an amazing revelation in the gentle art of billiards . . .

This quaint little portrait of Mr Fields does only faint justice to his beauty as he walks out on the stage in a scrubby beard and evening clothes that must have seen better days. They couldn't possibly have seen worse if they tried.

The 'quaint little [self] portrait' entitled, 'W. C. FIELDS, THE GREAT SILLY', shows a grotesque angular figure with a billiard cue. It was a sample of a new intriguing Fields sideline – a rush of lively cartoons, somewhat in the style of George McManus, creator of 'The Happy Hooligan' strip. All were self-portraits in various poses and costumes. The *Cleveland Plain Dealer* opened a revealing window on this new Fields some years later, in 1910:

10 Self-portrait of the artist, 1907.

How a man of the routine imposed upon W. C. Fields . . . makes to be lonely when his activities in the theatre take up most of his afternoons and evenings is surprising. Nevertheless, Fields confesses that he is the loneliest of men. When good books are not available Fields makes time merrily pass by drawing sketches. He has never taken a drawing lesson in his life, yet by instinct he is a clever workman with pen and pencil. When he can't wander about the streets sketching pictures of odd visages he sees, he retires to the theatre and makes copies of the details of the proscenium arch or a vista of the flyloft. Then too much time is taken up each week sketching on a single bristol board, impressions of the various acts on the bill. These Fields keeps as a pictorial diary of his vaudeville career.

Ronald Fields wrote that W. C. seriously contemplated a career as a newspaper cartoonist, but it was not to be. There was still no escape from juggling, though the road was now, despite his fame, harder, as once arrived, he had to keep his place against all rivals, new and old. Will Fowler told me that he believed Fields started drinking much earlier than many have thought, and therefore needed to find an alternative to juggling before his powers and skills might be compromised. Certainly he was emphasizing the comedy more and more, though the act was increasingly silent, until, in 1910, he officially renamed himself 'The Silent Humorist'.

In summer 1909 Fields returned again to England, for another gruelling tour. He had already switched his venue, late in 1908, from the Hippodrome to the Coliseum, another state of the art London theatre, first opened in 1904. The largest theatre in London, built by the impresario Oswald Stoll, it had the country's first revolving stage, a technological marvel, with a grand marble-pillared lobby and an electric carriage installed to take the Royal visitors, whenever they wished to visit, to the Royal Box. On its pilot flight, in 1905, King Edward VII stepped in the car and pressed the button, but it refused to budge. Muttering 'better walk then, what, what, what', the game monarch strode out past the sweating managers and squirming Stoll.

At his June appearance at the Coliseum, Fields appeared on the same bill as 'Occultos – A Riddle of the Universe'. This was a mechanical man who was assembled on stage, answered impromptu questions from the audience about life and politics, and was then taken apart and put back in his box. A less flattering fellow performer, at Newcastle-on-Tyne, was Consul, another damned monkey, who would enter his well appointed apartment in full evening-dress, put away his top-hat and gloves neatly, sit at the dinner-table and ring for his meal. Infuriatingly, he too, like the Congo pygmies, was invited to meet the King, as well as the President of the United States.

Fields' regular upstager, the ubiquitous Houdini, was also in town, having arranged to have himself placed, on the stage of the Oxford Theatre, in a galvanised iron milk can, naked, covered with water to the lid and sealed inside, with the audience invited to place the padlocks on the lid. Needless to say, he was not confined for long.

Bill Fields continued to consume this mixed diet of sweet fame and bitter herbs for another four years, constantly varying his act in small details. From June 1910 until March 1912, he toured Europe without returning to America, playing whatever circuits gave him work, wherever. In Britain he plied the heavy routes: not only the standards, Glasgow, Belfast, Manchester, but also backwaters like Preston, Sunderland, Croydon. He played every Empire hall in London: Hackney, New Cross, Shepherds Bush. In Autumn 1910 he crossed the Channel, to play Paris, Berlin, Brussels, Copenhagen. Then back to Britain, to play the Birmingham Grand in January 1911 with Zaleski 'The Golden Spider' and the Guatemalan Marimba Band which, *The Era* informs us soberly, 'produced a 9ft long instrument'.

A contract issued by Somers & Warner's Agency, 1 Tottenham Court

11 The Somers and Warner's contract.

Road, London, reveals a typical transaction. Fields signs, on 4 February 1911, to perform for one week at the Grand Theatre Bolton, commencing 10 April, at £70 per week, with one week in 1912 'at £75 a week to be mutually agreed by both manager and artiste'. Pencilled in is the agent's commission, at £5 16 shillings and eightpence, reducing the artist's take to £64.3.4. At a commission of one twelfth, this is a far better deal we would expect in our own grasping day and age. The paper is signed with the flourish 'W. C. Fields' whose 'Permanent address' is given as '15 Queens Road, Richmond, Surrey'. I do not know if this was a rented residence or a hotel. Fields' £70 salary, or around $300 at that time, was not bad cash for a week in so bleak a boondock as Bolton, but still, as we have noted, not top dollar.

This period in Europe has also given rise to more Fields' myth, such as his appearance on the same bill with Charles Chaplin at the *Folies Bergère*. As Chaplin was with Fred Karno's 'Mumming Birds' in Paris in the autumn of 1908, a period when Fields was booked solid in Britain, this tale too, must bite the dust. Fields did, on the other hand, share that stage with a very young Maurice Chevalier, who was being introduced in 1910–11 to the *Folies* by his older lover, the fabulous singer and mistress of ceremonies, Mistinguett. Theirs was a celebrated and, of course, scandalous partnership.

In May 1911 Bill was back at the London Hippodrome, appearing with the 'Moscow Aesthetic Dancers' (Madame Elena Knipper-Rabeneck, featured), the ubiquitous Bioscope, and the Bogannys in 'Fun in an Opium Den'. In June he crossed over to the Coliseum to appear, once again, with R.G. Knowles and with Sent M'ahesa's 'Suite of Old Egyptian Dances'. By this time the old theatre-loving King, Edward the VIIth, had died, and George the Vth had been enthroned. In Dublin, in July, Fields appeared at the Theatre Royal in a bill which included, intriguingly: 'Quinlan and Richards in their comedy "The Quack Dentist"' (a forerunner of the later 'Dentist Sketch'?), and a week later, at Edinburgh, *The Era* noted 'his expertness of manipulation being accompanied with a flow of pretty wit'. So the 'Silent Humorist' was still not silent all the time.

In September, W. C. Fields was at the *Folies Bergère* 'and needless to say, is "the" thing'. In October he was still in Paris, at the Alhambra. Then back to London for Christmas at the Coliseum.

In February he was at the Shepherds Bush Empire again, and some Spaniards in the audience, who had probably come to toast their countrywoman, 'the beautiful Spanish singer Carmen Turia', who was also on the bill, threw their hats on to the stage in appreciation of his juggling, as if he had just stabbed the bull, rather than the billiard table.

On 23 March the press logged his arrival back in New York aboard the mammoth steamer *Olympic*. He remained in the US until May 1913, once again crisscrossing the country, playing venues as wet and windy as Winnipeg, Canada or dry as dust as Salt Lake City, Utah, Lincoln Nebraska, Kansas City Missoura, Sioux City, Omaha, Denver, Milwaukee, Duluth. ('When I performed in Punka City,' grates a voice from the future, 'the house was so packed they couldn't applaud horizontally, they had to applaud vertically . . . ') The *San Francisco Examiner*, on 19 August 1912, wrote:

He is the first artist in his line, which is pantomime, juggling with subtle as well as violent forms of humor that keep his audience in an uproar. His famous pool game is up to schedule. He has a real pool table on the stage, with a mirror arrangement, so that the audience can see the balls. They run about as though compelled by some magic to serve the player's ends . . . It is impossible to tell whether Fields makes real or fake mistakes in his juggling. He will drop a hat apparently by accident in the middle of some difficult feat and catch it by another apparently accidental movement. It is the last word in juggling of this sort.

And Waldemar Young wrote, in the *San Francisco Chronicle*:

Fields is not only the best comedy juggler in the world today, without one single exception or lone rival, but he is also a comedian with more of the real spark of comic genius than almost any who styles himself so in the legitimate field. Were he to break an arm so that juggling would be impossible, I still believe that he could go right out as a comedian and finish in the first flight . . .'

The *San Francisco Call*, on 3 September, summed it up: 'The best that can be said of him is that he is original.'

No higher praise could be envisaged. And yet, in 1913, Fields was to breach another hurdle, and obtain his apogee upon the British variety stage, with, at long last, the full Royal imprimatur.

Chapter 15
'The House Beautiful';
or, Vaudeville's Last Illusion

By 1911, Vaudeville was already approaching middle age. It was no longer the new, vibrant medium of entertainment for the American mass. There was a new king in town. In 1911, the *New York Dramatic Mirror* signalled this shift by dramatically reducing its Vaudeville coverage, almost overnight, and replacing it with a much expanded section of 'Motion Picture News'. *Variety*, too, was following suit.

The development of the cinema as an art, rather than a specialty, or an experiment, was slow to come in America, but was already established in Europe, first in France, then in Sweden. In America, one of the foremost pioneers, Sigmund Lubin, had in fact exposed film in Fields' native Philadelphia as early as 1897, though his efforts, a horse eating hay and a pillow fight between his daughters, were pretty modest by any standard. There is no evidence Fields took any notice of this fledgling medium before he joined the stage. In 1904, the Edison-produced *The Great Train Robbery*, directed by Edwin S. Porter, made a stir (Lubin produced a prompt imitation). The Vitagraph Company, founded also in 1897, was going strong by 1902, producing a series of comic shorts based on the newspaper cartoon character, 'The Happy Hooligan'. Griffith was shooting films for the Biograph Studios from 1908. And we have seen, from the titbits in *The Era*, how British companies experimented both in documentary footage and short fiction films. In 1908, while Fields was playing the Empire circuit, Pathe Freres in London were offering such delights as 'Paddy Has Been Eating Horseflesh', 'The French Cupboard' and 'Vulture Hunting in Africa', subjects ranging in length from 478 to 676 feet.

But by 1911 the 'Bioscope' had migrated from the vaudeville halls to specialist theatres, dramatic subjects were common, and the American cinema had its first comedy star, the rotund John Bunny. A young singer and actor, named Mack Sennett, who had made his début in burlesque on the Bowery as the hind-legs of a horse, was directing for Biograph by 1910, but it was not until 1912 that he would hit on the formula which enabled his own Keystone company. At this time, young Charles Chaplin was still touring America with the Fred Karno troupe of players. His first movie would be made in 1914.

Famous names who would influence Bill Fields' career and many others had crossed his path almost unnoticed. In October 1907, when Fields was appearing on the same bill as Vesta Victoria at the New York Theatre, Keith's 125th Street was featuring a young man, Jesse L. Lasky, as a cornetist in Lasky's Military Octette. In the same week, a young playwright named Cecil de Mille, younger brother of the more famous William, was scoring a success in his 'stirring romantic playlet', 'The Man's the Thing'. In 1910, in the Bronx, Fields was on the same bill with Jesse L. Lasky's presentation of 'The Photo Shop, a snappy musical comedy'. This was only four years before Lasky, De Mille and another film pioneer, Samuel Goldfish (later Goldwyn), formed their own motion picture company to produce the first American feature film, *The Squaw Man*, in a Hollywood barn. Two years after that they would merge with Adolph Zukor's Famous Players to form Famous Players-Lasky, which was to become Paramount Pictures, producers of almost all W. C. Fields' films until 1938.

The writing was on the wall for vaudeville. The 'motion' picture, the medium that most expressed America's view of itself as a society of speed, mobility and endless dynamism, was the future. And yet, vaudeville was Bill Fields' world. He knew no other. It was the air he breathed. He soldiered on. In June he returned to England for his eleventh foreign tour in fourteen years. McIntyre and Heath were also in town, at the Hippodrome. Fields was at the Coliseum with George Robey and Hymack, 'the Chameleon Comedian'. The programme leaflet also announced:

Mme Bernhardt to play a season at the Coliseum with a Repertory Company to present Excerpts from her most Famous Plays.

Sarah Bernhardt was the grand phenomenon of the world stage. Famous since the 1870s – she had been around since the Paris Commune – she had branched out to conquer stages from Paris to the United States. She was probably the first example of what we would call today a Star: a peformer shimmering in the glow of celebrity, end-less media attention, and a cult-like worship. For some years now she had been broadening her appeal by appearing in short selections in variety theatres, a process frowned upon by the dourer critics. But the general audience adored her.

Fields' appearance at the end of September with Bernhardt – present-ing her selections from 'Le Proces de Jeanne D'Arc' – heralded a more significant date: 11 October, when the King and Queen, and other members of the Royal Family, were to give their patronage to Mme Bernhardt's 'Good Samaritan Performance, in aid of the French Hospital in London and Lord Lonsdale's Special Appeal for Funds for the Charing Cross Hospital. His Majesty,' the program added, 'has gra-ciously approved the Programme which will be of a unique character.'

The prices, too, would be unique, ranging from 5 shillings in the bal-cony to a top 10 guineas (£10 and 10 shillings, or over $40) in the 'Fauteuils'. Much has been made of La Bernhardt's largesse in appear-ing with Fields, due to her supposed aversion to jugglers, but in fact the only taboo in the Grand Dame's list of approved supporting acts was the brusque command to impresario Oswald Stoll – 'After monkeys not.' (On 10 September, just before Fields, she had appeared with his old juggling colleague, Tom Hearn.) At any rate, the occasion was grand enough.

Was this the only time – apart from his 1902 charity do for Queen Alexandra's Trust – that Fields performed before Royalty? His own claims co-opted the previous monarch, Edward the VII, into his circle of adoring fans. One of his cartoon self-portraits, executed in 1907, has the footing: 'As the Prince of Wales said when he took my hand: "Will is rough, and he's tough, and he's devilish slick – dev-ilish slick."' That Prince would have been the future King George. It is impossible to rule this meeting out entirely. Variety artists were occasionally invited to the Royal homes, including Buckingham Palace, to perform, but they were invariably British stars, such as the Scotsman Harry Lauder, or Imperial curiosities, like the Congo pygmies. These events were always reported. The Royals did attend the theatre and music-halls informally, and it could be that on one such occasion one of those august personages might have called the 'Eccentric Juggler' to the Royal Box for a special compliment. If it happened, it was not recorded. Perhaps it was the very first in a long line of those limp salutes that Fields would dub a 'hearty handclasp'.

The first official Royal Command Performance, at the Palace Theatre, was held in July 1912, when, as we noted, Fields was in the US. This marked a change in law whereby the music-halls were brought into line, in terms of status (and also censorship) with the 'legitimate' theatre. Music-hall was made respectable, and thereby, safe. Its days as a safety valve for popular pain were long gone. In 1912, two American jugglers, Paul Cinquevalli and Charles T. Aldritch, were on the bill. In 1913, Fields was the only American performer. Let us hie to *The Era* for an account of this benevolent occasion:

THE ROYAL PERFORMANCE AT THE COLISEUM.
THE HOUSE BEAUTIFUL.

To welcome his distinguished guests Mr Oswald Stoll has set his house in order, and what a lovely house it looked! From the base of the dome hung festoons of gold leaves. Leaves were everywhere, lit up by a myriad of electric lights in gold and silk shades, and the *coup d'oeil* from the royal box, hung with gold-coloured curtains, must have been magnificent, the charm of the decorative scheme being much enhanced by pink carnations embedded in greenery.

Their Majesties, accompanied by the Prince of Wales and the Princess Victoria, and attended by the Countess of Minto, the Lord Acton, and Colonel the Hon. Sir Harry Legge, arrived shortly after half-past eight . . .

The Era did not mention that, according to the *People* newspaper: 'As the Royal carriage approached the rear of the Coliseum . . . two suffragists came forward and said to their Majesties, "Women are being tortured in prison." . . . It was their intention to throw a number of handbills into the Royal carriage, but their attempt was frustrated.' *Plus ça change*. But back to the show:

Immediately their Majesties had reached the front of the Royal box they had a reception of the greatest cordiality from all parts of the house. The opening bars of 'God Save the King' brought everybody to their feet, and then Sir Alexander Mackenzie conducted his own 'Brittania' overture, a felicitous choice.

The parting of the new tableau curtains then revealed Miss Ellen Terry, our player-queen, who made her second appearance on the Coliseum stage, this time to read the deeply-touching verses of a specially written prologue from the graceful pen of Mr Owen Seaman, the Editor of 'Punch.'

At last, the evening's entertainment proper could commence. The French revue, *C'est Chic*, and songs by Madame Yvette Guilbert, opened. Then the English comic singer, Robert Hale, emoted, and Mr W. C. Fields 'represented American silent comedy in his display of remarkable pyramid shots, &c . . . the Royal party were evidently considerably amused by both comedians'.

Mme. Bernhardt's 'selections from Racine's tragedy of Phedre' closed the show, after which the audience sang the National Anthem, 'lustily', and, 'before the King and Queen left their box they were cheered again and again, the hearty demonstration of loyalty heard in the street as the great audience slowly departed at the conclusion of a night of happy memories . . .'

No one was invited back to Buckingham Palace, but the King's Privy Purse Officer, William Carington, wrote a letter of appreciation to La Bernhardt and the other performers on behalf of Their Majesties, noting that 'your good hearts will rejoice to feel that the noble work you did tonight will bring help, ease and comfort to many poor sufferers, who, without it, might fall uncared for and alone'.

A chorus of hearty handclasps all round.

Fields continued playing the Coliseum in November, with a little moonlighting at the Hackney Empire, and then reprised for the last time at the *Folies Bergère* in Paris before departing on his second and last world tour, to South Africa and Australia. In Paris he was on stage while comedian Harry Fragson was shot dead in his dressing-room by his mentally unstable father, an event which might have deepened Bill's misgivings about traditional family ties.

In my early notes about Fields' antipodean swan-song I assumed that this was a rather melancholy *déjà-vu*. Bill's letters to Hattie from the Southern Hemisphere are ill-tempered and reproachful. He appeared to be having a ghastly time in Johannesburg, castigating Hattie for sitting idle while

I am down here in Africa in the throes of a strike eating food that would not tempt the palate of a respectable canine. I haven't received any salary since the last day in January and my expenses will eat up a year's savings; yet I keep my own council . . . And please drop that 'Mrs W. C. Fields' on the back of the envelope just put Hattie Fields I like it better. A little thing like that might make me forget to send you my route. Love to Claude. Claude.

But, as usual with Claude, not all is at it seems. Having scoured the Fields scrapbooks for that year, I discovered that the juggler had fooled me again. The quickness of the hand deceives the eye. Never give a sucker an even break, particularly when he might be your biographer. The loneliness of Fields, on the road, has long been a staple of his legend, as exemplified by his oft-told tale of 'Why W. C. Fields Hates Christmas' – or 'Sleigh Bells Give Me Double Nausea':

> An actor on the road – as I was for so long – finds himself all alone on days when everyone else has friends and companionship. It's not so good to be in Australia, or in Scotland, or in South Africa, as I was on tour, all alone on a Christmas Day, and to see and hear a lot of happy strangers welcoming that two-faced merriment-monger Santa Claus, who passes you by . . .

In fact, W. C. Fields in South Africa and Australia, in 1914, was executing his latest illusion, a stunt worthy of Houdini himself.

Let us follow the dusty old trail: from Johannesburg Bill departed to Durban, where he played the local 'Hall-By-the-Sea'. By late February he was in Pretoria, where the local Afrikaaner rag gave him the accolade: '*W. C. Fields, de zwijgende humorist, de grote goochelaar heeft deze week de talrijke bezoekers van de Grand een reeks van prettige avonden bereid. Aller grappigst is Fields in het manupeleren met tennisballen, een biljartaffen, hoeden en zoveel andere voorwepen.*' In March, in Cape Town, he was threatening a local newspaper with libel action over a review which lumped his act with others under the heading PIGS AND OTHER ARTISTS. But by 4 April he had already crossed the ocean to Sydney, Australia, to open at his old haunt, the Tivoli:

1ST APPEARANCE AT THE MATINEE – DIRECT FROM EUROPE
– THE MAN WHO MADE KINGS LAUGH –
W. C. FIELDS, THE SILENT HUMORIST . . .

The Sydney *Daily Telegraph* wrote: 'After an absence of many years W. C. Fields, 'The Silent Humorist', renewed his acquaintance with Tivoli audiences on Saturday, and immediately sprang into favour . . .' From Sydney to Melbourne, from May until June, then on to Adelaide, from which he wrote to Hattie, on 25 June:

> Dear Hattie: – Enclosed please find $100.00. Hope you have received money up to date. Please do not send any more 'Destitute circumstances' cables. Give my love to Son, I hope he is well.
>
> Claude.

A man alone, in the antipodean summer. But what's this? In the scrapbook, dated 28 May, here is a long article in a column called *Table Talk*, from Melbourne, entitled 'W. C. Fields At Home'. The gossipy correspondent notes that W. C. Fields has the wanderlust and likes to travel while his wife prefers to stay at home. True enough. But as the eye travels down the newsprint, you find the following: 'Mr Fields is called away to the telephone and Mrs Fields says: "Although you would scarcely think it, he is a very nervous man, and he always says it is the nervous man who makes the best juggler . . . "' But isn't Mrs Fields away sending grumbling cables from the US? The article continues:

> Mrs Fields is herself very dark as to hair, but with a clear fair skin and an
> unusual contrast of light grey eyes. She is English, although here and there
> there is an inflexion which suggests America, but she has caught this from
> her husband, and says it is impossible to avoid doing so.

Surely some mistake? But, on the next page of the scrapbook, from *The Mail*, Adelaide, on 15 June, Mrs Fields tells the journalist about her husband: 'He is out playing golf and missed his engagement . . .' And from *The Critic*, on 17 June: 'Mr W. C. Fields and his charming wife are staying at the Grand Central Hotel, and it was there we had the opportunity for a chat.'

The chat is titbits and small-talk, such as Fields saying: '"The only danger attached to my turn is that I might get fat. I have to guard against that." "And yet he eats cream whenever he can get it," interposed Mrs Fields . . .'

But on 25 June Bill was sending Hattie $100 from Adelaide . . .

Can there be two Mrs Fields . . .? Bill remained in Adelaide through July, and then in August took ship across the Australian Bight to Perth, on the western coast, where he was due to play at the local Tivoli. En route, on the RMS *Orsova*, he dashed off another letter to Hattie, dated 10 August: 'Dear Hattie: – On account of the European war I may have some difficulties getting money to you . . . I tried to cable money before leaving Adelaide but the offices refused to take the money on account of the war.'

The conclusion is inescapable. Bill was travelling with a lady companion, and passing her off as Mrs W. C. Fields. Suddenly, we can read Bill's surly letter to Hattie from Johannesburg in a different light: 'Please drop that "Mrs W. C. Fields" on the back of the envelope just put Hattie Fields I like it better.' Was The Phantom Wife already with him then? And how long had they been together?

The mystery deepens when one sees, in the scrapbook, the brochure for the good ship TSS *Ventura* sailing from Sydney on 29 August 1914 for San Francisco, back via Pago Pago and Honolulu. Among the on board entertainments W. C. Fields is down for the men's singles Deck Quoits, as well as for the Potato Race. The passenger roster boldly lists 'Mr and Mrs W. Field [*sic*].'

Dramatic pause for the hollow laugh of the clown. So, indeed, at the end of his foreign tours, we can realise that Fields has been fooling us all along. In all probability, he was seldom alone. If he was audacious enough to travel openly with a companion down under, he may well have done likewise in Europe. But in Europe he would have no need for subterfuge: in London, Paris, Berlin or Milan, a gentleman's girl-friend or mistress was his own business, particularly in the 'loose' the-atrical world. The newspapers, unlike today's rapacious media, would pass no notice or judgement. We will find no smoking gun on this trail. But in provincial Australia, and particularly in buttoned-up towns like Melbourne or Adelaide, an openly unmarried couple could not pass. And thus the Phantom Mrs W. C. Fields, the English girl with a trace of an American accent, was born, embarked upon the TSS *Ventura*, and then vanished, nameless, leaving no trace, if it were not for the comedian's obssessive clippings, on the flows and eddies of history.

But, as Bill's letters to Hattie indicate, the outside world had inter-vened in his plans. Shots fired in Sarajevo, in Bosnia, on 28 June, when Fields was swanning in Adelaide, were to usher in the Great World War. On 3 August Germany declared war on France. On 4 August the German Army invaded Belgium, and England declared war on Germany.

The impact on the variety profession, as on everything else, was cat-astrophic and immediate. By 12 August, a reading of *The Era* shows variety artists accepting a halving of their salaries for the War effort. (In Perth, West Australia, on 14 August, W. C. Fields' performance was accompanied by 'a patriotic tableau entitled "Brittania and Her Overseas Sons"'.) By 26 August the first Patriotic plays are marching across the London stage, with productions like 'A Call to Arms' and 'Joan of Arc's Appeal'. *The Era* replaces its accounts of 'Amusements' all over the country with columns such as 'My Escape From Germany'. 'Patriotic Song Hits' are advertised at 6d per pack of six, including: 'Its a Glorious Thing to be a Soldier', 'We Didn't Want to Fight – But by

Jingo Now we Do!' and 'Don't Waste Your Time in Piccadilly – You'll Find Recruiting Offices Near the Fountains in Tra-fal-gar Square'.

The days of world tours and carefree ocean crossings were over. German U-Boats were soon roaming the Atlantic, hunting for Allied ships, military or civilian. Death and isolation was to replace life and commerce.

By 26 November 1914, W. C. Fields was home in America, with his phantom companion. Despite the fact that he had toured abroad regularly, since 1901, he never again set foot outside the United States, not for one single day.

Part III
In the Tent of Omar Khayyam

Chapter 16
Doing the Ziegfeld Walk

'Do you have any idea of what the Follies meant to a performer?' Eddie Cantor demanded. 'Opening night in the New Amsterdam on 42nd Street, you played to the best people in the country. The Whitneys, the Vanderbilts, the Goulds, the Harrimans, the Astors, they were all there. Everybody from the Mayor down, or from the Mayor up, was there. We played thirteen weeks in New York and out we went.

'On the road,' Cantor continued, 'when we came into Pittsburgh to play the National Theatre, or Chicago at the Colonial Theatre, or wherever we played – Philadelphia, Detroit, Cincinnati, Kansas City – we knew as long as we were in that town we would never see an empty seat. We were sold out in advance. Tickets were harder to get than for a world series. We stayed in the finest hotels, we were invited to the finest homes, people considered it a privilege if we *talked* to them.'

Cantor stopped bouncing long enough to submit a rhetorical question. 'Do you know what aristocrats are? We were aristocrats in the Follies, mister.'

Thus Eddie Cantor, at the age of sixty, being interviewed in Beverly Hills by journalist Norman Katkov, for Katkov's 1953 biography of Fanny Brice, *The Fabulous Fanny*.

It's not surprising to hear such an outburst from Cantor: little Isidore (Itchik) Kantrowitz, street urchin from the Lower East Side of New York, who won his first notice when, at the age of eight, he wrote a letter to Santa Claus via a New York *Evening Journal* competition saying, 'Dear Santa, I'm an orphan. I live with my grandmother who is very poor. I have no warm clothes. I would like a pair of rubber boots, an overcoat, and a sled. That is all I want for Christmas.' William Randolph Hearst sent the booty by return of mail. From then on, Itchik-Eddie's chutzpah never ceased.

Cantor's rise was classic rags to riches. When he appeared as a singing waiter, with an equally young piano player, Jimmy Durante, in

Carey Walsh's Saloon at Coney Island in 1909, they would perform any song on demand, even if neither of them knew the tune. If a customer asked for 'Springtime in Kalamazoo', they would go for it and, if the customer was sober enough to cry out: 'That ain't the song I know,' Eddie would open those wide innocent eyes and say: 'You mean there are *two* of 'em?'

Cantor went on to 'Dutch' acts, then 'Hebrew' acts, discovering the blackface make-up that would be his stock in trade, at the same time as another young Jewish boy, Al Jolson, was also blacking up for the stage. Cantor's big break came when he began singing songs by the new wunderkind of Broadway, Irving Berlin. But it was not till 1917 that Florenz Ziegfeld plucked him from the boondocks and propelled him into the big time.

The show Ziegfeld signed Cantor to join was already the most famous on Broadway. Its top-ranking players were the best known in their field: Ed Wynn, Leon Errol, Bert Williams, Fanny Brice, Will Rogers and W. C. Fields. Not to speak of the great beauties who led the glamorous 'Ziegfeld Girls' – Lillian Lorraine, Olive Thomas, Ann Pennington, Ina Claire, Mae Murray, Kay Laurell, Justine Johnstone and a whole host more.

When W. C. Fields joined the Ziegfeld *Follies* in 1915, it was the ninth annual show of that name. The path that Fields took to his *Follies* début is, once again, part of his myth. The story goes something like this:

While in Australia, Bill received a telegram from producer Charles Dillingham in New York, inviting him to return immediately for a major part in a new musical play which would feature the first complete score by Irving Berlin and star Broadway's favourite dancing couple, Irene and Vernon Castle. Fellow vaudevillian Frank Tinney would also be starring in this revue, which was entitled *Watch Your Step*. Due to German submarines in the Pacific (*sic*!) he had great difficulty finding a ship until he boarded a tramp steamer which took thirty-nine days to cross the ocean to San Francisco, followed by several more days passage to Syracuse, New York. Fields later made a great deal of this world record of his, travelling 'forty-nine days to play a one-night stand'. In fact, we know his passage was not the breathless dash of the legend, and we have seen that his creature comforts were not neglected. But it is true that, soon after the show opened, producer Dillingham decided to axe his part. This consisted, according to stage historian Stanley Green, of a scene at the Automat restaurant, where Fields performed his regular juggling act, with some patter. Dillingham decided to change the milieu to the 'Palais de Fox-Trot'. Nix the Automat and exeunt Fields.

Nevertheless, the audience for the opening night, so the legend goes, included Gene Buck, writer and impresario Flo Ziegfeld's right-hand man, who promptly cabled Ziegfeld to offer Fields a part in next summer's *Follies* show. This may be the sober truth, but it could also be that Fields had been looking for a *Follies* part for some time, given that *Ham Tree* writer George V. Hobart was writing some of the shows. Fields used to say he was always badgering producers for a speaking part, to no avail. He may have been swithering between the mixed blessing of supporting roles on Broadway and the certainty of stardom on the vaudeville trail. But, once the War in Europe put paid to the foreign tours, the choice was abundantly clear.

Between Syracuse and Broadway, Fields returned briefly to the vaud circuit in December 1914, dotting about from Toledo to Cleveland, from Chicago to Omaha, Sioux City, Des Moines and all points east. On 14 January 1915 he was 'obliged to terminate his Keith engagement Tuesday owing to a bruised hand, while playing his billiards game'. This turned out to be in the midst of an engagement in Columbus, Ohio, in which he shared the billing with a musical sketch entitled 'Home Again', featuring a wild young foursome rapidly rising through the ranks. In the words of a contemporary review: 'The Four Marx Brothers are featured at the head of a company of 13. The comedy, in two scenes, has little in the way of a plot, and the whole affair is rather nondescript.' This is the only known instance of W. C. Fields and the Marx Brothers on the same show. What occurred in the dressing-rooms must be left to our imagination, though Fields later wrote about his new rivals: 'They sang, danced, played harp and kidded in zany style. Never saw so much nepotism or such hilarious laughter in one act in my life. The only act I could never follow . . . I told the manager I broke my wrist and quit.' Groucho described the event thus to film historian Richard Anobile in 1971: 'He said: "You see this hand? I can't juggle any more because I've got noxis on the conoxsis and I have to see a specialist right away."' But on 23 January Bill was back at Keith's, Louisville, proceeding from town to town until his last known engagement, at the Temple, Detroit, on 29 April, from whence he embarked to New York City, to begin rehearsals for the Ziegfeld

Follies, due to open in the first week of June, 1915.

And so Claude Dukenfield's new life began . . .

When Eddie Cantor described the Ziegfeld *Follies* as the acme of social climbing, he was expressing, unconsciously, the guiding principle of his mentor, the Great Florenz Ziegfeld himself. The impresario's father, Dr Florenz Ziegfeld Senior, had been a student at Leipzig Conservatory and founder of the Chicago Musical College in 1867. Born one year later, the young Florenz Junior grew up in an atmosphere of austere Lutheran morals and classical music. When he was four years old the city of Chicago burnt down together with his father's College. It was rebuilt, but the boy soon shunned classical music and instead embraced popular culture. Buffalo Bill's Wild West Show was his earliest fad. The legend has him beating sure-shot Annie Oakley in a competition shoot-out, but new research by Paulette and Richard Ziegfeld has, as new research does, found that the dates of this story don't match. It was the first example of Ziegfeldian flim-flam, far from the last.

Whether young Flo ever ran away to join Buffalo Bill or not, the young man proceeded to dismay his Dad by running a string of cheap vaudeville shows. A possibly apocryphal example was 'The Dancing Ducks of Denmark', which, the SPCA discovered, had the poor creatures set on an iron grid lit below by concealed graduated gas flames, causing them to waddle to the music. Another was 'The Invisible Brazilian Fish', an empty bowl of water.

But great oaks from little acorns grow. When Ziegfeld Senior, still hoping against hope, sent his son to Europe to engage performers for the Chicago Columbian Exposition of 1893, Flo Junior returned with a bevvy of acrobats and jugglers, the Von Bulow Military Band and a Swiss mountaineering trio. But the act which changed everything for Ziegfeld was our old acquaintance, the Great Sandow, at that time twenty-three years old and performing at New York's Casino Roof Garden. He opened in August 1893 at the Chicago Trocadero and was an immediate sensation. Billed as 'Sandow, the Perfect Man', Sandow opened a safe with his teeth and lifted the pianist up with his piano. Ziegfeld's angle was to invite society women to get up on stage and feel the Strong Man's biceps for themselves. Thus began a series of carefully staged gimmicks, culminating in a wrestling match with the lion at San Francisco Zoo, a bout which was so stressful for the lion in rehearsal that it refused to perform for the actual show. Despite this débâcle, neither Sandow nor Ziegfeld looked back from that date. (In 1894, Sandow posed for one of the earliest Kinetoscopes, a single camera shot of the strongman flexing his muscles.)

After producing a successful play, *A Parlour Match*, with the vaudeville comics Charles Evans and Bill Hoey, Ziegfeld took the show to London, where he met a new, sensational singer from Paris, the Polish-French Anna Held. She had hit the big time singing a version of a German song, *Die Kleine Schreke*, translated as 'Won't You Come and Play Wiz Me'. Ziegfeld was smitten, and wooed the petite Held away from her Spanish gambler husband with promises of Broadway wealth and glory. By all accounts, Ziegfeld was a prodigious wooer. He was always able to make a woman feel she was the only person in the world, and to convince her he understood her innermost dreams.

But Ziegfeld had his own dream – to replace the easy vulgarity of vaudeville with a sophisticated, romantic entertainment which would reek of elegance and old world charm. At the age of twenty-nine, Ziegfeld secured his objective, and Anna Held became his new protégée in New York. A year later, she divorced her Spanish swain and married Flo.

Ziegfeld's selling of Anna Held was one of the great feats of the period, reminiscent of Barnum's marketing of Jenny Lind, half a century before. The greatest wheeze was to invent her custom of bathing in milk every day. A dairyman from Brooklyn was engaged to deliver over 400 gallons of milk to her suite at the Savoy Hotel. The twist was a legal suit brought by Florenz against the milkman on the grounds the milk was not fresh. This drove the newspapers wild. Even the revelation of the hoax couldn't stem the bandwagon, and streams of adoring young men followed Held everywhere. Ziegfeld starred her in several plays and they spent the profits indulging in the most opulent lifestyle that could be had: apartments furnished with antiques, paintings and sculptures, a boudoir in Louis XIV style.

The rise and rise of Ziegfeld was almost stemmed in 1906 when he lost 2,500,000 francs in one session at the Casino in Biarritz. But a new deal with theatre owner Lee Shubert saved his bacon. Ziegfeld was already planning the extravaganza which was from then on to bear his exclusive name. In 1907 he made a deal with Klaw and Erlanger to produce a *Follies*, based on the *Folies Bergère* of Anna Held's fame, set in the Roof Garden of the New York Theatre. Featuring sixty-four 'Anna Held Girls' as drummer-boys and then in a bathing-pool act, it was not an instant success. But it picked up on tour, and, back in New York, he engaged the star vaudeville singer Nora Bayes.

For the *Follies* of 1908 Ziegfeld engaged a new beauty, Lillian Lorraine, and put up the biggest electric sign ever: 80 feet long and 45 feet high. But it was the last hurrah of Anna Held for Florenz. Realising the new shimmer in his eyes for Lillian she departed from New York to Europe, leaving Ziegfeld to go on crying from strength to strength.

The Ziegfeld *Follies* of 1909 had Lillian Lorraine flying 'Up, Up In My Aeroplane' and the girls with hats shaped as lit-up warships. The *Follies* of 1910 introduced some completely new turns. This was the year Ziegfeld engaged two of his greatest talents, Bert Williams and Fanny Brice. Joined in 1911 by Leon Errol and featuring a new score by Irving Berlin and Jerome Kern, Ziegfeld was establishing his annual festival as *the* home of the popular stage's greatest names: 1913 featured Nat Wills and Frank Tinney; 1914 introduced Ed Wynn.

It was legendary that Ziegfeld had little sense of humour. He was generous to a fault to his friends, but demanded total loyalty, particularly when faced with such outlandish things as pay disputes. He was, in a cultural sense, a populist, who rarely read books, and then only mysteries, as well as magazines and newspapers. One of his biographers, Charles Higham, wrote: 'His driving force was one of demonic sensuality and a passion for vivid artifice. The *Follies* were astonishing demonstrations of the mind of a man who sought to release his need for women in displays of adulation for them.'

Ziegfeld admitted himself he never understood his comedians. His main concern was 'Glorifying the American Girl': the Ziegfeld Look, the Ziegfeld Walk, straight backed, breasts forward, a sexual tease and an untouchable icon. The critic Edmund Wilson wrote about the *Follies* dance scenes that they appeared to represent 'not the movement and abandon of emotion, but what the American male really regards as beautiful: the efficiency of mechanical movement'.

The other principle Ziegfeld applied was colour. He would brood and then say: this year's *Follies* will be blue. Or pink. In 1915 he found his ideal collaborator in the brilliant Viennese designer Joseph Urban, who designed the *Follies* sets from 1915. Urban used an Impressionistic style of *pointillage*, achieving in the mode of Seurat or Monet incredible effects with lighting. Combined with costumes by fashion queen Lady Duff-Gordon, and later, special *tableaux vivants* by society painter Ben Ali Haggin, the label 'Produced Under the Personal Direction of Florenz Ziegfeld' was to define an era not only on the American stage but in American popular culture as it lurched towards the 'roaring' twenties. For Ziegfeld's great gift was his ability to sniff out what the American audience wanted. And, although he knew they wanted his Girls, he also knew they wanted the singers, monologuists and comedians that leavened the show into something more than the mere sum of its parts. He was bored stiff by W. C. Fields. At first, he could not make head nor tail of Will Rogers. He didn't care much for Eddie Cantor, but saw how an audience rocked at his act. And so he gave these performers a platform, and by so doing, made them too into something more than they had been, dragging their acts around the circuits, or even round the world: he made them into stars.

12 *The Ziegfeld Follies*, 1918: W. C. Fields, Will Rogers, Lillian Lorraine, Eddie Cantor, and Harry Kelly.

Chapter 17
The Tomato Sauce of Fanny Brice

In the spring of 1915 the War in Europe was bogged down in the trenches of Belgium. At Ypres, the Germans first used poison gas on the battlefield. On 7 May, the ocean liner *Lusitania* was sunk by German U-boats in the Atlantic, with the loss of 1,198 lives.

The Ziegfeld *Follies* of 1915 were Blue. Act One was an aquatic extravaganza, 'Under the Sea', followed by 'Hold Me in Your Loving Arms' sung by Helen Rook and Chorus. Then came 'My Zebra Lady Fair', sung by George White and the Zebra Girls, and a sketch called 'The Catskill Mountains', featuring Leon Errol as Rip Van Winkle and Ed Wynn as 'Nut Sundae'. The next scene, 'Barker's Jungle', featured Bert Williams as 'O. Shaw Androcles' and Phil Dwyer as 'The Lion'.

W. C. Fields first turned up in Scene 9, 'Some Midnight Cabaret', as 'A Pool Player', with Ed Wynn as 'Al A. Cart' and the Oakland Sisters as 'The Onion Sisters'. Fields played in two more scenes in Act Two, one as Himself in a scene called 'Home of the Sun' and as one 'Adam Fargo' in a sketch called 'Hallway of the Bunkem Court Apartment', with Bert Williams, Ann Pennington and Leon Errol, among others.

Broadway had lost one of its luminaries, impresario Charles Frohman, on the *Lusitania*, and Ziegfeld (while no friend of Frohman) inserted a patriotic scene, 'America', with Carl Randall and Mae Murray appearing in front of a massive stars and stripes. But America, from the President down, was still isolationist. The patriotic motif, however, grew and grew.

The actual texts, the 'books', of the *Follies* shows have long been thought to be lost in the confusion which overtook the Great Ziegfeld's papers in the wake of his death in 1932. After a life of glitz and opulence, Ziegfeld died bankrupt, and the legal vultures stripped his assets bare. But the Library of Congress in Washington, which yielded up *The Ham Tree*, also yielded two drafts of *Follies* books, of 1916 and 1917, which we shall come to in due course. Overall, the texts are a powerful reminder of the ensemble work of the Ziegfeld team. While each of the comedians performed their individual skits – and we shall examine Fields' own sketches in detail – they also appeared on stage together for such acts as the 1916 Shakespearian Travesties, or the 'Recruiting' sketch, the 'Episode of the New York Streets and Subways', or the 'Travesty of Scheherezade'.

Eddie Cantor himself drew attention to the strong links that formed between the performers. In his first venture into autobiography, in 1928, he wrote gushingly of the 'Three Musketeers' – Will Rogers, W. C. Fields and himself:

> Probably at no time in theatrical history did three comedians in the same show work so harmoniously together. In a business where a laugh to a comedian is life itself and he usually begrudges every chuckle another comic gets, the Three Musketeers of the *Follies* were ready to lay down their laughs for one another. Will Rogers would watch my act from the wings or W. C. Fields' skit and offer changes in the lines or situations that invariably improved the original material. We tried to do the same for him whenever possible.
>
> One day, Will, Bill and I made a covenant among us and went further back than Dumas' musketeers for our idea of friendship. In fact, we went all the way back to Omar Khayyam, the original old soak of Persia. According to Fields, Omar had formed an alliance with two other tent-makers which provided that whatever might befall, any one of the three could always come to any one of the others and share his tent, his loaf of bread, and his jug of wine . . . Strangely enough, we have never needed to call on one another. To this day each of us has managed to do a fair business in his own tent.

Cantor was an unashamed sentimentalist, and the impression of generous camaraderie among the Ziegfeld Boys was not completely universal. The famous tale of Fields' contretemps with fellow comic Ed Wynn is a case in point. Once again, the legend goes: Bill Fields is wielding his billiard cue in his pool act, when he notices the laughs are all coming in the wrong places. He looks down and there is Ed Wynn, under the table, doing his own shtik and ruining the act. Bill allows this to proceed for a while and then, choosing his moment, whacks Ed over the head with the billiard cue, laying him out cold. Much mirth from audience, exit Wynn, dragged offstage by assistants.

Unusually, this tale is mostly true. But the event was not so spontaneous. An unsourced clipping in the Lincoln Center file, dated 16 November 1915, comments:

W. C. FIELDS SPEAKS!

For the first time in a long career on the stage which has taken him around the world, W. C. Fields, who plays his classic pool game in The *Follies*, is speaking. Sure enough, in his scene with Bert Williams in the Bunkem apartments he says words right out loud. When you can hear him, you hear a lovely voice which reminds you of stripping gears on a flivver. Incidentally, Mr Fields is losing some laughs in the pool game because Ed Wynn, who is funny too, is cutting up at the same time. Fields is comical enough to hold any stage . . . Wynn has plenty of opportunity to make em laugh during the entertainment and Fields would go better if Wynn left him alone. Trying to watch both is like trying to smoke two cigars at once, you don't enjoy either as much as if you could devote your time to them singly.

Fields always carefully read his reviews, savouring the good ones and spitting fire over any lack of acclaim. So he was simply taking the advice of the Fourth Estate in nipping this challenge in the bud.

As we have seen, the newspaper was wrong in claiming this show as Fields' first speaking part, but it was the first since *The Ham Tree*, in which he began working with scripts.

Cantor was right, though, to highlight another of the small coterie of mostly male friends which always formed around Fields. But there were more than three musketeers. Leon Errol had been in the tent since 1914. But another exclusion by Cantor is more typical of the period: that of the black comedian Bert Williams, who had joined the *Follies* in 1910, and had been there longer than any of them.

As a black American, Bert Williams could be an equal on stage, but offstage it was a different story. While staying in the same hotels as his white colleagues, he was forced to enter by the back, or tradesmen's entrance. When Ziegfeld first elevated Williams to the front rank, many of his white fellow actors threatened to walk off the stage. It is a tribute to Ziegfeld's colour-blindness (when he smelled talent) that he stood his ground and enabled the actor to become the first and, for a long while, only African-American to be a Broadway star.

One can only imagine the qualities required to breach the colour bar in this way. Many say Bert Williams was the greatest of them all. He had been in vaudeville longer than Fields, with his partner, George Walker, who died in 1911. Following such pioneers as Ernest Hogan

('The Unbleached American'), Williams and Walker worked their way through medicine shows and small time to arrive at Koster and Bial's Music Hall in the late 1890s. They appeared together in such variety shows as *A Lucky Coon, The Sons of Ham, In Dahomey, Abyssinia* and *Bandanna Land,* which crossed over from black to white audiences. *Bandanna Land* introduced Williams' most famous number, the song 'Nobody', which became his anthem. Williams said:

> Nearly all of my successful songs have been based on the idea that I am getting the worst of it. I am the 'Jonah Man,' the man who, even if it rained soup, would be found with a fork in his hand and no spoon in sight, the man whose fighting relatives come to visit him and whose head is always dented by the furniture they throw at each other . . . Troubles are only funny when you pin them to one particular indidivual. And that individual, the fellow who is the goat, must be the man who is singing the song or telling the story . . .

These truisms of comedy were clearly being absorbed by Fields as he watched his fellow comics perform. The melancholy lessons of the black American experience were conveyed on stage by Williams with an elegance which transcended the discomfort of the black man guying himself for the whites. Fields paid him tribute in a rare quote in a book about the great black star, from 1923:

> My good friend, Williams, met with so many unpleasantly limiting conditions . . . he would occasionally say, 'Well, there is no way for me to know this or that thing, which you say is going on – I'm just relegated – I don't belong.' It was not said in a bitter tone, but it did sound sadly hopeless and it did seem a pity that any artist who contributed so much that was of the best to our theatre, should be denied even the common comforts of living when on the road in cities like St Louis or Cincinnati.

Another veteran who preceded Fields to the *Follies* was Fanny Brice. She had appeared in the *Follies* of 1910 and 1911, but had then veered off to play vaudeville circuits and appear in a string of revues. In 1916 she was back in the fold.

Fanny Brice was a phenomenon of the stage. No beauty à la Lillian Lorraine, in fact, her looks were downright plain. She was made for the kind of burlesque which 'travestied' great acts and famous plays. Starting out as a teenager playing amateur shows and talent contests under the soubriquet 'the Brooklyn Favorite, Miss Fanny Borach', at fifteen, she had tried to get a dancing job in the chorus of George M. Cohan's *The Talk of New York*. But the fiery showman pointed at her and shouted: 'You – with the Saint Vitus Dance – back to the kitchen!' This convinced Fanny that she had to train to sing. Like Cantor, she was blessed with an immense chutzpah, and an unshakeable belief in her star. At the age of eighteen, a spotter for Ziegfeld, Jerry Siegel, signed her for the *Follies*, prompting her to run out of the office and stand at the corner of Broadway and 47th Street waving her contract and shouting: 'Ziegfeld signed me!'

Her first assignment was singing a 'coon song' for Bert Williams, 'Lovey Joe'. But she was to establish her own speciality in a broad Yiddish accented rendition of songs and comedy sketches. In fact, like W. C. Fields' imaginary traumas, her 'Yiddishness' was an act. Fanny's current biographer, Herbert Goldman, tells us that she never knew more than a hundred words of Yiddish. But she found an instantly recognisable ethnic character to represent her on the stage, under various guises, from 'Sadie Salome' to 'Soul-Savin' Sadie From Avenue A'.

Fanny's personal life was unusually tumultuous, even among show people. Briefly married to a barber, Frank White, at the age of eighteen, divorced at twenty, in 1912 she met a suave con man in Baltimore who became her passion and her curse for twenty years. Jules 'Nick' Arnstein would be her lover and later husband and father of her two children. In June 1915, when the Briceless *Follies* of that year opened with Bill Fields and Ed Wynn, Nick Arnstein was being sentenced to two years and ten months in Sing Sing for his role in what was called the 'Gondorff Ring'.

If Bert Williams was outside the gate, Fanny Brice was the fourth 'musketeer' in Eddie Cantor's band of comrades. The third, Will Rogers, was a highly unusual candidate for this post, given a background that differed dramatically from almost all his stage colleagues.

Bert Williams was of mixed race Caribbean origin. Eddie Cantor and Fanny Brice Jews of immigrant families. W. C. Fields, if we follow J.B. Priestley, was the man from Mars. But Will Rogers was a bona fide native American, 'one quarter' Cherokee Indian. He used to say his ancestors didn't come over on the *Mayflower*, they were waiting for the boat on the shore. A genuine cowboy, he had been brought up on his father's ranch in Indian Territory, later to become the State of Oklahoma. We have already noted his adventures in the antipodes, as he managed not to meet Fields in South Africa. Returning home, his reputation as a wizard with a rope grew apace. At the New York Horse Fair, in 1905, he was noticed by the press, and he began swinging his lariat on the vaud circuit soon after. At Keith's Union Square he was billed as 'The World Champion Lasso Manipulator', and audiences could see this claim was not baloney.

From the start, Rogers brightened up his act with laconic comments, such as 'I'm handicapped up h'yar, the manager won't let me swear when ah miss!' Like so many before him, he toured Europe, in 1906 and 1907, with his roping act. He was at a crossroads, pondering whether to join a larger troupe, when fellow vaudevillian Fred Stone encouraged him to continue solo. In 1911 he began delivering the ad libbed wisecracks which were to eventually transform him into the uncrowned seer of American political life.

An enormous amount of what is familiar in American populist political culture can be directly attributed to Will Rogers. He became, in the 1920s, a kind of *vox populi* for the Ordinary American. Lines like, 'Congress is so strange. A man gets up to speak and says nothin'. Nobody listens. Then everybody disagrees,' or 'Don't worry if a man kicks you from behind, it only proves you're ahead of him,' were amiable but unthreatening digs at the high and mighty. Rogers would read the daily newspapers, then comment upon them, extempore, in his show that night. If there was a famous person in the audience, even the President, that person was not happy till he was guyed by Will Rogers. In 1920 he began a series of essays which he called 'The Illiterate Digest'. It concerned such matters as 'Helping the Girls With Their Income Taxes', 'Prospectus for "The Remodelled Chewing Gum Corporation"', 'Lets Treat Our Presidents Like Human Beings', 'One Oil Lawyer per Barrel', and 'Settling the Affairs of the World in My Own Way'.

He had got his break with Ziegfeld, like Fields, due to the quick eye and ear of Gene Buck. But Buck hired him for a revue called The Midnight Frolic, a spin-off of the *Follies* proper. The *Follies* had moved in 1913 to the New Amsterdam Theatre, near the corner of Seventh Avenue and 42nd Street. At the top of this great Art Nouveau building, there was an 'Aerial Garden', which Ziegfeld conceived as a venue for a nightly post-*Follies* show. Here the patrons watched the acts from their tables, while they ate and drank the night away, until Prohibition came to dim the lights. Rogers, with his roping and wise-hick remarks, stole the show. In 1916, he was on the main stage.

All the featured acts between the Glorified Ziegfeld Girls were, in fact, ex-vaudevillians, who maintained their old camaraderie. The mythic image of W. C. Fields as a loner, hater of humanity, misogynist, grump, was never at greater variance with reality as in this period. There was Sam Hardy, with whom Fields would co-write and, in effect, co-direct his masterpiece *Man on the Flying Trapeze*, in Hollywood in 1935. There were comedians Carl Randall and Walter Catlett, who partnered him in various skits. There were Raymond Hitchcock, Jack Donahue, Don Barclay, Charles Winninger, and other stalwart partners like Ray Dooley and Edna Leedom, with whom he later did his 'Back Porch' and 'Bedroom' sketches. And his famous stooge/amanuensis/stage assistant/caddy – William Blanche, alias Shorty – was soon to appear on the scene. Not to speak of the girls of the chorus. Ziegfeldian Fields was not alone.

The Musketeers played practical jokes on each other, like the night of the Clay McGonigle joke. You ain't heard the Clay McGonigle story? Well, shucks, this is how it goes: Will Rogers often talked about his cowboy friends from the old days, particularly his old pal Clay McGonigle. A name like that was not one Fields could resist. One day Bill and Eddie concocted a letter Bill wrote out in a clumsy scrawl:

Dear Chickenchief,

Will be out front tonight watching your show. Will see you for the last time. Tomorrow I'm on my way to France. Whoopee!

Your old pal, Clay McGonigle.

That night Will Rogers dedicated his act to Clay McGonigle, playing and talking to his invisible friend in the audience. After the show he went to look for him in the lobby, and then spent the whole night scouring the city's hotels. The practical jokers were too shame-faced to ever tell Rogers the truth. It was a salutary lesson in Will Roger's strength – his genuine, unabashed and innocent loyalty. His motto: 'I never met a man I didn't like', would lead him into dangerous waters, as when he began to take certain politicians, like Benito Mussolini, at face value.

McGonigle, of course, was too good a name to waste, and fans will note his turning up, in Fields' own vintage character, The Great McGonigle, in his 1934 movie, *The Old Fashioned Way* . . .

*

Fields was rich enough now to indulge in his passion for motor cars, the best that money could buy. Cantor relates:

> When we were on tour we never traveled by train. It was always in Fields' open Cadillac. Sometimes we'd have Fanny Brice with us and Bessie Poole, Fields' girl during the *Follies* years. When the weather was mild Bill'd have the luggage compartment loaded with groceries and we'd stop in an open field and have a picnic. He had all the equipment Lewis & Conger stocks, the baskets, the thermos jugs. He'd build a fire and fry potatoes and broil steaks. It was fine traveling in good weather, but he didn't care what the weather, rain or shine. You don't know what cold is until you've traveled across country at seventy miles an hour in zero weather in Fields' open car. Fanny, Bessie and I would turn blue with cold while our host drove on, admiring the rigors of nature, declaiming on health and the state of the nation, all wrapped up in his big fur coat and heated from within. When my knees started knocking he'd wrap newspapers around my legs and fasten them with rubber bands. There was to be no talk about trains; fairies rode on trains. We'd stop for dinner along the way and Fields would have a couple of martinis. In him a couple of martinis had the same effect as one usher in Radio City Music Hall.

W. C. Fields would drive, and Fanny Brice would act as surrogate mother to this troupe of overgrown kids – despite the fact that she was twelve years younger than Fields. She took them to her hotel suite and cooked up her very own spaghetti with tomato sauce. But Fanny's maid had filled the jar of powdered cheese with Lux flakes by mistake. The boys' mouths were soon foaming with soap.

Such were the good days. But Fields was always looking onward. From the start of his Ziegfeld days, in 1915, he had had his eye on the new medium which was supplanting vaudeville. The twittering figures and paper cut-outs of George Melies' *Trip to the Moon*, which accompanied him in Melbourne in 1903, had become a force that could not be ignored. Shadowed throughout vaudeville by the 'Bioscope', Fields felt his time had come to conquer it. And so it was in the summer of 1915 that he signed up, with the British Gaumont Company, to make his first motion picture.

Chapter 18

'At the Picnic: Jealous Rivals for the Love of a Girl'

W. C. Fields' first film, the short *Pool Sharks*, is a dud. 1915 was early days in the development of silent movie comedy, but a lot was going on. John Bunny, the first movie comedy 'star', died in April of the same year. We do not know if Fields saw his movies, but if he did, the rotund figure of the henpecked father of an insatiable family, as in *The Troublesome Stepdaughters*, might have kicked off some ideas. Bunny often co-starred with Flora Finch as his on-screen wife. In *Bunny's Suicide*, she tells him in an intertitle: 'Take this rope and go hang yourself,' a task at which he singularly fails. The *Manchester Evening Chronicle* wrote, in its eulogy of Bunny on 28 April 1915:

> Bunny was lucky in having as a foil that aciduous female Flora Finch. Her sharp features and puritanical nose were an admirable contrast to the bulbous countenance of the inimitable John. When we saw him hen-pecked and dejected, seated at the breakfast table, withered by the bitter tongue of his formidable spouse, there was something more than laughter in our hearts. There was the least touch of pity, and this was a tribute to the truth and reality of his art.

We might well be reading an account of W. C. Fields' character in such painful family breakfast table scenes as those in *It's a Gift, Man on the Flying Trapeze* or *The Bank Dick*. This may be in the realm of coincidence, but perhaps not. Bunny made two or three films a week for the Vitagraph Company in New York between 1911 and 1915. He had begun in a minstrel show but graduated to the legitimate stage. Almost uniquely, he crossed directly from there to the cinema, bringing his roles a sophistication of gesture and movement that was recognised as special. Bunny also starred in an early film version of Dickens' *The Pickwick Papers*, shot in 1912. He is unknown today to all but film historians, but when he died one Dublin newspaper ran the headline: 'John Bunny is dead, the best-known man in the world.' He also earned up to $30,000 a year. If Fields was following the movies at all, and he must have, he could not have been ignorant of John Bunny. But this was another name that did not pass his lips.

To be cautious, one should point out that Fields could not have identified the gross, elderly figure of John Bunny with the trim, athletic thirty-something he was himself in those years. But early influences stick around for a long time, as Fields' entire life of vaudeville conservation demonstrates again and again. And Fields, like an elephant, never forgot any bit of business, stage or screen.

There were other names as obscure today, before 1915. Billy Bletcher played gay blades for Vitagraph. Fred Mace made comedies for Biograph. Billy Reeves, who had created the 'drunk' role for Karno that was later to be Charlie Chaplin's stepping stone to fame, fixed his flag to the ailing Lubin Company. Oliver Hardy, totally unknown then, also began at Lubin's. (Stan Laurel was still in vaudeville.) Another major clown, Max Linder, made literally hundreds of films for Pathe in France, and was a vital influence on Chaplin. And there was, of course Mack Sennett's Keystone, which introduced Ben Turpin, Harold Lloyd, Chester Conklin – who was to co-star with Fields in his vanished silent film trilogy – Mabel Normand, Charlie Chase, Snub Pollard, Fatty Arbuckle, Ford Sterling and, of course, Charlie Chaplin.

It was Chaplin who had transformed the low-class business of slapstick comedy into something else, a world-wide craze. He had made his first films for Sennett in February 1914, and by July 1915 he had made a full forty-three short films, the last nine for Essanay Films, which included *His New Job*, *A Night Out*, *The Champion*, *A Jitney Elopement* and *The Tramp*. It was 1915 that saw the great Chaplin explosion, as David Robinson writes: 'Every newspaper carried cartoons and poems about him. He became a character in comic strips and in a new Pat Sullivan animated cartoon series. There were Chaplin dolls, Chaplin toys, Chaplin books. In the revue *Watch Your Step* Lupino Lane sang: "In London, Paris or New York, Ev'rybody does that Charlie Chaplin walk!"' This is, of course, the same *Watch Your Step* that Bill Fields appeared in for one night only. Coincidences never cease.

It should come as no surprise, then, that Fields modelled his performance in his first motion picture, on Chaplin. It is a sad and regretful fact that W. C. Fields, in his first movie, was not playing the character he had spent so long developing on the stage.

The film opens with a girl sitting in a garden on a hammock. Fields moves into frame, screen left, twirling a cane. The cane hits his eye, Chaplin fashion. She laughs. He recovers. A boy, cleaning the steps of a house, sees Fields, pours out the water in his bucket and throws it at him. Fields, hit in the head, starts. A rival, flamboyant in a checkered jacket, enters frame right. They both sit in the hammock either side of the girl. The rival, having sat on a pin, draws it out (in close-up), then laughs at the burrs stuck to Fields' own pants. Fields dusts himself down, then all three sit on the hammock again. It collapses. The girl takes off, laughing. The rivals glare at each other. The rival wags a finger. Title:

AT THE PICNIC.
JEALOUS RIVALS FOR THE LOVE OF A GIRL.

The Fields who has thus lurched into the world of the movies is an unappealing character. He wears an ill-fitting silk jacket and pants, with white socks. His collar is sticking up around his neck. His hat is a light coloured, battered stovepipe. His cane is Chaplin-like. He has a short cigar stuck in his mouth. Underneath that nose, which was clearly always prominent – remember his brother Leroy referred to him, even in youth, as 'Big Nose' – there is a snub little moustache.

Even the most penetrating biography cannot enter fully into the recesses of its subject's mind. It must be counted a complete mystery as to why Fields adopted this excrescence, this fearful little clip-on brush that, Taylor claims, made its first appearance in Gene Buck's office, after the one night *Watch Your Step*. Nobody except Fields liked it, but it stayed, this dab of fungus, throughout Fields' run in the Ziegfeld *Follies*, through *Poppy*, and in all his silent films. A curious sidelight to this might be found in the Press Releases of Fields' 1928 film *Fools For Luck*, in which he co-starred with Chester Conklin, owner of a much more prominent fuzz. These publicity items were disseminated by the studios in the hope that lazy editors would fling them unchanged into their newspapers, which, more often than not, they did. This article was headed: 'Moustache Types Reveal Individual Preference: Both Fields and Conklin Loyal to Particular Growths Which Stamp Their Personalities':

'My mustache denotes comedy and, at the same time, it helps a lot in expressing pathos,' Conklin asserts. 'Being just a slight model, built low on the ground, the big mustache gets many a laugh . . .

'Getting a mustache that is applicable to both comedy and drama was a hard task and it took me years to work it out. Now I believe I have it down to perfection. At least Paramount has me and my mustache under contract.'

Fields differs slightly from Conklin, according to his own estimate.

'I can get just as many heart-throbs and laughs out of the bit on my upper lip as Chester can get with his great, blooming home-grown whiskers . . . I think the tiny misplaced eyebrow helps to stir an audience's sympathy. Furthermore it's easy to put on. Just a dab of spirit gum and it's there for all day long. It's not uncomfortable and hot. It is economical and it has personality. I'm just as loyal to mine as Chester is to his.'

Who were they both kidding? Of course, the above might well have been wholly concocted by a Paramount publicity agent with very little to say about a pretty shaky film. The Two Moustaches certainly never tickled the audience. But that is a tale yet to be told.

The problem with *Pool Sharks* is a combination of Fields' lack of experience of the medium, poor direction, by one Edwin Middleton, a script which seems to have been written on the back of an envelope (deriving from none of Fields' stage routines), an unattractive heroine (unnamed) and a positively repulsive – in the wrong way – rival, pug-nosed Bud Ross. Fields rampages through the movie, 'misplaced eyebrow' and all, like a kind of 'Happy Hooligan', which is perhaps what he was aiming for. Further high jinks at the picnic table include the unhooking of a small boy off his chair by Fields, followed by some nonsense rivalry with a plate of food, a carrot stuck in the eye, and much poking and shoving between the rivals. None of this has the flow and tempo of Chaplin's elegant sadistic manoeuvres. The small boy blows a pea from a peashooter at Fields, who pours coffee on the girl by mistake. The other guests at the picnic suggest 'A Friendly Game of Pool' to the rivals. This sets up the main arena of the action.

The pool hall sequence in *Pool Sharks* is a fake. Fields was shooting the movie in Long Island while performing nightly in the *Follies* with his trick pool table, and it was not feasible to transport the table daily between the New Amsterdam Theatre and the set. Thus an ordinary pool table was used, and a succession of shots done by trick photography: both Fields and Bud Ross hit all the balls round the table, into the pockets and back into the original stack. Ross hits all the balls into the pockets, with a title, 'See If You Can Beat That'. Fields hits all the balls in a neat parabola onto the racks on the walls. This is followed by more mutual rapping over the head with billiard cues and throwing of balls at each other. Fields' ball goes through the window and breaks the girl's goldfish bowl onto her head. The girl comes storming in for revenge. Ross dives out the window head first into a barrel. Fields rushes out through a trapdoor, down a flight of steps to find several crates of booze. The other guests fall down the steps in a pile. Fields locks down an outside trapdoor and walks off with the booze, pausing to tip Bud Ross back into his barrel. THE END.

Pool Sharks is full of continuity errors and inconsistencies. There is no clear sense of the central character, or what is supposed to be funny about Fields' hustling. Fields walks off with the bottle but then inexplicably loses it to have his hands free to deal with his rival. Then he walks out of frame without retrieving it, though he has been shown, when he discovers the crates, catching the bottle adroitly as it threatens to fall to the ground. This tiny bit of business and another flash of two seconds in which he juggles three balls before tossing them on the pool table are the only fleeting glimpses of his skill. But there is the sight of the man himself, young and vigorous, with a presence that cannot entirely be smothered by the imitative and awkwardly affected gestures.

The film historian William K. Everson has pointed out the elements of Fields' battles with the orneriness of inanimate objects, scattered through the film – the chalk, food, the garden hammock, and of course the billiard balls themselves. All the early comedians' first films were ropy, and Fields' début was no exception. The record shows that he made another film for Gaumont, *His Lordship's Dilemma*, directed by William 'Silent Bill' Haddock. Apart from being a name out of a possible Fields scenario, this pioneer lived to a great age, and Ronald Fields, in his filmography, quotes him in a 1963 interview with producer Sam Sherman reminiscing about those early days: 'A director had no assistant, had to write his own continuity, or shoot off the cuff, look up locations, make up his own prop list and sometimes act in the pictures.'

His Lordship's Dilemma was released in October 1915, by the Mutual Film Corporation – which had also distributed *Pool Sharks*; both films are listed as 'A Casino Star Comedy'. This is the first of Fields' lost films – a serious loss, as we might have seen Fields learning from the errors of his first film, and because it included his very first bar-room scene and the earliest version of his later famous golfing sketch. Bud Ross appeared once again, as his caddy, the first in a long line of suffering, moronic stooges. A surviving publicity still published by Ronald Fields shows Fields choking his caddy while a black child peeps out of his propped up golf bag.

Fields' film career, after this double burst, stopped abruptly, and did not resume until 1925. As noted, 1915 was the year of Charlie Chaplin, and any rival to the ubiquitous Tramp would have had to have done much better than this. Harold Lloyd was not to make his first 'Lonesome Luke' film till 1916, and the year after came Buster Keaton's first short film, *The Butcher Boy*, directed by and starring Fatty Arbuckle. W. C. Fields' two shorts did not catch on. It was the beginning of a long grudge fight in which Fields struggled to emerge from under the shadow of the Tramp, having been a 'Tramp' himself when Chaplin was ten years old and being discharged from the Lambeth Workhouse. 'That Goddamn ballet dancer' was always a thorn in Bill Fields' side, though it is pretty evident that he not only envied his success but admired his pantomimic skill and the professional qualities of his work.

Bill Fields' personal life, at this point of his breakthrough with Ziegfeld, is as unclear as the character in *Pool Sharks*. His son, Claude – by now, over ten years old – was, under Hattie's influence, becoming more estranged from his father. He wrote to her repeatedly offering 'to furnish one of my houses in Phila.' for her and Claude Jr., apparently property he had obtained in the city he is supposed to have ostracized. On 10 May 1915, he wrote to her sourly:

> Your low cunning and scheming will one day cause you no end of grief. You will never be happy as long as you practice your perfidy upon your young son. You have taught him a hymn of hate, likewise tried to make him a Christian, the two do not blend.

And, on 23 November:

> For ten years you have inculcated into the boy's mind stories of my atrocities, you used every artifice and cunning you could employ to turn him from me, and you succeeded, but! your success is empty, you have gained nothing.

'Let him prospect by himself,' he writes to her about their son, 'and when he gets to be about twenty he might look me up some day and want to know what it was all about.'

An open wound, scratched continually by the bitter and angry letters which Hattie, nevertheless, kept diligently. Despite it all, there was, there must have been, a memory of happier times, and of what might have been. Hattie remained a disappointed wife, a determined mother, dedicated to bringing up young Claude in a milieu free of the uncertainties and wanderings of vaudeville and the theatre. She would have her revenge on Bill by moulding her son into the kind of person he most despised – a respectable, accepted member of his community.

But Bill Fields had another life now. Disappointed in marriage, disappointed in his first stab at the movies, he threw himself back into his stage work, continuing his climb to the top, in the *Follies*, and finding new companions in the tent of Omar Khayyam.

Chapter 19
Arabian Nights in New York

The war in Europe could not be ignored, even by show people, in 1916. The famous 'neutrality' of President Wilson had presupposed a quick outcome, but as 1915 passed with the German, British and French armies still bogged down in trench warfare with cataclysmic loss of life, American isolationism wavered. With 1916 came a new Wilsonian motto: 'Preparedness.' After the *Lusitania*, Washington warned Germany about her submarine war in the Atlantic. War jitters increased the public rush to escape into theatres, and musicals and revues boomed. But on 6 April 1917, the United States Congress declared war on Germany, and by June local draft boards were registering over ten million male Americans to fight. On 13 June the first American regiments took ship for France, one day after the 1917 Ziegfeld *Follies* opened at the New Amsterdam in New York.

This was the year in which designer Joseph Urban surpassed himself, with a set of Chinese lacquer dissolving into showers of coloured water, and sixty girls in Chinese costumes climbing up and down red and gold ladders. Papier mâché warships sailed towards the audience, firing their guns and flashing the flag.

The nineteen scenes and a Finale of the show were constructed round an Arabian Nights type structure, with scenes entitled: 'The Episode of an Arabian Night in New York', 'The Episode of the Garden of Girls', 'The Episode of the Eddiecantor', 'The Episode of the American Eagle', 'The Episode of the Willrogersayings', and so on. W. C. Fields appeared in only two of these, 'The Episode of New York Streets and Subway', and his own original contribution: 'The Episode of the Tennis Match'. This was the first *Follies* in which he scripted his own scene, though he extended the New York Streets scene.

In the 1916 show he had inserted one of his stock acts, 'A Croquet Game' and played in three other sketches: in 'Recruiting', he played an aspiring ensign, one 'Reddan Greene', of whom, more later. In 'A

Travesty of Scheherezade' he played one O. Shaw, with Sam Hardy as The Sultan, Don Barclay as Zobeide, Norman Blume as a Eunuch and Bert Williams as 'Nijinsky'. Fanny Brice sang a song with male chorus. In Scene Four, 'Puck's Pictorial Palace', Fields played a dual role as Navy Secretary Josephus Daniels and as President Theodore Roosevelt, alongside Sam Hardy, Ina Claire and Bert Williams, with Ann Pennington as Mary Pickford and Fanny Brice as Theda Bara. The script, by George Hobart, has 'Theodore Roosevelt' prancing in and *singing*:

> I was going in the movies with my Moose! . . .
> But one day they raised the deuce
> They went and stole my fine old Moose,
> With salty tears my eyes are full,
> For I've nothing left now but the bull,
> My wonderful grand old Bull!
> (Roosevelt *dances* off.) [Author's italics.]

We must take this evidence of a singing and dancing Fields in good faith, if somewhat incredulously . . .

Ziegfeld himself was living half in and half out of his own fantasy. Anna 'Won't-you-please-come-play-wiz-me' Held had sued him for divorce in 1912, and his romance with leading lady Lillian Lorraine was famously tumultuous. On New Year's Eve 1913 he had met the brilliant and witty Billie Burke, whom he married in April 1914. Ziegfeld moved into the Burke family's palatial residence of Burley Crest, on the Hudson River, which the couple furnished in the most ostentatious style possible, with five chauffeurs to drive the five Rolls-Royces and a veritable zoo of poodles, pigeons, chickens, an elephant and Flo's pet monkey, Chiquita.

Given the Great Glorifier's example, it is amazing that most of his famous stars did not rush to emulate his lifestyle (if they could afford it). Will Rogers began to spend his money on shrewd land purchases in Los Angeles, which were to culminate in his immense ranch-residence at Pacific Pallisades and he remained married to his childhood sweetheart, Betty. Eddie Cantor, despite his breathless awe of the rich, also married an early love, Ida, who remained at his side to the end. Fanny Brice was stuck with supporting her gangster husband, Nick Arnstein, including prison visits to Sing Sing. In June 1917, the Governor of New York State pardoned Arnstein and he joined the menagerie of *Follies* actors travelling in Fields' car.

Arnstein fascinated Fields – one faker perhaps irresistibly drawn to another – though Fields never shared Fanny Brice's penchant for Nick's gangster friends, particularly the notorious gambling baron Arnold Rothstein. It was Nick Arnstein, according to Fanny's biographer Herbert Goldman, who provided the catchphrases which Fields later made his own: 'Never give a sucker an even break and never smarten up a chump.' (Other sources attribute 'never give a sucker' to legendary New York wit Wilson Mizner.) But Nick could also serve as a guide for these innocent show-babies in their brushes with reality. Once, when they were all together, Nick, Fanny, Bill Fields and Cantor in Bill's car, a man jumped on the running board and asked for a lift, claiming his car had broken down two miles away. Nick whispered to Fields that this was a stick-up man. Bill slowed down and told the man to jump, with Nick adding the appropriate threats. Bill himself embellished this tale later, in a 1934 newspaper interview headed 'Down Memory Lane':

> One night we were going from Cleveland to Detroit. I was driving my car with some friends, and we noticed that another car was passing us frequently, slowing down to permit us to pass, then going by us again. We figured it was a possible holdup, but didn't know quite what to do.
>
> We were getting to the outskirts of Detroit, and turned a bend in the road, when we saw the other car parked right across the road a few yards in front of us. It was a holdup.
>
> 'Want to take a chance with these thugs!' I yelled.
>
> Everybody agreed, so instead of stepping on the brake, I stepped on the gas. Two of the bandits had gotten out of the car and were standing in the middle of the road. The third was still at the wheel.
>
> I headed for the two feet of road that was behind the car, and gave my buggy all the gas it would take. Those two holdup men scattered as fast as they could – they didn't even stop to fire – and the driver shot his car in low, and then pulled out. We whistled by them at least 60 miles an hour, and I never took my foot off the throttle for miles.
>
> When I finally stopped to take a deep breath the first thing I noticed was the 'Prittiwillie Lumber Company.' That name impressed itself so much on me that I've used the name 'Prittiwillie' in a lot of my pictures.

Namely in his 1926 silent *It's the Old Army Game*. Who do you believe now, Bill Fields' version, or Fanny Brice? Of course, Fields censored all his famous friends' names out of the story, not to speak of 'never-give-a-sucker' Nick Arnstein. Bill's passion for narrative embroidery became a lynchpin of his inimitable style, as in this ramble from the 1939 *You Can't Cheat an Honest Man* (probably another bon-mot of Nick Arnstein's), an addendum to a monologue which became notorious (as we shall see in due course) as the 'Snake Story':

> Then suddenly from out of nowhere – bang bang! Two shots rang out in the clear home air – two blow outs and not a spare in sight . . . Two boa constrictors, whom I previously befriended, wrapped themselves around my naked limbs, and off we went again – Well, I go three hundred miles, on two tires and two boa constrictors . . . they left us in the outskirts of the city . . . a tow car came and pulled us into Punxhatauney . . .

Of course, context is all, and the tale is all the more pointless for being told in a roomful of stuck up society people who are not listening because they are ministering to Larson E. Whipsnade's prospective mother-in-law, who has fainted because she can't bear the very thought of snakes. But these echoes of old tales, old bits and bobs, trickle, as we have noted, down the years.

Fields' habit of pressing down on the throttle almost brought him and his colleagues to a sticky end, as his car, en route from Baltimore to Washington for a *Follies*, overturned – when Fields was trying to pass a motorcycle, or, in his own version, having hit a rock or had a blowout – distributing his passengers all over the landscape. Will Rogers sustained a broken leg, but Fields got away with 'a bump on my head, about twice the size my head normally was. And I didn't even think I had been hurt!'

But Fields was really cooking with gas, at this point, and he had also made up for his much-exaggerated loneliness, by finding a new partner, following the Great Flo's footsteps, from the beauties in the show.

The girl's name was Bessie Chatterton Poole. She is the first verifiable name to emerge out of misty shapes which constituted Bill's extra- or rather, post-marital girlfriends. The elusive Grace George and the Phantom Mrs Fields of Australia never emerged from their veils, but, starring on Broadway, Fields was firmly in the limelight now. Nevertheless, it is noteworthy how discreetly Fields' alliances have been treated, until the last, with the feisty Carlotta Monti. Carlotta met Fields in 1933 and claimed to have been his closest confidante from then on until his death. We shall examine her claim, in her 1971 book (co-authored with Cy Rice), *W. C. Fields and Me*, in due course. But her statement that Fields, contrary to his own self-nurtured woman-hating image, had had a regular flow of girlfriends before her, turns out to be substantively true.

Bessie Poole was one of the tens of thousands of stage-struck girls who dreamed of Broadway and one of the hundreds who struck it lucky for a while. She got on the first rung of the ladder and never managed to climb any higher. Bessie's mother, Mrs Bessie Adelaide Witherell, who told her tale over thirty years later, in 1949, in an interview in the Los Angeles *Examiner* of 29 April 1949, said:

> Bessie went to Broadway when she was 16. There she met Mr Fields and fell in love with him.
>
> They teamed up in vaudeville between annual editions of the Ziegfeld *Follies* in which they both played. He visited my home with her often and sometimes came to dinner. He ate at least 15 scallop dinners that I cooked for them – how that man loved scallops!

Well, that last point at least rings true. Mrs Witherell said: 'He would not marry her, but she remained mad about him.' Of course, Fields could not marry Bessie Poole even if had wanted to, though newspaper gossip claimed, falsely, that they did tie the knot. The problem arose soon after, as related in an unusually well-informed *Sunday News* story about Fields' affairs with women, published on 26 June 1949:

> Mrs Faye Bunny, then Faye O'Neill of the *Follies*, tells how it all started with Bill and Bessie.
>
> 'Bessie and I,' she recalls, 'were in the opening number of the Ziegfeld show which was called "The Birth of Elation", and I remember when Bill, the gentlemanly juggler, came on stage for the "Blushing Ballet" number.
>
> 'He paused in the anteroom of the harem and took a second look at Bessie. He smiled and she smiled and that was it. Nobody was surprised because Bessie was the best dancer of us all. She had long beautiful legs and was so fresh and attractive.
>
> 'From then on Bessie was Bill's girl. Her dressing table was always crowded with flowers, perfume and other gifts from him . . .
>
> 'I remember the night Bessie went to the hospital for what we thought was an appendicitis operation. I asked Bill how she was and how the operation had come out. He laughed and said: 'Operation, hell! She had a turkey in the oven.'

The programme for the 1916 *Follies* verifies the presence both of Bessie Poole and Faye O'Neill in 'The Birth of Elation' prologue. (Faye O'Neill came on as '*Follies* Girl of 1907' and Bessie Poole as '*Follies* Girl of 1915'.) But, just to make things awkward, the *Follies* programme of 1915 shows Bessie Poole already present, in the 'Silver Forest Scene' – 'A Girl For Each Month in the Year', as May. (Faye O'Neill was not in that *Follies*.) And so Bill might have plucked up Miss May a year earlier. But back to Faye's tale: according to her account, she was living with Bessie in a hotel in 1917, while Bessie was obviously pregnant. The child was duly born on 15 August. There Miss Bunny's tale stops, as she did not see Bessie again until 1920, when, she claimed, Bessie was still together with Bill.

The baby born on 15 August 1917 was to become one William Rexford Fields Morris, and would turn up, as we have noted, as a claimant at the great Fields Inheritance Grudge Fight of 1947–54. There is no proof that he was W. C. Fields' illegitimate son, as, unlike Chaplin's famous paternity fight with Joan Barry, no blood tests were ever taken. The whole affair was handled under wraps. Bessie, a poor girl with no resources in a strict and merciless age, gave the child in care to a Mrs Rose Holden, in New Jersey, who brought him up as her own son. In his evidence in 1949 Mr Morris, then thirty-one, an airline employee living in Dallas, Texas, said he had known Fields and Poole as 'Uncle Bill' and 'Aunt Bessie', and that he only found out 'Uncle Bill's real identity in 1934. (This sounds a bit stretched, as Fields was nationally famous from the mid-twenties at least, if not from 1915.) Morris said:

> As time went on, I began to suspect something . . . Mrs Holden had another son, and she favored him a lot . . . I talked it over with Mrs Holden's Aunt, and she told me some. Then I told Mrs Holden, 'You're not my mother, are you?' She said, 'Of course, I am. If you took a child and brought him up and gave him love and devotion, that is the same as being a mother, isn't it?' Some time later she told me Aunt Bessie was really my mother and W. C. Fields was really my father.

The court did not accept Morris's claim, due to a document produced, with Bessie Poole's signature, renouncing any future claims on Fields and swearing that the boy was not his son. This affidavit was drawn up in 1927, in return, it appears, for a $20,000 cash settlement which Fields paid Bessie at a time when she was virtually destitute.

This was not Bill Fields' finest hour. Faye Bunny said, in her 1949 interview, that Bill 'used to bring the baby to his performance and he used to chuck it under the chin'. Bill discreetly paid $50 weekly for the kid's upkeep, whether out of obligation or goodwill to an errant girl-friend is up to anyone to guess. Across the depths of time, it is not possible for us to know whether Bessie Poole was a star-struck innocent or whether she had other affairs. We do know that she came to a sad and early end. She died in 1928 as a result of a brawl at the Chez Florence night club, in which she was beaten badly by a 'prominent business-man'. (Names later named were Joseph Whitehead, millionaire soft-drinks heir, and Robert Keilly, another 'beverage firm executive'.) The official cause of her death was given as alcoholism, but the immediate cause appears to have been a haemorrhage due to a strong blow on her nose. This was covered in typically cynical New York style by the press, which reported:

GIRL LEAVES RING TO W. C. FIELDS; ROMANCE BARED OF COMEDIAN AND DANCER WHO DIED FOLLOWING NIGHT CLUB BRAWL: SHE FORGOT TO DUCK.

Dr Henry Gilbert, who attended Miss Poole, said she complained to him of an injury to her nose, and when he questioned her as to what caused it, she replied: 'I guess I forgot to duck.'

The newspapers in 1928 made brief whoopee with the tale of Bessie Poole's pathetic will, filed in the Manhattan Surrogate's Court, which left Fields a diamond ring and a letter saying:

Dear Bill: Mr K has the key to my vault. Now there are some of my letters and things in there which you would not want anyone to get. So in case I die, why, June will give them to you as I have given her written notice to open said vault.

I have also left my diamond ring to you, so you will have something to remember me by. And darling, I love you and have never loved anyone else and I never will. And all the luck and love in the world to you, dear, is my last wish. Bessie.

Bill's response to this publicity was to fire off a statement saying Bessie Poole was just a friend he had been helping after she had gone broke and that 'some years after I first helped her she began demand-ing money. I got threatening letters from her and a lawyer. I concluded she was being made the tool of blackmailers. Her son is now 10 years old but I never met her until six or seven years ago.'

This was, alas, not true, as we have seen. Years later, in his suit, William Rexford Fields Morris produced a letter in Fields' unmistakeable handwriting dated 1926 and addressed to Rose Holden, asking her to forward her new address so he could 'keep payments up'.

A brief coda: as both Carlotta Monti and Will Fowler attest, young William Rexford Fields Morris did turn up one day on the doorstep of W. C. Fields' palatial residence in De Mille Drive, Hollywood. According to Fowler: 'The comedian's butler announced that Morris claimed to be his illegitimate son, and was waiting to meet Fields downstairs. Fields replied to his butler: "Give him an evasive answer: tell him to go fuck himself."'

Whatever the biological facts, it's clear that Fields behaved with a contradictory mix of ruthlessness and goodwill. On the one hand, he denied a possible offspring, and took vigorous evasive action at his ex-girlfriend's death. On the other hand, he paid out a regular sum to keep mother and child above water, though there may have been an element of force majeur there. Acknowledging a bastard son might well have given Hattie a lethal weapon in the war to keep Claude Jr. from him, although that war was already lost. Despite the $20,000 settlement with which Bessie Poole signed her claims away, Morris later claimed some payments continued, and that when he was married, in 1941, Fields sent him $100. The Los Angeles Court disentangling the Fields inheritance eventually awarded him a special payment of $15,000, to be made out of the widow, Hattie's entitlement, barely enough to cover his legal costs. The ghost of Bessie Poole was still troubling the family conscience, thirty years on.

We can view the Bessie Poole affair more poignantly in the light of Fields' years of frustration over the estrangement of his son Claude. Here was one child, blocked off, denied to him, and another, unwanted, or not even his, offered. The absurdity of this position must have rankled. It may well have deepened the syndrome that made him portray small children as eternal enemies, a hammer in the hand of ornery nature. At any rate, whatever the facts of William Rexford Fields Morris's paternity, Bill Fields made damn sure he would not be caught out in future. Whatever the means, he managed, with his later-girlfriends, to evade any procreation.

*

Bessie Poole was never a replacement for Hattie. Nor were any of Bill's other known 'regular' girlfriends, who numbered, from Bessie to Carlotta Monti, about five. Fields' affairs with women, at least from this point on, appeared to follow a very particular pattern: he avoided teaming up with any woman who was his intellectual – or financial – equal. Gene Fowler reported rumours that he had been sweet, in 1909, on the great comedienne and singer Nora Bayes. But he was not in her league then. And when he reached that league, he went for solace to the chorus: Bessie Poole, from the *Follies* of 1916. Linelle Blackburn, from the chorus of *Poppy*, in 1923. Fay Adler was a featured dancer in Earl Carroll's *Vanities* in 1928.

Both Linelle and Fay were cited, as we have noted, in Hattie Fields' claim for Bill's estate in 1947, along with Grace George. Maude Fenwick and Mabel Roach were other names of women who figured in his will, though Mabel Roach was an old family friend from Philadelphia. Fields certainly wasn't the stingy, mean-hearted curmudgeon of myth with any of his lady friends.

This whole matter of W. C. Fields' lovers undermines another peculiar legend about Fields, his alleged pathological fear of syphilis. This sprang, according to Robert Lewis Taylor, from an anti-venereal disease film he saw in an unnamed mid-Western town, some time in his twenties. The film featured such fearful revelations, according to Taylor's fancy, as: 'Eighty-two per cent of all white, Protestant males between the heights of five feet two and six feet eight are exposed to syphilis on an average of eleven times a year in public drinking places.' Carlotta Monti did quote, in her book, some nervous Fieldsian jokes on the subject, such as his answer to an interviewer asking: 'Have you ever been exposed to great risk?' 'Yes, sitting on a toilet seat after Greg La Cava just got off.' But we cannot be sure how far back this anxiety goes. Fields in his last decade was a very different person from the one he was ten years before. At any rate, these common and not unjustified fears for that era did not stop him from having all the other longstanding relationships of his Broadway days.

Louise Brooks, who co-starred with Bill in *It's the Old Army Game* in 1926, and appeared with him in the *Follies* in 1925, wrote a chapter about Fields and his troubles with women in her 1974 book, *Lulu in Hollywood*. The peerless Brooks has been noted for her sharp and insightful observations of tinseltown, but her chapter on Fields is, in fact, misleading. Louise Brooks wrote about Fields:

Bill adored beautiful girls, but few were invited to his dressing room. He was morbidly sensitive about the eczema that inflamed his nose and sometimes erupted on his hands, so that he had to learn to juggle wearing gloves. After several devastating experiences with beautiful girls, he had decided to restrict himself to girlfriends who were less attractive, and whom he would not find adrift with saxophone players.

How did she get it so wrong? As I have tried to set out at the beginning of our journey, the salutary fact to know of W. C. Fields' private life is that, at every point of his life, very few people knew him well. Everyone else around him only knew the tall stories that accumulated like clouds of twinkling fairy dust. Louise Brooks knew Fields at the tail end of his shaky relationship with Bessie Poole, at a time at which he was clearly determined to keep his sexual affairs as discreet as possible. She was not – to Fields' eternal loss – in his inner circle. Else how could she write:

Years of traveling alone around the world with his juggling act taught him the value of solitude and the release it gave his mind. He abhorred bars, nightclubs, parties, and other people's houses. He seems to have left no diaries, no letters, no serious autobiographical material. Most of his life will remain unknown.

So many pitfalls. Brooks herself was probably too hot and too sought after for Fields to contemplate. (Some thought she should be renamed 'Louise Brooks No Restraint'.) But we can turn back to the *Sunday News*' very different version of Bill Fields' social life, to quote a vintage memory flash dating from two or three years after Louise Brooks was pitying him for his loneliness:

By now Bill's romance with Maude Fenwick was dying the seven year death, and he was interested in Linelle Blackburn, a Texan beauty. Bill was still in the courting phase when they were motoring one time through Florida after a sojourn at Dazz Vance's resort near Homosassa. Dazzy was a pitcher for the Brooklyn Dodgers and a great pal of Fields.

Bill Grady (Fields' agent) was driving Bill's $13,000 Locomobile while the lovebirds sat in the back holding hands. 'Bill was in the wooing stage,' Grady recalls, 'and he would put himself out a lot for a girl when he was still in love with her.'

The following incident, recounted by Grady, was the basis for one of Fields' best known laugh-pulling jokes: 'Linelle expressed a desire to have a cool drink from a famous spring in the Everglades and Bill volunteered to get it for her. He pushed his way down through the thick undergrowth and in a few minutes he came back yelling at the top of his lungs. He said a giant alligator had attacked him. His finger appeared to be bleeding from a scratch from one of the thorny bushes, but he swore it was an alligator bite.

'Linelle pretended to believe him and all the afternoon he was made a hero because he had dared an alligator to get her a drink. I heard him elaborate on that story many times after that and it finally got so good he was able to describe a hand to hand tussle with a giant man-eating crocodile.'

Bill Fields, in the 1910s and 1920s, was, despite the occasional eczema on his hands and nose, a trim, athletic and even handsome man – when the light fell in a certain way: not too tall – five foot, eight – with his faculties increasingly battered but not overcome by liquor, at the height of his creative powers. A Broadway star with the latest automobiles is unlikely to be lonely. And his female companions certainly couldn't complain of a lack of non-stop entertainment.

Chapter 20

'Now Stand Clear and Keep Your Eye on the Ball!' – The Vaudeville Sketches of W. C. Fields, Part 1

But let us step back to Ziegfeld and the *Follies*. In an aforementioned interview, 'Down Memory Lane', Fields related his strained relationship with his demanding mentor:

> 'Ziggy' was a great guy, and a great producer, but he didn't have a lot of use for comedians. He considered them more or less a necessary evil, yet he had every comedian of any prominence in his shows . . . I remember, I wanted to do my golf act in one of the 'Follies.' I went to Ziegfeld, and outlined the idea to him. He was enthusiastic.
>
> 'It's a great idea, Bill,' he said, 'I think it will be a hit. There is only one little thing. We have a beautiful yacht set . . . all full of beautiful girls. Now if you will only change your golf gag to a fishing gag it will be a sensation.'
>
> I thought I had figured out how to handle Ziegfeld, so I agreed with him. He went ahead with the plans for the yacht – with all the beautiful girls – and I went ahead with my part of the act. He wanted to see it, but I'd never show it to him. I told him everything was working out perfectly. I would start with a fishing gag, then go into the golf act. That satisfied him.
>
> When the final tryout came, I did my golf act, no more. Even though it was on a yacht. The act got over all right, but Ziggy was in tears. But he had to give in. He finally compromised. I could do the golf act, but he would have at least one girl in it. He would have one of his beauties walk across the stage, leading a Russian wolfhound.
>
> I knew that would ruin my part of the show completely, but I couldn't argue him out of it. To Ziggy, an act wasn't worth putting on unless he had one of his girls in it.
>
> So opening night I started my golf act. In the middle of it this beautiful girl, gorgeously costumed, walked across the stage leading this handsome

wolfhound. I stopped. They walked from one wing to the other. 'My,' I said, 'what a beautiful camel.'

That got a laugh, and the act was a success.

The golf act was introduced in the *Follies* of 1918, though it was clearly extant in 1915, as the vanished second Gaumont film attests. In another magazine article, for *The American*, in 1934, Fields told the tale a little differently. The article, 'Anything For a Laugh', opens a window into the comedian's trial and error, the painstaking process of finding out which gag and what line works best. At first, he says about the incident with Ziegfeld, he tried using the word 'horse': 'I experimented night after night to find out what animal was the funniest. I finally settled upon "That's a very beautiful camel."' Fields continued:

The funniest thing about comedy is that you never know why people laugh. I know what makes them laugh, but trying to get your hands on the why of it is like trying to pick an eel out of a tub of water . . .

You usually can't get a laugh out of damaging anything valuable. When you kick a silk hat, it must be dilapidated; when you wreck a car, bang it up a little before you bring it on the scene.

It is funnier to bend things than to break them – bend the fenders on a car in a comedy wreck, don't break them off. In my golf game, which I have been doing for years, at first I swung at the ball and broke the club. Now I bend it at a right angle. If one comedian hits another over the head with a crowbar, the crowbar should bend, not break. In legitimate drama, the hero breaks his sword, and it is dramatic. In comedy, the sword bends, and stays bent . . .

I know we laugh at the troubles of others, provided these troubles are not too serious. Out of that observation I have reached a conclusion which may be of some comfort to those accused of 'having no sense of humor.' These folks are charming, lovable, philanthropic people, and invariably I like them – as long as they keep out of the theatres where I am playing, which they usually do. If they get in by mistake, they leave early.

The reason they don't laugh at most gags is that their first emotional reaction is to feel sorry for people instead of to laugh at them.

I like, in an audience, the fellow who roars continuously at the troubles of the character I am portraying on the stage, but he probably has a mean streak in him, and, if I needed ten dollars, he'd be the last person I'd call upon. I'd go first to the old lady and old gentleman back in Row S who keep wondering what there is to laugh at.

Of course, many comedians did get laughs out of breaking, rather than bending things, for example, Laurel and Hardy. But Fields always had strained relations with objects that got out of shape, or appeared on the scene misshapen from the source. The very building blocks of his reality were skewed. Thus, as J.B. Priestley observed, even when he stopped juggling as an act, he still had to juggle with life itself, with every small thing, at every corner.

As the *Follies* liberated him from the juggler's routine, he began devising his own scenarios. It was long since he had confessed to O. K. Sato his clumsiness at the typewriter and the recalcitrant pages. We don't know when Fields began writing his 'vaudeville scripts', some of which may have predated the *Follies*. But it was during the *Follies* that he sat down, in his hotel apartment, and began methodically churning them out.

Where do comedians get their material? The answer is usually, from other comedians. Comedians found their jokes in joke books and humourous magazines and revamped them to fit their act. George Burns wrote:

> Performers would take material from anyplace they could find it. Harpo [Marx] told me about a theatre the Marx Brothers played in Fargo, North Dakota; the manager had hung up a big sign in the wings listing about 100 jokes and the warning, THESE JOKES HAVE ALREADY BEEN USED IN THIS THEATRE – DO NOT USE THEM. And nobody used them there, but everybody wrote them down and put them in their act for the next booking.

Nat Wills, one of vaudeville's greatest draws, was known to have been a regular subscriber to *Madison's Budget*, a joke magazine published between 1898 and 1918. It sold for one dollar and was a treasure house of comedy gags and situations. Later the author, James Madison, sold complete sets of his old journals to comedians like Eddie Cantor and Fred Allen.

In the vaudeville days, the only way a comedian could protect material was to seal it in an envelope and send it to Pat Casey, of the Vaudeville Managers' Protective Agency. But this was not a foolproof method. Fields, like other professionals, lived in a constant anxiety that carefully worked out routines would be pilferred by rivals. From 1918 onwards he began registering his sketches with the Copyright Division of the Library of Congress in Washington. These were eventually to comprise the sixteen sketches now in the Library's W. C. Fields' box. In

1920 Fields became embroiled in a conflict with Ned Wayburn, director and producer of the Ziegfeld *Follies*, over plans by Wayburn to stage a production in London which would include 'A Game of Tennis' and 'A Game of Golf'. Fields wanted arrangements made to copyright his Tennis sketch in Britain and Canada, and further armour-plated the Golf sketch by having an International Copyright (No. 109) issued to him in Australia under the name of 'An Episode on the Links'. The copyrighted sketches in Washington are the following (some are filed in several versions):

An Episode on the Links (Registered 1918)
An Episode of Lawn Tennis (1918)
Just Before the Battle, Mother (1919)
The Mountain Sweep Steaks (1919)
The Family Ford (1919, 1920)
An Episode at the Dentist's (1919, 1926, 1928)
The Pullman Sleeper (1921)
Off to the Country (1921, 1922)
What a Night! (1921)
The Sport Model (1922) (variant of The Family Ford)
The Caledonian Express (1922)
Ten Thousand People Killed (1922)
The Sleeping Porch (1925)
Stolen Bonds (1928)
My School Days Are Over (1928)
The Midget Car (1930) (another car sketch variant)

These sketches have been considered, up to now, the bedrock upon which Bill Fields built the routines which he performed on stage, many of which he was to insert into his films in future years. Further digging around establishes, however, that there were many more manuscripts than these. Will Fowler, the last survivor of the Fields ménage of the late 1930s, handed me a list of fifty-three original Fields sketches (including versions of the ones above) which had been loaned to certain radio performers, for whom Fowler had been writing material, in the early 1950s. Some of these cannot be found, but between Will Fowler, the family archive, and other collections, a fuller picture of the facts can be realized.

Throughout his Ziegfeld period, and on to the end of the 1920s, Fields dashed out dozens of these sketches, synopses, outlines, ideas, of different lengths, ranging from one to twenty pages, many typewritten, others in handwriting, on notepaper, headed hotel paper, or anything else that came to hand. They might have totalled over one hundred. I have counted thirty-one additional concepts apart from the twenty-odd that have been noted so far. These include intriguing titles like: 'Hip Hippo', 'The Sharp Shooter', 'The Patriotic Politician', 'Professor Kamo (in his Series of Marvellous Impersonations)', 'Chapeau Shopping', 'Baseball Game', 'The Vanishing American', 'A Born Dancer', 'The Mormon's Prayer', 'Bisbee (a concept developed into the movie *So's Your Old Man*)', 'The Sea Gull', 'In the Park', 'Into the New Flat', 'Boat Sketch', 'Elevator Scene', 'Seerist Act', 'Gerald Geoffrey', 'The Porter', and 'Fido the Beautiful Dog'.

These sketches form a unique and incomparable insight into their creator's mind. The vaudeville sketches are the very heart of the art of W. C. Fields, and were the base metal which he was constantly labouring, in later years, to transform into motion-picture gold.

'Fido, the Beautiful Dog' is a random example of an unformed sketch, in rambling handwriting over thirteen pages, which casts doubt on another enduring Fields myth – his canine phobia. (Any fondness for the critters is subject to the deepest Fieldsian denial, but, nevertheless, grandson Ronald Fields has shamelessly revealed that Bill did keep a dog, in the late 1920s, and Carlotta Monti testifies to other pooches well into the 1930s. Fans will note 'Buster the Dog' in *It's a Gift*.) The sketch is outlined: 'Big and frightfully dopey looking dog. Mr. and Mrs. Cunningham try finally to get rid of it. They give it away – take it away. It always comes back. People find it and bring it home to the Cunninghams. Cunningham finally decides to get a bag and mark it: property of First National Bank.' And so on.

Some of the handwritten outlines, like the 'Boat Sketch', are marked with Fields' inimitable little drawings. An interesting insight can be gleaned from the many magazine and newspaper cuttings which he collected. Pages of cartoons from 'Life' would be clipped out, as seeds of later ideas. A spread from June 1923 shows various gentlemen trying to wrestle with the cramped bathrooms of a railway Pullman sleeper, a clear germ of a later Fields sketch of that name. Another has a harassed gentleman trying to carry parcels, umbrella and a lunch-counter snack together, and has a pencil scrawl by Fields: 'Elevator Scene'. Another clipping, from January 1926, shows a family jammed together in a bag-laden Ford bound for a cross-country

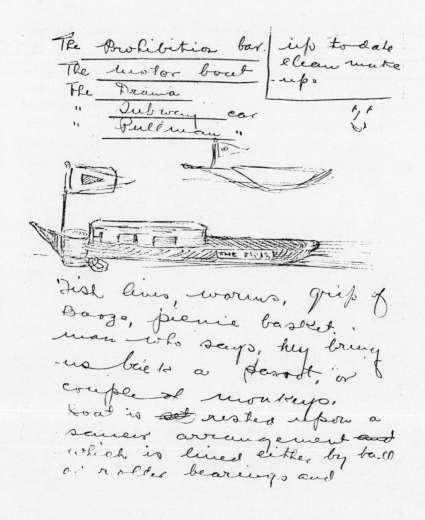

The Prohibition bar. / up to date
The motor boat / clean make
The Drama / -up.
"   Subway car
"   Pullman "

Fish lines, worms, grip of
Booze, picnic basket.
man who says, hey bring
us back a parrot, or
couple of monkeys.
boat is set rested upon a
science arrangement and
which is lined either by ball
or roller bearings and

13 The Boat Sketch (courtesy Will Fowler/Tim Walker Collection).

run, with camping outfit and family dog attached – the exact image of the motor car in many of his later sketches and in the movie, *It's a Gift*.

In the 'Seerist Act', a four-page handwritten sketch, Fields presents a manager's monologue –

Ladies and gentlemen, I have great pleasure in presenting to you this evening, Madam Bertha Cropfin, world's foremost seerist and soothsayer. Madam Cropfin has astounded the scientific world times out of number. Madam has been engaged by Mr. Ziegfeld at the highest salary for an animal act. Madam has appeared at nearly every court in Europe, and has so impressed those before whom she appeared that they have insisted upon her remaining. On many occasions from three to six months. Once she got a year and a half . . .

There then follows the most crashingly obvious exchange as the manager prompts Madam with the most outrageous promptings: '"What has the lady on her head?" – "A hat." "Don't let this stick you." – "A hat pin." "Is there no end to Madam's talent?"' But, as far as we know, this draft never went further, and was never performed on stage.

Another unperformed sketch – probably Fields thought better of it – was 'The Patriotic Politician'. This was an unusually political sideswipe at that familiar American institution: 'I want to say as Lincoln said when he stood at Valley Forge, "If this be treason make the most of it." . . . For the benefit of the children of these Great and Glorious United States of Ours [a phrase repeated *ad nauseum* in the text] we have arranged a pie-eating contest.' But this early sample of the politician striking small pie-stealing boys on the head with his gavel, bit the dust, and was recycled elsewhere.

The unperformed and outlined sketches are of course the icebergs whose tips are the sketches which Fields presented on stage. These went through various versions and became more elaborate as time went on. Fields was a tireless and obssessive reworker of monologues, dialogues and sight gags. We know that he drew on other texts and examples, such as McIntyre and Heath's *The Ham Tree* routine, or Harry Tate's 'Motoring'. He also had the example of the Ziegfeld *Follies* sketches by Gene Buck, Channing Pollock, George Hobart and others. But the comparison of their texts and his reveals the unique direction of Fields' own brand of comedy.

The basic sketch, from which all other Fields' sketches sprang, was his pool act, that unique brand of patter and pantomime which he had honed since 1903. It was his featured role in his first *Follies*, in 1915. In the *Follies* of 1916 he performed a version of 'A Croquet Game'. 1917 introduced 'The Episode of the Tennis Match', copyrighted by Fields in 1918 as 'An Episode of Lawn Tennis'. This is the first of Bill's detailed sight-gag scripts:

SCENE: *Back drop shows side of wire fence, enclosing court. Tennis Net runs up and down stage about four feet from wings – stage left – two benches each about six feet long are placed against back drop to right of net. A ground cloth marks the court. Several raquets are discovered on bench. At rise of curtain Mr. Itch is discovered on stage eating a banana. He tosses the peel on stage centre; and walks up stage to bench to collect another raquet. Mr Squash enters carrying a dozen raquets under his arm . . .*

Of course, the inevitable occurs. The tennis sketch was wholly pantomime, consisting of a crazy match between Bill Fields and Walter Catlett, and two women, Peggy Hopkins (later to co-star as Peggy Hopkins-Joyce with Fields in his 1932 film *International House*) and Allyn King. Much business was made of trying to catch hold of dropped tennis rackets and hats at the same time, and Fields perennial gag of putting his hat back on the handle of his racket (or his cane, or any other protruding object) instead of his head was refined here. The gag with the failure to put his hat on became almost a Fields signature. It was surely the acme of the juggler's war with the cosmos that even his own head failed to be where it should be at these crucial moments. It is one of the oldest attributes of the clown that his own body does not obey his will, let alone anything else in the universe.

The second sketch in which Fields appeared in 1917 was 'The Episode of the City Streets and Subways', which has been described from memory by playwright Marc Connelly in his memoir, *Voices Offstage*. In Hobart's draft text, Walter Catlett, as Mr. Wooley, a stranger from the West, arrives in the helter-skelter of New York City and is nonplussed by its confusion. He protests: 'Every robber in the world is loose. If you go into a hotel restaurant and ask for a sliver of pie it costs you eight dollars to get back on the street . . .' After a deal of banter with check-room girls, taxi-drivers and newsboys, Catlett cries out:

> WOOLEY: Is anybody on the level in this town? (*Enter* PIETRO *[Fields] with small pushcart – containing peanuts and a peanut roaster which whistles . . .* WOOLEY *goes to* PIETRO) Say, can you tell me where I can get a drink after one o'clock in this town?
>
> PIETRO:* Peanuts!
>
> WOOLEY: No, no; a drink – highball! – cocktail!
>
> PIETRO: Stranger?
>
> WOOLEY: Yes, I'm a stranger and I want to tell you St Joe, Missouri, can put it all over this burg.

* Pietro became 'Wise Acres, a pushcart man', on the stage.

PIETRO: After one o'clock see me. (*Lifts up top part of peanut cart revealing a small but fully equipped bar – bottles, syphons, etc.*)

Marc Connelly's memory of this scene is radically different, reflecting the kind of developing or ad-libbing Fields indulged on stage (those who saw his shows always said he never repeated the same lines twice).

FIELDS: Seeking sustenance from peanuts, friend? Those small yet succulent morsels of tastiness? . . .

STRANGER: I'm a friend of Charley Bates. He said to mention his name.

FIELDS: Bates? Bates? Charley Bates? Christened Charles, I presume?

STRANGER: Yes, sir. Of St Joe.

FIELDS: Of St Joe, you say?

STRANGER: Yes, sir. He was here last month. Charles G. Bates.

FIELDS: Ah yes, Charles G. Bates. A bell seems to tinkle. I concede the name might in truth be familiar. Perchance you too have a monicker?

STRANGER: Yes sir. Gus Ferderber. (*He offers a calling card, the surface of which* FIELDS *thumbs suspiciously.*)

FIELDS: You'll pardon me, I trust. Mountebanks could easily have such things printed to fleece honest merchants in the goober trade.

STRANGER: But I *am* Gus Ferderber. I just got to town today.

FIELDS: I see. And where is your permanent abode?

STRANGER: St Joe.

FIELDS: Come, come. Don't tell me there are *two* people in St Joe! (STRANGER *offers his hat, and* FIELDS *examines the hat-band, murmuring:*) Joe Zilch, Gents Furnishings, Paris, London and St Joe . . . I welcome you to our little settlement. Any friend of brother – whatshisname – again? Charlie Bates? is a friend of mine. Just a second, doc. (FIELDS *presses a lever and the peanut machine is turned into a completely stocked bar.*) Name it, brother.

Note the 'Micawberian' tone here, the huckstering Eustace McGargle of *Poppy*, still to come, in embryo. As usual, though, we have to take this memoir under advisement, as Connelly remembers it as a comment on Prohibition, from 1920, whereas the record shows it predates the nationwide ban on alcohol, perhaps anticipating it, in 1917.

In 1918, Fields appeared in two *Follies* sketches (alas, still missing), as Senator La Follette, in 'The Lower Regions', and as Bunkus Manyan, a Patent Attorney, who has to contend with Eddie Cantor's invention of an elaborate contraption to wake the entire household up whenever a mouse appeared. An unpublished outline suggests that this, too, was a now vanished Fields text. The *Follies* of 1918 (the 12th) was marked by a massive war tableau staged by Ben Ali Haggin entitled 'Forward Allies!', with numerous Allied troops bayonetting cowering Huns, and nubile maidens Kay Laurell, Dorothy Leeds and 'Dolores' wrapped in the French, British and American flags, respectively. A 5 August programme reveals, in the small print, Bessie Poole still present in the chorus of Lillian Lorraine's 'Starlight' number. In another Lillian Lorraine number, 'Any Old Time at All', the male supporting chorus included Will Rogers, Eddie Cantor and W. C. Fields, all warbling together.

The 1918 *Follies* was a smash hit, particularly as November brought the long delayed Armistice in Europe, prompting exuberant relief throughout the Allied nations. But another, perhaps smaller boost for mankind, in that show, was the unfurling, as we have related at the start of this chapter, of Fields' long prepared, lovingly crafted Golf Sketch.

The Golf sketch, first performed in the lost silent short *His Lordship's Dilemma* in 1915, was, the pool act apart, Fields' favourite routine. He was able to insert it into the silent film, *So's Your Old Man*, and again into its sound remake, *You're Telling Me* (1934), as well as reprising it in his first sound short, *The Golf Specialist* (1930), which is the most faithful rendition we have of a Fields sketch as it was performed on stage. As 'An Episode on the Links' it is well worth transcribing in full, with all its typographical errors preserved:

AN EPISODE ON THE LINKS
BY
W. C. FIELDS

CHARACTERS:

COL. BOGEY – *A Golfer*

WILLIE SNIFF – *A Caddy*

SNOW – *Another Caddy*

MISS GREEN – *A Golfer*

MISS MORSE – *Out for a stroll with her dog*

MISS QUIET – *A horse woman*

MISS STOPIT –

WILLIE STOPIT – *Her brother*

FRED SHOOTOM – *A Hunter*

HENRY GOTYEA – *A Sheriff*

SCENE: Back drop depicting golf course. Centre of stage a green about ten feet in diameter. A lawn mower is laying at up-stage end of the green. An oil can is lying just in front of handle of lawn mower and the green. Keeper's lunch just behind the lawn mower. A golf club is lying on the down-stage end of green. The hole is indicated on the green with flag in same. The first hole on Saint Mike's golf course.

Enter Miss Green – stage left – followed by Col. Bogey, speaking to Miss Green. 'I haven't played since playing in the Canary islands many years ago.' Colonel Bogey beckons Sniff and Snow, the caddies. 'Come on, boys.'

Enter Sniff and Snow from stage left. Sniff carrying a large golf bag, containing a number of clubs – a stuffed rabbit and a motor horn – Snow a small bag containing not more than two club – .
  Colonel Bogey speaks – 'In the early days in the Canaries, we used to tee up on one Island and drive to the other –' Miss Green asks – 'How far is it from one Island to the other?' Colonel Bogey – 'O! about four or five miles.' Colonel Bogey swings golf club which he finds too flexible – turns to caddy – 'Caddy, there is too much whip in this club.' Walks to boy to get another club. Finds the dead rabbit and the motor horn in the bag, which he throws upon the green, giving Sniff a reprimanding glance. Picks club from bag and speaks to Miss Green – 'You know, I haven't played for so long. I'll hardly know what ball to use for this hole.' Takes chalk from pocket and proceeds to chalk club as though it were a billiard cue. 'Caddy, give me a ball.'

Sniff hands Colonel Bogey pint bottle of whiskey. Colonel Bogey – 'Not that kind of a ball – you know I don't smoke. Give me a golf ball.'

Sniff hands Bogey a golf ball. Bogey places abll on green, hits ball whcih strikes an iron angle about three feet distant, rebounds and drops into

Sniff's hat. Colonel Bogey hits Sniff on back and Sniff allows a rubber ball to drop from his mouth, which Colonel Bogey catches in his hand. Replaces it on green and is about to hit it when Sniff interrupts with – 'Wrong club! Try this putting niblick' – and offers club to Bogey.

Colonel Bogey asks 'a whating whichlick,' Sniff – 'A putting niblick.'

Bogey takes club, drops hat – catches same before it falls to stage. Sniff tries to catch hat. Bogey replaces hat on head – it falls again. Bogey catches it as before but drops club. Sniff tries again to catch hat, misses it, then reaches for club, which Bogey retrieves with his foot. Bogey drops club and walks to boy taking out a club with load shaft – He walks back to Miss Green saying – 'I lost a very dear friend in the Canary Islands – A chap named Herbert Pothlewistle.' He stoops to pick up ball, accidentally steps on head of club which flies up and strikes him in back. He jumps away in great indignation and scowls at Sniff – He again tries to pick up ball, steps on head of club with the result as before. He steps to Sniff and knocks his hat off saying – 'How dare you?'

Lopking at Miss Green, Colonel Bogey says – 'Yes, young Pothlewhistle was killed in the Canaries – He was kicked to death by two ferocious Canary birds.' He then prepares to swing at ball and club bends. He looks at club with great disgust, throws it on green and takes club from Sniff. Colonel Bogey prepares his grip on club and Sniff discovering the green keeper's lunch proceeds to open same, which is wrapped in some very crisp paper and makes considerable noise.

The Colonel is irritated by the noise and grabs the paper from Sniff, leaving him the lunch. The Colonel separates the paper and throws it off towards stage right and walks back to ball. The paper blows back to the Colonel, who again throws it to stage right, and it is again blown back to Colonel Bogey. Colonel Bogey adjusts his hat and remarks to Miss Green – 'Quite a breeze.' He is about to hit the ball again when Sniff walks to piece of paper farthest away – picks it up and walks across stage with it and drops it. Sniff has a pair of shoes with whistles in the heels and every time he puts his foot down the shitles screech. When he returns after disposing of paper, Colonel picks up large oil can and oils Sniff's shoes, remarking, 'just keep your out out closed whilst walking over those links.'

Colonel Bogey is about to play again when Sniff drops the green keeper's pie on green and starts again for the paper. Bogey halts him and cautions him to be quiet. Walks over toward golf bag after him and steps on pie which clings on to Bogey's foot. He tries to extricate it, finally using club. The pie clings to club. Bogey steps on one of the pieces of paper which clings to his foot. He removes the pie from end of club and it sticks to his glove. He then places head of club on another piece of paper which also clings. He finally gets Sniff to put his foot on pie in order to release it from his glove. Bogey shakes paper from both foot and club and finds his hand caught on club. Releases hand from club, takes silk handkerchief from pocket, wipes his hands, replaces handkerchief in pocket and handkerchief sticks to glove; after all efforts to replace it in pocket fail, he throws both handkerchief and glove away. Colonel Bogey goes back to ball to putt when Sniff again causes annoyance by trying to get the pie off his foot. Bogey becomes most irate, goes to Sniff, tears off his shoes with pie clinging to it and throws both off stage. He returns to pick up club and sees Sniff working his big toes up and down. Sniff's sock is torn and great toe is plainly visible. Bogey crawls near Sniff and brings the club down with considerable force upon Sniff's toe. Sniff jumps and groans. Bogey retruns again to ball; just as he is about to putt, Miss Morse, a smart looking girl with grayhound, saunters across stage from stage left to stage right. Bogey sees her, bids her good day and remarks – 'Fine looking camel you have with you!' Turning to caddy says 'stand clear, caddy.' Is about to putt again and is interrupted by Miss Quiet, a horse woman, crossing from stage left to stage right, wearing a riding habit, and carrying a quirt. She does not see Bogey and as she passes in front of him stops and says – 'O! I've forgotten something.' She then turns and walks to stage right. Bogey looks at Miss Green and says – 'She's probably forgotten her horse.' Miss Quiet stops again, meditates and says – 'O! I won't need it' and walks to stage left – steps on golf club which is lying on green in front of Bogey – and breaks it. Bogey picks up club, looks off stage after her and shouts 'No, you won't need it, but we will,' then turning to Sniff says – 'put that in the bag, caddy.' He takes his stanch behind ball and says – 'Stand clear, Caddy, and keep your eye on the ball.' Miss Stopit enters from stage right followed by her brother, Willie Stopit. Willie sees rabbit, picks it up and says to his sister – 'O! sister, look what I've found.' Miss Stopit looks at Willie and says – 'O! Willie, how can you. Throw the dirty thing in the ash can.' Both start to exit left. Bogey runs to bag and hurriedly removes rabbit. Turns to Willie before he exits and says – 'thank your sister for the rabbit.' Willie replies – 'go to hell.' Willie exits left. Bogey shouts 'you are a great hulking boy! There, I've slanged him.' Bogey goes to ball and prepares to hit it, cautioning caddy to 'stand clear and keep your eye on the ball.' He draws back to hit ball when Fred Shooter, a hunter, enters right, looks into the flies, aims and fires gun. A prop turkey falls and hits Bogey on the head, knokcing him on the green. Shooter, frightened, runs off stage left. Bogey gets up and staggers from the effects of the blow, holds his head, then reaches to his hip and pulls oil can from same. He stumbles over handle of lawn mower, stoops and picks it up, catching the end in Miss Green's dress. Miss Green screams and extricates it. Bogey, looking into the flies, explains 'I wish those aviators would fasten themselves in more securely.' Picking up turkey – remarks – 'A robin red breast.'

'Now stand clear, caddy,' he says, as he again approaches ball. As he is about to strike Sniff says – 'try this baffy' and hands Bogey a rashie which had a telescope shaft. Bogey tries to use club and shaft collapses. He is most annoyed with Sniff and grabs former club from Sniff. He is about to putt again when he is interrupted by Sniff stepping upon a motor horn. All look off stage right as though motor car was coming. Bogey goes back to ball and is about to strike when he is interrupted by Sniff. Bogey says, 'I'll tee it my dear.' He is about to putt again and is interrupted by Sniff who asks him if he would like to hear a riddle. 'Ah, ah,' says Sniff. Bogey reprimands Sniff and Miss Green tries to tee ball. Bending with back to Bogey, Bogey swings without looking and almost hits her.

Bogey says - 'No. I do not care to hear your riddle.' Sniff says, 'Gee, I'd like to tell one' – Bogey says – 'Well, if you must tell one – tell it, but don't let me hear it.' Sniff says – 'we have a black hen at my house that lays a white egg' – Bogey says 'I don't see anything remarkable about that.' Sniff says – 'You can't do it.' Bogey, most annoyed, leaves club on green and is about to reprimand Sniff when a dog runs from stage left and steals ball. All chase dog off.

Curtain.

Chapter 21
The Vaudeville Sketches of W. C. Fields, Part 2

The Golf Sketch reveals the great detail in which Fields crafted his every move and gesture. Although people who saw Fields perform used to say that he varied his act slightly from night to night, much of what was set out in 'An Episode on the Links' in 1918 was performed to the last nuance in *The Golf Specialist* of 1930. All the business with the caddy, the wrapped lunch and the pie is exactly as set out twelve years earlier. A number of minor characters, such as the Stopits, were cut. But how meticulously Fields turns a straightforward golf session into a saga of frustration and pain . . .

The dialogue, too, is an early precursor of those rambling monologues, which begin in absurdity and tail off into the outer edges of the implausible, a twilight zone of the surreal. It was a given twist of these long pointless stories that they were addressed to a stooge who wasn't listening, whether it was the society snobs of *You Can't Cheat an Honest Man* or the human bar-room props of *My Little Chickadee*, *Never Give a Sucker an Even Break*, et al.

While the end of the Great War, in November 1918, put paid to the gross military displays of the *Follies*, Fields continued to work on a long sketch, set in an air corps recruiting office, entitled 'Just Before the Battle Mother', co-written with one Mortimer M. Newfield. It gives us a rather rare insight into Bill's inner thoughts on war and peace, beyond the patriotic façade. The sketch may well have been sparked off by the campaigns of aerial warfare which American air squadrons had joined for the first time in the spring of 1918, and was probably a version of a skit performed in that year's *Follies* with Eddie Cantor as a thick-headed Bronx recruit, perhaps the 'R. U. Strong' of the typescript.

It is also similar in tone to an earlier *Follies* sketch, 'Recruiting', which was performed in 1916. In the original 'Recruiting' sketch, which featured Bert Williams, Don Barclay and Sam Hardy, Hardy was the Recruiting Officer interrogating the would-be soldiers who came staggering off the street. The sequence seems to be set in the era of Pancho Villa, which provided a host of Ziegfeld gags. George Hobart's script proceeds:

(*Enter Reddan Green* [Fields], *a bum* ...)

SPANN [Hardy]: What do you want?

FIELDS: I want to see General Funston.

HARDY: General Funston is in the front.

FIELDS (*goes to footlights – pages*): General Funston, please!

HARDY: Here, what are you doing? General Funston is in Mexico.

FIELDS: I thought you said he was out front . . .

HARDY (*to colleague*): Shoot him!

FIELDS: Wait, don't be cross with me. Let me join.

HARDY: What qualifications have you?

FIELDS: While marching through a dry country I'd be a great help to the other soldiers.

HARDY: How is that?

FIELDS: I don't drink water.

HARDY (*to colleague*): Shoot him!

This is not vintage stuff. In fact, much of the Ziegfeld text is like this, pretty tenuous, with scattergun jokes. Tickling the audience's funny bone while they waited for the girls. Only the Travesty of Othello, with Bert Williams, rises to dizzier heights. But Fields saw possibilities in these routines which he developed on paper.

'Just Before the Battle, Mother' runs to nineteen typescript pages. Entitled 'A farce comedy in three acts', it features characters called Willy Weekin, a Private; R. U. Strong, a Private; Lieutenant Loot, a Soldier; Lieutenant Ballup, a Souse; Major Zaminem; and I. M. Bungdup, another Private, probably played by Fields. Act One takes place 'Outside Camp Chare, Texas', and Act Two, in the 'Examination Room' of the camp, involves an insurance examination for aviation recruits. As Major Zaminem enters, Lieutenants Loot and Ballup rise to salute, and Loot catches his foot in a pail, prompting the corny gag:

ZAMINEM (*to* LOOT *who is trying to extricate foot from pail*): Keep your foot still. You'll kick the bucket soon enough . . .

Enter WEEKIN *right.*

ZAMINEM: What do you want?

WEEKIN: Insurance.

ZAMINEM: Lieutenant Loot, take charge of this man . . .

LOOT: Do you want insurance? (*proceeds to question* WEEKIN) What is your name?

WEEKIN: Willy Weekin . . .

LOOT: Do you consider drinking a habit, an art, an inheritance or a talent? (WEEKIN *looks at* LOOT *bewildered.*) Do you enjoy good health?

WEEKIN: Certainly. Who doesn't?

LOOT: Are you a prohibitionist or do you mind your own business?

The examination then proceeds, Weekin having suddenly turned into Strong, perhaps due to heavy adjournments by both writers for liquid refreshment . . . Zaminem sends Strong over to Ballup's desk.

BALLUP: What kind of work did you do before you joined the army?

STRONG: I was a strikebeaker when the conductrettes walked out until a great big hulk of an Irish woman crowned me with an oblong piece of petrified mud. After that I blacked my face and became a black cross nurse in a colored hospital.

BALLUP: That's enough. I'll put you down to carry boxes of ammunition . . .

Enter PRIVATE BUNGDUP *left wearing overseas outfit. His right leg is heavily swathed in bandages. He limps to the personnel table.*

BALLUP (*looks at his leg, astonished*): Were you hurt?

BUNGDUP: No, I have got the gout. This army is too rich for my blood.

BALLUP: Got your number?

BUNGDUP: No, but I got yours . . .

BALLUP: What do you want?

BUNGDUP: A transfer.

BALLUP: Where to?

BUNGDUP: Home.

BALLUP: I can transfer you to Washington.

BUNGDUP: I know he's dead the same as you.

BALLUP: What er – ah –

BUNGDUP: I didn't mean you're dead. I meant the greatest service you can do the country is to die.

BALLUP: Why you – er – um.

BUNGDUP: Aw what's the use tryin' to explain. Where do I get my insurance money?

BALLUP *refers* him *to* ZAMINEM, *who throws a file at* BUNGDUP's *leg.* BUNGDUP *jumps about in great pain.*

ZAMINEM: What have you in there? . . .

BUNGDUP: A piece of German shrapnel.

ZAMINEM: Take it over to the ammunition department.

BUNGDUP: But it's in my leg. I was wounded in France.

ZAMINEM: Wounded in France, eh? Does it hurt?

BUNGDUP: No. How could a piece of shrapnel in your leg hurt?

ZAMINEM: I suppose you want to collect your insurance money.

BUNGDUP: Yes sir.

ZAMINEM (*Looks up* BUNGDUP's *application card. Glances at it.*): Humph – you can't collect a penny. We ought to court martial you for perjury . . . Next time you apply for insurance, please don't lie.

BUNGDUP (*bewildered*): Lie? I? How –

ZAMINEM: I find in this insurance application that when you were asked what the habits of your great, great grandfather were in his early youth, you said he was found [*sic*] of playing marbles. We have traced it down and find he never played marbles until he reached the mature age of 22. You also said your great, great grandmother was a ballet dancer in the chorus of Eva Tanguay's second farewell tour. We find that at this remote date ballet dresses were not made. So be on your way.

BUNGDUP *walks to stage right. Nods to* LOOT. *Opens trap door in top of bandage on leg. Removes bottle of whiskey therefrom; takes glass from pocket; hands bottle and glass to* LOOT. LOOT *paws floor with toe as if endeavouring to locate brass foot rail.* BUNGDUP *takes a collapsible cuspidor from pocket, places it on floor near* LOOT *who deposits cigarette butt in same.* BUNGDUP *then spreads some sawdust on floor before* LOOT *and hangs picture of nude woman round* BUNGDUP*'s neck.* LOOT *places foot on rail, pours out drink, swallows same.* BUNGDUP *replaces bottle in lame leg, picks up cuspidor and bar rail. Exits right.*
Curtain.

There are a host of delicious echoes here. We have an early hint of the follies of insurance, later to surface in *It's a Gift*. We have some digs at the coming Prohibition, and another version of the liquor-bar-room gag in the 'City Streets' sketch. Hints of strikes (soon to break out as the great Equity Strike of 1919), an early version of a perennial Fields line: 'Of course not, how can a piece of shrapnel in your leg/being thrown on your head/ etc hurt?' and an intriguing vaudeville reference (vis. Eva Tanguay). Note the anti-military bias and the unusual dig at George Washington. We can't tell what input 'Mortimer M. Newfield' had into the text. But it lifts a veil, where elsewhere there is silence.

Another influence which should be noted at this point is the underlying impact of newspaper cartoon strips on the jokes and argot of the day. Wes Gehring has pointed out the influence of early comic strips on silent screen comedy, citing 'The Katzenjammer Kids', 'Mutt and Jeff', 'Bringing Up Father' and 'Krazy Kat', dating from 1897 through to the 1920s. The jagged images and surreal language of George Herriman's 'Krazy Kat' are particularly interesting, given the banal nature of present-day American strip cartoons. These strips, often transferred to the silent animated film, were full of wild, anarchic energy. A few years hence, Fields would meet a journalist and playwright intensely involved in this comic-strip world, who would propel his own creativeness in a new and fruitful direction. This man's name was Joseph P. McEvoy, but we shall get to him in due course.

A 1919 sketch which shows the influence of comic-strip thinking with an unusual twist is 'The Mountain Sweep Steaks'. Subtitled 'A Moving, Talking, Eastern, Western, Society, Dramatic Spectacular Comedy Motion Stage Picture', this is a spoof on a host of current silent film-stars with a cast of characters like Jack Cass Fairbanks – an Aviator; Anna Polly Pickford – a Country Girl; Lew 'Left Foot' Chaplin – a Wag; Martin Fetlock Keanan – an Adventurer; Molta Zikrantz Barra – a Vampire; and Bohunk Rogers Hart – a Cowboy. The playlet is in the manner of a broad pastiche, with Country Girl Pickford sauntering out of her house to say 'How sweet the birds sing' several times until a stage propman imitates some bird song. Villain Keanan saunters up to her and says:

KEANAN: Marry me and the mortgage will be yours. Refuse me and your Papa and Mama, your brother Jack and you will be kicked into the gutter.

PICKFORD: Why you poor fish, you roll off my knife . . . Boy, if Dug were here he would knock you for a goal.

KEANAN: Who is Dug?

PICKFORD: Dug is my sweet patootie. He flies with the mail between New York and Washington every day. I expect him over the house any minute.

KEANAN: If I see him I will shoot him down as I would a clay pigeon.

The plot, such as it is, concerns Dug's effort to win the car race known as the Mountain Sweep Steaks to save Polly's mortgage. 'Lew' Chaplin is a pantomime role, with the 'Wag' wooing vamp Barra and then winning the race by beating the cars. The whole affair is intended to be highly stylised, with cartoon-like characters, silhouettes and paper cut-out motor cars. The sketch, thirteen pages long, does not seem to have ever been performed. It remains a tantalising clue to Fields' preoccupation with the successful stars of the screen and his own inability, so far, to break into this crucial medium. His ambivalence to Chaplin is reflected in the ending, when the silent 'Wag' runs off with the sweepstakes winnings.

Denied the screen, Fields continued to develop his own brand of craziness. In 1919 he shifted from the *Follies* upstairs to the *Midnight Frolic* on the roof, continuing to work, by day, on his scripts. He was working at the *Frolic* when the first ever general strike of Broadway actors was called. Actor's Equity had a long simmering dispute with producers over pay for rehearsals and holiday shows. The chorus girls were particularly disadvantaged. Eddie Cantor was a leading light of the union, and called the Ziegfeld actors off the stage.

According to Cantor, Bill Fields was exempt from the strike call, as the *Frolic* was classified as 'vaudeville', but he left the show to join his friends on the picket line. He also played the Equity benefit week at the Lexington Opera House, with a cast including Ethel and Lionel Barrymore, Frank Tinney, Ed Wynn, and most of the *Follies* performers. Cantor relates that Fields joined him and the strike committee in a car which they stalled in front of theatres which refused to shut down: 'We pretended to be fixing the car and clowned around until the prospective ticket-purchasers were attracted by us. We entertained them so well on the street corner that they willingly missed the show inside. The policemen were in sympathy with us, so was the public, and we invariably captured the day for Equity.'

An unpaid benefit which W. C. Fields certainly never mentioned in any of his essays. Faced with the unusual solidarity of highly paid stars with the lower ranks the managers caved in, conceding extra pay for holiday gigs and for rehearsals that lasted more than four weeks. It was a small gain, but significant for any union in 1919.

Fields' freebie car routine intriguingly echoes his registration, that same year, of the earliest known version of his motoring sketch, 'The Family Ford'. In this vintage script, George Fliverton (a 'flivver' was a slang name for the Ford) and his wife are driving in the country when their engine stalls. Also with them is Henry Eitzel, Mrs F.'s daffy father. Other characters who turn up as 'Friends' include Elsie May, and Adel Smith – both first names of Fields' own sisters. There is also Kate Hoofnagle, 'a nurse girl' (remember Kate, Bill's mother) and one James Cunningham, 'a blind man'. Fliverton vainly attempts to restart the car, but the engine dies again –

MRS FLIVERTON: My God you ain't going to blame that on me are you? (*crying*) I never saw anything like it in all my life, I get blamed for everything. I'll never go out in this car again . . .

MR FLIVERTON *raises hood and looks into engine. A shot is heard, and the whistle follows. The right tire has punctured.* MR FLIVERTON *removes his head from under the hood, walks to rear tire.*

MR FLIVERTON: O gee, what are you doing now?

MRS FLIVERTON: (*begins crying*): I never did a thing, I was standing there and I never said a word to it.

MR FLIVERTON: Shut up! Where's the jack?

MRS FLIVERTON: Here. (*Hands* MR FLIVERTON *her pocket book.*)

MR FLIVERTON: The jack to jack the car up.

MRS FLIVERTON *takes small jack out of her stocking.*

MR FLIVERTON: Where's the handle?

MRS FLIVERTON *takes small rubber handle out of her bust.*

This is our very first introduction to a Fields staple – the nuclear family in its atomic decay. Fields' stage vengeance on Hattie and all his marital humiliations starts right here. But, if we cast our minds back, we might recall the English music-hall comedian Harry Tate's Motoring Sketch of 1908. The similarities, down to the shot heard off-stage, are evident. And Fields was to produce an even closer version to Tate's in a later rewrite called 'The Sport Model', later still to be revived on screen for 1934's *It's a Gift*. Another precursor of *It's a Gift* is a small scene with a blind man, who, ignoring the motor horn, 'steps over into car and pokes the right front headlight glass out; he then strikes the car violently as he passes trying to feel his way offstage right'.

MR FLIVERTON (*looks over side of car and inspects damage*): Why don't you look where you are going?

MRS FLIVERTON: The way you went over those bumps today I'll bet a lot of people thought this was a flying boat. This ain't Automolibing, it's a trip through the clouds.

MR FLIVERTON: Never you mind what they thought it was, you keep your hands off the machinery.

Fields was inordinately fond of his Motoring Sketch and lovingly polished it up in different versions, culminating in 'The Midget Car', for Earl Carroll's *Vanities* in 1928. But it was first performed in the Ziegfeld *Follies* of 1920 with Fanny Brice as Mrs Fliverton. By then Bill had added to the above cast a young daughter, Baby Rose, played by the petite comedienne Ray Dooley. The father-in-law, now called Henry Steel, was played by a short-statured actor called William

Blanche, hitherto known as 'Shorty', who had been first engaged as a caddy in the golf sketch, and then became Fields' on-and-behind stage 'stooge', dresser and general amanuensis, to the end of his Broadway days.

In the 1920 *Follies,* Bill and Fanny Brice played husband and wife in another number, 'In the Theatre', with Mary Eaton, Charles Winninger and Carl Randall. This was a forum for the 'Six Little Follies Girls' to do a water act. Fields' role was to pay too much attention to one of the beauties in the chorus, until he got dragged by Fanny off the stage.

Art was already echoing life.

Fanny was having serious trouble, again, with Nick Arnstein, whom she had finally married in June 1919, after his divorce from his previous wife came through. Two months later their first child, Frances, had been born, coinciding with the Actors' Equity strike. Nevertheless, early in 1920, Nick Arnstein absconded from another charge of fraud and went on the run. From his hideouts, he entrusted Fields with the task of passing messages to his distraught wife. Bill would turn up at Fanny's dressing-room with an envelope postmarked Akron, Ohio, and a note reading: 'You remember the rides in your car with our friend. Tell her I've left the stage and am working in a brassiere shop on Second Avenue.' It's a wonder Fields could figure out where his stage act ended and so-called real life began.

But by now he was on top of the world. He had achieved the major ambition of his early juggling days, to earn $1,000 a week. He was, as Eddie Cantor put it, in the aristocracy of show business. The movies had devoured vaudeville, but Fields kept it alive in his small but highly prized corner of the Broadway stage.

This was the Jazz Age, with New York as the rough hub of the wheel. The times were crazy: The Volstead Act, inaugurating Prohibition, came into operation on 16 January 1920, and all America went officially dry overnight. In reality this promulgated the era of even harder, ever more desperate drinking, bootleggers and organised crime. By 1922 New York had over 5,000 'speakeasies', in back rooms, apartments, 'tea rooms', drugstores and 'novelty shops'; some said that by the end of the 1920s there were 100,000 such dives in New York. Everyone learned the new routine, knocking twice on the door and muttering 'Joe sent me.'

It's clear that, for those people who were already boozing, like Fields, Prohibition provided a challenge that could not be refused. And even those who might not have been heavy drinkers before felt obliged to join this clandestine culture. We are all aware how it permeated the American cinema, showing its influence long after the Act itself was repealed in 1933. Prohibition also gave a big boost to the night club, the speakeasy's respectable richer sister. White musicians raided black Harlem for the syncopation of the age. Everyone had mogo on the gogogo. Another fad, the 'dance craze', swept America, culminating in the massive, gruelling dance marathons which lasted well into the Depression.

This was also the era of rabid tabloid journalism, of the paranoid fear of Bolshevism, of witch-hunts on anarchists, notably the trial of Sacco and Vanzetti. But Broadway seemed a world away from all that. Of course, there was another Broadway, in the shadow of Ziegfeld's glitz. John Barrymore played Richard the Third in 1920, and a dazzling Hamlet in 1922, at the Plymouth Theatre. In 1920, a fringe playwright, Eugene O'Neill, won the Pulitzer prize with a Broadway production of his first full-length play, *Beyond the Horizon*. It ran for 111 performances. The Ziegfeld *Follies* of 1920 ran for 123.

What did William Claude Dukenfield do with his new-found status? We have already seen his love of automobiles. He did not buy any real estate – to the end of his life Bill only rented, never bought any of his homes. While working in Manhattan he lived in the appropriate hotels for members of his caste, the Somerset and later the Astor in Times Square, the very acme of swank and prestige. At some point he joined the Lambs Club, New York's oldest and most prestigious theatrical club, at 128–130th West 44th Street. In the late 1920s, his letters show he was using this as his address. One might assume that for a time he was actually living in its accommodations. The Lambs was New York's premier venue for what we today call the 'gliterati'. Members included writers, poets, mayors, governors, champion pugilists, baseball stars, ministers, generals, even priests. At the Lambs, it was normal to find George Gershwin, or Irving Berlin, tickling the ivories. Almost all the famous names of the city propped up the bar at some time or other, sipping their sarsaparilla ('What flavour?' you hear a familiar barman ask, and that rasping nasal voice, replying: 'Oh, horseradish, spinach, anything . . . '). All the Barrymores were *habitués*, with their illustrious uncle, John Drew. It might well have been here that the seeds of friendship between the two prodigious imbibers of the sauce, John Barrymore and William Claude, were sown.

In short, The Lambs was an unlikely place for an anti-social, lonely misanthrope to hang his hat. The myth finally crumbles and dies here. Bill Fields, in Rome, did as the Romans, ate and drank and revelled at their revels. The building at 130 West 44th is still there today, untouched, as yet, by the Times Square destroy and rebuild boom. But it has an ironically different function now: it houses New York's Church of the Nazarene. One wonders what voices devout parishioners hear when they bow in solemn prayer.

In 1921, Bill Fields and Fanny Brice took the stage again together for Ziegfeld, to present another vintage Fields sketch. This one was called 'Off To the Country', and was a reunion of the Fliverton Family. Once again Mr and Mrs F. are saddled with daffy offspring – Ray Dooley as their daughter and Raymond Hitchcock as son Sammy 'Sap' Fliverton. The scene is a subway station, and the Fliverton family rush down the steps to the train bowed down by 'impedimenta of every sort'. Sap carries a small phonograph, a tennis racket, a baseball mask and bat. Fliverton carries folding fishing rods, a mandolin in a case, several bundles, a parrot cage and hat box. Mrs F. carries a hat box, a grip and a bird cage, and baby Ray carries a big doll, a teddy bear, some balloons, 'an all day sucker' and a can of worms.

Here is an early tussle of Pop Fields with 'his' child, as he belts her for making them miss the train –

MRS FLIVERTON: You let her alone! She hasn't done a thing!

FLIVERTON: She has too! She keeps dropping those worms and I keep slippin' on 'em! (*Hands can of worms to* SAP. SAP *begins to pout and finally cries louder and louder, holding worms away from him*) What's he crying for?

MRS FLIVERTON: You know he is frightened at worms.

MR FLIVERTON *grabs can away from him and places it near the parrot's cage. The parrot eats worms.* FLIVERTON *takes candy cigarette from* SAP.

RAY (*screams*): The parrot is eating the worms!

FLIVERTON *kicks cage over and removes can.* SAP *picks up cage.* FLIVERTON *leans over to pick up worms. Bird protrudes its head through cage and bites* FLIVERTON *in the back.* FLIVERTON – *to wife.*

FLIVERTON: What kind of bird is that, he bit me in the head.

MRS FLIVERTON: Woodpecker.

A whistle blows, the Fliverton family run for their bundles, but are pushed back by exiting crowds. The train pulls out, leaving them on the platform. Another whistle and they grab their bundles again. It's the wrong train on the wrong track. At one point, arguing with a guard about their tickets, with Baby Ray babbling, Fields has inserted in handwriting – the only handwritten notation on the typescript – the line: 'RAY *screams and jumps up and down.* FLIVERTON: That's right – show your mother's disposition.' Finally they crowd on board a train, leaving Sap behind by mistake –

MRS FLIVERTON *screams, again and again – runs up and down platform.*

FLIVERTON: What's the matter?

MRS FLIVERTON: Sap, Sap, Sap! Where are you? He's killed! He's killed!

FLIVERTON: He isn't killed. He hasn't enough sense to get killed!

RAY: Sap! Poor Sap! Sap was left on the train!

MRS FLIVERTON: Sap was left on the train. It has taken him away and you don't care – and he is your own flesh and blood.

FLIVERTON: Yes, you are a lot of saps. He has gone off the train he will be back from the next station.

SAP *is heard crying. Enters, running downstairs, arms outstretched.* FLIVERTON *picks up bundle, kicking his own hat off and hits* SAP *in the face with the bundle.* RAY *runs to* SAP. SAP *runs to his mother, who is standing just before* FLIVERTON's *hat.* MOTHER *pats* SAP, RAY *runs and hugs him. Jumps up and down on* FLIVERTON's *hat unconscious of what she is doing.* FLIVERTON *sees* RAY, *hits her again, picks up hat. Drops it and is after both kids once more . . .*

Whistle again.

FLIVERTON (*shouts*): Hurry up!

All enter platform. They grab bundles. FLIVERTON's *hat is on grip with* RAY's. *They exchange hats in the confusion.* FLIVERTON *grabs refuse can*

along with grips etc. Two birds escape from the cage. All chase birds. FLIV-
ERTON *gets caught on fishing line. Drops rod. Finds he is caught. Starts to
release hook.* RAY *picks up pole, trying to get birds.*

FLIVERTON: Let go of that pole! Let go!

FLIVERTON, MRS F *and* RAY *get bundles together, rush in train; doors are
closed leaving* SAP *on platform. Train pulls out,* SAP *cries at top of voice.
Curtain.*

Here is the Fields family fully blown, the harridan wife, the ungrateful brat, the useless son. It is easy to see the echoes of Hattie and little
Claude Junior in these grotesque caricatures. But we should also know
that this kind of portrayal of the nuclear family was already a familiar
staple in American popular culture, most notably in the crazy world of
the strip cartoons. In 'Bringing Up Father' a 1918 panel has the anti-
hero, Jigger – an Irish-Yankee bricklayer who had won the sweepstakes – dressed in top-hat and spats, rattling the door-knob of the
room his socially-climbing wife has locked him in while she's gone out
to the opera, saying: 'By golly . . . I'd have more freedom if I wuz in
jail!' Mutt and Jeff, perennial favourites, reprised endless screwy wife
jokes, with Mutt visiting Jeff to play cards and Jeff saying: 'Sh-h-h!
What was that? Gee, it's my wife. She hates you and you gotta get out
before she sees you!' Some panels further on, the bony wife exclaims:
'In bed with your clothes on, eh? Up to the attic for you, you freak.
You can't be trusted a minute!'

Cultural historian Ann Douglas has written about the era as one in
which men rebelled against a matriarchal ethos prevailing before the
'crusade' of the First World War. Certainly a kind of 'matricidal'
impulse and rather fierce gender warfare was in the cultural air. This
fitted in well with Fields' own marital grievances. But there might also
have been another origin for the characterization of Mrs Fliverton.
Both 'Off to the Country' and 'The Family Ford' were surely written
with Fanny Brice in mind. The outgoing, loud, mothering role she took
on with the boys in the Ziegfeld band might have played a part here.
Ironically, when Fanny went on radio, years later, the role she was
most successful in playing was of the worldly wise 'Baby Snooks'. But
Fields obviously saw her in a very different light. At any rate, it's an
intriguing thought what might have happened if they had ever partnered on the screen. Fanny did star in three film vehicles, one in 1928
and two in 1929, as well as supporting roles in four other movies, but

her films never caught on, and are consigned to oblivion.

Bill and Fanny appeared in two other sketches in the *Follies* of 1921 – a spoof on the Barrymore family, 'Lionel, Ethel and Jack in *Camille*', with Raymond Hitchcock as Lionel, Fanny as Ethel and Bill Fields as Jack (John) Barrymore. This sketch – written by Channing Pollock – is missing. The second sketch, also lost, was a pastiche of the recent Jack Dempsey – Georges Carpentier World Heavyweight Championship fight, with Fanny Brice as Carpentier, Ray Dooley as Dempsey, and W. C. Fields as the Referee. The *Follies* girls provided the fight fans. In Act Two Fanny sang her signature song, 'My Man', with all its echoes of her crazy love for her gangster spouse.

Fields continued to turn out his 'vaudeville' scripts, throughout the 1920s. Often they would include his inimitable drawings, stage instructions, asides on bits and pieces of business. (As complete as possible a list can be found in an appendix.) They reflect a restless mind, a search for the perfect gag, the perfect version of old routines. This obsessiveness lies at the heart of Bill Fields. Of course, he craved the adulation of the audience. Of course, he wanted to be rich and famous. Of course, he wanted to get the best girls. But behind all that – there was always the naked creative urge, that fire within that never went out, despite the quenching downpours of reality.

Chapter 22
The Purple Bark Sarsaparilla – The Birth of Eustace McGargle

14 *Poppy*: W.C. Fields and Madge Kennedy.

To many, the Ziegfeld *Follies* are identified with the 'roaring twenties'. But in a sense, by 1922, Ziegfeld was a dinosaur. His shows were still big business but he was getting deep into debt, and new contenders for the crown of Theatosaurus Rex were springing up to challenge him. One of these was an ex-Ziegfeld dancer, George White, who opened his first challenge, called 'George White's *Scandals*', at the Liberty Theatre in 1919. A New York East Sider who had hoofed for nickels and dimes in the Bowery's music halls, George White's stated aim was to put on the most beautiful girls in town, to out-girl Ziegfeld. But, like Ziegfeld, he knew that a revue could not survive without variety acts.

Bill Fields, ever restless, was looking to move on. He still wanted to break through into the movies but the movies had leapt forward since 1915, and were now an established empire in Hollywood. Ziegfeld fought hard to prevent his actors from moonlighting in the rival medium. George White offered Fields more money and a licence to make movies if he could. Fields took the plunge and joined the cast of the *Scandals* of 1922.

Fields performed four sketches in the *Scandals*: 'Terrific Traffic', a version of the motoring sketch with comedienne Winnie Lightner, a baseball sketch called 'The Big Leaguers', a parody of early radio called 'The Radio Bug', and a 'W. C. Fields Speciality', a revival of his juggling act. But the reviewers did not warm to these sketches and the movie offers failed to materialize. The *Scandals* were to continue sporadically till 1939 (the last show featured the Three Stooges), making millions for White, who spent it all at the races and died broke in 1968. But Fields, in 1922, quickly realized that he was going backwards, not forwards. Just as he had sniffed out when vaudeville was dying, he could sense the decline of the revue.

Ever fearful of being caught in a rut, Bill was looking for a chance to break into 'book musicals', plays in which he could star alone. In 1923 a good angel, producer Philip Goodman, came up with a perfect proposal.

The play was *Poppy*, by the actress Dorothy Donnelly. It was a romantic weepie, about a young girl who grows up in a carnival after her mother has died, set in small-town Connecticut in 1874. The girl, Poppy, is looked after by a roguish carnival grifter and card sharp, who tries to pass her off as an heiress to a rich family, so as to ensure her future. The twist in the tale is that she really is the heiress, as her mother was the rejected daughter of the strict old judge who had turned her out in the past.

The part of the fairground drifter was perfect for Fields. Not surprisingly – as it was specially reworked for him, from the original script, by an uncredited co-writer, Howard Dietz. Dietz (who was to become one of Broadway's most famous songwriters, author of shows like *The Bandwagon*) had been assigned by Goodman to adapt a German operetta, *Die Beiden Nachtegallen,* into a revue called *Sylvia*. The show was never produced. But a character in it, of a country faker and patent medicine seller, was thought ideal for Fields by Goodman. And so Dietz grafted it into the text of *Poppy*.

At last Fields could spread his wings. The producers were not yet ready to give him star billing, and the play was presented as a vehicle for the popular stage and screen actress Madge Kennedy. She related her memories of Fields, fifty years later, to film historian Anthony Slide:

> Poppy was a . . . 'Cinderella' story. And of course, anything to do with W. C. Fields was fascinating, and I remember he was so good . . . he would do the most incredible things. He would come on in that funny coat and stood alone and they arrested him, we were what you call grifters, and I would say to the Constable, 'Look at him, he's just a child, you can't take him away.' And I would look at him so – It was a very touching moment, really. One night he would come on, and from under this coat he would take out a lollipop that he had made. Well of course the audience and everybody else but the players was out the window. I said, 'Bill, if you'll play that one scene and mean it, it won't matter what you do.' He said, 'Daughter, you're right.' And we'd be all right for another month, and so he'd come out with a trumpet, or something . . .

Everything suddenly clicked for Bill in *Poppy*. The medicine shows and fairground barkers of his youth, the tricks of Bill Dailey and the shell and peas 'old army game', the strutting mannerisms and supreme self-confidence against the odds of Dickens' Micawber, gelled into a character which he was to reprise, in one form or another, for the rest of his life. Eustace McGargle and Fields, as David Robinson has pointed out, 'came together and set to recreating each in the other's image'. The play became the basis for two of Bill's most successful films: 1925's *Sally of the Sawdust,* directed by D. W. Griffith, and the 1936 sound version, *Poppy,* directed by Eddie Sutherland.

Poppy is another allegedly lost text which is unlost, as there are two copies in the W. C. Fields family archive. The play opens with the scene of a country fairground. Signs on the stage indicate: 'Professor Caro, knife acts and torch throwing', 'The Only Human Lady Pin Cushion – weight 435 and a half lb'. 'Professor' McGargle comes in quite late, on page 13, with Poppy, surveying the setting of the carnival –

PROF: This is evidently the scene of our future labors.

POPPY: Labors is right.

PROF: My child, how often must I correct your manner of speech. 'Labors are right,' my darling! Remember your grammar.

POPPY: I was too busy remembering my shoes. My left one split this morning.

PROF: Shoes! Pshaw! When our ship comes in, you shall be shod in satin . . .

POPPY: Pop, you're awful good to me.

PROF: No one could ever·call me parsimonious . . .

POPPY: Pop, can't we give up grafting? I hate to see you trimming these poor farmers.

PROF: My dear, they deserve it. I pride myself on being a modern Robinhood. Like him, I take from the rich and give to the poor.

POPPY: What poor?

PROF: Us poor.

Soon after, McGargle introduces himself to his fellow-plotter, Amos Sniffen:

PROF: I am Professor Eustace McGargle, at your service. I dispense healing roots and herbs in company with my daughter, Miss Poppy McGargle, the well known cantatrice and song-bird, professionally known as the girl with a double larynx . . . She is half-elf and half humming bird. I have to coax her to eat. Her sensitive tissue recoils at the thought of coarse food – the white of an egg beaten up in a spoonful of cream, some strained honey, some grated sponge cake – that is all.

SNIFFEN: I suppose its the double larynx that makes it hard for her to swallow . . .

Here is a Fields instantly familiar to viewers of his great sound movies – *The Old Fashioned Way, You Can't Cheat an Honest Man, My Little Chickadee*, and *Poppy* itself. The Great Huckster is born in all his glory:

PROF: Now, ladies and gentlemen, this wonderful remedy cures hoarseness. It cures hoarseness . . . (*takes drink, voice grows louder*) IT CURES HOARSENESS! Now ladies and gentlemen, those who would know the future have their opportunity at hand . . . Ladies and gentlemen, this stupefying secret of our presence before you has not been unveiled. It is purple bark sarsaparilla, the greatest discovery in the scientific world of medicine since Hypocracies discovered the onion . . . We will conclude our performance by playing on this solid, black ivory xylophone, presented to us by Adelina Patty. You may listen without charge . . . (*to* POPPY *aside*) Take the suckers! Take the suckers!

Of course, we have 'the old army game' – the shells and the little peas: 'Remember, it is not a game of chance. It is a game of science and skill. A boy can play as well as a man . . .'

The *Evening World* wrote: 'W. C. Fields makes "Poppy" gorgeously funny. He turned the trick of his life at the Apollo Theatre by scoring a bigger hit than his hat as a genuine comedian. He is a whole side show in himself.' Eight months into the tour of the play, Madge Kennedy was replaced for a short while by her understudy, and Fields became the featured star of the show – returning to co-star billing when the leading lady returned. A news clipping of 3 June 1924, revealed the moment of triumph:

W. C. Fields . . . became a star last night in this musical comedy and in the first speaking role [*sic*] of his career . . . In his case stellar honours are well deserved. Will Rogers dropped in at Apollo last night to congratulate Mr Fields. The cowboy comedian read wires wishing the new star well from Fred Stone, Eddie Cantor, Leon Errol, Harold Lloyd, Al Jolson, Walter Catlett, Oscar Shaw, Raymond Hitchcock, Jerome Kern, Buster Keaton, Lee Shubert, E. F. Albee and others. Prior to the reading Mr Rogers christened Mr Fields 'Star' by cracking him over the head with a bottle of ginger ale. The operation didn't hurt him as it was a soft drink.

Ginger ale my foot! Ronald Fields reports that Bill's mother, Kate Dukenfield, also attended that 2 June show. Fields was now being acclaimed not only by his peers, which must have caused him supreme satisfaction, but by the most influential critics of the day. Heywood Broun wrote, in the New York *World*: 'At the moment, we can't remember anybody who has ever made us laugh more. It is first-rate clowning, but that is only the beginning of the job which Fields has done. In additional to his familiar but none the less hilarious stunts he gives us a real and complete portrait of as merry a rascal as the stage has seen in years.'

Alexander Woolcott wrote in the *Herald*: 'His jaunty and shameless old mountebank has the flavor of someone astray from one of Mark Twain's riverboats or one of Mr. Dickens' groups of strolling players.' Both Broun and Woolcott were *habitués* of what would come to be called the 'Algonquin Round Table', that informal collection of celebrities which included Dorothy Parker and Robert Benchley. The significance of Fields' work as a performer was being recognised not only in theatrical circles but by New York's intellectual élite.

There is no record of Fields attending the Algonquin circle – he preferred to take his 'purple bark sarsaparilla' at The Lambs – but he was certainly no stranger to them, rubbing shoulders and tinkling amber glasses with Ring Lardner, H. L. Mencken and even, Ronald Fields reports, Gertrude Stein – whom he was to lampoon a decade later in the breakfast scene of his 1935 movie, *Man On the Flying Trapeze*.

Madge Kennedy continued to share in the limelight, and gossip columnists got in on the act, reporting that:

'POPPY' STAR ALWAYS BEING CLAIMED AS LONG-LOST CHEE-ILD – ACTRESS SAYS THREE FATHERS A WEEK ARE OFTEN EMBARRASSING.

It turned out that complete strangers, old men and women from all corners of the United States were writing to Miss Kennedy claiming her as their long-lost daughter. This raw nerve which *Poppy* touched in certain lonely or unhappy old people was clearly echoed by the nerve it touched in Fields: it is from *Poppy* that we can date the fantasy relationship of father and daughter which was to become a staple of so many Fields films. The self-sacrificing father with the beautiful and vulnerable daughter stood in contrast to the real-life sundered relationship between the father and his estranged son. The long-dead mother-wife was so convenient a substitute for the very alive and very demanding Hattie.

Bill's verbal war with Hattie had continued unabated throughout his

Ziegfeld period, as his bitter letters attest. From February 1920: 'You have been a lazy, ignorant, bad-tempered, arguing troubling making [*sic*] female all your life. You [will] find yourself friendless in your old age . . . I haven't one good thought or memory of you . . .' In February 1922: 'You have so much character – Your letters sound as though you were using dope . . . I am tired and sick and have many troubles and I do not care to hear your continual complaining and asking for money – You get your full share every week.' And in October 1923, after *Poppy* had opened: 'Enclosed please find cheque for $50 duly signed – I can imagine what a great annoyance it must be to you to have me forget to sign one cheque in about eighteen years. Tough.'

These testaments to a more familiar Fields – grouchy, irascible and complaining – continued to be the undercurrent below the social Fields carousing in the watering holes of Jazz-age Manhattan. Other witnesses, work colleagues, attested to that itchy, untrusting side, embattled with his managers, employers, agents. But this was a 'normal' show-business trait – the constant anxiety about the future, about the size of names on billings, about the fleetingness of fame. Fields was far from the worst case of this syndrome. Of Al Jolson, Broadway's biggest star and most prickly ego, it was said that it was easy to keep Jolson happy, you just had to applaud him for breakfast, applaud him for lunch and keep it up till after midnight. Anything less was tantamount to treachery.

But when one looks at the published record – the interviews, news clips and features about Bill Fields throughout the twenties – the downbeat Fields is wholly absent. It is only later, in the thirties, when he transformed this grouchy side into his stock in trade, that the press-wagon began to roll. And then it was Fields himself who lovingly polished up this facet, ascribing it, again and again, to the imaginary hardships of his Dickensian childhood. When one strips away all the excuses, however, we have to conclude that it was his marital strife, above all, that initially hardened his shell.

From *Poppy* onwards, W. C. Fields was a full-fledged Broadway star. But behind the success, his parental wound throbbed continually. And so Fields took refuge in a wonderful fantasy family: the daughter, or adopted daughter, always sweet and adorable, loving her 'Pop,' willing to do anything for him. And he, ready to sacrifice everything – sneaking out at the end so as not to disturb her new-found life of happy marriage and luxury. This phantasm appears in fifteen of Field's forty-five movies, as we shall see. The other component of the fantasy, the once-loved wife, usually a circus trapeze artiste, who was killed in an accident in the little daughter's infancy, was a theme Fields was continually trying to insert into his movies to the bewilderment of studio heads, producers and writing teams who couldn't figure out where on earth this was coming from and what it could possibly have to do with their stories.

Poppy introduced a number of Fields' famous routines: the shell game, the brazen and self-righteous fakery, the poker game in which, worming his way in with no money, he manages to scoop the pot with a flush of fours –

PROF: I love stud poker, although I've only played it once or twice – I forget which . . .

BILL: Lets cut for deal.

PROF: Aw! The old pain – inderstitial, vegititus. The moptic gland of the iris becomes ostracized . . . Has anybody ever tried to cheat you at this game? (*To* POTTLE) Have I ever told you the story of the two blackamoors?

POTTLE: Deal the cards. Deal the cards . . .

And, a short while after –

POTTLE: Well, I win, I have three kings.

PROF: No good, I have four little fours.

POTTLE: Well, what do you know about that?

PROF: Its all science and skill. Its the old army game.

As Madge Kennedy recalled, he varied his act as he pleased, relishing the role that life had prepared him for, so that audiences returned again and again, to see what new tricks he had up his sleeve. *Poppy* ran for 346 performances, a good showing, if far from a Broadway record.

Another outcome of the play was that flamboyant costume: the shabby frock-coat, the stovepipe hat, the checkered pants, the spats, which became as recognisable as Chaplin's tramp, or Harold Lloyd's round, glassless spectacles. Even today, if you seek an image of Fields, that is the first that springs up. It is the image on the memorabilia mugs, the little rubber stamps you may buy in souvenir shops in Hollywood and Beverly Hills. *Poppy* inaugurated Fields as a merchandisable image.

Florenz Ziegfeld, always drawn to success, wanted Fields back in the *Follies*. But Bill had shown that he could carry an entire show on his shoulders, and began looking for another star vehicle. It was not long before he found it, in an unproduced revue by a Chicago journalist whose first full-length play, *The Potters*, had just completed a long run on Broadway. Once again, by happenstance, Fields had come upon material which would profoundly affect his work from that time on. He had met a kindred, equally combative spirit: an ebullient Irishman named Joseph Patrick McEvoy.

Chapter 23
J. P. McEvoy and 'The Comic Supplement'

How fleeting is fame. When I was searching for background for my short booklet on W. C. Fields' 1934 film *It's a Gift*, I noted the opening credit: from 'The Comic Supplement' by J. P. McEvoy. The same credit appears on the titles of the 1926 silent version of the same story, *It's the Old Army Game*. This was intriguing, since Fields was not prone to crediting others for his material, unless they were his own inimitable aliases: Charles Bogle, Mahatma Kane Jeeves, or Otis Criblecoblis. But I had never heard of J. P. McEvoy.

Nevertheless, in his own day, he was well known. From the early 1920s to the mid-1930s, McEvoy wrote and produced half a dozen plays and revues, including three versions of a musical, *Americana*, whose 1932 edition introduced the song, 'Brother, Can You Spare a Dime?' which became the anthem of the Depression. He also published novels, one of which, *Show Girl*, became both a Ziegfeld musical and a movie, leading to a sequel, *Show Girl in Hollywood*, in 1930. He wrote prolifically for magazines like the *Saturday Evening Post* and the *American*, ending up as a roving editor for the *Reader's Digest* until his death in 1958.

He had been born in 1895 in New York, but his earliest jobs were as a reporter for the *South Bend* (Indiana) *News* and two Chicago papers. At a tender age, by his own account, he became a writer of greeting-cards, a job which kept the wolf from the door while he married and begat a family and wrote a volume of poems, published in Chicago in 1919 under the title *Slams of Life, With Malice For All, and Charity Towards None*. These early rhymes provide an early insight into a man who shared certain preoccupations with his future collaborator. For example:

A PLEA FOR CHICAGO HUSBANDS:
An open season once a year

When husbands could be shot,
As in the case of game and deer
Would be a happier lot,
But wives, we beg you hesitate,
Your daily shooting cease,
For we would like to molt and mate
And raise our young in peace.

Other ditties, like 'Never Argue With a Woman', or 'The High Cost of Licker', 'Beware of the Geezer With Something to Sell', 'The Brilliant Iceman' or 'There Ain't No Cure for Golf' ('Written after reading a news story in which a doctor advocated golf as a cure for the inmates of insane asylums') uncannily echo other Fieldsian fixations. None more so, perhaps, than the ode of a weary father to his new child: 'No sweeter baby in the block / Than you, my darling little gem / But why arise at four o'clock / A.M.? / No grouch am I, nor yet a crank / But you have put me on the blink / You cut it out or Paw will spank / You pink.'

This obscure volume did not make McEvoy's fortune, but another idea he managed to sell to the Chicago *Tribune* did. This was a series of illustrated dialogues, little vaudeville vignettes, set in an all-American family named 'The Potters'. A slice of American life, the sketches featured Pa Potter as the paterfamilias who can never live up to his own financial schemes, with Ma Potter as his hen-pecking wife. The strip achieved a wide syndication, to over sixty newspapers, and when McEvoy developed it into a play, Richard Herndon produced it on the stage, with Donald Meek as the ineffectual fortune-seeker.

A critic for the Philadelphia *Inquirer*, Mark Wilson, wrote about *The Potters*:

> The most important factor in the play is the character of Pa Potter, who represents in his brave, if misdirected, efforts the constant struggle of thousands (of) middle class Americans to provide for the family for which they are responsible. Mr McEvoy is a realist. He has given us in 'The Potters' the unvarnished truth, the commonplace of everyday life, and, the strange part of it all is . . . that the things and people we rub elbows with daily are, in many instances, screamingly funny, when viewed in perspective by a disinterested spectator. Personally, I know hundreds of Pa Potters, in fact, whole Potter families and their friends and neighbours, but I never dreamt they were comic till I saw the show at the Lyric.

Pa Potter appears to be a blood-brother to another newly famous character of the day: the anti-hero of novelist Sinclair Lewis's *Babbitt*, published in 1921. Babbitt is a creature of small-town America. Proud of his prejudices and ignorance, Babbitt is a pillar of his community, but he is tormented by a sense of inner emptiness and failure. He worships the clockwork efficiency of industry, but dreams of romance and an escape from it all. Lewis describes 'his luxurious custom to shave while sitting snugly in a tubful of hot water. He may be viewed to-night as a plump, smooth, pink, baldish goodman, robbed of the importance of spectacles, squatting in breast-high water, scraping his lather-smeared cheeks with a safety-razor like a tiny lawn-mower, and with melancholy dignity clawing through the water to recover a slippery and active piece of soap.'

In chronology, Potter preceded Babbitt, which suggests that this kind of character was in the air, a common symptom of industrial America outgrowing and ingrowing at the same time. It is uncanny how, physical features apart, Lewis's Babbitt in the bath prefigures W. C. Fields shaving in the bathroom as we can view him in 1934's *It's a Gift*. This scene was first played by Fields in his filmed version of *The Potters*, his vanished silent movie of 1927, based on McEvoy's play.

I do not know when Fields and McEvoy first met, but it must have been an instant recognition. Contemporary snapshots of McEvoy reveal a brash, confident young man of Fieldsian demeanour, with a (genuine) moustache and a cigar in his mouth. The overall tale might be somewhat like this: a brilliant vaudeville and revue performer, who dabbled in writing his own short but pungent scripts, met a man who shared many of his own views on life and the family and was a seasoned writer, who understood the structure both of short pieces and of a full-length work. They fused – and something new was born.

In early 1924, when Fields was still in the run of *Poppy*, McEvoy had completed the first draft of a satirical revue, based around a Potter-esque family, which he called *The Comic Supplement*. Florenz Ziegfeld, eager to find a way to entice Fields back into his fold, was prevailed upon, by Gene Buck, to commission its production, despite his suspicions of McEvoy, whom he saw as an unwashed hairy hooligan. Julian Mitchell was brought in to direct the show and Norman Bel Geddes to design it.

Two versions of the script of *The Comic Supplement* are extant, and the differences between them show the bent of McEvoy's original ideas, and the impact of Fields' collaboration with him. The first, 1924 draft, is McEvoy's work alone. The '1925 version', which was that produced on stage, was written by McEvoy and Fields.

McEvoy's original concept, as relayed to press agent Bernard Sobel, was this:

I am not making any efforts to adapt comic supplement technique to the stage or materialize comic supplement characters, rather I am going back to the original idea of caricaturing life which all the cartoonists started out with . . . 'The Comic Supplement' is an honest effort to reflect the absurdities, comicalities and the wistful futilities of American life in a multicolored panorama of story, song, ballet and pantomime. I am striving to achieve in 'The Comic Supplement' continuity of interest and idea, speed, fun, beauty and, above all, the bounce of vitality with the steadying certitude of a definite viewpoint.

In other words, McEvoy had a specific satirical and even political attitude to what was generally seen as a purely escapist genre. In the 1924 version this is expressed through sixteen scenes, in two acts, with titles such as 'The Bathing Beach', 'The Drug Store', 'The Cafeteria (Ballet)', 'City Apartment', 'City Street', 'Outline of American History', 'The Movie', 'City Life', and so on. The play opens with a Potter-style family in their apartment – Father, Mother, son Johnny and little daughter Gertie, who is climbing all over Papa's neck as he reads the funnies:

GERTIE: What's this one about, Dad? Read this one. Isn't this funny? Look at this one.

FATHER: Beat it, will you, the both of you.

MOTHER: Why don't you take a little interest in your children's welfare. You're their father, aren't you?

FATHER: Don't rub it in. I was young and I didn't know.

This domestic bliss is interrupted by a radio broadcast of the Reverend William Jones on 'What we American Christians Should Do for the Benighted Peoples of Other Lands.' McEvoy's stage instructions then read:

Scene changes to 'comic supplement interior', the family in vivid cartoon style colored dress, a brutal pantomime interrupted only by 'Zowie's',

'Oook's' 'Pow's' etc, *as various members of family are hit with bricks,*
clubs, etc. General pandemonium, during which Radio Sermon proceeds
with unctuous deliberation . . .

RADIO: I am sure, my friends, you all remember the story of Cain and Abel,
and how when Cain became jealous of Abel he struck him on the head with
a club and killed him. Ah, the violence of those primitive days. How fortunate we have become more civilized . . .

The radio spiel continues as the scene changes back from cartoon
violence to the real family, as Father finishes off reading out from the
comic supplement page:

FATHER: Blooie . . . Blam . . . Blupp, blupp . . . Gag . . . Pow . . .

Lights out.

Next in the script is the Drug Store scene. This has always been considered one of W. C. Fields' most basic sketches. It would be first filmed
in his silent feature, *It's the Old Army Game,* in 1926, then lovingly
reprised in the 1933 Mack Sennett short, *The Pharmacist,* revamped
and revised in *It's a Gift,* and even reconstituted as a radio sketch in
1938. It became one of Fields' favourite routines, but the record shows
that its originator was J.P. McEvoy alone. In McEvoy's draft, the
Proprietor of the store is 'the pathetic father of the comic supplement
family. A boy of all work is sweeping the floor . . .' A haughty woman
comes in and wants to see the telephone directory. A brisk businessman wants a two cent stamp. A flapper comes in and engages the
counter boy in 'a long unprofitable talk'. An 'excited woman' rushes in
and wants some medicine for her coughing baby. Then 'a mannish
looking woman enters' –

MANNISH WOMAN: Are you the proprietor of this business? (*points accusing*
finger at cowering DRUGGIST *who nods assent*) I represent the Society for
the Prevention of Cruelty to Armenians.

DRUGGIST: But I haven't been cruel to any Armenians.

WOMAN: Perhaps not, although I would not put it past you. The point is,
have you done anything for them? If not, why not? If so, when? I'll tell you
when. Now, now is the time to come to the aid of the poor Armenians.
Your quota is ten dollars . . . Did you know that one dollar will feed two
Armenians and a half for eleven days? . . .

Other people come in wanting to use the telephone. Someone phones and wants a box of cough-drops delivered. Then loud shouts are heard from the street, and two policemen bring in a woman who has fainted on the street.

Fields was to develop the Drug Store sketch further, adding all manner of little embellishments along the way. But the bulk of the sketch is the same. The woman collecting for Armenians, the businessman with the stamp, the fainting woman, and a line where the policeman hesitates to give her a swig from a bottle, saying: 'It's a shame to give this to anybody that's unconscious.' The 1925 draft has some lovely new lines, like the woman who comes in to demand: 'I would like to see some of your invisible hairnets at once.' There is a 'foreigner' who comes in mouthing gobbledegook and wanting something removed from his eye. In his later screen versions, Fields was to add bits of business like the businessman wanting his two-cent stamp from the middle of the sheet, or embellish the cough-drop gag: 'What's that? A box of Smith Brothers cough-drops? No, I'm sorry we can't split a box. Can't separate the Brothers. Yes, we can deliver – I'll send our truck right away.'*

The framework family, the long-suffering Pa, hen-pecking Ma, the soppy baby child, all derive from McEvoy's original text, but fit perfectly with Fields own *Follies* family of Fanny Brice and Ray Dooley. Modes of operation of the two collaborators, despite the similarities, are different, and not what we might expect: McEvoy paints with broad strokes, befitting his journalistic and comic-strip experience (he was also to write a long-lasting syndicated comic strip called 'Dixie Dugan' [the original *Show Girl*]). His voice is loud, his gabbiness Irish. Fields' contribution is to the subtleties, the little points, the absurd trivia. McEvoy's 1924 version is unashamedly political in its satire – 'A City Street' features a War Parade, with banners saying: 'DO YOUR BIT, HELP POOR LITTLE JUGO SLAVIA, SHE WILL NEVER FORGET', and other banners, of clashing marchers, under the strains of the 'Star Spangled Banner': 'HURRAY FOR THE KU KLUX KLAN – ONE HUNDRED PER CENT AMERICAN', 'DOWN WITH THE KU KLUX KLAN', 'NO MORE IMMIGRANTS', 'DOWN WITH THE CAPITALISTS', 'DOWN WITH LABOR'. The stage instructions read: '*Lights changing . . . dusk . . . cops wildly gesticulating and whistling . . . groups of workmen appear and start to tear up the street,*

* *It's the Old Army Game.*

beginning to sing in tune with sledges . . . workers chorus changes tone and tempo to denote protest and then a primitive, helpless rage . . .'

This was a hot time in American politics – the so-called 'Teapot Dome' scandal, concerning corruption of government in oil company loans, erupted in March 1924. A bill limiting immigration was passed in May. But all these political strains in McEvoy's manuscript were cut from the 1925 version.

The 1925 *Comic Supplement* is a much expanded and very different revue. There are forty-four scenes, more song and dance numbers, more beach numbers, more Fieldsian specialties. Two songwriters, Con Conrad and Henry Souvaine, were brought in to beef up, or rather thin out, the gruel with such ditties as 'Cafeteria Chow', 'The Cop and the Nurse', 'Goo Goo Goo', 'The Scrubwomen's Ballet' and 'The Sunday Poipers'. Baby-talk courting between daughter Myrtle and suitor George is brought to the forefront of the show. It has been Ziegfeldized, with a Bathing Beach Tableau, Comic Supplement Ballet, Kissing Number and full stage Cabaret.

Ziegfeld reportedly bought the script for $3,000 and gave Fields carte blanche to write his numbers. Bill took full advantage of the opportunity, setting one of his latest 'vaudeville' scripts – 'The Back Porch', at the opening of the work, as an 'Alley Scene', and adding a Billiard Scene, an Elevator Scene and 'The Joyride', later known as his 'Picnic Sketch', as well as developing lines and business throughout the entire text. Taking McEvoy's original 'Pa Potter' type and moulding it and expanding it to suit his purposes. 'Pa Jones', in *The Comic Supplement*, became the second side of the W. C. Fields of the future, to complement Eustace McGargle. An additional element, deriving from a Julian Street short story called 'Mister Bisbee's Princess' – which was to be the basis for his films *So's Your Old Man* and *You're Telling Me* – would later flesh out 'Pa' and make him into the iconic Fields of *It's a Gift, Man on the Flying Trapeze* and *The Bank Dick*.

The Back Porch scene was to be another Fields staple, revived on screen for the silent *It's the Old Army Game* and brought to genius in *It's a Gift*. 'Pa' is trying to sleep on a swing on the back porch while a host of nuisances combine to drive him crazy. In *The Comic Supplement* the added pain is that of a raging toothache. It is dawn. The Milkman stomps up and down the stairs with wooden shoes and his crate of 'musical bottles'. A dog howls. Alarm clocks go off all over the place. The iceman comes with a huge block of ice. Bill was clearly paying back one of his teenage grudges.

ICEMAN: ICE! ICE!

PA: I heard you!

ICEMAN (*louder*): I C E !

PA (*trying to hide under covers*): OH! MY GOD!

ICEMAN: Where do you want it? Huh?

PA: Put it in the box. Where do you suppose?

ICEMAN: Where's the box?

PA (*indicating*): There!

ICEMAN: Where'll I put it?

PA: In the box!

ICEMAN: SAY LISTEN, IF YOU FEEL THAT WAY ABOUT IT BOZO, YOU CAN PUT IT IN YUSSELF.

The iceman leaves the ice behind and Pa grapples to put in the box, but it keeps slipping, finally falling away through a stage drop. Pa returns to bed but the alley is alive with men shouting. A scissors grinder, fish peddlers, vegetable peddlers, coal peddlers, etc. The script says: '*Lay it on thick.*' Ma comes in, wheeling their baby in a buggy. The baby wails. Pa wheels it off into the alley then goes back to his swing, but is woken again by Myrtle and Ma talking:

MA (*in a loud voice*): Myrtle! Myrtle!

MYRTLE (*louder*): What do you want?

MA: Do you know what you're going after now?

MYRTLE: You said you wanted a loaf of bread, didn't you?

MA: Better get two loaves, while you're at it.

MYRTLE: Won't one be enough?

MA: No, better get two.

MYRTLE: One's enough.

MA: All right then, bring one.

MYRTLE: I can bring two just as easy.

And so on. Ah, the enraging fickleness of women! The predelictions of both Fields and McEvoy were apparent in this dialogue, which was to reappear in a slightly different form nine years later in *It's a Gift*. Pa's next ordeal is a routine of courting couple George and Myrtle, with little Gertie pouncing on them from behind –

MYRTLE: Does itsi-witsi like Georgie-porgie?

GERTIE: Ga, ga, ga, ga.

A surfeit of this would goad Saint Francis to murder, not to speak of the 'Goo Goo Goo' song. The 'Alley Scene' crescendos with a Grind Organ playing a medley of old music and a dance of alley kids. This leads directly to the 'Sunday Papers' number, which leads in turn to 'The Comic Supplement Family', which is a rewrite of McEvoy's opening scene from 1924. This openly posits a supporting cast of 'Comic Strip Characters: Krazy Kat, Ignatz Mouse, Mutt & Jeff, Happy Hooligan, Abe Kabbible, etc.,' but the radio voice, instead of presenting McEvoy's anti-religious satire, is now offering 'Madam Casaba who will now sing a simple little Russian folk song, "Yutska Gazutska."'

In Fields' 'vaudeville' sketch, named 'The Sleeping Porch' – which may be either the origin or a spin-off of the 'Alley Scene' – the action is set out mainly in pantomime, as a vehicle for the familiar 'Mr Fliverton' of 'The Family Ford' and 'Off to the Country'. As in the Golf sketch, the business is set out in meticulous detail:

At rise of curtain Fliverton is discovered on his sleeping porch trying to sleep. A newsboy with hair all slicked down and bright, highly shined shoes that squeak as he walks, ascends stairs leading up to sleeping porch, passes porch upon which F. is sleeping and continues to floor above. As he passes floor upon which F. is trying to sleep., F. awakened from his sleep looks hazily about the porch in quest of the strange noise.

Fliverton not being able to locate same returns to his pillow for further rest. The newsboy having delivered his paper on the upper floor, descends stairs passing floor upon which F. is trying to sleep. F. bestirs himself this time making a more detailed inspection of the sleeping porch, ultimately going into the house bringing with him a rat trap, and placing it in corner of porch. F. returns to port swing, as he sits upon edge of swing, rafters overhead groan under his weight. F. looks about him with some misgivings as to the security of the hammock supports. When comfortably settled in the swing, the right support gives way permitting hammock to drop about a foot, then almost immediately following, the support drops further, entirely, permitting that end of hammock to drop to floor.

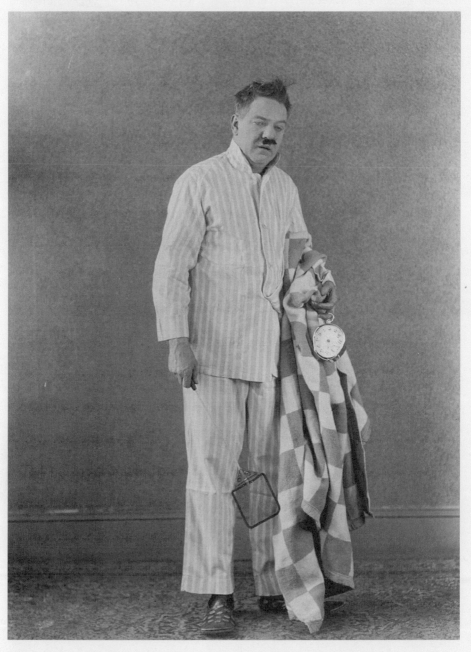

15 *The Comic Supplement*: Pa Jones stocking up for the back porch.

Here there are elements unused in *The Comic Supplement* but which echo down to *It's a Gift* in 1934. A particular disturbance in the sketch version is a 'Holland hired girl' who runs upstairs in heavy sabots. She is calling out for 'Mrs Fuchwants!' – a name that will echo, too, down the years until it would play the most astonishing part in Fields' war with the Hollywood censor over *Never Give a Sucker An Even Break*, *circa* 1941! The baby carriage, the vegetable vendor, and the iceman all feature.

The 1925 Drug Store sketch, as we have seen, is largely unchanged. But there is more tussling, at home between Pa and little Gertie, who introduces herself to her newly hired Nurse by emptying her purse, kicking her and running out with Ma in hot pursuit. Pa says to the Nurse: 'Isn't she a friendly child? Always like that. As playful as a mountain lion.' In his movie career, Fields would find Baby Le Roy to replace Rae Dooley's Gertie, and the person being kicked would always be himself. However, his much-famed war with tiny tots starts in earnest here, accompanied by the particularly savage comment, in the later 'Joyride' scene, to Ma:

PA: I'm beginning to understand those animals you read about where the mother has got to hide the young so the father won't eat 'em.

Another sequence, included in the 1925 text, but never produced on the stage, is entitled 'American Bar'. In the scene Ma and Pa Jones are exiting from 'a Harrigan and Hart' show, in evening dress. The show prompts Pa to remember the good old days – 'the old Metropole and the Fifth Avenue Bar and the old songs and stories!' The bar then materializes before him, and an entire sequence of old Harrigan and Hart songs are played within while Ma bends down to retrieve a glove – perhaps the glove that a woman had to pick up in Philadelphia if she were not to be accused of 'strip-teasing'. Though one can't be sure, the odds are the scene was written by Fields, in an unusually candid nostalgic mode. The stage instructions read:

In the entire scene Pa is an unhappy outcast. He is in, but not of the past. The gay, roistering men of the old days are having a rollicking good time but this should be done as though this was a memory rather than a reality. No one should speak to Pa or be conscious of his presence.

Pa leaves the bar, 'sad and thoughtful', while Ma is still frozen in the act of picking up her glove. She says to him: 'You are not paying attention to me. I asked you if you did not think it was much better now without those nasty old bar rooms they used to have?' To which Pa answers: 'I was just thinking, dear . . . just thinking . . .'

But the nostalgic stuff was cut from the show. Fields was compensated with his more familiar Billiard Scene, which was tied in to Pa Jones's role as civic leader of the 'Royal Sons of Arcola Parade'. An early sample of the tiny Masonic jokes sprinkled through some of Bill's texts: 'This is the first time the Royal Sons of Arcola paraded since I was elected exalted keeper of the Royal Wampus.' In the parade scene, later on: 'Band appears, followed by Pa . . . wearing a tremendous red sash round his shoulders and a sword that is much too long hanging on a heavy belt.' A cop tries to stop them parading without a permit, and little Gertie urges Pa to stab the cop with his sword –

GERTIE: Cut his gizzard out Pa.

PA (*feels around him and succeeds in getting* GERTIE *by throat*): But listen the band is here and our parade and our float with all our prize-winning pretty girls on it.

COP (*gallantly*): Oh, that's different. Bring on your parade. I'll watch it myself.

Vanity, thy name is Ziegfeld. But the pretty girls did not, in the end, save the day. *The Comic Supplement* was a lavish production, but it was doomed to be short-lived. As was the custom with New York shows, it opened out of town, at the National Theatre in Washington, DC, on 20 January 1925, then moved to Newark, New Jersey, on 26 January, where it played for three weeks, and closed on 14 February. It never opened on Broadway. Ziegfeld closed the show, proclaiming it a failure. The audiences, he said, were not responding. This is only partly borne out by the reviews. The *Star* commented:

Florenz Ziegfeld waved his wand at the National Theatre last night and brought vividly to life the boisterous, flamboyant comic supplement of America's Sunday newspapers, immersed in the trappings and pulchritude of a Ziegfeldian revue . . . W. C. Fields' . . . Pa Jones was robustly comical, rollicking, and at times his pantomime brought shrieks of laughter . . . (But) somehow the idea of the whole, with its heterogeneity, failed to strike home . . . There is almost as much machinery as in a circus: Freak radios, a trick automobile, a whole apartment in a folding piano, automatic pool tables, a huge Riverside bus with wheels that go round, and a row of elevator doors.

Certainly the staging of the piece was highly ambitious, and designer Norman Bel-Geddes was acclaimed as a 'unique genius' for his extraordinary designs. Another clipping described the work as 'undoubtedly . . . the greatest extravaganza ever assembled on the stage. A three-ring circus, in comparison to "The Comic Supplement," is totally devoid of attractions.' Norman Bel-Geddes, in his autobiographical book *Miracle In the Evening*, takes up the tale:

> As far as Ziegfeld was concerned, the only reason anyone came to any of his revues was to see his girls. Men came to see their bodies, and women came to see their clothes, if any. The comedians in his shows were there only to entertain the vulgarians who did not, or could not, sufficiently appreciate his girls. At no time during the rehearsals or after did Ziegfeld read the script. His sole knowledge of what his show was all about derived from what Gene Buck told him or what he picked up as he wandered in and out of rehearsals . . . In the first few days of rehearsal . . . he threw out four comedy sketches and ordered me to design four new, full-stage settings for new girl numbers to replace them . . .
>
> But it all went in. Opening night at the National Theatre, the final curtain came down at one-thirty in the morning. W. C. Fields and Rae Dooley, instead of appearing, as stars customarily did, a half-dozen times during the performance, were in ten of the thirty-one acts. The surprising thing was that all the material looked excellent. It was, perhaps, the laughingest show ever seen. The audience was howling to the bitter end, and beyond.
>
> Ziegfeld was horrified. He had spent most of the performance in the lobby, wincing, and had come in at one point to find the audience laughing at one of his chorus numbers. This was the height of disrespect . . .

Ziegfeld went home and wired a series of his typically vitriolic telegrams to McEvoy. McEvoy wired back. Ziegfeld wanted to close the show. Bel-Geddes was horrified. He had created a ground-breaking design, which would later be the basis for choreographer Busby Berkeley's stunning dance numbers. The New York *Telegraph* raved that 'his Times Square is gorgeously contrived with pencil gray structures spinning back, like a huge divided wave, into such a blue as will lift you from your seat'. Bel-Geddes approached Fields and offered to buy the show off Ziegfeld with himself as producer. Fields agreed. Bel-Geddes offered Ziegfeld $100,000. According to Bel-Geddes, Ziegfeld agreed, but then went off and closed the show anyway. He had spent $150,000 on *The Comic Supplement*, but he was willing to write it all off.

For good or ill, Ziegfeld always followed his hunches. He understood his *Follies* formula. But any whiff of satire knocked him cold. McEvoy's contempt for his formula was clearly evident. No matter that the show might have been a hit in New York. Ziegfeld could not accept any ego but his own in charge of one of his attractions.

In 1932, an interview with McEvoy about his show, *Americana*, was headlined: 'J. P. MCEVOY NAILS HIS HOPES ON EXISTENCE OF INTELLIGENCE: Author of "Americana" Believes There Are Many Persons Who Like Their Humor Whetted to Fine Edge, So He Makes His "Mosaic of a Thousand Details".' Walter Winchell called *Americana* 'a jokeless revusical', and McEvoy was slowly eased off Broadway. He had been rich and successful in his mid to late twenties, had acquired a home at Woodstock and a pack of St Bernard dogs. He puffed Havana cigars 'from shower-bath to pyjama time'. He had his day in the sun.

McEvoy's influence on Bill Fields was profound and long-lasting. He brought the world of comic strips, of journalistic observation and economy of style, of the combination of realism and exaggeration, into a much sharper focus for his partner. Bearing in mind Fields' early dabbling in cartoons, he was as steeped as any other American newspaper reader in the wacky world of the 'funnies'. And he had himself said, in an interview in the New Jersey *Herald*: 'There are many little incidents . . . in a street car or elsewhere that are full of natural humor, and I want to crochet them together into acts.' But Bill's overwhelming influences were from the actor's life, the stage, the self-contained world of vaudeville and music-hall. McEvoy supplied a much needed boost, and then faded out, but not completely. Bill was to bring him back to script one of his sharpest 'Pa Jones' characterizations, as Sam Bisbee, in *You're Telling Me*, in 1934. The social satire, which McEvoy laid on so thickly in the 1920s, becomes, in Fields' later work, a backdrop against which the Fieldsian character wends his rocky, troubled way.

Curiously, but perhaps not so suprisingly, Fields never wrote about McEvoy, and McEvoy, in his blizzard of magazine articles, only wrote two about his old colleague: 'He Knew What They Wanted', and 'W. C. Fields' Best Friend', in which he describes Fields in his Hollywood mansion, and recounts the usual childhood myths. It's clear that McEvoy's relationship with Fields was solely professional, and that he never got beyond the outer skin.

After Ziegfeld killed *The Comic Supplement*, he lured Fields back to

16 J. P. McEvoy (standing, left) with W. C. Fields, Cary Grant, Carl Brisson with Henry Wilcoxon, Queenie Smith, Emanuel Cohen, Katherine de Mille and Mary Boland at a banquet for Cohen, Paramount's head of production, 1934.

the 1925 *Follies* – in a special 'Spring Edition', by including four of the 'Comic Supplement' skits: 'The Drug Store', 'A Back Porch', 'A Road – the Joyride' and 'The Picnic'. The New York Sunday *Times* called it 'the best Follies in years'. The *Times* added:

> The outstanding feature of the new production is W. C. Fields. Not so long ago Fields was known only as a limited specialty comedian – last night he clearly proved his right to be called one of the supreme comedians of our time. His is the comic spirit that is able to play upon his audience's sense of the ludicrous as well through his delivery of his lines as through his physical actions. And the New Amsterdam was filled last night with the hysterical gasping of its patrons . . .

Fields could afford to mark a strategic retreat from solo stardom, because he had already broken through on the front which had thrown him back into the trenches in 1915. He had made his first appearance since that year in a cameo role in a movie, *Janice Meredith*, and had been approached with an offer he could not refuse to translate his stage hit, *Poppy*, into film. He was about to embark upon his next adventure, a far cry indeed from the abortive *Pool Sharks*. Both Ziegfeld and producer Philip Goodman wanted to sign him to long-term contracts, but Bill saw his star in another portion of the heavens.

In order to climb that stairway, however, he had to lose his voice. And thereby lies the wry twist in the tale . . .

Part IV
Voiceless in Eden

Chapter 24
'Under Which Shell is the Little Pea?'

The hardest thing to put into the movies is a human being . . . People in real life do very human things just by acting natural. The moment you get them to try to *act* those things, they usually become artificial and strained . . . People who are funny are people who are sincere . . . The easy, free laughter that is the true reward of real comedy never comes from self-conscious or insincere acting. Real comedy must be the most human of all acting, for it portrays inevitably the weaknesses and absurdities of life. The insincere can pretend the strengths of human nature and realize more or less success in their playing; but comedy will infallibly expose the insincere . . . Probably none of us is so familiar with the strengths of human nature as with its weaknesses. That

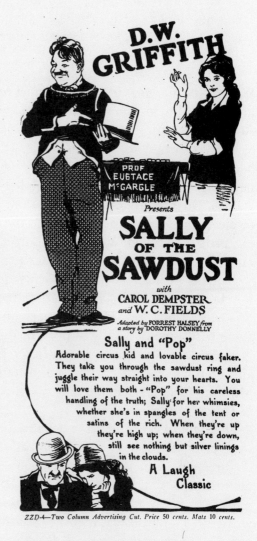

17 Poster for *Sally of the Sawdust*.

259

is why the public is quicker to detect the unreal in comedy than in serious drama.

We have fortunately captured many laughs in *Sally of the Sawdust*. It was done without great effort. That is because the characters of Sally McGargle and her lovable old 'Pop', the great Prof. Eustace McGargle, are real.

Miss Dempster has played the role with sincerity and W. C. Fields, who plays the professor, is undoubtedly one of the greatest comedians, whether on stage or screen.

It is his earnesteness and sincerity that makes Fields great. Never have I directed a more charming person nor a harder worker. He is the drolleries and the laughter of life itself. Two minutes in his presence, and one is laughing. Yet he works as diligently and far harder than any bricklayer.

D. W. Griffith, in Press Notes for *Sally of the Sawdust*

Sally of the Sawdust was a good start for Bill Fields as a movie star in his own right. In *Janice Meredith*, a two and a half hour epic of the American Revolution, he had turned up for three minutes as a British Sergeant flirting with Marion Davies who is getting him drunk to free her lover, an American spy. The overblown film was a production by newspaper baron William Randolph Hearst for his young protégée, Davies. Directed by one E. Mason Hopper, it is not a neglected masterpiece. But Fields landed a part in the movie, due to a young managing producer called William Le Baron, who was director-general of Hearst's Cosmopolitan Pictures at the time.

William Le Baron was Bill Fields' most important and influential fan. Louise Brooks described him as 'the most extraordinary man who was ever in pictures. He was a very intelligent man, a very tall handsome Irish type . . . He was born in Illinois, and then he came out to New York and he was more or less a playwright and a play adaptor, and then Mr Hearst gave him a job and he produced the first movie Marion Davies ever made that was a success, *When Knighthood Was in Flower*.'

That would certainly have delighted Hearst. Cosmopolitan's movies were being distributed by Adolph Zukor and Jesse Lasky's Paramount Pictures, and when Zukor allowed the generally unprofitable Hearst pictures to be taken over by his ex-partner Goldwyn, Le Baron remained as an associate-producer with Paramount. From then on, whenever Le Baron was in any position of power, W. C. Fields worked at Paramount, and all his silent pictures were made for or in conjunction with their studios. This fortune continued into the sound era, when fourteen of Fields' twenty starring role features were produced by Le Baron.

In 1925 Paramount had two major studio complexes: the grand lot in Hollywood and a new purpose-built studio in Long Island, completed in 1920, which has today become the American Museum of the Moving Image, at Astoria, Queens. It was the largest film studio on the East Coast, and Fields' first six silent features were all shot there.

D.W. Griffith, the silent cinema's most famous director, was also transferring to Paramount. Griffith had become disillusioned with United Artists, the company he had founded 1919 with actors Charles Chaplin, Mary Pickford and Douglas Fairbanks, and had turned to Zukor and Lasky. But before signing with Paramount, he decided to mount his own independent production, at Astoria. The story he chose was W. C. Fields' stage hit, *Poppy*.

It was a strange alliance. Griffith had directed, since 1908, every conceivable kind of picture, as well as transforming the cinema forever with his epics *Birth of a Nation* in 1915 and *Intolerance* in 1916. But comedy was not his forte. He was, above all, the master of melodrama, in the finest sense of that word. Since the early 1920s his star was waning, and he was looking for new directions to explore. His own 1924 epic of the American Revolution, *America,* had bombed, and his next project, *Isn't Life Wonderful?*, a tale of Europe's economic woes shot in Germany, was not having much impact. So adapting *Poppy* may have been a welcome diversion.

But Griffith was Griffith after all, a battered but not unbowed master. It was probably he who changed the name of the show from 'Poppy', to reflect the changes he wanted to make to the story. The main attraction of the story was the leading female role, which he thought was tailor-made for twenty-three-year-old actress Carol Dempster, with whom he was completely besotted. Griffith tried to build her up, claiming that she had reached 'a very high standard of screen appeal' in this movie, but she did not shine outside his embrace. It appears she resented being upstaged by Fields, and, after seeing the film in the cutting-room, prevailed on Griffith to shoot some extra, gratuitous close-ups of her.

Griffith threw himself into *Sally of the Sawdust* with characteristic intensity. The film opens with the big show riding into town: the elephants, the lions in their cages, the acrobats, the cootch-dancers doing

18 Professor McGargle and the cigar-box trick: with Carol Dempster in
Sally of the Sawdust.

their fling. The action has been updated from the carnival era of the
1870s to modern times – 1920. Professor Eustace McGargle and the
young girl, Sally, mingle with the crowd. McGargle sits on the elephant's podium, but is pushed off by its trunk. Sally nuzzles the pachyderm. A title:

SALLY – A CIRCUS WAIF –
WHOSE ONLY HOME HAS BEEN THE BIG TOP.

We fade, after this introduction, to the first scene of W. C.
Fields/McGargle in action. He leaps forth, upon a side-show stage,
dressed in a tight-fitting jacket and those baggy checkered pants, with
light top-hat, and that 'misplaced eyebrow', juggling vigorously with
three rubber balls.

This is our first proper sight of Bill Fields since 1915. He is manifestly
in top form. He is forty-five years old but looks much younger, his figure still in good trim, his pale eyes shining with a kind of mischievous

delight. A ball bounces off the stage, to be caught by a short awkward man with a large cap, in the front row, who climbs on the stage and hands back the ball. Fields throws the balls up behind his back, as the stooge's head bobs up and down, and then pushes the rube off the stage. This is one of only two sightings on film – the other is in *So's Your Old Man* – of Fields' long-term stage valet, 'Shorty', alias William Blanche.

Those who saw Fields in the theatre are divided as to the manner of his act on the stage. Some say his forte was a languid casualness, the typical juggler's trick of making it all seem so easy. But we have also seen him develop his sassy and disgruntled act, Pa Jones or Mr Fliverton, as well as dancing and even singing for his Ziegfeld gold. The screen Fields has, already in his first proper role, a jaunty optimism, an aura that expresses a vigorous belief in his own star, that showbiz adage, that every cloud has a silver lining. His movements already suggest a man caught between a natural grace of the spirit and the innate clumsiness of his own body, that threat from the material universe to his blithe dreams.

The Professor introduces Sally, who does a graceful dance, eyed lustfully by an acrobat, Leon. Deprived of words, McGargle mouths them anyway, emoting his bright glee at the performance of his ward. A title concludes his unheard peroration:

STEP INSIDE AND SEE THE GREATEST SHOW ON EARTH!

There follows a bit of business where McGargle lifts an old man's wallet, but loses it to the elephant, so that the victim can retrieve it from its trunk. McGargle moves on, inevitably, to the shell game, intertitled – 'It's not a game of chance – it's a game of science and skill – the old army game! – Your eyes against my hand! – Under which shell is the little pea?' One of the yokels tempted is a youthful Tammany Young, later to replace 'Shorty' as Fields' main stooge in sound films. A fight develops, with fists and cudgels, and Sally raises the age-old circus cry of 'Hey rube!' – calling the general alarm.

Nursing her black eye in her tent, Sally is attacked by Leon, who tries to kiss her. McGargle enters and chases him away. A title: 'McGargle, whom Sally has always worshipped as a real father, suddenly realises a father's responsibility.' He fondly takes out an old photograph, triggering a flashback to Sally's dying mother, years before: 'Since my husband was taken, you have been my only friend, McGargle. Do what is best for Sally.'

This is the only instance in which Fields was able to insert the scene of the dying 'wife' who bequeathed him his adoring 'daughter'. It is not surprising that it was Griffith, alone, who allowed him to do this. The scene was not in the stage *Poppy*. Some writers about Fields have assumed that Fields' and Griffith's systems of working were opposites – Griffith's discipline clashing with Fields' ad-libbing – but we now know that Fields was the most disciplined of actors, when he was working with those he respected. Louise Brooks wrote about Field's work in *Sally*, in her book, *Lulu in Hollywood*:

> He paid no attention to camera setups. For each shot, he would rehearse the same business to exasperating perfection while his co-star, Carole Dempster, and the Director D.W. Griffith sat bored and limp in chairs beside the camera. Long shot, medium shot, two-shot or close-up, Bill performed as if he were standing whole before an audience that could appreciate every detail of his costume and follow the dainty disposition of his hands and feet. Every time the camera drew closer, it cut off another piece of him and deprived him of some comic effect . . . As he ignored camera setups, he ignored the cutting room, and could only curse the finished film, seeing his timing ruined by haphazard cuts.

But elsewhere, when interviewed for the Astoria Studio's oral histories, Louise Brooks said that 'Griffith would leave Bill alone, and then, when Carol Dempster, when it was time to direct her, then he was all attention. But she was not a friendly girl, in fact she was very withdrawn . . .'

That Griffith and Fields clicked is affirmed by the fact that Griffith cast him again in his next film, *That Royle Girl*. But one has only to look at *Sally of the Sawdust*, in the mint print at New York's Museum of Modern Art, to realise that this was, in fact, Fields' best-directed picture.

Griffith was drawn to *Poppy* because the story mirrored his own taste for tales of redemption through an unselfish love, set against the self-destructiveness of snobbish, moralising puritans. McGargle is not Sally's father, but he sacrifices all for her. Sally's real surviving relations are her grandmother and grandfather, the stern old judge who wants to send her and her 'Pop' to jail as common carnival cheats. Sally is another quintessential Griffith heroine, plucky but battered by an uncaring world, like Mae Marsh in *Intolerance*, or Lilian and Dorothy Gish in *Orphans of the Storm*.

To provide the love interest Griffith cast Alfred Lunt, a star of the legitimate stage, as the young and rich Peyton Lennox, whom Sally will marry at the end. The whole story has a very Dickensian tone, with echoes of *Oliver Twist* and *Little Dorrit*. This was another mutual interest that drew Griffith and Fields together. Eustace McGargle was a new departure for Griffith, and so the great director gave the actor his freedom to create the character as he saw fit. Griffith was the only director whom Bill Fields ever openly praised, despite his personal friendship with several of his later directors, like Gregory La Cava and Eddie Sutherland. Ronald Fields quotes Bill on Griffith: 'He gives actors credit for having some brains. He is one of the finest men I had ever met.'

Further paralleling Dickens, Griffith slewed the story away from the circus comedy and further towards the melodrama, though he gave Fields a great intertitle when McGargle first meets the stern old Judge Foster – 'Got a face that looks like it's worn out four bodies.' There is a neat gag with a little dog and a watering can that enables Fields to kick a canine for the first time on screen. In the same sequence, McGargle dissuades Sally from throwing a small stone at the snobbish Fosters' house, handing her, after a pause, a much larger rock.

Griffith also changed the central premise of *Poppy* – that McGargle is unaware that Poppy is, in fact, the heiress of the rich couple he is trying to swindle into thinking she is. This was too cynical a ploy for Griffith. In *Sally*, McGargle knows all along the Judge is her real grandfather, and has in fact taken her to the Judge's town, Green Meadows, to reunite them, but, when he sees how harsh the Judge behaves towards mendicant circus folk, a title states: 'McGargle quiets his conscience with the thought that Sally would be happier in ignorance of her parentage.'

Another title sees him 'Determined to keep the secret and hold Sally for himself.' This idea is reinforced at the end, when McGargle reveals the papers that prove Sally to be Judge Foster's grandchild and says: 'It was I, your Honor, who wrote you of her tragic demise.' Pause, and another title: 'But, somehow, I forgot to mention the child.' One can see the echoes of the frustrated father leaking out again, the fantasy daughter easing the pain.

Before this sentimental finale there is a satisfying amount of business allowing Fields to display his routines, mainly at the 'Annual Carnival for the Benefit of Homeless Orphans'. We get a brief, tantalising glimpse of the cigar-box act which we shall not see again until *The Old Fashioned Way*, and an appearance, in a backyard, of the peanut roaster-cum-liquor cart first seen in the *Follies* of 1916. The little cart, a converted baby carriage, came complete with a portable brass footrail and sawdust to sprinkle on the ground. Incidentally, a recent book on Walt Disney's silent animation days reveals that Disney, having seen this gag in *Sally of the Sawdust*, copied it in one of his 'Oswald the Rabbit' films, to create a mechanical Blind Pig, which opened up to allow one Putrid Pete to dispense bootleg liquor from its insides. Thus did the strip cartoon influence come full circle.

Arrested for gambling, McGargle escapes down the suburban streets of 'Green Meadow' in a rug and Indian feathered head-dress, a perfectly surreal moment. The Sheriff arrests Sally as McGargle's accomplice, and we end with a typical Griffith cross-cut between her trial for vagrancy and a rush by Fields across country in a car purloined from some crooks, culminating in his line, as he dashes into the courtroom with the telling documents that save Sally: 'I'd have been here sooner, but I was thrown by a Ford!'

Redeemed and justified, McGargle walks off, Chaplinlike, down an empty road, but he is dragged back by Sally and her new family. The film ends on an un-Chaplinesque but very Fieldsian note: McGargle, now richly attired in fur coat, bowler hat and cigar, is motoring down with Sally and the Judge to show them his new enterprise, a giant sign proclaiming:

J. EUSTACE MCGARGLE – REALTOR.
CHOICE LOTS FOR SALE.
EVERY INVESTOR SHARES IN PROFIT.

Pointing to which, with his cigar, the Professor exclaims: 'The old army game!' The car reverses out of frame, and fade.

The entire movie was shot on the stage of the Astoria Studios and on locations further along Long Island. *The Great Neck News* for Saturday 23 May 1925, recorded with pride that David Wark Griffith had chosen Russell Gardens, Great Neck's newest development, to use for his latest movie. Presumably this was referring to the epilogue scenes. Great Neck and Bayside were becoming ideal suburbs for wealthy New Yorkers itching to get away from the blare of Manhattan, and many theatrical stars were moving there too. Mary Pickford, Eddie Cantor and Groucho Marx bought houses here, and

Fields too found it a congenial escape – there was a fine golf course nearby. Eventually he was to move into a house at 35–25 223rd Street in Bayside, and commute from there to the studio or to his hotel haunts in New York City when theatrical engagements required.

Sally enabled Bill to go back to his oldest forte in acting: pantomime. Having been performing mime when Chaplin was in short pants he saw no reason why he could not compete with the giants of silent screen comedy. In an interview following the release of the movie, Fields told Ruth Waterbury of *Photoplay*:

> I prefer pantomime [over dialogue] . . . It's the better medium, much funnier than speech can ever be. The laughs can come quicker. In spoken comedy, you must wait for the laugh . . . In pantomime, the laughs can come as fast as an audience can shake them out of their throats. That's why I believe so firmly in the great future for the movies. There are no racial, language, time or distance barriers for them. That's why I'm so excited about having landed in them at last . . .

The film also gave Bill an opportunity he had not had before to see himself as others saw him. The stage actor can only feel his way through the audience's response, but in this medium, Fields told the press publicists: 'I can be my own severest critic. If there is a defect in my work – when a gag or a situation doesn't "click" – I need not fear the silence of an unresponsive audience. I can see what's wrong, analyze my own shortcomings and improve my work.' Not, of course, if the movie is already in the theatres.

Indeed, *Sally* was an auspicious beginning, but it was not a great hit. Sime Silverman, founder and editor of *Variety*, wrote in his review of 5 August 1925:

> 'Sally' is not a great picture nor is it a great comedy, but it's a fine film comedy release, that must get over at any house, albeit the 104 minutes are much too long . . . Mr Fields has put in bits of business and gags that will make the Chaplins and Lloyds bawl out their gag writers. And Fields plays them as well as though on the stage. He gives a smoothness to his comedy stuff and his playing that cannot be missed.

In *Sally of the Sawdust*, Griffith gave Fields what would remain his most sympathetic role in motion pictures. It was a role in which Bill was acting, not himself, or his own familiar stage persona, but a defined fictional character. It was ideal for Fields, allowing him to combine the role that Dorothy Donnelly and Howard Dietz had created with his particular quirks and routines. It gave him an opportunity to hone the character of the scoundrel who nevertheless has 'warmth and human sympathy underneath his rogueries. The immortal types of comedy,' Fields declared 'are just such men.'

It was clear where, in his own mind, he was heading. But his path towards that goal was far from smooth . . .

Chapter 25

It's the Old Army Game! – Elmer Prettywillie, Bisbee, Potter and Finch

W. C. Fields' next film, *That Royle Girl*, again directed by D.W. Griffith, is missing. It is one of five W. C. Fields silent features which have disappeared, despite diligent archive searches, and have not been seen for over fifty years.

Films of that period were printed onto nitrate stock, which is flammable, and prone to deterioration. In order to be available for normal screening, they have to be copied onto modern, inflammable film stocks, a process that often involves laborious reconstruction of damaged negatives or prints. Thousands of silent films, if not tens of thousands, not deemed worthy of preservation, have either been allowed to rot in warehouses piled high with rusted cans, or simply to vanish in the many reorganisations of studios and film production companies. Up until the 1960s it was thought that all Fields' silent films, apart from *Sally of the Sawdust* and *Pool Sharks*, were missing, but since then prints of *It's the Old Army Game, So's Your Old Man* and *Running Wild* have turned up. This leaves *That Royle Girl, The Potters, Two Flaming Youths, Tillie's Punctured Romance* and *Fools for Luck* still missing, as well as the second silent 1915 short, *His Lordship's Dilemma*.

This is a massive hole in the life and art of such a man as Fields. As we have seen, in all his works there was a progression, a building, step by step, of gags, of characters, of situations, which were polished up, reused, filed away and resurrected years if not decades later. Fields was an artistic elephant who never forgot. But we have to manoeuvre round the potholes. The most irksome loss is that the missing list includes all the three films Fields made teamed up with Chester Conklin, one of the funniest graduates of the Mack Sennett school of comedy. Of the trilogy – *Two Flaming Youths, Tillie's Punctured*

Romance and *Fools for Luck* – one title has left a comprehensive script, which enables us to recapture some of its flavour.

That Royle Girl was released in January 1926, to a sour review in *Variety*:

> It is just a long-winded film which gets mixed up in the middle, starting with a melting pot theme and then forgets all about it . . . It is the poorest thing Griffith has turned out in a great many years . . . In a vain effort to make a comedy, Griffith has dragged in W. C. Fields as the girl's father, but he doesn't belong in the picture, no matter how you look at it. He has nothing to do, and does it just like a man with nothing to do would do it.

Many of *Variety*'s reviews of films we now consider classics were sour, but there was definitely a problem with *That Royle Girl*. The story was based on a Hearst serial and book by one Edwin Balmer, and told the tale of a girl, Daisy Royle, born of the Chicago slums, who swings with the boys in the 'jazz zone' of the city. She falls in love with a bandleader, Fred Ketlar, whose estranged wife is murdered, and he is put on trial. Daisy defends him, but he is condemned to death owing to the zeal of a Prosecutor, Calvin Clarke. Now here's the twist: the Prosecutor falls in love with Daisy, but still pursues his duty, until she goes underground to unmask the gangsters who really committed the crime. After a mad dash to beat the scaffold, clearly echoing the famous scene in *Intolerance*, Ketlar is saved, but Daisy marries the upright Prosecutor.

Griffith was trying to make his own comment on the 'jazz age', but it was an unwise choice of subject for a man whose nineteenth-century morality co-existed with his mastery of the twentieth-century movie camera. The age of the flapper, sexual laxity and experimentation with strange weeds could only fill him with disdain. Gangsters, drugs, sex and music all got mixed up in his mind.

Fields' presence in the movie is clearly an afterthought, a boost from Griffith who wanted to direct him again. He comes on as Daisy's alcoholic father, and production stills show him, tantalisingly, swigging a bottle by the side of a baby carriage with a crying baby, an early precursor perhaps of the 'Back Porch' scene of later years. Since the film is missing, it is impossible to tell how much of the 'Back Porch' Bill sneaked in. He also sneaked in, apparently, another bit part for 'Shorty' Blanche, but this cannot be verified.

Griffith obviously sensed, in production, that things were awry. His other solution, apart from Fields, a flask of booze, and a baby, was to conceive a spectacular finale for Daisy's flight from the gangsters, a great cyclone which would lift the punters from their seats. The girl, again, was Carol Dempster, struggling womanfully with the wind stirred by twenty-four aeroplane propellers blowing the water from four fire hose nozzles. An entire village, with fields and trees, was constructed on a football field by the Astoria Studios to take the blast. According to the film's press book, Fields was in the scene hiding in a wagon blown along by the wind. His part was mostly shot in the studio, with a traditional wind-machine blowing dirt and sand into his face. This put him off cyclones for life.

The cyclone could save neither Griffith nor Carol Dempster, who left him soon after to marry an investment banker. No amount of studio hype, with words like 'Melodramatic, heart-throbbing, flashy, funny, pathetic, gripping!' could save the film from a nose-dive. Griffith's career was all downhill from then on, involving his bizarre travails with *The Sorrows of Satan* and six other films before his death, in 1948, forgotten and neglected by the industry he had done so much to build. Piquantly, he survived his junior, Bill Fields, by two years.

Bill, however, was not badly damaged by *That Royle Girl*, in which he had not starred. The film had been produced for Paramount, and his powerful fan, Bill Le Baron, was in the driving seat at the Astoria studios. Le Baron offered Fields a deal for three pictures a year, for five years, at $4,000 a week, providing he finally quit his job with the stage. Fields signed and Florenz Ziegfeld sued him. Two other plaintiffs were also suing Fields at the time, *Poppy* producer Philip Goodman, who claimed *he* had a five-year contract with Fields, and a Griffith casting-director named Charles Walton, who claimed 10 per cent of the actor's earnings because he had got him his first jobs in the movies. Litigation, from that point on, seemed to follow Fields like a swarm of marauding wasps, zooming from left and right field to attack him again and again.

For their first production, Paramount and Fields agreed to adapt his favourite sketches from *The Comic Supplement* into a feature narrative, *It's the Old Army Game*. The screenplay was commissioned from Thomas J. Geraghty, who was to be a firm friend of Bill's from then on. The film was to be directed by Edward Sutherland, a vigorous thirty-year-old, who had served his apprenticeship as an assistant to Chaplin, and had directed one feature to date, entitled *Wild, Wild Susan*. Le

Baron thought he would be ideal for Fields. In the event he would direct four future Fields' movies, *Tillie's Punctured Romance, International House, Mississippi* and the remake of *Poppy*, as well as one of Fields' last guest appearances in the 1944 dud *Follow the Boys*. He also became a close friend, though subject to what would become familiar tirades from his irascible star. The third bonus Eddie Sutherland got from *It's the Old Army Game* was to marry the leading lady, Louise Brooks.

It's the Old Army Game was Louise Brook's fourth movie role, following her start in the chorus of the Ziegfeld *Follies* and George White's *Scandals*. Despite her modest origins as a freckled teenage dancer from Cherryvale, Kansas, her career became a legend, mainly due to her starring role in the German director G. W. Pabst's tour-de-force *Pandora's Box*, made in 1929, a role which made her *the* movie face of the 1920s. But in 1926 this was still ahead of her, as she flitted about in a minor key as Fields' assistant in his drug store, fending off the advances of out-of-town confidence trickster William Gaxton.

Louise Brooks has left us a fascinating glimpse of Paramount's east-coast operations at that time: the film was shot in Ocala, Florida, and its plot line had Fields as the drugstore owner Elmer Prettywillie (remember the crazy car ride escaping the roadside hijackers?) getting unwittingly drawn by Bill Gaxton into a scam to sell Floridans non-existent land in New York. This was the period of the great Florida lot racket, when New Yorkers were falling over each other to buy land in Florida which either didn't exist or was swamp. (The Marx Brothers first movie, 1929s *The Cocoanuts*, also revolved around the same deals.) Louise Brooks recalled the filming in *Lulu in Hollywood*:

> In February, 1926, Paramount sent the production unit to Ocala, an inland farming town in Florida. About six miles away was Silver Springs, which (had a) basin ... filled with tropical fish, surrounded by tropical plants and flowers. The iridiscent beauty was viewed from a glass-bottomed motorboat, which Eddie used for a love scene between William Gaxton and me. The Citizens of Ocala, hoping to make Silver Springs a rich tourist attraction, welcomed our company ... We were treated to so much Southern hospitality that the script got lost and the shooting schedule wandered out of sight. Nobody in Ocala seemed to have heard of Prohibition. And if ever there was a company that needed no help in the consumption of liquor it

was ours. Eddie and Tom Geraghty (the writer) drank; William Gaxton, Blanche Ring, the crew, and I – everyone drank. Bill Fields, apart, drank his private stock with his girlfriend, Bessie Poole; his manager, Billy Grady; and his valet, Shorty.

This tells us, by the way – unless Brooks is completely mistaken – that Bessie Poole was still living with Fields at this time, ten years at least after their first meeting. But (according to Faye O'Neill) Bill had already met the next but one of his girlfriends, Linelle Blackburn, in the chorus of *Poppy*, not later than 1924. So it might well be that Bill was running his girlfriends concurrently, and not consecutively as hitherto assumed. Two will get you four, four will get you eight . . . Not all the questions have answers, in the world of Fieldsian flim-flam.

Despite all the Southern hospitality, *It's the Old Army Game* still looks pretty coherent. Although J. P. McEvoy does not seem to have been involved in the film, the material from *The Comic Supplement* was used faithfully. As in the stage revue, the Drug Store is the central hub from which all the action flows. Fields reprised four of the stage sketches performed in *The Comic Supplement* and in the Ziegfeld *Follies* of 1925: 'The Back Porch', 'The Drug Store', 'The Joyride' and 'The Picnic'. The main difference is the major change of setting from the New York streets to small-town USA, as the opening title of the movie reveals:

This is the epic of the American druggist – a community benefactor. His shop is at once the social center, the place of countless conveniences and the forum of public thought. It is the druggist we seek in hours of suffering and adversity, and day and night he is oft the agency between life and death . . .

A car shoots across the countryside at speed, cutting dangerously ahead of a rushing train, to stop at the house of Elmer Prettywillie, 'apothecary and humanitarian'. Out of the car steps Elise Cavanna, in the first of the roles in which the languid and angular commedienne would serve as Bill Fields' foil, or wife, in the later Mack Sennett shorts. She has awoken the druggist to call for a two-cent stamp, but rushes out without paying. Searching for a mailbox she sets off the fire alarm by mistake, bringing the fire brigade to poke about Elmer's store and cash box in the vain hope of finding a fire.

The Prettywillie ménage includes a nagging sister, an obnoxious small boy, Mickey – 'a combination of Peck's Bad Boy, Gyp the Blood and Jesse James', and the counter assistant, Marilyn – Louise Brooks.

Fire breaks out in a cigar box after the firemen leave, but Elmer manages to put it out. There are still the echoes of the circus showman McGargle in this harassed small-town chemist. Having chased the firemen away from Louise Brooks, Elmer settles down in a hammock on his porch for some rest.

The screen Back Porch, deprived of sound dialogue, nevertheless follows the stage version closely: a woman wheels out a large crying baby (Fields' stage 'child', Ray Dooley, has been replaced by an uncredited actress). Elmer tries to stuff a sheet in its mouth. The baby pushes it out. Elmer hands it a mirror and a mallet but the child wallops him over the head. He leaps up, breaking the railing over the second-floor landing, and is dangling the child over the edge when mother returns to save her tot. Much ado with an immense safety-pin follows, and attempts by Elmer to manoeuvre baby into its pram with his boot clamped down on its hand. After being beaned with a milk bottle Elmer gives up, with a spoken title, as he walks away: 'Uncle will give you some nice razor blades to play with.'

The vegetable vendor is next, crying his wares. Elmer rushes indoors, coming out with a rifle, but the vendor has gone. A scissors-grinder calls out: 'Scissors to GRIND!' The iceman leaves him with a slippery block. After vain efforts to get it in the ice box Elmer throws it in the trash can and returns to his hammock, only to knock down the rifle, which goes off, bringing the whole hammock down.

In the Drug Store scene a nasty little twist has the druggist offering to get a speck out of a distraught woman's eye by offering her a swab onto which a cockroach has climbed. Elise Cavanna is back, asking to see the telephone book, and a man comes in asking, 'Have you got something for the hip?' Fields wields a small fan to push open the visitor's lapel to see if a tell-tale Sheriff's star lurks behind it. Another irascible customer asks for a two-cent stamp – 'A clean one – out of the middle.' 'Shall I send it?' asks the helpful apothecary, breaking away to take a telephone order: 'What's that? A box of Smith Brothers cough-drops? No, I'm sorry but we can't split a box – can't separate the brothers. Yes, we can deliver them – I'll send over our truck right away.'

The gags come thick and fast, and the intertitles are funny, but they lack the impact of the spoken word. It was 1926, a year after Chaplin's *The Gold Rush* and Harold Lloyd's *The Freshman*, a year before Buster Keaton's *The General*. All three were pure cinema – the visual gag their sole creative source. Each derived comedy from something implicit in their central characters – Chaplin's lost innocence, Lloyd's urge to succeed, Keaton's mad love. Fields' comedy, at this time, derived from his own and McEvoy's observations of the life that swirled around them. The small accumulations of human frailties, failings and eccentricities informed all the *Comic Supplement* sketches. Elmer Prettywillie reacts to the cut and thrust of adversity. He is an anti-hero long before his time.

Eustace McGargle has become a harassed urban grouch. Interestingly enough, the script makes no attempt to create any special 'fatherly' relationship between Fields and Louise Brooks; his only family connections here are grisly and cacophonous. This is the family of 'The Family Ford', 'Off to the Country', the Flivertons without Fanny Brice. The nagging wife has become a nagging sister here, played by Mary Foy. I am not sure if this was Mary Foy of the famous vaudeville 'Seven Little Foys', the children of the turn of the century star, Eddie Foy. Blanche Ring, though, who played the pest who troubles Elmer with a speck in her eye, was in her day a great vaudeville singer, starring on stage when Fields toured and juggled.

According to Louise Brooks, Fields and Eddie Sutherland argued incessantly on the set. Fields later would refer to his director disparagingly as 'an ex-chorus-boy still in his teens'. Louise Brooks remarked: 'Eddie Sutherland said you had to argue, the first few days on a Fields picture you had to talk him out of using all his stock scenes, you know, the . . . pool-table sequence, the golf sequence and some of his other favourite sequences.' But once at work, Bill needed no direction, 'because he'd done all his routines before for 40 years'.

It's the Old Army Game was moderately successful at the box office, but, once again, not a smash hit. The Paramount press office did what it could to build Fields up, in a grotesque but familiar process of what we today call hype. These stories, issued in official Press Books, and mostly made up by press agents, wove round the stars whatever special aura the studio hacks thought would draw crowds. The Paramount publicists, in those early Fields productions, were unsure how to present their new star, resorting to all kinds of drivel, which they would wire to all the newspapers.

EXTRA! WHITE-ROBED MEN CAUSE TROUBLE AT RESORT.
Fields Heads Big Parade From Barber Shop as Tiny Skunk Enters. When two dignified men dash out of the exclusive Hotel Alba, Palm Beach, with

white sheets wrapped around their necks and faces, a crowd gathers . . .
The two white-draped runners were Thomas J. Geraghty, supervising editor of Paramount Productions, and W. C. Fields, former 'Follies' star, who
was in Florida for scenes in his first Paramount starring picture, 'It's the
Old Army Game,' (Meaning 'Never Give a Sucker an Even Break'), which
comes to the —— on ——.

Fields and Geraghty hurried into the Alba barber shop about 8:30 in the
morning – a remarkable early hour for Palm Beach – and seated themselves
preparatory to the morning shave. The bootblack suddenly went crazy,
according to Mr. Fields. He hurled his brush across the shop. All the barbers followed suit with assorted bottles of hair tonic and lotions. One even
tossed a steaming towel. There was a rush for the exits. On their way out,
Mr. Fields grabbed his nose and Geraghty a towel. Mr. Fields expressed the
opinion that it was the only skunk that had ever tried to break into society.
Business was very dull for the rest of the day.

I'll bet. Such desperate scribblings showed that Fields was not yet
a clearly defined commodity. (Although, if there was any basis for the
incident, might it not have sparked the barber shop routines of
Fields' later Mack Sennett short?) Unlike Chaplin, Keaton or Lloyd,
Fields had still not gelled, had not found himself in motion pictures.
But he was to take a great step forward in his next movie, which
introduced him to yet another new director who was to become a
lifelong friend.

This newcomer was Gregory La Cava, who was to match Fields blow
for blow in the domain of both booze and bellicosity. La Cava had
entered movies as a producer of animated cartoons – drawn by Walter
Lantz – of William Randolph Hearst's newspaper comic strips such as
Mutt and Jeff and *The Happy Hooligan*. He then scripted and directed
a number of comedy shorts and had already helmed six feature films
by the time he met Bill Fields. He was to become Bill's most constant
golf partner and, later in the 1930s, his neighbour in Los Angeles. (Cue
the line in 1940s *The Bank Dick*: 'That must be the Cava's calling for
their lawn mower. Tell 'em we haven't finished with it yet.') They
rowed incessantly, and La Cava was the butt of endless Fieldsian ribbing, calumny and mocking derision. A typical letter, of Second World
War vintage, has Fields commenting to another boozum buddy, Gene
Fowler (whom he addressed as 'Nephew') –

Bel-Air
6 A.M. Pacific Standard Time,
6 P.M. U.S.S.R. time at Usk.

Dear Nephew,

In response to your query is Mr. LaCava of the cinema still off H²O, last evening I had occasion to test his poison liquor and eat his food, such as it was. I must say he provides excellent bread of which I ate my fill. When we were sitting on his sandpile at the rear of his leanto at the beach, he, unsolicited, informed me a few days previously he had seen a submarine, either of German or Japanese registry, cruising off his home . . .

I could not glean from the fragments of his conversation whether he was drunk or not. He later fell asleep and a comely concubine came out and suggested if we modulated our voices Mr. LaCava could sleep more comfortably on his improvised flop, comprising of two chairs and a brass cuspidore. He was out when I left and I didn't care to disturb him; therefore, I cannot answer your question – is LaCava still drinking?

– Your dear Uncle

Bill's beloved 'Dago' directed two of his silent movies, *So's Your Old Man* and *Running Wild*, but did not, alas, direct any of his sound films. This may be counted a serious loss, as La Cava directed one of the 1930s most biting satires, *My Man Godfrey*, in 1936. His eccentricity is most apparent in his 1933 film, *Gabriel Over the White House*, in which a crooked President, played by Walter Huston, is visited by the aforementioned archangel and turns into a reforming zealot, determined to execute racketeers and force world peace by methods suspiciously like those of Mussolini.

La Cava and Fields feuded on the set but nevertheless produced a minor gem of comedy. *So's Your Old Man* was the only silent film which was remade for Fields by Paramount almost scene for scene as a sound movie in 1934, as *You're Telling Me*. The only difference in the plot was the replacement of the hero Bisbee's unbreakable windscreen with a puncture-proof tyre.

'The story of a glazier that can be seen through and laughed at!' was the Paramount Press Book's take on *So's Your Old Man*: Samuel Bisbee is the local 'optometrist, optician, occultist and optimist' of the small town of Waukeagus, New Jersey. He has invented an unbreakable glass windshield for motor cars but no one will believe him, not even his drinking buddies, until he demonstrates it to them by running his car repeatedly into a tree. His snobbish wife despairs of him ever making good. His daughter, Alice, 'convincing evidence that even poor people can have attractive children', is in love with Robert Murchison, son of the 'bell cow of the Waukeagus social herd', Mrs A. Brandewyne Murchison.

Bisbee gets his chance to demonstrate his invention at an automobile convention: 'Stand by boys! This brick may bounce!' But his car is switched and he throws his bricks through ordinary windscreens. In despair, on the train back home, he plans to end his own life by drinking poison but it spills from his grasp. Seeing a beautiful woman in another carriage with a bottle of iodine marked 'Poison' (and a cut hand), he mistakes her motives and talks her out of her imagined error. She turns out to be a real-life socialite, the Princess Lescaboura, who, bemoaning her rich but empty life – 'If only I could be of service . . . to help some poor person . . .' devises a plan to turn up at his home town to seek her 'old friend, Sam Bisbee', and show that he is, in fact, the *crème de la crème* . . .

The story was loosely based on a short story by Julian Street, 'Mister Bisbee's Princess', which had won the O. Henry Prize for short story of the year in 1925, and which William Le Baron rightly thought would fit Fields like a glove.

Looking at the film, a biography of the screen Fields begins to emerge: replacing the New York Mr Fliverton, who was named after the mass produced Ford, or 'flivver', we have Sam Bisbee of Waukeagus, New Jersey. Fields wrote several versions of sketches using this name, for stage or screen ideas. A small-town dreamer, his everyday life is a litany of humiliations, frustrations and thwarted ambition. His wife has despaired of him ever rising to her level. She has married beneath her. As the quintessential scene from the sound version, *You're Telling Me*, exemplifies, when rich Mrs Murchison comes to visit the dowdy Mrs Bisbee, to discuss her son's infatuation with Bisbee's daughter:

MRS MURCHISON: In short, the whole affair's absurd, and I've come to –

MRS BISBEE: Why is it absurd that your son should want to marry my daughter? The women of the Warren family have always been above reproach. That is history.

MRS MURCHISON: The Warren family? You don't mean the Warrens of Virginia?

MRS BISBEE: My grandfather was General Robert Henry Warren of Virginia.

MRS MURCHISON: Not really!

Mrs Bisbee brings out the family album. Mrs Murchison is suitably impressed, until Sam Bisbee enters in his undershirt, rolling a car tire and talking about his invention.

MRS MURCHISON: I take it Mr Bisbee did not come from Virginia.

MRS BISBEE: N-n-no.

SAM: So Abigail's been telling you her family history, hey? Well, you ain't seen a thing. Wait till I show you the Bisbee clan. We were all Union men.

MRS BISBEE: Sam, I don't think Mrs Murchison would be interested in those pictures.

SAM: Aw, sure she would. Real down to earth people. Speak our language. Now, there's Uncle Bean . . . Bean Bisbee, the tiger. Fight at the drop of a hat, and yet underneath it all as tender hearted as a baby lamb. Look at those eyes. Oop! Wrong picture! That was Uncle Jim. He was the black sheep of the family until he got into politics. Now he's got a big home up at Passamaquoddy. And that's . . . (*revealing chorus girl*) Aunt Minnie. An angel of mercy if ever there was one, and there was. Known from California to Maine and back again. Stayed up all night taking care of the boys, night after night . . .

For the 1934 movie, J. P. McEvoy was brought in to write this dialogue, but it closely mirrors the same scene in the silent *So's Your Old Man*, in which Sam shows Mrs Murchison portraits of his cousin Sadie, 'the best dancer in burlesque until she lost her voice', and tells her, mumbling through a mouthful of crackers: 'I knew your old man when he had just one pair of pants.' Of course, this puts the kibosh on the marriage. In the 1934 sound version, Sam tells his distraught family: 'You've got nothing to worry about. I got a letter from the National Tire Company right here in my pocket.' His daughter Pauline replies: 'Well isn't that just dandy. Now I suppose I can marry a balloon tire.' To which Mrs Bisbee ripostes: 'Well, I've been married to one for twenty years, and a flat one at that!'

Both versions highlight Bisbee's antecedents: working class and show business, and the pretensions of Mrs Bisbee. What we never find out in this fictional biography is how Mr and Mrs Bisbee ever got to meet and mate, across the yawning divide. But everyone in the Bisbee world is a social climber, and all rose from the same earthy dirt. Someone is putting on airs, someone – or rather everyone, is dissembling, except Sam Bisbee, the only honest man in the den of thieves.

Bisbee, in his distant past, was McGargle. But in place of the circus ex-wife, 'Gorgeous', he has married Mrs Fliverton, alias Fanny Brice, who fantasized herself as Salome, Scheherezade, or Ethel Barrymore, a thespian of impeccable lineage. There are hints, in later films, that Mrs Fliverton, alias Mrs Bissonette, for example, may have had a show-business background herself, but it has been vigorously covered up.

Stripped of masks, Bisbee is living the reality principle. The connection of all this to Fields real-life traumas with Hattie and Claude Junior is glaringly obvious, down to the old 'Lees of Virginia' argument. The boy-brats scattered about the 'Bisbee-Fliverton-Bissonette' films are further evidence, and the even more brattish Baby Le Roy enters the scene only to round out the syndrome. Above all, the fantasy daughter, 'Poppy-Sally-Betty-Pauline-Hope' offers a balm lacking in life. In three instances, in Fields' episode of *If I had a Million*, in *Six of a Kind*, and in *Tillie and Gus*, we are offered a glimpse of a surviving and grown up 'Gorgeous', in the shape of fellow dipsomaniac Allison Skipworth, an equal helpmeet that might have been. And only in one movie, *My Little Chickadee*, does McGargle-Bisbee-Twillie come into conflict with a female rival of matching huckstering skills, in the shape of Mae West.

Bisbee's fantasy triumph in *So's Your Old Man* enables him to join the smart set on the Waukeagus golf-course for our first filmed glimpse of the Golf Sketch. The caddy is played by William 'Shorty' Blanche. The impact of the rustling paper and squeaky shoes gags is blunted by the lack of sound, and the plot soon intervenes, in the shape of the chairman of the automobile convention, who has found Bisbee's car, tested the windscreen, and is offering him a million dollars. Chasing Bisbee – who mistakes the motives of the waving worthy – down the golf-course, he falls in the lake and is fished out by our hero, who smooths out the sodden contract and obtains an instant signature on the dotted line.

So's Your Old Man was moderately successful and got good reviews, though *Variety* said it was 'no great outstanding comedy wallop, but it is a series of humorous situations and laugh compelling bits that follow along in an endless train . . . Fields is great and one doesn't have to say any more.' The film also introduced a young actor, Charles 'Buddy' Rogers – who later became Mary Pickford's husband and the male lead in William Wellman's air war epic *Wings* – as the suitor, Bob Murchison. His memory of playing with Fields was rather limited, as recorded in his Astoria Studio 'oral history' interview with Anthony Slide, several decades later: 'They sent me out to a golf course where W. C. Fields was making this picture . . . and he put me in front of the camera right then without knowing anything, 'cause it was silent and Fields said mumble mumble . . . "you're going to marry my daughter in the film"; that's about all he ever said to me . . .'

Slide: 'Was Fields sort of difficult to work with?' Rogers: 'I just remember him being a funny, sweet guy . . . timid as I remember . . .'

For his next picture, Le Baron proposed to Fields another dip into the McEvoy file, picking out McEvoy's 1923 stage hit *The Potters* for adaptation to the screen. This was shot in the latter part of 1926 and released in January of 1927.

The Potters is lost, so all we have are production stills and synopses. As in the play, Pa Potter is an urban dreamer who spends the family's mortgage money on fake leases for oil wells which turn out to be real gushers in the end. The loss of the film is all the more tragic as it clearly gave Bill Fields another defined role which was pivotal in developing 'Sam Bisbee' that much further. The film was directed by Fred Newmeyer, who also directed Harold Lloyd's masterpieces, *Safety Last* and *The Freshman*. (According to *The Potters*' Press Book, Newmeyer and Fields had met before, in Denver, Colorado, on the same vaude-ville bill, when the young Fred was acting in a Shakespearian vignette from *As You Like It* . . .)

Highlights of the lost film included an embryonic bathroom scene in which Pa and his son, Bill, are trying to shave at the same time at one small mirror. This was a scene Fields would reprise in 1934's *It's a Gift*, as well as in a number of variants of his 'Pullman Sleeper' sketch. The scene where Pa is hooked by the confidence trickster would also have been one to savour. Fields was quoted in the Press Book, as commenting on his role:

In my first picture, 'Sally of the Sawdust', they let me cut up at my old tricks, but since then I've been cast as the innocent object of my former vil-lainies. In 'The Old Army Game,' 'So's Your Old Man' and now in 'The Potters,' my role is that of the dumb guy in the brown derby who always gets it in the neck . . . Making you laugh at the hard-boiled three card monte man who is trimming a sucker is one thing – and not so easy – but making you laugh at the sucker is something else . . . In 'The Potters' I fall for an oil stock swindler who takes me for everything but my eye teeth. On the stage I'd have played the swindler, but in the movies I have to make you laugh at poor, old buncoed Pa Potter.

The stage *Potters* had coincided with the eruption of the so-called 'Teapot Dome' scandal and the film version coincided with it's denouement: the sorry tale of how President Calvin Coolidge's Secretary of the Interior, Albert Fall (unlucky name, unlucky guy) had leased two major oil reserves to businessmen who paid him back in kickbacks. Despite fake oil leases being a hot subject, the film was not a box office hit. But Fields was becoming an established screen presence, despite his nagging hankering for a return to salad days. The Press Book of *The Potters* includes a poignant item on the still stage-struck Fields:

If you should happen to be in New York and see a man with a hungry look in his eyes roaming Broadway, a long, black cigar in his mouth, snooping in and out of theatre lobbies, listening, moving on again, like one in a trance, you'll know who it is . . .

If you should ask him what he's doing, roaming thus anxiously about in the old haunts where in his pre-movie days he was a laugh getter in the Ziegfeld Follies and other Broadway musical productions, he would tell you that he couldn't sleep, that he was listening for the ghostly clapping of hands and the once familiar roars of laughter.

'The hardest thing for a former stage player to get used to in movie work,' says Fields, 'is to do your stuff minus applause or encouragement before a handful of cameramen and technical directors. You wonder if you're getting across, and there's no way of finding out. Moreover, for one who has played on the stage some thirty years, never getting to bed before two or three in the morning, it's hard as the dickens to turn up for work each day at nine. I tried my darndest, but I couldn't do it. So, now I spend my evenings on the old camping ground. I can generally find a theatre showing one of my pictures . . . and I drop in to listen for the laughter and applause I missed while making the film.'

This, of course, contradicts the upbeat assessment Fields was quoted as making for his screen début in *Sally of the Sawdust*. But perhaps it also reflected the press agents' awareness that, even after four feature films, W. C. Fields was still known to the public primarily as a stage actor. That Fields still yearned for the direct contact with the audience is borne out by a small ad in *The New York Times* in 7 July 1929, announcing, in a revival of *So's Your Old Man*, that 'Mr. Fields will make personal appearances at matinee and evening performances today.'

Bill's last picture for the Astoria Studios was another Gregory La Cava piece, *Running Wild*. This was a lost film too for many years but is now extant, and even available on video. Once again, Fields was set in the gladiatorial arena of the American home, this time as Elmer Finch, a put-upon clerk in 'Harvey's Toys and Novelties', where his best friend is a nodding toy donkey. Finch has not had a pay rise for over twenty years. His home consists of a mercilessly henpecking second wife, a saintly daughter from his first marriage, and a hideous bloated teenage son of his present wife's previous marriage to the moustachioed Chester, whose steely portrait overlooks their misery. The final straw is the family dog, Rex, who sinks his fangs into Elmer Finch's fetlocks at each and any opportunity. In a complicated comedy of errors, Finch ends up thrust onto the stage of a variety theatre in the middle of the hypnotist's act. Hypnotised into thinking he is a lion, and clad in boxing gloves, Finch breaks out of the theatre, runs back to his office, triumphs over his bewildered colleagues, and rushes home to turn the tables on his boorish family by whipping Junior with a belt, smashing Chester's portrait and delighting his daughter by showing them all who's boss.

This was Fields as Jekyll and Hyde, all meek and wimpish one half of the film, insufferably aggressive in the latter half. It was a comedy misjudgement, despite intriguing scenes in which an unusually agile Fields bounces about the family furniture crying out 'I'm a lion! I'm a lion!' His own instinct that the meek and bold should co-exist in the same soul was overridden by a poor script. The story was originally La Cava's, so he must take the primary blame. But Fields was not yet clear enough, in his own mind, exactly who Bisbee-Potter-Finch was, and exactly how he should be facing the world. He knew his gags back to front, but not yet the character who would wield them in the world.

One bonus of the film was the meeting between Fields and Mary Brian, a young Texan actress (original name Louise Dantzler), who became his favourite screen daughter and was cast again in *Two Flaming Youths* and in the 'remake' of *Running Wild* – *Man on the Flying Trapeze*, 1935. The latter film was far more than a remake, as we shall see in due course.

Running Wild was the last silent film to be made at the Astoria Studio. Gregory La Cava completed his direction of the movie and left for Hollywood on 28 April 1927, the last of the Paramount executives to leave. Paramount had decided to cut its losses from the East Coast operations and move all production to the West. Production would return to Astoria with the talkies, in 1929, beginning with newsreels and continuing with the Marx Brothers' first film, *The Cocoanuts*. Ronald Fields wrote:

> In 1927 most of Paramount's contract players based in New York, including W. C. Fields, started the hegira to the promised land – Hollywood. Many of them felt they would not see New York again. Fields packed his belongings into his Lincoln touring car and in late June drove to California with his girlfriend Bessie Poole . . . At Ziegfeld's New Amsterdam Theatre, where the lobby housed photographs of the *Follies'* top stars who had performed over the past decades or so, someone had put black crepe paper underneath W. C.'s picture with a sign underneath, 'Gone to Hollywood.'

But, as it turned out, the mourning, or the celebration, was premature . . .

19 *Running Wild*: Fields as hen-pecked Elmer Finch, with fantasy daughter Mary Brian.

Chapter 26
'The Side Show'

20 The lost double-act: W. C. Fields and Chester Conklin in *Two Flaming Youths*.

All three of the silent films Bill Fields made in Hollywood are lost. What lies behind that kind of statement? Books go out of print, but one can find, in a library somewhere, some copies. Songs are sung and remembered. Plays survive in fading playscripts. But the film is a performance that was recorded once only. If that recording is gone, the art is truly vanished; all that we can retain are echoes.

Two Flaming Youths, Tillie's Punctured Romance and *Fools For Luck* all starred W. C. Fields and Chester Conklin. All were shot at Paramount's Los Angeles studios. Their credits tell us they were produced by John Waters for Paramount, by the 'Christie Film Company', and by Paramount Famous Lasky Corporation, respectively. One name is absent from all three: William Le Baron, of the now defunct East Coast studios, did not seem to be involved.

The pairing of Fields and Conklin, the two moustaches, was the brain child of anonymous Hollywood executives. The studio, with both under contract, felt that neither could break through alone. They twinned them three times, registered three strike-outs, and then booted them off the lot. The public did not fill the theatres, the distributors hated the pictures, the critics gave them lukewarm reviews. In 1928, Bill Fields' optioned contract came up for renewal. The Paramount executives passed. No one bothered to preserve the negatives or prints of the films. If any exists out there, in some warehouse or garage, it has not yet been found.

But in the files of the Academy of Motion Pictures' Margaret Herrick Library, among the folders of Fields' Paramount scripts, there lies one vital echo – a script, or rather three different script versions of the first of the trilogy, *Two Flaming Youths*.

A silent film script is a clumsy artifact. Without the film, it is difficult to tell whether it is an early or a final draft. The sound script folders usually include a Dialogue Continuity Script, which is the version of the movie released to public viewing. The file contains a Shot Continuity Sheet, a list of shots with the final intertitles. Put beside the longer, annotated scripts, a version can be reconstructed that corresponds as closely as possible to the film as it was shot and shown.

The final credits of the film list two screenwriters: Percy Heath and Donald Davis. The longer typescript has a pencilled note on the title page: 'Contributions by Grover Jones' – a name that will crop up later on in relation to Fields' talkies. The film was directed by John Waters, a craft director in the Paramount stable. B. P. Schulberg was Associate producer. The final intertitles were written by Jack Conway and Herman J. Mankiewicz: the first already a veteran director who had started out with Griffith's stock company, the second a young writer who would have more business with Fields in the future, and who would later enter legend as the disputed author of Orson Welles' *Citizen Kane*.

Adolph Zukor and Jesse Lasky presented Fields and Conklin in *Two Flaming Youths*. But the script had a different working title: 'The Side Show'. With so many cooks it might be expected to be a stale broth. But in fact, a reading reveals it to be a vital part of Fields' evolution. It is the missing link between Eustace McGargle in *Poppy* and two of Bill's greatest movie creations: the Great McGonigle of *The Old Fashioned Way* (1934), and Larson E. Whipsnade of Universal's *You Can't Cheat an Honest Man* (1939).

Where *Poppy* and *Sally of the Sawdust* were set in a circus world, 'The Side Show' is set at the seedier end of the travelling show – the 'dime museum', the kind of world in which Harry Houdini began his career as the 'Wild Man of Mexico'. For this tale Paramount had scoured California for an appropriate cast of circus freaks. They collected a strong man, John Serresheff; a 395-pound lady, Anna Magruder; a human pin cushion, Chester Moorten; an 8 foot 9 inch giant, John Aasen; and a 4-foot-high midget, William Platt. A boxing kangaroo and a group of hula-hula girls completed this menagerie, and a tantalising roster of vaudevillians in cameo roles included, according to the cast list, Joe Weber and Lew Fields, Moran and Mack, Wallace Beery and Raymond Hatton, Savoy and Brennan and the Duncan Sisters.

The story is as follows: Gabby Gilfoil is the owner and manager of 'Gilfoil's Nonpareil Circus' which, according to the opening title, 'attracted bad weather, sheriffs, and bill collectors – everything except cash customers'. The script proceeds:

1. EXT. CIRCUS LOT . . . LONG SHOT . . . FADE IN . . .

A drizzling, depressing rain is falling as the circus makes ready to move . . . Under the direction of a sheriff and his deputies, the circus equipment is being taken down and loaded on wagons. Other wagons, already loaded, are starting away from the lot. (Insert a series of CLOSE-SHOT FLASHES) showing, in order, (1), a driver 'snaking' his long whip over the backs of his striving horses and urging them to greater effort, (2), the mud-dripping wheels of a circus van rotating slowly, creaking through the heavy mud, (3) the hooves of a team of straining circus horses, as they are planted in the goo, withdrawn, and set down in a new place . . .

2. MEDIUM SHOT . . . *A crew of canvas men leveling a small tent and carrying it out of scene. As the tent comes down* GABBY GILFOIL *is disclosed. He is seated behind it, on an upended suitcase, watching the work going on around him with mild interest – but his expression is altogether lacking in any suggestion of despondency or depression.*

SUBTITLE 2: Gabby Gilfoil felt that all he needed was a radio set – his public had already given him the air – W. C. FIELDS.

3. SEMI CU *of* GILFOIL. *He is smoking a cigar, and as he blows the smoke from his mouth it forms a ring. Immediately he becomes more interested in the manufacture of smoke-rings than in the activities proceeding around him. He grins happily as he succeeds in making another ring . . .*

4. EXT. ANOTHER SMALL TENT. MEDIUM SHOT.

A flash as a crew of canvas men, led by a sheriff's officer, advance upon the tent and begin to take it down. The SHERIFF *parts the flaps of the tent and looks inside.*

5. INT. THE TENT . . . FULL SHOT . . . MARY GILFOIL *is putting on her hat.*

SUBTITLE 3: MARY GILFOIL, born in a tent, had longed all her life for a home that wouldn't fold up – MARY BRIAN.

6. SEMI CU *of* MARY. *She turns to face the intruder. Her expression indicates disappointment, despondency. She has been quietly crying.*

Gilfoil and his 'circus' are being evicted for the usual non-payment of bills. Mary asks him: 'What are we going to do without the circus, Daddy?'

SPOKEN TITLE: 'It's all right, honey. The sun is bound to shine for us.'

12. MEDIUM SHOT. *As he finishes the title he points up. A ray of sunlight, breaking through the clouds, touches them. Mary sighs with resignation, but nods her head as though agreeing to do as* GABBY *says. He pats her tenderly saying 'Atta girl!'* MARY *glances off and sees:*

13. LONG SHOT *of the freaks approaching in a body.*

14. MEDIUM SHOT – MARY *rises and calls her father's attention to the*

approach of the side-show performers. These (the freaks), include the FAT
WOMAN, *the* HUMAN SKELETON, *the* STRONG MAN, *the* WILD MAN *and one or
two others. They march into the scene in a body, headed by the* HUMAN
SKELETON. *Their manner marks them as a delegation come to make certain
emphatic demands and determined to get what they have come for.*

15. GABBY, *thinking the freaks have come to say goodbye, grins and offers
to shake hands. The* HUMAN SKELETON *who acts as spokesman for the
group, says:*

SPOKEN TITLE: 'We may be freaks, Gilfoil – but even freaks crave food!'

Gilfoil tries to make a little extra cash with the shell game, but the
local sheriff chases him off: 'If I catch you in my territory again, I'll
lock you up.' Adding: 'And if you stop in Arkosa county, you'd better
watch your step. Sheriff Holden over there is as hard as they make
'em.'

29. LONG SHOT – *the truck bumping along the uneven road. The sun light
disappears. The rain pours down.*

We fade to Arkosa, to the Mansion House, an inn which 'can boast
of everything that makes a hotel prosperous – excepting guests.'
Madge Malarkey, the proprietress 'is looking into the face of a mortgage foreclosure which threatens to send her back to the burlesque
stage.' The bellboy is quitting, with the line: 'I been here for ten days
and I ain't even got a tip on the weather.' While outside, 'Simeon Trott,
financial magnate of Arkosa, can hardly wait for the day when the law
will permit him to foreclose on the Mansion House.'

Next, in the Sheriff's office, Ben Holden (Chester Conklin) is looking
at himself in the mirror – 'his hair has been carefully brushed and the
ends of his moustache have been waxed'. Sheriff Holden is courting
Madge, who rejects him. Meanwhile the evicted circus folks approach
the hotel:

79. EXT. MANSION HOUSE. LONG SHOT.

The street is deserted. Along it comes the Gilfoil truck. GABBY *is at the
wheel,* MARY *beside him. The freaks, a tired, dispirited lot are huddled in
the body of the truck. As the truck arrives in front of the Mansion House it
comes to a dead stop.*

80. INSERT CLOSE UP *of gasoline gauge showing arrow indicating* EMPTY.

Gilfoil decides they'll stay in this hotel, telling Mary: 'We'll honor this hostelry with our patronage – the best is none too good for you, kid.' A comedy of errors occurs in the hotel lobby as Madge, hoping for paying guests, gestures Sheriff Holden to pretend to be the bell boy. Gilfoil presents Madge with his card:

'J.G. Gilfoil – Sole Owner of the World Renowned Gilfoil's Non-Pareil Circus.'

MADGE (SPOKEN TITLE): 'I'm always glad to meet anyone in the profession. I used to be in burlesque myself.'

GABBY (SPOKEN TITLE): 'I might have known it. The stage could not afford to overlook such beauty.'

The scene is set for the rivalry between Gabby Gilfoil and Sheriff Ben Holden. At the same time Mary is being courted by the Sheriff's young cousin, Tony Holden, played by Jack Luden. These are the 'Two Flaming Youths' of the title, in case you were wondering. The situation will be reprised, in a different configuration, in 1934's The Old Fashioned Way, in which Jan Duggan, alias Cleopatra Pepperday, the rich widow of the town, is courted both by Fields as the Great McGonigle and the local sheriff, leading to Fields having to sit quietly through three choruses of La Pepperday singing 'Gathering Up the Shells Upon the Sea Shore'.

But in this instance we are still with the freaks, who climb off the truck, the giant dropping the dwarf over the side and the fat woman falling on top of Sheriff Holden, who is trying to help her climb down. 'Her weight suddenly applied to the rear end of the truck sends the front end up into the air.' Ben, badly shaken, enters the hotel with the freaks and Madge, still casting him as bellboy, hands him the room keys. Surlily he shows the freaks up, trying to evade the flirtatious attentions of the fat woman, who tells him:

SPOKEN TITLE: 'You smell like my late husband – he was a chorus man.'

Gilfoil soon discovers that the 'bell boy' is in fact the Sheriff of Arkosa, as the Sheriff warns him:

SPOKEN TITLE: 'You keep away from Miss Malarkey! She's my fiasco – if you'll pardon my French!'

Gilfoil's daughter Mary, having met Tony, yearns to stay and settle down. She tells her Dad: 'Wouldn't it be great if we could live here all the time? . . . But tomorrow they'll find out about us, and then we'll be eating dust again . . .'

Responding to her dreams, Gilfoil redoubles his efforts to flirt with Madge Malarkey, who has stated that she will marry the man who finds the money to pay her mortgage. In the hotel lobby, that night, he juggles to amuse her, while Sheriff Holden tries to impress her with his prowess upon a musical saw. (Oh, for sound! But we are still in silents . . .) Ben returns to his office, to find a telegram:

REPLYING TO YOUR WIRE MAN CALLING HIMSELF GILFOIL MAY BE CHICAGO MIKE IF HE HAS TWO GOLD WISDOM TEETH ARREST HIM. SAM TURNER CHIEF OF POLICE.

The Sheriff returns to the hotel, trying to get Gilfoil to sing so he can look into his mouth, but he is unable to catch a glimpse of his teeth. A strange dream sequence follows, in the script, in which Ben Holden dreams of cracking a whip over Gilfoil, who acts as a performing dog. I do not know if this scene was in the final film. But the next sequence was certainly featured: Gilfoil has opened a local dime museum in a building he has rented from Simeon Trott. Surviving stills bear witness to the unique nature of this sequence in Fields' work – a loving reconstruction of the old freak shows of the past:

229. INT. MUSEUM – FULL SHOT.

This is a long and narrow room. The rear end of it has been transformed into a small stage by the simple process of setting up a fairly high platform, and masking the back stage area from the auditorium with a couple of scene 'flats' or mangy portieres. The freaks occupy lower platforms set at intervals along the side walls.

GABBY *is on the platform beside the tattooed man calling attention to the picturesque beauties of the exhibit's epidermis. The small audience is listening to him with rapt attention.* MADGE MALARKEY *is in the very forefront of the audience and* GABBY *is directing his talk to her as tho' she were the only other person present.* BEN *is standing beside her.*

Leap forward to Larson E. Whipsnade in 1939, introducing the 'Punkwat Twins – they baffle science!' . . . Sheriff Ben tries to prove the freaks are fake, but gets stuck with a pin from the human pincushion, while Gilfoil introduces the Wild Man: 'Single handed and armed only with a lassoo I pursued this monster to his jungle home and captured him after a combat lasting three hours!' Sheriff Holden gives up for the moment, and Gilfoil receives an invitation to a grand carnival at another town, where he can't fail to clean up. We fade out and in to the carnival grounds at Boynton –

367. A FLASH *of the wheel of fortune, and its operator.*

368. A FLASH *of a ring game concession.*

369. A FLASH *of a hula dancer operating on a platform in front of a tent.*

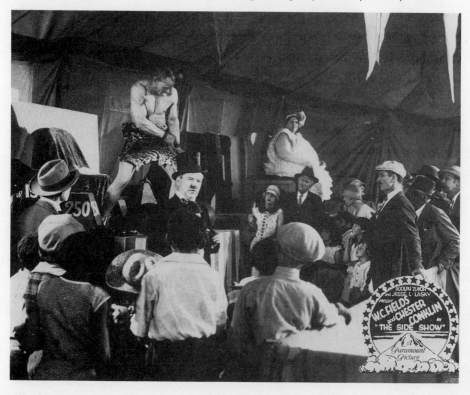

21 *Two Flaming Youths* a.k.a. *The Side Show*: Gaby Gilfoil with the performers of 'Gilfoil's Non-pareil Circus'.

370. LONG SHOT. *In the central space between the tents a shallow artificial lake. On the edge of it a tamer for a diving horse act. A uniformed trumpeter appears and beside him a man with a megaphone. The trumpeter blows a resounding blast to attract the attention of the crowd . . .*

377. MEDIUM SHOT *of Gilfoil's tent. A canvas sign across the front of the tent announces it as the show place of*

GILFOIL'S

Congress of Human Caricatures.

Entertaining – Educational – Extraordinary.

But the Sheriff is stalking Gilfoil. He produces a warrant and arrests him for being 'Slippery Sawtelle' (a change from 'Chicago Mike' in the previous title). He produces the cuffs, but the fat woman once again falls on top of him and Gilfoil escapes. The Sheriff pursues him. They run past the animal acts:

415. EXT. ANIMAL SHOW – LONG SHOT

In front of the tent the barker is making his spiel, the girl with the performing bear is helping him out. GABBY *slips into the tent.* BEN *comes along and does exactly the same thing. CU sign: 'AUSTRALIAN BOXING KANGAROO World's Champion.'*

416. EXT. REAR OF ANIMAL SHOW – LONG SHOT

GABBY *emerges from the rear of the tent, slips around a corner and proceeds in the direction of his own tent. A moment later* BEN *appears. He spots* GABBY. *In the opening of the tent the boxing* KANGAROO *(wearing his gloves) appears – on* BEN'S *trail. Ben sees the* KANGAROO *and runs – in pursuit of* GABBY. *The kangaroo hops after him.*

417. EXT. CARNIVAL GROUNDS – FULL SHOT *(Gabby's tent in background)* GABBY *runs across the center space pursued by* BEN, *who is, in turn, followed by the* KANGAROO. *The audience is surprised and amused, and some of them follow the* KANGAROO.

The kangaroo pursues Ben Holden into the 'Wild Man's tent, where he falls into the pit. As the freaks scatter before the kangaroo the beast leaps into the pit and takes a swing at the Sheriff, knocking him down. Sheriff Ben fights back and all the freaks gather. Gabby watches this scene, which gives him a great idea. He exits the tent:

423. EXT. TENT – LONG SHOT

GABBY *mounts his box and goes into a loud-voiced, fervid ballyhoo of the 'show now going in inside.' The crowds attracted by his eloquence surge around him.*

424. CLOSE SHOT of GABBY as he talks:

SPOKEN TITLE: 'The battle of the century – a struggle between man and beast – a finish fight between the boxing kangaroo and the sheriff of Arkosa!'

Everyone crowds round, eagerly putting money in Gilfoil's hand. At this point the crooked bellboy who had quit the Mansion House hotel, and who is the real 'Slippery Sawtelle', is spotted in the crowd by the local, Boynton Sheriff, who arrests him, while:

432: INT. TENT – LONG SHOT OF PIT

Continuing the match between the KANGAROO *and* BEN. *Suddenly the* KANGAROO *lands an upper-cut on* BEN's *chin and lifts him clear out of the pit. He is caught by members of the uproarious audience.* BEN, *unhurt, fights his way from the clutches of his captors and struggles through the crowd to the front of the tent.*

Sheriff Ben realises he has been after the wrong man. But a chase now ensues between himself and Gilfoil to reach Madge Malarkey in time to pay off her mortgage and win her hand in marriage. In the final scene, at the hotel, Mary and Tony rush in to announce they've been married. Gilfoil realises that he has no need to wed Madge in order to ensure his daughter's happiness. He therefore relinquishes his claim in favour of the Sheriff, who can pay the mortgage with the reward money he gained from apprehending the real crook (courtesy of his Boynton colleague). Gilfoil tells Mary:

SPOKEN TITLE: 'Everything's happening for the best, my dear. You nearly had me married to that burlesque queen – now I can split it up!' He turns to Sheriff Holden: 'Take her, my boy – and may all your troubles be midgets!'

BEN, *overcome by emotion, grabs* GABBY's *hand and thanks him . . . But (landlord Simeon)* TROTT *steps to* MADGE's *side and gesticulates to* BEN *to stand off.*

SPOKEN TITLE (TROTT): 'She got tired of waiting for you four-flushers – and so she married a real man!'

This has the effect of a bombshell on the gathering. MADGE *faces them defiantly and says:*

SPOKEN TITLE (MADGE): 'I couldn't count on either of you false alarms making good – so I married Mr Trott to save my hotel.'

SHERIFF BEN *turns to* GABBY (SPOKEN TITLE): 'You tried to do a fine thing for me – so we're square.'

SPOKEN TITLE, GABBY TO BEN: 'There's no future for a sheriff in this town. How'd you like to become a partner in Gilfoil's Nonpareil Circus?'

BEN *hands his handcuffed crook over to* TROTT –

578. FULL SHOT –

The crook grinning at the amazed and indignant TROTT. MARY *and* TONY *laughing in background.* GABBY *motions to* BEN *to come on. They link arms, and, swaggering, start for the front door.*

579. EXTERIOR HOTEL – AT DOOR – CLOSE SHOT

GABBY *and* BEN *enter from the hotel, arm in arm. They stop dead still, staring straight in front of them.*

EXTERIOR HOTEL – MEDIUM SHOT

The freaks, in their show costumes, weary and worn, muddy and dishevelled, grouped at the edge of the sidewalk. The giant, trudging, is pushing the dwarf in a wheelbarrow. Calmly he upsets the wheelbarrow, dropping the dwarf to the road. The dwarf lies where he falls, without movement or protest. The giant collapses into the wheelbarrow and the wheelbarrow breaks.

SEMI CLOSE UP

GABBY *and* BEN. *They look from the freaks to each other and begin to laugh.*

FADE OUT.

In the silent films, in particular, we do not know the extent of Fields' own involvement in the development of the draft scripts. 'The Side Show' was certainly tailor-made for his long-established concern with the world of show business and its labouring cast. The freaks, in particular, were the most poignant examples of the harshness of this kind of life. Not for nothing does Tod Browning's landmark horror film, *Freaks*, shot five years after *Two Flaming Youths*, inspire an uncanny pity to this day. Fields is well known for his prejudices, his foibles and complaints, but what is less apparent, until one looks a little closer, is his boundless compassion for showpeople at the bottom rungs of the ladder. We can only guess whether the impact of the movie itself enhanced this feeling, or might convey it today. The reviews were mixed, but box office was lousy. Though *Variety* commented, tantalisingly, that 'Fields' native talents for juggling are consistently introduced. His capabilities with the cigar boxes, balls, shell game, etc., are neatly dovetailed into the action under the intelligent direction of John Waters.'

So it seems that it was not directorial incompetence which poured the film down the plughole. Perhaps, after our close look, we might speculate that the film was altogether too weird; its setting too surreal, its characters too disturbing to be popular, despite the hokey tale woven around its stars.

There seems little doubt, though, that Fields two next movies with Conklin were weary and dishevelled vehicles. *Tillie's Punctured Romance*, trumpeted as a remake of the famous Mack Sennett hit of 1914, with Charlie Chaplin and Marie Dressler, was a ramshackle affair about a circus which is taken over to Germany to amuse the troops and wins the war when the lions escape to ravage the Huns. Eddie Sutherland directed, but Louise Brooks has written:

> I was still married to Eddie during the preparation and production of *Tillie*, which was the worst mess of filmmaking that I have ever observed . . . It was filmed with groans, previewed with moans, shown in a few theatres, and then buried in the vaults. Poor old *Tillie* had not a single mourner.

Bill had fallen under a truck during the filming of the final chase scene of *Two Flaming Youths*, and fractured his third cervical vertebra. A stuntman named Johnny Sinclair saved his life by dragging him just in time from under the wheels. Fields hired him from then on in every movie he made until Paramount put him on the general payroll. (Ronald Fields notes that in *Million Dollar Legs* [1932] he even had a part, as the Secretary of Labor.) In *Tillie* Bill had more trouble, being almost blown up in a minefield and almost eaten by the lions, who were let loose before he had cleared their cage. Fields made sure that from then on the only animals that co-starred with him were ostriches, cats, small dogs or children.

The third film of the trilogy, *Fools For Luck*, is the most obscure. No one can seem to make much sense of the plot. It involved Fields in a Potteresque exchange with Conklin, as two businessmen who row over oil wells. Paramount's Press Book for the film tried desperately to convince the punters that 'This scintillating comedy of the professional promoter's adventures in a small town is an entertainment master-piece,' but surviving script treatments do not bear this out. The talent was there, but not the material. Charles Reisner, the director, had worked with Chaplin and directed Buster Keaton in the superb *Steamboat Bill Junior.* Fields and Conklin played together in a reprise of Field's pool act. But nothing could save the film. This was more dev-astating to Chester Conklin than it was to Bill Fields. Unlike Fields, he never returned to movie stardom, and eked out his living in cameo roles. He appeared with Fields once more, in *Her Majesty Love*, in 1931, but only in a very minor part. He shone briefly as Charlie Chaplin's workmate, in *Modern Times*, in 1936, who digs Charlie out of the machine. Chaplin used him again, in *The Great Dictator*, as a customer in the little Jew's barber shop. He turns up in Preston Sturges' *Hail the Conquering Hero*, in 1944, and in tiny, flitting moments thereafter. His last sighting was in a 1966 western called *A Big Hand for a Little Lady*, a poker game movie, which starred Henry Fonda, Jason Robards and Joanne Woodward. He died, aged eighty-three, in 1971.

He had the best moustache in motion pictures.

Bill Fields was banished from Hollywood. But, as he turned his back, salvation was beckoning. In October 1927, in *The Jazz Singer*, Al Jolson had opened his mouth on the screen and emitted the immortal words: 'Wait a minute, wait a minute, you ain't heard nothin' yet . . . '

Chapter 27
Vanities, Vanities – The Show Must Go On

Bill Fields' personal life, during his silent film ventures, continued to run on a familiar groove. He continued to send money to Hattie, and in 1927 arranged with the Harriman National Bank to have a sum of $75 available for her weekly on an indefinite basis. A letter from Los Angeles, in April 1928, resounds grouchily to her demand that this allowance should rise according to his rising salary:

> I have been badly handled and am now out of movies. I have worked sixteen weeks in the last thirteen months. Have had two big law suits, lost both and am entering upon a third. After income tax, lawyer's fees, agent's comms. and damages have been deducted from my income there is little if anything left. I am coming back now to work on the stage again, if my chest will permit it. So 'drive easy, the road is muddy' as McIntyre and Heath used to say.
>
> Claude

At this point, Bill was also in occasional touch with his son, Claude Junior, who, according to family lore, had visited him, probably at Hattie's goading, to ask him for help in getting through College. His father told him to stand on his own two feet, as he had, but it seems their communication was amiable, if distant. On 15 August, Bill sent his son, from New York, a cheque for $200 and a hearty handclasp for his graduation from Columbia University law school.

Bill gave his New York address to Hattie, in this period, as 130 West 44th Street – his old watering hole of the Lamb's Club. In May 1928, he wrote in hand, on the letterhead of the nearby Hotel Astor on Times Square, to his good friend Tom Geraghty, in Los Angeles, a typically elliptic Fieldsian epistle:

> Dear Thompson,
>
> Your good letter read, but your description of the manner in which you are

swinging the Dover egg beater leads me to believe you are not in groove. Further, the implement is a combination egg beater and waffle iron and should never be taken into the garden . . . I have signed with Carroll and will start emoting about Aug. 15th, but have permission to do movies and talkies. Also have some backers for a Co. of my own and have Elmer Pearson telling me Harold Lloyd will hurl untold wealth into a talking picture for the two black crows and myself.

This is the sabbath and it is raining. What a great country for the farming, but you can't raise a thing in my room at the Astor Hotel, consequently I am very low . . . about weather conditions. We have had one nice day since we left Los Angeles. They can have New York and 'stick it.' . . . It is nearing the hour of five so I must leave you to go to Leones and get pissed. The real joy of the day. We send our very best to you all. Words fail me when I try to tell you how we miss you all and baby. I think I told you I nicked Earl Carroll for fifty two hundred per week. I think it is next to the record. Jolson outsalaries me.

All for now. Save 'The Scar' for me. If the Co. comes into existence we will do that after or before The Great McGillicuddy. Write when you get the time. Keep your eye on the ball. Always your friend,

Bill Fields

As ever, the real Fields behind the myth is an intriguing surprise, if not shock. The warm salutations to his friend are so far from the misanthropic grouch of legend. What is all this stuff about gardening? Who are 'We?' Is Bill still with Bessie Poole, or with another girlfriend, Linelle Blackburn, she of the chorus of *Poppy*? Louise Brooks, in her memoir, has left us a description of Bill's plots to get rid of Bessie Poole in Los Angeles, by pretending to go on a business trip to San Francisco with his agent, Bill Grady, so as to send her a ticket back to New York from there. Brooks describes the two plotters waving to Bessie on the platform, from the observation car: 'Goodbye, Bessie! Goodbye, my dear – my little rosebud! Take care of yourself!'

A later letter to Geraghty, naming Linelle as Bill's companion, suggests that she had, at some point, replaced Bessie Poole in Los Angeles. It seems likely that Bessie did return to New York alone, a separation which may well have caused her to hit the bottle and spiral down towards her dismal demise in Chez Florence in the late autumn of

1928, leaving Fields with her unhappy will and woeful epitaph – 'I forgot to duck . . .'

The letter does tell us that Bill was continuing his search for the Holy Grail of his own production company, first mooted in 1907, in vaudeville. The hint that Harold Lloyd was a prospective partner shows us that Fields was not the hostile rival to everyone else that has been assumed; Chaplin, of course, excepted. (A letter to Gene Fowler from November 1940, commenting on *The Great Dictator*, notes sourly: 'I hope Chaplin's picture is as bad as the critics say it is.') But, alas, nothing came of the Harold Lloyd deal.

Other projects which never came to fruition crop up in press reports and other letters. A script, *The Wild Man of Borneo*, is reported by Ronald Fields to have been extant as early as 1926, written by Herman Mankiewicz: 'The rollicking tale of a dapper boarding house Romeo who poses as a Broadway star greater than Booth or Irving and who really was *The Wild Man of Borneo* in a cheap Broadway sideshow'. Another version of the same project spoke of a role for Lillian Gish as a native dancer with W. C. Fields as 'the shipwrecked yachtsman'. I have seen, in the family archive, a later version of this script, dated May 1933, credited to Herman Mankiewicz and Marc Connelly, writer of the famous *Green Pastures*. *The Wild Man of Borneo* was eventually served up as a certified turkey in 1941, with Frank Morgan and Billie Burke instead of W. C. Fields and Lillian Gish.

The Great McGillicuddy is a more intriguing shadow. Like *Two Flaming Youths*, it is another missing link between Eustace McGargle and the Great McGonigle of *The Old Fashioned Way*. A surviving treatment, with handwritten annotations by Fields, is prefaced:

> The Great McGillicuddy is the owner and chief actor of an 'Uncle Tom's Cabin' company . . . [he is] an actor of the old school fast disappearing from the face of the earth. He is at once self-confident, pompous and dignified whether he is revelling in success or sinking to the depths of despair. We love him for his faults and blunders as well as for the tenderness he shows when his big heart is so easily touched.

A clear manifesto of the character that Fields, with various collaborators, was aiming to create. The film was going to end in a spectacular scene, echoing the real life 'Uncle Tom's Cabin', in which the Great McGillicuddy leads the people of the small town where he is performing across a river of ice, to save them from a dam which is about to burst. The usual stock characters abound: Peggy Wells, McGillicuddy's ward and the apple of his eye; Mrs Jenkins, wardrobe mistress of the troupe whose advances towards the Great Man make his life a constant misery; and there is a great role for Shorty – clearly intended for William Blanche – as valet-cum-mediator-cum-deputy manager. The scrawled annotations by Fields on various pages suggest 'Turkey egg and ale gag here', or 'poker game here instead' of a pool-room scene, or 'Small boy from fence gives McGillicuddy the bird, That's what they all say – greatest show on earth . . .'

But *The Great McGillicuddy* never got to first base, let alone to production. *The Scar* must have been another such abortive project, lost in the messy transition of movies from silents to sound. But it is clear that Fields' short stay in Hollywood, despite his failure there, whetted his appetite for California. He became hooked on the sun and the wide open spaces of an as yet unspoiled Los Angeles. The rain on the window-panes of New York – despite later folderol about how he loved the pitter-patter of raindrops on the roof – is only giving him the willies.

Nevertheless, financially, Bill had fallen on his feet again, courtesy of Broadway producer Earl Carroll. This was another of the flamboyant showpeople, like George White, who had set himself up to out-Ziegfeld Ziegfeld. Having begun as a songwriter, Carroll determined to out do the Great Glorifier by fielding even more glorious girls. At the beginning, in 1923, he tried emulating George Cohan by writing his own material, as well as the songs. But he soon discovered, like Ziegfeld, that he had to vary the talent if he wanted to draw the audience in. Joe Cook, Jimmy Duffy, and the double act of Moran and Mack (the 'two black crows' referred to in Fields' letter to Geraghty), appeared in the four shows until 1926. Thereafter, Carroll suffered a setback of sorts, as he was hauled in by New York's finest for cooking the books, and earned a stretch in the Federal Penitentiary at Atlanta, Georgia. Unabashed, he bounced back in 1928, with even more money, and rushed to California to entice W. C. Fields to star in his newest, brashest revue to date.

As Bill wrote to Geraghty, it was an offer he could hardly refuse, allowing him to make movies – if he could get any assignments – and paying him over five thousand a week. Ziegfeld himself was still producing – the *Follies* of 1927 was mostly a vehicle for Eddie Cantor. But thereafter there was no *Follies* until 1931, his last, and a mere echo of former glories.

So let us return to Broadway, 'the Great White Way', where, in 1928, 264 plays and revues were in production, an all-time peak. Fields was, briefly, back home, on the stage, in the year of the final, deceptive glitter of a golden age which was soon going to die.

The Earl Carroll *Vanities* of 1928 were practically a showcase for Fields, as the show's featured star. His Broadway audience clearly remembered him fondly, and his movies had only whetted the appetite to hear the voice as well as see the man. Bill appeared in seven numbers, including three sketches – 'The Stolen Bonds', 'The Caledonian Express' and 'The Dentist' – which were to be immortalised in the movies. A fourth sketch, 'School Days', I have quoted earlier. Three other skits: 'All Aboard', 'Mrs Hubbard's Cupboard' and 'The Mormon's Prayer' have evaded my questing eye.

For some of these numbers, Bill was reunited with his old 'baby' foil from Ziegfeld, Ray Dooley, and her brother Gordon. Joe Frisco was the other featured male comedian. And of course, there were all the dazzling dames, led by Dorothy Knapp, 'The Most Beautiful Girl in the World'. Dorothy Britton – Miss Universe; Vanita Carol – Miss Denmark; the Misses Cleveland, Pittsburgh, Long Beach and Bronx; and Miss Australia, Blanche Satchel, added lustre. And a significant name lurks in a number called 'The Dance Marathon', whose 'Couple No. 41' presented one Fay Adler, whom we have noted featuring in Hattie Fields' deposition for Bill's estate in 1947.

Freed of Florenz Ziegfeld's patronising strictures, Bill felt he could experiment more freely, and so there is a quantum change in the nature of the sketches Bill wrote for the *Vanities*. The curtain goes up, on 'The Stolen Bonds,' to –

Scene showing interior of old country farmhouse made of logs in Canadian northwest. Living room left – small bedroom right. At rise of curtain two Indians with blankets over them are sitting in front of the fireplace.

Scene opens wind is howling, falling snow can be seen thru the window. Door opens. SNAVELY *(a trapper) enters living room from upstage right. As he opens door velocity of wind can be heard more plainly and a quantity of snow is blown into the living room. Dogs can be heard howling outside. Room is dimly lighted.* SNAVELY *is carrying one gold nugget about the size of a human skull (a gilded automobile sponge). He carefully deposits same on table with thud.*

SNAVELY: Hello thar, hello thar, hello, hello.

Walks to telephone, says – 'Hello.' Walks stage left sees Indians. Indians rise.

FIRST INDIAN: How Mr. Snavely.

SNAVELY: How chief.

SECOND INDIAN: How.

SNAVELY: And how. Vamoose! Ewscray!

INDIANS *exit.* SNAVELY *closes door behind them.*

SNAVELY: It ain't a fit night out for man nor beast and it's been astormin for over a fortnit.

He looks about the room furtively, goes to electric light nearest door pulls the cord to light same and electric light at opposite side of window flashes on. He goes to lighted lamp pulls the cord and the opposite light flashes on.

MRS SNAVELY (*voice off*): Who's thar?

SNAVELY: S'me ma.

MRS SNAVELY *enters from door stage left.*

MRS SNAVELY: Did you find any gold down in the gulch?

SNAVELY: I found a nugget. Thar it be on the table.

MRS SNAVELY *sees nugget on table and effusively exclaims:*

MRS SNAVELY: A nugget, a golden nugget.

She picks it up with great care and deliberation.

MRS SNAVELY: A golden nugget, just what you have combed them thar hills for for nigh on thirty years. It must be worth almost a hundred dollars.

Aficionados will not fail to recognise the unmistakeable words and movements of Bill's 1933 Mack Sennett short *The Fatal Glass of Beer.* Of all Fields' movies, this, *The Golf Specialist* apart, is the most faithful rendition in the oeuvre of a Fields' stage skit. The scripts of stage and screen are almost word for word identical, with a minor switching of the order of the scenes. This is Fields at his most surreal, parodying the Frozen North and, probably, his rival Chaplin's rendition of it in *The Gold Rush*, in 1925. It also contains another dig at a wayward son, Chester, who left his Pa and Ma for the city, and was tempted by the demon liquor. Imprisoned for stealing money from his bank, Chester is released to return to his dear old parents, having thrown out 'all of that tainted money', but only 'to sponge on us for the rest of your life!' they protest as they throw him back out in the snow.

Playing the zither with his mitts on, going out to milk the elk, the monosyllabic Indians, and eating his lead dog, who 'was mighty good with mustard', Fields plumbed new heights of the topsy-turvy absurd. All attempts to analyse the sketch's 'social significance' disappear into the buzz of its anarchic play on meaningless postures and juxtapositions. The handful of snow in the face, every time a door or window is opened, to the rolling mantra of 'It ain't a fit night out for man nor beast', is more Lewis than Earl Carroll. Mark Twain would have rolled on the floor, had he seen it.

As usual, the sketch was meticulously rehearsed and prepared. A press release from the 'Vanities' revealed that, according to Fields' own estimate –

> . . . he has used 175 pints of soup in which to dunk 175 loaves of bread, and at the same time, has stopped just exactly one ton of artificial snow in his 'Stolen Bonds' sketch. All of these materials are actual waste and represent the cost expended for the sake of laughs. The specially diced paper used for snow, costs $14.00 a ten-pound bag because it must be fireproofed. Another item of expense for laughter in the Vanities has been 200 boxes of soda crackers which Fields munches during one of his acts . . .

In *The Caledonian Express*, which sprang from some weird memory Fields retained of his vaudeville travels in Scotland, Bill played four separate roles as Guard, Conductor, Station Master and Policeman, all in different variants of Scottish accents, trying to dissuade an American, played by Joe Frisco, from taking over a Lord Derby's compartment. English Lords were always a good butt for jokes. Fields was inordinately fond of this sketch, which he chose to bring out of mothballs for his very last appearance in film, in *Sensations of 1945*. But it would hardly play in Glasgey.

Two of the lost *Vanities* sketches, 'All Aboard' and 'The Mormon's

Prayer', were apparently written by Thomas Tarrant and Herman Meyer, respectively, the latter with Fields as Brigham Young surrounded by a bevvy of Earl's greatest beauties. The third vanished skit, 'Mrs Hubbard's Cupboard', with Ray and Gordon Dooley, is a mystery. But the crowning glory of the show was without doubt 'An Episode at the Dentist', perhaps W. C. Fields' greatest sketch of all time, which became *The Dentist* for Mack Sennett productions.

Several versions of the Dentist Sketch are extant. The Library of Congress file has three different versions. Fields lovingly crafted and recrafted it, adding new gags and characters, truncating old ones. An early version includes the following cast list:

CHARACTERS:

DR O. HUGH HURT – *A dentist*

MISS MOLAR – *A patient*

BUTS BENFORD – *A boy with a mean tooth*

K. O. DROPP –- *A prize fighter*

WILHELMINA JAZZ – *A chorus person*

LYCURGUS WAGSNIFF – *A dentist's assistant*

MISS GLUFUSS – *Just Miss Glufuss*

DUCKIE – *Brother of Miss Glufuss*

MIKE PICK – *A plumber*

MISS GLENN – *Just Miss Glenn*

MISS DALE – *Just Miss Dale*

MR FOLIAGE – *A nature lover*

SCENE: *the dentist waiting room stage right, occupying one third of stage. The dentist office occupying two thirds of stage left.*

DR HURT (*pulling tooth of* MISS MOLAR): Now there honey it's out.

MISS MOLAR: Yes I see it's out, and you are out too. You said it wouldn't hurt and you just tried your best to hurt me and I hate you.

LYCURGUS WAGSNIFF *enters office from door left, walks to closet, takes out book and reads.*

K. O. DROPP (*sits in dentist chair*): I want this whole cluster on the right-hand side out.

DR HURT: Will you remove your hat. (*Finds it is the protuberance he has mistaken for his hat*) I beg your pardon. Do you want gas, friend?

K. O. DROPP: Nothing stirring, you can blast for all I care; some yegg gives me a stick of dynamite to chew on and tells me it is sassasfras root and it blows the whole left side out.

DR HURT *operates with a boxing glove on* K. O. – *lets a haymaker loose from hip which connects with* DROPP's *jaw.* DROPP *staggers to basin and spits out teeth.*

DR H *throws boxing glove which contains a couple of horse shoes on stage.*

Later, Mr Foliage enters –

DR HURT: That is a very becoming moustache you have.

FOLIAGE: Yes, it is becoming and beautiful because it is natural. I live close to nature, I sleep in the fields, the little birds are my friends.

DR HURT: I'd like to keep all the golf balls I find in here. (*Makes careful search for mouth*) He must have a mouth or he couldn't talk – just keep on talking sir. Lycurgus just hand me that stethoscope.

WAGSNIFF *hands stethoscope to* DR. DR HURT *tries various parts of head, back of neck and body to find location of mouth.*

DR HURT (*finally*): Lycurgus, just take this gentleman out in the yard and run the grass mower over his face once or twice.

LYCURGUS *and* FOLIAGE *exit door left.*

In a later version, the Doctor, now called Dr Pain, seats Foliage in the chair and gets to work on him with the drill –

DENTIST: You didn't feel anything that time.

FOLIAGE: Nothing but pain.

More grinding, patient spits out crockery in bowl. DENTIST *wipes instrument on* PATIENT's *tie.*

DENTIST: You say you have never had your teeth filled before, yet I find some gold on my instrument.

FOLIAGE: You must have struck my back collar button.

After some more drilling, Foliage pushes the dentist away. When the dentist does reach him a bird flies out of Foliage's beard.

FOLIAGE: Never mind, don't bother, I'll fill it myself. Teeth are hell. (*Exits*)

DENTIST: Yes, we come into the world without them and go out of it without them. The interval belongs to the dentist.

In yet another revised version, copyrighted on 1 November 1928, while the *Vanities* was in full swing, Fields first assays the immortal line, to Miss Minkey (who was played on stage by Ray Dooley, and her equivalent on film, in 1932, by Elise Cavanna): 'Have you had this tooth pulled before?' adding, as he stops in mid-pull to fan himself with a palm leaf – 'How's business in the Capitol this week?' The Foliage scene, in this version, has Fields cutting away the patient's beard from around the mouth:

DENTIST: Now just where is the trouble?

FOLIAGE: The trouble is in Mexico. You see I'm joining the Mexican Army and I want my teeth fixed.

DENTIST: Are you going to bite the enemy?

DENTIST *fixes drill and turns on juice. Drills in* FOLIAGE'*s mouth.* FOLIAGE *arises and spits out beans.* DENTIST *examines* FOLIAGE'*s beard again and bird flies out.*

DENTIST *then quickly grabs hunting cap from table and puts it on and picks up gun then pokes gun into* FOLIAGE'*s beard. He backs away and throws golf ball into* FOLIAGE'*s beard as though to scare up a covey of birds.* FOLIAGE *leaps out of chair and starts towards door.*

FOLIAGE (*furious*): Never mind I'll fix it myself . . . (*Runs out, shouting*) You'll never catch me again!

DENTIST (*shouting back*): I'll set a mousetrap for you.

As in Bill's 'School Days', the other added factor in the Dentist Sketch is a certain smutty humour, as when the Doctor tells another patient, Miss Doodab (played on the stage by the peerless Dorothy Knapp), when she prattles on about a dog that bit her on the ankle – 'You're lucky it wasn't a Newfoundland dog that bit you.' Or, in a previous version, with Miss Molar –

DENTIST: Would you like gas?

MISS MOLAR: Well gas or electric light. I'd feel nervous to have you fool around me in the dark.

Well, it was 1928 . . . Though this kind of thing was going to get Bill into hot water with the censorship boards, in Hollywood, as we shall relate in due course . . . But we can see how Fields' verbal imagination is already in full swing.

The Dentist Sketch builds, of course, on foundations which are extremely old and venerable in comedy – surely jokes about quacks made cavemen laugh. One 1912 English music-hall sketch, entitled 'Dentistry', has the exchange – Patient: 'I'll have the gas.' Dentist: 'We haven't any gas, it's all electric light here.' Clearly an old staple of burlesque. Certainly laughing gas would be out of the question in Doctor Pain's surgery. Anything to reduce the dentist's unshakeable, and mistaken, faith in his own ability to extract teeth painlessly would be ruled out of court.

Fields' dental adventures in Earl Carroll's *Vanities* had one more curious spin-off. The gag with the canary was prefaced by Fields blatantly producing the canary from his pocket to stuff in the patient, Foliage's beard. At one performance, on 13 September, two enforcers from the Humane Society climbed on stage and arrested Fields for cruelty to the canary. It was alleged that at this performance the bird had flown into the audience and knocked itself dead on a backdrop. The case was heard on 14 September 1928, before the Hon. George Simpson, City Magistrate. The resulting court transcript is published in Ronald Fields' 1973 volume, *W. C. Fields By Himself*, and would do justice to Mark Twain, Lewis Carroll or W. C. Fields himself –

Q: Have you got the beard here that was on the unknown man's chin?

A (Fields): No.

Q: How long a beard would you say it was?

A: The beard was this long (*indicating*), but the bird does not touch the beard. I held the bird, and the beard is there.

Q: You do not place the bird in the beard?

A: Just underneath the beard.

And so forth. But the court accepted the defence submission that the bird had in fact been asphyxiated by the smoke from photographers' flash-bulbs, set off while the Humane officer was holding the bird in his hand. Fields – 1, Humane Society – nil. It may well be, however, that this whole affair was a publicity stunt cooked up by Fields and the *Vanities* press staff. Some things are too good to be true.

Bill continued to develop his sketches, the last of this decade, registered in 1930, being yet another version of his age-old Motoring sketch, 'The Midget Car'. The characters in this short piece are set down as Charlie Bogle, Mrs Bogle, and 'A man'. Charlie Bogle arrives on stage in a tiny car, honking for Mrs Bogle, who enters laden down with props – including a bird cage with two canary birds, a set of golf clubs, a large mandolin in a case, two grips and a black cat – note the strong canary bird motif. Trying to climb into this contraption – 'It's too small to call a car and its too big to call a roller skate and it can't be a scooter because it has four wheels,' says Mrs Bogle. The mandolin is crushed, and familiar Goodbyes are exchanged with offstage neighbours. The engine, of course, stalls.

More familiar business trying to start the car, with neighbours shouting offstage: 'Goodbye! Goodbye!'

BOGLE (*getting out of car . . . removes engine and dusts it with a feather duster*): Hand me that shifting spanner . . .

MRS BOGLE: What's the matter?

BOGLE: The nuts are loose.

MRS BOGLE: The what are loose?

BOGLE: The nuts! The nuts!

MRS BOGLE: Well, don't lose your temper . . . (*head protruding thru top of car*) There's not room enough in here for a couple of canary birds, let alone two human beings.

BOGLE: Will you remove that bird cage from my seat?

(BLIND MAN *enters from stage left tapping cane. Strikes car violently with cane as he proceeds along feeling his way. Exits stage right.*)

BOGLE: Why in hell don't you look where you're going?

MRS BOGLE: You fool, he's blind.

BOGLE: He must be. (*Blow razzberry horn twice* ... BOGLE *and* MRS BOGLE *get out of car and begin throwing the broken golf clubs and broken bird cage out.* MRS BOGLE *runs all around the car bewildered and excited. She has lost something. She is very excited.*)

MRS BOGLE: Where's pussy? Where's pussy?

BOGLE: What?

MRS BOGLE: I've lost pussy. Where's pussy?

BOGLE: How do I know where's pussy? (*Look around and discover cat.*) Here's pussy. (*Hold up dead black cat.*)

Renamed as 'The Baby Austin', this sketch was performed on stage in the short-lived 1930 play *Ballyhoo*. But portions of the skit would turn up eleven years later in *The Bank Dick*, and other bits of business, including the pussy, would turn up in the 1932 talkie, *International House*, where the unlucky feline would spark off a war between the censor and Paramount Studios that would have far-reaching consequences ...

But other, even more powerful forces than the censors or the Humane Society were about to show their hand ...

Chapter 28
Spitting in the Gulf Stream

In April 1929, Bill wrote his friend, Tom Geraghty, again, from Great Neck, Long Island:

> Have just returned from Fla. where we did enjoy good sunshine. My how he does love Florida he must hate New York in the winter . . . I have several offers to do talkies including one from Famous to do some shorts and two longies 'IN N.Y.' But I want to get to California. I have a former mngr. named Goodman who has a company formed to make pictures. He wants to start immediately but his stories are no good. Will you please send me on a copy of the Great McGillicuddy at your earliest convenience, I am sure I can get him interested in it. How is your golf? I did 79 Sunday, 82's Monday & Tuesday. Not too bad.
>
> Well Tom I suppose you have met our old friend Charlie Mack and love him as everyone does. Don't tell him I played a 79, or he will throw his clubs away and I want him to continue the game he is worth money to me. I wouldn't sell him for $250 per week cash paid in advance. Will leave you now dear old Thompson. Linelle and I are always talking about you, Ethel and your children; you are all wonderful and were all so kind to us. Goodbye before I break down and sob like a babe.
>
> Write soon as convenient, Bill.

After his Florida break with Linelle Blackburn, chasing alligators with Bill Grady, he returned to the 1929 run of the *Vanities*. In these later shows, Bill added his tried and true Golf Sketch, with William 'Shorty' Blanche as his obstructive caddy. His salary rose to $6,000 a week. When the *Vanities* closed, Bill played the New York Palace with the 'Golf Sketch' and 'The Stolen Bonds'. This was his last appearance on a straightforward vaudeville bill.

Despite Bill's hopes, there were still no takers for *The Great McGillicuddy*, and he was forced to rethink his refusal to make movies on the east coast. Once again it was William Le Baron, his benefactor of the Astoria Studios, who got him back in the groove. Le Baron had moved on, to become Vice-President in charge of production for RKO Radio Pictures. One Louis Brock was then in charge of short subjects at the studio, and had announced plans to shoot a series under the title of 'Broadway Headliners' at the Ideal Studios in New Jersey. Brock allowed Fields to choose his own material. He chose the Golf Sketch.

The Golf Specialist was Bill Fields' first sound film. For the first time we can hear The Voice, nasal and grating, with that know-it-all-tinge coupled with an eternal ennui. Apart from a completely tacked-on opening and closing scene, the movie is a carbon copy of 'The Episode on the Links' as transcribed heretofore. The caddy's squeaky shoes, the wrapping paper, the sticking pie, the bent clubs, the languid watching girl, all are followed to the last tic and mumble, although there are little changes of emphasis. Alas, it is not 'Shorty' Blanche who appears as the caddy but an unidentified stand-in.

The point of Fields' golf game is, as in one version of the pool sketch, that the player never actually connects with the ball. In the movie, the character has a new name, Effingham Bellweather, a kind of dandified con man, who is seen, in the prologue, trying to wrest a money-bank from a little girl. It is a sign of the importance Fields attached to painting his character in less than glowing colours. As we have quoted him in talking of his silent roles: it is quite a challenge to make you like the scoundrel, the man you would normally want to hiss. To make it sharper, Bellweather is flirting with the girl whose husband, the thuggish house-dick of the lakeside hotel which is the action's backdrop, has just tied another pest into a ball and rolled him out of the lobby.

Bellweather's villainy is emphasized at the end when a Sheriff reveals to the house-dick a wanted poster with his face in the 'Stolen Bonds' Alaskan fur hat and a list of heinous accusations:

Bigamy.
Passing as the Prince of Wales.
Eating spaghetti in public.
Using hard words in a speakeasy.
Trumping partner's ace.
Spitting in the Gulf Stream.
Jumping board bill in seventeen lunatic asylums.
Failing to pay instalments on a strait-jacket.
Possessing a skunk.

Revealing the facts of life to an indian.

As an early Talkie, the movie's limitations as photographed theatre are its particular strengths, enabling us, perhaps for the only time, to see a Fields sketch as it would have been seen on the stage. For these are the first spoken words of W. C. Fields that we hear, as he enters the hotel lobby singing off-key – 'Happy days are here, la-dee-dee . . .' and querying the desk boy: 'Any telegrams, cablegrams, radios, television? Oh, a little note, eh . . .' Reading it and tearing it in little strips – 'silly little girl'. A useless pretence, as we have seen it dictated as a demand for payment by 'Deep Sea McGurk, alias the Slaughterhouse Kid', an uncredited Irish stage heavy. The business with the little girl also allows Bill to reprise a gag from *Sally of the Sawdust*, with a watering can wetting his pants and a little dog – only this time the dog is a stuffed toy, and Fields' kicking it all the more absurd.

Much has been written about Fields' voice and some of it the usual nonsense besides. The cracked tones resulting from that frozen childhood in the Philadelphia streets, it has been said. The whiskey drawl, it has been mooted. But Ronald Fields was told by his Great-Aunt Adel that Claude Dukenfield's mother, Kate, had the same accent, a result of bad colds clogging the sinuses. Much of it, too, is clearly affectation. A surviving clip from a home movie shot at Bill's De Mille Drive home, in the late 1930s, shows that The Drawl was not his normal tone. As time went on, the act had become defined and calculated – the voice, the walk, the look, the gestures, all were elements of the self-created man. The Great Silly, refined and re-invented. The juggler juggling with his own character, keeping all the balls revolving in the air.

The Golf Specialist was released on 22 August 1930. Between the shooting and release Bill returned to the theatre, for a highly paid but short engagement of a completely unique kind. He had signed to play the leading role of Cap'n Andy in a new production of *Show Boat*, the spectacular musical play Ziegfeld had first produced in 1927. The show had been adapted by Jerome Kern and Oscar Hammerstein II from Edna Ferber's best selling novel, which was published in 1926. Some say Jerome Kern developed the role with W. C. Fields specifically in mind, but this is unlikely, as in late 1926 he was already in the midst of his multi-film deal for Paramount.

Be that as it may, Cap'n Andy, a role made famous by Charles Winninger first on stage and then in the 1936 movie version, was an ideal one for Fields. Showboats, like the early circuses, carnivals and dime museums that featured so broadly in his repertoire, were another glorious reconstruction of variety's golden past. The 1930 production, the first not produced by Ziegfeld, was to be presented in the huge open air space of the Saint Louis Municipal Opera House, which had ten thousand seats. Given the size of the theatre, the show did not run long, opening on Monday 11 August and closing on Sunday 24 August 1930.

It was for this show that Fields wrote his publicity piece about playing Saint Louis in his burlesque days, back in 1898. Bill received $4,000 for his two weeks' work, and this included the salary of his sidekick, William Blanche, who played one 'Rubber-face', presumably at Fields' insistence. This and the subsequent *Ballyhoo* were the last appearances of 'Shorty' Blanche in the annals, and thereafter he disappears completely from sight. According to Ronald Fields, he died in Santa Monica shortly after accompanying Fields upon his second Hollywood pilgrimage, but there seems to be no trace of his passing, not even a *Variety* obituary. Only his two fleeting screen appearances remain to hint at his contribution to Bill's act on the stage.

Meanwhile, at the same time as Bill Fields was cavorting in 'The Stolen Bonds' in the *Vanities*, a more global and deadly kind of Vanities was being performed in the streets of lower Manhattan. On Tuesday 29 October 1929, Wall Street 'laid an egg,' and failed investors began jumping out of windows. Believers in the gospel of Stocks and Shares and the perpetual upward trend of the market were cast down into the pit of despair. One such rudely awakened sinner was Florenz Ziegfeld, who spent the entire day of the Great Crash in court suing an electrical sign company over a trivial bill of $1,600. All his assistants and office staff were with him in court, and there was no one to answer the phone as his brokers frantically tried to call him to sell his assets. By the time Ziegfeld left court, the newspaper headlines told him he was ruined. Ziegfeld never recovered from this blow.

Fields himself lost money in the Crash, as he related to Hattie in a later letter, in 1932: 'The little nest egg I had cached for inclement weather almost entirely disappeared.' But as we now know, he had money stashed in other bank accounts, though not the hundreds conjured up by myth. It was not so much his personal as his professional fortune which suffered in the aftermath.

The multiple bank and business failures which followed the Wall Street Crash sunk Broadway, as well as the country. The number of productions dropped and continued to plummet throughout the 1930s – never recovering, in fact, to this day. Audiences declined as ordinary people lost their money or became unemployed. Five thousand actors lost their jobs. The creative theatre of Eugene O'Neill, Maxwell Anderson and Marc Connelly continued to function, in fact in some ways prospered, but the days of glitz and glamour were over.

One of the typical casualties of this new age of austerity and grief was Bill Fields' next, and last Broadway show, *Ballyhoo*. This was an original revue produced by Arthur Hammerstein, written by Harry Ruskin and Leighton K. Brill, based on the 'bunion derbies', or transcontinental footraces, staged by a real-life eccentric, C. C. Pyle. Pyle promoted a string of marathon dances, and even tried to establish his own football league. This time the main character of the play, renamed Q. Q. Quale, was definitely written for Fields. No one else could play this souped-up Eustace McGargle. It was a Fields day from start to finish. As Quale, he was 'a genial and ingratiating rascal, who goes happily across the country selling shares in his great enterprise until he has sold several hundred per cent of it, and selling, too, anything else of no value on which he can lay his hands'.

Q. Q. Quale was definitely a man of the moment, and perhaps too close to the bone to wow an audience of people who might face imminent ruin because of his kind. It may have been the wrong time to get laughs from such a person. But Quale also takes us back to an old literary role-model, Mark Twain's honey-tongued Colonel Sellers, with his talk of buying up 'a hundred and thirteen wild-cat banks in Ohio, Indiana, Kentucky, Illinois and Missouri . . . buy them all up, you see, and then all of a sudden let the cat out of the bag! Whiz! the stock of every one of those wildcats would spin up to a tremendous premium before you could turn a handspring . . .!' Or, on a smaller scale, to the real-life Bill Dailey, master of the old army game.

Bill Fields seized on Quale as a distillation of everything he had been building up to for years. Every night, on the stage, with faithful 'Shorty' by his side, he dominated the theatre, throwing in all of his old specialties – he juggled, he played pool, he did the cigar-box trick, he cheated a group of cowboys at poker in a reprise of *Poppy*, he won a hosecart from a fire-company in a backgammon game, he revived the Drug Store sketch, he played 'The Baby Austin'. One reviewer noted:

From the moment that he rolls on the stage enthroned in a magnificent chariot equipped with a calliope, in Shamokin, O., making the Mayor's speech as well as his own and presenting himself with the keys of the city, this leisurely comedian with the diagonal moustache is pretty much the whole show . . .

But the fall, from these heights, was all the harder. *Ballyhoo* opened on 22 December 1930, and closed after only two and a half weeks. Business was terrible. On New Year's Day 1931, Bill wrote to Arthur Hammerstein, suggesting revisions and tightening of the script and conveying an offer by members of the cast to take half salary until the show was back on its feet. But business was lousy all over Broadway. Hammerstein, with losses totalling $1,300,000 from his last eight productions, decided to close the show. Reporter Ward Morehouse wrote that four other shows closed on Broadway on the same night, including the latest edition of the *Vanities*. He related: 'Exactly four persons were in orchestra seats at one of the Broadway theatres at 8:50 o'clock last night and the management held the curtain, hopefully waiting for more. A half dozen more did arrive, and the show went on . . .'

Still determined, the actors reopened the show on their own, in 'a cooperative manner'. 'Scenes have been combined, acrobats have been taken out of hallways and the fire eater no longer satisfies his appetite in the patio of the hotel.' For a while, this was the talk of Broadway. Perhaps this was the new way to keep the Street open? Fields was now the producer, not only the star, of the show. Every evening the box office take was brought to his dressing-room, and anyone was free to examine the proceeds. But this actors' revolution did not last either. *Ballyhoo* closed, with a sigh and a whimper, at the end of February 1931.

Ronald Fields wrote:

W. C. had nothing to do now. He would walk Broadway at night and see other shows closing . . . The big Broadway names were packing up and heading for Hollywood, hoping to find work there. Fields waited. He would sit in Leone's eating their delicious Italian food and afterwards stay very late, sipping red wine and entertaining his friends at his table. But the lights were dimming in New York City . . . Fields could wait no longer. In June of 1931 he decided he had to try the movies one more time. He had no offers, he just had to go to California and hope.

William Claude Dukenfield was fifty-one years of age. He looked back on a stage turning to ashes. But W. C. Fields, his own personal phoenix, was about to be reborn once again.

Part V
Man on the Flying Trapeze

Chapter 29
The Largest Insane Asylum in the State

22 The myth in action: marital relations in Mrs Wiggs of the Cabbage Patch (with Zasu Pitts).

GREENE: Good morning. What can you give me for some shattered nerves? I got the inside mimis, the jitters.

SOUSÈ: Charles, the gentleman has butterflies in the stomach. I suggest a dash of Rover in it – (*to* GREENE) uh – dog – absinthe – its very good for the nerves.

GREENE (*downs drink, while* SOUSÈ *and bar companion look on nervously*): My name's Green, Mackley Q. Greene, and a man more beset by trouble you'll never see. (*To* BARTENDER) Again. I'm out here in Lompoc on a movie location. My director started on a bender last night and that's usually good for ten days. We've got a thirty-six hour schedule and a stinko script. It's a one reeler and a bupke and it opens in this very town the day after tomorrow.

SOUSÈ: Aw, you're yellin' right down my alley. In the old Sennett days I used to direct Fatty Arbuckle, Charlie Chaplin, Buster Keaton and the rest of 'em. I can't get the celluloid outa my blood. Nights I used to tend bar . . .

GREENE: Would you entertain a proposition to direct this picture?

SOUSÈ: Uhhh . . .

GREENE: Take a gambler's chance on a percentage of the profits basis?

SOUSÈ: Uhhh, just a moment . . . (*To* BARTENDER) Was I in here last night and did I spend a twenty dollar bill?

BARTENDER: Yeah.

SOUSÈ: Oh boy, what a load that is off my mind. I thought I'd lost it . . . (*To* GREENE) I've got a script that I've had in mothballs for twenty years. I read it to Irving and Milton who run the Gem Cinema down here. They said to me, they said – Souse, it's better than Gone With the Wind . . .

GREENE: My car's outside, let's get down on the set.

SOUSÈ: O.K. (*Turns to go, turns back to clear four glasses of liquor off the bar. To* BARTENDER) I'll bring the glasses back later . . .

> *The Bank Dick*, 1940, original story and screenplay
> by Mahatma Kane Jeeves

Bill Fields' second coming to Hollywood has been described in suitably mythic (and almost Wagnerian) terms: How he motored alone across the desert, stopping along the way to take on beverages, then arriving at the front of a troupe of bearers staggering with his portmanteaus and trunks to the lobby of the most luxurious hotel he could find in Los Angeles, tapping with his cane on the receptionist's desk, demanding the bridal suite, while promising to supply the bride forthwith. He had arrived in Oz, to be the Wizard.

Of course, he was no stranger to Munchkinland. His friends, Tom Geraghty, Greg La Cava, and Eddie Sutherland, were there, and other drinking partners, like the veteran western star, W. S. Hart. He went to parties and juggled with the cutlery. He soon moved from his hotel suite to a rented house at Toluca Lake, just above Universal Studios and just across the lake from the exclusive Lakeside Golf Club. Thus Bill could row across to play and row back when the day was done. The great apocryphal tales of W. C. Fields, such as his Gargantuan tussles with the Toluca Lake swans, and other marauders, begin at this point.

It was not a life of great deprivation. But Hollywood is, of course the land of make-believe. In reality, Hollywood of the early Talkies was an industry in deep crisis. Despite the overwhelming popularity of the new synchronized sound pictures, the movie business was not immune to the economic Depression. In the year of the Wall Street Crash, studio profits had soared, particularly of Warner Brothers, producers of *The Jazz Singer*. In 1929 one hundred million people per week paid to see a movie in the United States. But profits began dropping dramatically in 1930, and in 1931 movie theatres cut their prices to win their customers back. Warner Brothers' slid from a profit of 17.2 million dollars in 1929 to a loss of 7.9 million in 1931.

At Paramount, Jesse Lasky commented that Americans were weary and Depression-ridden and only 'new ideas' would bring the audiences back. But 1932 proved an even worse year than the previous, and Paramount, the most successful studio in the silent era, was technically bankrupt in 1933. Boardroom battles led to Jesse Lasky himself being turned out of the studio he had helped to found. RKO and Universal Pictures were in the hands of receivers, and Fox was soon to be swallowed by a smaller company, Twentieth-Century. In 1933 nearly a third of all movie theatres in the United States had shut down.

The solution was Comedy – and lots of it. But, paradoxically, comedy, too, was in crisis. The transition to sound meant that silent comedians had to rethink the basic concepts of their art. Pantomime was no longer the be-all and end-all of comedy. The spoken word, which had dominated the lost world of vaudeville, was suddenly king once again.

Some comedians refused to recognise this reality. Chaplin, above all, made the boldest choice to ignore it altogether. Pantomime, the universal language of the Tramp, had made him famous throughout the world. It was unthinkable that the Tramp should suddenly shrink to one language, one culture. What accent would he speak? Chaplin's London English? New York style? The early Talkies seemed to some a fad, an aberration, with their cumbersome sound-boxes which enclosed and confined the camera. Chaplin said, as late as 1931: 'I'll give the Talkies three years, that's all.' To be fair to him he was echoing the sentiments of none other than Thomas Edison himself, who, aged seventy-nine, proclaimed in 1926 that 'the idea (of talking pictures) is not practical . . . Americans require a restful quiet in the moving picture theatre.' Chaplin proceeded to complete *City Lights*, begun in 1927, as a silent film with synchronized sound effects and music, in January 1931. It was a hit. But Chaplin, with his unique control of his own productions, was a rarity in the film business.

Harold Lloyd, another shrewd manager of his own career, weathered the change to sound with more difficulty. His remake of his silent classic, *Safety Last*, as *Feet First*, in 1930, was a flop, and later productions, though more successful, never returned him to his silent peak. Buster Keaton, whose grasp of movie technology might have made him a perfect candidate for survival, foundered on the rock of the determination of MGM, and producer Irving Thalberg, to control his future work. The sound pictures MGM chose as his vehicles, some teamed with Jimmy Durante, were horribly misjudged, and Keaton fell out of sight and into deep personal crisis.

Harry Langdon, who had rivalled the Big Three in the silent era, notably in *The Strong Man*, directed by Frank Capra, dropped out of sight even more steeply, and his name even disappeared from some reference books by 1933. All in all, when one hears tales of the paranoias and anxieties of W. C. Fields in the 1930s, it's clear he had good reason to feel the terror of Hollywood's short memory and ruthless disdain for failure.

The winners were clearly going to be a new breed of funnies, who could play with words, as well as with bodies. A prime cross-over success were Laurel and Hardy, as yet appearing only in shorts (and baggy pants). Crossing over directly from the stage, the four sons of Minnie Marx, who had wowed Broadway with their mad revues, *I'll Say She Is* in 1924, *The Cocoanuts* in 1925 and *Animal Crackers* in 1928, were tailor-made for the early, static Talkies. *The Cocoanuts*, in 1929, was the first film to be shot at the re-opened Paramount east-coast studios at Astoria, Queens. Their second movie-of-the-revue, *Animal Crackers*, was also shot there, and then they too, like everybody else, decamped to Hollywood, for *Monkey Business*, in 1931.

Los Angeles, then as now, was a byword for all kinds of 'monkey business', mad excess, grotesque and gross behaviour. In New York, even Eddie Cantor's showbiz aristocrats lived in the real world and real streets. In Los Angeles, they often fell over the edge of reality into the sump of earthly desires. In 1921, the Fatty Arbuckle scandal, in which the overweight comedy star was accused of the rape and murder of a model, Virginia Rappe, at a wild San Francisco party, had already put the Hollywood movie colony on notice by the guardians of America's morals. In 1922, an ex-postmaster general in the administration of Warren G. Harding, one Will H. Hays, was made the President of the Motion Picture Producers and Distributors of America, a hastily formed body that included most of the colony's founding fathers: Carl Laemlle, Marcus Loew, Adolph Zukor, William Fox, Samuel Goldwyn and the brothers Lewis and Myron Selznick. Hays' brief was to clean up Hollywood's act. He declared:

> The potentialities of motion pictures for moral influence and education are limitless. Therefore its integrity should be protected as we protect the integrity of our children and our schools . . . This industry must have towards that sacred thing, the mind of a child, towards that clean and virgin thing, that unmarked slate . . . the same responsibility . . . that the best teacher or the best clergyman, the most inspired teacher of youth, would have . . .

Movie makers, producers, directors and actors, were not clergymen, nor even teachers, but the MPPDA made sure, throughout the 1920s, that they toed the line, as far as their product on the screen was concerned. In their personal life the movie people continued to lapse to the extent that their fabulous salaries allowed. In 1924, the movie studios adopted the 'Hays Formula', by which they agreed to submit any material intended for the screen to a panel of readers, who would rule according to a long list of matters that should not appear in motion pictures. These ranged from profanity and nudity through any 'wilfull offence to any nation, race or creed', any material sympathetic to criminals or hostile to the institution of marriage, any scene showing a man and woman in bed together, the use of drugs or 'excessive or lustful kissing'. This list was administered, like castor oil, by a Public Relations Committee under the serendipitously named Colonel Joy.

Eventually, producers began to chaff at this bit and ignore some of the Committee's advice, but when sound came the potential threat to censorship expanded: new writers and actors came from a less restricted stage tradition, and ad-libs on set made the prior approval of the script a less than watertight barrier. A new gun was brought in to tame the unruly west, one Martin Quigley, a devout Catholic and publisher of the *Motion Picture Herald*. Quigley proposed to Hays a new 'Code to Govern the Making of Talking, Synchronized and Silent Motion Pictures', which was adopted by the MPPDA in February 1930. The General Principles governing the Code included the cavils that 'no picture shall be produced which will lower the moral standards of those who see it', and 'Law, natural or human, shall not be ridiculed, nor shall sympathy be created for its violation.'

The movie producers did not immediately knuckle under to the Code, and several battles were fiercely fought, notably over Warner Brothers' crusading *I Am a Fugitive From a Chain Gang* and Mae West's risque *She Done Him Wrong*. As the Depression set in, and movie studios were weakened, the forces of censorship marched on in the shape of the Catholic Legion of Decency. These pressures led Will Hays to appoint a new, zealous deputy, one Joseph Ignatius Breen. In the fall of 1933, Breen entered the hot seat as the secular Vicar of Hollywood. Breen declared war on every whiff of sin, immorality and transgression in each and every film made in Hollywood throughout the 1930s, and indeed, he was still in the saddle, albeit on a weakened horse, well into 1956. His battles with producers, writers and directors were legion and legendary. His war against Chaplin has been well documented. But little has been said about his feud with another comedian, whose sins were more subtle than Chaplin's, but who equally aroused Breen's ire on an ongoing basis, throughout his Talkie career . . .

Fields, on his first sojourn in the mad house, had failed to be adopted as an honorary lunatic, and had returned to his staple home on the stage. At his second stay, he displayed the single-mindedness which always attended one of his strategic choices. Knuckling down to some serious golfing at Lakeside, he sent his agent Bill Grady scuttling about to raise whatever film offers he could from the Depression-hit studios.

Fields was certainly not the only Broadway star looking for a new career in the California sun. Fanny Brice had gone to Hollywood in 1928 to make *My Man*, at Warner Brothers, a part-silent, part-sound film that bombed instantly. A second vehicle for her, *Be Yourself* (1929), for United Artists, hadn't fared any better. Fanny returned to the New York stage. Another ex-sojourner in the Tent of Omar Khayyam, Eddie Cantor, had done better with *Whoopee* in 1930 and would continue to make movies, which have not stood the test of time. But the fourth comrade of Ziegfeld days, Will Rogers, was, as Fields would be, reborn with sound.

Will Rogers had preceded Bill Fields to Hollywood, acting in a string of cowboy features produced between 1918 and 1922, alternating with his work on the stage. Throughout the 1920s, he had continued to develop the cracker-barrel philosophy expressed in *The Illiterate Digest*, with homilies such as 'Settling the Affairs of the World in My Own Way'.

Since then, Will had travelled to Europe, meeting various luminaries such as Lady Astor, Sir James Barrie, and Benito Mussolini in Rome. He had decided that Mussolini was 'a regular guy' and they shared a joke about castor oil. He went to Moscow but mercifully did not meet Stalin, whom he described as a 'two fisted fighting egg from down in the Caucasian Mountains'. On his return to the US he stayed in the White House with President and Missus Calvin Coolidge. In 1929, realizing the strength of the Talkies, he began a second career in Hollywood, beginning with *They Had to See Paris*, directed by the veteran craftsman Frank Borzage. In all, Rogers was to make twenty features, at Fox, with directors like Henry King, James Cruze and John Ford, films which were to catapult him to the top rank of box-office earners, until, in 1934, he was number one. Having invested earlier on in Los Angeles real-estate, he became fabulously rich, settling with his family on a vast ranch at Pacific Pallisades, north-west of Santa Monica. From there he could dispense his gentle wisecracks to a people desperately seeking for some good news in the dark Depressive days.

Two other stage stars who would play a future role in Bill Fields' life were also set on conquering Hollywood. John Barrymore, a drinking partner from the Lamb's Club in New York City, had been making movies since 1913. Scion of the great stage family, he was a child of the theatre, but the big money was in Los Angeles. As assiduously as he wooed the audience of his Richard the Third and his great Hamlet, he wooed the motion-picture producers. In 1926 he starred in *Don Juan*, for Warner Brothers, the first movie with a fully synchronized music track. In 1930 he was shooting *Moby Dick* – a film that chilled moviegoers with his screams as Ahab suffering the cauterization of his severed leg, a scene that had somehow not occurred to author Melville ('The public loves torture,' said Barrymore) – and meanwhile lavishing huge sums on Bella Vista, his dreamland Los Angeles mansion.

Another defector from the stage, Mae West, had begun her career, like Bill Fields, in variety. Beginning in small-time burlesque, she had stunned New York by writing and starring in her own radical shows, which tested the moral guardians of the 1920s to breaking point. Her first play, *Sex*, was closed by the New York Mayor's office, and got her dispatched to jail for ten days for 'corrupting the morals of youth'. Her second play, *The Drag*, which opened in April 1926, was about the life of homosexuals in the theatre. Her third play, *Diamond Lil*, was a sensation in 1928, described by Bernard Sobel as 'one of the few authentic stage pictures of tenderloin night life'. But she too was knocked out by the fall of Wall Street and joined the hegira to Hollywood. When she reached LA in 1932, to join Bill Fields and the Marxes at Paramount, the celluloid really began to sizzle. But there was no sign yet of West and Fields' bacon sizzling on the hot plate together.

Fields was not, in fact, idle for very long, despite his later protestations. Either Bill Grady's ministrations had paid off, or, if one accepts his own version for once, chance favoured him by a casual meeting in his hotel with a colleague of Ziegfeld days, Marilyn Miller. She too had trekked west and signed a contract with Warner Brothers, to star in a movie remake of an early German talkie, *Ihre Majestat die Liebe*, as a bar-girl at a Berlin cabaret, who lived with her widowed father – a role played at Ufa by S. Z. Sakall (later to be known in Hollywood as 'Cuddles' and best remembered as the barman in *Casablanca*!). *Her Majesty Love* seemed tailor-made for Bill's old specialty – Bisbee with a teutonic twist.

Bill was back on his feet once again.

Chapter 30
'Just What I Suspected – The Country Starving and You With Gold in Your Teeth!'

'I think of baby when nights are long . . . I think of baby when things go wrong . . .'

Thus warble the drunken *habitués* of the 'Berlin Cabaret', a veritable cornucopia of old vaudevillians hoping for a new break in life. There is Leon Errol, Bill Fields' old partner on the Ziegfeld stage, complete with stage monocle as the Baron Von Schwarzdorf. There is, believe it or not, Ford Sterling, Mack Sennett's first big star and chief of the Keystone Kops, looking well fed, if desperate, as Otmar Von Wellingen. Chester Conklin is waiting in the wings for his last – and only surviving – appearance with Fields; behind the bar, happily wielding a cocktail shaker, is Ziegfeld's own Marilyn Miller, who sang 'Mine was a Marriage of Convenience' at the *Follies of 1918,* 'dressed in a pink frilly and ruffly costume that creates havoc in the hearts of the audience'.

Her Majesty Love was a recycling job from top to bottom. The director, William Dieterle, an apostle of stage director Max Reinhardt from Berlin, had been specialising in Hollywood in making German language versions of American films, and here he was given the opportunity to turn the job around. Two of his later films, *A Midsummer Night's Dream* (which he co-directed with Reinhardt) and *The Hunchback of Notre Dame*, with Charles Laughton, were to become classics, but in 1931 he was only feeling his way in Hollywood. *Her Majesty Love* is a pretty stilted and rather ponderous effort, but it gave Fields a chance to try a variant on his 'Pa Jones' character, leaning more heavily towards pathos, and cutting the harshness out entirely. A rather gentle, avuncular Dad – Bela Toerek – is awakened in bed by a phone call from his daughter, Lia (Marilyn Miller), to tell him she has just become engaged to young Fred, heir of the Von Wellingen Ball

Bearing Company. He sits up vaguely, attired in pyjamas and an authentically teutonic moustache – the 'misplaced eyebrow' having sprung new shoots:

DAD (*sleepily*): Hullo . . . hullo . . . What? Who? Oh its you. What? You're engaged? In the middle of the night? Two o'clock in the morning? With whom? Oh, to him. Who's him? He? And who's he? I see. Him and he are the same. I think you're a little tipsy. Never mind. It's a very good omen for marriage. I was half stewed when I proposed to your mother. What? No, sure I'm glad. Sure dear. Tell him I send you both my blessings and a good old fashioned hug. Good night . . . Oh – one question – does he really love you?

Following a mundane script by Robert Lord and Arthur Caesar, Fields took no great liberties with his role. At a reception given by the Von Wellingen family for their jubilee and their son's engagement, he embarasses his daughter and shocks the stewed prunes present by revealing that she is a barmaid and he is a barber, who had once been a vaudeville juggler. He throws an eclair onto Chester Conklin's spoon and demonstrates his juggling prowess, giving us a tantalising glimpse of The Silent Humorist at work. Plates fly and break, balls pop against the brow of the shrewish Aunt Harriette (a coincidental name?) and there is a delicious moment when his hands paw after the balls, only just preventing them from getting away. This scene among the snobs will be echoed, eight years later, in *You Can't Cheat an Honest Man*, when Larson E. Whipsnade recounts the Snake Story to the society nobs whose son his daughter has rashly agreed to wed. But by that time Bill was too unsteady to juggle, except with life, the universe, and his own cosmic metaphors.

Like fading echoes, vaudeville memories reverbrate through *Her Majesty Love*, as Fields comments to Lia: 'I haven't seen such roses since I was in vaudeville; my public used to send them to me,' and 'once in vaudeville my assistant handed me a porcupine instead of a rabbit . . .' Lia, rejected by the Von Wellingens because of her inferior status – as Vicky Whipsnade will be by the Bel-Goodies in 1939 – succumbs to the wooing of the multiply-divorced Baron Von Schwarzdorf, egged on by Dad: 'He's rich, he's old, what else do you want? – and you can always look forward to a happy widowhood . . .' Leon Errol, as the Baron, was also trying to revive a flagging career, but he was not destined to reach the top in movies, and we will meet him again in a rather forlorn supporting role in Fields' *Never Give a*

Sucker an Even Break, in 1941. He was perhaps best known in movies for a series of 'Mexican Spitfire' vehicles in which he co-starred with Lupe Velez, who had been married to Johnny 'Tarzan' Weissmuller and whose carefully planned romantic suicide in 1944 was ruined by her drowning in the toilet bowl in a last desperate attempt to cough up a huge dose of Seconal. Errol died in a more dignified setting in 1951, outliving his stage colleague by five years.

Lia marries and divorces the Baron, thus enabling herself to be married to young Fred, who signed an oath never to marry Lia Toerek, but not to shun the Baroness Von Schwarzdorf. Sleaze and romance meld in the Berlin Cabaret, and Papa Toerek can have rich in-laws after all.

On 14 December, Bill Fields wrote to Elise Cavanna, the angular pest from *It's the Old Army Game*:

Dear Elise,

Just received your letter of Thursday and appreciate it to the fullest. I'm glad you liked me in the picture. I hadn't a hell of a lot to do, but in these depressing times a fellow is glad to get anything. I haven't done anything since 'Ballyhoo' laid an egg last February. I was about to apply for a position as chauffeur or dresser when this thing came up. I tried to get hold of you for Maude Eburne's part [this was Aunt Harriette Von Wellingen], but did not know your address, but I have it in my book now and won't lose it.

Would like to have you and Mrs Seeds over some night for provender and bellywash and to meet the new Krud. If you can squeeze me in sometime this, or next week, phone Gladstone 6801, or drop me a line to 9950 Toluca Lake Avenue, Toluca Lake, North Hollywood.

Best to you and your Mother always,

Brinzel J. Opalgangle,

[signed] Bill Fields.

'The new Krud' sounds like another Prohibition code for booze. This letter inaugurated a correspondence with Elise Cavanna that lasted over the years. She was to play Bill's foil in three of his four Mack Sennett shorts, in 1932 and 1933, and his wife in two of them, *The Pharmacist* and *The Barber*. In 1934 he wrote to her: 'Dear Elise: – You are the most appreciative long piece of string I've ever met and you're just as full of inferiority complex as an egg is goodie!' And in 1937, from his Bel Air home at Funchal Road, under the heading:

'THE OUT HOUSE' INN
PROF. W. C. FIELDS
UNDER THE MANAGEMENT OF CARLOTTA MONTI.

An open letter to 'Armetage, Cavanna, Seeds' hook-up. Tea and Crumpets will be served any Monday, Tuesday, Wednesday or Thursday. At the above address by giving one day's notice in advance.

Doors open any time after six. Light aperitif, and refreshments served immediately. Tabs drawn about 7:30.

FOR SOLIDS
SUBJECT

and in honor of –

'THE RETURN OF THE JUMPING BEAN'

Claude W.

We can see another Fields myth dying here, in the living proof of his ability to maintain affectionate relationships with women who were not his lovers – once again his love and respect for fellow show-people is evident.

Her Majesty Love was not box-office gold and Fields waited another six months for his next part. His old benefactor at Paramount, William Le Baron, was still running the east-coast studio, and the memory of Bills' silent flops still lingered in Hollywood. He hunkered down at Toluca Lake, golfed, and continued to rail against the swans. But Bill was not entirely friendless at Paramount, where Herman Mankiewicz, the producer in charge of the Marx Brothers – the most thankless task in the Northern Hemisphere – was an old fan, having co-written the intertitles for *Two Flaming Youths* and the unproduced *The Wild Man of Borneo*. Joe Adamson describes Mankiewicz as 'a Promethean wit bound in a Promethean body, one of the most entertaining men in existence . . . called the "Central Park West Voltaire" by Ben Hecht'. A long-time writer for the *Chicago Tribune, New York Times* and every other quality newspaper, he had been, in New York, an honorary Algonquinite and intimate of Dorothy Parker, Heywood Broun, Marc Connelly and George S. Kaufman, before landing on the Marxian team. His younger brother, Joe, had been another Fields fan since Bill had given him an interview for his high school magazine when, as a callow youth, Joe had been smit by *Poppy*. Joe Mankiewicz had written a script for Jack Oakie, a Paramount contract star who had also transferred from vaudeville. He had written into this script a role tailor-made for Fields, and this time brother Herman was in a position to see it through into production.

And so *Million Dollar Legs* was born. It is now a seldom shown film, but people who saw it twenty and thirty years ago often remember it with a glow of wonderment and disbelief. A precursor of the Marx Brothers' *Duck Soup* (1933), also overseen by Herman Mankiewicz, it represents one of those rare moments in Hollywood where, in the words of *Helzapoppin* – 'anything can happen and it probably will', in which anarchy triumphed over bureaucracy, the leash was slipped, and the dogs of comedy relieved themselves all over the astounded lot.

Fields is the President of Klopstokia, presented in the opening credits as

> A Far Away Country.
> Chief Exports: Goats and Nuts.
> Chief Imports: Goats and Nuts.
> Chief Inhabitants: Goats and Nuts.

This is a Ruritanian fantasy land, perhaps with some prescient hints of what Nazi Germany – not yet born then – would become. The Fuller Brush magnate Baldwin, approaching a ship's gangway in the port, says to an official at the pier: 'I want to get out of this country. I have the feeling I'm being spied on.' The official replies: 'Everybody in this country feels like that. But I can't understand it. Spying is impossible in Klopstokia.'

The spy, wrapped in a black cape, is Ben Turpin, Mack Sennett's famous cross-eyed star, who is present throughout the picture, in fireplaces, in hidden doors behind bookcases, and even inside portraits. The film, in fact, is a Sennett treasure-box, with Ben Turpin joined by Hank Mann, Billy Engle, Eddie Baker, Vernon Dent and walrus-lipped Andy Clyde. Joe Mankiewicz played on these personas lovingly, but he wrote real gold for Fields. The first entrance of the President into his cabinet meeting nicely lampoons Bill Fields the tireless self-promoter – as he marches in, a one man band, literally banging his own drum and tooting his own horn, to the tune of 'We're in the Army Now . . .'

PRESIDENT: Any of you mugs been playing my harmonica? It's busted.

23 *Million Dollar Legs*: The President of Klopstokia blows his own horn.

(*Proceeds to arm wrestle with the Secretary of the Treasury [Hugh Herbert], who retires defeated, cursing under his breath.*)

PRESIDENT: The usual oath of allegiance to me, and no stalling!

CABINET (*with fingers crossed behind their backs*): We pledge our allegiance to you. Long may you live.

PRESIDENT: I thank you. (*As he clasps a knuckleduster at his side*) I in turn will always extend to you the hearty handclasp of friendship!

Note the first appearance in text of 'the hearty handclasp', like another Joe Mankiewicz phrase, 'my little chickadee', later to become a Fields staple.

Klopstokia is, of course, bankrupt, like Depression USA, but Fields cuts short the Cabinet's complaining by rushing forward to seize hold of the Secretary of the Treasury's mouth, crying out: 'Just what I suspected! The country starving and you with gold in your teeth! Get out!'

He proceeds to throw his own bodyguards out. Klopstokia, it appears, is a country where every inhabitant is an athlete of Olympic status, as Fuller Brush salesman Oakie soon finds out. They jump, run, throw faster and wider than anyone else, apart from their other peculiarity, that every woman in the country is called Angela and every man, George.

Oakie is in love with Angela (of course), the President's daughter, and comes up with a brilliant plan to make Klopstokia's fortune: entering a team for the Olympic Games in Los Angeles. Angela will enter for the diving championships and her Dad for the weight-lifting contest. Andy Clyde, the President's Major-Domo, is the fastest runner in the world.

This plot provided a cheap way to incorporate found footage, of the 1932 Olympic Games, into the movie, and a motive for the subversive conspiracy of the President's cabinet to bring him down by assigning the slinky Mata Machree – 'The Woman No Man Can Resist (Not Responsible For Men Left Over Thirty Days)' – to seduce the entire Olympic team. A sure cue for the exchange:

SECRETARY OF THE TREASURY (*at Mata's castle*): I want to see this woman no man can resist.

BUTLER: Sorry, Madam is only resisted from 2 till 4.

This was also the first instance of a Fields picture running foul, in a minor way, of the censors. Will Hays objected first of all to the title, writing to Paramount's chief, Adolph Zukor, on 27 April 1932: 'In re: "Million Dollar Legs" . . . Pursuant to the action of the Board of Directors at the meeting of December 10th, 1930, it is suggested that the above title be not registered.' But on 25 June producer Lamar Trotti wrote to Governor Carl Milliken: 'Despite this title this is not a sex picture. The legs belong to Andy Clyde who is entered in the Olympic Games.'

Hays might have been alerted by the Press Book and posters, which did feature a shapely pair of female pins with all the principals ogling it, Ben Turpin in particular looking in a direction that might give cause for severe offence. The studio hacks also announced a 'Million Dollar Legs Contest – Which Girl in Your City Has the Most Beautiful Legs? To Which Nationality Does She Belong? – Which nation produces girls with the prettiest legs? The English? Irish? American? Russian? French? Italian? – The girls are to be assembled on your stage . . . behind a drop or curtain RAISED ONLY to THEIR KNEES . . . This stunt may be worked with or without the cooperation of a newspaper

'. . . Cooperative ad tie-ups with shoe and hosiery stores are obvious.'

The Board's objection to the title was waived, but with the following points suggested to be cut:

1 The line 'Where should a Privy Councillor be?'

2 In the scene on the train when Mata says she is going to demoralize the athletes the tag line, 'My compliments.'

3 The underscoring in the phrase, 'That is all I can do in public.'

The first point related to the exchange between Fields and Andy Clyde as his Major-Domo.

PRESIDENT: Take this to the Privy Councillor.

MAJOR-DOMO: Where is he, your excellency?

PRESIDENT: Where would a Privy Councillor be? – If he's not there he's with my daughter.

Clearly Adolph Zukor and Paramount did not see fit to take Will Hays' advice on this one, and the movie did go out with all three lines uncut. Nevertheless, in Pennsylvania, they didn't like the following dialogue in Reel 4: 'Mata: "I know why you are here. I know everything. I even know what you think – *you beast*." Also her song lines: "It's terrific when I get hot. It's something terrible the gift I got." In Ohio, on the other hand, the movie was approved without cuts, an astonishing aberration, as we shall see in due course.

The Board retired to lick its wounds. But it would be back, very soon . . .

Million Dollar Legs was directed with great panache by Eddie Cline, who had cut his teeth on Mack Sennett's Bathing Beauties and gone on to direct Buster Keaton's *Three Ages* (1923) and *Sherlock Junior* (1924). He would return to shape three of Bill's Universal pictures: *My Little Chickadee*, *The Bank Dick*, and *Never Give a Sucker an Even Break*, i.e. – Bill trusted him to allow him to get on with the job. This was not, apparently, the way things were at the outset: Fields and Cline rowed initially over the usual Fields ad-libs, while Mankiewicz was very protective of his brother's precious lines, but Cline learned to trust Bill's instincts for the comic stuff.

We can see that Bill is now in his element in the movies. Despite playing second fiddle to Jack Oakie, he is revelling in the discovery of his new Talkie persona – despite the unusual role. Bisbee has clearly re-invented himself as President, with regulation daughter and sappy suitor, and a whole crowd of villainous politicians to quell. His love of the absurd is compelling, asking his Major-Domo, while he juggles with dumb-bells, allowing one to conk him on the head:

PRESIDENT: How many customers did we turn away today?

MAJOR-DOMO: Twenty-four, sir.

PRESIDENT: Ah, we're slipping. I guess business is bad all over the world.

Fieldsisms and harbingers of *Duck Soup* include a row of Presidential call-buttons inscribed: 'CALL THE GUARD. AM I IN? SHOW THE AMBASSADOR IN. SHOW THE AMBASSADOR OUT. SHOW THE SECRETARY IN. THROW THE SECRETARY OUT. MAJOR DOMO. TEA. HAM ON RYE. WITH MUSTARD. WITHOUT MUSTARD. DAUGHTER'S SUITORS.' In the final Olympic shoot-out between Fields and his Treasury Secretary at the Weight-Lifting contest, Fields throws a 1000lb weight clear out of the arena, thus winning the Shot-put contest at the same time. At the end the Fuller-Brush magnate Baldwin, who has sponsored the Klopstokian team, shakes the President's hand and throws him in an arm-wrestle, prompting the closing line from Fields: 'It's the ultimate! I've been drinking too much orange juice!' FADE OUT.

Another ultimate and earth-shaking event which occurred in *Million Dollar Legs* was the abandonment by Bill of his 'misplaced eyebrow'. The clip-on moustache, which had served him throughout the Ziegfeld *Follies* and his silent movie career, was cast away, not before time. This was a lucky omen. Though some critics were as puzzled by the film as the audience – *The Nation* wrote: 'One cannot help regretting that the film fails to rise to its opportunities' – the *Motion Picture Herald* wrote that the film-makers 'have gone back to the dark ages of motion picture production and adapted in this picture all those great laugh-creating ideas that made motion pictures the fourth greatest industry in the country'. While the *New York Herald Tribune* wrote, on 31 July 1932, about Fields' performance –

Perhaps he doesn't exactly belong down here among the blondes, but it provides as good an opportunity as any to remind the world that, in 'Million Dollar Legs', heaven bless it, he proved that he is as magnificent a comedian on the screen as he is on the stage. Now, if Hollywood doesn't take advantage of that discovery, its guilt is not on my soul.

The enthusiastic scribe need not have worried. Fields was on his way. But Paramount was not, as yet, completely won over. Despite his hopes for a long-term contract, the moguls spooned out work with a long handle. Once again, the Mankiewicz clan came to his aid. The famous director of suave and sophisticated comedy, Ernst Lubitsch, had been put in charge of a portmanteau film of eight episodes, revolving round an eccentric dying millionaire who resolves to send a million dollar cheque to eight different people picked at random out of the telephone book. The film was to be a showcase for Paramount talent, casting Gary Cooper, George Raft, Charles Laughton, Jack Oakie, Charlie Ruggles, Frances Dee, Mary Boland, with James Cruze, Norman McLeod, Norman Taurog, William A. Seiter, H. Bruce Humberstone, Stephen Roberts and Lubitsch himself directing the various segments.

W. C. Fields, way down the list, was to be teamed with Alison Skipworth, a chubby British character actress who had just starred in *Raffles* (1930) with Ronald Colman, in an episode written, once again, by Joe Mankiewicz. This was a story very much to Bill Fields' heart. As an ex-vaudevillian, Rollo La Rue, he is joint owner of a Tea Shoppe with his long-term wife and vaudeville partner, Emily. They have just taken possession of their new car and have barely taken it round the block when it is totalled by a reckless driver. They return, Emily in tears, to the Tea Shoppe to find the cheque to Emily for a million dollars. Their immediate response is to buy a fleet of cars and hire a host of tough chauffeurs, so that they can drive out around town in convoy to locate the 'road hogs' and crash into them one by one.

Here was Mankiewicz knowledgeably honing in on a host of Fieldsian obsessions. It is the only film where his passion for motor cars and loathing for all other drivers is brought out with such ferocious glee. It, intriguingly, imagines a life in which Bill and Hattie did remain married (though no hints of offspring, Joe knew where and when to steer clear), and pursued their joint career into retirement as a loving, perfectly matched couple. The episode's opening scene fondly captures the small world of ex-artistes, with the dialogue of Emily with her friend, Agnes:

AGNES: When was it we played together last? Was it Wilkesbarre, in '23?

EMILY: '24, my dear. I shan't forget that year. That was the winter Rollo had that bad cold. Why, I had him in mustard and vinegar for two months.

AGNES: (*laughs*) I remember that egg. He was the juggler kept hangin' around you. You sure were lucky to lose him.

EMILY: I didn't lose him. Rollo is here with me now, partner in this tea room . . . It's been wonderful, having this place for our own to settle down in. You know, Agnes, after thirty years of it – one night stands and split weeks – that's about all you ever dream of . . . a place of your own.

ROLLO *enters, with chef's ladle, to relate the coming of their new motor car –*

EMILY: Oh, Rollo, let's go and look at it! Oh, excuse me, I forgot. You know Agnes Du Pont.

AGNES: Hi, Rollo.

ROLLO: Agnes Du Pont, Queen of the high wire. What are you playing these days, revivals?

AGNES: I'm headlinin' bills they wouldn't even let a juggler on.

EMILY: Oh, Rollo, Rollo, let's go look at it.

ROLLO: Coming, my little chickadee.

24 *If I had A Million*: Fields with helpmate Alison Skipworth as ex-vaudevillians, Rollo and Emily.

Fields was so fond of that little phrase that he took the trouble to buy it off Joe Mankiewicz. Ever mindful of vaudeville's old larceny, and jealous as he was of his own copyrights, he took care when dealing with friends. In an earlier draft of the script, the vaudeville banter between Rollo and Agnes continues, with Agnes commenting to Emily:

AGNES: If I was gonna pick a chauffeur, I wouldn't pick a juggler.

ROLLO: For a woman who has spent the last sixty years of her life on a tight rope, you seem to know a great deal about what goes on in the world.

AGNES: I know enough not to trust a juggler any further than I could throw him.

ROLLO: You never met the juggler you could throw.

In the released film, he says:

ROLLO: I find it very difficult at this time to remember that you're a woman.

AGNES: I wish you'd forget it. I'd like nothing better than to knock your ears down into your neck. Goodbye, Emily. (AGNES *exits.*)

ROLLO (*calling after her*): I suppose you forget the day I busted you in the nose in Cincinatta . . .

Alas, this was the last collaboration between Bill Fields and the Mankiewicz brothers. All three would go on to fame and fortune. Joe would progress from writer and producer to Oscar-winning director and writer of *A Letter to Three Wives* in 1949 and *All About Eve* in 1950. His later credits included *Julius Caesar, The Barefoot Contessa, Guys and Dolls, The Quiet American, Suddenly Last Summer*, and *Cleopatra*. None of these were comedies (not even the last named), but he returned to a quirky comic renaissance in the filmed play *Sleuth*, with Laurence Olivier and Michael Caine, in 1972. His legacy is as one of the most intelligent craftsmen in the Munchkin City. His elder brother, Herman, after penning *Citizen Kane* for Orson Welles, never shone so brightly afterwards.

It is a moot speculation what might have been had Joe Mankiewicz continued to write for Fields. Plied with inferior collaborators, from this point on, Bill came to rely more and more upon his own material, as was his wont and his fundamental ambition, but if . . .

If I Had a Million was a hit, but Bill had to share the glory with too many illustrious rivals. He excelled in the film, but so did Charles

Laughton, Charlie Ruggles, and George Raft. Bill needed starring vehicles. Paramount was still not ready to award that elusive long-term deal. Unwilling to be idle again, Bill found a temporary solution. Out of the chaotic voices of Hollywood he picked out the siren call of a veteran, the old, undisputed King of Comedy, father of the Keystone Kops – Mack Sennett.

Chapter 31

'And It Ain't a Fit Night Out for Man
nor Beast . . .'

The four short films W. C. Fields made for Mack Sennett are the 'essence' of Fields, like distilled water, with all the impurities siphoned out. This fitted perfectly with the first principle of the Sennett movie: pure comedy, the gags above all.

The name of Sennett is synonymous with the rough vulgarity and boundless, anarchic energy of early silent pictures, when the movies were still seen as simple fodder for the lower classes and immigrants. The 'slapstick' story, the speeded up action, the train rushing towards the heroine tied across the railroad tracks: Mack Sennett was the motion in the motion picture. He was also the great teacher whose pupils surpassed him, and left him, one by one, for greater glory. Sennett employed 'Fatty' Arbuckle, Mabel Normand, Hank Mann, Chester Conklin, Slim Summerville, Edgar Kennedy, Ford Sterling, Ben Turpin, Harold Lloyd, Harry Langdon, Frank Capra, Marie Dressler, and, of course, Charles Chaplin, to name but a few. He had joined D. W. Griffith at the Biograph Studio, in 1909, where he met the love of his life, Mabel Normand; followed Griffith from the east coast to Hollywood in 1910, and finally settled there in 1912 to form his own movie company, Keystone.

By the 1920s Keystone was in decline, but Sennett survived, having bought, like Will Rogers, land in Los Angeles, mainly 304 acres in Griffith Park, not to speak of a gold mine in Grass Valley. He bought a farm and populated it with hogs to eat up the rampaging snakes. He entered the Depression financially fortified, and built a new studio in the San Fernando Valley, fully equipped for sound, at a cost of $500,000. After the Mack Sennett Company was no more, it would become Republic Pictures.

Sennett's own tale of how W. C. Fields came to work for him is full of the usual pitfalls. Lapses of memory, or ego, lead him to claim that he had written those four short films for Fields, whereas all the movies Fields made for Sennett were written by Fields alone. Mack and Bill had been golfing buddies since the Ziegfeld days, and they had discussed collaboration then, but nothing came of it. Sennett wrote about their reunion, in 1932:

> I ran across him at Lakeside. He said:
> 'Mack, I'm fed up with my frivolous existence. Why don't I come out to your studio and do something – anything. Gag, write, direct – any little chore. Money's no object. I just want to be busy.'
> Since money was no object, I arranged an appointment for the following morning.
> 'You've never been in pictures, Bill,' I said [!]. 'Lets forget the gags and the writing and the directing and put you in a comedy.'
> 'Well, Mack, that's fine. My regular salary for *acting* is $5,000 a week.'

Bullied and 'anesthetized' by Bill's salary demand, Sennett gave in, and Bill waltzed out 'and had a martini breakfast. He always talked business cold sober.'

Thus far the Keystone version. But as we have often found, the facts are different. Like Fields himself, Mack Sennett was a man of infinite pride, who never liked to play second fiddle. He had to be the boss, even when he was fast becoming a discarded Hollywood footnote. Louise Brooks describes him, as of 1936, as a big, healthy, 'wonderfully handsome and virile man' of fifty-one, sitting in the lobby of the Roosevelt Hotel, smoking his cigars and watching the people go by. Brooks asked: 'How could *he* have allowed himself to be discarded to die on the Hollywood rubbish heap?' But, as we know, Hollywood has no memory, and little sense of its own heritage.

But, in 1932, Bill Fields came to Sennett as an equal, as much an asset to the tired old factory as an old friend in need of a job. The four short films Fields made for Sennett – *The Dentist, The Fatal Glass of Beer, The Pharmacist* and *The Barber Shop* – released in 1932 and 1933, were all, save the last, faithful adaptations of his old stage routines: 'The Dentist Sketch' and 'The Stolen Bonds', from Earl Carroll's *Vanities*, and 'The Drug Store Sketch', from *The Comic Supplement*. *The Barber Shop* was a version of material developed for the *Vanities*, with bits and pieces from other sources.

The twenty-minute length of the films enabled them to play perfectly to the strengths of the condensed comic skit. In *The Dentist*, an opening scene has been tacked on to show the oral craftsman's home life: unusually, he has a spoilt daughter, rather than the adoring fantasy of other films. Her determination to marry the iceman, the ultimate insult in the Dukenfield eye, is countered by Dad's growl of: 'Get that iceman outa here! I'm going to order a fridgidaire.' His attempts to put a block of ice into the icebox (allowing it to melt on the gas ring to an appropriate size), echo the iceman gag of 'The Back Porch'. The Dentist then exits to a game of golf, shot at his very own Lakeside Golf Club – with fine views of Toluca Lake itself – in which various fandangles with dropped and thrown balls are enacted. There is a boorish caddy again, to be ordered about: 'Never mind where I told you to stand! You stand where I tell yer!' Further failures to land the ball anywhere but into the lake prompt Fields to throw bag, clubs, caddy and all into the water.

Fields has laid the ground for the dental skit proper. All the old stalwarts of the stage sketch are here: the woman patient who was bitten on the ankle: 'You're fortunate it wasn't a Newfoundland dog that bit yer'; the bearded patient, aka Foliage, herein a silent presence, but still

25 The Dentist: 'Have you had this tooth pulled before?'
(with Zedna Farley and Elise Cavanna).

342

with birds in his beard. Elise Cavanna has been finally summoned by Fields to be his main foil in the dentist's chair. Plying his dental tongs in her mouth, she wraps her legs around his back as he pulls her out of the chair. These shots were later cut for TV transmission in the 1950s and 1960s and have only recently been restored. The dentist (unnamed in the film) is a new kind of character: he is Bisbee triumphant, Elmer Prettywillie with the sentiment taken out, Pa Jones of *The Comic Supplement* with, as it were, teeth. This is already the Fields we will come to know in his future films: the 'little' man ranged against the universe of ornery offspring, recalcitrant golf balls and caddies, thick-headed golfing buddies who insist on the rules, dental patients who are unable to trust the infallible skill and fearsome tools of the doctor. This is Elmer Finch as the lion, bolstered by the certainty of his own invulnerable strength. There is a hint of the tyrant in this man, who is getting his own back against the slings and arrows of life.

In *The Fatal Glass of Beer*, Bill's second short for Sennett, the stage skit 'Stolen Bonds' is presented, as I have noted before, almost without change. The episode with the Indians is shoved a little further back in the story, which begins with some stock snowy forest footage followed by a knock on the door of prospector Snavely's wood hut. 'Who's thar?' 'Officer Postlewhistle of the Canadian Mounties.' 'Hullo officer . . . is it still snowin'?' 'Ah don't know,' says the officer, dusting half a ton of flakes off his coat, 'to tell you the truth, ah never looked.'

I have developed, in writing this book, a clinical approach to watching Fields movies on screen and video, anxious not to miss the nuances and shades. But I still find it impossible to view *The Fatal Glass of Beer* without collapsing in insane laughter. The staginess of the film, which made it, at the time, a box-office disaster, seems to show a wonderful contempt for the motion-picture conventions, which fits our 'postmodern' conceits. This is Fields truly as the Great Ham, rising dramatically to deliver such homilies as 'Once the city gets into a b-hoy's sy-hy-stem, he loses his a-hankerin' for the ca-hountry,' as the tale of woe of his son Chester unfolds. It is a cornucopia of Fields' greatest remembered lines: 'Figurin' on goin' over the rim tonight.' 'I think I'll go out and milk the elk.' 'He won't get Bozo, my lead dog, cause I et him. He was mighty good with mustard.' And the repeated refrain, most famous of all: 'And it ain't a fit night out for man nor beast!' as a handful of snow is thrown offscreen into his face.

The Fatal Glass of Beer was directed by Clyde Bruckman, one of the silent cinema's best helmers, who had worked with Buster Keaton (*Sherlock Junior, The Navigator* and *The General*) and with Harold Lloyd (*Feet First* and later *Movie Crazy*). But there is little sign of movie directing here. Presumably Bruckman just sat behind the camera and laughed like crazy. This is all Bill's own staging, meticulously lampooning the old style of melodrama and higher humbug: 'As my Uncle Ichabod said, speakin' of the city: it ain't no place for women, gal, but pretty men go thar.' The film deliberately has the feel of the oldest of all silent dramas, before Griffith and others crafted screen style acting, complete with honky-tonk piano on the soundtrack. Here is our only instance of a two verse W. C. Fields song – 'You wouldn't consider me rude if I played with ma mitts on?' – strumming upon the old zither: 'There once was a poor boy / and he left his country home / and he went to the city to look for work . . .' No wonder officer Postlewhistle is weeping at the plaintive dirge of the luckless Chester, who took the Fatal Glass of Beer and 'staggered through the door with delirium tremens'. All this in the heightened drama of flashbacks, as Chester, having wickedly broken a Salvation Army gal's tambourine, is set on the road to crime which leads him to the stolen bonds.

This is the first instance in film of Fields abiding love for the puritanical temperance sermons of his youth, the delicious lampooning of his own era's Prohibitionists in the hackneyed argot of the nineteenth century. It was to return in his meticulous recreation of the 1840s temperance drama, 'The Drunkard', in *The Old Fashioned Way*, one year later.

The Fatal Glass of Beer reduces the hallowed American frontier into an arena of meaningless, absurd postures. This may be part of the reason why the film, released in March 1933, was met by general consternation. Theatre owners reported: 'Two reels of film and 20 minutes wasted' – J. E. Weber, Princess Theatre, Chelsea, Michigan. 'This is the worst comedy we have played from any company this season. No story, no acting, and as a whole has nothing' – J. J. Medford, Orpheum Theatre, Oxford, North Carolina. Sennett hated the film. He had forced Fields to shoot the flashbacks of the song, which Fields thought would ruin the work (it didn't), and Fields wanted out of his contract. Ronald Fields quotes from Bill's letter to Sennett at this point: 'When I have the stage all set for a Fields picture and you come in and have everything changed to a Sennett picture you . . . render me helpless . . .

I do not believe our business relations are going to be successful. I wish you would agree to terminate the contract and we continue our friendship of yore.'

But Sennett must have known he was on to a good thing. If Fields could only steer clear of his more surreal and non-realistic ideas he was surely destined for glory. And indeed, Bill was scared off trying to foist this side of his comedy on producers until much later – towards the end, when he went for broke with *The Bank Dick* and *Never Give a Sucker an Even Break*. Still, it was a tantalising glimpse of an even wilder W. C. Fields than audiences had seen till then.

Bill remained with Mack to shoot *The Pharmacist* and *The Barber Shop*. And Elmer Prettywillie was reborn as Mr Dillweg, proprietor of the small-town Drugstore. Here, Bill returned all the way to J. P. McEvoy's original Jones family, at breakfast, complete with brattish daughter, Priscilla, the bane of her Dad's life: 'Is Papa's little angel going to sit down? . . . Or will Papa bust you over the head with this stick?'

Priscilla is choking because she has eaten the canary bird. Dillweg's wife is Elise Cavanna, languidly presiding over this bedlam. An older daughter, Ooleota (a name Bill will return to in *Never Give a Sucker*) is in love with one Cuthbert, the first appearance in Fields' repertory company of the shambling and amiable Grady Sutton: 'I never knew a Cuthbert in my life that wasn't a sissy. When I was a kid I licked every kid in school named Cuthbert.'

Downstairs, in the shop, we are back on the Ziegfeld stage. 'Hello . . . yes . . . yes . . . this is Dillweg's Drug Store . . . What's that? A box of cough drops . . . Yes . . . No, I'm very sorry, we can't split a box . . . Yes . . . we can deliver them . . . Uh huh . . . eighteen miles straight onto Route 96 . . . turn to Route 13 . . . Yes . . . all right . . . I'll send our truck out with them right away . . .' We have been here before. The lady who wants to use the telephone and takes away the free gift, the florid gentleman untempted by 'Read Mother India? Sex Life of the Pollyp? Rover boys in . . . Cake a la mode? . . . Old Moscow in winter . . . Could I interest you in a stamp?'

Fields is at the top of his form, working with familiar material, happy at last with the pace and space of the motion picture; he has transformed the stage act into a reality. Dillweg's world is surreal and very recognizable at the same time, the world of the smallest, and the largest, frustrations. In *The Barber Shop*, Dillweg has become O'Hare, the town's barber, once again with Elise Cavanna as his helpmeet. The opening shot, with a banner 'YOU ARE NOW ENTERING FELTON CITY – 2ft Above Sea Level,' hints that we are in a very personal Dukenfield mode here – remember Kate Felton, Bill's Maw? Voices behind the banner strike the right note: 'Pretty good town you have here!' 'You bet we have – a public library and the largest insane asylum in the State . . .' Cornelius O'Hare, stropping his razor outside his shop, responds to the passersby with the kind of mumbling he heard his mother utter on her porch at home:

'Hello O'Hare, whadayaknow?' 'Not a thing, not a thing. (*Aside*) That lunk tells his wife everything he knows . . . I should tell him anything . . . Good morning Mrs Scroggins. How's Mr. Scroggins?' 'He ain't feeling so well this morning.' 'That's too bad. (*Aside*) Guess he was on one of his benders last night again . . . Boy, how he can drink that raw alcohol and live, I don't know . . . Fine mayor he is . . .'

This time the Fields ménage includes a young son, Ronald, regaling him at the breakfast table with some familiar riddles:

RONALD: Why is a cat's tale like a long journey?

O'HARE: I'm afraid you have me, Ronald, why is a cat's tail like a long journey?

RONALD: Cause its fur to the end . . . har har har . . .

O'HARE: Very good, Ronald, very good, you are absolutely side-splitting . . .

An old McIntyre and Heath joke sure does go fur . . . 'Eat your spinach . . . Eat your spinach . . .' The barber O'Hare is a much more amiable figure than either the Dentist or Dillweg. Perhaps playing his cello, 'Lena', does the trick. His wife, oddly enough, is a vegetarian, but this is an in-joke I am not able to trace. There is a furore in town over a bandit who robbed the bank at Cucumonga City, for whom a two thousand dollar reward is offered.

O'HARE: I would like to get that dough. If I wasn't so busy I'd go over there and choke that guy to death . . .

Taking a shave with O'Hare is as hazardous as taking your aching teeth to Dr Payne: 'That a mole?' 'Yes, I've had it all my life.' 'Uh huh . . . you won't have it any more . . .' A fat man comes in to take some weight off in the steam-room. A Mrs B. brings in a baby to be watched.

A customer is treated to a typical monologue:

CUSTOMER: Say, what is that dog doing in here?

O'HARE: That's a funny thing . . . the other day a man was in here . . . I was shaving him . . . the razor slipped and I cut his ear off . . . the dog got it . . . ever since he's been hanging around . . . get away, get away . . .

The fat man is trapped in the steam-room and emerges shrunk as Stan Laurel: 'I'll have the law on you for this!' The bank robber rushes in, demanding to be shaved. O'Hare escapes from the shop and comandeers a bicycle. The thief gives chase. From the yard the kid, Ronald, bats a baseball, which knocks the bandit and O'Hare, who have gone full circle, back into the barber shop, O'Hare still feebly protesting: 'I didn't try to catch yer . . . I like bandits . . . Some of our best friends are bandits . . . The President of the Bank comes up to our house . . .'

O'Hare claims to have captured the bandit and earned the $2,000 reward, but the cops come up with the real hero, his son Ronald. 'Are you hurt, Mr O'Hare?' 'Not physically.' The crowning humiliation is the discovery that his cello, 'Lena', and a friend's cello which has been left beside her for safe keeping, have given birth to a brood of little fiddles. 'Lena, how could you . . .' He kicks in the offending cello and throws it out: 'You dog, you . . .' FADE OUT.

The Pharmacist and *The Barber Shop* were both directed by Arthur Ripley, another veteran, who had worked with Harry Langdon. All four screenplays were written by Fields, free of the studio teams of writers who were stubbornly assigned to him, again and again, in his later Paramount films. *The Barber Shop*, particularly, provided Fields with more freedom to experiment in blending 'real life' with the surreal. The film has a nice flow of events that just might make sense but somehow don't, in the cosmic condundrum of life. Three years earlier, in France, the young surrealist Luis Bunuel, with Salvador Dali, had produced his provocative and bizarre masterpiece, *L'Age D'Or*, 'The Golden Age', in which scorpions fought, live cardinals became skeletons and a blind man was kicked by the hero. But O'Hare-Dillweg's small American town is just as full of strange acts. Why should not two cellos mate, a fat man lose all his girth, and the hero ride a bicycle off frame right to arrive back where he started from frame left?

Bill's long expressed desire to take the 'many little incidents . . . that are full of natural humor' and 'crochet them together into acts'; the long, painstaking process of the scribbled notes and multiple drafts of the vaudeville sketches, tied together with McEvoy's influential satire, had flowered forth, at last, upon the Talkie screen.

Bill Fields had regained his voice. Mack Sennett gave him, as he had given so many others before him, a testing ground upon which to hone his craft. The Fields persona that we know was knitted together in these four short films. Now began the search for the material which would allow Bill to express and develop his character in the more demanding realm of the talking feature film . . .

Chapter 32
'What Isn't Crosswise in China?'

Bill, at Toluca Lake, was becoming quite a Hollywood magnet. If we believe previous accounts, he lived the life of a recluse, increasingly eccentric, drunk and misanthropic. Taylor tells an apocryphal tale (one among so many) of Mack Sennett motoring up to Toluca Lake to find Fields crouching in a clump of azaleas, hiding from Earl Carroll, who 'was sending his brother up here to try and borrow $8,000 to start a restaurant with'. The next day, so the tale goes, Fields turned up at the Sennett studios with a false beard and dark glasses, eventually check-mating Carroll by pretending to be in bed 'beginning a long illness'.

But the myth, in its multiple errors and inventions, has brought a much later Fields, sick, crusty, and paranoid, into the earlier, ebullient period. In fact, Fields' house at Toluca Lake, and later at Encino, where he rented a large ranch with several acres of land, was a Mecca for many Hollywood newcomers. Broadway, in its decline, had emptied out west, towards Los Angeles, a horde of expatriate actors who craved a meeting place of like minded folk.

The Depression had changed the political map of America. The age of cosy Republican rule, of Coolidge and Hoover, had given way to a new doctrine. In the elections of November 1932, a new man, Franklin Delano Roosevelt, was swept by a landslide into the White House. The Democrats were back in power. On 4 March 1933, a day after the release of *The Fatal Glass of Beer*, Roosevelt was inaugurated as the United States President.

Most of Hollywood rejoiced. Show-people, many of whom had climbed up from the lower ranks of society, responded to the Roosevelt New Deal. Will Rogers embraced Roosevelt as a saviour, although he himself had been mentioned as a Presidential candidate. This was the heyday of populist politics, which had already produced the dema-gogic Senator Huey Long in Louisiana, but Rogers, mercifully, did not crave power. Another influential ex-vaudevillian, Eddie Cantor, also greeted Roosevelt with open arms. As President of the Screen Actors Guild of America, he had been swimming in political seas for some time, and even went to Rome to ask Mussolini for permission for American crews to make movies in Italy. But he was tactless enough to ask Musso's son-in-law, Count Ciano: 'What's this unholy alliance between Mussolini and Hitler?' Show-people are nothing if not naive.

Cantor loved Roosevelt, and was the man who suggested to him the slogan of the 'March of Dimes', to raise money to fight polio. A different intervention he made, representing the Screen Actor's Guild, was to try and talk the President out of his plans to limit actors' incomes to a maximum of $25,000 a year. Roosevelt relented, but there were some famous actors who never forgave him for that proposed act of highway robbery.

Bill Fields was one of them. In the intervening years, between Ziegfeld and Sennett, something had happened to his political viewpoint. Remember George Burns' words, about the apolitical nature of vaudeville folk? Show-people's bread and butter was the general audience, which came from all walks of life and all parties. Some performers wore their heart on their sleeve and were none the worse for it. Others were fanatical in their refusal to commit themselves to any political creed. Fields was supposed to have said that the world's political problems should be worked out by their leaders being forced to fight each other in sporting arenas with sackfuls of dung. In reality, as we have been told by Cantor, he was far from ignorant of the world of politics and the events of the day.

Fields was an omnivore, who devoured information, recycling it into his own material, using it in his own peculiar way. Always concerned, during his stage years, with the well-being of his fellow vaudevillians, he was happy to be counted among the White Rats, their union, and, we might remember, he stood with Eddie Cantor and the Equity strikers of 1919. But his life-long fear of the intermittent nature of the performer's life was taking its toll, more so, paradoxically, as he became more affluent. When we are young, we are more willing to accept the uncertainties of our chosen path. As we grow older, we crave security. This, I believe, is what happened to Fields. Having begun his second movie career at the age of fifty-one, he was determined to defeat the here-today gone-tomorrow nature of Hollywood success. Louise Brooks wrote about his 'clutching fear of being discarded to die on the Hollywood rubbish heap', increasing all the more as time went by, but clearly present at the start.

Bill Fields, who had never espoused this or that party – and lampooned them all, at one time or another – was, in his private soul, becoming a Republican. This never seemed to have been manifested when that party was in power, but, almost as soon as the Democrats became the establishment, he embraced the opposition.

Income Tax was the big bugaboo. Roosevelt's administration was the first in the Western industrial world to adopt what are today called 'Tax and Spend' policies by their opponents. A spectacular raft of legislation provided credit for agriculture, industry, home financing, Federal relief and a host of special projects for recovery. All this would have to be paid for. In 1936, the government passed a specific Wealth-Tax Act, levied against the 'unjust concentration of wealth and economic power', increasing surtaxes on yearly incomes of over $50,000.

And Fields' wrath waxed sorely. He had begun his career in a period when income tax was a mere gleam in governments' eyes. Now, when he was beginning to get the rewards of a life's labour, he resented like hell any depletion of the fees he had to fight like a tiger to receive. Bill's battles with the Federal Tax authorities became legendary. In 1939 he was still fighting against tax and penalties claimed for the years 1933, 1934 and 1935, claiming such exemptions as necessary expenses for 'sleight-of-hand training', payment for a trainer to build up his health, even, at one point, his liquor bill. All this crystallised into a series of articles on 'How to Beat the Federal Income Tax', collected in his only book, *Fields For President*, in 1940. To wit:

> March 15 is always a day of rare rejoicing and unbridled revelry throughout the nation. For that is the day when all the citizens of our fair land may practice their inalienable rights of sending a fat slice of their yearly increments to Washington; in return, our Congressmen will forward packages of radish seed or intimate candid-camera shots of themselves weeding their farms or kissing their grandchildren. Most Congressmen are very human, if nothing else.

The style of these essays might be called Will Rogers with extra bile thrown in. For this was a war Bill fought until his dying day, and indeed beyond. His resentment of Roosevelt turned into an unreasoning hostility, which spread, in later years, to the President's wife, Eleanor, and was to take a bizarre turn . . .

Another transformation which affected Bill's politics was the familiar one of employee to employer. Once Bill had taken on palatial residences, with an entourage of gardeners, cooks and servants, he began an instant fulmination against their incompetence, disobedience and downright treachery. This would be expressed in many outbursts and complaints, but most ironically, perhaps, in a later version of the Barber Shop sketch, proposed but unused in his movie *The Big Broadcast of 1938*, in which Fields has become the suffering customer rather than the working man, and the actual barbers of the ship he's travelling on have gone on strike, leaving the kitchen's butchers to take up the slack.

Hollywood was, for stage people, a kind of gilded isolation. After the crowded bar of the Lambs, the bright lights of Broadway, the direct hug of audience and stage, the wide, open plan sunny climes of Los Angeles tended to separate rather than connect. The Broadway exiles found new watering holes: the Masquers' Club, Chasen's restaurant. New groups formed, clustering around, if not for warmth, for the company of like with like, to spend their money and to complain about the morons and charlatans who were paying the bills.

New recruits, joining the self-exiled actors, were the incoming Talkie writers. Journalism had provided many of Broadway's toughest scribes, men such as Ben Hecht, Charles MacArthur, J. P. McEvoy. Hecht and MacArthur had written the famous newspaper satire *The Front Page*, in 1928. In their original play, the man due to be hanged for political glory was a suspected Communist. In the later movie versions, the victim would be demoted to a common alleged killer. Broadway into Hollywood: Q.E.D.

As journalists, these were hard-talking, hard-drinking men, natural boozing partners for Bill Fields. But another ex-reporter, already trailing his own legend, had just hit Hollywood and was to become Bill's closest confidant and friend. This man was Gene Fowler.

Fowler was born in Denver in 1890. Like many of his generation, he was a self-taught man who blended a hard-nosed knack for sports and physical prowess with a broad self-achieved education; in Fowler's case, an early interest in Egyptology and foreign lands. Such a man was tailor-made for journalism, first with the Denver *Republican*, then the Denver *Post*, where he interviewed Buffalo Bill Cody, then in boozy retirement in Colorado. During these early years Fowler also devoured the classics, from Tolstoy through Rabelais, Mark Twain, Dickens. Recruited by Damon Runyon to work on William Randolph Hearst's

New York *American*, in 1916, he remained there for over ten years. His expense accounts, as well as his reporting, became legendary, notably the heading *Flowers for bereft bitch – $1.50*, to cover the story of a heroic lead-dog's death in Alaska. Fowler was also famous for his affairs, with Mary Astor and, allegedly, with Queen Marie of Roumania. Gene's wife, Agnes, was a long-suffering critic of these escapades.

In his late thirties, Fowler began a long planned second career as a novelist, publishing his first novel, *Trumpet in the Dust*, in 1930. The following year another novel, *Shoe the Wild Mare*, appeared. Gene's prowess as a writer travelled west, probably via his friends, Hecht and MacArthur, and in 1931 he received the summons to occupy a screen-play-writer's office in Hollywood at a salary that could not be refused. The assignment – a script for his friend, John Barrymore, in a film entitled *State's Attorney*.

Another project Fowler was working on brought him directly to Fields. He had been commissioned to write a biography of Mack Sennett, to be called *Father Goose*. It was probably at the Sennett studios that the crucial first meeting occurred. At any rate, it did not take long for the two self-made men to meet, mingle, and share their contempt for the grand moguls of Hollywood.

Hollywood's treatment of writers is well documented. The studios needed craftspeople to string words together, but they did not want them to wield any power. The producers were Hollywood's real Generals, with the studio heads as their Field-Marshalls. Writers were NCOs, and actors the common soldiers, the cannon-fodder of the box-office wars. Even the most powerful of stars were vassals. The result was a smouldering hatred in the ranks for the bosses, especially the studio heads, the Midas knuckleheads, who could turn careers on and off with a flick of their fingers.

Almost all of these studio heads were Jews. And almost all were still the same pioneers who had immigrated from Eastern Europe and sprung from a background of small trade. Adolph Zukor had started out in the fur business. Shmuel Gelbfisch, a glove salesman, became Samuel Goldwyn. Carl Laemmle had begun as a bookkeeper. Louis B. Mayer started out in scrap-metal. Harry Cohn, the most hated mogul in Hollywood, was a tailor. A legendary riposte, some say delivered by John Barrymore, others by Gene Fowler himself, to Harry Cohn wagging his finger in anger, was: 'Don't wag that finger at me – I remember that finger when it wore a thimble!'

Resentment of the moguls always risked tipping over into anti-Semitism. The moguls themselves were acutely aware of this, and responded by becoming more gentile than the gentiles, to the extent of exiling the new genre of Yiddish-speaking Talkies to the East Side ghetto of New York. Most critics of the studio heads, like Fowler, were never tempted by prejudice, but some, like Fields, in private, vented some unpleasant spleen.

Fields' attitude to racial prejudice was ambivalent. We have seen that he was a man of his time. Brought up in an age when black-white divides appeared natural to most whites, he took on board other common baggage. But his own personal experience – despite 'Ubangis in the fuel supply' – taught him that all races and creeds mixed in his beloved vaudeville, and racial bias was inherently wrong. In 1925, he wrote to Hattie, accompanying the usual cheque, a telling remark: 'You should not speak so disparagingly of C.C. (Country Club) and its Jewish attendancy. There are many wonderful Jews. I know of no race finer.' But much later, in 1942, he is writing to his good friend Paul Jones claiming jokingly that Louis B. Mayer and 'Franklin Disraeli Rosefeld' are one and the same, or, also in 1942, commenting in a letter to Elise Cavanna: 'I got an infected big toe which the doctor says was due to kicking those Jews in the can over at Fox.' On the other hand the correspondence, through the 1930s, abounds with friendly letters to both Fanny Brice and Eddie Cantor ('Dear Rabbi' or 'Dear Christ-Killer') and at least one of his aborted projects, a treatment called 'Motel', is about a Jewish delicatessen owner, Mr Goldberg, who sets out for California to be a cowboy (thirty years before Mel Brooks . . .).

An apocryphal tale about Fields, told in many versions, has him railing about the Jews at RKO, and responding, when told that the people at RKO are Baptists – 'That's the worst kind of Jew!' In his attitudes to black people, Fields was probably influenced by white intellectuals like H. L. Mencken and other New Yorkers who saw the black contribution to America's popular culture as positive and integral: Blacks were not foreign. They had been brought here against their will. For better or worse, they were native Americans.

Whatever his prejudices, Fields was always careful to keep them out of his work. Apart from the mild 'Ubangi' jokes, he steered clear of stereotypes – why should he need them, since he was lampooning everyone? The real story, I believe, is that Bill Fields recognized two distinct categories of human beings: show-business people, and all the rest. To fellow showmen and women he was almost always open, friendly, and generous to a fault. To others, he gave at best a 'hearty handclasp', and at worst, the full blast of his wrath.

That Fields could blow both hot and cold at the same time is exemplified by his long correspondence with Hattie, which continued throughout this period. Despite the separation, he is still keeping in touch. On 5 May 1932:

Dear Hattie,

I am in receipt of yours and Claude's letter. I note the derogatory rumors concerning my use of alcoholic stimulant and lavish living. It is the penalty of greatness . . . I would have sworn, when those rumors reached you, that you would have retaliated as did Lincoln, when informed by some nosy parker, that Grant was continually in his cups, 'Find out the brand of whiskey he drinks and send a barrel to each of my Generals.' . . . I have never failed you with the bacon and all the money I sent you was for your own use, as Claude testifies in his letter that he has done everything himself. It is an admirable trait in him, and I can well appreciate it as I have kept myself and others since reaching the tender age of eleven . . .

Trust you are both well,

Claude

In this letter Bill slips, imperceptibly, into the mask of Eustace McGargle, or the Great McGonigle, soon to be born. The process whereby character and performer merge was accelerating, in the Never Never Land of 1930s Hollywood. The boozing, too, was, despite his protestations, slowly taking its toll. It was badly complementing a chronic illness which had been plaguing him for some time. The respiratory ailment of the early 1900s, his apparently self-cured TB, was recurring as bouts of chest pains and grippe. In 1929 he complained to Hattie of four attacks in that year. There was a constant fear of pneumonia. A dose of whiskey might have done the trick in Edinburgh in 1904, but rivers of gin defiantly flowing down the gullet during Prohibition were not proving beneficial. Nevertheless, he continued along this road, drawing sustenance from his drinking partners, new and old.

Why did Fowler, Fields and their friends drink so much? Today we know a fair amount about addiction. But this was not just a matter of a tautology: they drank because they drank. There was something else, expressed in inimitable style by Gene Fowler in an essay written some time in the mid-1930s, but not published until 1962; he called it, after De Quincey, 'Confessions of a Celluloid Eater'.

This monograph has to do with the disintegration of an intellect. It is the unholy record of a scenario writer who became enslaved to a narcotic . . . The drug of which I write is celluloid . . . I had written a play, the merit of which was earmarked when its potential sponsor committed suicide during dress rehearsal. The manuscript was laid in camphor balls, to be exhumed only after Sol Effendi, a motion picture magnate, deemed it sufficiently inferior to be produced cinematically for the peanut munchers of the great American wilderness . . .

In the beginning I was unaware that I had set foot in a bottomless quagmire. Yet I can see it all now in retrospect – the successive stages of mental castration. First the lulling wave of economic ease which breaks over the bathers on the nepenthean shore. Next, the delusions of grandeur that impel shanty-bred hacks and half-baked hams, who have eaten of the drug, to set up seraglios, engage regiments of butlers, second men, chauffeurs, footmen and maids, acquire Tiberian swimming pools, six-car garages with seven automobiles per domicile . . . and to retain bodyguards with perfumed mustachios and platinum shields . . .

Was it a part of my invidious dream? Or did I actually repeat after the Grand Inquisitor verses from the 23rd Psalm as follows: *Will Hays is my shepherd, I shall not want. He maketh me to lie down in clean postures. He purgeth me with bilge-waters.*

He forecloseth my soul . . .

Surely mediocrity and pelf shall follow me all the days of my life; and I will smell in the house of art forever . . .

Self-doubt, even self-loathing . . . One had to have a drug, to counter the drug. And so the work, on the nepenthean shores, continued.

In the spring of 1933 Bill Fields returned to Paramount. His old mentor, William Le Baron, had moved west from Astoria, and his old director buddy, Eddie Sutherland, was putting together a movie-revue to showcase a range of comedy stars, many of whom who had become known on radio: George Burns, Gracie Allen, Franklin Pangborn, Rudy Vallee, Baby Rose Marie, Colonel Stoopnagle and Bud (who they?) and, from Ziegfeld days, Peggy Hopkins, now Peggy Hopkins

Joyce. W. C. Fields was written in as Professor Quail, eccentric inventor of the autogyro – an early helicopter – who has landed by mistake in Wu-Hu, China, and joins the crew of celebrities at the International House Hotel, who have gathered to bid for a new invention – a radioscope (which we now call television) – developed by the Chinese eccentric Dr Wong.

International House is a strange and uneven concoction. The George Burns-Gracie Allen routines are vintage, for die-hard fans. (George: 'There's a man outside with a rash in the rotunda.' Gracie: 'Well, it takes all kinds to make a world.') But Fields breezes through at full power, from the moment he lands in the ballroom, with the immortal words: 'Is this Kansas City, Kansas, or Kansas City, Missouri?' prefacing the following exchange:

QUAIL: Hey, where am I?

PEGGY: Wu Hu.

QUAIL: Wu Hu to you sweetheart. (*To Pangborn*) Hey, Charlie, where am I?

MANAGER: Wu Hu.

QUAIL (*taking flower from pocket and throwing it away*): Don't let the posy fool yer. Where am I?

MANAGER: This is the roof garden of the International Hotel.

QUAIL: Never mind the details. What town is it?

MANAGER: This is Wu Hu, China.

QUAIL: Then what am I doing here?

MANAGER: Well, how should I know?

QUAIL: Well, what is Wu Hu doing where Kansas City ought to be?

MANAGER: Maybe you're lost.

QUAIL: Kansas City is lost! I am here!

The derivation of Quail from the Q. Q. of *Ballyhoo* is the clue to this new twist of Bisbee. The inventor is now abroad, cutting a swathe through pomposity and pretensions with his own brand of haughty familiarity: 'Send up a bird's nest and a couple of two hundred year old eggs boiled in perfume,' he instructs room service, having negotiated the lobby with its treacherous maze of loose switchboard cables: 'Looks like a Chinese noodle swamp!' His exchange with Dr Wong, who offers him a shared bed in the quarantined hotel, in the mistaken belief he is the buyer from the American Electrical Company, is particularly poignant:

WONG: Where are you going to sleep tonight?

QUAIL: I'm going to sleep on my right side with my mouth open . . .

WONG: I always sleep on my stomach.

QUAIL: Don't you find it gets all wrinkled?

But in the end he opts to sleep, unbeknownst to her, in Peggy Hopkins Joyce's bedroom, prompting a jealous fit from her ex-husband, Bela Lugosi as General Petronovitch, who is watching with binoculars from across the street. The flim-flam climaxes with Quail's escape from the hotel with Peggy in a midget car (re-Earl Carroll's *Vanities*) where their attempts to settle down are disturbed when she says:

PEGGY: I'm sitting on something.

QUAIL: I lost mine in the stock market.

(*Cat meows off.*)

QUAIL: Ahh!

PEGGY: What's that?

QUAIL: Sounds like a body squeak . . .

After tightening the nuts ('The what?' 'Nuts! Nuts! Nuts!'), they drive into the autogyro, where Peggy still says:

PEGGY: I tell you I'm sitting on something. Something's under me. What is it?

QUAIL: It's a pussy.

Small cat is revealed, and, at the end, as they take off, a whole litter, which Peggy views with bewilderment.

PEGGY: I wonder what their parents were?

QUAIL: Careless, my little nut cake, careless.

None of this scene was in the original script, and its appearance in the movie prompted a veritable blizzard of condemnation from the MPPDA's censors, who had already been perturbed by some of the dialogue in the film. On 8 May 1933, the Board member James Wingate wrote to Paramount executive A. M. Botsford, categorising *International House* as 'a type of picture with which censor boards recently have been dealing severely, with particular reference to double-meaning lines and gags'. From the standpoint of the code, wrote Mr Wingate, there were six items which the board thought should be deleted:

1 The line by Grace Allen when she is sitting on the stethoscope, stating that she can 'hear her heart beat.'

2 Fields' line 'Don't let a flower deceive you' – as an inference of sex perversion.

3 The shot in the dance routine in which the girls are bent over and the camera is focused on their posteriors.

4 The line when Fields looks into the keyhole, 'What won't they be trying next.'

5 Fields line 'What isn't crosswise in China?'

6 Fields tag line 'Careless' in reference to the parents of the cats . . .

Mr Botsford wrote back protesting about deletions which would 'eliminate considerable comedy . . . which is, we believe, entirely innocuous.' Concerning Fields' 'flower' line he wrote:

Fields' line 'Don't let the flower deceive you' indicates merely a 'sissy' reaction. It would take an expert in abnormal psychology to wheedle out of that an inference of sex perversion . . . Fields line into the keyhole, 'What won't they think of next' is smutty only in the minds of persons who want to construct smut out of it.

Botsford did concede deletion of the 'crosswise in China' line, but insisted that 'the "careless" line with reference to the parents of the cats is, we believe, merely innocuous in this day and age.' Mr Wingate wrote back, accepting the 'crosswise in China' deletion as a deal, but internal memoranda between the censors show that this was not the end of the matter. On 22 June, Carl E. Milliken, Secretary of the MPPDA, wrote to Joseph Breen:

> . . . I happen to note today the following elimination from INT. HOUSE by one of the stag censor boards:

> Reel 7: Eliminate words: 'What are you feeling about for?' Eliminate underscored words: '<u>I tell you I am sitting on something.</u>' '<u>It's a pussy.</u>'

> This caused me to look up the file on this particular picture. The whole picture is vulgar and borders constantly on the salacious according to the comments of the public groups. Originally our west coast office required six deletions under the Code. The studio gave them an argument on all of them and they finally insisted on only one. This deletion was not made, as evidenced by the report of the reviewer who saw the print in New York.

> The elimination referred to above apparently escaped the notice of our office and of the public group reviewers. The dirty minded lout who put it in the picture knew perfectly well, however, what he was doing and undoubtedly gained something by getting away with it. I wish that Kuykendall or somebody whose words would carry weight could manage to give him an impression of the opinion that is rapidly developing throughout this country regarding him and his kind.

> With all good wishes, I am, sincerely yours,

> Carl E. Milliken.

Further memos try to recall what the scene had originally been and how the Board could have got gypped. Mr James B. M. Fisher thought the line in the script had been: 'It's a cat', rather than 'pussy'. He continued: 'If it is true that the scene has been changed so as to make it play differently from the way it went in the version which we saw, it is my opinion that Paramount should certainly be called to account. For from various comments, it appears we are taking a terrific beating in allowing something to pass which is unmistakably vulgar.'

We might find it astonishing that grown men can get into such a tizz about such a frivolous matter, but the Board's wrath was not to be laughed off easily. In October 1935, Paramount was asked to withdraw its application for Code of Approval Seals to permit the reissuing of a number of pictures, including *No Man of Her Own, Pick Up, Devil and the Deep* and *International House*. In 1950 Breen, still in situ, is demanding deletions of scenes from another reissue: 'Delete the

line: "You spent half the night feeling in the dark for nuts and bolts."
. . . Delete underlined words in the line "I can't go to bed, I'm not married yet." . . . Delete action of Fields looking in keyhole, including line,
"What won't they think of next."' And of course, the whole pussy sitting scene, once again.

At its initial release, the film was approved without cuts only in two
states – New York and Kansas. In Pennsylvania they eliminated the
underlined words – 'Tommy, don't you see we'll never be married; you
– you just can't take the strain.' In Virginia, the nuts and bolts had to
go. In Maryland, they didn't like the line 'Oh, doctor, I can hear my
heart beat.' In Ontario – 'Don't let the posy fool you.' In Ohio, 8 deletions, including Quail's line to Peggy, when he tells her he'll come back
to collect her: 'Don't forget, tap on the window as soon as the chumps
leave.'

It should be noted that America was far from the only country
seething with puritanical fever: in Australia, the censors were even
more cautious, deleting – 'I'll be down as soon as I take off these pyjamas.' And in Japan, they took umbrage at Peggy Hopkins Joyce taking
some shorts out of a suitcase and saying to the besotted Tommy: 'I
packed these by mistake in the desert.' In Sweden the whole film was
'CONSIDERED UNSUITABLE – Story too artificial and absurd.'

When we watch *International House* today, we are struck at the
carefree innocence of these 1930s comedies, with all their silly twists
and turns. But it is salutory to realize with what horror such high jinks
were regarded by the censorship boards of the day. From that point on,
Breen had Fields' number, as an unconscionable vulgarian, who would
get away with murder, obscenity and every other transgression in the
censor's book, if only he could. The battle lines had been quite sharply
drawn.

Chapter 33
Bringin' in the Sheaves . . .

Just how far the censors were in tune with popular taste, then as now, was proved by *International House* becoming a big hit. Now at last Paramount was willing to forget the silent flops and offer Fields a multi-picture contract. After much haggling, Bill emerged with a deal for $100,000 a movie, three films a year, for three years. A tiny fraction of the sums box-office stars expect today, but very tidy at that time. Bill had entered his golden years. Between the summer of 1933 and the summer of 1936 he would appear in eleven films, and star in eight of them. It was by far his most prolific period, accounting for four major works: *You're Telling Me, The Old Fashioned Way, It's a Gift* and *Man on the Flying Trapeze*, as well as the more minor *Tillie and Gus, Six of a Kind, Mississipi* and the 1936 remake of *Poppy*. Cameo appearances in *Alice in Wonderland* (1933) and *David Copperfield*, add to the list, and the dismal *Mrs Wiggs of the Cabbage Patch*, which he valiantly pepped up in a couple of scenes, rounds it up. This was the movie equivalent of Bill's juggling heyday, or his ten years in the tent of Ziegfeld Khayyam.

It was also the period when W. C. Fields, the invented man we all know so well, was constructed, both by himself, in many magazine pieces, and by the tireless press publicists of the Paramount staff. Foremost among these was Teet Carle, for whom Fields was a publicist's dream. Unlike other stars, he didn't care what the Publicity Department published about him as long as it fed the mythic image. Carle had first met Bill on the set of *Two Flaming Youths*, back in 1927, but became his chief press scribe from *If I Had a Million* in 1932.

Fields related to Carle all his fondness for strange names of people and places – Officer Postlewhistle, Eustace McGargle, Dr Otis Guelpe, Sneed Hearn, Figley E. Whiteside, and later Cuthbert J. Twillie, Mrs Hermissilio Brunch, Egbert Souse, Ogg Ogilby ('sounds like a bubble in a bathtub'), J. Pinkerton Snoopington, Larson E. Whipsnade, as well as Cucumonga, Punxhatauney, Lake Shosho Cocomo, Pismo Beach, Lompoc and so on and so forth. These may well, as Carlotta Monti later claimed, have derived from his beloved Dickens – from the echoes of Pecksniff, Mrs Gamp, Uriah Heep, Mr Spottletoe, Chevy Slyme. Some of the personal names were of real people – Bogle was a common Philadelphia name, Mr Muckle of *It's a Gift* was an old neighbour. Harold Bissonette, Fields' character in that film, was in fact, a fellow member of the Lakeside Golf Club in North Hollywood, though his name, as Ronald Fields discovered decades later, was not pronounced 'Bissonay'. Twillie, Ogilby, Dunk and McGonigle, James Smart of Philadelphia informs us, could also be found in the Phila. directories of the 1890s. Mahatma Kane Jeeves, author of *The Bank Dick*, had another source – 'my hat, my cane, Jeeves'. Bill Fields purloined all kinds of bits and pieces. As he comments, as Humpty Dumpty in the 1933 *Alice in Wonderland*:

HUMPTY-DUMPTY: When I use a word, it means what I choose it to mean, neither more nor less.

ALICE: The question is whether you can make words mean different things.

HUMPTY-DUMPTY: The question is which is to be the master, you or the word, that's all.

But Fields did not care what words Teet Carle and other publicists made up for the movie Press Books. He was already vending his own myth, as in 1935, to Alva Johnston for the *New Yorker*. He told Teet Carle the same story of his harsh early days, so that Carle and his staff had no problem writing, in the Press Book of *Six of a Kind*:

W. C. FIELDS: 'Born of poor but American parents,' according to his own testimony, he left home at the age of eleven, because his father's alarm clock annoyed him . . . Today he lives in solitary grandeur in his Hollywood hacienda, and sleeps when he is not working . . .'

Well, not quite solitary . . . We may have noticed a dropping out of the female names which accompanied Bill, certainly throughout his stage years and his first Hollywood sojourn. But none seem to have accompanied him the second time. Perhaps he felt too financially vulnerable to support his girlfriends in the manner to which they had grown accustomed. Contrary to Louise Brook's memoirs, and the usual legends, he did not shun parties, as long as he was giving them, though he did not mix with the Hollywood colony's established upper crust. He was, as we saw, forming his own colony, which was to set forth, on a sea of alcohol, upon a voyage into its own battered psyche. But he did not remain bereft of female company for long.

It happened during the shooting of publicity stills for *International House*. These were staged events, much like the newsreel-style one-reelers like *Hollywood on Parade*, in which Bill featured in 1933 and 1934, with various stars in tiny sketches (in the first of these, Tammany Young, a noted Hollywood gate-crasher, appeared for the first time as Fields' stooge). In the publicity photographs, out of work actresses were often called up to pose with the movie's stars, just to add some spice. One of the ladies chosen at this occasion was a twenty-four-year-old Hispanic-American beauty named Carlotta Monti (née Montijo). According to her own account she had just broken up with her boyfriend, but dried her tears to go to work. Let us follow her story:

> 'Mr Fields,' the assistant director said, 'this is Miss Monti, who will be doing the stills with you.'
>
> Instantly doffing his grey stovepipe hat, W. C. Fields placed it over his breast and bowed low before me. 'It is a pleasure, my dusky beauty,' he murmured . . .
>
> In 1932, the mumbling comic with the scratchy voice was blond, trim-figured, and handsome, with an unblemished complexion and bright blue eyes. Such a flattering portrait may seem incredible to those familiar with the movies he made during the 1940's, at which stage of his life his face resembled a relief map of some coal mining district, suffering from perpetual hard times . . . He must have been thirty years my senior – but that was a mere triviality. He looked cute and cuddly. I wanted to mother him, smother him with attention, please him . . .

Wo, Rover! (She was mighty good with mustard . . .) Carlotta Monti is the only one of Bill's lovers to have left us with a testament (which was even filmed, in 1976, with Rod Steiger). But her book, *W. C. Fields and Me*, leaves us with a whole raft of problems.

I just missed meeting Carlotta Monti, who died in 1994, at the age of eighty-eight, apparently lucid and active till the end. Her book was published in 1971, co-authored with a professional writer, Cy Rice. As an entertainment, it is a pleasant and often funny read, but as a historical record, it is full of obvious errors. Carlotta met Fields in 1933, not 1932, and her subsequent description of being driven up to meet him at Encino is suspect, as he was not yet living there at that time. Her claim to have been his closest confidante, companion and lover during the entire period from 1933 until his death is countered by other testimony. Another actress friend, Mary Brian (Bill's screen daughter in *Running Wild* and *Man on the Flying Trapeze*) told historian Anthony Slide that she had never seen Fields in public with Monti. Carlotta, in her book, never once mentions Bill's secretary, Magda Michael (aka 'Mickey Mouse', of whom, more anon), who was living in Field's houses for some years. There are many other omissions and distortions.

The fact is, Bill developed, during these years, a rigorous ability to compartmentalize the various aspects of his life. Just as he had kept his love affairs and long-term relationships with women discreet to the point of invisibility for so many years (remember 'Mrs W. C. Fields' in Adelaide?), he kept his private and business life separate. People who knew Bill in his film work knew very little of his life off set. General acquaintances who might turn up for parties or sit at the table at Chasen's while the Great Man gave forth, knew almost nothing of his inner circle. Even his closest drinking partners, as Will Fowler has told me, were not intimately aware of his day to day struggles on the film sets. And almost no one was aware of the long correspondence with Hattie, the matter of his estranged son, Claude, or anything directly about the Dukenfield clan. The public, aware only of the flim-flam of press puffs, knew only the W. C. Fields of myth.

And thus the secrets were kept, even from his biographers, for so many years and decades.

These compartments were yet another symptom of the highly organised nature of the man. Throughout this period, the scrapbooks continued to be rigorously kept, though now Bill had an official clippings agency collecting every jot of promotion and reviews. The scrapbooks of this period are massive broadsheet affairs. In addition, Bill kept all his financial records, which were later organised by his live-in secretary, Magda Michael. Bill was an enthusiast for the early technology of personal sound recording, and Miss Michael had been hired as a temporary assistant to transcribe his dictaphone notes. Eventually she was to become his Woman Friday, his typist, business confidante and also, on occasion, a collaborator – the 'Motel' idea appeared to have been a joint project.

'Mickey Mouse' moved with Fields, in 1934, to the ranch in Encino, with its seven and a half acres of land. Fields wrote an uncharacteristic piece about his new home for the *Hollywood Reporter*'s fourth anniversary issue, in December 1934, entitled 'Now I'm a Gentleman Farmer', enthusing about his 'gorgeous trees of all kinds', his tennis court and goldfish pond. This is a compartment of Fields we have not known so far! Thrilling to the stalks of corn and wheat pushing through the ground into the light. Talking tongue in cheek about his farming experiments:

> For one thing I am watering my orange trees with gin instead of water. Then all I have to do is squeeze the juice into a glass.
>
> I am crossing the asparagus with raisins. The iron in the raisins will cause the asparagus to assume an erect position and it will be a joy, rather than a feat fit for a contortionist, to eat.
>
> When I am through with these little things, I plan to develop a water-melon with the seeds in the center like a cantaloupe and also an ear of corn with handles.
>
> Being busy in a picture, I haven't time to devote to these scientific achievements, however, but just give Fields a chance. What he starts, he finishes.

Or darn well knocks himself out trying. Fields' house at Encino became a preferred watering hole for the growing colony of east-coast expatriates. Carlotta Monti seemed to weave in and out of favour. In May 1934 Bill's name was linked romantically with a young actress, Judith Allen, who played his daughter in *The Old Fashioned Way*. And still photographs of the period show him turning up at Hollywood premières with other, less prominent starlets. Whatever Carlotta thought of these dalliances, she never mentioned them in her book. Her fondest hope was for Bill to help in her career. In fact he cast her twice in his movies, once in *Man On the Flying Trapeze*, in 1935, as his secretary, and again in 1941, as Franklin Pangborn's receptionist, in *Never Give a Sucker an Even Break*. Her other ambition, to become a singer, was less to his liking, and her attempts to warble led to a distinct cooling at times. He called her 'Chinaman', after her penchant for Chinese gowns, or possibly because he first met her in Chinese costume for the stills session of *International House*. She called him Woody, for reasons which are obscure, in her own words:

> It – it just fits because you're cute. Like – like a bear. I know that sounds silly.

'A bear can be very ferocious,' he said. 'Such as a grizzly, for example . . .'

Their relationship could get quite tempestuous. A typical event occurred in 1937, as reported by the *New York World Telegram*, on 24 September:

Police Called as Two are Hit in Row at W. C. Fields' Home. Cops Are Puzzled, However, as to Who was Struck in Wrangle.

Hollywood Sept 24 – Someone got hit early today at the home of W. C. Fields, the comedian, but police, who were called twice by Mr Fields, said they weren't sure who it was or what it was all about.

Mr Fields said someone popped him with a cane. Miss Carlotta Monti, his pretty secretary, said she too, got hit. The butler, name undisclosed, told police he didn't own a cane.

The police got in on the play when Fields telephoned. He said his secretary and butler were arguing and that he wanted it settled. Patrolmen Earl Case and E. C. Stebbins found only the butler when they arrived. Fields and Miss Monti were in their rooms. The butler said some mistake must have been made and the police departed.

They were back in a few minutes, and this time they found the trio in a hallway. Fields was arguing with his employees.

'It is all right to argue in the daytime, but I want peace and quiet at night,' Fields yelled, 'She came here, awakened the butler and . . . started the row.'

Miss Monti said that was not so. 'Mr Fields let me in and started the argument,' she said, 'the butler merely tried to soothe him. And besides, I got hit.'

Fields said he got hit, too. The butler kept silent.

As well he might. Being hired help to W. C. Fields must have been like being an air-conditioning salesman in Hades. In the earlier years, this was not yet apparent. As far as Carlotta Monti was concerned, she gave as good as she got. But she must have known, in her heart, that the compartment she had been designated was marked Sex, and that was all.

The department of friendship, on the other hand, was a wide one, although the inner circle was exclusively male. It was in this period – 1933 to 1934 – that Will Fowler, teenage son of Gene, came to know the man he was to call 'Uncle Claude'. In lieu of off-stage and off-set stooges, Will became his caddy for a while, at the Lakeside Golf Club. Will wrote:

Demoniacally intense in his professional moods, Fields was contrastingly amiable in his hours of leisure – especially on the golf course, where he dressed nattily in delicately tinted silk shirt and tightly knotted flower-designed necktie after the fashion of Walter Hagen. While 'The Haig' ambled about the links with hair Vaselined flat, Fields promenaded, wearing a white cap to protect his Klaxon-horn nose from the sun's rays. When he addressed his ball on the first tee, Fields appeared as immaculate as a Beverly Hills surgeon about to make an expensive opening.

Bill's regular golfing partner was Gregory La Cava, his old mate and director from the silent days. Intensely they accused each other of cheating, and Fields, as ever, loved to distract his rival's game by absurd and playful manoeuvres. 'The Golf Specialist' of 1930 was turning into a documentary. But their friendship remained an abiding one. To Will Fowler, Bill was a force larger than life, a man as funny off-screen as on, an eternal ham, as he chased away the Toluca Lake swan climbing on to his property with the cry: 'Either shit green or get off the lawn!' In later years, when he reached the age of sixteen, Will would often be the driver conveying his carousing father and friends from house to house in their enchanted circle; they thought he was sober enough for the job. He was – sometimes. Today, he still remembers the physical grace of Bill Fields, even in later years, when his health was failing – the delicate smallness of his hands, the way his fingers crooked, pinkie stuck out, the hand permanently poised in the way it holds a Martini glass.

Another two recruits to the inner circle were actor John Barrymore and painter-designer John Decker. Barrymore had known Bill from Broadway days, legend has it from 1909, when, some say, they were rivals for the charms of vaudeville singer-star Nora Bayes. The story goes that, hearing that Bill Fields was his rival, Barrymore went to see him juggle, and said: 'I'm not in love with Miss Bayes now! Hell, I'm in love with W. C. Fields!' This is probably apocryphal. But Jack (as John Barrymore was called by his friends) and Bill were surely drinking partners at the Lambs Club. Jack was, by all accounts, an even more prodigious drinker than Bill, having dived into the sauce as early as his fourteenth birthday. Unlike Bill, who was never seen to be classically drunk, and was said to get funnier the more he drank, Jack Barrymore often became violent and threatening, particularly towards his wives. Mercurial in temperament, easily bored, restless, he was even nicknamed, by his best friends, 'The Monster', due to his

Jekyll and Hyde personality when in his cups.

During 1932 and 1933, Jack appeared in starring roles in ten movies, for MGM, RKO and Universal Pictures. In all he appeared in fifty-seven films, most of them either mediocre or downright trashy, his electrifying presence always lifting up a dire script. All the money he made he sunk into his real-life Xanadu in Beverly Hills – 'Bella Vista' – an unfinished folly of 55 rooms, greenhouses, zoos, old Spanish mission and cantina doors and a great stone fireplace from a Scottish castle, adorned with the made-up Barrymore crest – a crowned serpent. Here he ensconced himself with his third wife, Dolores Costello, a young actress who had begun her career, as an 'English Tea Girl', in the chorus of the same 'George White's *Scandals*' of 1922 in which Bill Fields had starred. Another great expense was a 106 ft yacht, the *Mariner*, which he bought in 1926 for $100,000, to cruise about the Caribbean. Barrymore sank more than one million dollars into his palace, and was destined for bankruptcy and disaster. In 1933, he was already manifesting the signs of the illness which would cause him to black out on sets, and affect his memory, raising in his mind the terror of suffering the same fate as his father, the great Maurice Barrymore, who died of syphilis, raving in the asylum. As it was, Barrymore did not have syphilis, but the deterioration of his liver, caused by alcoholism, was to hasten his decline.

Gene Fowler, too, had problems with illness, a cardiac condition which would lead to heart attacks. Bill Fields was beginning to suffer, as well as from his grippes and chest problems, from aggravation of the back injury he had sustained falling under the truck in *Two Flaming Youths*.

All these rebellious late-middle-aged men banded together to raise their spirits high. In time, they found a central node around which to revolve in their binges, an eccentric artist of somewhat mysterious origins, John Decker, whose house on Bundy Drive became a kind of rugged Algonquin, where a select group of temperamental boozers acted out their terminal passion play, venting their defiance of the Hollywood system until the bitter end.

But we are still in the good years. *Tillie and Gus* was the first fully-fledged star vehicle for Bill, although he was twinned again with Alison Skipworth, in an attempt to repeat the episodic success of *If I Had a Million*. As Augustus Q. and Tillie Winterbottom, they play fake missionaries summoned to share in the will of their dead brother. Their brother's son and daughter, Mary and Tom, are in debt to the crooked family lawyer, Phineas Pratt, who has stolen their inheritance. Their only chance to get it back is to compete with him in the riverboat business, by entering a battered old boat, the *Fairy Queen*, in a race to win a lucrative franchise. Tillie and Gus, in effect Mr and Mrs Eustace McGargle, leave their respective gambling and card-sharping careers to help the young people out in their noble cause.

The movie enabled Fields to reprise his poker game act out of *Poppy* – 'You must forgive the ignorance of a novice,' says Gus, as he allows himself to be enticed into the game, producing the requisite four aces, and walking off with Tillie, singing ecclesiastically: 'Bringing in the sheaves . . .'

This was also the movie which introduced Fields to another deadly rival – Baby Le Roy, who was to star with him in two other films. Despite the baby's best endeavours to lose the riverboat race, Fields is forced to rescue him in the end. We have seen Bill adopting the trick of bullying a child since *Pool Sharks*, and notably in *The Golf Specialist*, when he wrestles the little girl for her piggy-bank. Later, referring to

26 With Baby Le Roy in a typically intimate moment.

the scene in *The Old Fashioned Way* (1934) in which he kicks the Babe in the butt, he said he was playing on that secret longing every father had to kick his kid – speaking very obviously about himself and his own frustrations with Claude Junior. The challenge was all the greater for the kid being a three-year-old, rather than a thuggish ten, and so cutely bouncy and gurgling.

Le Roy Overacker, the Baby in question, was to have a short career in the movies. As soon as he stopped being cute and gurgly, he was out, and in later life, I am told, he became a lifeguard in Los Angeles. In all interviews he gave, in his adulthood, about those years, he admitted he simply had no clear memories of his brief fling at stardom. Of Fields he said only that he could not recall the actor ever being mean to him. The legends of Bill spiking his orange juice with gin, on the set of *It's a Gift*, may well be true, but Fields may have been simply initiating him thus into his inner circle. Certainly he was keen to have the Baby on board, as his most effective and challenging straight man. Production stills from *Tillie and Gus* show Fields holding the legendary brat on his shoulders with cheerful sang-froid.

Fields was not keen to pursue a long-term partnership with Alison Skipworth, but the studio teamed them again, in his next film but one, *Six of a Kind*. The film, another showcase for Paramount's comedy stars, Charlie Ruggles, George Burns and Gracie Allen again, among others, was directed by Leo McCarey, who had cut his teeth with Laurel and Hardy and was to spar with the Marx Brothers, in the following year, in their comic masterpiece, *Duck Soup*. McCarey was a Fields fan and friend, and allowed him to present, for the first time on screen, his age-old billiard-table routine. Working with his new stooge, Tammany Young, Fields – playing the Sheriff of Nuggetville, Nevada – fiddles with the cue, hesitates, moves the ball, knocks the cue ball off the cushion onto his head, fiddles some more, then sticks the cue into the table and exits without having potted a single ball, having delivered a running patter in answer to the planted question: 'Tell me, Sheriff, how did you ever get the name of Honest John?'

SHERIFF: At the time of which I speak, I'm tendin' bar up at Medicine Hat. Well, a guy used to come in there with a glass eye. I used to wait on him. Wasn't a bad guy. (*Pause as billiard routine*) He used to take this glass eye out and put it in a tumbler of water. Wait'll I break these balls. (*Crash*) He comes in one day and he forgets the glass eye. (*Ball hits table and bounces back to Sheriff*) Don't stand so near the table, will you? (*More fiddling with cue*)

27 *Six of a Kind*: Fields with Tammany Young: 'But tell me, why do they call you Honest John?'

DOC: But tell me, how did they come to call you Honest John?

SHERIFF: As I was saying, one day he forgot his glass eye. I found it. The next morning when he came in, I said, 'Young man, here's your glass eye,' and I gave it back to him. Ever since that time – (*Crash – routine ends, they exit*) Ever since that day, I've been known as Honest John.

The script, by Walter De Leon and Harry Ruskin, also gave Bill some of his best lines with Alison Skipworth as 'The Duchesse', proprietess of the local hotel, who chides him for his drinking: 'According to you, everything I like to do is either illegal, immoral or fattening.' (A good counter-blast at one remove to Hattie . . .) Other lines also resonate: 'I feel as though the Russian army had been walking over my tongue in their stockinged feet,' or 'I'm about as busy as a pickpocket at a nudist colony.' Hard to tell whether these were the script's, or his own. But certainly the pool-room monologue is not in the original script version on file at the Academy Library in Los Angeles.

Between these two films, Bill played Humpty-Dumpty in Paramount's prestige production of *Alice in Wonderland*, directed by Norman McLeod. Richard Arlen, Gary Cooper, Leon Errol, Louise Fazenda, Cary Grant, Edward Everett Horton, Charlie Ruggles, Alison Skipworth, Ned Sparks and Ford Sterling were all featured, among other stars. As a highly made-up face sitting on a wall, he has not much to do, and the press agents were hard put to find some publicity story to fit him, finally coming up with the following nonsense:

'CRAZY!'

W. C. Fields, Paramount's funny screen comedian, dashed out of his Toluca Lake home one morning at a tremendous speed.

'Help! help!' ejaculated Mr Fields, loudly, 'there's a crazy man in there!'

'Crazy?' query the neighbours.

'He's trying to measure me for an egg!' roared Mr. Fields indignantly.

Poor old Teet Carle. *You're Telling Me*, Bill's next film, was, of course, an easier vehicle to present, being the sound remake of *So's Your Old Man*. The dialogue for this was written by J. P. McEvoy, who had been brought in to write a sequel to *Six of a Kind*, using the same characters, a project which never got off the ground. McEvoy worked on *You're Telling Me* with scriptwriters Walter de Leon and Paul Jones, whose repeated presence belies some of the familiar myths regarding Fields' hatred of writers: De Leon also co-wrote *Tillie and Gus* and *Six of a Kind*, and Paul Jones was an old friend of silent days. In fact, Fields was building up another secret compartment of his multi-layered life: a coterie of gag writers, who were to serve him faithfully in the coming spate of Grade A golden eggs.

Chapter 34
Three Epitomes of a Motion Picture

28 Poster for *The Old-Fashioned Way*.

Three films can be said to show the full development of the fictional W. C. Fields in the mid-1930s, the golden age of Hollywood sound comedy: *The Old Fashioned Way, It's A Gift*, and *Man on the Flying Trapeze*. Bisbee had found his voice, and now Eustace McGargle, alias The Great McGonigle, would strut the stage, followed by more Bisbee alter egos – Harold Bissonette and Ambrose Wolfinger.

The Old Fashioned Way is Fields' greatest tribute to the lost theatrical world of his youth. As the Great McGonigle, he heads a seedy repertory company, which tours the small towns of middle-America performing a temperance play, *The Drunkard*, and skipping each town one step ahead of the local sheriff with his writs for unpaid boarding house bills. Evolving out of *Poppy, Sally of the Sawdust* and *Two Flaming Youths*, *The Old Fashioned Way*'s portrayal of the wandering life, the fear of poverty and abandonment, the grotesque inns on the road, the melodramatic acting and burlesque skits, all are vintage Heritage Fields. It is the only movie in which he performs his juggling act, almost complete, on the screen, including the cigar-box trick of the early 1900s. Tammany Young is the stooge and assistant in place of Harriet or Walter Fields, and the liveried footmen are in the background. It is an authentic window into the past, to the Silent Humorist, older and stouter, but just as ebullient as he appeared before the vaudeville audiences of Ponca City, Keith's Fifth Avenue Theatre, the London Hippodrome, the *Folies Bergère*, the Berlin Wintergarten, the Théâtre Variété Prague, or the Circo Parish Madrid.

Released in the summer of 1934, *The Old Fashioned Way* was produced by William Le Baron, and directed by William Beaudine, a prolific workhorse whose credits range from *The Cohens and the Kellys in Paris, The Crime of the Century, Kidnapped* to *Lassie's Greatest Adventure* and, alas, *Billy the Kid versus Dracula* (1966). The screenplay is credited to Garnett Weston and Jack Cunningham, based on 'a story by Charles Bogle'. But the history of its writing provides a fascinating example of the tortuous road a Fields' script (or many Hollywood scripts, for that matter) travelled towards a rendezvous with the public.

In the beginning there were two different 'original' stories: the first was 'Grease Paint', the tale of a clown with a broken heart, penned by H. M. 'Beanie' Walker, writer of many of Laurel and Hardy's Talkie routines. The second was a treatment by Fields (aka Charles Bogle) entitled *Playing the Sticks*, which was a Talkie rewrite of *Two Flaming*

Youths with elements of the long yearned for *The Great McGillicuddy*.

Ronald Fields has published the long version of *Playing the Sticks* in his 1973 book of W. C.'s essays, sketches and letters, *W. C. Fields by Himself*. Described on its title page as 'an epitome of a motion picture story', the tale is set in 'about 1898'. A previous, shorter draft still clung to McGillicuddy as the character, but later he became 'Mark Antony McGonigle'. The cast of characters includes one Percilla, his daughter; her boyfriend, Jack Pepperday, son of Confederate Colonel Tyler Pepperday (replacing the Chester Conklin figure in *Two Flaming Youths*); Cleopatra Pepperday, his wealthy spinster sister (aka Madge Malarkey in the silent film); and one Baby Ivar, a child actress in the treatment, who will mutate on screen into Baby Le Roy.

The treatment opens in the boarding house of Mrs Wendleschaffer, the 'hard-boiled, angular landlady' who oversees her profligate actor guests with steely eye, and exchanges a familiar banter with McGonigle:

MCGONIGLE: On our last appearance here the house was so crowded they couldn't applaud horizontally, they had to applaud vertically (*fits the action to the words*).

MRS WENDLESCHAFFER: I suppose you never had them so packed in they couldn't laugh, ha ha they had to laugh, he he.

MCGONIGLE: That happened on several occasions in Ponca City, Oklahoma.

Playing the Sticks is a convoluted treatment, spread over more than twenty pages, containing dialogue only in the first two. The other 'original' script, *Grease Paint*, started out with one Lionel Livingston as the head of the Livingston Opera Company, which becomes, in the second full-script version, The Great McGonigle Repertory Company. This second script is close in feeling and intent, though not yet in detail, to the final product on screen.

The conflicts between Bill Fields and the studio screenwriters are legendary. One myth is that he could never remember lines. But we have heard from Eddie Cantor of Fields' prodigious memory for details, which is borne out by all the meticulous bits and pieces of show-business lore that crop up all over his work. Bill refused to remember lines that he had not written, unless their writer was his beloved Dickens, or Lewis Carroll. The studio routine however, even under Bill Le Baron, was to appoint teams of writers to productions, even in the teeth of what they already knew full well about Fields.

Carlotta Monti quoted Fields as saying that he could devour a writing team in seven minutes flat, but that 'they were hard to digest because all those semi-colons and exclamation marks pricked the lining of his stomach'. A reading of his own *Playing the Sticks* treatment, however, shows that in 1934 he had not yet mastered the knack of feature-length structure. A writer such as Jack Cunningham (who was also credited with *It's a Gift*), would be able to contribute that technical experience. In the silent era he had written 1923's *The Covered Wagon*, and *Don Q Son of Zorro* for Douglas Fairbanks. In 1938 he would write Harold Lloyd's *Professor Beware*. Screenwriters like this, in Hollywood, were script doctors. Often they came in to save movies that were heading for the knacker's yard. Gene Fowler was to become rich and much sought after in the business for just such a talent, earning big bucks for such forgotten barnyard creatures as *The Roadhouse Murder, Union Depot, The Way to Love, The Mighty Barnum, Shoot the Works, Call of the Wild, Career Woman, Half Angel* and *Ali Baba Goes to Town*. (His most lasting title is probably *What Price Hollywood*, the precursor of the later versions of *A Star is Born*.)

Bill needed these craftsmen, but railed constantly against them. His rejection of them is certainly part of his myth. But if we look at the full credits of *It's a Gift*, for example, we find eight writers listed as 'contributors to treatment' and 'contributors to special sequences' – among them names that are familiar from the credits of other Fields pictures: Garnett Weston, who co-wrote *The Old Fashioned Way*; Claude Binyon, who worked on *The Old Fashioned Way* and *Mississippi*; Harry Ruskin had co-written *Six of a Kind* and Field's last stage play, *Ballyhoo*; John Sinclair was the stuntman who had pulled Bill from under the truck during the shooting of *Two Flaming Youths*, and was at his side in many of his movies; Paul Gerard Smith had co-written dialogue with Fields in Earl Carroll's *Vanities*. Eddie Welch, Lou Breslow and Howard J. Green were other writers under contract to Paramount.

In short, like everyone else in the business, W. C. Fields used gag writers, who often received no credit on screen. Four uncredited writers – J. P. McEvoy, Garnett Weston, Paul Jones and Claude Binyon – worked for Paramount on *The Old Fashioned Way*. As time went on, and Bill became more sure of his own touch, and less tolerant of corporate interference, he would be known to take the day's script pages and crumple them in a ball to throw away. But in practically every case, a close look at the different script versions of Fields' Paramount movies shows the changes he made on the set.

In the final written version of *The Old Fashioned Way*, for example, on the train taking the McGonigle company out of the clutches of the writ-serving Sheriff and towards another engagement, McGonigle tries to calm his quarrelsome troupe:

> MCGONIGLE: Come, let us have done with petty bickering. I have a telegram here from the manager of the Bellefontaine Opera House. He says: 'House sold out for the performance. Whole town crazy to see you. Special reception arranged. Signed, the manager.'

In the actual film, the lines are:

> MCGONIGLE: I have a telegram here that will warm the cockles of your heart. I received it last night in Pocatello. 'The Great McGonigle, America's leading Tragedian.' Its headed that way . . . 'Train number forty-two . . . upper berth . . . uh, private car number three. Dear sir, in reply to your telegram, the advance sale indicates the wor – the best business this theatre has ever known . . . signed, Sneed Hern. The Manager.'

This is clearly no ad-lib, but lines written by Fields for this scene, bypassing the official script. This would be his procedure in practically every movie. Changes were constant, as we have seen from the many drafts of his vaudeville scripts. There was never a final script for Fields until he spoke the lines that he chose to deliver, on the set.

The scene on the train is prefaced by a classic piece of Fieldsian comic business, at the station, as the film opens: McGonigle, hurrying to catch the train, sets fire to the Sheriff's writ from behind and then lights his cigar from the startled official's burning paper before immediately climbing aboard. 'Thanks for the light!' he calls, as the stupefied Sheriff remains with the burnt ash in his hand. There follows a rigmarole with a dropped sleeping-car ticket which McGonigle picks up, usurping the real owner's sleeping berth and even admonishing him as he argues with the attendant about his lost ticket: 'Quiet please, quiet! What is this, a cattle car? Drat!'

The scenes in the sleeping car are yet another twist on 'The Pullman Sleeper' sketch of 1921 – 'Quiet please! Quiet please, lets have a little order on this train!' Echoes, too, of 'The Caledonian Express' (1922) –

Secretary: 'Do you mean to say you will not get out of this compartment?' Breeze (Fields): 'Go away or I'll kill you . . .' It is also a variant on a bathroom shaving sequence from the silent *So's Your Old Man*.

A cherished bit of business has Fields getting down in the morning from the upper berth into the nightshirt of a sleeping giant foreigner below: 'What are you, Chinese peoples?' – 'Vot's de idea, valking around in my nightshirt?' 'What's the idea having a nightshirt big enough for people to walk around in?' This culminates in Fields borrowing a little boy's polo mallet to wreak an unseen revenge, handing the weapon deftly to the boy's irate father, who is left to be strangled while Fields exits the car. This scene would be reprised in 1941, in *Never Give a Sucker an Even Break*. As Humpty-Dumpty said in *Alice Through the Looking Glass*: 'When I make a word do a lot of work like that . . . I always pay it extra.'

As always when Fields is in control, the comic business, the gags, always illuminate character, and all comedy stems from the character, not from some mechanical plan. The plot is simply a clothesline on which to hang the comic elements. The Great Man is the source of all that flows . . .

Speaking of words with many uses, this may be the place to mention Fields little pocket 'dictionary', which he apparently carried with him always, and in which he set down words he had made up and their meanings. This priceless artefact turned up for auction at Christie's in 1989, in a batch named the 'Magda Michael Collection', a sale which was stopped by legal action of the Fields family. The items in that collection were scattered and the dictionary has disappeared from sight, leaving some tantalising quoted samples, such as '*Philanthroac:* One whose mission in life is to take care of drunks who don't want to be taken care of'; '*Bibliodemon:* One who looks through your volumes of classics for uncut pages' and '*Squeemudgeon:* Director who calls an actor down to the studio at 8 a.m. and doesn't use him till 11.'

The Old Fashioned Way is full of incidental delights, not least the meticulous reproduction of its play-within-the-play, the McGonigle Repertory Company's *pièce de resistance* – 'The Drunkard'. The lay audience probably assumes, especially today, that this absurd puritanical morality piece was made up by Fields or his screenwriters. But 'The Drunkard; or, The Fallen Saved' was, in fact, a real play, first performed in 1844 at the Boston Dime 'Museum'. The original writer of this harangue is unknown, but it was none other than the Prince of

Humbugs, Phineas T. Barnum himself, who used it to draw the public to his own American Museum in 1853, so they could see the play and then immediately sign The Pledge. Barnum wrote:

> In the first act we see the Moderate Drinker. In the second act, we have his progress, step by step, to ruin, his increased appetite for strong drink; the distress of his relations; the embarassment of himself and his family. In the third act, we have his drunken orgies on Broadway, his bar-room debauchery, the degradation of himself and vileness of his associates . . . In the fourth act, we have Despair and Attempted Suicide, and in the fifth act, his restitution to sobriety amd society by the aid of a Temperance Philanthropist.

In 1844, when 'The Drunkard' was first performed, it was the first American play in history to run for over 100 consecutive performances. By the twists of fate, it returned, unchanged, but now as unintentional satire, to the stage, in the wake of the repeal of Prohibition in 1933. Student and theatre groups everywhere took it on the road, and it was tailor-made for Bill's loving lampoon of the way things used to be. The entire scene, the dressing of the stage, the set, the ambience, the stylised acting, echoes the world that Pa Jones, in the unproduced segment of *The Comic Supplement*, walked into in his glowing dream – with himself as Squire Cribbs, entering with the inevitable line: 'It ain't a fit night out for man nor beast!'

> CRIBBS: Ah, my proud beauty! You are in my power! Tis late. You are unfriended!
>
> *Screams. William enters.*
>
> WILLIAM: Well, squire, what's the lowest you'll take for your rotten carcass now?
>
> CRIBBS: Curse you! I shall be revenged for this, if there is law or justice!
>
> WILLIAM: Aw, get out!
>
> WILLIAM *shoves* CRIBBS *off scene, crashing, banging off.*

No wonder Fields has to kick Baby Le Roy in the behind, to balance up this stuff! Behind the scenes, we can eavesdrop on his constant sparring with the rich old spinster Cleopatra Pepperday, whose rival suitor, the Sheriff of Bellfontaine, is a remnant of Chester Conklin's Sheriff in *Two Flaming Youths*. Having promised her a part in his play, and stoutly resisting the idea that she should perform her terrifying rendition of 'Gathering Up the Shells Upon the Sea Shore' in public, The Great McGonigle keeps her waiting offstage, rehearsing her only line: 'HERE COMES THE PRINCE!' which is, in fact, not in the play at all.

This is another instance of Fields re-using even the most obscure leftovers from older material. 'Here Comes the Prince' is the title of an unproduced sketch, author and date unknown, intended for use by Fanny Brice, with Fields as the Backer of a musical show. The sketch is set in a dressing-room, and everyone is suggesting to the lead girl, Flora (written for Brice) how to enunciate her only line – you guessed it – 'Here comes the Prince!'

At the end of the movie, we have another sample of the script changes from written to performed version, when McGonigle, caught sneaking out of the boarding house with Tammany Young and his trunk, avoiding payment, rapidly thinks up the scam of pretending to be bringing the baggage of another man in.

Script version:

MRS WENDLESCHAFFER: What's this? What's going on here?

MCGONIGLE: It's all right, Mrs Wendleschaffer. We're just bringing in the trunk of a friend of mine. He's going to stay with me as my guest for several days.

MRS WENDLESCHAFFER: I don't want any more of your kind in my house – take it out, do you hear – take it out! . . .

MCGONIGLE: Very well, I'll do just as you tell me.

And in the film:

MRS WENDLESCHAFFER: What's going on here?

MCGONIGLE: Oh! Ah, my dear Mrs W, I regret having awakened you at this unearthly hour, but a friend of mine, Charlie Bonheur, the top-mounter of the Grinzeratti family . . . is coming to spend a few days with me. We're bringing his trunk in. (*To* GUMP) Come, come!

MRS WENDLESCHAFFER: No, you don't!

MCGONIGLE: Huh?

MRS WENDLESCHAFFER: I've had enough of your kind. Take that trunk right out of here.

MCGONIGLE: Oh, Mrs Wendelschaffer! . . . However, you are mistress of this establishment (*gestures* GUMP *to move trunk back down stairs*) Poor, dear Charlie! How my heart bleeds for him! Hurry, hurry, hurry! Go on! I wonder where he'll sleep tonight. (*To* MRS WENDLESCHAFFER) You'll regret this in the morning . . .

MCGONIGLE *and* GUMP *exit.*

His subterfuge successful, McGonigle exits the boarding house, leaving his daughter, Betty (played by his probable lover, Judith Allen), to carry on the show now that her suitor Wally's rich father has been won round to their marriage. We can now fade in to McGonigle/McGargle, on his own, ensconsed at a busy fairground, reprising the old quack medicine shows of William Claude Dukenfield's youth (and a similar scene from the stage *Poppy*) above the sign

YACH'WEE INDIAN MEDICAL DISCOVERY. PINE TAR REMEDIES.
MCGONIGLE: Ladies and gentlemen. It has been my great privilege . . . many years ago, whilst traveling through the mountains of Paraguay, to find the Yach'wee Indians drinking the juice of the cactii . . . the only real cure for hoarseness known to medical science. I have here tonight a few bottles which I am selling for one dollar. It cures hoarseness. It'll cure the most stubborn cases of hoarseness. I have been a martyr to hoarseness for many years. This malignant disease, whenever speaking in public as I do, and I (*coughs*) – It cures hoarseness. It'll cure the most stubborn cases of hoarseness (*whispers*) One little sip of the bottle – (*croaks then roars*) IT CURES HOARSENESS!! (*Confused voices*) Who'll be the first to buy a bottle? *Fade out. The End.*

Having attended to the memories of his distant youth, Fields returned to the recycling of his vaudeville sketches in his next classic, *It's a Gift*. A broadened remake of the silent *It's the Old Army Game*, this consisted, once again, of a reprise of several of *The Comic Supplement*'s most enduring skits: 'The Back Porch', 'The Drug Store', 'The Picnic Sketch' and a version of the multi-faceted motoring sketch. Another sketch from the *Follies* of 1925 – 'The Nagger' or the bedroom sketch, was fitted in as well. Other recycled routines included the bathroom sequence from the vanished silent *The Potters*, in which family-pecked small-town New Jersey grocer Harold Bissonette struggles with his daughter's hair-brushing, a cut-throat razor and a recalcitrant mirror in the lethal battlefield of his own *salle-de-bain*.

The classic nagging family here consists of a small boy, played by Tommy Bupp, a grown-up problem daughter, played by Jean Rouverol, and his most Hattie-like wife, Kathleen Howard, who first played his won't-help-mate in the Bisbee Talkie, *You're Telling Me.* Here she is, deploying to devastating effect the vocal cords and commanding presence of her previous career as an Opera singer and Fashion Editor of *Harper's Bazaar, circa* 1928.

> MRS BISSONETTE: Don't smoke at the table! Don't throw matches around! ... Harold, I want one thing settled. If you get the money from Uncle Bean you are not going to buy an orange ranch with it!
>
> HAROLD BISSONETTE: Oh, no, no, no ...
>
> MRS BISSONETTE: Don't try that innocent look with me! We need THINGS in the house, I haven't a STITCH to my back, the children need clothes, and we should have a car.
>
> HAROLD: Oh yes a car by all means ...
>
> MRS BISSONETTE: I don't know where you get the idea you can make money raising oranges when you can't even run a corner grocery store ...

Harold's grocery store is his cross, as he is dreaming of using the money from Uncle Bean's will to go into the orange grove business in California. This is Pa Jones who has already set his sights on the American commandment: go west, young man! Elmer Prettywillie is no longer happy with his lot. 'The Drug Store' sketch has been expanded and completely recast to encompass Tammany Young as his useless assistant; Baby Le Roy as Baby Dunk the Great Molasses Vandal; Mr Muckle the blind man who destroys all in his path but is himself invulnerable to passing cars or fire-trucks; and the fuming good citizen Jasper Fitschmueller, with his insistent demand for 'Ten pounds of cumquats!'

The immortal 'cumquats' are another example of Fields' constant quest for the right comedy pitch. In the first version of the script – originally titled 'The Back Porch' – the line is 'Give me ten pounds of granulated sugar!' In the second version, Jasper says: 'I'm in a hurry here! A dozen eggs – you're sure they're fresh?' Then, consulting his list, he asks for sugar, and then – 'five pounds of cumquats.' But Fields' unerring Humpty-Dumpty eye for the proper double-barrelled word brought him to reduce it all to 'CUMQUATS! C-U-M-Q-U-A-T-S!

QUATS! QUATS!' And Harold's refrain: 'Uh, coming, coming, coming, coming . . .' as he tries to stop Mr Muckle's swinging cane from wrecking his shop and smashing every light bulb in sight.

'The Back Porch' sketch itself is recast as well. This time Fields hunkered down to develop the scene to its utmost, grinding the plot to a halt and going for a full eleven minutes of the ultimate battle between W. C. Fields and the universe. Bill often encouraged his press hacks to put out stories like:

W. C. FIELDS VIEWS SLEEP AS PRIME ACHIEVEMENT

W. C. Fields is a great respecter of sleep . . . A victim of insomnia, Fields tosses and turns, twists and twirls, while the clock ticks off the hours. Like a true showman, Fields has turned his adversity into fortune. He gets some of his biggest laughs from sleep scenes in his pictures . . .

'I am,' says Fields, 'full of admiration for those people who can slumber peacefully at any and all times. I consider them favored above ordinary mortals. They are a race set apart, and my envy for them occupies most of my waking hours, which are considerable . . . The worst nightmare I ever experienced is that I am being awakened from the best sleep I have had in years . . . There is nothing more descriptive of man's inhumanity to man than the awaking of a slumberer from his dreams . . .'

This was no flim-flam. Some time before, Bill had bought, in addition to his fleet of cars, a specially outfitted trailer, in which he would travel from his home to the studio or location. Rising from his unsteady slumber, he would go into his trailer in his pyjamas and emerge, reasonably refreshed, in more ways than one, for the day's opening scene. This furnished him with a combined travelling car, dressing-room and retreat for stocking up or for confabs with his directors, or other actors. It became a famous sight around Hollywood, and more and more vital to Fields as his various ailments combined, in 1935 and 1936, to sap his previous agility and vigour.

In *It's a Gift*, Harold Bissonette's attempts to escape his hen-pecking wife and sleep on the porch as morning dawns is doomed by familiar interruptions: the milkman's bottles, the yakking neighbours, the vegetable vendor (the iceman and the scissors grinder were cut out of the Talkie version), Baby Dunk squeezing grapes and then a screwdriver through a hole in the floor above onto his face, and of course, the Insurance Salesman, prompting the immortal exchange:

SALESMAN: Is this 1726 Prill Avenue?

HAROLD: No.

SALESMAN: Is there a Prill Avenue in this neighborhood?

HAROLD: I don't know.

SALESMAN: Do you know a Mister Carl La Fong? Capital L, small a, capital F, small o, small n, small g. Carl La Fong!

HAROLD: No, I don't know a Mister Carl La Fong, capital L, small a, capital F, small o, small n, small g. And if I did know Carl La Fong, I wouldn't admit it.

SALESMAN: Well he's a railroad man and he leaves home very early in the morning.

HAROLD: Well, he's a chump.

SALESMAN: I hear he's interested in an annuity policy.

HAROLD: Ah, isn't that wonderful.

SALESMAN: Yes, it is . . . (*Bounds up the stairs, undeterred by the obstructive drawl.*) The public are buying them like hot cakes. All companies are going to discontinue this policy after the 23rd of this month . . .

HAROLD: That's rather unfortunate . . . (*He has withdrawn beneath his blanket but the* SALESMAN *stands over him, oozing enthusiasm.*)

SALESMAN: Yes, it will be. Say, maybe you would be interested in such a policy!

HAROLD: No I would not.

SALESMAN: Say, what's your age?

HAROLD: None of your business.

SALESMAN: I'd say you were a man of about fifty.

HAROLD: Ah, you would say that.

SALESMAN: Let me see . . . (*Thumbing through his notebook*) Fifty, fifty, fifty . . . Here we have it. You can, by paying only five dollars a week, retire when you're 90 on a comfortable income . . .

MRS BISSONETTE (*entering through door*): Harold, if you and your friend wish to exchange ribald stories, please do it downstairs . . .

HAROLD: My friend???! (*Rushes into house.*)

SALESMAN: And should you live to be a hundred . . .

HAROLD BISSONETTE *emerges with raised cleaver.* SALESMAN *beats a hasty retreat down the stairs.*

HAROLD (*calling after him*): I suppose if I live to be 200 I'll get a velocipede . . .

It may well have been Bill's real-life insomnia, particularly due to his increasingly aching back, which sharpened *It's a Gift*'s Back Porch sequence into such a painful classic. It had nothing to do with the orange-grove buying plot, but, as a coherent, self-contained segment, it remains probably the greatest of all Bill Fields' movie routines. And, as he charges up the stairs to strangle little Baby Dunk, finally, in Bissonette's words – 'Even a worm will turn . . .'

Bill would need all his wormlike persistence, as the censorship board returned to the fray, albeit half-heartedly, over *It's a Gift*. The Breen office proposed that 'there should be no objectionable exposure of Mrs Dunk's Person in scene C-9' and the business of 'the old lady thumbing her nose' should be changed. Also, 'Mr. Fields' routine gag about being wet by a spray and turning round and kicking the dog should *not* be used in this sequence.' There were objections to the use of the word 'bums' and 'lousy'. On 25 October 1934, Mr James Wingate of the board proposed four points for deletion:

1 The reaction of the girl after ordering a round steak to Fields line 'Off the rump' should be deleted.

2 The sea gull gag indicated by Fields line 'guess I made a mistake – it was the Navy.'

3 The action of Fields walking out to the dilapidated out-door toilet should be deleted.

4 The daughter's line 'Father, please stop at the first clean gas station' should be deleted.

James Hammell, a Paramount executive, wrote back to Wingate in puzzlement. 'There is no sea gull gag in our finished picture,' he stated, the nearest thing being the gag where Fields splits a can of tomatoes with a cleaver, saying he learned how to do this in the Army, then, as the contents spurt out, says 'I guess I made a mistake – it was the

Navy.' But there was no seagull flying overhead, and 'no "takeum" by Fields to indicate that the splash of tomatos has come from above.' Eliminations 1, 3 and 4 were accepted.

Script dialogue which is not in the film for other, unknown, reasons, is part of the recycled 'Picnic Sketch' from It's the Old Army Game. The Bissonettes, en route to California and orange glory, trash the lawn of a rich man's estate. As the outraged owner's footmen shout at them to get off the grounds Harold dismisses their protests as: 'It's a moving picture theatre – they have (them) all over the countryside in California . . .' Mrs B. says: 'What are they waving for?' Harold: 'Probably the matinee is about to begin.' As the owner turns up with the police to threaten them with arrest, Harold's wife says: 'Don't have him arrested – he's not a man who understands social amenities.' The owner answers: 'I can see that, Madam,' and Amelia, Mrs B., adds: 'He doesn't – well, you know – I'm a Thistlewaite – the New Jersey Thistlewaites, you may have heard of us . . .' But this Bisbee-esque dig at Hattie's pretensions is not in the released film.

In fact, it was at about this period that Hattie and Bill called a truce after their thirty years of long-distance bickering. The hateful letters ceased as the news of Bill's mounting health problems softened the edge of resentment. In his other compartments, Bill continued to live his other lives – business, work, friendships, sex with Carlotta Monti. Bill continued to drink, and spent the money that was now rolling in on his old passion – motor cars, of which, at that time, he had seven, his most prized possession being his 1933 Lincoln roadster. He would set forth with friends, in convoy, on his more modest passion of Ziegfeld days – picnicking. Other friends would be summoned to the picnic spot and arrive to find Fields ensconsed, with his trailer, hampers of hot and cold food being unpacked, and the appropriate libations.

At his Encino ranch, amid the tiled patios and lush lawns, Bill's real-life orange grove provided the setting for the finale of It's a Gift, where Bissonette, having sold his useless purchase to some racetrack moguls and thus enriched his moaning family, sits squeezing oranges into a tall glass. This routine, in real-life, was a hallowed ritual: Bill and his close buddy, Sam Hardy of Ziegfeld days, put together a portable bar made out of a child's coaster-wagon with an old wood icebox fitted in it. The ice bucket, dozen bottles of various nectars, cocktail and highball glasses, were towed along from the lawn to the tennis court and all over the estate.

In his drinks, Bill had a timeless passion for Martinis. An undated and unsourced clipping in one archive file quotes from his only, alleged, published poem, entitled – 'A Drink With Something In It'.

> There is something about a Martini,
> A tingle remarkably pleasant;
> A yellow, a mellow Martini;
> I wish that I had one at present . . .
> There is something about an old-fashioned
> That kindles a cardiac glow;
> Its soothing and soft and impassioned
> As a lyric by Swinburne or Poe . . .
> Then here's to the heartening wassail,
> Wherever good fellows are found;
> Be its master instead of its vassal,
> And order the glasses around . . .

But Fields could not forever remain the master of his wassailing brew. Both his face and his figure were already changing, as can be seen from the difference in his looks between the Mack Sennett shorts and *It's a Gift*, made only two years later. The man is still vigorous and full of life, but the old trimness has gone. The famous Fields nose, which, like all his troubles, he would elevate into his comic material, was already fleshing out. It had always been prominent, but a skin ailment, which Louise Brooks had mentioned as affecting his hands, was becoming more apparent. Assumed to be a symptom of the drinking, it is now known to have been a condition called 'rosacea', a chronic, waxing and waning ailment which can cause severe, disfiguring blotches. Fair-skinned persons like Fields are the most common sufferers.

Another cause of the famous Nose was revealed by Bill's son, Claude Junior, in an interview in 1969, when he claimed that his father had, at some stage, had an operation to remove the cartilage, thus causing the nose to be soft and flabby. This eventually became the bulbous protuberance which prompted so much self-lampooning.

Notwithstanding these complaints, Bill continued his work: 1934 was rounded out by two further movies, the less than lustrous *Mrs Wiggs of the Cabbage Patch*, with Zasu Pitts, and *David Copperfield*, which was released in 1935.

In *Mrs Wiggs* (shot between *The Old Fashioned Way* and *It's a Gift*)

Fields comes in close to the end of the picture to rescue a mawkish, tear-jerking sermon about a poor family uplifted by love. It was the third of four versions of this story, the first two having been silent films. Venting it in the Depression years was sheer folly. Fields appears as a mail-order, ex-vaudevillian husband, desperately stirring a few jokes into the movie.

Better fare, however, was on the way. MGM's young mogul, David O. Selznick, was casting for the big prestige production of *David Copperfield*. Fields, by all accounts, lobbied hard for his ideal role, as the eternally bankrupt Mr Micawber. The original choice for the role, Charles Laughton, was not well cast, and preferred to bow out.

Fields *was* Wilkins Micawber. No one else should have imagined

29 Bill Fields dispenses wisdom to surrogate son: with Freddie Bartholomew in *David Copperfield*.

taking the part. Bill had drawn on Micawber and other Dickens characters, mainly Pickwick, to flesh out the fairground grifter McGargle. His only regret in the part was Dickens' foolish omission of a poolroom scene. As Bill teeters over the rooftops of a Hollywood-studio

London, with a painted Saint Paul's in the background, in McGargle-white spats and grey stovepipe hat dangling as ever over his cane, evading his creditors to arrive through the skylight to greet his wife and brood of children with that nasal call: 'I have thwarted the malevolent machinations of our scurrilous enemies – in short, I have arrived!' – we know in fact that he has. In his scenes with Master David Copperfield, played by Freddie Bartholomew, there is no trace of the child-hating ogre of legend – generous affection flows from every pore of the penurious optimist's being, and there is no Fieldsian scene-stealing from the young star: 'All that we have is yours, Master Copperfield. Our domestic comfort, quiet, the privacy, call them your own. Count on us now and forever.'

Playing a beloved classic, the irascible Fields was a veritable lamb in the hands of director George Cukor. A number of ad-lib scenes involving high jinks with a bathroom razor were apparently filmed, but lost in the cutting-room. Fields was working among some of the best talent in Hollywood, Lionel Barrymore, Elsa Lanchester, Basil Rathbone, and Roland Young as the definitively 'umble Uriah Heep, although his own scenes were pretty self-contained, and completed in about ten days.

After this job, Bill went back to one of his own vehicles, *Mississippi*, to co-star with another top-grossing Paramount asset, Bing Crosby.

Based on a play by Booth Tarkington, *Mississippi* was not wholly a Fields vehicle, despite his old friend Eddie Sutherland taking the helm. Playing a riverboat Captain – Commodore Orlando Jackson – Bill was once again in a vintage historical setting, the old South of the plantation era. Crosby played Tom Grayson, a young Philadelphian in love with the daughter of the rich plantation owner. At one point he is rehearsing a song called 'Swanee River', which the Commodore pooh-poohs, telling him, 'It'll be forgotten in two weeks. People can't remember the tune.'

This is the movie in which Fields tells his passengers the tall tale of his exploits among the Shug Indians. In another scene, at the bar, the card-sharping Commodore and drinking partners are discussing a notorious Colonel Steele, who has just killed a man because 'the fellow had four aces and the Colonel didn't like it'.

FIRST MAN (*laughs*): Uh – where did this Colonel Steele come from, anyway?

COMMODORE: From Texas.

SECOND MAN: I thought it was Philadelphia.

COMMODORE: No, he was born in Phildelphia, but raised in Waxahatchie, Texas . . . uh – shot a man's nose off down there many years ago.

FIRST MAN: Shot a man's nose off?

COMMODORE: Yeah. The man had a rather prominent proboscis, after the fashion of all eminent men. Stood on the corner, pulled out his shootin' iron an' says: 'I'm gonna shoot that man's nose off.' Shot it off as clean as you could cut it with a buzz saw.

FIRST MAN: Wasn't he arrested?

COMMODORE: Oh, yes, he was arrested. Jury was out one minute.

FIRST MAN: What was their verdict?

COMMODORE: The verdict? The verdict was he was the best shot in Texas.

Fields was now becoming more than famous, an object of spin-offs, souvenirs and merchandising. The first of several animated cartoons with Fields-like characters was made in December 1934 (1938 would see the best of these, Frank Tashlin's W. C. Fields pig on ice skates, with bartending Saint Bernard, in Warner Brothers' *Cracked Ice*). Fields as an animated cartoon is a fascinating full circle from the Fields whose peanut-liquor vending contraption inspired the young Walt Disney in 1925, as we have seen. The final closure would be affected by Fields – whose 'Potteresque' antics were inspired, via McEvoy, by the early newspaper strip cartoons – becoming a character called 'The Great Gusto', in a strip called 'Big Chief Wahoo', in 1938 and 1940. (In the 1960s the Fields family tried to revive this tradition, in a 'W. C. Fields' strip syndicated by the *Los Angeles Times*, but it did not last.) Cigarette cards with his image had already appeared in the late 1920s, and the now famous W. C. Fields dolls were eventually to follow, in 1938, based on his most characteristic costume, in *Poppy*.

Bill was making money for the studio, and so the studio was ready to indulge him as they had not been prepared before. He had been elevated to the front rank by *David Copperfield*, but his films were still cheap to make. Eddie Sutherland once described his principal elements: 'All he had was ugly old man, and ugly old woman, and a little brat of a child.' In the summer of 1935 Bill returned to these primal elements, resulting in perhaps his most neglected masterpiece, *Man on the Flying Trapeze.*

When, in researching this book, I met Bill's eldest grandson, also Bill (W. C. Fields III), we discovered that we both shared *Man on the Flying Trapeze* as our favourite Fields picture. The only thing that jarred on Bill III in this most stinging of all satires on the 'nuclear' American family was that the surrogate son in the movie, Claude Nesselrode, is portrayed as a 'cissy'. 'My father was never a cissy,' said Bill Fields, still a little hurt even sixty years after . . . And indeed Claude Junior, Bill and Hattie's son, was, to all accounts, an amiable and good-hearted man, who in his adult years adored and respected his father, and was eager to mend the long rift between them.

But Claude Nesselrode is definitely a horror, the second and most intolerable of the son, stepson, or suitor characters created by Grady Sutton, that ungainly, suet-pudding of a young man plucked by Fields out of obscurity in *The Pharmacist.* Lying about on the sofa, exhausted by an entire day of not looking for work, stealing Bill's ticket, or berating him mockingly – 'drunk again, and lying in the gutter!' – he is the cruelest of all the caricatures created by Fields to cauterize the itching traumas of his past.

Once again, like *The Old Fashioned Way*, this was a 'Charles Bogle' story. At the base, it was another remake of a silent comedy, this time of 1927's *Running Wild.* But unlike the previous two remakes, only the barest skeleton of the original film was used.

Ambrose Wolfinger is a henpecked clerk who has worked for the same firm for twenty-five years without a single day off. At home he lives with his wife, mother-in-law and her shiftless son, Claude. But when Claude steals his ticket for the wrestling match between Tosoff and Meshobab, the stage is set for confrontation . . .

The film was a collaboration between Bill and his old Ziegfeld buddy, Sam Hardy, who partnered him in, among other sketches, his croquet act in the *Follies* of 1916. Hardy was down on his luck in Hollywood and Fields persuaded William Le Baron to take him on as his co-writer. There was the usual writing team, including stuntman Johnny Sinclair, and a congenial director, Clyde Bruckman, probably still reeling from *The Fatal Glass of Beer.* According to Ronald Fields, Le Baron intended to direct the picture himself, but both he and Bruckman caught the grippe and so Bill Fields and Sam Hardy more or less directed the picture as they saw fit.

O happy chance! The film opens with one of W. C. Fields' greatest sequences, the 'burglars in the cellar' routine. It is prefaced by another Fieldsian bathroom scene, with Mrs Ambrose Wolfinger – Kathleen Howard in her most nagging role – calling out from the bedroom:

MRS WOLFINGER: Ambrose!

AMBROSE: Yes my dear.

MRS WOLFINGER: What are you doing in the bathroom?

AMBROSE: Brushing my teeth dear.

MRS WOLFINGER: I don't know what's come over you. You're always in that bathroom brushing your teeth!

AMBROSE (*hiding flask*): Yes dear.

MRS WOLFINGER: Are you sure you're brushing your teeth?

AMBROSE (*gargle gargle*): Uh, yes dear – (*comes into bedroom*) do you want anything dear?

MRS WOLFINGER: *Please* come to bed and put that light out!

Returning to the bedroom, Ambrose commences the most infuriating domestic routine of all time: taking off each sock, blowing into it and rolling it up very slowly and meticulously. Carlotta Monti has omitted to tell us whether this was an authentic Fields procedure.

MRS WOLFINGER: Hurry up and come to bed!

Ambrose pauses to take up flyswatter to swat fly, before recommencing the routine with his second sock.

MRS WOLFINGER: Please come to bed and put the light out!

Ambrose gets into bed, Mrs W. switches off the light.

Meanwhile, down in the cellar, full of the barrels in which Ambrose stocks his home-made 'applejack', a burglar crawls in, shining his flashlight on a second burglar who is already there:

NEW BURGLAR: Legs!

FIRST BURGLAR: Willie the Weasel! What are you doing here?

NEW BURGLAR: Steve sent me over here to lift some silverware.

FIRST BURGLAR: Eh, he's off his nut, he sent me over on the same job.

The burglars are Tammany Young and a very young Walter Brennan. There follows their testing of the applejack as I have described in an earlier chapter, singing the song they remember from the old 'Orland Social Club' – 'On the banks of the Wabash, far away . . .'

Back in the bedroom, Mrs Wolfinger wakes up: 'Ambrose, did you leave the radio on?' But she soon realises the sound is coming from the ventilator shaft:

MRS WOLFINGER: Wake up, Ambrose, there are burglars singing in the cellar . . .

AMBROSE (*sleepily*): What are they singing?

MRS WOLFINGER: What difference does it make what they're singing? Get up and see what it's all about! . . . Don't just sit there like a bump on a stump. Go down and throw them out! Hurry, hurry Ambrose . . .

AMBROSE: What are they singing down there for?

MRS WOLFINGER: It doesn't matter what they're singing. Go down quickly, Ambrose. We're in danger, I tell you . . .

AMBROSE: The more haste the less speed. I'll be down there.

MRS WOLFINGER: Oh, Ambrose, my poor mother! My poor, helpless old mother! My darling!

AMBROSE: She's upstairs, they won't find her.

Of course Ambrose has to find his socks, unroll and unblow them, put two on the same foot and then scout around for the second, swat another fly, listen to the singing down the ventilator shaft: 'Oh what rotten voices,' rummage in the drawer for a gun, coming triumphantly up with: 'Look at that. There's the gloves that you lost two weeks ago!' and 'Say, what are these doing in here, all these walnuts?' which are knocked from his hand to the floor, as he tries to untangle the gun from a belt, muttering, as his wife fidgets: 'Nothing to be frightened of. It's unloaded . . .' Bang! Mrs Wolfinger screams and falls on the bed.

AMBROSE (*a little eagerly*): Did I kill yer?

MRS WOLFINGER (*groaning*): Oh, leave me in peace, leave me in peace . . .

AMBROSE (*gleefully*): Good, good, I didn't kill yer. (*Laughs*) That's fine . . .

Enter Mrs Nesselrode, shrew par-excellence (played heroically by Vera Lewis), her son Claude, and Ambrose's daughter from a previous marriage, Hope – played, as her equivalent was in *Running Wild*, by Mary Brian, whom Fields insisted on casting from New York for the picture. Ambrose's domestic predators, Mrs Nesselrode, Claude and Mrs Wolfinger, gang up to demand he goes down by himself to check out the intruders in the cellar.

AMBROSE: Think I'll just brush my teeth first.

MRS WOLFINGER: No you don't, you just brushed your teeth.

Ambrose decides to call the neighbourhood patrol ('What am I paying five dollars a month for?'), but gets a wrong number first, responding: 'I'm sorry Mrs Crud, but we have burglars singing in the cellar.' Mrs W., in a reprise of the bedroom scene in *It's a Gift*, ripostes: 'Who's that woman you were talking to?' Wolfinger replies with a cascade of mumbles.

Eventually, as they wait, a cop arrives, climbing into the cellar and handcuffing the crooks, but then joining them in applejack and song. Mrs Wolfinger: 'Now there are three of them singing!' Ambrose, still hesitant, suggests a little nip of applejack before setting off downstairs, prompting the immortal exchange from his female loved ones:

MRS WOLFINGER: Ambrose Wolfinger, you know perfectly well my mother detests alcohol!

MRS NESSELRODE: When I was a young and pretty girl, I always vowed to my parents that lips that touched liquor would never touch mine.

AMBROSE: Oh yes, pretty sentiment, very nice . . .

Ambrose descends with the gun, trips on the stair carpet and breaks through the cellar door, landing on a plank with a nail: 'Why couldn't I fall on a small dull one?' The gun has gone off, causing more mayhem. The cop picks him up and soon they are all drinking from the liquor, humming . . .

COP: Remember that tune?

AMBROSE: We used to sing it up at the Tahachapee Glee Club many years ago. Brings back fond memories . . . before I was married . . .

MRS WOLFINGER (*upstairs*): It's a quartet! Merciful heavens, he's singing with them now!

She shouts down the shaft. Ambrose suggests the cop lets the crooks go, but the cop has to take them in. All climb out through the window, staggering and singing down the road.

Structure, character, dialogue and gags have all meshed here. Fields has knitted his nightmare of marriage, his sense of the meaninglessness of family ritual, his observation of the smallest gestures and the widest metaphysical implications into his cosmic drama of the absurd.

The story rolls on its inexorable path: at the police station, the Judge releases the burglars but sentences Ambrose to thirty days for manufacturing applejack without a permit, thus landing him in a cell with a homicidal maniac who is in jail for killing his wife.

MANIAC: And then, I took my scissors . . . and stuck straight into my wife's t'roat . . . Like dat . . .

AMBROSE: Uh, uh uh . . . You tickle me . . .

MANIAC: Wouldn't you do the same under the circumstances?

AMBROSE: I'd do the same thing, I guess, or probably worse . . .

MANIAC (*putting his huge mitt on Ambrose' shoulder*): You're my friend.

AMBROSE: Uh hum.

MANIAC: I had three wives.

AMBROSE: Oh, yes.

MANIAC: But this is the first one I have killed in all my life!

AMBROSE: Oh, that's in your favor, yes . . . They have no more case against you than a sheep has against the butcher.

Finding humour in the bleakest of situations, Fields glories in the realistically surreal. Even the censor was unable to understand what Fields was getting at in this film, and passed the picture, amazingly, without any fuss or cuts.

At home, Claude, who has stolen Ambrose's ticket to the wrestling match, crows at the news that he's landed in jail. Daughter Hope bails Ambrose out, so he can return home to bed for an instant's lie-down before the alarm clock rings, prompting his fatalistic comment: 'Quite a snooze.'

There follows another of Fields' breakfast table calvaries, reprising the mundane agony of *It's a Gift*:

HOPE: Is the toast warm, Dad?

AMBROSE: No dear its cold. But it's all right. I've been eating cold toast for eight years now. I like it.

Still determined to go to the wrestling match, despite the stolen ticket, Ambrose asks his boss for the afternoon off, giving the reason that his mother-in-law has died of poisoned liquor. His secretary, played by Carlotta Monti, sympathises: 'It must be hard to lose your mother-in-law.' Ambrose: 'Yes it is, very hard, almost imposs . . . oh yes . . .'

The boss informs the staff of Ambrose's sad bereavement, calling for floral tributes and an announcement in the press. Ambrose sets off in his battered car to the wrestling match between Tossof, 'the Russian Behemoth', and Meshobab, 'the Persian Giant'. After convoluted flim-flam with traffic cops on the way, he arrives to find the last ticket sold.

A Fieldsian denouement is now inevitable: Meshobab throws Tosoff clear out of the ring onto Ambrose, who is knocked cold outside. Carlotta rushes up to cradle his head, while stepson Claude emerges to gloat. Back home, the Nesselrodes are aghast at the newspaper announcement of Mrs N.'s supposed death. Claude runs in with the latest news of Ambrose's ultimate humiliation. Ambrose arrives, dishevelled, with a black eye and a futile peace offering: 'A little nose-candy, uh, nosegay . . .' But only his daughter Hope defends him against the rampaging Nesselrodes. Claude threatens Hope, and is knocked unconscious by Ambrose, who, for good measure, takes a swing at Mrs Nesselrode, chasing both her and his wife out of the room, as Hope tries to hold him back.

AMBROSE: Let me go! I'll knock em for a row of lib-labs!

MRS WOLFINGER (*thru door*): Leave this house and never cross this threshold again! And take your ungrateful minx of a daughter with you!

HOPE: Dad, come on!

AMBROSE: I'll exterminate the three of 'em!

Throwing a small wreath onto Claude: 'Rest in peace . . .' he fiddles with his hat, and exits.

Man on the Flying Trapeze is Fields' most autobiographical vengeance, and his darkest vision of the slams of life, the ungratefulness and injustice, the meanness behind the American 'Momist' myth. Al Jolson sang 'Mammy', but only Fields would try and belt her in the puss. He may even have been directly commenting on the one remaining obstacle between himself and the real Claude Junior, his son's hurt over his open relationship with Carlotta Monti. There was nothing in Fields' life that could not be recycled into his raw material.

We have, of course, an obligatory happy ending – Ambrose proves indispensable to his firm because no one else can fathom his eccentric filing system, allowing his daughter Hope to negotiate him a vastly improved position, while Mrs Wolfinger rebels at last against the lazy Claude. We finale in a family ride in Ambrose's new car, with Mrs Nesselrode and Claude caught in the open back seat in the rain. 'These sandwiches are very good,' murmurs Ambrose, cosy and dry in the front. But despite this, *Man on the Flying Trapeze* is Fields Agonistes, Fields naked, Fields battered mercilessly by the elements, his triumph just a fantastic dream . . .

Chapter 35
The Sun Never Sets on Purple Bark Sarsaparilla . . .

Bill Fields' real-life troubles, however, were not fantasies. Soon after filming *Man on the Flying Trapeze*, Bill checked into Soboba Hot Springs, a health spa in the San Bernardino Mountains. He was reported to be suffering from back pain, bouts of the grippe and pneumonia. But this was the first of several unsuccessful attempts to dry out. The summer of 1935 was full of bad omens. On 15 August, Will Rogers died in a plane crash flying over Alaska. He was fifty-five years old and had just completed filming *Steamboat Round the Bend*, with John Ford. Will had developed a passion for flying and had arranged to accompany a veteran pilot, Wiley Post, on an experimental survey of a passenger route between the United States and Russia via Alaska. The local Eskimos saw the plane fall and found the bodies. The country was in mourning, and Fields was devastated. Later, in November, he wrote an appreciation of Rogers: 'I was with him for years in the Follies, and he did an entirely different monologue every night, a thing I have never known in my 37 years of trouping. Rogers was the nearest thing to Lincoln that I have ever known. His death was a terrible blow to me.'

In the autumn, Bill was dealt a second blow, when his friend and collaborator Sam Hardy died. Fate seemed to be beckoning. Death, whom Bill named as 'The Man in the Bright Nightgown', began to be a chilling real presence. By October, Ronald Fields writes, he was too sick to work, and had to cancel the third film in his contract. He filled part of his time that year writing letters and frivolous essays, such as 'Life Begins at Twenty, Says W. C. Fields', published in *Motion Picture*, in September:

> I came to the stage all of a sudden. My mother's brother was a Swiss Bell
> Ringer. He dressed like an actor, and was always hungry. He came to our

home each day in time for meals. One time he hurt my mother's feelings by not eating the crust of a pie she had baked. He claimed that people who ate pie crusts caught measles easily in Philadelphia, where I had the bad luck to be born . . .

And so on. Another text from this period, which remained unpublished until unearthed by Ronald Fields in 1973, was the now famous 'Why Alcohol Has Taken the Place of the Dog as Man's Best Friend, by W. C. (D. T.) Fields, with a forward and backward by A. Edward (Bayboo) Sutherland and Gregory (One Punch) La Cava . . .'

The astonishing news that I have gone on the water wagon was disclosed recently in the public prints. This, I must sadly confess, is at least partly true . . . Alcohol, of course, can take care of itself, which is more than a dog can do . . . What would Omar Khayyam have been had he not extolled the jug of wine, and the little girl, her name escapes me for the nonce, who went tripping along singing 'Little brown jug how I love thee' . . . There is no question as to whether whiskey or the dog is man's best friend . . . Whiskey does not need to be periodically wormed, it does not need to be fed . . . you have to train a dog. But you never have to train a bottle of grog. A dog will run up and lick your hand. No bottle will do that. If the whiskey ever starts licking your hand, I would advise that you lay off for a while, say five or ten minutes . . .

Fields, as ever, followed his own advice assiduously. But this was not helping him return to work. He had, in proper Hollywood style, changed his agent, to the prestigious Charles Beyer (his long-term agent, Bill Grady, had left the profession to become a casting director at MGM). But although various projects were mentioned in the press, all failed to materialize. The most tantalising of these was a script called *Farike the Guest Artist*, which was written by Ben Hecht and Gene Fowler for Fields, but I have not been able to find any trace of it. On 26 October 1935, the New York *American* published an intriguing item:

FIELDS TO ENACT PRINCIPAL ROLE IN PICKWICK PAPERS, BY JERRY HOFFMAN (PINCH-HITTING FOR LOUELLA PARSONS) . . . Paramount has scheduled 'Pickwick Papers' for Bill's first picture when he returns to the studio. That isn't all. Bill, whose recovery is almost complete . . . will find two other grand stories awaiting him. Following 'Pickwick Papers,' Fields is to make 'Rip Van Winkle' and after that 'Don Quixote.'

Undoubtedly quite a few liberties will be taken with the last two tales but if they make good pictures, who cares?

None of these wonderful things came to pass. Ronald Fields mentions another two titles: 'Don't Look Now' and 'The Count of Luxemburg', with Irene Dunne, neither of which ever materialized.

Finally, in March 1936, Fields was well enough to work, and began shooting another sure-fire remake, this time of his great stage success, *Poppy*. This was to be a return to the original – minus the song and dance numbers – rather than a reprise of Griffith's *Sally of the Sawdust*. Freed from Griffith's moralising eye, Bill restored the swindling character of Eustace McGargle, making him again the witting agent of the scam to present the young girl, Poppy, as the heiress, only to find, at the end, that this is fact, not fake. Lines from the original play are restored, such as, 'My little plum, I'm like Robin Hood, I take

30 Poster for *Poppy*.

from the rich and I give to the poor.' 'Which poor?' asks Poppy. 'Us poor.' As well as the expected new Fieldsisms: 'What a gorgeous day, what effulgent sunshine . . . It was a day of this sort that the McGillicuddy brothers murdered their mother with an axe . . .'

As usual, Bill added bits and pieces of stuff to the story: selling a 'talking dog,' whose last words are 'Just for selling me, I'll never speak another word as long as I live!' ('He's a stubborn little fellow,' says Professor McGargle to the confused buyer, as he moves towards the door, 'I'm afraid he'll keep his word.'); a vintage routine at the hot-dog stall, piling on the 'mutard' and horseradish ('you haven't a little foie gras to rub on these things?'), and telling the vendor: 'I'll pay you at the conclusion of our engagement.' When the outraged vendor gets him to put down his three-quarter eaten sandwich, exclaiming 'Listen, you tramp – how am I gonna sell these again?' McGargle has the ultimate response: 'First you insult me, then you ask my advice concerning salesmanship! You sir, are a dunce! Dunce, sir! D-u-n-c-e, how do you spell it . . . Come, my little plum . . .'

Once again, McGargle is selling his patent medicines: 'Purple Bark Sarsaparilla, good for man or beast. Will grow hair and also remove warts. The sun never sets on Purple Bark Sarsaparilla . . .' Bald headed man: 'Will it really grow hair?' 'Grow hair on a billiard ball!' 'It won't grow hair on a pool-ball, will it?' 'All except the eight-ball . . .'

When entering society Fields presents his Croquet Game, unplayed since Ziegfeld 1916: 'Professor, do you play croquet?' 'No, I do not. I used to do a little tatting on trains . . .' He also plays his beloved kadoola-kadoola – 'I have the honour of rendering for your approval this evening the first Dugijigg of the Opera Schrekensach by Gilka Kimmel and Ossip Pippitone . . .'

At the end of the movie Bill reprised the stage version closely:

POPPY: Pop, what do you think, I'm really the heiress!

Semi-closeup, POPPY *and* PROFESSOR.

PROFESSOR: Wonderful. So you're finally getting some sense, eh?

POPPY: Isn't it grand? Now we have a beautiful home and we can settle down.

PROFESSOR: That's marvellous. And if we should ever separate, my little plum, I want to give you one little bit of fatherly advice.

POPPY: Yes, Pop.

PROFESSOR: Never give a sucker an even break.

They embrace. POPPY *exits.* PROFESSOR *crosses to chair, picks up the Mayor's hat and cane from chair, puts on hat, crosses to table, gets cigars from box and exits through doorway. FADE OUT.*

The shooting of *Poppy* was a physical agony for Bill. He had to wear a kind of corset to keep his back straight, but to cap it he fell off the penny-farthing bicycle he rode to escape the police and broke a vertebra. Soon after the shooting, while he was still recovering, he apparently fell down the stairs at his home and broke his tailbone. The legend goes that he fell clutching a Martini glass, and commented proudly, as he lay in agony on the floor, that he hadn't spilled a single drop.

This was incredibly bad luck, as the shooting of *Poppy* truly marked his arrival at the top. The press campaign for *Poppy* went to town, capitalizing on the now familiar costume – the frayed coat, the checkered pants, the spats, the stovepipe hat, the pelican-headed cane, which is still kept by his grandson Everett, in Los Angeles. The Paramount Press Book suggested that movie theatres should convert their box-offices into a comically enlarged head of W. C. Fields by dressing it with a hat, collar and necktie. Still cut-outs, a 'strolling figure costumed to look like W. C. Fields, carrying a sandwich board made of "Jumbo" telegram blanks lettered with "gag" copy,' an old-fashioned calliope, 'make up a man as Fields' double with a putty nose' – all were touted. In the *New York Times*, Hollywood correspondent Idwal Jones described Bill's presence on the set in an almost awed tone:

In the last two years Fields has become a sort of myth or legendary character, entitled, therefore, to make his entry in a hush. All this while he had been basking in the sun, sunken in a canvas chair, wearing spectacles and with a cap pulled over his face. He has a genius for immobility. This is just as well, for he is still recovering from that exquisite malady, a displaced sacro-iliac . . . So he rose with great wariness and flanked by two bodyguards and a valet carrying a bottle of restorative and two canes . . . Then the cameras turned in a burst of light and Fields was himself again. You saw the pea trickle under the walnut shell, but you did not see it shoot back into his palm . . .

Bodyguards on set, Carlotta Monti, transformed into his nurse, in the home. It is difficult to be certain how constant was her presence, as Fields tended to sack her and throw her off the premises, a habit he was prone to with the rest of his staff. Bill was now too ill to work, and it must have irked him beyond endurance to be in this state at the exact moment when his box-office potential, and movie fame, was at its height. Richard Watts had written, in the *New York Herald Tribune*:

> Because they are the two outstanding clowns of our generation, it is only natural that there should be comparisons between Fields and Chaplin. As I have often said, for sheer fun it seems to me that Fields is superior. He can handle pathos with the best of them when there is any need for it, and there is a certain battered and bewildered meekness about him that invariably makes for the proper degree of sympathetic appeal. Essentially, it is, however, the sheer, hearty, racy humor that bubbles out of the man which supplies his greatest quality.

Bill must have been especially pleased by this, as his rivalry with Chaplin was unabated. Chaplin's continued physical grace and agility must have pained him all the more in his semi-paralysed state.

But in mid-1936 the roof fell in on Bill. Although he was recovered enough in May to be 'hosting his friends at the pleasant, rambling house in the San Fernando Valley that has become one of the picture colony's favorite watering places', according to the *New York World Telegram* of 29 May, by 16 June the *New York Sun* reported:

> W. C. Fields . . . the ex-vaudeville juggler, has been confined in an oxygen tent since he entered Riverside Community Hospital last Friday, seriously ill. His temperature ranged between 101 and 102, the nurse said. Dr. Jesse Citron, the actor's personal physician, consulted with Los Angeles specialists on the case last night. Their judgment was that Fields was 'doing as well as could be expected.'

'The Man in the Bright Nightgown' was beckoning again. Fields had collapsed while undergoing two weeks of treatment (presumably drying out again) at the Soboba Hot Springs, but apparently he spent much of his time there playing golf with the said Dr Citron (or Citrone), taking surreptitious nips from his hip flask while the quack struggled with the unfamiliar game. After his collapse, Fields sued Dr Citrone over a bill for $12,000 which the doctor rendered for his two weeks of golf study. Fields sued for $25,000, alleging that Dr Citrone's treatment had in fact set back his recovery, perhaps due to his failure to stand clear and keep his eye on the ball. This would be a long-running legal battle, to commence in court the following year.

In the hospital, Fields' rosacea erupted, blotching his face and turning his nose a bright, flabby red. Just as another patients' friends might bring him flowers or chocolates, Bill's friends smuggled in a flow of booze. The DTs were an inevitable consequence. He began to suffer from double-vision, and could not read. In his affliction he turned to the radio, listening to old vaudevillians like Fred Allen, Jack Benny, George Burns and Gracie Allen. Radio was providing them with a living and with nationwide fame at a time when movies were not too kind to these stalwarts. Fields described his amazing discovery of the wireless medium thus:

She (the nurse) set it down by my bedside and it looked me right in the eye, yes, yes, an eye that once looked upon better days – the good old days when they gave you a free lunch with a stein. Throwing all caution to the winds, I lunged at it boldly and seized it by the throat with one hand while tweaking its nose with the other . . .

31 Fields discovers radio: 'I lunged at it boldly and seized it by the throat . . .'

Fields' voice had in fact had its radio premier some years earlier, in 1933, in a long forgotten guest appearance on a CBS 'California Melodies' show. Bill's second broadcast, from his bed, in January 1937, was as part of a Paramount Silver Jubilee programme, dedicated to Adolph Zukor. The audience loved the gravelly, drawling voice. When, in April, Bill left the hospital, he was approached by Chase and Sanborn, a coffee company, to appear in their sponsored weekly show, which then starred a young ventriloquist, Edgar Bergen, and his obnoxious dummy, Charlie McCarthy.

The radio show became a life-raft for Fields. Radio was then, as television is now, the mass communication medium of the day. Millions of people went to see films, but tens of millions listened to the radio every day. When old-timers MacIntyre and Heath had been approached, in the early 1930s, to transform their blackface routine into radio, they refused, being too weary to start anew, and thus made way for another team – Amos 'n' Andy, who became a household name.

Edgar Bergen's success was particularly curious, since the whole point of ventriloquism is lost on radio. The secret was in the character of Charlie McCarthy, played as a wisecracking, mischievous ladies' man. In 1937, Charlie even won an honorary degree from Northwestern University, as 'Master of Innuendo and the Snappy Comeback.' But he is best remembered for the feud which Bill Fields kindled between himself and the little wooden scoundrel.

As another surrogate child, an arboreal 'Claude', or grown up Baby Le Roy, Fields recognised that he could plumb new depths of hostility because of Charlie's essential non-humanity. He could kick Baby Le Roy, but he could not threaten to throw him, or Claude, into the fireplace:

FIELDS: Tell me, Charlie, is it true that when you slide down a bannister the bannister gets more splinters than you do?

CHARLIE: Why, you bugle beak, why don't you fill your nose with helium and rent it out as a barrage balloon?

FIELDS: Listen, you animated hitching post, I'll sic a beaver on you.

BERGEN: Listen Bill, you'll do no such thing, you'll not harm a hair on this boy's head.

FIELDS: That's not the end I'm going to work on . . .

32 Fields and wooden
rival: 'I have a warm
place for you, Charles.'
'In your heart, Bill?' 'No,
in my fireplace.'

The Fields-versus-Charlie routines became a staple of American
folklore. Listening to the shows, one feels a kind of slackness, perfectly
suited to radio, which Bill adopted for this phase of his life. Dick
Mack, who was supposed to write Bill's dialogues, gave way to Field's
ad-libbing. But ad-libbing came naturally in this medium, and fumbled
or fluffed lines only added to the cosy, private nature of the thing. Bill
was able, in this format, to reprise many of his old vaudeville routines,
with new twists, in the show. The Drug Store Sketch, aka 'The
Pharmacist', was a typical example, as a customer inquires: 'Say, by the
way, what's that big sign you got out there, souvenirs with every purchase?' 'Oh, yes, pardon me. Souvenirs . . . here they are right up here
. . . you wish a 404 elephant gun? pair of mounted silver tusks? electric
pocket watch or a spoon with Baby Snooks head on it?' (Fanny Brice's
child creation was already a wow on the airwaves.)

In 'The Golf Game', Bill inducted Bergen and McCarthy into his specialty, with Don Ameche, who often joined them, as an added attrac-

tion. Jokes on alcohol and drunkenness abounded: 'Would somebody get me a sedative, with an olive in it . . .' 'What's the score, caddy, how do I stand?' Charlie: 'I often wonder . . .'

The most famous of all Fields' radio routines was to be the 'Temperance Lecture,' recorded much later, in 1945, which features in most collections of vintage Radio Classics –

Throughout the Middle Ages the use of liquor was universal . . . and drunkeness was so common it was unnoticed . . . They called it the Middle Ages because no one was able to walk home unless they were between two other fellows . . . I was the middle guy . . . How well I remember my first encounter with the devil's brew . . . I happened to stumble across a case of Bourbon, and went on stumbling for several days thereafter . . . Of course now I touch nothing stronger than buttermilk . . . ninety proof buttermilk . . . I look on my days of revelry with scorn and reproachment and shudder . . . When I recall going to the corner saloon and tugging at my Daddy's coat-tails and saying, Father, dear Father, come home with me now . . . and bring a jug with yer . . .

Now many of you in the audience are giggling and scoffing and saying that I have given up strong drink only because the stuff is so hard to get nowadays . . . But you are in error . . . my basement is loaded . . . as I am . . . My friends, you set a bucket of beer in front of a pig and he'll grunt and walk away . . . so should you . . . or would you rather be a duck? Back in my rummy days I would shake and tremble for hours upon arising . . . it was the only exercise I got . . . Now don't say you can't swear off drink – it's easy . . . I've done it a thousand times . . .

Another famous talk of late vintage was 'The Day I Drank a Glass of Water' – 'I haven't had a drop of water on my tongue since the gold rush days . . .' But already in his 1937 dialogues, Bill, as ever, was making his pain into his material. The shows enabled him to claw his way out of the doldrums, to reinvent himself yet again, rising like a phoenix out of his own ashes. W. C. Fields became a household name, and his vitriolic insults aimed at Charlie McCarthy became known to countless millions: 'Quiet, you termite's flop-house . . .' 'I'll cut you down to a pair of shoe-trees . . .' 'I'll always have a warm place for you, Charlie . . .' 'Where, in your heart?' 'No, in my fireplace . . .'

Bill's future co-star, Mae West, also tried her luck at the Chase and Sanborn Hour, in December, 1937, but caused a celebrated scandal. Her dialogue skit of Eve and the Snake in Eden caused uproar and denunciation as 'an insolent caricature of religion and the Bible'. But Fields was not involved in this divine region, not yet . . .

Nevertheless, radio was just a stop-gap for Bill, despite its crucial boost to his popularity. He still yearned to return to Paramount, to pick up his contract and make more films. But the only way the studio would accept him back now was in a spin-off movie of radio's famous stars. Paramount had already made two portmanteau movies of this kind – after *International House* – called *The Big Broadcast* and *The Big Broadcast of 1936*. As ever with Hollywood, the moguls adored sequels, since they didn't have to think of anything new. In late 1937 they finally signed Bill to return to the screen, in *The Big Broadcast of 1938*.

Chapter 36

'You're Going to Lose My Trade!' – The Last Paramount, and the Vaudeville Sketches Revisited

By early 1937 Bill had left his dream ranch in Encino, due to the return of its absent owner. Bill offered to double the rent, but the owner refused. Unlike either Will Rogers or John Barrymore, Bill had a peculiar fear of owning real-estate. The only thing he would spend money on was his cars, purchasing, in 1938, a brand-new 16-cylinder Cadillac which he fitted with its own portable bar. He moved to another rented house, in Bel Air, west of Beverly Hills, at 655 Funchal Road, where he remained until late 1939. Carlotta Monti was present, and in charge of the catering, as witness his invitation of 27 July to Elise Cavanna, previously quoted, for 'Tea and Crumpets' at the 'OUT HOUSE' INN, UNDER THE MANAGEMENT OF CARLOTTA MONTI.

Here he returned to his hobby of gardening, with particular attention to flowers, his passion for which he was at great pains to hide from posterity. At a later date Gene Fowler would chronicle his occasional habit of sticking notes addressed to his rosebushes on his personal billboard: 'Bloom, you bastards! Bloom!' For public consumption, he made light of his troubles, telling his interviewer for *Liberty*:

> 'Now I'm full of *joie la vie* – in spite of Charlie McCarthy . . . I've been in the clutches of science . . . It has not only put the old chassis back in the used car market but it has actually stepped up the motor . . . I can now stop or start on a dime.'
>
> . . . There are two things he doesn't like about hospitals, Fields says. Three, if you include doctors. But the two pet grievances are beds and ceilings.
>
> 'I am a connoisseur of beds,' he says. 'I consider myself an outstanding

savant on the bed and its numerous benefits to mankind . . . As a youngster, I didn't have a bed to sleep in; and in my more virile years (now, for example) I am troubled with insomnia. So I know about beds: I have slept on everything from park benches to barber chairs, and from Louis XV specials to a bunk in my trailer. I would place the hospital bed somewhere in the middle. And somebody other than Mr. Fields in the middle of the bed . . .'

Having replenished his creative batteries by his year of radio sketches, Bill was ready to get back into the movies. In fact, he had already been working on a number of sequences he was going to propose for his part in the forthcoming *Big Broadcast of 1938*. These sequences, tidily typed (presumably by Magda Michael), and dated 18 August 1937, represent the last extant versions of Bill's vaudeville-type routines. Only three of these seven sequences found their way, much truncated, into the final film. The rest remained to languish on paper, unfilmed, and unpublished until now.

The 1937 'Comedy Sequences' show a Fields increasingly out of sorts with the world. Although the world was always a painful and strange place to him, it was never quite as prickly as this. Fields, for the first time, was venting a very particular anxiety, a despair, against a kind of modernism that he had never so eschewed.

In the first episode, Fields arrives at a Gas Station manned by a battalion of smartly dressed attendants. In the film, he was supposed to play a double role as S. B. Bellows, a straightforward shipowner, and his twin brother T. Frothingell Bellows, millionaire playboy and ne'er-dowell. But in the typescript he is always 'Fields', the first time Bill refers to himself in the third person, as a character in his own right. He draws up to the gas pumps to demand a refill for his cigarette lighter, and goes directly into an anti-Rooseveltian diatribe against all the symptoms of the New Deal:

FIELDS: How much?

ATTENDANT: Two cents.

FIELDS: Tch, tch! The price of gas has sure gone up!

ATTENDANT: Yes, sir, I'm sorry sir. It has advanced one cent since you were in here last. All our customers are complaining – but you see, with all the taxes: Social security, unemployed, street lighting, etc etc . . .

The attendants, flustered, leave the air pumping into Fields' tire, until it is so huge the car is raised off the ground. Fields protests:

FIELDS: Hey, what kind of service is this? Look at that fly speck on the windshield!

ATTENDANT: Sorry, sir, it shan't happen again, sir . . .

FIELDS: Excuses, always excuses! You're a lazy lot of louts!

ATTENDANTS (*in unison*): Yes, sir!

FIELDS: Never saw such service! Drat you – all of you! You're going to lose my trade!

The scene is then to dissolve, into the Golf Routine. Here, in the manuscript, Bill inserts a revealing paragraph:

(NOTE: *pardon me for reiterating here: The Fields' character is sort of a composite character study, as might be reproduced in magazines like 'Life' and 'Look' – done rather with pictures and pantomime than with dialogue. The dialogue should be more in the nature of captions than actual conversation. I think this will be entertaining, and is a departure from the orthodox picture comedy – my aim being to make this slightly different.)*

Fields rolls up to the Club House, making a grandstand entrance, before a mass of members and caddies. A 'Club Member' engages him in conversation, as Fields looks at his watch:

FIELDS: Be quick! What do you want? I can only give you a minute!

CLUB MEMBER: How's your wife?

FIELDS: Don't know. Haven't seen her for months.

CLUB MEMBER: How are your children?

FIELDS: Both dead, thanks – and everybody I know is feeling lots better.

He proceeds. Other Club Members are 'in various stages of dishabille,' as Fields disrobes and orders drinks. Fields writes: 'QUICK FLASHES of several Club Members, as Fields passes on his way towards the links – in as scanty attire as the censors will permit . . .' Alas, the studio never took the chance. A feature of this sketch which survives into the film is Fields' 'Scootmobile', an all-purpose golf buggy. But the whole written sketch is full of a vigorous bile and craziness:

FIELDS *hires a flock of caddies – who will be ready at all times with the proper clubs . . . (one of them) to be a sort of Norman Taurog, puffing type, out of breath, and walks as though on hot bricks . . .* FIELDS *hits the ball – hops on his Scootmobile – and beats the ball to the first hole, looking back to be sure that it is following . . .*

In the course of the game he passes several of his caddies lying on the grass – bags strewn about them – utterly exhausted. FIELDS, *disgusted, runs up a little hill.*

FIELDS (*yells*): Shoot out another caddy!

A Shot of the Club House. At the direction of the Caddy Master, one of the caddies crawls into the great cannon and is shot into the air.

CADDY MASTER (*to* ASSISTANT): Shoot him out to Boomer, on Number Four!

The fuse is ignited – and the CADDY *is catapulted out through the cannon's mouth.*

SHOT OF CADDY *flying in mid air. He hears* FIELDS *call: Putter! Caddy, as he hangs to his parachute, selects a putter. Before he has hit the ground,* FIELDS *has grabbed the putter from him. Just as he hits the ball, the 'Gigantic's' whistle can be heard again.*

CADDY: That's the last whistle, Mr Boomer. You've missed the boat!

FIELDS: Quiet!

FIELDS *hops aboard the Scootmobile – presses a trick button – wings sprout out of the handle-bars of the motorcycle, and* FIELDS *takes off into the air, shouting back instructions, what to do with his automobile, where to collect the fees for the game, etc.*

The next sketch is a 'Barber Shop Routine' on the ship. The earlier Sennett movie setup is reversed: Now Fields is the customer. A strike is in progress. The strikers are sitting idly in the barber shop chairs. The barbers have taken over the kitchen and the meat carvers are acting as barbers. 'Outside the shop,' writes Fields, 'pickets are marching in circles, bearing signs on their backs: "This shop is unfair to Union Labor."' Bill Fields, having long ago left the world of the working Joe and climbed up the ladder, vents his spleen about recalcitrant servants:

Stewardesses crowd in with food and drinks for the striking barbers. One stewardess kisses a striking barber, after supplying him with a nice piece of chicken, some toast, pickles and a bottle of beer.

PICKET (*yelling*): Bring me a Scotch and soda! Make it Old Heather Picker – very little soda.

ANOTHER PICKET: What about a little entertainment?

STRIKE LEADER: Patience, gentlemen – we're having some talent sent in. Some of them are arriving now.

(*Then follows entertainment – girl doing Mae West impersonation, etc.*)

Perhaps Bill knew very well that this would never be filmed . . . There follow some rough notes on a 'Dentist gag' and an 'Occulist gag', with Fields unable to read the letters until the Occulist produces a tiny label in the smallest print: 'Royal Scotch Whiskey', which Fields reads perfectly.

The next scene is a 'Pool Room Routine': Fields plays snooker with a daffy English nobleman, Lord Droopy. Fields writes in his script: '*Fields has several pieces of business with cue and shooting the balls, which would be difficult to describe on paper.*' In which case I shall not presume . . .

The last sketch Bill proposed for the movie, but which was never filmed, was an 'Orchestra Routine'. Once again: '*In this routine there are many and divers pieces of business difficult to explain on paper. (The scene was fully described to both Mr Harlan Thompson, the supervisor, and Mr Mitchell Leisen, the Director, and met with their approval.*') Alas, Bill was deluding himself, because the 'Orchestra Routine' exists only on paper. We can only imagine the loss to the screen. Bill listed his required props:

1 trick trombone
1 coronet
1 bass violin
1 bassoon
½ dozen trap drums, with paper used in lieu of gut
Several cheap trick violins
½ dozen trick batons
2 trick bass drums
1 set of musical sleigh-bells
3 prop drumsticks (to be used in connection with bass drums)

1 trick xylophone
1 sliding microphone
All of which will be described by Mr Fields to the prop man. These scenes will be developed, as usual, on the set.

The scene was to be composed of various sight gags on the instruments – Fields bending the trombone, wrecking a $200,000 Stradivarius, trying the bassoon and advising its player: 'Don't eat onions tomorrow night!' and finally taking hold of the xylophone and accompanying the orchestra in Sousa's 'Stars and Stripes Forever,' with two hammers in each hand. Fields: 'Now you know what I want – let's have it right!'

Fields notes: 'Although the musical number is one grand discord, the musicians must at all times be kept on their dignity, apprehensive of what they expect may happen any moment.'

I have become increasingly aware, navigating the mass of Fields' unmade, unshaped raw material, that what we have inherited on the screen, in Fields' forty odd movies, is a mass of scattered fragments. The tip of a giant iceberg of comedy, which floats serenely on, below the surface, waiting for the *Titanic* of the studio heads to strike and hit the life-rafts, keening loudly. *The Big Broadcast of 1938* is indeed one

33 Buck Fields Rides Again: Returning to work on *The Big Broadcast of 1938*.

such vessel, a ponderous piece of fluff, although directed by Mitchell Leisen, who would go on to make the peerless *Midnight*, with Claudette Colbert. It seems a final answer to the age-old question of what is heavier, a ton of lead or a ton of feathers. The capricious Fields/T. F. Bellows, is sent by his staid twin brother, S. B., owner of a super-liner, the *Gigantic*, to scupper the chances of a rival ship, the *Colossal*, in a Transatlantic race. But the capricious Bellows joins the *Gigantic* by mistake and proceeds to wreak havoc on the wrong ship. Aboard the vessel, various stars such as Martha Raye, Dorothy Lamour, Leif Erickson, and Bob Hope, in his first feature role, cavort to no appreciable purpose.

The gas station sketch, the golf sketch, and the pool sketch, survive, though altered and tamed. There is no anti-New Deal rant, no cannon-ball caddies, and a confused Lord Droopy, played by Lionel Pape, whom Fields adopts as a crony ('Meet me down at the bar, we'll drink breakfast together'). A particularly bilious moment is added to the golf scene, when Fields picks up a frog from the hole, and comments: 'That reminds me, I have to send the little lady her alimony.' Other lines are as lacklustre: 'We're just passing the bar.' 'Keep right on going, we'll stop at the next one.' . . .

Fields and Mitchell Leisen did not get on at all. Leisen was a directing director, Fields could take no instruction. It was bad news. Fields became more irascible. His prop man remembers having to bring him his bottles of whiskey on the set, a breach of all rules. A little newsreel item shot on set, 'W. C. Fields acts again,' shows Fields, Leisen and Bill Le Baron joking together, though one can tell there's an edge. It then shows us a scene from the golf course, with the wind machine blowing sand around Bill's ankles. All seems, on the surface, hunky-dory.

But it was the end of the road. Fields was weary with Paramount, and Paramount were weary with him. In fact, he was not the only star whom Paramount was shaking loose. Mae West, who had practically saved the studio from bankruptcy with *She Done Him Wrong* and *Belle of the Nineties*, in 1933 and 1934, did not get on with Ernst Lubitsch, who had become production chief at the studio. She formed her own production company and started looking elsewhere for finance. Marlene Dietrich, too, had left Paramount, where she had made her greatest pictures, the latest being *Angel*, with Lubitsch. Lubitsch seemed to be causing a stampede at Paramount. Across Hollywood, a newly aggressive Universal Pictures was ready to gobble up these great exiles. Fields would have stayed with Paramount had they made him an offer for another picture. But they declined to do so. He cast about elsewhere. An old project, mentioned in his letter to Tom Geraghty of 1929, linking up with Harold Lloyd, was revived again. But this was just speculation. Harold Lloyd was not getting anywhere either. Laurel and Hardy had peaked, and were heading towards such turkeys as *The Flying Deuces*. Buster Keaton and Langdon had disappeared. The Marx Brothers had just made the dud *Room Service*. Abbott and Costello were about to be born. The Golden Age of Comedy seemed to be heading for a date with The Man in the Bright Nightgown.

Bill Fields was ill, insomniac, and tired to death of studio battles. And yet, he burned, as ever, with the old flame of certitude. The burning passion of the juggler. Keep those balls in the air! Practice, till your hands, your feet, your eyes and your soul bleed.

Amazingly – the best was yet to come.

Part VI
The Universal Twilight; or,
You Can't Cheat an Honest Man

Chapter 37
Why Is a Cat's Tale Like a Long Journey?

It is Christmas night. The wind outside is howling. The clown rests, hunched in his writing chair, pillows propping his aching back, his fingers on the old typewriter keys:

Dear John [Barrymore],

I have been having a few drinks and I thought I would drop you a note. About this time of year I usually take a moment to write a few letters to my good friends; the time when I remember all the good things and indulge myself to the extent of getting a little sentimental.

It is a blustery evening, but here in my Den it's coz-zy and confuable. I'm sitting before a nice open fire with my typewriter, John, sort of haff lissning to the radio and sllowly sipping a nice, very dry double martini . . . I just made up a big pitcher of Martinis . . . So now I'm all set and here goes. Besides Mratinis are great drink. For some reson they never seeme to effec me in the slightest. and drink thrm all day long. So here goes. The greateest think in tje whole wokld, John, is friendship. Anebelieve me pal you are the gertests pal anybody ever had. do you remember all the swell times we had together 'pal??/ The wondderful camping trisp. I'll never forget the time yoi put the dead skunnk in my sleeping bag. Ha ha Bow how we laughued didn we. Never did the skin kout ouut od it . . . But what the heck & after all you still my beset old pal john, and if a guy can't have a luaghg on good treu friedn onc in a whiel waht the heck. Dam pitcher is impty so i just went outand ma deanotherone and i sure wisch you wee here old pal to hel me drink these marotomi . . . jjhon Barrymroe best pal i goo Off course why a pal would do a dirty thinb liek puting a skunnk in nother pals sleping bagg I&m dash if I kno. That was a lousi thing for anybodyhdy todo an only a frist clas heel would di it . . . And if you thininkit funny your a dirty lous anasd far as Im concrened you can go plum to helll and stya ther you dirty lous. To hel with ouy.

Yours very truly, Bill Fields

Scripts, essays, treatments . . . Painfully, the comedian drags himself down, or rather, gets his chauffeur and bodyguards to drag him down, to the studio, to proceed with his latest picture, *You Can't Cheat an Honest Man*, while behind the scenes, the studio executives are already tearing out their hair.

Universal Pictures.

Production Notes: Weekly Status Reports of Pictures in Production: November 25 1938:

#932 Marshall (AA-2)

To: Mr Cliff Work   From: M. F. Murphy. (Martin F. Murphy)

Mr Matthew Fox   (Studio & Production Manager)

Mr Milton Feld

Mr H. S. Brewster

This production started Monday, November 21st, also operating without script.* Progress has been exceedingly slow and we have no way of determining just when shooting may be completed and how much this production is likely to cost.

Up to and including Friday night, November 25th, the company has completed: 6 1/2 pages. 6 Mins. 15 secs. of dialogue.

Dec 10: This picture finishes the 17th shooting day tonight and progress has been exceptionally slow. Due to lack of script we are not in a position to prepare schedule or budget or in any way forecast a probable finishing date or final cost.

Up to Friday Dec 9th – 26 1/4 pages shot, 24 Mins. 50 Secs. of dialogue.

Dec 17: After a very lengthy session with George Marshall and Lester Cowan, which continued until late last night, we finally obtained a form of script which both these gentlemen agreed would be adhered to after a fashion. This is considerable encouragement to us because it at least gives us some idea of where this show is going and what they are likely to require . . . We feel pretty definitely certain, after our conversation with Marshall, that we will be grossly misleading ourselves to expect this picture finished before January 28th. Progress during the past week has been very poor, the

---

* The other film operating without a script at the same time on the Universal lot was *Son of Frankenstein*, where time was being taken off for the birth of Boris Karloff's first born!

company averaging about one page per day . . .

On 31 December:

Progress on this picture continues to be very disappointing and the entire setup far from a commercial proposition. The constant change of routines and lack of a real, definite continuity makes it impossible for us to intelligently lay out any schedule or figure what the probable final cost might be. We do feel if the show winds up by January 28th, the probable final cost will be around about $700,000 . . .

Jan 7, 1939:

We believe the action taken during the past week in acquiring the services of Edward Sedgwick as an additional director will tend to show a marked improvement on this situation. Starting today we are operating with two separate units – Marshall working on scenes with Bergen and Sedgwick devoting his time to sequences with W. C. Fields. While we are striving to have all shooting completed by January 21st, we feel it will take until Janury 28th to wind up the show. Lack of script and the temperaments of various elements involved in the set-up makes it very difficult to arrive at a definite estimate on the picture.

Jan 14th:

We have just passed through a most eventful week on this production – Sedgwick finishing up as director on the Fields unit on Monday night and Eddie Cline replacing him Tuesday morning. Since then the Fields unit has shown a very definite improvement on both quantity and quality of work. The Marshall unit met with a setback through the illness of Bergen and have spent the last two days making production shots without principals, such as the circus wagon train en route over country roads and long shots of circus tents and midway, etc. Arrangements have been made whereby salary will be deducted for Bergen on all days he has been unable to appear. We are still very much in haze with reference to the remaining scenes of this picture . . .

January 21:

Cline is being closed today and the unit operating on the sequences with W. C. Fields was disbanded last night. After the meeting with Marshall, who will handle the show from now until the finish, we mapped out a tentative schedule whereby it looks possible to wind up all the remaining scenes with Bergen by Saturday, Jan 28th . . .

Indeed, the studio was able to wrap the production on 28 January with a total of fifty-seven shooting days, having shot 1 hour, 48 minutes, 45 seconds of dialogue, 174,450 feet of negative exposed. The production ran $5,000 over budget, a sum which included $1,700 the irate studio execs were unable to deduct from Edgar Bergen's salary for his two days off sick. But due to credit received on cast insurance, this shortfall was made up.

From Mr W. C. Fields,

to Mr Cliff Work, Universal Pictures Corporation –

I am advised that recently, and at a time when I was available, you employed a double for me in certain important scenes in a picture 'You Can't Cheat an Honest Man.'

The use of a double for an acknowledged star has by custom and practice in the motion picture industry been limited to instances in which it is desirable to protect the actor from danger, or where the actor is unable to perform the required services . . . None of these conditions existed . . .

My only wish is to make this picture one that will stand out and without a story it is meaningless. My character is shot. The picture now is a jumble of vaudeville skits – Bergen and Fields in their vaudeville skits. The play which I had written in has been written out . . .

Cliff, it looks to me like sabotage. Someone with the reins in their hands, is ruining this fine picture . . . The humaness and the truth have been deleted . . .

'As my grandfather Litvok said, before they sprung the trap: You can't cheat an honest man. Never give a sucker an even break or smarten up a chump . . . Step this way, folks, the Big Show is about to begin . . .'

From the office of Joseph Breen, Motion Picture Producers and Distributors of America, 30 November 1938:

. . . Care must be taken with the costume of Princess Baba, to avoid rejection. Her person should be fully covered, and her appearance in no way offensive or suggestive. The entire upper portion of her body must be covered with opaque material. The use of breast plates, suggestively emphasizing the appearance of her breasts, is unacceptable . . .

Page 5: The business of Charlie (McCarthy) looking toward the breast plates, panting and breathing rapidly, must be dropped . . .

(Note: Breen is concerned about a lustful dummy . . . !)

Dec 20 –
Pages 33 et seq.: Whipsnade should not be shown bare to the waist.
There should be no offensive exposure of his person while taking a
shower. It should suffice to show his head and shoulders . . .

Once again, like Sisyphus, the long journey, rolling the stone up the
hill, only to have it rolled down again by studio writers, producers,
directors. Leaving, indeed, the consolation of friends . . .

The final years of W. C. Fields are a mixture of engaging triumphs
and besetting ills. The move to Universal did not immediately solve the
problems of the power struggle in the war of comedy ideas. Universal
had promised Bill his choice of scripts and more freedom to interpret
them on the set, but was reluctant to deliver on its pledges. His new
producer, Lester Cowan, unlike William Le Baron, was no easy touch
for the creative mind. And yet, Fields' four feature movies made at
Universal were to be his most successful and enduring, the titles most
familiar and most accessible to present-day fans: *You Can't Cheat an
Honest Man, My Little Chickadee* with Mae West, *The Bank Dick* and
Never Give a Sucker an Even Break.

Already in *You Can't Cheat an Honest Man* Fields amazes with his
vim and vigour, given what we know about the ill-health of the man.
He bounces forth, cluttering about in his ticket-booth, ringing his bell,
knocking his bowler hat over, putting his foot through the floor and
fleecing Grady Sutton, as 'Colonel Dalrymple's nephew Chester', of fifteen bucks a week for not even bothering to teach him about the circus. Again, Bill tried to insert into the film the story of Gorgeous, his
ex-wife and trapeze artiste, 'the lady with the most perfect figure on
earth and the two million dollar legs', who fell off the high wire and
died, leaving him with a son and a daughter. None of this flashback
story survives in the movie. The daughter, Vicky (played by Constance
Moore) decides to save her debt-ridden father's circus by marrying the
rich and snobbish Roger Bel-Goodie, sparking off the clash of
Whipsnade and Society reminiscent of the little barber Toerek in *Her
Majesty Love.* Featuring the Snake Story, told as Mrs Bel-Goodie faints
in the background, to be fussed over by the penguin-suited hoi-polloi,
who are dismissed by the muttering Whipsnade as 'Chinese people . . .'

WHIPSNADE: I had quite an experience up Lake Titicaca . . . I had a wonderful experience with a rattlesnake . . . This rattlesnake was imprisoned

425

under a rock . . . I took the rock and rolled it off the little feller's back . . .
To show his appreciation he followed me to the wickieup . . . I took my
socks off and put em over the snake . . . During the night a marauder
crawled through the window . . . The snake, in order to show its appreciation . . . sank its teeth into the marauder's fetlock . . . Then it stuck its tail
out the window and rattled for a Constable . . .

Four years later, a New Jersey hardware merchant, one Harry
Yadkoe, sued Fields in open court for plagiarism in re-using the Snake
Story in a radio show. Amazingly, Fields lost the case:

Hollywood (UP). W. C. Fields, who brought a keg to court for use in an
emergency, tapped its contents yesterday because a jury found him guilty of
plagiarism and awarded an amateur gag writer $8,000 . . . Fields ignored
Yadkoe's offer to shake hands. Instead, he hoisted the red rubber cask he
had brought with him. 'This is an emergency,' he muttered, and tapped the
cask, filtering an unidentified liquid through dry ice at the top . . .

Fields was continually being sued by women who claimed to be his
wives and to have borne him several children, a blessing he was continually having to keep at bay. In his own real-life family, however,
there had been a change, following his illness, and the correspondence
with Hattie becomes more and more polite, and then downright
friendly. Hattie writes, on 7 March 1939, to 'Claude Willie Dukenfield',
that she had seen his latest picture and 'it certainly was fine, congratulations. I want to see you, very very soon. Best luck, keep well, Hattie.'
In 1938, Claude Junior had married Anne Ruth Stevens, and this event
drew father and son back together.

Back in the privacy of his study, Bill continued his habit of clipping
out items from newspapers, some as sparks for comedy ideas, others
just stuff that took his fancy. An undated clipping: 'FATHER MEETS SOL-
DIER SON AFTER 27-YEAR WAIT,' with a picture showing 'Finally united
– Carl R. Rittenhouse as he greeted soldier son, Pvt. Ralph W.
Rittenhouse, at Pasadena Regional Hospital.' Other clippings were less
upbeat – from the *Los Angeles Herald and Examiner* (?) – 'MOTHER
ACCUSED – HURLS SON INTO SEA,' over which there is Fields' pencil
scrawl: 'mother is a boy's best friend'. Other cuttings, which he would
send to Gene Fowler, boosting his obsessions, would include '110
GLASSES WATER FATAL TO GIRL – NEWARK, NJ.– Twelve year old
Margaret Boylan died today a few hours after drinking 110 small
glasses of water in a drinking contest with her brother and sister. Dr

Harrison Martland, Essex County medical examiner, issued a tentative verdict of "death from internal drowning." Another note to Fowler enclosed a Ripley's Believe It Or Not type drawing of 'Baby Carl Yenson, Age 2, Smokes 10 Cigars a Day,' with his comment: 'Dear Nephew (his normal form of address to Fowler), Those kids of yours are just cissies.' Yet another postcard has a paste-up of a small cutting proclaiming 'I Licked My Constipation,' upon which Bill has added:

'Evidently a contortionist . . .'

BABY CARL YENSON
AGE 2
SMOKES 10 CIGARS A DAY
Oneonta, N.Y.

W. C. FIELDS

Dear Nephew
Those kids of
yours are just
sissies — love
Uncle

34 Baby Carl Yenson.

Chapter 38
Useless, Insignificant, Poetic . . .

It was in this period that the eccentric artist, John Decker, painted a portrait of W. C. Fields as Queen Victoria. In the world outside the Hollywood cocoon, World War II had broken out – on 1 September, Germany invaded Poland, and on 3 September, Great Britain declared war on Germany. But this was happening quite far from Los Angeles.

John Decker, none the less, had more cause than most of his friends to worry about events in Europe since, as he would later reveal to Gene Fowler, he was in origin a German national, whose real name, he claimed, was Leopold Wolfgang von Decken. Son of a German Baron and his San Franciscan bride, he had fallen foul of a mix up in the First World War involving a forger of Old Masters, from whom he had learnt his craft of copying, and who, as a sideline, sewed messages to Berlin in the double-canvases of his forgeries. As a result, Decker had spent the war in an English prison camp on the Isle of Man as a suspected spy, and his friends, after the war, had arranged his passage to America by means of a fake passport. Now he was living in a hillside studio in Hollywood earning his keep by painting stars like Clark Gable, Fanny Brice and Harpo Marx in the manner his disastrous mentor had taught him. (But without the secret messages.) The outbreak of war was to kindle his old fears of internment.

Neither Gene Fowler nor anyone else was able to verify this shaggy Hun story. But Decker's studio, which was soon moved to a new property in Bundy Drive, Brentwood, was to become the central hub for the coterie of dilapidated old masters such as Bill Fields, Gene Fowler and John Barrymore. The Queen Victoria portrait was requested by Gene Fowler, who hung it in his office, resisting Fields' poignant cry of 'Sabotage! Decker has kicked history in the groin!'

Fowler remembered the day he hung the portrait well, because it was also the day on which he adopted an even stranger new member of the Old Boys' convocation: the crazy Japanese-German Sadakichi Hartmann.

In 1954, Gene Fowler published his memoirs of this period, entitled *Minutes of the Last Meeting*. Fowler's book is by far the most distinctive account that has come down to us of the private side of W. C. Fields' last years. It is not a biography of Fields, since Fowler had ceded this task to Robert Lewis Taylor. Having already written his biography of Barrymore, *Goodnight, Sweet Prince*, Fowler decided to focus on the extraordinary Sadakichi as the hub of his tale of the Twilight of these Hollywood Gods.

Sadakichi, in fact, was probably known to both Fields and Barrymore from their drinking days in the Lambs Club. Sadakichi Hartmann was the son of a German father and Japanese mother, born in Nagasaki in 1867. His father took him to Germany to be educated and from there he travelled to America in 1885, where he specialised in the history of art. He became a kind of unpaid secretary to Walt Whitman, who later cast him out for revealing his caustic views on fellow artists. Back in Europe, he became acquainted with Mallarmé and Verlaine. A grade-A leech, he set out on a life-long career as a celebrity groupie. Bill Fields said of him scathingly: 'He has been a peeping tom, a cap-and-bell interloper at all the art shrines.' But Barrymore adored him, as the ultimate offender against the pretensions of high society, and dubbed him 'the last of the Pharaohs, and nicely mummified at that'.

Sadakichi knew no boundaries. He was the ultimate egotist, who would yell, when told that a toilet was around the corridor: 'Bring it to me!' Or he would cry out: 'Other people talk and talk about dying. I'm doing it!' At the turn of the century, he had been the self-styled 'King of Greenwich Village', and had in fact published two volumes of an important *History of American Art*. He had pioneered the appreciation of early photographers, such as Stieglitz, Henry Havelock Pierce and Frank Scott Clark, as well as publishing a blasphemous book called *The Last Thirty Days of Christ*, in which Christ was enamoured of Mary Magdalene. He was well ahead of his time, but by the late 1920s he was already an established sponger. By the early 1940s, he was a physical wreck, staggering about with a homemade truss which supported a great scrotal hernia.

Sadakichi's perverse admirers called him The Gray Chrysanthemum. But Fields, who hated him, as he hated all pretension, called him

'Itchy-Britches', 'Hoochie-Koochie', 'Itchy-Scratchy' or 'Catch-a-Crotchie', and said he belonged in the pages of Steckel or Krafft-Ebbing.

When I first ran across the name of Sadakichi, I assumed he was a fictional construction invented by Gene Fowler to pep up his book, but the man was real enough. In 1939, he was living in an Indian reservation near Banning, and when war broke out with Japan and the order came to intern all Japanese domiciled in the United States, Fields' friends, Decker, Fowler and Barrymore, succeeded in shielding him from the authorities.

John Barrymore himself was leading no less strange an existence in this *Götterdämmerung* period. Having been the great heart-throb of female America in his halcyon days, the booze had thickened and coarsened his famous profile and utterly scrambled his memory. In his last films he had to read his lines from huge idiot cards held over the camera, although, Fowler claims, he could still recite *Macbeth* word for word. He told Fowler: 'I remember Shakespeare's words because he was a great writer. I can't remember Hollywood lines; just as I may well recall a wonderful meal at Delmonico's many years ago, but not the contents of the garbage pail last Tuesday at Joe's Fountain Grill.'

In their convocations, the Twilight Knights indulged in crazy behaviour, Shakespearian charades and drunken ribaldry – Barrymore suggested Fields as Lady Macbeth. At the gate to his house Decker had hung the motto of these dissolute companions: 'USELESS, INSIGNIFICANT, POETIC.'

Gene Fowler wrote about his friends:

As I looked on, it became clear to me, if not to the men themselves, that they were severally enacting the final scenes of a tragedy – no matter the comic masks they wore. Each in his own fashion had lived too much in conflict with his God-given talents, as well as against the world of thou-shalt-not; and so they now must walk in the long shadow; but never for outsiders to see them except in their cap and bells. They were their own executioners.

The whole point about this group was its almost monastic maleness, despite Decker's risqué art which was hung all over his walls (and certain samples of which would create a strange connection between W. C. Fields and J. Edgar Hoover of the FBI, as we shall see ...). As Will Fowler tells it, this was a sanctuary where the men could get away from women. The only woman present, according to Will, was Decker's wife, Phyllis, who was so silent that Will called her 'an ambulatory case of sleepy sickness'. Members of this group were adopted neither by rank nor status, but only by general acclaim. They would include, over the years, actors Thomas Mitchell, Roland Young ('Uriah Heep'), Alan Mowbray, Norman Kerry, John Carradine and a few younger initiates – Anthony Quinn, Vincent Price, Errol Flynn and of course Will Fowler himself. Errol Flynn, in his often fanciful and self-serving autobiography, *My Wicked Wicked Ways*, referred to the group as the 'Olympiads', and mentioned at least one other woman present.

W. C. Fields held forth about his vaudeville days. Since he and Jack Barrymore were pretty much contemporaries, Jack would interrupt with a story that hinged on one Fields might be telling. Fields was called Claude, for C. He had a gloriously tall and willowy secretary who hovered in the background, serving him, taking care of his needs, anticipating his requirements. He had a hobby of clipping newspapers, taking out bizarre items and sending them to his friends with his own comments, such as, *There, you see what a stupid world it is.*

Note, the presence – if the tale is true – of Magda 'Mickey Mouse' Michaels, not of the distinctly petite Carlotta.

Useless, insignificant, poetic . . . Nevertheless, 'Uncle Claude' was never one to waste too much of his time in frivolity. We have realized by now that his public clowning masked a man of the most serious purpose. Kept from his primary work, he had increased, since his illness, his output of letters to both friends and enemies, renewing old acquaintances and airing his multitudinous gripes. As a spin-off of his popular magazine articles, he was also compiling, in the Fall of 1939, a book, which was to be entitled *Fields for President*. A joke candidacy had already been proposed, back in 1936, according to the *New York World Telegram*, which spoke of:

. . . talk of a Presidential candidate to be selected from the entertainment world. W. C. Fields, the Major Hoople of Hollywood, is the unanimous selection. Originally sponsored by the West Side Riding and Asthma Club, Fields planned to make the race on the slogan of 'A chickadee in every pot.' Lately, though, he has been having twinges of doubt, together with even stronger twinges of neuralgia, neuritis, rheumatism and a sacroiliac ailment. He has packed all these with his golf clubs and notes on his next picture, and by the time you read this he will be touring the desert and all available hot springs . . .

Fields' book – his only published prose volume – was an avowed expression of his by now hallowed principle: never give a sucker an even break (a sentiment he attributed to the Tammany Hall scoundrel, Boss Tweed's lesser known brother – Harris Tweed). The book was to appear in time for the run-up to the 1940 election in which his *bête noir*, Franklin Delano Roosevelt, would-be-taxer of actors, was standing for an unprecedented third term. Fields proclaimed:

> I am truly a candidate with both my feet on the ground . . . And when, on next November fifth, I am elected chief executive of this fair land, amidst thunderous cheering and shouting and throwing of babies out the window, I shall, my fellow citizens, offer no such empty panaceas as a New Deal, or an Old Deal, or even a Re-Deal. No, my friends, the reliable old False Shuffle was good enough for my father and it's good enough for me.

The book was formed out of a number of pieces Bill had already written or was writing for the magazine *This Week*: 'How to Beat the Federal Income Tax', 'My Views on Marriage', 'How to Succeed in Business', 'My Rules of Etiquette', 'The Care of Babies' and so on. All resound with the inimitable Fields voice, particularly in his typically jaundiced views on women:

> *Never try to impress a woman!* Because if you do she'll expect you to keep up to the standard for the rest of your life. And the pace, my friends, is devastating . . .

The 'Fields Formula For Fretting Females', his daily schedule for the ideal wife, proposed '7:00 – 8:00: Arise quietly, shake down furnace, stoke it, prepare breakfast – eggs exactly four minutes, two lumps in the Java! 8:00 – 8:10: Awake husband *gently*, singing *sotto voce* . . . 9:00 – 10:00: Drive husband to station, do marketing for dinner, and be sure not to order anything husband might decide to have for lunch. 10:00 – 12:00: Mow lawn, wash clothes, iron husband's shirts, press his suits, paint screens, weed garden, swat flies . . .' And so on. At the end, after collecting husband from work and cooking meal – 'keep busy – keep smiling – for, as every man knows, the husband is tired'. (Fields' advice was, in fact, not far from the real-life homilies offered to women in such works as '101 Things For the Housewife To Do', familiar well into the late 1950s . . .)

Fields For President reverbrates with the comedian's own peculiar philosophy, and, while it is of course a joke book, this is no reason, as countless academics have discovered, not to make at least some effort to hang the jokes out to dry and peel off a few layers. As in his films, the Fields persona – the Eustace McGargle candidacy – is based upon a self-lampooning, without which the character would be insufferable. It is the self-awareness of McGargle/Whipsnade as huckster which makes our submission to his wiles a matter of our own gullibility, our desire to believe, despite all the evidence, that 'two will get you four, four will get you eight – a boy can play as well as a man'. It's the old army game, and the oldest army game of all is politics:

> The reason Columbus discovered America was that he wished to find India. Abraham Lincoln liberated the slaves because he wanted to make all men free and equal. My cousin Haverstraw married a tattooed lady for art's sake alone.

Unlike most political credos, Fields' is totally honest. While shamelessly re-inventing his past in the usual way: 'I was born in a humble log cabin a scant stone's throw from Grant's tomb, the second son of a lowly cord-wainer', he has always kept a 'memory-basket': 'each August 18th – in commemoration of the day I smoked my first marihuana cigarette – I run through this precious memory basket item by item'. No wonder *Fields For President* became a smash reprint in the early 1970s! Apart from dispensing good advice on employment – 'Never show up for an interview in bare feet' – and telling the story of Old Tom, the only common house fly to receive a degree from Harvard Medical School, Fields' political platform is refreshingly candid: 'Remember folks, cast a vote for Fields and watch for the silver lining. Cast several votes and watch for the police.'

The problem with Fields' book is that, funny as it is, it lacks resonance unless read aloud in that unequalled voice. For Bill Fields, every text was a means to an end: the Performance. Without the Performance, it is only a blueprint, a mere shadow, detached, like Peter Pan's, from its source. It is only ever a might-have-been . . .

But this was a sideshow, and Fields returned vigorously, despite his rebelling body, to the main course. After his initial débâcle with Universal, he pleaded for a second chance. But the studio felt the best way to tame Fields was to reduce their dependence on him, by proposing a unique collaboration – with an equally cantankerous, equally untameable female partner. With an almost sadistic eye to his intransigent spirit, they decided to twin Fields, the scourge of the female sex, with Mae West, the scourge of the male . . .

Chapter 39
'Could We Be Lonesome Together?'

The legend of the war between Mae West and W. C. Fields is probably the best known of Fieldsian tales. Ronald Fields has covered it copiously in his filmography and in *W. C. Fields by Himself*, in which he published most of the painful correspondence between Bill Fields and the studio. A summary will suffice: Universal Studios, having struck box-office gold with the cod-western *Destry Rides Again*, with James Stewart and Marlene Dietrich, thought, as studios always do, that a repeat with a different, similarly odd couple would continue their lucky run. Mae West had abandoned Paramount and was direly in need of a comeback film. Since the Hays Code had clipped her wings in 1933 after *She Done Him Wrong* and *I'm No Angel*, her subsequent films, *Belle of the Nineties* (1934), *Going to Town* (1935), *Klondike Annie* and *Go West Young Man* (1936), and *Every Day's a Holiday* (1937), were mere shadows of what might have been. By 1939 Mae was aged forty-seven, a sex-pot in manner more than substance. Her attitude to Fields was ambivalent. She clearly appreciated his technical comic skills, but her taste in men ran to athletic hunks rather than ageing roués, and she hated his drinking. Fields, on the other hand, recognized a rival, but also realized that he might have a formidable ally, a fellow artiste, to fight the studio bosses.

Each side wrote their own screenplay, and submitted it to the studio. Bill's proposal was another of his 'epitomes', *December and Mae*. This was a tale set in a rough saloon in a Colorado mining town, where Mae West, proprietress of the 'Elite Café', presents 'Variety and Specialty Acts' with her spouse of convenience, Fields. Bill suggested Gene Fowler to write the screenplay, and his repertory regulars Eddie 'Rochester' Anderson, Jan ('Here comes the Prince!') Duggan and Elise Cavanna as the supporting cast. A later version, *Honky Tonk* or *Husband in Name Only*, included yet another attempt by Bill to insert the tale of his dead trapeze artiste wife, Gorgeous. Other proposed

435

treatments were entitled *Her Man*, *The Little Lady*, or *First Lady of Lompoc*.

The studio responded by commissioning a screenplay from Grover Jones, which turned out to be a straightforward western, denounced by Fields as 'a cross between The Drunkard and Nick Carter'. He lampooned this version in a mock-treatment he entitled 'Corn With the Wind, a Cinema "Epic-Ac" of Long, Long Ago. Based on the novel idea that movie audiences have the minds of 12 year olds.' Adding: 'This is NOT a Motion Picture. "Read it and Weep."'* Lester Cowan, for Universal, responded aggressively that Fields' contract did not include 'story approval'. Cowan threatened to sue Fields for over $100,000 (his acting salary), if he did not knuckle under. Bill's response was: 'Just dropped into town for a snack at Chasen's . . . COME UP AND SUE ME SOMETIME.'

Bill appealed to Mae West to support him against the studio. He even agreed to support her own version against that of Cowan, Eddie Cline and Grover Jones. (Cline, the designated director, was now the third offender.) Mae claims that she then wrote the screenplay which was eventually filmed as *My Little Chickadee*. In fact, Bill continued to revise his own versions, until the studio was ready to capitulate. He clung stubbornly to his own dialogue, she clung to hers, and they collaborated in those scenes which they shared. To complicate matters still further, Lester Cowan has claimed, speaking to Mae West's biographers, that he was the screenplay's real author.

> I took the plot from Ferenc Molnar's 'The Guardsman' and made it into a Fields-West version. The masked bandit whose kiss is his signature is the key. Read Molnar's play . . . I swiped the idea and helped Grover Jones with the screenplay. In the script Jones turned out, there was a bird puppet that sat on Fields' shoulder and talked to him. Brilliant show-woman that she is, Mae immediately spotted this as an original scene stealing gimmick that would turn her into Fields' leading lady instead of his co-star.

Be that as it may, the film ground into production on 30 October 1939, astounding the wary production managers by progressing not far behind schedule, as their notes reveal:

> While progress on this show has not worked out strictly in accordance with our pre-arranged plans, we can at least feel somewhat content that it has

---

* Full version in Ronald Fields.

moved along for three weeks without major catastrophes, which might easily be expected on a set-up of this type.

In fact the film came in on 5 January 1940, after a fifty-six day shoot – fourteen days over schedule – but $5,000 under the original budget of $630,000. In the Hollywood factory method, the film was cut as shooting progressed, with a preview within three weeks of the end of filming, in this case a second preview already on 27 January, with the film's general release set for 9 February! Director and editor were totally separate functions, which explains John Ford's famous penchant for 'cutting in the camera', shooting in such a way that the film could only be cut the way he wanted.

But *My Little Chickadee* did not reach the screen without the intervention of another, concealed screenwriter: Joseph Breen, of the MPPDA censorship board. Already on 29 September 1939, while Fields was still arguing about the script with Lester Cowan and co-producer Cliff Work, Breen wrote to executive Maurice Pivar informing him that 'I regret to be compelled to advise you that, while the story is technically within the provisions of the Production Code, there are a number of details spread throughout the script which, quite definitely, are *not* acceptable.'

Breen directed Pivar's attention to the 'revealing white blouse' worn by Miss West in Scene 12, cautioning that it 'must *not* expose her breasts'. In the same scene, the quatrain, 'He who sins, and runs away, must die in sin, another day', was verbotten, as was 'the entire speech regarding the travelling salesman'. Scene 51: 'The acceptability of this scene with the dancing figures on rubber, will depend entirely on how it is shot.'

Scenes suggesting a sex affair between the girl and the Indian were quite beyond the pale. Mae matching the Indian music with 'graceful motion' should not imply suggestive movements. Any response of the watchers in this scene breaking out in sweat cannot be approved.

Scene 158, page 55: . . . Please note that the word, 'tramp,' when applied to a woman, is always deleted by the British Board of Film Censors in London . . . (also) the words 'punk' and 'lousy.' Scene 207: Please eliminate the business of the woman belching.

Any film involving Mae West was bound to attract the censor, but Breen was also put on notice by an anonymous letter which was sent him on September 8 from a 'listening post' in Hollywood:

Dear Mr Breen, (Personal)

You are the worthy clean-up man for our national screen. Here's what you want to know, in these days of smut and general filth. Eddie Cline, director, is right now engaged in connection with a so-called comedy production for Universal, starring Mae West and W. C. Fields. They have been instructed to 'make it plenty dirty' so that 'success' may be assured.

The writer happens to *definitely know* that one gag man and his wife (the latter connected with Paramount) are engaged solely in the writing of smut gags, in the hope that they can so treat it that the filth will only be 'smelled' by those patrons who enjoy and hunt it.

If some of the 'gags' I have unintentionally heard talked over are allowed to get by your cautious office, the picture will be a planned success for the sloppiest and nastiest batch of downright manure that this demoralised business has had to undergo . . . Cline is clever at hiding such covert filth.

Wish I could sign my name, but I have a job which supports the wife and kids, so I must as usual play dumb. Sorry, Joe.

In October, Breen was still valiantly fighting a revised script, from which he took exception to a number of Fields gags, in particular, the scene of Cuthbert J. Twillie 'getting into bed with the goat, fondling it, remarking about its smell, etc.' There must also be no exposure of Twillie in the bathtub. Director Eddie Cline made some revisions. Breen then found another bone of contention, the song sung by Mae in the film: 'Willie of the Valley'. He objected strenuously to the Coda: 'Willie was a good man / Too bad he had to go / I said he was a good man / and I ought to know . . .' This eventually was agreed as: 'Willie was a good man / The best man that I've found / I said he was a good man / He should have hung around . . .'

Breen was nothing if not tenacious. Having cleaned up the song, he moved on to 'the Samson and Delilah' scene, which must be omitted as 'an attempt to burlesque a Biblical reference'. Also, he told the studio to drop the line 'Snow White was all right but she drifted,' sighing: 'It is an old gag, and has always been cut out.'

When the film was done, with the usual evasions which at least preserved some of Bill's high jinks with the goat, Breen took exception to another line in his dialogue, prompting an irate personal letter from Fields:

Mr Joe Breen,
c/o the Hays Office,
5504 Hollywood Boulevard,
Hollywood, Calif.

Dear Joe Breen,

Thanks for your graciousness and kindly counsel to Charlie Beyer this afternoon concerning the line in 'My Little Chickadee': 'I know what I'll do, I'll go to India and become a missionary. I hear there's good money in it, too.'

I'm still prepared to sacrifice a valuable part of my anatomy to keep the line in but if the short-haired women and the long-haired men are back in the driver's seat again, I guess there's nothing to be done.

Will this also have to be deleted from the European version or does that not come under your jurisdiction? I've got to get a laugh out of this picture somewhere even if it's down in India.

My best wishes and sincere thanks,

Bill Fields

P.S. I'm going to have Dave Chasen throw an Indian tsetse fly in your soup the next time you dine there for this overt act.

B.F.

Breen sent Fields a soothing reply, telling him he didn't need the line, as he has seen the picture and enjoyed it. Conscientiously, he explained that the production Code forbade anything 'suggestive of an unfavorable, or derogatory, or comedy, reflection on the gentlemen of the cloth'. Breen concludes: 'Long life to you – and may your shadow never grow less.' Bill wrote back in similarly cordial vein that 'I shall henceforth hold my peace.' But Breen, like bullies everywhere, only took this as a sign of weakness, and was yet to return to the fray. At any rate, in British Columbia and Australia, the censor boards did delete the goat. In New York, they only deleted the 'pear shaped ideas' and the line: 'Go back to the reservation and milk your elk.'

The story that eventually emerged on the screen is, on analysis, much more Fields than West, but with Cowan-'Molnar' still framing it to no particular avail: Flower Belle Lee (Lita in the original script) is sent out of town after her liaison with the masked bandit – who has kidnapped her, but, like a good Breen boy, done nothing that would breach the MPPDA Code – and is en route by train to Greasewood City. On the way the train is stopped by an Indian on a horse trailing the slumbering Cuthbert J. Twillie ('Novelties and Notions') behind him. The Indian is George Moran, Bill's old vaudeville comrade of Moran and Mack, still desperately in need of a job. Well, he had played a black man for thirty years, and, we may recall, had already been an Indian in *The Fatal Glass of Beer*. On the train, introduced by Flower Belle's chaperon, Miss Gideon (Margaret Hamilton, who had just played the Wicked Witch of the West in *The Wizard of Oz*), Twillie offers his hand in matrimony to Flower Belle, who, mistaking his bag of fake money for the real thing, welcomes a sucker to stamp her as a respectable citizen of the Wild West.

'New squaw?' says Moran. 'New is right, she hasn't even been unwrapped.' In the town, Twillie fails to consummate his marriage, as Flower Belle is eager to renew her abduction with the masked bandit. Twillie retires to the bar and another variant of his poker act: 'I'll give you my personal i.o.u., a thing I seldom give to strangers.' Jeff Badger, the saloon owner, is sweet on Flower Belle, and offers to make Twillie sheriff, the town's shortest lasting job. Another sucker, Carter, the town's newspaper editor, gets Flower Belle to try her talents at teaching in the town's school. ('I am a good boy. I am a good girl. What is this, propaganda?') Back in the saloon, she sings Breen's version of 'Willie of the Valley'. At night, Twillie, once again trying to consummate, finds himself in bed with a goat, despite the MPPDA's objections: 'You better take your coat off, dear, you won't feel the good of it when you go out.' Discovering the substitution: 'Beelzebub! Shadrach Meshach and Abednego!' Having discovered that Flower Belle is meeting with the masked bandit (who has revealed himself as Jeff Badger), Twillie dresses up as him to try and steal a kiss. (His call: 'Chiquita!' prompted censor's gripes that his mis-pronunciation was an affront to the Mexican nation.) Caught by the townspeople, Twillie is arrested as the masked bandit, who has already robbed the local stagecoach. This prompts some of Fields' most famous lines: 'I was at a masquerade party impersonating a Ubangi!' And as the rope tightens round his neck:

TWILLIE: Hey, what's this thing doing? It's ruining my necktie! Who's going to pay for my laundry?

OUTRAGED CITIZEN: Have you anything to say?

TWILLIE: Yes, this is going to be a great lesson to me.

MISS GIDEON: You villain! I'd advise you to make your peace with the here-after!

TWILLIE: I'm not thinking of the hereafter, 'm thinking of the present!

MAN: Have you any last wish?

TWILLIE: Yes, I'd like to see Paris before I die! (*as the rope tugs*) Philadelphia will do! (*Raises hat as rope tugs further*) Vote for Cuthbert J. Twillie for Sheriff!

At this point Flower Belle shoots the rope off his neck and the masked bandit rides in, throwing down his stolen loot and escaping in the mêlée. Twillie is rehabilitated and, it turns out, his marriage to Flower Belle is nul because it was carried out by a gambler, Amos Budge, impersonating a minister of the cloth on the train. Twillie heads back east, to sell stock in 'hair-oil wells,' while Flower Belle heads upstairs, as they switch bylines:

FLOWER BELLE: What a man!

TWILLIE: If you get up around the Grampian Hills, you must come up and see me sometime!

FLOWER BELLE: Oh yah . . . I'll do that, my little chickadee . . .

The 'Grampian Hills' have a poignant significance in Fields' own private mythology. In *You Can't Cheat an Honest Man*, Whipsnade escapes from the snake-phobic Bel-Goodies with his son and daughter, urging them to 'Run for the Grampian Hills, children!' And when his daughter Vicky asks: 'Where are these Grampian Hills, Dad?' 'I wonder, I wonder . . .' Clearly on the other side of the delirium tremens rainbow . . .

My Little Chickadee is a cornucopia of Fields gags and one liners: 'Is this a game of chance?' 'Not the way I play it.' 'Is he a full-blooded Indian?' 'Quite the antithesis, he's very anemic.' 'Sleep, the most beautiful experience in life . . . except drink . . .' 'I understand you buried your wife recently.' 'I had to – she died.' As well as one of his great bar monologues, about the time he tended bar in the East Side of New York:

TWILLIE: A tough paloma comes in there by the name of Chicago Molly. I cautioned her: None of your pecadilloes in here . . . There was some hot lunch on the bar comprising succotash, asparagus with mayonnaise and Philadelphia cream cheese . . . She dips her mitt into this melange, I was yawning at the time, and she hits me right in the mug with it. Well, I jumps over the bar and I knocks her down . . .

SQUAWK MULLIGAN (*also tending bar*): You knocked her down? I was the one that knocked her down.

TWILLIE: Yes, that's right, you knocked her down, but I was the one who started kicking her . . . (*To customer*) Have you ever kicked a woman in the midriff who had a pair of corsets on?

CUSTOMER: No, I just can't recall any such incident at this time.

TWILLIE: Well, I almost broke my great toe. I never had such a painful experience.

CUSTOMER: Did she ever come back again?

SQUAWK MULLIGAN: I'll say she came back, she came back a week later and beat the both of us up.

TWILLIE: Yeah, but she had another woman with her, an elderly lady with grey hair . . .

Mae West's own scenes, in comparison, are lacklustre, and her affair with the masked bandit is pretty tame. The problem with twinning Fields and West was that, though both were mavericks, they cast their nets in different directions. Mae West always promised more than she would deliver, and Fields played a man who could no longer deliver anything, but swept through life as if he had it all. While women admired Mae West's self-sufficiency in a world of male power; men, particularly in the wake of the Depression, responded to the general air of male helplessness that Fields, in his Bisbee persona, generated. Cuthbert J. Twillie, on the other hand, was McGargle gone to seed, the old reprobate reduced back to carnival days – back to Bill Dailey and the 'old army game'. Novelties and Notions – as he answers Flower Belle's question: 'What kind of notions?' – 'You'd be surprised . . . Some are old, some are new . . .'

But in fact they were all old notions which had stood the test of time.

*

442

35 Bill and Mae bill and coo: 'What kind of notions?' 'Some are old, some are new . . .'

At the end of 1939 Fields had moved house for the last time, renting a bijou residence in the heart of Hollywood, at 2015 De Mille Drive, between Los Feliz and Franklin Avenue, just south of Griffith Park. This estate was described thus by the realtors when put on the market in 1985:

FORMER W. C. FIELDS ESTATE: This unique gated estate sits atop the hills of Hollywood. The French style residence features 5 bedrooms, 11 baths, formal dining room, library, maids apt., pool and spa. A glass elevator separates the main house from the recording studio, offices, full floor bar, tennis court and observation deck.

A well-known comedienne lives there now. It is a private Drive, locked off from the main roads by electronic gates and all the usual Keep Out Armed Response This Means You signs. The maid's apartment was the separate quarters which Carlotta Monti occupied, at times when she was not being fired.

Bill was not particularly happy to be living in a street named after

Cecil B. De Mille, who was in fact his neighbour, but he had long coveted the house. In the event, he managed to rent it for the ridiculous price of $250 a month. Later the landlord tried to increase the rent, offering to pay for much needed renovations. But Fields, according to Gene Fowler, refused, on the principle that 'All landlords should go to the electric chair . . . Not one cent for tribute,' Bill declared, 'let the joint fall apart.' Wrote Fowler: 'As a consequence of this deadlock the mansion took on the appearance of the House of Usher. Where the wallpaper had not fallen off, it hung like the tattered battle standards of Napoleonic campaigns. When the ground jiggled, as sometimes happens in California, plaster flecked the pool table in the drawing room . . .'

In the kitchen an electric refridgerator on wheels was attached to a long cord, so that ice could be available at short notice. One room doubled as a barber's emporium, with a barber's chair which Fields had long used to sleep in during his worst attacks of back pain. At one point Sadakichi Hartmann fell asleep in this hallowed seat while, as Fowler describes, Fields stood about looking like 'a Frans Hals burgomaster', in his white bathrobe, 'in one pocket of which he kept perhaps thirty keys on a chain, and in the other a fat roll of currency. Whenever he stirred he sounded like the Prisoner of Chillon.' Fields had locks on every chest and the doors of his storerooms, to guard against his servants stealing his booze. He also installed an intercom system, so that he could call the servants from any room in the house. Once, when railing against them to Fowler, he forgot to switch the system off, prompting a mass walkout. In his house, Bill complained, 'It's capital versus labor all the time.' Both Fowler and Carlotta confirm that Bill would often take catnaps in the garden, while one of the servants sprayed water from a hose onto the canvas shelter to simulate rain.

Upstairs, there was an exercise room, with equipment installed by his personal trainer, Bob Howard. There was a rowing machine and a stationery bicycle, which, Carlotta wrote, faced a bar 'well stocked with potables, and with the sight of the bottles as an incentive, Woody would pedal fast and furiously'. But he would catch up with the bottles in the end, and any benefits of all the drill were offset by the continued drinking.

Carlotta Monti told the story of another hired strong man, dubbed 'The Chimp', whom she said was hired as a butler. When 'The Chimp' installed a makeshift gym in the garage, Bill loosened one of his ropes, causing the muscle-bound flunkey to fall on his head, enabling Fields to fire him on the spot. Believe It Or Not. But Bill's staff quit as often as they were fired. On 20 April Bill wrote a peeved handwritten letter to Magda 'Mickey Mouse' Michael, who had given him notice over a pay dispute. He accused her of always striking when he was ill or downcast.

You struck once at Las Encinas when I was still very ill and now in the middle of writing what will probably be my last picture . . . Yes I told you I think you can write and should write. And I would be sorry when that time arrives because I would lose your valued services and enjoyable sallies. I know a lot of people who I think can write, it is a hard arduous work and requires concentration. Little time for games or vacations. If you decide to follow such a course and ever get stymied, and you think I can help you – call upon the old pautata.

The script Bill was referring to was to become *The Bank Dick*, though it, too, went through a few stages. For a while Bill toyed with a film based on the comic strip 'Little Lulu', with child star Gloria Jean, but this was to emerge in a different form in his next film but one. The other idea was yet another variant on the Bisbee/Bissonette/Ambrose Wolfinger character, which at one point Fields wanted to call 'The Great Man'. He continued working on this until July.

From his cavernous study, with its 'W. C. Fields Filing System' desk, he also continued to hurl letters forth to all and sundry. To Jack Warner, refusing to help fund his Community Chest; to his son, Claude Junior, ever more friendly; to Dave Chasen, complaining that his chef had served him beef stew instead of roast beef hash; complimenting the Manager of the Del Mar Turf Club; to Greg La Cava, discussing the War in Europe: 'I am ready to take up arms at a moment's notice. The legs we can take up later.' To George Moran, and Fanny Brice, and to Bill Dailey, his primal manager from Philadelphia days, who had written him from Canada – 'Remember how we talked over giving a benefit for W. C. Felton née Dukenfield in the saloon situated in Batley Hall? Bill, that was my first real money . . .' And to a Mrs Paul Tresk, in Flushing, Long Island: 'Do you recall the "Monte Carlo Girls" disintegrating in Kent, Ohio, Jim Fulton and Eva Swinburne running out on the show, salaries unpaid . . .' Bill never forgot his vaudeville days.

It was in this house that Fields' famous and probably apocryphal feuds were fought out, with child star Deanna Durbin, who lived down the street, and whom he was supposed to fear finding singing in his garden, and with Cecil B. De Mille, especially after America entered the war, and Cecil became the local air-raid warden. Again according to Carlotta, Bill confronts Cecil, sneaking across his lawn in his warden's helmet, with a shotgun, accusing him of being a lost German paratrooper: 'You speak English well for a Nazi!' 'I was born here!' 'Another Benedict Arnold,' cries Fields. 'I pay your salary,' ventures the peeved De Mille. 'Leave a check in the mailbox and beat a hasty retreat,' says 'Woody.' Believe It Or Not. (Of course, Bill was not working for De Mille's Paramount at that point, so another fine tale bites the dust.)

But in 1940 Fields was still busy with the main chance, with his next script, which he was determined to shoot his own way, and not knuckle under any more to the bosses. In July, the script of *The Bank Dick* was submitted to the studio and by the studio to the Breen office. It attracted the usual list of caveats. Scenes of a bank robbery were deemed too explicit and transgressing the code on portraying criminal acts.

> All the play between Egbert (Sousè) and the girl's legs is very questionable from the standpoint of political censorship . . . political censor boards will delete the shot showing the nude figure of the girl standing near the lake . . . the expression 'nuts to you' in Egbert's speech, to be deleted; ditto the bartender putting powder into a highball; the word 'stinko' should be changed; likewise the word 'hell'; likewise the reference to 'castor oil'; the names of 'Irving and Pincus Levine' should be changed to avoid identifying them with any particular race; and, most vitally – nix the reference to the 'Black Pussy Café'. It would, however, be acceptable to say 'Black Pussycat'.

Fields then entered into another correspondence with Breen, assuring him that no obnoxious vulgarity was intended, reminding him that the word 'hell' was used in *Gone With the Wind* and offering a 'hearty handclasp'. Breen must have written back in a friendly vein, because Bill's next letter is conciliatory, ending with 'love to you from Old man Fields, The Crab'. Meanwhile the studio was up to its old tricks and assigned a writer to tidy up the script, who, of course, rewrote it completely. Bill appealed to the President of Universal, Nate Blumberg, who intervened to stop his underlings' antics. *My Little Chickadee* had made the studio money. The penny had finally dropped, and the powers that be realized that it was best to allow Fields a free hand.

For the first time in his life, Fields had control of his destiny. He had a movie to juggle the way he chose to juggle it.

This time there were no fumbles, and no dropped balls.

Chapter 40
The Hearty Handclasp; or, Bisbee's Last Stand

I've changed everything – instead of an English drawing room dray-ma, I've made it a circus picture . . .

The Bank Dick

Bill Fields' last two starring features, *The Bank Dick* and *Never Give a Sucker an Even Break*, are perhaps best seen as two sequential parts of a single, final testament. *The Bank Dick*, with its many echoes of *Man on the Flying Trapeze*, *It's a Gift*, and *The Pharmacist*, wraps up all the Fields movies coming from the 'Pa Jones/Potter' stem. In fact, its references to the original *Comic Supplement* revue are in some ways stronger than the previous films. Egbert Sousè has two daughters, the older Myrtle and younger Elsie Mae Adele Brunch Sousè (Claude Dukenfield's sisters were Elsie May and Adel), while Pa Jones in McEvoy's *Comic Supplement* has two daughters, the older Myrtle and the younger Gertie, who, like her later counterpart, is apt to go in for acts of grievous bodily harm. In *The Comic Supplement* – 1925 – Myrtle greets her boyfriend, George:

MYRTLE (*to* GEORGE): My, he is all dressed up today.

GEORGE (*tugging at necktie and eager to make impression*): Oh, I don't know? Do you think so?

MYRTLE: Oh, you look swell, you look so manly!

In 1940, this has become more formal: 'Father, this is Og Oggilby.' 'Og Oggilby . . . sounds like a bubble in a bathtub . . . I'm mighty glad to have met yer . . .'

Oh, bring back the 1920s . . . But this is a harsher age. McEvoy's original comic-strip family has become a dark, grotesque spectre, Norman Rockwell out of Heironymous Bosch. The fussy Kathleen Howard has been replaced by Cora Witherspoon as the sloppy Agatha

Sousè, with Jessie Ralph as mother-in-law Mrs Hermisillo Brunch. Breakfast is the usual smouldering inferno, which Egbert Sousè adroitly avoids, only pausing to steal the child's *Detective Magazine* and exchanging a kick on the shin, slap on the head and ketchup bottle thrown unerringly on the Sousian sconce.

Pa Jones-Potter-Bisbee-Finch-Bissonette-Wolfinger is no longer employed. He has no grocery store, no twenty-five year sinecure in the ball-bearings company, no small-time business prospects. He just drinks and smokes in his room and hangs about in the Black Pussy Cat Café – it should have been the Black Pussy, but Joseph Breen insisted on the feline emphasis – with his cronies: the ubiquitous Bill Wolfe, silent and gaunt, propping up the bar, and, behind the counter, barman Shemp Howard, who was to replace his brother Moe as one of the Three Stooges, in 1947. The arrival of harassed film producer Mackley Q. Green sets him up in his short-lived career as film director, to replace the sozzled A. Pismo Clam.

The Sousès are Fields' most dysfunctional family. Where previously Kathleen Howard held the family together by matriarchal tyranny, this seedy lot are characterized by the distorted chords of 'No Place Like Home' which wails and wows on the sound track. Mrs Brunch complaining that 'the house just smells of liquor and smoke', and 'imagine a man who takes money out of a child's piggy bank and puts in i.o.u.s'. Even daughter Myrtle, schooled evidently in the Breen tradition, is going to starve herself to death because her Sunday school teacher, Mr Stackhouse, told her that he 'saw my father coming out of a saloon the other day, and that Dad was smoking a pipe!'

Set in Lompoc, a mythical Fields town which just happens to have the same name as Lompoc, a sleepy Californian town adjacent to the Vandenberg Air Force base, this all-purpose borough doubles as a movie location, in which Bill can lampoon all the slings and arrows of his own travails in the business. The drunk director, ill-matched stars, tall Francois and tiny Miss Plupp ('is she standing in a hole?'), irrelevant script and incompetent production, mirror all Bill Fields' movie sorrows. To cap it all, he is beaned on the nut by his own little daughter, and wanders off the set to follow his bartender back into the Black Pussy Cat Café.

The Bank Dick is Bill's most structured movie, although it, too, differs on screen from the script, which has been published. An entire opening scene on the river has been omitted – two boys and Fields sitting in a rowboat with a fishing rod, talking to a raven, Nicodemus, which is perched on the gunwhale. Egbert Sousè is introduced in this script as 'a scholar, gentleman and judge of good grape'.

EGBERT (*to the bird*): Life, my ebony friend, is a simple proposition. (*He scowls off at the interruption [by the boys]*) . . . Quiet, please, you'll scare the fish. (*Continuing to* NICODEMUS) As I said, life is . . .

NICODEMUS (*unexpectedly*): What fish, Egbert?

EGBERT: Ah, the realistic touch! You know there are no fish in this lake – and I know it. But fortunately the suckers aren't as wise as we are.

NICODEMUS: They never are.

We might remember Lester Cowan's words about writing a talking bird-puppet for Fields in 'his' version of *My Little Chickadee*. Might this have been, after all, a Fields idea in a script version which has not come to light? At any rate, here it is, promptly vanishing again onto the typing-room floor. The whole affair seems built up so that Nicodemus can call out, when Egbert takes a swig from his flask: 'Quoth the raven – nevermore!'

Having caught a sea-bass in this fishless lake, Egbert announces: 'I shall repair to the bosom of my family – a dismal place I admit – and with this tasty token . . . I shall clout the first member of the tribe who contends – as is usual upon my return – that I am a loafer, ne'er-do-well, and double gaited soldier of misfortune!'

There is a dissolve indicated from the fish in Egbert's hand to the fish bones picked clean on his breakfast table, proving that he is, despite it all, a provider. But here the movie as we know it begins. Throughout the unfilmed script there is a host more dialogue than finally turns up in the film, proof that Bill had long learned the virtues of economy when dealing with the screen and not the stage.

Another sequence which dropped out before the cameras rolled occurs in the Black Pussy Café, when the sight of a fly on the bar prompts a monologue on Old Tom, the fly who 'used to drive in the chariot races in the circus', and who featured in *Fields for President* as the recipient of a degree from Harvard Medical School. In this instance, Old Tom saved Sousè one day when he was arrested for stealing a watch in Hoosic Falls, 'dragged off to the local bastille and held in durance vile', but 'Old Tom, the fly, stuck his hind leg into the Governor's inkwell, dragged it above the dotted line, forging the

Governor's signature. The Governor's secretary, unaware of the hoax, inadvertantly picked up the document, gave it to a messenger and sent it to the warden who released me with profuse apologies. I love that fly.'

He sure did, because he tried to insert the story again into the next film, *Never Give a Sucker*, as censor files reveal. In fact, Bill's modus operandi, as far as shooting *The Bank Dick* was concerned, was clearly to make up his lines day by day, holding his cards very close to his chest in his poker game with the studio, and springing them on his unwitting fellow actors on the set, as Reed Hadley, playing François, revealed in a later interview, quoted by Ronald Fields:

> Working with Bill . . . each take was different. Here I was, having studied the script, expecting a specific cue from Mr. Fields. But he would usually say something quite different, and the first few times actors would be a little startled. But whatever he said, Bill would usually express the general idea of what was actually written in the script . . .

Looking at the published script, and at the film, it becomes clear how fine Bill's instincts were on the set. While the script contains many funny sequences, as outlined above, it is unwieldy, and lacks a proper pace. But the life-long juggler understood the rhythm and flow of a gag, a line, a gesture, a bit of comic business. For the first time one does not get a sense of comic episodes strung together for the sake of convenience, but a coherent whole, knit together and flowing from point to point with the inexorable logic, not of real life, but of Egbert Sousay.

A reprise of the robbery sequence from *The Barber Shop*, which occurred offstage in the Drug Store scene of *The Comic Supplement*, moves the plot further along. Repulsive Rogan (aka 'Filthy McNasty', banned by Breen) and Loudmouth McNasty, played by George Moran (the original character names were erroneously placed in the credits), rob the State Bank of Lompoc and get into a fight behind a bench towards which Egbert is heading to pursue his morning read of the 'Lompoc Picayune Intelligencer'. (Alas, this fine journal has never been produced in Lompoc, but is now the title of the official newsletter of the W. C. Fields Fan Club.) As Og Oggilby alerts the police to the chase, Egbert is knocked over onto the fallen bankrobber and, in a twist on *The Barber Shop*, is hailed as a hero.

The stage is set for Egbert to be offered the job of Bank Dick by Mr Skinner, Bank President, in a scene which offers us the 'hearty hand-clasp' first aired in *Million Dollar Legs*. The merest touch of the fingers on an outstretched palm, it is the token of so much false promise by the rich and powerful to the ordinary man in the street. Accompanied by the gift of a calendar of 'Lompoc in spring' – 'doesn't look unlike the Mona Lisa', comments Sousè – the main plot of the movie can now unfold.

Of all W. C. Fields' films, *The Bank Dick* has the greatest density of Fieldsian lines and dialogue, so that a mere summary can do it little justice. Eddie Cline, the director, allowed Bill to do his own thing and placed the camera where it would be to his best advantage. The story continues to purloin bits and pieces from past Fields films: the salesman unloading what he thinks are worthless stocks derived first from *The Potters* and then reprised, with Fields as the con man, in *Fools for Luck*. Here the grifter is J. Frothingham Waterbury, unrolling his long spiel about his five thousand shares in the Beefsteak Mines in Leapfrog, Nevada:

> These shares sell for ten cents. It's simple arithmetic – if five'll get you ten, ten will get you twenty. Sixteen cylinder cars – big home in the city – balconies upstairs and down – home in the country – big trees, private golf course – streams running through the rear of the estate . . . I'd rather part with my dear grandmother's paisley shawl or her wedding ring than part with these bonds . . .

It's the old army game once again! But when Fields comes to relate the patter to poor Og, to suggest that he 'borrows' a little money from the bank against his coming bonus to buy the shares, he gives us the Fields Rendition of that land that lies beyond those mysterious Grampian Hills:

> SOUSÈ (*to* OG): Beautiful home in the country, upstairs and down. Beer flowing through the estate over your grandmother's Paisley shawl . . . Fishing, in the stream that runs under the arboreal dell . . . A man comes up, from the bar, dumps three thousand five hundred dollars in your lap for every nickel invested, says to you, 'sign here, on the dotted line,' and then disappears, in the waving fields of alfalfa . . .

The importance of this grifter's spiel is underlined by the fact that it follows, word for word, the script version, and is clearly a hallowed piece of business. Of course, the consequence of Og's 'borrowing' the money is the appearance of nemesis in the shape of the Bank Examiner, J. Pinkerton Snoopington, alias Franklin Pangborn, in perhaps the best of his many fusspot roles. With his multiple eyeglasses, forestalling their grinding underfoot by clients with something to hide, Pangborn is the ultimate face of stringent authority and, naturally, the most attractive sucker to be denied an even break. Slipped a Michael Finn in the Black Pussy (Cat) Café, he is stalled in bed for a while, but returns to his duties despite being warned by Sousè about 'malta fever, beri beri and that dreaded of all diseases – Mogo on the gogogo'. In the event, Og Oggilby is only saved by the revelation that the Beefsteak Mines are not worthless, but 'a bonanza' after all.

36 'J. Pinkerton Snoopington, bank examiner?' (with Franklin Pangborn).

In a dynamic coda, a clear tribute to the old Sennett days, Repulsive Rogan returns to try and rob the bank again and escapes in a car with Egbert driving. In the published script this leads to a scene by Lake Talahasee where Egbert and the raven Nicodemus meet up again, but in the movie it is just a hair-raising, back-projection chase up the grittier roads of Griffith Park and other environs, with cops and others in pursuit, bits of the car falling off one by one, windshield, handbrake and steering wheel coming loose amid a plethora of laconic Fields comments: 'Lot of traffic around here for a country road, don't you think?' 'Lake Shosho Cocomo is right over the top of this mountain.' 'The resale price of this car is gonna be nil after all this,' and, as the car comes to a jarring stop at the Lake edge: 'Have to take the boat from here on anyway.'

Sousè is a hero again, recipient of another 'hearty handclasp', and Mackley Q. Green turns up with a cheque for ten thousand dollars for a story Egbert told him while making the earlier picture, which the studio bosses are crazy about. Finally Egbert trips down past the breakfast table of his newly acquired mansion, fawned over by loving wife and mother-in-law, in a reprise of the ending of *It's a Gift*: 'Judkins, has Mr Sousè had his Café rhum a-la-baba?' But, as he strolls off through his garden, he spots the bartender going by, and rushes out after him, towards greener pastures . . .

The Bank Dick, released on 29 November 1940, got Bill his best reviews, though critics still carped about the 'poor story and thin situations'. Today we find both story and situations perfect for the surreality of the character which Fields had built. And it is a creation, this Sousay, made out of the building blocks of so many previous characters, Potter, Bisbee, Bissonay, Finch and Wolfinger, not forgetting a soupcon of Mr Snavely, the Arctic prospector of *The Fatal Glass of Beer* – although the Californian weather does not force him to play with his mittens on. Cutting loose from the social-reality of J. P. McEvoy, and the realistic settings that William Le Baron urged upon him, Bill was free to let his fancy drift along in the arboreal dells of his mind, flowing over his grandmother's Paisley shawl, and running off in the waving fields of alfalfa.

It is salutory at this point to look at Fields the writer, free, by hook or by crook, of the leaden hand of studio hacks. We have always seen that Fields was master of his own lines, but here for the first time we can judge the lines and nuances that he has created for the other characters: the finely judged pernickety J. Pinkerton Snoopington, or the awkward innocence of Og Oggilby, the perfect foil for Sousè's scams. The women, too, are drawn with vivid strokes, perfect creatures out of Thurber cartoons. Despite the archetype, there is always a logic given to a Fields wife or mother-in-law, within her own stubborn terms. She dreams, like Mrs Bissonette, of a better world, or is resigned, like Agatha née Brunch, to having sacrificed her life for a Sousè. But the battle lines are drawn between equals – they always give as good as they get. Like Margaret Dumont with the Brothers Marx, they achieve the greatness of their grotesque single mindedness; in Dumont's case, her patrician innocence, in the Fields women – their imperious intensity, their defiant loyalty against all the odds.

Fields himself is a self-contained vaudeville character, with his own set of responses to the hostile world, his own peculiar mask. No wonder, then, that in his next film he dropped the multiple faces he adopted till now, and became who he was, his own fictional self in its own right – a fully fledged imaginary character, called, what else? – W. C. Fields.

In the second scene of Fields' last starring picture, he is revealed staring at a vast billboard advertising W. C. FIELDS IN THE BANK DICK. Two small boys, Butch and Buddy, pass by, one saying to the other: 'Was that a bupkie!' Fields does an angry double-take: 'You're about to fall heir to a kitten's stocking!' 'What's a kitten's stocking?' 'A sock on the puss!' 'Another bupkie!' says the kid, as both brats make their escape.

Bill prepared what turned out to be his last artistic testament between December 1940 and April 1941. Once again, he entitled it 'The Great Man'. Once again, he inserted his own film-making traumas, only this time they took centre stage. The framework was simple: W. C. Fields, an ageing comedian, is trying to sell his script to Franklin Pangborn, producer for Esoteric Studios. In Pangborn's office, the producer insists on reading the script for himself, and most of the remainder of the film is the madcap story that Fields is trying to sell. The script included a part for Gloria Jean, a teenage singing star who seemed to strike Bill as his ultimate doting fantasy daughter. It was also to include, once again, an attempt to sneak in the story of Gorgeous, the beautiful trapeze artiste – in this case the daughter of his long dead brother, Tom, who left Gorgeous and Gloria Jean in his care. This part was, once again, dropped in the movie and mutated into a short opening scene in which Gorgeous and her daughter Gloria Jean throw a horseshoe at a pile of bottles. Then Gorgeous disappears from the story. But in the original script, Gorgeous lies stricken in her bed while the cries of the circus resound outside: 'Get your hot dogs! Jumbo brand peanuts! Pretzels! Candy! Hot gubers!' Fields snaps at a clown: 'Shut him up!' Then enters the tent where Gorgeous is dying:

FIELDS: Would you like a glass of water, dear? . . .

GORGEOUS (*smiling*): Thank you, Bill . . .

FIELDS: You know now you've positively got to quit this circus business . . . You know I wanted you to quit the circus even before Tom died. And Tom wanted you to quit too.

GORGEOUS: I know he did, Bill, but you know how difficult it is to quit the circus after the sawdust once gets into your blood . . . (*Withdraw camera to include* FIELDS *seated by the bed. He puts his hand on hers and pats it gently . . .*)

GORGEOUS: If anything happens to me, I know you'll see that Gloria Jean won't get the worst of it.

FIELDS: Before my brother Tom died, you know I assured him that I would take care of you and Gloria Jean as though you were my own kids. I even wanted to adopt you both. (*Withdraw camera to include* GORGEOUS. *She smiles gratefully.*)

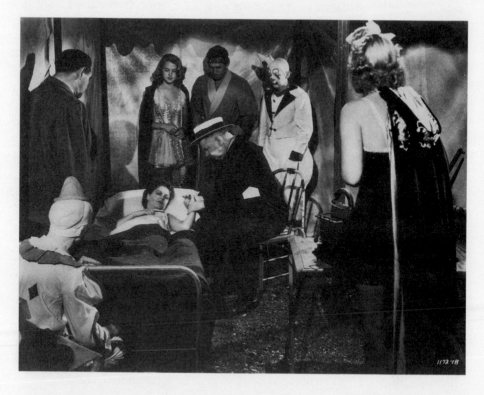

37 *Never Give a Sucker an Even Break*: Fields with the dying trapeze artiste, Gorgeous, in a scene cut from the film.

FIELDS: You know that I have never married and it would give me something serious to think about to take care of you two children.

GORGEOUS *looks understandingly at him, and half closes her eyes, a grateful smile on her lips.*

FIELDS: I'll be right outside here, if you need me . . .

Outside the tent, Fields tells his friend, Schlepperman, aka his old friend Leon Errol –

FIELDS: You know, if anything happens to Gorgeous, I'm going to fold this tent like the Arab, go to Mexico and sell some wooden nutmegs to a colony of Russians who established themselves there many years ago and have never changed their costumes or customs since. They love grated nutmegs on their caviar.

SCHLEPPERMAN: In Riga, we never thought of the idea, but it sounds good.

But a woman performer calls them back to the tent. It is clear that Gorgeous has died.

In this unfilmed version, Gloria Jean was the sister, not the daughter of Gorgeous. But maybe Fields wanted to preserve at least a glimpse, an unsung hint, of his long-cherished fantasy. Another long scene, in Pangborn's office, was pruned for the released movie. In the film, Bill walks into the office just as the producer's secretary is on the phone. She is speaking to someone else, but Fields thinks she's speaking to him, as she scolds:

SECRETARY: You big hoddy-doddy! You smoke cigars all day and drink whiskey half the night! Someday you'll drown in a vat of whiskey.

FIELDS (*to himself*): Drown in a vat of whiskey . . . death where is thy sting . . .

The hidden irony is that the secretary is played by Carlotta Monti, her second and last appearance in a Fields movie, relishing her obviously heartfelt lines. She has fleshed out a bit since 1935, and is no longer the very trim 'Chinese peoples' of yesteryear, but she is clearly still on the scene. She finishes her tirade with 'Goodbye!' prompting Fields to begin walking out the office, mumbling: 'Shortest interview on record.' But she sees him now and ushers him into Pangborn's inner sanctum. An unfilmed scene follows in which Fields and Pangborn exchange repartee about Fields' new script:

PANGBORN: What's the title of the picture?

FIELDS: The Noble Red Skin Bites the Dust.

PANGBORN (*turns to secretary*): Wasn't there a picture out about fifty years ago by that title? . . . Look up that title and see if it's still in the public domain. Or wait a minute — we'd better call Putshwantz over at Demopublic Studios and see if they haven't a first call on that title. (*He turns to* FIELDS) These things are very important.

FIELDS: Well, use any title. I don't care what title you use. Instead of using 'The Noble Red Man Bites The Dust' make it – 'Dust Bites Indian.'

PANGBORN (*thinking it over*): Don't you think that's too close to 'Gone With The Wind?'

FIELDS: What's the similarity?

PANGBORN: Well, the wind blows up the dust and it bites the Red Man in the face. There's an element of wind in it and we've got to keep as far from well-known titles as possible. (*To secretary*) Contact the legal department and see if we can use that title.

SECRETARY: Yes, sir. (*Exits.*)

PANGBORN *gets to his feet, picks up the putter, and, during the following dialogue, he unsuccessfully tries to knock several balls into the putting tin, which* FIELDS *watches in an interested manner.*

PANGBORN: We'll have to submit those titles to the sales department. They can only sell certain titles, no matter how good or bad the picture is. We had a sales manager here the other day and we had a fine story all written – was called 'Fun at the Equator.' The sales manager said he couldn't sell the title, but he could sell 'Perry's Last Voyage to the North Pole' – and we had to rewrite the first and last sequence, change the names of the characters, and buy three thousand dollars worth of gum drops and feed the company. They all played Esquimos. The leading man got sick at his stomach and sued the company. That's why we've got to be careful . . .

Pangborn's wife, an actress, comes in, and dialogue ensues about her playing in the picture with a beard – some of which is in the final film. ('You then go to the local barber shop, get shaved, and play the rest of the picture with an absolutely clean face.') This is interrupted in the movie by the charlady, Mrs Pastrome, taking a call from her husband about the evening's ravioli dinner, on Pangborn's phone. In the original script, Fields continues to try and pitch his story:

FIELDS: There's this Irish character –

PANGBORN (*interrupting*): I'm Irish. The Irish are a very sensitive people and no matter what kind of character he is, good or bad, there's always the possibility of an objection arising.

FIELDS (*inquiringly*): What about a Chinaman?

PANGBORN: With China at war, the Burma Road closed tighter than Dick's hat band, I think you're skating on pretty thin ice.

They then all take time off to listen to the two o'clock races on the radio, Fields murmuring: 'I owned a horse one time – a race horse. He only had three legs, but he could run all these beetles this guy's mentioned over the fence.' As they turn the radio off, a cameraman enters, speaking rapidly:

CAMERAMAN: Pardon this intrusion, but I just want to tell you that if Miss Wilde is in this picture that lets me out as cameraman. I couldn't light up her left profile in the last picture and I'm not going to try to do it in this one. I got a reputation to uphold. I won the Academy Award in 1921.

All this delicious spoofing of the madness of the motion-picture business is absent in the final movie, *Never Give a Sucker an Even Break* – a studio title which Fields claimed the marquee signs would cut down to 'W. C. Fields – Sucker.' His contemptuous ending to the sequence is also absent, a glance at the clock: 'Is that the right time?' 'Of course,' says Pangborn. 'Excuse me,' says Fields, 'I promised to lend a fellow a hundred dollars and I don't want to keep him waiting.' Exit.

This version of the script was credited to 'John T. Neville and Prescott Chaplin, Based on an original story by Otis Criblecoblis', Fields final and most obtuse pen-name. The original screenplay was basically Fields' own dialogue with the two writers simply organising the text to his instructions. But when it was submitted for approval to the MPPDA censor board it attracted Joseph Breen's longest and most spectacular tirade. A six-page letter, addressed by Breen to Universal executive Maurice Pivar, this reveals Breen to be – unwittingly – one of the greatest humorists of the American prose tradition, an equal of Fields himself and even Mark Twain. Breen wrote:

Dear Mr Pivar,

We have read the script, dated April 15, 1941, for your proposed picture titled THE GREAT MAN, and regret to report that, in its present form, this script is not acceptable from the point of view of the production Code.

Breen averred that the script was filed with 'vulgar and suggestive scenes and dialogue', innumerable jocular references to drinking and liquor; sixty scenes laid in a cocktail lounge, in addition to numerous other scenes set in bars and saloons, all of which would have to be deleted or changed. Breen then got down to detail, beginning with familiar objections to scenes in which 'Fields is shown looking at girls' legs or breasts and reacting thereto', the business of Gloria Jean hitting Fields on the head with a brick, which was 'the sort of scene which will undoubtedly give offence to parents and organisations dealing with child training generally', and the various scenes dealing with drunkenness and drinking. Concerning the scenes with Pangborn, Breen was concerned that,

> If Pangborn plays his role in any way suggestive of a 'pansy', we cannot approve any scenes in which this flavor is present . . . It will be acceptable to play the Pangborn character as a definite fuss-budget type, if offending dialogue and action now present in this script are omitted . . . In Pangborn's dialogue, the name 'Fuchschwantz', because of its sound . . . should be deleted or changed. The line 'tighter than Dick's hat band' is questionable. A child's line: 'Ma-ma – I gotta go home,' is unacceptable [!].

As Breen proceeds, we become aware of an interesting, if unsurprising, phenomenon, of the censor gradually losing his mind, as he progresses to more and more paranoid heights of delusion in his search for transgressions:

> Scene 168: In Fields' speech, the word 'physiology' should be deleted or changed.

> Scenes 195 – et seq.: At all times, Ouliotta Delight must be costumed adequately, so that there is no unacceptable exposure of her person. Any suggestion at any time that she is preparing to take a nude sun bath, or is in the nude, will not be approved in the final picture. This same caution as to costuming applies as to her mother, in scene 211, and as to all women shown at any time in the picture.

Scene 232: Mrs Haemoglobin's reference to 'playing' is unacceptable, and should be changed.

Page 76: Ivan's exclamation 'Utsna!' is unacceptable, and must be deleted or changed.

Scene 276: The Indian's remark, 'My name – <u>Falling Water</u> O'Toole,' is unacceptable as to the underlined words, which must be deleted or changed.

Scenes 279 and 280: The four uses of the word 'buzzards' may be deleted by some foreign political censor boards. Note, also, page 110.

Scenes 281, et seq.: Any and all dialogue and showing of bananas and pineapples is unacceptable, by reason of the fact that all this business and dialogue is a play upon an obscene story.

Scene 302 – et seq.: All of this business dealing with the 'chamber pot' gag is completely unacceptable, and must be omitted.

Scene 366: The business of the man taking out his false teeth strikes us as a piece of business which will give offense to mixed audiences.

Scene 367 (cont'd), page 121: Fields' remark, 'did you ever gondola . . .' and Mrs Hemagloben's (sic) answer are unacceptably suggestive, and should be rewritten.

Scenes 411 – et seq.: You will have in mind that we cannot approve scenes of comedy in connection with marriage ceremonies. It is permissible to have some comedy *before* a marriage ceremony begins, but once begun the ceremony must be played straight. This applies with reference to the speeches of the Justice of the Peace, in scene 423, and there must be no comedy in scene 427. Scenes 432 and 433 are unacceptable scenes that deal with comedy as Fields and Mrs Hemagloben are married. This scene can be saved if the Justice of the Peace is out of the scene and some comedy takes place involving the marriage ceremony and the actual business of Fields and Mrs Hemagloben being pronounced man and wife in the midst of this confusion is omitted . . .

We shall be glad to read a revised script which will overcome the objections set forth above.

Cordially yours,

Joseph Breen

Chapter 41
Towards the Grampian Hills . . .

A brief flashback: on Christmas Eve 1940, Gene Fowler relates, he, John Decker and John Barrymore decided to visit Uncle Claude and bring him some of the 'Tom and Jerry' batter which Decker had made at his Bundy Drive studio. 'If we hurry,' Decker said, 'we can reach his place before the sun begins to set.'

The approach to W. C. Fields' house in De Mille Drive was a long, cloister-like path under a pergola covered with wild vines. The door-knocker was carved in the form of a woodpecker, and a loudspeaker over the door enabled Bill to call out insults or encouragement to his visitors, or simulate some grotesque argument within to scare off unwanted callers. On this day there was silence, and Gregory La Cava answered the woodpecker's call, informing the friends that there had been another servants' strike, and Bill was resting from an upsetting experience. A lady who lived up the road had been pestering him with fan mail for a long time, asking to meet him. The day before, her Filipino butler had called, saying his employer was dying to meet him. Bill dressed up in his 'heartbreaker's' outfit and went over, to find the lady's house empty and quiet. Then the butler showed him into the parlor, where the lady lay, dead, in her coffin. The butler leaned over her body and said: 'Mr Fields, this is my madam . . . Madam, meet Mr Fields.'

Bill's deep dudgeon at this was not assuaged even by his closest friends. 'Why do these things happen to me?' he moaned to Gene Fowler. 'Fate simply hates my guts!'

On the way home, after helping Uncle Claude to drown his sorrows, Fowler relates, Decker was stopped by cops and taken to the station for a sobriety test. The police doctor, a very short man, asked him his profession. 'I'm a portrait painter,' said Decker. Could you paint a portrait of me in your present condition? asked the small doctor. 'No,' Decker replied, 'I don't paint miniatures.' Fowler ends this tale: 'This remark cost the artist's friends three hundred dollars.'

When *Never Give a Sucker an Even Break* was released, in its inevitably bowdlerized form, critics were puzzled, if not downright hostile. Getting grumpier by the month, Bill responded by sending furious letters to the *Hollywood Reporter* and to the *Christian Science Monitor*, which had accused his film of being a 'rehash of old business' or 'the usual atmosphere of befuddled alcoholism'. 'Wouldn't it be more terrible,' Bill wrote the latter sinner, 'if I quoted some reliable statistics to prove that more people are driven insane through religious hysteria than by drinking alcohol'?

But Bill could not escape the fact that the film was, indeed, a reprise of so many of his old routines: the 'Pullman Sleeper' act transferred from train to aeroplane with 'open air rear observation compartment', the entire sequence with the 'Turk' and the mallet from *The Old Fashioned Way* also replayed, as well as the crowded bathroom scene from *So's Your Old Man*. Boozing scenes in the saloon, transposed, après-Breen, to an ice-cream parlour: 'Give me a drink, I'm dying.' 'What'll it be?' 'Jumbo ice cream soda.' 'What flavor?' 'Oh, I don't care, spinach, horseradish . . . anything you've got there . . .' And of course: 'This scene was supposed to be in a saloon, but the censor cut it out. It'll play just as well.'

The entire film within the film oozes Bill's contempt for the scenario-hacks of the Hollywood studios. A crazy confection of Mexican cantinas and Russian carts with singing gypsies, it also featured the clifftop residence of the fearsome Mrs Hemogloben (Margaret Dumont borrowed, with extra mascara, and fangs, from the Marx Brothers) and her Great Dane, standing guard over her innocent daughter, Ouliotta, who has never before seen a man. 'Have you ever played the game of Squidgilum? . . . Now close your eyes and pucker your lips . . .' The many personal in-jokes might puzzle the present-day viewer as much as they did the Christian Scientists: Fields falling in a basket several hundred feet down the cliff and breaking his flask, muttering 'what a catastrophe', mirroring his own legendary Humpty-Dumpty fall down the stairs breaking his tail-bone and worse, spilling his drink. The expected Fieldsian *bons mots* abound: his cure for insomnia: 'Get plenty of sleep.' And the famous lines: 'I was in love with a beautiful blonde once . . . She drove me to drink. It's the one thing I'm indebted to her for.'

At the beginning of the film, Bill settled his scores with all the shabby studio cafeterias he had to suffer in his life. At its end, he couldn't resist another Mack Sennett car race, this time a mad rush, tangling with fire engines and ladders, to get a woman he mistakenly thinks is just about to give birth to the maternity hospital. Gloria Jean rushing up to Bill as he climbs out of wrecked car, sighing: 'My Uncle Bill! But I still love him!'

Gloria Jean Schoonover remembered Bill with affection in a television interview:

> I was just a kid at the time, but it was an experience I'll never forget. I felt that he was playing his own life. He said to me, I wish I had a daughter like you. He said, all my life I've wanted someone like you. You can't imagine how good that made me feel . . . Many times he'd say, come over here and talk to me, I'm lonesome. And I'd watch him and I felt that he was a lonesome man . . .

As she was a minor on the set, Bill was forbidden to have alcohol anywhere near her. At one time her schoolteacher minder thought she had caught Fields out, but his drink turned out to be mouthwash. Bill's secret is now out: He loved children, and often amused them in his own garden when the parents among his close friends brought them along. In 1942 a tragedy occurred on his grounds, when the two-year-old son of Anthony Quinn, who was married to De Mille's daughter, drowned accidentally in his small lily pond. Bill withdrew into his house and would speak to no one for many hours. In 1943, when his first grandson, Bill Fields III, was born, Bill doted on the baby and used to prop him up on his desk as he banged away at his typewriter with his now arthritic fingers.

Never Give a Sucker an Even Break, 'directed' by Eddie Cline again, was released on 10 October 1941. On 7 December the Japanese bombed Pearl Harbor, and on 8 December the United States entered World War Two. An oft-told tale of Fields and his cronies, related reliably by Gene Fowler, has the four musketeers, Fowler, Fields, Decker and Barrymore, answering the call to register for home defence by staggering into the army office in Santa Monica. Fields, said Fowler, 'looked like the wrath of John Barleycorn'. The young woman who gave them the forms to fill in for their registration queried: 'Gentlemen, who sent you? The enemy?'

Another tale of Pearl Harbor has Barrymore and Fields sojourning together when the news of the attack comes through. Barrymore sees Bill make a surreptitious phone call, and some time later a truck comes and unloads forty-two cases of gin. Why only forty-two cases? asks Jack. Because I think it'll be a short war, drawls Bill. Believe It Or Not.

Bill's drinking increased the more unwell he felt. It had become such an integral part of his myth, recounted again and again to newspapermen: '"I have a hangover, from 42 years of drinking about $185,000 of whiskey . . ." Fields said that in all the years he spent drinking whiskey he could never get drunk. He turned to rum and pineapple juice. This made him fat. He switched to Martini cocktails in water tumblers. He even hired a night watchman so he could have a drinking partner until 4 a.m . . . "but I remained sober". Two years ago, Fields said, he quit drinking briefly, because he almost died of pneumonia. "And what happened?" he asked, "I'd hardly quit liquor, before I got the d.t.s. I'd see little men with whiskers and high hats, sitting on bulls, and they'd charge me. They almost got me one afternoon. This was in a hospital. My best friend died of drinking too much. His was a case of internal drowning . . ."'

But Bill could not flim-flam his way out of his failing health and the strict reluctance of the studios to give him more work. In January 1942 he put in five days of work (for $50,000) in another portmanteau film, à la *If I had a Million*, entitled *Tales of Manhattan*, for 20th Century Fox. The film was the tale of a tail-coat as it passes from one owner to another. Charles Boyer, Thomas Mitchell, Charles Laughton and young Henry Fonda all featured. Fields was society hustler Postlewhistle who buys the coat at Phil Silver's second-hand schmutter shop, to wear to his lecture about the virtues of cocoanut milk and the evils of alcohol at Mrs Langahankie's stately home. Meanwhile Mr Langahankie dumps a load of booze into the cocoanut milk (shades of Chaplin's famous short: *The Cure* . . .). While the guests unknowingly tipple, Fields proceeds, before an anatomical chart, to lecture on the 'battle against Old Nick's brew,' noting:

This is the oesophagus . . . the first part of the anatomy to feel the shock of the concoction of Lucifer – Bee-eelzebub! And here we find the liver – very good with bacon – this majestic organ falls easy prey to these misguided moments of liquid Saturnalia . . . (*Pointing to intestines*) Here is the Burma Road. I remember the journey well. A storm blew up and our little party stopped at a wayside inn . . . a little girl called Ming Toy waited upon us . . . She was a vision of loveliness . . . She had more curves than the road itself . . . I continued my journey on a crude cart . . . (*Chart lifts to show picture of Fields flanked by dusky beauties*) Uh oh . . . This brings our journey to a very happy conclusion – my assistant will now pass the buck – uh, plate . . . I am allergic to the sound of silver . . . I thank you . . .

But Bill's entire part, with Margaret Dumont as Mrs Langahankie, was cut from the released film. The French director, Julien Duvivier, and Bill did not get on, and even the mediation of Buster Keaton and director Mal St Clair (everyone in Hollywood seemed to be in on this turkey) failed to patch things up.

Bill's appearance in the surviving clip is dire – the make-up barely manages to conceal the rosacea blotches on his puffy face. Only the voice is undimmed. The studio bosses looked at him and decided that his day had gone. No new offers of work materialized that year, and not till December 1943, when he got a walk on part in a vaudeville format film, *Follow the Boys*, to carry out his pool act. The film was made to entertain the troops, but was another Christmas turkey for all concerned. Nevertheless, it is the only screen performance of W. C. Fields' original pool act, with his old table brought out of mothballs, complete with the final stroke driving all fifteen balls simultaneously into the pockets. 'They don't build billiard tables today like they used to do in grandfather's day . . .' drawls Bill as he starts his act. The Hollywood press reported his comeback thus:

LIQUOR SHORTAGE GETS AROUND AT LAST TO PARCHED
W. C. FIELDS, by Fred Othman.
Hollywood Dec. 3 – W. C. Fields returned to work in the movies without liquor, nothing to drink around his house except fly spray, mouth wash, imitation vanilla extract, two quarts of green enamel, the stuff in the coils of his refridgerator, a half bottle of liquid shampoo, an unopened jug of furniture polish and the squeezings from his Christmas pudding. The desperate Fields said he had wrung out this pudding, like a wet chamois skin, but that the amount of the brandy so rendered was negligible. He said that his blood was becoming viscous and his tissues dehydrated from lack of moisture.

The Man in the Bright Nightgown was edging nearer and nearer. Bill's virtual blood-brother, John Barrymore, had died on 29 May 1942, finally succumbing to his many illnesses. As he lay dying in the Hollywood Presbyterian Hospital, a priest received him back into the Catholic Church and gave him the last rites. But Jack lingered, and told the priest, a few days later, that he still had carnal thoughts about the nurse. His brother Lionel, Gene Fowler and John Decker were in constant attendance. Fields sent a telegram: YOU CAN'T DO THIS TO ME.

Jack had sixty cents in his pocket when he died. He had wasted all his money on his house and his yacht and had neglected to pay most of his tax. The next day, while Fowler was grieving, Sadakichi Hartmann telephoned him from his hideout in Banning, to tell him his latest artistic discovery: 'Holbein was left-handed.' Fowler wrote that this display of indifference covered up Sadakichi's genuine sense of loss. In a way this was typical of the Bundy Drive boys. Death was, after all, knocking on all their doors. Fowler wrote:

> When a circus tent is struck in the night, the carnival moves on to another town. The scavengers come early the next morning to try their luck among the leavings at the fun-deserted scene: they poke solemnly in the trodden sawdust for stray peanuts, or perhaps a lost coin, or a wrinkled baloon cast aside by some tired child. As the young attorney read the Barrymore will I sat thinking of Jack's life as a circus that had moved on in the night . . .

As it would for others . . . Decker and Gene Fowler wanted Uncle Claude to be a pallbearer, but Fields demured, saying, 'The time to carry a pal is when he's still alive . . . Why should I hoist a graveyard box?' Well, Decker suggested, if it gets dark 'your nose would make an excellent tail light'. Bill was not amused. He refused to travel in the black funeral limousine, arriving in his own car, with fully stocked bar. As the requiem mass was completed, Bill whispered to Gene that they should adjourn to his portable wake. A crowd of noisy autograph seekers followed them out, demanding Fields' signature. He repulsed them angrily. One of the kids shouted: 'We'll never go to another one of your pictures!' Bill shouted back at them: 'Back to the reform school, you little nose pickers!' In Fieldsian legend, this would become a kind of general credo, but, Fowler shows us, it derived from a moment of extreme stress. Another distortion on the road to myth.

'I'm going to be cremated,' said Uncle Claude, 'and have my ashes thrown like confetti all around the nineteenth hole of the nearest golf club.'

The friends opened up the icebox, and Fields ordered his chauffeur to pull over so they wouldn't spill their drinks. A police car drew up and a sergeant came out to ask them why they had double-parked.

Fields said, famously: 'We are sitting at the crossroads between art and nature, trying to figure out where delirium tremens leaves off and Hollywood begins.'

Exiled from film work, Bill continued to write and send his letters and try and plan a comeback. He was now reconciled with his son – who had married Anne Ruth Stevens in Providence, Rhode Island on 4 August – and was eager to meet the bride and groom as soon as they could come to California. He kept contact by letter with his own siblings, Adel and Walter, on the East Coast. The letters to Hattie are now friendly enough to have them both reminiscing about times past – 'I always recall your Joke "man in the room in Berlin" on my birthday 21st. It is raining and I enjoy it in Calif. as it washes the air,' writes Bill. 'I am sorry I do not remember birthdays – males seldom do. I hope you keep well and happy for many years . . . Claude.'

His jaundiced views about President Roosevelt and the Democrats did not, however, soften one wit. In the Fall of 1942 an incident occurred which is still shrouded in some mystery. Fowler recounts, without dating the event, that at some point an FBI man turned up at Bill's doorstep, not, as the comedian feared, to arrest him for his Tax affairs, or to demand the whereabouts of Sadakichi Hartmann, but to inquire about a series of portraits, painted by John Decker, which were, in Fowler's words, 'caricature studies of a Washington woman whom Fields passionately disliked'. In fact, these were obscene cartoons of Eleanor Roosevelt, which, when turned upside down, revealed her as an open vagina. Somehow J. Edgar Hoover himself had got wind of this stunt. This seems to have resulted in a personal visit by Hoover to Fields – it might be that the FBI man Fowler mentioned was in fact the legendary Director himself. At any rate, the archives contain a curious letter sent by Fields to Hoover at the Department of Justice, Federal Bureau of Investigation in Washington, dated 6 October 1942, in which Bill states that he was proud and happy to get Hoover's invitation to visit him in Washington and 'I was very happy to have you visit me during your stay in Hollywood. If there is anything I can do for you in either a private or business way, I am yours to command.' As a sweetener, Bill added that he had received a postcard from Germany soliciting food for American POWs, which he suspected was a scam. Hoover wrote back on 17 October on FBI letterhead, saying, 'You may rest assured that we will not hesitate to call upon you in the event a situation should arise requiring your services. It means so much to me to know that the Bureau can call upon loyal friends like you in time of need.' However, he pooh-poohed the significance of the German letter.

The veiled threat behind this exchange can only be appreciated in the historical hindsight of the FBI's long interest in Hollywood and in the political views of its denizens. Hoover loved to have a hold on people, and the Eleanor portraits served that need. What on earth he might have expected from Uncle Claude in his dotage, apart from imaginary sightings of Japanese submarines off Santa Monica or Malibu, one can only wonder.

Uncle Claude never forgave Roosevelt for wanting to tax actors, and his prejudice against Eleanor was a typical revenge. He disliked the idea of a woman in politics and accused Eleanor in private of corruption in her travels abroad. In one particularly nasty letter, in October 1943, written to his sister Adel, he accused the Roosevelts of getting America into 'this terrible mess' of the war in the first place. Bill's patriotism was definitely of the isolationist variety. He probably savoured his little encounter with Hoover. Earlier in 1942 he had already got himself 'inducted into service' as a United States Marshall and Los Angeles County Deputy Sheriff. He was probably attracted by the name of the LA sheriff – Eugene Biscialuz.

Bill continued to write to vaudeville survivors like Eddie Cantor and Fanny Brice, remembering their old friends Will Rogers and Sam Hardy. In November 1942 he made a return to radio, recycling the Fields-Edgar Bergen-Charlie McCarthy skits. It appears he made a rare trip to New York, but the record does not show whether he detoured to Washington to report to his new pal, the other Edgar . . . Fields was still taking, in public, a completely neutral stance:

FIELDS: Sometimes I was in the Confederate Army, Charles, and sometimes in the Union. I still have my Union card. But I'm a little tardy with my dues.

EDGAR: What have you been doing since you got back from the front, Bill?

FIELDS: I have been a greeter at picnics . . . the Elks, the Eagles, the Lambs, the Moose . . .

CHARLES: You haven't been to any pink elephant's picnics, have you?

FIELDS: Very good, Charles, very good . . .

The radio shows enabled Bill, again, to recapture some of the verbal knockabout of the old vaudeville shows, shorn of Hollywood studio interference. At one point in a subsequent skit, published by Ronald Fields, he sings 'Just before the bottle, mother', a fading echo of his unperformed 1919 skit – 'Just before the *battle*, mother'. 'That's some voice you have there,' says the dummy Charlie. 'In my younger days,' says Fields, 'I . . . had a range of four octaves – and ten Martinis – not counting the olives . . .' Charlie then plays off singing: 'Wait for the wagon and we'll all take a ride . . .'

But it was far too late for that: 1943 was a dismal year for Bill. It had begun with the plagiarism suit by Harry Yadkoe against his re-use of the 'snake story' in one of his radio spots, and continued with him nervously seeing his son off to fight for Uncle Sam in the Pacific. A proposal from producer Arthur Freed to appear in a forthcoming Technicolor revival of the 'Ziegfeld *Follies*', with William Powell as Ziegfeld, fell through due to his continuing illness. (Fanny Brice was the only one of the old guard to appear in the movie.) Bill was isolated for most of the year. Gene Fowler was writing his book on John Barrymore, mostly in his house on Fire Island, New York. Uncle Claude continued to send Gene his news clippings, with personal comments in the margins. A poignant sample is a page from *The San Quentin News*, the prison journal, billed as 'The Other Side of "The Inside"'. Perhaps the news item 'State Prison to be Turned Over to Women' caught his fancy. Or 'Former Michigan Prison Doctor Held Captive by Japs.' Upon the forbidding photograph of the prison's main gate and walls ('This is the first, and last, sight to greet all men here,') Bill had drawn an X on one of the tiny cell windows and scribbled above: 'Having wonderful time wish you were here. X marks my room, Uncle Claude.'

Bill was now spending a great deal of time at Las Encinas, the drying-out clinic which had become his second home. His arthritis was worsening, and cirrhosis of the liver was an inevitable outcome of all those years of championing 'the grape'. Early in 1944 Gene Fowler, now back in Los Angeles, wrote to him in De Mille Drive in sympathy:

Dear Uncle Willie,

Thank you for your note. I am passing through a period of slight melancholia, and my recourse to the bottle only heightens it.

I hope to see you soon and join you in your old Crow's Nest so that we can sit and look out on the world and despise it thoroughly.

Meanwhile, the best to you,

GENE FOWLER

On 6 May, Fowler was even more melancholy: 'Dear Uncle Claude, I am confined in a tunnel with guards at the door . . . Hope that you are okay. With best regards . . .'

The doom-laden whispers of the Man in the Bright Nightgown . . . After *Follow the Boys*, Bill continued to look for any way to return to work. In May 1944 entrepeneur Billy Rose, who had been Fanny Brice's second husband (until 1938), cabled Bill an invitation to appear in a musical review by George S. Kaufman at the Ziegfeld Theatre, but Bill had to decline. He had been commissioned to make his last two movie appearances, in two more brief cameo roles. The first was in *Song of the Open Road*, a mediocre vehicle for a new singing star, Jane Powell. Bill, Edgar Bergen and Charlie McCarthy replayed their radio feud, but it was a pale shadow of the past. The second, and Fields' last, appearance in a movie, was in another variety type revue, *Sensations of 1945* ('A touch of tomorrow, today!') released, confusingly, at the end of June 1944.

Director Andrew Stone had been in touch with Bill since 1943, to perform his old Pullman train sketch. Stone wanted Bill to do a scene in the bathroom where he shaves entangled with a six-foot Marine. But Fields wrote back saying that this 'would be most hilarious done by a younger man'. Instead, Bill suggested 'The Caledonian Express', his sketch from 'Earl Carroll's *Vanities*' of 1928. In this late version he reduced the four different parts he had played then to only one, the drunken passenger who takes over the carriage.

In the film, the old trouper C. Aubrey Smith introduces Bill upon the stage: 'My great good friend, W. C. Fields, will do a sketch for you . . .'

Onto the railway carriage set walks Fields, moving painfully in a great fur coat, with straw hat and suitcase, accompanying young actress Louise Currie. She recalled that his eyesight and his memory were so bad he had to read his lines off big blackboards, necessitating take after take.

FIELDS: Aren't you cold, dear? You're so scantily clad.

GIRL: As a matter of fact I am cold.

FIELD: Aw, put your arm right in there – that's it. Here's a compartment.

GIRL: Oh, but look at the placard, it's 'reserved for Lord Robert R. Roberts.'

FIELD (*removing sign*): It isn't reserved for him now – here put it right in there dear.

A couple of drunks turn up, and proceed to fight half-heartedly. Fields ad-libs vaguely as they thrash about: 'Didn't screw his legs on right this morning I guess. There he goes – look out – look out! The dying swan . . . here you are – you're all right now. Now you're both all right . . . Aw, don't do that you'll hurt him . . . Oh! That's terrible – I must try that on my wife. Oh – You broke his throat. Now he's got butterflies in the throat. I've had them in the stomach but never in the throat. What's he going to do now – oh, no – no! No! Ouch! Mother of pearl . . . (He slaps the drunk) I guess I don't know my own strength . . .'

GIRL: Oh, dear – oh, dear! Oh, dear!

FIELD: Yeah, aren't drunks repulsive. Come my little Poppinjay.

End of sketch – APPLAUSE.

These were the final lines of W. C. Fields on stage or screen. He looks exhausted. There is an air of humiliation about exploiting his weakness in this way. Comedy has finally turned into tragedy. Even the publicity book of the film played on his troubles: 'MATCH W. C. FIELDS' SCHNOZOLA AND WIN "SENSATION" CONTEST.' A $25 war bond was to be presented to 'the owner of any nose which most matches in size, coloration and general decorative effect the bulbular projection of Mr Fields'. Old and new stars – Eleanor Powell, Sophie Tucker, Eugene Pallette, Cab Calloway and his band are there to witness the swansong. To see an era come to an end.

Bill continued to write to his friends, and increasingly, to his family. Magda Michael remained his constant companion. Carlotta Monti was intermittently in and out of the picture, despite her own claim that she was always by his side. She had certainly earned her keep, particular in the last years, when Bill still craved his sexual release but was increasingly infirm, and paranoid about her other affairs. Sometimes, Will Fowler told me, Bill would send her for a medical VD check-up before he was prepared to have sex. But despite the benefits that she accrued from being close to so famous a celebrity, I have no doubt that she loved him deeply. She never deserted him, despite the fact that he cast her out, more than once. In July 1944, he wrote to his sister Adel: 'Miss Monti, who has been a paramour on and off, is at present doing her stuff in a chapeau emporium in Santa Barbara . . . After a short visit there, she will head for Mexico City where she has a prospective job singing in a cabaret.'

He was well enough then to head for the races at Tijuana with Dave Chasen, Gene Fowler and John Decker, in September. In October, Carlotta is back, and Bill is complaining that he can't finance her Mexican and New York trips any more, inviting her to return to a 10 a.m. to 6 p.m. routine of 'cutting clippings and furnishing occasional gags . . . I have got to knuckle down to a real business routine.'

But there was no business coming Bill's way. From his Crow's Nest, Bill could see the rest of the world approaching the end of its own long dark road. While the United States was bleeding in the Pacific, and the War in Europe ground to its exhausted end, the comedian's voice had gone silent. The world of Hitler's bunker, and the world ushered in by Hiroshima, was not the world of William Claude Dukenfield, of W. C. Fields, 'the Great Silly'. Only the echoes could remain . . .

It is a terrible time, the dotage of the clown. Bill was spending more and more days and weeks at the Las Encinas sanitarium, in Pasadena. Soon he abandoned the house on De Mille Drive entirely, on the pretext of refusing to pay more rent to renew his expiring lease. He moved, lock stock and barrel, to Las Encinas. The time had come to prepare for the final act. Bill was now attending to a subject which had long been an issue of banter among his friends, his long-discussed Last Will and Testament.

This document was to be the cause of the long drawn-out battle waged by Hattie to overturn its curious terms. Long before, Bill had confided in Gene Fowler his intention to leave most of his money to found a home in Philadelphia for orphans. At the outset, this was to be for Negro orphans, because, Fields told Fowler: 'The little devils need help; besides, it will drive some people I know off their rocker.' But in the event, Bill was offended by one of his servants, who was black, and who, allegedly taking advantage of the fact that household help was scarce in the war years, was being insufficiently subservient. Bill declared to Fowler:

'Just for that' – and he spoke with some heat – 'I'm changing my will. No colored orphans!'

'That's a mistake,' I told him. 'Such a narrow gesture will make you misunderstood and much disliked.'

'I've always been misunderstood,' he rasped, 'Besides, did you ever hear of a corpse complaining of unpopularity?'

The proposed 'W. C. Fields College for Orphan White Boys and Girls, where no religion of any sort is to be preached', never came to be. Challenged by Hattie, the clause was disallowed by the judge, who stated that 'Mr Fields in his lifetime could have discriminated against other races, but he cannot in death.' The various small allowances and sums of money to Carlotta, his sister and brothers, and a range of old friends who were to receive between $500 and $5,000 – including Mabel Clapsaddle, the bank clerk whose name he had 'fallen in love' with, in Will Fowler's words – were eventually paid out in part. The remainder of the estate, calculated at a total of $771,428, was fiercely fought over by Hattie; William Rexford Fields Morris, Bessie Poole's son; and Edith Williams, the crazy blind woman from Chicago who claimed Fields had married her in 1893.

In her testimony to the court, Magda Michael, who was the executor of the will, revealed some sad facts about the last days at Las Encinas. In a discussion about the disposition of Fields' remaining stock of liquor, valued at $1,553, she admitted that she had delivered to Fields at the sanitarium one case of gin, half a case of vermouth and a case of beer, every week, from a stash hidden in the cellar of his agent, Charlie Beyers. The sanitarium authorities frowned on this practice, but knew there was no point trying to prevent it. The judge ruled that the liquor should be divided between the three heirs to the estate decreed by Fields: his brother and sister, Walter and Adel, and Carlotta Montejo, alias Monti.

In the sanitarium, Bill had a bungalow, in landscaped surroundings, green lawns and tall trees. But this was not a place of repose. In his last months, in De Mille Drive, he had already been subject to shaking fits in the night, and had to be fitted with a kind of makeshift cot, to prevent him falling out of bed. Added to his sufferings were bouts of polyneuritis, which made his entire skin unbearably sensitive to the lightest touch. Magda Michael continued to be in attendance, with Carlotta pleading to be allowed access. Perhaps she was only after her salary, as he complained in a letter of 9 June 1946, giving her one month's notice. 'Perhaps you were thinking of someone else when you called me a stingy bastard,' he wrote plaintively. 'I had in mind to advance you to $12.00 a day which is $84.00 a week and your regular $50.00. Your duties would be giving me a pill every four hours . . . You should have accepted it for divers reasons but you were too busy . . .'

Bill accused Carlotta of pestering him, stealing money from his pockets and reading his private mail. But still she persevered. She told in her book how she would spray a hose on the roof of the bungalow in the hot summer, just as she had in his garden in De Mille Drive. 'I would say, "It's rainmaking time," and he would say, "What would I do without my little Chinaman?"' But in May he was writing to Gene Fowler from Las Encinas:

Dearest Nephew,

Thanks for yours undated. I am sorry I had to clap the little lady in the bastille on that marijuana rap . . . From now on I'm going to confine all my activities to musical directors. Tell Agnes not to give it another thought.

My love to you all,

Bill Fields

Agnes was Gene Fowler's wife, whom Bill was always promising to include in his will, though he never did. On 12 November he wrote what may have been his last letter, to Gene:

Dear Nephew,

This Gideon J. Pillow friend of yours is not a 'Pillow;' his proper name is 'Wetblanket.'

Agnes is still in the will and will remain there until after I examine my Christmas tie.

Your loving Uncle, Claude

On 7 December Bill sent a Christmas card to his son and daughter-in-law, who then visited him in the bungalow. On Christmas Day 1946, according to Carlotta Monti, just before noon, Bill said to her: 'Grab everything and run. The vultures are coming.' Three minutes later he called her, 'Chinaman . . . Goddamn the whole frigging world and everyone in it but you, Carlotta.' And then he was shaken by a violent stomach haemorrhage, his last moves on this earth.

A month before Christmas, according to Will Fowler, the surviving Bundy Drive boys, Gene and Will Fowler and John Decker, visited Bill in his bungalow, to be offered the usual libation from his extremely well-stocked bar, though he himself, amazingly, Will Fowler testifies, had drunk nothing but ginger ale for the past month. A nurse came to take his temperature and turn on the radio to Christmas songs. 'Turn it off! Cease!' cried the hater of Christmases. 'I'm changing my will. Nobody who observes Christmas will be mentioned in my last testament. Not a farthing for them, man or boy!' Later in the month, he lapsed into a coma. Magda Michael and the nurses kept the death watch. On the morning of Christmas Day, December 1946, according to Ronald Fields, he awoke. Only Magda Michael and a nurse were in the room. Wrote Ronald: 'He brought his forefinger to his lips to signify quiet, winked, then closed his eyes; and "the Man in the Bright Nightgown" took him away.'

38 Christmas card sent to Gene and Will Fowler
(courtesy of Will Fowler/Tim Walker collection).

Coda

Hattie Hughes-Fields died on 7 November 1963, in Beverly Hills, aged eighty-five, survived by her son, W. Claude Fields Jr., his wife Ruth, and five grandchildren, William, Everett, Harriet, Ronald and Allen Fields.

When the Man in the Bright Nightgown called for Hattie – I envisage him as being played by Franklin Pangborn, complete with a set of five spare scythes, in case some are broken by reluctant clients – I see him taking her up the winding path towards the pearly gates, when they are brought to a stop by a familiar voice holding forth from the bar just outside the entrance. The call reverbrates, enjoining them to 'Hide the egg and gurgitate a few saucers of Mocha Java . . .' They enter, through the old-fashioned swing doors. It is a familiar old saloon, with the rows of bottles glistening on shelves behind the polished table, and a couple of dozen tables with chairs, leading up to a stage, with an old backdrop of an arboreal dell in summertime. Fields is at the bar, holding forth over a collection of mugs, tumblers and glasses, from which he is sampling as he proceeds. The man he is talking to, Bill Wolfe, cadaverous as ever, props up the bar in his usual solemn silence. There is a hot lunch on the bar, comprising of succotash, asparagus with mayonnaise, and Philadelphia cream cheese . . .

The music strikes up from an old piano in the corner. These are the honky-tonk tunes of long ago: 'Mulligan's Daughter Nell', 'Frankie and Johnny', 'The Hog's Eye Man', 'Everything in the Garden's Lovely' and 'Some Things Are Better Left Unsaid'. Above the stage is a large notice, left over from Harrigan and Hart:

ler's

GO TO HELL Wonder

Theatre

The acts roll up upon the stage, a host of many familiar voices and faces: there are Weber and Fields, poking each other in the eye amid their quickfire repartee: 'I am delightfulness to met you!' 'Der disgust iss all mine!' There are Duffy and Sweeney, with their Irish patter. Cinquevalli, tossing plates around as the juggling waiter. Nat Wills, the 'Happy Tramp', in his monologue. McIntyre and Heath, as Hennery and Alexander: 'If I ever get back to that livery stable, the first man tells me I got talent, I'll stick a pitchfork in 'im . . .' Houdini, as the Wild Man of Mexico. Frank Tinney, playing his cornet, and the Keaton family – Joe and Myra throwing little Buster on his head all over the stage. Eva Tanguay, plump and dissolute, in burlesque queen tights, singing 'It's All Been Done Before But Not the Way I Do It'. And Bert Williams, coffee coloured through his burnt cork make-up, standing stock still in the spotlight, to deliver one of his ineffable monologues:

Where I'm livin' now is a nice place, but you got to go 'long a road between two graveyards to get to it. One night last week I'm comin' home kinda late, and I get about half way home when I look over my shoulder and I see a ghost followin' me. I started to run. I run and run till I was just about ready to drop. And then I looked around again. But I didn't see no ghost, so I sat down on the curbstone to rest. Then out of the corner of my eye I could see somethin' white, and when I turned square around, there was that ghost sittin' right beside me. The ghost says: 'That was a fine run we had. That was the best runnin' I ever saw.' I says to him: 'Yes sir, and soon as I get my breath back, you're gonna see some more.'

39 'Soon as I get my breath back, you're gonna see some more.'

Afterword: W. C. Fields and Me

I discovered W. C. Fields in the late 1960s, at a time when the great comics of the 1930s were being recast as anti-authoritarian rebels. Fields, the Marx Brothers, even Laurel and Hardy were seen as the ancestors of the generation which was urged to 'be practical – dream the impossible!' Stan and Ollie were eternal children. The Marx Brothers were anarchy times-three-or-four (who wanted to bother to count?). And W. C. Fields was the ultimate rebel 'inside the system', who blew it apart with the dynamite of its own lack of logic.

Beyond that, I came to see him as the funniest of all clowns, his achievement the greater for his being alone against all the odds. The Marx Brothers could spark off each other, Stan and Ollie reinforce each other's incomprehension at the slings and arrows of life. W. C. Fields stands alone, against the family, against sheriffs and bailiffs, against the flow of the traffic, against bathroom mirrors and billboards and banks.

When I began to research this book, I had no reason to question the perception of Fields as the one comedian whose life on screen and off was identical, who was the character we saw in his films: the misanthrope, the hater of children and dogs, the miserable kicker against the pricks whose primary source was his own harsh, Dickensian childhood. While writing a previous, short booklet on Bill's 1934 movie, *It's a Gift*, I discovered Ronald Fields' *W. C. By Himself*, of 1973, which offered a revised view of the clown's origins, but I did not realise how far revision could reach.

As I began retracing the clown's footsteps back through time, through his vaudeville days, I discovered that Bill Fields' attitude to authority was quite different from that I had assumed long ago. The previous version of young Claude's rebellion against his father and his life in the streets made him a perfect 1960s hero. But since we now know that was untrue, a very different picture emerges of Bill's true social attitudes. In fact, I came to realize, Bill had a great fear of antagonising authority, and like many kids who fear being bullied, by a parent, or by other kids, he took refuge in his inner world of creation. He took refuge in jokes.

Young Claude's raw talent would have made him quite an enigma to his father, James, the first generation American. Like so many of his period, James saw hard work as the key to advancement in the New World. He must have tried, like so many fathers throughout the ages, to thump a little sense into this stubborn child. I found no reason to believe that James did not love his son, although he did not understand what made him tick, nor did he comprehend the nature of the creative explosion which would soon be set off. Nevertheless, he certainly recognised the boy's strong will, and did not, in the end, stand in his way. In 1904, as we have seen, he even accompanied his son, daughter-in-law and baby grandson on part of their European tour.

The boy Claude was certainly not alone. He had a brother and two sisters (the second brother, Leroy, was born when he was fifteen), and a mother whose humorous bent supplied him a relief from Dad's narrow expectations. He had a grandmother who covered for him, aunts and uncles. Like so many kids in a less protected world than ours is (for some), he responded to his father by standing on his own two feet as early as possible. Not by hiding in a hole in the ground, as legend went, but by taking odd jobs, building his independence while he carved out his stubborn path to his art.

Show-people, in the main, develop an ambivalent attitude to power and authority. To succeed, they must be popular, they must follow the crowd, but they must also lead, in expressing the crowd's secret desire to rebel. The clown, from his very beginnings in culture, transgresses: the court jester could mock the King, and say what no one else dared to say. But he was still the court jester. He lived by authority's patronage. And so the clown becomes the Great Dissimulator, the one who tells the truth by means of many lies. He never confronts authority, but always dances around it, throwing pepper and sand in its face. There are exceptions – like Chaplin, who found a synthesis between his art and his strong political views. Chaplin was able to do this because he controlled his own productions, he was the owner of his own art. Fields never owned his art: he had to fight his way to it, through battlefields of producers, music-hall entrepeneurs, the studio-factory of Hollywood with its armies of executives, house-writers and hacks.

As he flailed on through this minefield, Fields became more and more aware of the need to never let down his guard, to always maintain his mask, in public. Therefore his private life receded further and further into the background, carefully covered up, concealed, like a dog burying its bones everywhere. The Act became the Life, nurtured, cultivated and watered with the rains of publicity. The studios, always eager for clear images to differentiate their properties one from the other, were only too happy to oblige.

In digging up the buried bones, I have been aware of a voice calling truculently from behind the celestial curtain: Cease! Miscreant! Varlet! Godfrey Daniel! Spawn of Beelzebub! And sometimes even: get that damn Jew out of here! Like many people who spend their life eliding authority, Bill Fields had his own strong authoritarian streak. There was more of his father in him than he would ever admit: like James Dukenfield, he didn't believe in something for nothing. He continually lectured his estranged wife and his own son on the virtues of self help and independence, and the long-suffering, self-made *pater familias* he plays in his movies, especially in his Bissonette mode, has more than a whiff of his Dad: the man whose wife made him give up the saloon business so he would not be a bad example to his children. Bill even tried, as we have noted, to sing, occasionally, in that tuneless, perhaps inherited voice . . .

Fields had risen to success, against all odds, by hard work and his own talent, and he saw no reason why everyone else should not follow the same hard path, with no easy short cuts. In politics, he admired Will Rogers, whose populist themes could be used to deflect attention from the abuse of power by those who really held it. Like many self-made men, he became a reactionary, a man who, paradoxically, adopted the hard world of his father as a model, at the same time as he disparaged that same world as the source of his woes, which he had overcome. Anyone who appeared to adopt a 'special pleading' – welfare dependants, trade unionists, foreigners, sometimes blacks and Jews, became suspect in his eyes. He came, eventually, to take a perverse pride in his prejudices, which kept do-gooders and other nuisances from his door. He kept his virtues hidden and his sins displayed, imaginary as they often were. He cherished his reputation as a curmudgeonly miser, while sending money to many ex-vaudevillians in trouble, and often keeping his lady friends and lovers in the manner to which they aspired. He had no great business sense, although he cultivated his own business, and spent his money on those he loved, on his liquor, and on his other passion, motor cars.

Paradox was his stock in trade. The essence of the characters Bill created, be they McGargle or Bisbee, the Great McGonigle or Bissonette, Whipsnade or Sousè, was their creator's knowledge of the absurdity of their ambitions and desires. Egbert Sousè, like Bissonette and Bisbee, dreams the American dream of suddenly striking it rich out of worthless 'Beefsteak Mine' stock, so that he can sit at home, with his doting family, or at the bar, counting the incoming dollars. By the magic of the movies, the fairy tale, it happens, but like the Wizard of Oz, these are only puffs of smoke. The Great McGillicuddy, in his unproduced treatment, strikes out boldly across a frozen river, rescuing the townspeople who have failed to believe in his star. The cosmic juggler tosses the balls and hats and cigar boxes of life in the air and catches them with consummate ease. All fifteen billiard balls leap into the pockets. The world can be controlled, but only by illusion.

Politicians try to control the world and risk plunging it into misery. The clown is terrified of causing harm. He pretends to be an ogre – 'Do you like children?' 'I do if they're properly cooked!' But, offstage, off-screen, he dreams of his own curtailed paternity. And so we all become the clown's children, following him into the magic circus tent. The big show is about to begin. If we hurry we can get a seat right up in front of the elephants . . .

Fields' great bogeys, his prejudices and his pet hates, were the mumbling echoes of his personal frustrations. These were not, as I have tried to convey, the traumas of his youth, or even of the long-term pain caused by his conflict with Hattie, for I have come to believe that history has given her a bum rap, as a foil to his misanthropic jests. She deserves more credit for the crucial support she supplied in those first five years, when he was lean and hungry. The first years of learning his craft, when legend has him alone, but when she was, day by day, night by night, at his side. Bill tried to find many substitutes for her, but, despite the venomous nature of so much of their correspondence, something linked them together, over the decades of their stubborn separation: their son, his patrimony, a real Baby Le Roy whom he so yearned to kick in the pants.

In fact, Bill and Hattie were perfectly matched, in strength of will, in total stubbornness and a determination to battle on to the end. She was his hidden other half, brooding in the shadows, and right at the end of his life they might both have realized that perhaps their long feud had been a folly, and both wondered at what might have been. Why else would she have kept all his angry letters, his lovingly compiled scrapbooks, every piece of paper, hundreds of photographs and souvenirs? As I have shown, versions of a Hattie that might-have-stayed crop up in Fields' movies, either as an old faithful, Alison Skipworth type, or as the fantasy trapeze girl, Gorgeous.

As time passed, Fields turned sour inside because, at the height of his movie success, he fell ill, and never recovered his full health. Fate had conspired to strike him down at the pinnacle. This, above all, fuelled his ire. But there was something else, beyond his ill-health, and the increased boozing to drown the pain, which only made it worse: there was, throughout his life, that metaphysical search for the perfect joke, the perfect gags.

Fields raged inside because, I believe, he felt, at his core, that he was not being funny enough. Ronald Fields, his grandson, published a number of scribbled notes which accumulated from Bill's final years, pencilled notes on 3 by 5 inch notepaper. Scraps like

Dr Dont worry about your heart
it will last as long as you live

and

I need these characters to work with.
Its my act – if you take away my tools I'm not me.
Billowy Sands
wind

The clown's death is tragic because he has not achieved his aim of making the world a happier place. But he has achieved it, for his fans, in a host of small moments, which are of incalculable value.

For this, a hundred thousand thanks. But no, I will not buy a bottle of Purple Bark Sarsaparilla, even if it does grow hair on billiard balls!

Appendices

W. C. Fields – Chronology & Itinerary

I. Burlesque & Vaudeville, 1898–1915

1898

13 January: Natatorium Hall, Philadelphia.

11 March: Programme of the First Grand Concert and Hop of
Lady Meade Lodge, Peabody Hall, Philadelphia.

29 April: Third Grand Concert of Manhattan Athletic Club,
Batley Hall, 2748 Germantown Avenue, Philadelphia.

13 June: Benefit: 'Select Vaudeville Entertainment,'
Batley Hall, Philadelphia.

1 August: Plymouth Park, Norristown, J. Fortescue – Proprietor.

August–September: Fortescue's Pavilion, Atlantic City, New Jersey.

September 19: Opening of Monte Carlo Girls.

October: Gaeity Theatre, Albany; New York, Star Theatre, Troy, New York;
Hersker's Opera House, Mahanoy City, Pennsylvania; etc.

November: Altoona, Pennsylvania.

1899

28 January: Miner's Bowery Theatre, New York City.

February–June: Monte Carlo Girls cont'd, New York, Massachussetts,
Pennsylvania, New Jersey, Washington DC.

(Note: The full itinerary of W. C. Fields' American engagements between
October 1898 and December 1900 can be found in David T. Rocks' *W. C.
Fields, an Annotated Guide*, MacFarland, 1994.)

July: 'Murphy and Gibson's American Minstrels', Steel Pier,
Atlantic City, New Jersey.

26 August: 'Irwin's Burlesquers' – People's Theatre, Cincinnati, Ohio.

September–October: Irwin's Burlesquers, Milwaukee, Chicago, Cleveland.

28 October: Miner's 8th Avenue Theatre, New York City.

November–December: New York, Maryland, Pennsylvania.

16 December: Irwin's Burlesquers at Trocadero, Philadelphia.

30 December: Miner's Bowery Theatre, New York City.

1900

January: New York; Cincinnati, Ohio; Louisville, Kentucky.

10 February: Empire Theatre, Indianapolis, Indiana.

17 February: Standard Theatre, St Louis, Missouri (*see* 'It's a Tough Spot').

18 March: First solo performance on Orpheum circuit – San Francisco.

21 April: Orpheum, Los Angeles.

May–June: Orpheum, Kansas City, Missouri; Omaha, Nebraska, Cleveland, Ohio; Buffalo, New York.

16 June: Koster & Bial, New York City.

June–December: Keith's Orpheum Circuit, New York City, Chicago, Philadelphia, Boston, Toledo, Cincinatti, Providence. (Full list in Rocks, ibid.)

1 December: Orpheum, Kansas City, billing 'Mr & Mrs W. C. Fields'.

13 December: Orpheum, Omaha, Nebraska.

1901

1 January–February: Opens at Wintergarten, Berlin, Germany.

23 February–16 March: Palace Theatre, London.

23 March: Tivoli, Birmingham.

30 March: Tivoli, Leeds.

13 April: People's Palace, Bradford.

18 April: Kristalpalast, Leipzig.

4 May–1 June: *Folies Bergère*, Paris.

6 July: Tower Circus, Blackpool, England.

(5 August – sails by RMS *Majestic*.)

24 August: Keith's, New York City.

7 September: Keith's, Providence, Rhode Island.

October: Shea's, Toronto; Duquesne's, Pittsburgh; Columbia; Cincinatti.

November: Olympic, Chicago; Columbia, St Louis; Opera House, Chicago; Grand Opera House, Indianapolis.

December: Empire, Toledo; Shea's, Buffalo.

1902

15 February: Orpheum, Omaha, Nebraska.

March: Duquesne's, Pittsburgh; Olympic, Chicago.

April: Haymarket Chicago; Columbia, St Louis; Empire, Cleveland.

May: Orpheum, Brooklyn; Keith's, Boston; Keith's, New York City.

June: Electric Park, Baltimore; Shea's, Buffalo.

12 July: Brighton Beach, L.I.

15 August–20 September: Wintergarten, Berlin, Germany.

20–31 October: Orpheum, Vienna, Austro-Hungarian Empire.

1–30 November: Théâtre Variété, Prague, ditto.

December: Hippodrome, Leicester Square, London.

27 December: Queen's Dinner for soldier's widows & orphans,
Alexandra Trust Buildings, London.
Guest appearance at Hippodrome pantomime: *Dick Whittington.*

1903

17 January: Empire Palace, Birmingham.
24 January: Empire, Leeds.
7 February: Keith's, Providence, Rhode Island.
14 February: Keith's, Boston.
March: Keith's Philadelphia; Orpheum, Kansas City; Orpheum,
New Orleans.
April: Orpheum, San Francisco; Orpheum, Los Angeles.
May–June: On board SS *Sonoma* to Australia.
3 June: Auckland Racing Club ('Dead Heat').
18 June: Opera House, Melbourne.
11 July: Adelaide.
21 July–29 September: Tivoli, Sydney.
19 October–November: Opera House, Melbourne, shares billing with film by
Melies: *A Trip to the Moon.*
(November–December: To South Africa.)
14 December: Standard Theatre, Johannesburg, South Africa.
25 December: Tivoli, Cape Town.

1904

January–February: Tivoli, Cape Town.
(March – Sailing to England.)
2 April–30 April: London, Hippodrome – with Sandow, Houdini, Elephants.
11 June: Empire, Edinburgh.
18 June: Empire, Glasgow.
25 June: Empire, Bradford.
2 July: Empire, Liverpool.
9 July: Empire, Newcastle.
16 July: Empire, Leeds.
23 July: Palace, Hull.
30 July: Empire, Sheffield. Birth of son – telegram.
13 August: Palace, Manchester.
20 August: Empire, Shepherds Bush, London.
22 August: Empire, Holloway, London.
27 August: Empire, Hackney, London.
10 September: Empire, Nottingham.
12 September: Empire, Leicester.
24 September: Empire, Cardiff.
1 October: Empire, Stratford, London.

8 October: Empire, New Cross, London.

12 October: Ad WCF TOURING THE WORLD – Olympia, Paris.

6 November: *Folies Bergère*, Paris (shares bill with La Belle Oterita).

26 November: Alcazar, Marseille.

17 December: Eden, Milan, Italy.

December – to Prince's Theatre, Manchester, for Pantomime:
  Cinderella.

1905

January–March – Prince's Theatre, Manchester – *Cinderella*.

January – Benefit for Manchester's Jewish Working Men's Club.

18 January: Benefit for poor children, Manchester. Juggling.

25 March: Scala Theatre, Copenhagen, Denmark.

8 April: Wintergarten, Berlin.

18 April: Kristlapalast, Leipzig.

6 May: Ad: W. C. Fields to go to Moscow, Russia.

27 May: 'Fields will not go to Russia.'

May–June: Hansa Theatre, Hamburg.

June: Circo Parish, Madrid, Spain.

22 July: Arrived back in New York aboard the *Deutschland*.

August: Opening of *The Ham Tree*, New York City.

August 1905 – May 1907: Touring in the US with *The Ham Tree*.

1907

Juggling act resumed:

18 May: Lyceum, Rochester.

25 May: Chestnut Street Opera House, Philadelphia.

28 May: Opening of Jardin de Paris, New York City.

22 June: Nixon Theatre, Pittsburgh.

29 June: Jardin de Paris, New York City

(28 June: misleading item: 'W. C. Fields to tour the Orient . . . ')

6 July: Music Hall, Brighton Beach, L.I.

17 August: Morrison's, Rockaway Beach.

14 September: Shubert Theatre, Newark.

28 September: New York Theatre, New York City.

7 October: Tremont Theatre, Boston.

19 October: Forrest, Philadelphia.

26 October: Academy, Montreal.

November: Chicago, Kansas City, St Louis.

30 November: Keith & Proctor's Theatre, 125th St, New York City.

December: Buffalo, Syracuse, Rochester.

1908

January: Washington DC, Detroit.

15 February: Hammerstein's Theatre, New York City.

7 March: Colonial Theatre, New York City; Keith's, Boston.

April: Hartford, Newark.

May: Lowell Massachusetts, Boston.
  (Fields departs for Europe)

2 June: Grand Theatre, Birmingham.

6 June: Empire, Shepherds Bush, London.

20 June: Empire, Coventry.

29 June: Empire, Leeds.

6 July: Empire Palace, Liverpool.

15 July: Ardwick Empire, Manchester.

27 July–end August: London Hippodrome.

7 September: Empire, Hackney, London.

14 September: Empire, Holloway.

21 September: Empire, New Cross.

28 September: Empire, Stratford.

5 October: Empire, Bradford.

12 October: Empire, Sunderland.

19 October: Her Majesty's Theatre, Walsall.

26 October: London Coliseum.

1–7 November: Royal Palace of Varieties, Oldham.

(13 November – sails from Britain to US.)

23 November: Colonial, New York City.

30 November–5 December: Hammerstein's, New York City.

December: Grand, Pittsburgh; Temple, Detroit; Cook's, Rochester, New York.

1909

January: Shea's, Buffalo; Bennett's, Montreal; Grand, Syracuse, New York.

February: Keith & Proctor's 5th Avenue, New York City; Keith's, Boston; Keith
  & Proctor's 125th St, New York City; Keith's, Providence R.I.

March: Orpheum, Brooklyn; Keith's, Portland Maine; Keith's, Boston,
  Keith's, Providence R.I.

April: Orpheum, Brooklyn; Alhambra, New York City; Orpheum, Brooklyn;
  Majestic, Johnstown PA; Majestic, Chicago.

8 May: Colonial, New York City (shares bill with Eva Tanguay).

24 May–5 June: London Coliseum.

19 June: Empire, Dublin.

24 June: London Coliseum.

3 July: Palace, Hull.

10 July: Hippodrome, Manchester.

17 July: Grand, Birmingham.

24 July: Olympia, Liverpool.

14 August: Empire, Newcastle-on-Tyne.

21 August: Empire, Glasgow.

4 September: Empire, Leeds.

18 September: Ardwick Empire, Manchester.

9–23 October: Colonial Theatre, New York City.

30 October: Alhambra, New York City.

6 November: Keith's, Philadelphia, then Lawrence, Mass.

13 November: Keith's, Boston.

20 November: Keith's, Providence.

27 November: Keith & Proctor's, 5th Avenue, New York City.

4 December: Greenpoint, Brooklyn.

11 November: Keith & Proctor's, 5th Avenue.

18 December: Proctor's, Newark, New Jersey.

25 December–1 January: Hammerstein's, New York City.

1910

8 January: Shea's, Buffalo.

15 January: Toronto, Canada, then Detroit.

12 February: Keith's, Cleveland, then Keith's, Columbus.

26 February: Grand, Syracuse, then Bennet's Theatre, Montreal.

12 March, Orpheum, New York City.

15 March: Harrisburg PA.

24 May: New Haven, Conn.

28 May: Alhambra, New York City

13 June: Pavilion, Glasgow, Scotland.

20 June: Hippodrome, Belfast.

16 July: Hulme Hippodrome, Manchester.

23 July: Hippodrome, Preston.

13 August: Empire, Sunderland.

September: Paris

31 October: Palais d'Ete, Brussels, then Berlin.

13 November: Copenhagen.

3 December: Empire, Nottingham, England.

10 December: Empire, New Cross, London.

17 December: Empire, Hackney, London.

31 December: Hippodrome, Manchester.

1911

7 January: Grand, Birmingham.

14 January: Empire, Shepherds Bush.

28 January: Empire, Leeds.

4 February: Empire, Leicester.

12 February: Empire, Glasgow.
18 February: Ardwick Empire, Manchester.
27 February: Olympia, Liverpool.
11 March: Empire, Newport.
18 March: Hippodrome, Croydon.
25 March: Empire, Newcastle-on-Tyne.
4 April: Grand, Bolton.
15 April: Empire, Cardiff.
22 April: Empire, Sheffield.
15 May: Hippodrome, London.
12 June: London Coliseum.
(24 June: Coronation of King George V and Queen.)
22 July: Theatre Royal, Dublin.
29 July: Theatre Royal, Edinburgh.
16 September–14 October: *Folies Bergère*, Paris.
28 October: Alhambra, Paris.
9 December: Empire, Bradford, England.
18 December–January: London Coliseum.

1912

6 January: Empire, Hackney.
(January: Presentation of Dickens' centenary plays at Court Theatre.)
13 January: Hippodrome, Manchester.
20 January: The New Middlesex Theatre, London.
27 January: Empire, Shepherds Bush, London.
12 February: Palladium, London.
17 February: Grand, Birmingham.
23 March: Returns to America on steamer Olympic.
20 April: Keith's 5th Avenue, New York City.
27 April: Orpheum, Brooklyn.
11 May: Shea's, Buffalo.
25 May: Alhambra, New York City.
June: Bushwick, Brooklyn; Keith's, Boston;
    New Brighton, Brighton Beach.
29 June: Hammerstein's, New York City.
July: Orpheum, Winnipeg, Canada.
3 August: Orpheum, Seattle; Orpheum, Portland, Oregon.
24 August: Orpheum, San Francisco (for three weeks).
September: Orpheum, Oakland; Orpheum, Los Angeles;
    Orpheum, Ogden, Utah.
October: Orpheum, Salt Lake City; Orpheum, Denver;
    Orpheum, Lincoln, Nebraska; Orpheum, Kansas City, Mo.
November: Orpheum, Des Moines; Orpheum, Omaha Neb.;

Orpheum, St Paul, Min.; Orpheum, Duluth.
December: Majestic, Milwaukee; Palace, Chicago.

1913

January: Orpheum, Memphis, Ten.; Orpheum, New Orleans;
   Keith's, Cincinatti.
February: Keith's, Indianapolis; Keith's, Louisville, Kent.;
   Hippodrome, Cleveland.
March: Grand Opera House, Pittsburgh; Orpheum, Montreal, Canada;
   Keith's, Boston.
(1 March: special performance at Atlanta Federal Prison.)
April: Poli's, Hartford Conn.; Orpheum Brooklyn.
3 May: Colonial, New York City.
10 May: Hammerstein's, New York City.
17 May: Keith's, Philadelphia.
24 May: Alhambra, New York City.
(Departure to Europe and last world tour.)
10 June: Leicester?
14 June: London Coliseum (for 3 weeks).
7 July: Tivoli, Hull.
14 July: Empire, Wood Green, London.
21 July: Hippodrome, Bristol.
28 July: Empire, Sunderland.
20 August: Hippodrome, Leeds.
3 September: Empire, Sheffield.
10 September: Empire, Newcastle-on-Tyne.
29 September: London Coliseum.
11 October: London Coliseum – Mme Sarah Bernhardt's
   'Good Samaritan' performance in presence of His Majesty King George V.
10 November: London Coliseum.
27 November: Empire, Hackney, London.
30 November: *Folies Bergère*, Paris.

1914

3 January: *Folies Bergère*, Paris (Harry Fragson shot offstage).
(Fields sails to South Africa.)
26 January–5 February: Empire, Johannesburg.
10 February: Hall-By-The-Sea, Durban.
16 February: Apollo, Germiston.
24 February: Grand, Pretoria.
(March: Sails for Australia.)
7 April: Tivoli, Sydney, Australia.
28 April–2 June: Tivoli, Melbourne.

25 June–1 August: Adelaide.

(10 August – sailing via Australian Bight to Perth.)

13 August: Tivoli, Perth (shares bill with 'patriotic tableau').

(29 August – sails on TSS *Ventura* to San Francisco.)

26 November: Opens at Empire Theatre, Syracuse, New York, in revue
   Watch Your Step. (Cut out of play, November 29.)

December: Resumes Vaudeville circuit:

26 December: Grand, Syracuse.

1915

January: Temple, Detroit; Keith's, Columbus Ohio (with 4 Marx Bros.); Keith's,
   Louisville, Kentucky; Keith's, Indianapolis.

February: Orpheum, Grand Rapids, Michigan; Keith's, Toledo;
   Palace, Chicago; Columbia, St. Louis.

March: Majestic, Milwaukee; Orpheum, Sioux City; Orpheum, Omaha.

April: Orpheum, Kansas City; Orpheum, Des Moines; Orpheum, St Paul.

12 June: Opens at New Amsterdam Theatre, New York City,
   in Ziegfeld *Follies* of 1915.

II. The Ziegfeld *Follies* & other stage appearances, 1915–1930

The Ziegfeld *Follies* of 1915 (including 'Pool Act').

The Ziegfeld *Follies* of 1916 (including 'A Croquet Game').

The Ziegfeld *Follies* of 1917 (including 'Tennis Sketch' and 'The Episode of the
   New York Streets and Subway').

The Ziegfeld *Follies* of 1918 (including 'A Game of Golf'
   aka 'An Episode on the Links').

Ziegfeld 'Midnight Frolic' – March 1920. (Also 1919.)

The Ziegfeld *Follies* of 1920 (including 'The Family Ford').

The Ziegfeld *Follies* of 1921 (including 'Off to the Country').

George White's *Scandals* of 1922 (including sketches 'Terrific Traffic', 'The Big
   Leaguers' and 'The Radio Bug').

Poppy 1923 – New Apollo Theatre & tour.

The Comic Supplement – December 1924–February 1925.

The Ziegfeld *Follies* of 1925 (including 'The Drug Store', 'A Back Porch', 'The
   Joy Ride', 'The Picnic', 'The Nagger'.)

Earl Carroll's *Vanities* of 1928 (including 'The Stolen Bonds',
   'The Caledonian Express', 'School Days', and 'An Episode at the Dentist's').

Last vaudeville acts, at the Palace Theatre, March 1930:

'The Stolen Bonds' and 'Golfing'.

Earl Carroll's *Vanities* of 1930 – Fields claimed 12 weeks work though he was not on the cast list.

August 1930: *Showboat*, St Louis Municipal Opera.
(Two weeks as Cap'n Andy.)

December 1930–February 1931: *Ballyhoo*, Hammerstein's Theatre.

III. Radio performances, 1933–1943

10 May 1933: guest on CBS show 'California Melodies'.

7 January 1937: NBC programme honoring 'Adolph Zukor's Silver Jubilee'.

May–September 1937: NBC 'Chase and Sanborn Hour',
with 'Charlie McCarthy', Edgar Bergen & Don Ameche.

1938: Guest appearances on NBC 'Chase and Sanborn Hour'
and CBS 'Lucky Strikes' Your Hit Parade'.

1942, 1943, 1944, guest appearances on NBC, Chase and Sanborn's
'Charlie McCarthy Show'.

1944, Christmas, Armed Forces Radio Service 'Christmas Special'.

28 October 1945: CBS Campbell Soup's 'Request Performance', broadcast of
'The Temperance Lecture' & 'The Day I Drank a Glass of Water'.

W. C. Fields—Filmography

1. Silent pictures

Pool Sharks. 1915. Short, 10 minutes.
Released by the Mutual Film Corporation, 19 September 1915. A Casino Star
  Comedy. Produced by the Gaumont Company. Director: Edwin Middleton.
Cast: W. C. Fields, a pool shark; Bud Ross, his rival.
Fields as pool hustler battles rival for fair lady and bottles.

His Lordship's Dilemma. 1916. Short, one reel. Lost film.
Released by the Mutual Film Corporation, 3 October 1915. A Casino Star
  Comedy. Produced by the Gaumont Company. Director: William Haddock.
Cast: W. C. Fields, remittance man (?); Bud Ross, his valet.
Fields' first version of his golf sketch.

Janice Meredith. 1924. 153 minutes.
Released by Metro-Goldwyn-Mayer, 8 December 1924. Produced by
  Cosmopolitan Pictures (William Randolph Hearst, prop.).
Directed by E. Mason Hopper. Screenplay by Lillie Hayward.
Cast: Marion Davies, Maclyn Arbuckle, Robert Thorne, Harrison Ford (not
  that one, guys), Holbrook Blinn, W. C. Fields as a British sergeant.
Cameo by Fields as a redcoat flirting with Marion Davies in 1776 dud.

Sally of the Sawdust. 1925. 104 minutes.
Released by United Artists, 2 August 1925. Produced by D. W. Griffith, Inc.
  Shot at Paramount's Astoria, New York, studios. Directed by D. W. Griffith.
  Based on the 1923 stage play *Poppy*, by Dorothy Donnelly. Adapted by
  Forrest Halsey. Photographed by Harry Fishbeck & Hal Sintzenich. Art direc-
  tor: Charles M. Kirk. Editor: James Smith.
Cast: W. C. Fields, Professor Eustace McGargle; Carol Dempster, Sally; Alfred
  Lunt, Peyton Lennox; Erville Anderson, Judge Foster; Effie Shannon, Mrs
  Foster; Charles Hammond, Mr Lennox Sr.; Roy Applegate, detective;
  Florence Fair, Miss Vinton; Marie Shotwell, society woman; Glenn Anders,
  Leon; Tammany Young, yokel; William "Shorty" Blanche, stooge.
Griffith's version of Fields' great stage hit; first sight of Eustace McGargle.

That Royle Girl. 1925. 114 minutes. Lost film.

Released by Paramount, 7 December 1925. Produced by D. W. Griffith for
Famous Players-Lasky. Presented by Adolph Zukor & Jesse L. Lasky.

Directed by D. W. Griffith. Based on 1925 *Cosmopolitan* magazine serial and
novel by Edwin Balmer. Screenplay by Paul Schofield. Photographed by Harry
Fishbeck & Hal Sintzenich. Art director: Charles M. Kirk. Editor: James
Smith.

Cast: Carol Dempster, Joan Daisy Royle; W. C. Fields, her father; James
Kirkwood, deputy district attorney Clavin Clarke; Harrison Ford, Fred
Ketlar; Paul Everton, George Baretta; George Rigas, his henchman; Kathleen
Chamber, Adele Ketlar; Florence Auer, Baretta's girlfriend; Ida Waterman,
Mrs Clarke; Alice Laidley, Clarke's fiancee; Dorothea Love, Lola Nelson;
Dore Davidson, Elman; Frank Allworth, Oliver; Bobby Watson, Hofer;
William "Shorty" Blanche, supporting role (?).

*Fields is Dempster's dissolute Dad in allegedly creaky tale of dance bands and
bootleggers.*

It's the Old Army Game. 1926. 72 minutes.

Released by Paramount, 24 May 1926. Presented by Adolph Zukor and Jesse L.
Lasky. Directed by Edward Sutherland. Associate producer: William Le
Baron. Screenplay by Tom J. Geraghty & J. Clarkson Miller. Based on *The
Comic Supplement,* by Joseph P. McEvoy. Titles by Ralph Spence & W. C.
Fields. Photographed by Alvin Wychoff. Supervising editor: Tom J. Geraghty.
Assistant director: Paul Jones.

Cast: W. C. Fields, Elmer Prettywillie; Louise Brooks, Marilyn; Blanche Ring,
Tessie Overholt; William Gaxton, George Parker; Mary Foy, Elmer's sister
Sarah; Mickey Bennet, nephew Mickey; Elise Cavanna, morning customer;
Josephine Dunn & Jack Luden, society bathers; George Currie, artist;
Expanded sketches and plot from The Comic Supplement.

So's Your Old Man. 1926. 67 minutes.

Released by Paramount, 25 October 1926. Produced by Gregory La Cava for
Famous Players-Lasky. Presented by Adolph Zukor and Jesse L. Lasky.

Directed by Gregory La Cava. Associate producer: William Le Baron.
Screenplay by J. Clarkson Miller. Adapted by Howard Emmett Rogers &
Tom J. Geraghty from Julian Street's *Mr Bisbee's Princess*. Photographed by
George Webber. Edited by Ralph Block & Julian Johnson.

Cast: W. C. Fields, Samuel Bisbee; Alice Joyce, Princess Lescaboura; Charles
"Buddy" Rogers, Kenneth Murchison; Kittens Reichert, Alice Bisbee; Marcia
Harris, Mrs Bisbee; Julia Ralph, Mrs A. Brandewyne Murchison; Frank
Montgomery, Jeff; Jerry Sinclair, Al; Charles Beyer (later Fields' agent), Prince
Lescaboura; William "Shorty" Blanche, caddy.

Inventor Bisbee's unbreakable windshield wins out in the end.

The Potters. 1927. 71 minutes. Lost film.

Released by Paramount, 15 January 1927. Produced by Famous Players-Lasky. Presented by Adolph Zukor and Jesse L. Lasky. Directed by Fred Newmeyer. Associate producer: William Le Baron. Based on *The Potters,* by Joseph P. McEvoy. Adapted by Sam Mintz & Ray Harris. Screenplay by J. Clarkson Miller. Photographed by Paul Vogel.

Assistant director: Ray Lissner.

Cast: W. C. Fields, Pa Potter; Mary Alden, Ma Potter; Ivy Harris, Minnie Potter; Jack Egan, Bill Potter; Richard "Skeets" Gallagher, Red Miller; Joseph Smiley, Rankin; Bradley Barker, Eagle.

J. P. McEvoy's play of an embattled middle-class father and dreamer.

Running Wild. 1927. 68 minutes.

Released by Paramount, 11 June 1927. Produced by Gregory La Cava for Famous Players-Lasky. Presented by Adolph Zukor and Jesse L. Lasky.

Directed by Gregory La Cava. Associate producer: William Le Baron.

Adaptation and screenplay by Roy Briant. based on a story by Gregory La Cava. Photographed by Paul Vogel. Edited by Ralph Block.

Cast: W. C. Fields, Elmer Finch; Mary Brian, Elizabeth Finch; Marie Shotwell, Mrs Finch; Claud Buchanan, Jerry Harvey; Barney Raskle, Junior; Frederick Burton, Mr Harvey; J. Moy Bennett, Mr Johnson; Frank Evans, Amos Barker; Ed Roseman, the hypnotist Arno; Tom Madden, truckdriver; John Merton, cop; Rex the Dog by himself.

Meek and henpecked Elmer hypnotised into becoming victorious paterfamilias.

Two Flaming Youths. 1927. 55 minutes (?) Lost film.

Released by Paramount, 17 December 1927. Produced by John Waters for Paramount Famous Lasky Corp. Presented by Adolph Zukor & Jesse L. Lasky.

Directed by John Waters. Screenplay by Percy Heath & Donald Davis. Based on a story by Percy Heath. Titles by Jack Conway & Herman J. Mankiewicz. Photographed by H. Kinley Martin. Fields-Conklin unit supervised by Louis D. Lighton.

Cast: W. C. Fields, Gabby Gilfoil; Chester Conklin, Sheriff Ben Holden; Mary Brian, Mary Gilfoil; Jack Luden, Tony Holden; George Irving, Simeon Trott; Cissy Fitzgerald, Madge Malarkey; Jimmie Quinn, Slippery Sawtelle; John Aasen, giant; Anna Magruder, fat lady; William Platt, dwarf; Chester Moorten, human pincushion; Lee W. Parker, tattooed man; John Serresheff, strong man; Jack the boxing kangaroo as himself; famous stage acts as themselves: Bobby Clark & Paul McCullough; George Moran & Charles Mack; Wallace Beery & Raymond Hatton; Clarence Kolb & Max Dill; Savoy & Brennan; Baker & Silvers; Benny & McNulty; Pearl & Bard; the Duncan Sisters.

The missing link: Fields' elegy for the travelling freak show.

Tillie's Punctured Romance. 1928. 57 minutes. Lost film.

Released by Paramount Famous Lasky Corp., 3 March 1928. Produced by the Christie Film Company. Presented by Al Christie. Directed by Edward Sutherland. Screenplay by Monte Brice & Keene Thompson. Based on the play *Tillie's Nightmare,* by Edgar Smith. Photographed by Charles Boyle & William Wheeler. Edited by Arthur Huffsmith. Assistant director: Paul Jones.

Cast: W. C. Fields, the ringmaster; Louise Fazenda, Tillie, a runaway; Chester Conklin, circus owner Horatio Q. Frisbee; Mack Swain, General Pilsner, Tillie's father; Doris Hill, trapezist; Grant Withers, wireless operator; Tom Kennedy, property man; Jean "Babe" London, strong woman; Billy Platt, midget; Kalla Pasha, axe thrower; Mickey Bennet, bad boy; Mike Refetto, lion tamer; Baron Von Dobeneck, German officer.

Circus brought to entertain the boys in the trenches gets lost behind enemy lines and wins the war. Vot iss diss, Chinese peoples?

Fools For Luck. 1928. 60 minutes. Lost film.

Released by Paramount, 7 May 1928. Produced by Paramount Famous Players Corp. Directed by Charles F. Reisner. Screenplay by Sam Mintz & J. Walter Ruben. Based on a story by Harry Fried. Titles by George Marion.

Photographed by William Marshall. Edited by George Nichols, Jr.

Cast: W. C. Fields, Richard Whitehead; Chester Conklin, Samuel Hunter; Sally Blane, Louise Hunter; Jack Luden, Ray Caldwell; Mary Alden, Mrs Hunter; Arthur Housman, Charles Grogan; Robert Dudley, Jim Simpson; Martha Mattox, Mrs Simpson.

Smooth-tongued Fields sells oil well to Conklin. Reputed to include Fields' pool routine.

2. Sound pictures

The Golf Specialist. 1930. Short, two reels.

Released by RKO, 22 August 1930. Produced by Louis Brock. Presented by Radio Pictures. Directed by Monte Brice.

Cast: W. C. Fields, Effingham Bellweather. Girl, caddy, etc, unknown.

Faithful rendition of 1918's An Episode on the Links.

Her Majesty Love. 1931. 75 minutes.

Released by Warner Brothers-First National, 15 December 1931. Produced by Warner Brothers. Directed by William Dieterle. Screenplay by Robert Lord & Arthur Caesar. Based on the German film *Ihr Majestat die Liebe,* from the play by Rudolph Bernauer & Rudolph Oesterreicher. Dialogue by Henry Blanke & Joseph Jackson. Edited by Ralph Dawson. Art director: Jack Okey. Photographed by Robert Kurrle. Lyrics by Al Dubin. Songs: "You're Baby

Minded Now," "Because of You," "Don't Ever Be Blue," "Though You're
Not the First One."

Cast: Marilyn Miller, Lia Toerrek; Ben Lyon, Fred Von Wellingen; W. C. Fields,
Bela Toerrek; Ford Sterling, Otmar Von Wellingen; Leon Errol, Baron Von
Schwarzdorf; Chester Conklin, Emil; Harry Stubbs, Hanneman; Maude
Eburne, Aunt Harriette Von Wellingen; Harry Holman, Dr Jeisenfeld; Ruth
Hall, factory secretary; William Irving, third man; Mae Madison, Elli;
Clarence Wilson, cousin Cornelius; Virginia Sale, Laure Reisenfeld; Alfred
James, lawyer; Elsa Peterson, cabaret woman; Lynn Reynolds, cabaret girl;
Florence Roberts, grandmother; with Frank Darien, Donald Novis, Eddie
Kane, Irving Bacon, Leonard Carey, Oscar Apfel, Gus Arnheim and His
Coconut Grove Orchestra, and Ravero's South American Tango Band, as
themselves.
*Fields as ex-vaudevillian barber tangles with daughter's love life and Berlin ball-
bearing barons.*

Million Dollar Legs. 1932. 64 minutes.
Released by Paramount Publix Corp., 8 July 1932. Supervised by Herman J.
Mankiewicz. Directed by Edward Cline. Screenplay by Henry Myers and
Nick Barrows. Based on a story by Joseph L. Mankiewicz. Photographed by
Arthur Todd. Songs: "Klopstokian Love Song," "When I Get Hot in
Klopstokia."
Cast: Jack Oakie, Migg Tweeny, brush salesman; W. C. Fields, president; Andy
Clyde, Majordomo; Susan Fleming, Angela; Ben Turpin, mystery man; Lyda
Roberti, Mata Machree; Hugh Herbert, secretary of the treasury; George
Barbier, Baldwin; Dickie Moore, Angela's brother; Billy Gilbert, secretary of
the interior; Vernon Dent, secretary of agriculture; Teddy Hart, secretary of
war; John Sinclair, secretary of labor; Sam Adams, secretary of state; Irving
Bacon, secretary of navy; Ben Taggart, ship's captain; Hank Mann, customs
inspector; Chick Collins, jumper; Sid Saylor & Hobart Bosworth, starters;
Ernie Adams, contestant; Charlie Hall, Herman Brix, Bruce Bennett, Billy
Engle, Klopstokian athletes; Eddie Dunn, coachman; Al Bridge & Heinie
Conklin, spies in capes; Herbert Evans, butler; Eddie Baker & Edgar Dearing,
train officials; Don Wilson, stationmaster; Tyler Brooke, Olympics announcer.
*In the crazy Republic of Klopstokia, President Fields battles to survive in office
as leader of a nation of Olympic-level athletes.*

If I Had a Million. 1932. 88 minutes.
Released by Paramount Publix Corp., November 1932. Production supervised
by Ernst Lubitsch. Associate producer: Louis D. Lighton. Directed by Stephen
S. Roberts, James Cruze, Norman Taurog, Norman McLeod (Fields segment),
H. Bruce Humberstone, Ernst Lubitsch, William A. Seiter. (Uncredited direc-

tor: Lothar Mendes.) Based on the novel *Windfall,* by Robert D. Andrews. Screenplay of Fields segment, *Road Hogs:* Joseph L. Mankiewicz.

Cast of segment: W. C. Fields, Rollo La Rue; Alison Skipworth, Emily; Cecil Cunningham, Agnes.

Dying millionaire sends one million dollars apiece to eight people chosen at random from the phone book. Emily La Rue, wife of retired vaudevillian Fields, spends hers with Fields buying a row of cars to hunt down road hogs after her long-desired car has been wrecked.

The Dentist. 1932. Short, two reels.

Released by Paramount, 9 December 1932. A Mack Sennett Star Comedy. Produced by Mack Sennett. Directed by Leslie Pearce. Screenplay by W. C. Fields. Based on *An Episode at the Dentist* stage sketch.

Cast: W. C. Fields, the dentist; Babe Kane, his daughter; Zedna Farley, his assistant; Elise Cavanna, Miss Mason; Bud Jamison, Charley; Dorothy Granger, Miss Peppitone; Billy Bletcher, "Russian" patient; Bobby Dunn, caddy; Arnold Gray, the iceman; Harry Bowen, Joe; Emma Tansey, old lady.

Fields' stage sketch from Earl Carroll's Vanities *of 1928.*

The Fatal Glass of Beer. 1933. Short, two reels.

Released 3 March 1933. A Mack Sennett Star Comedy. Produced by Mack Sennett. Directed by Clyde Bruckman. Screenplay by W. C. Fields. Based on *The Stolen Bonds* from Earl Carroll's *Vanities* of 1928.

Cast: W. C. Fields, Mr Snavely; Rosemary Theby, Mrs Snavely; George Chandler, Chester; Rychard Cramer, Officer Posthlewhistle; Jack Cooper, officer; George Moran & Artie Ortego, Indians; Marvin Lobach, bartender; Gordon Douglas & Ernie Alexander, college students.

'And it ain't a fit night out for man nor beast!'

The Pharmacist. 1933. Short, two reels.

Released by Paramount, 21 April 1933. A Mack Sennett Star Comedy. Produced by Mack Sennett. Directed by Arthur Ripley. Screenplay by W. C. Fields. Adapted from *The Drug Store* sketch from *The Comic Supplement* and the Ziegfeld *Follies* of 1925.

Cast: W. C. Fields, Mr Dilweg; Babe Kane, his daughter; Elise Cavanna, his wife; Grady Sutton, Cuthbert; Lorena Carr, older daughter; Si Jenks, checkers player; Joe Bordeaux, gunman; Emma Tansey, old lady; Efe Jackson & Jack Cooper, bit parts.

'Gimme a clean stamp from the middle!'

The Barber Shop. 1933. Short, two reels.

Released by Paramount, 28 July 1933. A Mack Sennett Star Comedy. Produced by Mack Sennett. Directed by Arthur Ripley. Screenplay by W. C. Fields.

Cast: W. C. Fields, Cornelius O'Hare; Elise Cavanna, his wife; Harry Watson, Ronald O'Hare; Dagmar Oakland, Hortense the manicurist; Fay Holderness, little girl's mother; John St Clair, Mr Flood; Cyril Ring, bandit; Frank "Fatty" Alexander, steam room victim; Harry Bowen, officer; George Humbert, Jose, fiddle salesman; Joe Bordeaux, bit part.

'Is that a mole?' 'Yep, had it all my life.' Swipe! 'Well, you don't have it any more.'

Hip Action.

Short in *Bobby Jones, How to Break 90* golf series. Released by the Vitaphone Corp., 24 June 1933. Directed by George E. Marshall.

Cast: Bobby Jones, W. C. Fields, Warner Oland, William B. Davidson, as themselves.

International House. 1933. 70 minutes.

Released by Paramount, 2 June 1933. Directed by Edward Sutherland. Screenplay by Francis Martin & Walter DeLeon. Based on a story by Neil Brant & Louis E. Heifitz. Music and lyrics by Ralph Rainger & Leo Robin. Photographed by Ernest Haller. Song: "Reefer Man." (!!!)

Cast: W. C. Fields, Professor Quail; Peggy Hopkins-Joyce, as herself; Bela Lugosi, General Petronovitch; Stuart Erwin, Tommy Nash; Sari Matitza, Carol Fortescue; Edmund Breese, Dr Wong; Franklin Pangborn, hotel manager; Harrison Greene, Von Baden; Henry Sedley, Serge; James Wong, Inspector Sun; featuring George Burns & Gracie Allen, Colonel Stoopnagle & Budd, Sterling Holloway, Cab Calloway & his orchestra, Baby Rose Marie. With Ernest Wood, Edwin Stanley, Clem Beauchamp, Jerry Drew, Norman Ainslee, Louis Vincenot, Bo-Ling, Bo-Ching, Etta Lee, Lona Andre, Andre Cheron.

Fields lands in Wu Hu, China, instead of Kansas City, and demands two hundred-year-old eggs boiled in perfume.

Hollywood on Parade (B-2).

Promotional short released by Paramount, 8 September 1933. Starring W. C. Fields, George Burns, Gracie Allen, Jack Haley, Irving Pichel, Bing Crosby, Mary Brian, Adolphe Menjou, Katharine De Mille, Cecil B. De Mille, Cary Grant, Dale Van Sickel, Jean Rogers, Gertrude Michael, Tammany Young, Henry Wilcoxon.

Tillie and Gus. 1933. 58 minutes.

Released by Paramount, 13 October 1933. Produced by Douglas MacLean. Directed by Francis Martin. Screenplay by Walter De Leon and Francis Martin; adapted from a story by Rupert Hughes. "Contributors" to script:

Grover Jones, William Slavens McNutt, Ray Harris. Photographed by
Benjamin Reynolds. Art directors: Hans Dreier & Harry Oliver. Song:
"Bringing in the Sheaves."

Cast: W. C. Fields, Augustus Q. Winterbottom; Alison Skipworth, Tillie
Winterbottom; Baby LeRoy, the "King" Sheridan; Jacqueline Wells, Mary
Blake Sheridan; Clifford Jones, Tom Sheridan; Clarence Wilson, Phineas
Pratt; George Barbier, Captain Fogg; Barton MacLane, Commissioner
McLennan; Edgar Kennedy, Judge Elmer; Robert McKenzie, defense attorney;
Master Williams, Hard Card Harrington; with William Irving, Ivan Linow,
Lon Poff, James Burke, Frank Hagney, Lew Kelly, Irving Bacon, Billy Engle,
Joe Glick, Chick Collins, Brooks Benedict, Cyril Ring, Ferris Taylor, Ed
Brady, Harry Schultz, Jerry Jerome, Frank O'Connor, Eddie Baker.

*Fields and Skipworth teamed again in riverboat race, first skirmish with Baby
LeRoy.*

Alice in Wonderland. 1933. 90 minutes.

Released by Paramount, 22 December 1933. Produced by Louis D. Lighton.
Directed by Norman McLeod. Based on Lewis Carroll's "Alice" books.
Screenplay by Joseph L. Mankiewicz and William Cameron Menzies.
Photographed by Henry Sharp & Bert Glennon. Music by Dimitri Tiomkin.

Cast: Charlotte Henry, Richard Arlen, Gary Cooper, Jack Duffy, Leon Errol,
Louise Fazenda, W. C. Fields as Humpty Dumpty, Skeets Gallagher, Cary
Grant, Raymond Hatton, Sterling Holloway, Edward Everett Horton, Roscoe
Karns, Baby LeRoy as the Joker, Mae Marsh, Polly Moran, Jack Oakie, Edna
Mae Oliver, Charlie Ruggles, Alison Skipworth as the Duchess; Ned Sparks,
Ford Sterling.

Fields plays egg but sticks to scripted yokes.

Six of a Kind. 1934. 65 minutes.

Released by Paramount, 9 February 1934. Produced by Douglas MacLean.
Directed by Leo McCarey. Screenplay by Walter DeLeon & Harry Ruskin.
Based on a story by Keene Thompson & Douglas MacLean. Photographed by
Henry Sharp. Art directors: Hans Dreier & Robert Odell. Music by Ralph
Rainger. Edited by Le Roy Stone. Sound recorded by Eugene Merritt.

Cast: Charlie Ruggles, J. Pinkham Whinney; Mary Boland, Flora; W. C. Fields,
Sheriff "Honest John" Hoxley; Alison Skipworth, the Duchess; George
Burns, George Edwards; Gracie Allen, Gracie Devore; with Grace Bradley,
Bradley Page, William J. Kelly, James Burke, Dick Rush, Walter Long, Leo
Willis, Lew Kelly, Alfred P. James, Tammany Young, Lee Phelps, Irving
Bacon, Paul Tead, Henry Bernard, Robert McKenzie, George Pearce, Verna
Hillie, Florence Enright, William Augustin, Kathleen Burke, Neal Burns.

'So tell me, how did you get to be called Honest John?'

You're Telling Me. 1934. 67 minutes.

Released by Paramount, 6 April 1934. Produced by William Le Baron. Directed by Erle C. Kenton. Screenplay by Walter De Leon & Paul M. Jones. Adapted from "Mr Bisbee's Princess," by Julian Street. Dialogue by J. P. McEvoy. Photographed by Alfred Gilks. Art directors: Hans Dreier & Robert Odell. Music by Arthur Johnson & Sam Coslow. Edited by Otto Lovering. Sound recorded by Earl S. Hayman.

Cast: W. C. Fields, Sam Bisbee; Joan Marsh, Pauline Bisbee; Louise Carter, Mrs Bessie Bisbee; Larry "Buster" Crabbe, Bob Murchison; Kathleen Howard, Mrs Murchison; Adrienne Ames, Princess Lescaboura; James B. "Pop" Kenton, Doc Beebe; Robert McKenzie, Charles Bogle; George Irving, president of tire company; Jerry Stewart, Frobisher; Tammany Young, caddy; Louise Cavanna, gossip; with Del Henderson, Nora Cecil, George MacQuarrie, John M. Sullivan, Vernon Dent, Lee Phelps, Dorothy Vernon Bay, Edward Le Saint, Eddie Baker, James C. Morton, Billy Engle, George Ovey, Al Hart, Frederic Sullivan, William Robyns, Harold Berquist, Frank O'Connor, Florence Enright.

Retread of So's Your Old Man, *with unbreakable windshield replaced by puncture-proof tire.*

Hollywood on Parade (B-10).

Promotional short released by Paramount, 27 April 1934. Starring W. C. Fields, Groucho & Chico Marx, Jack Oakie, Jack LaRue, Buster Crabbe, Richard Arlen, Mitchell Leisen, Claudette Colbert, George Raft, Mary Pickford, Dick Powell, Mae West, Jimmy Durante, Clarke Gable, Walter Huston, Ruth Etting, Max Baer, Rhea Langham as themselves.

The Old Fashioned Way. 1934. 66 minutes.

Released by Paramount, 13 July 1934. Produced by William Le Baron. Presented by Adolph Zukor. Directed by William Beaudine. Original story by Charles Bogle (W. C. Fields). Screenplay by Garnett Weston & Jack Cunningham. "Contributors" to script & treatments: J. P. McEvoy, Paul Jones, Ralph Ceder, Hal Yates, Lex Neal, H. M. Walker, Claude Binyon, Walter De Leon. Photographed by Benjamin Reynolds. Music by Harry Revel, lyrics by Mack Gordon. Songs: "Rolling in Love," "A Little Bit of Heaven Known as Mother," "The Sea Shell Song." Art director: John Goodman. Sound recorded by P. G. Wisdom.

Cast: W. C. Fields, The Great McGonigle; Judith Allen, Betty McGonigle; Joe Morrison, Wally Livingstone; Jan Duggan, Cleopatra Pepperday; Baby LeRoy, Albert Pepperday; Nora Cecil, Mrs Wendleschaffer; Tammany Young, Marmaduke Gump; Oscar Apfel, Mr Livingstone; with Jack Mulhall, Joe Mills, Samuel Ethridge, Emma Ray, Ruth Marion, Richard Carle, Lew Kelly,

Adrienne Ames, Clarence Wilson, Billy Bletcher, Robert McKenzie, Dorothy Ray, Davidson Clarke, Marvin Lobach, Oscar Smith, Sam Flint.

The Great McGonigle plays the sticks with his old-time theatrical travelling troupe. Featuring the authentic rendition of The Drunkard.

Mrs Wiggs of the Cabbage Patch. 1934. 80 minutes.

Released by Paramount, 19 October 1934. Produced by Douglas MacLean. Presented by Adolph Zukor. Directed by Norman Taurog. Screenplay by William Slavens McNutt & Jane Storm. Based on a story by Alice Hegan Rice & Anne Crawford Flexner. Photographed by Charles Lang. Art directors: Hans Dreier & Robert Odell. Songs: "Comin' Thro' the Rye," "Glow Little Glow Worm," "Wait Till the Sun Shines, Nellie," "Listen to the Mocking Bird," "Swanee River." *(Godfrey Daniel!)*

Cast: Pauline Lord, Mrs Elvira Wiggs; Zasu Pitts, Miss Tabitha Hazy; W. C. Fields, C. Ellsworth Stubbins; Evelyn Venable, Lucy Olcott; Kent Taylor, Bob Redding; Charles Middleton, Bagby; Donald Meek, Mr Hiram Wiggs; with Jimmy Butler, George Breakston, Edith Fellows, Virginia Weidler, Carmencita Johnson, George Reed, Mildred Glover, Arthur Housman, Walter Walker, Sam Flint, Edward Tamblyn, Dell Henderson, Lillian Elliott, James Robinson, Bentley Hewlett, Al Shaw, Sam Lee, George Pearce, Earl Pingree, Anne Sheridan, Tyler Brooke.

Fields arrives late to enliven dire sentimental farrago. 'Do you want to grow up and be dumb, like Zasu Pitts?'

It's a Gift. 1934. 73 minutes.

Released by Paramount, 30 November 1934. Presented by Adolph Zukor. Produced by William Le Baron. Directed by Norman McLeod. Screenplay by Jack Cunningham from a story by Charles Bogle (W. C. Fields). Based on *The Comic Supplement,* by J. P. McEvoy. "Contributors" to script and treatments: Eddie Welch, John Sinclair, Lou Breslow, Harry Ruskin, Garnett Weston, Claude Binyon, Paul Gerard Smith, Howard J. Green. Photographed by Henry Sharp. Art directors: Hans Dreier and John B. Goodman. Sound by Earl S. Hayman. Song: "On the Banks of the Wabash."

Cast: W. C. Fields, Harold Bissonette (pronounced Bissonay); Kathleen Howard, his wife; Jean Rouverol, daughter Mildred; Tommy Bupp, son Norman; Tammany Young, Everett Ricks; Morgan Wallace, Jasper "Cumquats" Fitschmueller; Charles Sellon, blind Mr Muckle; Baby LeRoy, Baby Dunk; Josephine Whittell, Mrs Dunk; Diana Lewis, Miss Dunk; T. Roy Barnes, insurance salesman; Jerry Mandy, vegetable man; with Spencer Charters, Guy Usher, Patsy O'Byrne, Del Henderson, Edith Kingdom, William Tooker, Billy Engle, Jack Mulhall, Bud Fine, Eddie Baker, Jane Withers, Chill Wills and the Avalon Boys, and Buster the dog.

Remake of It's the Old Army Game—*the* Comic Supplement *sketches in sound dialogue. 'Even a worm will turn.'*

David Copperfield. 1935. 133 minutes.
Released by Metro-Goldwyn-Mayer, 18 January 1935. Produced by David O.
  Selznick. Directed by George Cukor. Based on the novel by Charles Dickens.
  Adaptation by Hugh Walpole. Screenplay by Howard Estabrook.
  Photographed by Oliver T. Marsh. Art director: Cedric Gibbons. Wardrobe:
  Dolly Tree. Music by Herbert Stothart. Edited by Robert J. Kern. Sound by
  Douglas Shearer.
Cast: W. C. Fields, Wilkins Micawber; Lionel Barrymore, Mr Peggotty; Jessie
  Ralph, Nurse Peggotty; Maureen O'Sullivan, Dora Spenlow; Freddie
  Bartholomew, David the child; Jean Cadell, Mrs Micawber; Madge Evans,
  Agnes Wickfield; Lewis Stone, Mr Wickfield; Elizabeth Allan, Mrs Clara
  Copperfield; Roland Young, Uriah Heep; Basil Rathbone, Mr Murdstone;
  Violet Kemble-Cooper, Mrs Murdstone; Elsa Lanchester, Clickett; Lennox
  Pawle, Mr Dick; Una O'Connor, Mrs Gummidge; John Buckler, Ham; Hugh
  Williams, Steerforth; with Ivan Simpson, Hugh Walpole, Mabel Colcord,
  Herbert Mundin, Fay Chaldecott, Florine McKinney, Marilyn Knowlden,
  Harry Beresford, Renee Gadd, Arthur Treacher, and Frank Lawton as the
  older David.
Fields' only straight dramatic interpretation of a classical role as Micawber.

Mississippi. 1935. 80 minutes.
Released by Paramount, 22 March 1935. Presented by Adolph Zukor. Produced
  by Arthur Hornblow Jr. Directed by Edward Sutherland. Screenplay by
  Francis Martin & Jack Cunningham. Based on Booth Tarkington's 1923 play
  The Magnolia, adapted by Herbert Fields & Claude Binyon. "Contributors"
  to treatment: Dore Schary & Herbert Fields. Photographed by Charles Lang.
  Art directors: Hans Dreier & Bernard Herzbrun. Music by Richard Rogers,
  lyrics by Lorenz Hart. Songs: "Soon," "It's Easy to Remember," "Down by
  the River," "Roll, Mississippi," "Swanee River." Edited by Chandler House.
  Sound by Eugene Merritt. Second unit director: Marshall Neilan.
Cast: Bing Crosby, Tom Grayson; W. C. Fields, Commodore Orlando Jackson;
  Joan Bennett, Lucy Rumford; Queenie Smith, Alabam'; Gail Patrick, Elvira
  Rumford; Claude Gillingwater, General Rumford; with John Miljan, Edward
  Pawley, Fred Kohler Sr., John Larkin, Libby Taylor, Harry Myers, Paul Hurst,
  Robert McKenzie, Oscar Smith, Harry Cody, Forrest Taylor, Warner
  Richmond, Ann Sheridan, Jean Rouverol, Jules Cowles, Theresa Maxwell
  Conover, Charles King, King Baggott, J. P. McGowan, Molasses & January as
  themselves, and The Cabin Kids as themselves.
Gamblin' an' croonin' on ole man river. They was mighty good with mustard.

Man on the Flying Trapeze. 1935. 65 minutes.

Released by Paramount, 26 July 1935. Presented by Adolph Zukor. Produced by William Le Baron. Directed by Clyde Bruckman (and unofficially by W. C. Fields & Sam Hardy). Screenplay by Ray Harris & Sam Hardy. Based on a story by Charles Bogle (W. C. Fields). "Contributors" to script and treatment: Bobby Vernon, Johnny Sinclair, Jack Cunningham. Photographed by Alfred Gieks. Song (in key of Eek): "On the Banks of the Wabash."

Cast: W. C. Fields, Ambrose Wolfinger; Mary Brian, daughter Hope; Kathleen Howard, Mrs Wolfinger; Grady Sutton, stepson Claude; Vera Lewis, mother-in-law Mrs Nesselrode; Lucien Littlefield, Mr Peabody; Oscar Apfel, Malloy; Tammany Young, Willie the Weasel; Walter Brennan, Legs the second burglar; Arthur Aylesworth, judge; Lew Kelly, cop; Michael S. Visaroff, maniac in jail; Carlotta Monti, secretary; Harry Ezekian, Kookalluka Mishabob; Tor Johnson, Tossoff, the Russian Behemoth; David Clyde, J. Farnsworth Wallaby; with Ed Gargan, Eddie Chandler, James Burke, James Flavin, Sarah Edwards, Sam Lufkin, Helen Dickson, Lorin Raker, Heinie Conklin, Harry C. Bradley, Rosemary Theby, Jack Baxley, George French, Billy Bletcher, Mickey McMasters.

Fields agonistes. Loose remake of Running Wild *presents Fields' most dysfunctional family.*

Poppy. 1936. 75 minutes.

Released by Paramount, 19 June 1936. Presented by Adolph Zukor. Produced by William Le Baron. Directed by A. Edward Sutherland. Associate producer: Paul M. Jones. Screenplay by Waldemar Young & Virginia Van Upp. Based on the 1923 stage play *Poppy,* by Dorothy Donnelly. "Contributors" to script: Jack Cunningham & Bobby Vernon. Photographed by William C. Mellor. Art directors: Hans Dreier & Bernard Herzbrun. Costume designer: Edith Head. Music by Ralph Rainger, Leo Robin, Sam Coslow & Frederick Hollander. Musical director: Boris Morros. Songs: "Poppy," "A Rendezvous with a Dream." Edited by Stuart Heisler. Sound by Earl S. Hayman and John Cope.

Cast: W. C. Fields, Professor Eustace McGargle; Rochelle Hudson, Poppy; Richard Cromwell, Billy Farnsworth; Granville Bates, Mayor Farnsworth; Catherine Doucet, Countess De Puizzi; Lynne Overman, Attorney E. G. Whiffen; Maude Eburne, Sarah Tucker; with Bill Wolfe, Adrian Morris, Rosalind Keith, Ralph Remley, Wade Boteler, Tom Herbert, Dewey Robinson, Tom Kennedy, Ada Mae Moore, Tammany Young, Charles McMurphy, Cyril Ring, Eddie Waller, Del Henderson, Nora Cecil, Harry Wagner, Frank Sully, Malcolm Waite, Dick Rush, Grace Goodall, Gertrude Sutton, Johnny Sinclair as Fields' double.

Remake of Sally of the Sawdust *returns to the original* Poppy *story.*

The Big Broadcast of 1938. 1938. 97 minutes.

Released by Paramount, 18 February 1938. Presented by Adolph Zukor. Executive producer: William Le Baron. Produced by Harlan Thompson. Directed by Mitchell Leisen. Screenplay by Walter De Leon, Francis Martin & Ken Englund. From a story by Frederick Hazlitt Brennan. Adapted by Howard Lindsay and Russell Crouse. Additional sketch material (uncredited) by W. C. Fields. Photographed by Harry Fishbeck. Art directors: Hans Dreier & Ernest Fegte. Costumes by Edith Head. Musical director: Boris Morros. Songs: "Thanks for the Memory," "You Took the Words Right Out of my Heart," "Zumi Zumi," "Brunnhilde's Battlecry," "The Waltz Lives On," "Mama, That Moon Is Here Again." *(Mother of pearl!!)* Edited by Eda Warren & Chandler House. Cartoon sequence by Leon Schlesinger. Special effects by Gordon Jennings. Additional scenes directed (uncredited) by Eddie Cline.

Cast: W. C. Fields, as T. Frothingell Bellows and his brother, S. B. Bellows; Martha Raye, Martha Bellows, his daughter; Bob Hope, Buzz Fielding; with Dorothy Lamour, Shirley Ross, Lynne Overman, Leif Erickson, Grace Bradley, Rufe Davis, Tito Guizar, Lionel Pape, Virginia Vale, Russell Hicks, Leonard Kinskey, Patricia Wilder, Shep Fields & his Rippling Rhythm Orchestra, and almost everyone else out of work in Hollywood at the time.

Fields in double part as millionaire playboy and responsible magnate flim-flamming aboard an ocean-going liner.

You Can't Cheat an Honest Man. 1939. 76 minutes.

Released by Universal, 17 February 1939. Produced by Lester Cowan. Directed by George Marshall. Assistant director: Vernon Keays. Additional scenes (uncredited) directed by Eddie Cline. Screenplay by George Marion Jr., Richard Mack & Everett Freeman. Based on a story by Charles Bogle (W. C. Fields). "Contributors" to script: Henry Johnson, Lew Lipton, Manuel Seff & James Seymour. Photographed by Milton Krasner. Art director: Jack Otterson. Musical director: Charles Previn. Songs: "Hi, Charlie McCarthy," "Camptown Races." Edited by Otto Ludwig. Production assistant: Cliff Work.

Cast: W. C. Fields, Larson E. Whipsnade; Edgar Bergen, himself; Charlie McCarthy, dummy (himself); Mortimer Snerd, another dummy; Constance Moore, Vicky Whipsnade; John Arledge, Phineas Whipsnade; Mary Forbes, Mrs Bel-Goodie; Thurston Hall, Archibald Bel-Goodie; James Bush, Roger Bel-Goodie III; Grady Sutton, Chester Dalrymple; Eddie Rochester Anderson, Cheerful; with Ivan Lebedeff, Frank Jenks, Lee Phelps, Ferris Taylor, Irving Bacon, Jan Duggan, Evelyn Del Rio, David Oliver, Ed Thomas, Edward Woolf, Bill Wolfe, Billy Engle, Blacaman the lion tamer as himself.

Fields returns to form as circus owner and snake-story raconteur.

My Little Chickadee. 1940. 83 minutes.

Released by Universal, 9 February 1940. Produced by Lester Cowan. Uncredited producer: Jack Gross. Directed by Edward Cline. Screenplay by Mae West & W. C. Fields. Photographed by Joseph Valentine. Art director: Jack Otterson. Music by Frank Skinner, directed by Charles Previn. Song: "Willie of the Valley," music by Ben Oakland, lyrics by Milton Drake. Edited by Edward Curtiss. Sound by Bernard V. Brown.

Cast: Mae West, Flower Belle Lee; W. C. Fields, Cuthbert J. Twillie; Joseph Calleia, Jeff Badger/masked bandit; Dick Foran, Wayne Carter; Margaret Hamilton, Miss Gideon; George Moran, Indian; Si Jenks, deputy; James Conlin, Squawk Mulligan; with Bud Harris, Russell Hall, Eddie Butler, Bing Conley, Anne Nagel, Ruth Donnelly, Fay Adler, Jan Duggan, Bob Burns, Bill Wolfe, Morgan Wallace, Robert McKenzie.

Mae West and Fields twinned in western hi-hokum. 'I'd like to see Paris before I die! Philadelphia will do!'

The Bank Dick. 1940. 74 minutes.

Released by Universal, 29 November 1940. Supervised by Jack Gross. Directed by Edward Cline. Screenplay by Mahatma Kane Jeeves (W. C. Fields). Collaborating director: Ralph Ceder. Additional material written by Dick Carroll. Photographed by Milton Krasner. Art director: Jack Otterson. Musical director: Charles Previn. Sound by Bernard B. Brown.

Cast: W. C. Fields, Egbert Souse; Cora Witherspoon, Agatha Souse; Unna Merkel, Myrtle Souse; Evelyn Del Rio, Elsie Mae Adele Brunch Souse; Jessie Ralph, Mrs Hermisillio Brunch; Grady Sutton, Ogg Ogilby; Shemp Howard, Joe the bartender; Franklin Pangborn, J. Pinkerton Snoopington, bank examiner; Richard Purcell, Mackley Q. Greene; Russell Hicks, J. Frothingham Waterbury; Pierre Watkin, Mr Skinner; Al Hill, Repulsive Rogan; George Moran, Loudmouth (alias Filthy) McNasty; Jack Norton, A. Pismo Clam; Pat West, assistant director; Reed Hadley, Francois; Heather Wilde, Miss Plupp; Harlan Briggs, Dr Stall; Bill Alston, bank teller; Eddie Dunn, chauffeur; Jan Duggan, Mrs Muckle; Bill Wolfe, Otis; with Bobby Larson, Patsy Moran, Charlie Sullivan, Emmett Vogan, Fay Adler, Nora Cecil, Dorothy Vernon.

'I've got a script I've had in mothballs for twenty years. I read it to Irving and Milton who run the Gem Cinema down here. They said to me—Souse, it's better than Gone With the Wind . . .'

Never Give a Sucker an Even Break. 1941. 70 minutes.

Released by Universal, 10 October 1941. Directed by Edward Cline. Screenplay by John T. Neville & Prescott Chaplin. Based on a story by Otis Criblecoblis (W. C. Fields). Associate director: Ralph Ceder. Photographed by Charles Van Enger. Cameraman: Jerome Ash. Art directors: Jack Otterson & Richard H.

Riedel. Music by Frank Skinner. Musical director: Charles Previn. Songs: "Estrellita," "Comin' Thro' the Rye," "Ochi chorniya," "Here Comes the Bride." Edited by Arthur Hilton. Sound by Bernard B. Brown.

Cast: W. C. Fields, himself; Gloria Jean, herself as his niece; Leon Errol, Schlepperman; Margaret Dumont, Mrs Haemoglobin; Susan Miller, Ouliotta Delight; Franklin Pangborn, producer; Mona Barrie, his wife; Carlotta Monti, receptionist; Minerva Urecal, Mrs Pastromi; Anne Nagel, Gorgeous (scene cut from film); Irving Bacon, Tom the soda jerker; Jody Gilbert, waitress; Jack "Tiny" Lipson, Turkish peoples; Billy Lenhart & Kenneth Brown as Butch & Buddy; with Bill Wolfe, Charles Lang, Emmett Vogan, Leon Belasco, Dave Willock, Billy Wayne, Harriet Haddon, Marcia Ralston, Duke York, Claud Allister, Michael Visaroff, Eddie Bruce, Emil Van Horn as the Gorilla and Prince the Great Dane as himself.

The Great Man's swan song: 'This scene was supposed to be in a saloon, but the censor cut it . . . it'll play just as well . . .'

Tales of Manhattan. 1942. 118 minutes.

Released by 20th Century Fox, 30 October 1942. Produced by Borris Morros & Sam Spiegel (as S. P. Eagle). Directed by Julien Duvivier. Screenplay & stories by Ben Hecht, Ferenc Molnar, Donald Ogden Stewart, Samuel Hoffenstein, Alan Campbell, Ladislas Fodor, Lazlo Gorog, Laszlo Vadnai, Lamar Trotti, Henry Blankford. Uncredited stories by Buster Keaton, Ed Beloin & Bill Morrow. Photographed by Joseph Walker. Art directors: Richard Day & Boris Leven. Music by Sol Kaplan. Edited by Robert Bischoff. Sound by W. D. Flick & Roger Heman.

Cast in W. C. Fields segment: W. C. Fields as Postlewhistle; Margaret Dumont as Mrs Langahankie; X the unknown as Fields' stooge, Schicklegruber. Segment cut from released film but restored for video release, 1997. Cast in other sections includes: Charles Boyer, Rita Hayworth, Thomas Mitchell, Eugene Pallette, Henry Fonda, Ginger Rogers, Cesar Romero, Charles Laughton, Elsa Lanchester, Edward G. Robinson, George Sanders, Mae Marsh, Paul Robeson, Ethel Waters, etc.

Tales of a tailcoat which passes from hand to hand. Fields lectures on the demon rum: 'This is the liver, very good with bacon . . .'

Follow the Boys. 1944. 118 minutes.

Released by Universal, 5 May 1944. Produced by Charles K. Feldman. Directed by Eddie Sutherland. Screenplay by Howard Breslow & Gertrude Purcell. Photographed by Dave Abel. Art directors: John B. Goodman & Harold H. MacArthur. Musical director: Leigh Harline. Edited by Fred R. Feitshans Jr. Sound by Bernard B. Brown.

Cast: George Raft, Vera Zorina, W. C. Fields with Bill Wolfe, Jeanette

MacDonald, Marlene Dietrich, Dinah Shore, Donald O'Connor, Arthur Rubinstein, the Andrews Sisters, Lon Chaney Jr., Gloria Jean, Andy Devine, Gale Sondergaard, Randolph Scott, Orson Welles' Mercury Wonder Show, etc.

Vaudeville format tale starring everybody who was available in Hollywood. Fields' only authentic reconstruction of his original pool routine.

Song of the Open Road. 1944. 93 minutes.

Released by United Artists, 21 June 1944. Produced by Charles R. Rogers. Directed by S. Sylvan Simon. Screenplay by Albert Mannheimer. Photographed by John W. Boyle. Art director: Bernard Hertzbrun. Musical director: Charles Previn. Edited by Truman K. Wood.

Cast: Jane Powell, Peggy O'Neil, Bonita Granville, Charlie McCarthy, W. C. Fields, Edgar Bergen, Jackie Moran, Reginald Denny, Bill Christie, Rose Hobart, etc.

Jane Powell vehicle includes Fields sequence with Edgar Bergen & dummy.

Sensations of 1945. 1944. 87 minutes.

Released by United Artists, 30 June 1944. Produced & directed by Andrew L. Stone. Screenplay by Dorothy Bennett. Based on a story by Frederick Jackson & Andrew Stone. Photographed by Peverell Marley & John Mescall. Art director: Charles Odds. Musical director: Mahlon Merrick. Music by Al Sherman, lyrics by Harry Tobias. Edited by Jimmy Smith.

Cast: Eleanor Powell, Dennis O'Keefe, C. Aubrey Smith, Eugene Pallette, Mimi Forsythe, Lyle Talbot, Hubert Castle, W. C. Fields, Louise Currie, Bill Wolfe, Sophie Tucker, Dorothy Donegan, The Christianis, Cab Calloway & Woody Herman bands, etc.

Fields' last film, a guest appearance presenting a version of his "Caledonian Express" sketch of 1922, with Louise Currie and Bill Wolfe. A sad goodbye.

List of Extant and Missing Vaudeville Sketches

1 Registered at the Library of Congress

'An Episode on the Links' (registered 1918)
'An Episode of Lawn Tennis' (1918)
'Just Before the Battle, Mother' (1919)
'The Mountain Sweep Steaks' (1919)
'The Family Ford' (1919, 1920)
'An Episode at the Dentists' (1919, 1926, 1928)
'The Pullman Sleeper' (1921)
'Off to the Country' (1921, 1922)
'What a Night!' (1921)
'The Sport Model' (1922) (variant of 'The Family Ford')
'The Caledonian Express' (1922)
'Ten Thousand People Killed' (1922)
'The Sleeping Porch' (1925)
'Stolen Bonds' (1928)
'My School Days Are Over' (1928)
'The Midget Car' (1930)

2 Missing sketches listed by Will Fowler

'Elevator Scene' (probably as performed in *The Comic Supplement*)
'Episode in the Apartment House'
'Picnic Scene' (probably as performed in *The Comic Supplement*)
'Bisbee' (approximately 1924)
'Hip Hippo' (Notation at top: 'Give Hippo 1/2 peanut. Got his foot caught in mouse trap.')
'At the Osteopath's' (23 June 1919)
'The Train Leaves in Half an Hour' (*c.*1928)
'The Sharp Shooter' (*c.*1922)
'Traffic Sketch' (1922, probably as performed in George White's *Scandals*)
Untitled 'Butler' sketch (*c.*1923)
'Professor Kamo (In his series of Marvellous Impersonations)'
  (Fields note on one page: 'These things grow on you . . . No . . .

Not the hats . . . the imitations . . . ')
'Chapeau Shopping'
'Cinema' (*c.*1920 – a grievous loss, this, whatever it was)
Untitled sketch between Fields and 'Josephine', Napoleon's wife.
City Street Scene' (*c.* 1920, possibly the one quoted by Marc Connelly)
'Baseball Game' (1 August 1922)
'The Vanishing American' (*c.* 1920 – another grievous loss. Fowler's note reads:
    'This is believed to be the original concept of Mr. Fields' drinking sketch.')
'All Absent-Minded' (*c.*1923)
'The Master Mind' (*c.*1928)
'A Born Dancer' ('Shortly after 1923')
'City Park Scene' (*c.* 1921, possibly early draft of 'Comic Supplement' sketch)
'The Master Wind' (*c.*1927)
'Dressing Room Scene' (*c.*1924)
'Gerald Geoffrey' (*c.*1924. Fowler's note reads: 'A fifteen page
    sketch said to be one of Mr. Fields' favourites because he had
    the opportunity to show his ability as a great pantomimist.')
'Keep Right on Dancing' (*c.*1928. Possibly a draft for sequence later
    used in *Ballyhoo*.)
'Pool Table Scene' (Fowler: 'Before the sketch with Ed Wynn.')
'Bimbo Lodge' (4 pages. Fowler: 'Glass stain on first page . . . ')
'Shimmy Melodrama' (*c.*1924)
'The Mormon's Prayer' (*c.*1924. Possible early draft of sketch in Earl Carroll's
    Vanities, attributed there to Herman Meyer)
Untitled sketch of 'Boy and Girl at Anapolis during a parade' (*c.*1924)
'The Girl in the Golden Vest' by Ed Wynn – four characters all to be directed,
    supervised and acted by W. C. Fields

3 Sketches from Will Fowler/Tim Walker collection (mostly early handwritten drafts)

'The Patriotic Politician'
'Fido the Beautiful Dog'
'The Seerist Act'
'Rehearsal'
'Thieves in the House'
'Foot O'Play'
'Walk-Through'
'Patent Office' (synopsis)
'Big Duke & Shorty Duke' (early draft of 'What a Night,' above) Routine for
    Moran & Mack
'Go!' (Chapter headings: Peanut Scene, Baby Scene, Golf scene,
    One minute dramas, Subway)
'Old Gentleman in Hall'

'Motor Boat'
'Automobile Act'
'The Sea Gull'
'Into the New Flat'
'The Porter'
'Boat Sketch'
'Porch Scene'

**4 Sketches performed in George White's *Scandals*
of 1922**
'Terrific Traffic'
'The Big Leaguers' (Baseball sketch)
'The Radio Bug'

Notes on Sources

Abbreviations

Archives and Collections

AMPAS: Academy of Motion Picture Arts and Sciences, Margaret Herrick Library, Los Angeles, California.

AS: Astoria Studios, American Museum of the Moving Image, Queens, New York. (Handwritten oral histories – interviews conducted by film historian Anthony Slide.)

BLLC: British Library, Lord Chamberlain's Manuscripts Collection.

BLNP: British Library Newspapers & Periodicals.

FLP: Free Library of Philadelphia Theatre Collection.

JTW: James T. Walker Collection, California.

LCMD: Library of Congress, Manuscript Division, Washington DC.

LCMP: Library of Congress, Motion Picture Division, Washington DC.

LCRB: Library of Congress, Rare Books Division, Washington DC.

MK: Miles Kreuger's Institute of the American Musical.

NYPA: New York Library of the Performing Arts, Billy Rose Collection, Lincoln Center, New York City.

TM: Theatre Museum, London.

USC: University of Southern California, Doheny Library, Los Angeles.

WCFA: W. C. Fields family archive, Los Angeles, California.

Books

CM: Carlotta Monti, *W. C. Fields and Me*, Prentice-Hall, Englefield, NJ, 1971.

FA: Fred Allen: *Much Ado About Me*, Brown & Co., 1956.

MOLM: Gene Fowler, *Minutes of the Last Meeting*, The Viking Press, New York, 1984.

RFF: Ronald Fields, *W. C. Fields, a Life on Film* (filmography), St. Martin's Press, New York, 1984.

RFWC: Ronald Fields, *W. C. Fields by Himself*, Prentice-Hall, Englefield, NJ, 1973.

RLT: Robert Lewis Taylor, *W. C. Fields, His Follies and Fortunes*, New American Library, 1949, 1967.

516

Newspapers and Magazines

NYDM: *New York Dramatic Mirror*

NYS: *New York Star*

NYT: *New York Times*

Note: Quotations from script dialogue unsourced below are transcribed from on-screen dialogue, from prints or videos of the respective films.

Prologue

p.4 'ALEXANDER: I don't like that theatre acting . . .' George Hobart, *The Ham Tree*, LCRB 1905

p.5 'Enter SHERLOCK BAFFLES . . .' Ibid.

Chapter 1

p.7 'He requested his friends . . .' Will Fowler, *The Second Handshake*, Lyle Stuart Inc., Secaucus, NJ, 1980, p.116.

p.8 'While we favoured burial in the ground . . .' *NYT*, 31 December 1946.

p.8 'the niche where Uncle Claude . . .' Will Fowler, personal interview, 1995.

p.8 'A little man . . .' AMPAS clipping file, 3 January 1947.

Chapter 2

p.13 'Master Duffy . . .' *NYDM*, 4 November 1899.

p.14 'I like a man who knows when to stop . . .' George Burns, *All My Best Friends*, G. P. Putnam's Sons, NY, 1989, p.82.

p.14 'CIRCUS PERFORMER . . .' *NYDM*, 9 October 1909.

p.15 'It reminded me of the time . . .' *NYDM*, 8 November 1902.

p.15 'Paid for hearing the musical glasses . . .' etc. From *The Billboard*, 28 May 1904.

p.16 'Is it a lower order of MAN . . .' A. H. Saxon, *P. T. Barnum, The Legend and the Man*. Columbia University Press, NY, 1989.

p.17 'the four-legged girl . . .' etc. FA, pp.82–3.

p.18 'was the breeding ground for . . . great comics . . .' Ann Corio, *This Was Burlesque*, Grosset & Dunlap, NY, 1968, p.39.

p.18 'The opening chorus goes . . .' Bernard Sobel, *A Pictorial History of Burlesque*, Bonanza Books, NY, 1956, p.52.

p.19 'MIKE: I am delightfulness . . .' Armond Fields & L. Marc Fields, *From the Bowery to Broadway*, Oxford University Press, 1993, pp.82, 106.

p.22 'a Chinese, holding a trombone . . .' etc. E. J. Kahn, Jr, *The Merry Partners, the Age and Stage of Harrigan and Hart*, Random House, NY, 1955, pp.28–9.

p.25 'Don't miss this greatest show . . .' Douglas Gilbert, *American Vaudeville, Its Life and Times*, McGraw Hill, 1940, pp.199,NY, 203.

p.25 'NOTICE TO PERFORMERS . . .' Edwin Milton Royle, *The Vaudeville*

Theatre (1899), quoted in *American Vaudeville As Seen By Its Contemporaries*, Charles W. Stein, Ed. Alfred Knopf, 1984, p.24.

Chapter 3

p.28 'I never heard that story . . .' FLP clipping, *Philadelphia Inquirer*, 1980.

p.30 'I'm glad my poor father . . .' NYPA, W. C. Fields clippings file.

p.30 'As someone more eloquent . . .' Ibid.

p.30 'an old fashioned homebody . . .' *Sunday Bulletin Magazine*, NYPA, W. C. Fields clipping file, 23 March 1969.

p.32 'The Philadelphia law of laws . . .' John Lukacs, *Philadelphia, Patricians and Philistines*, FSG, NY, 1980, p.43.

p.33 'from our front step . . .' *Sunday Bulletin Magazine*, NYPA, W file, 23 March 1969.

p.35 'MY SCHOOL DAYS ARE OVER . . .' LCMD.

p.36 'One afternoon . . .' etc. *New Yorker*, 2 February 1935.

p.37 'The Philadelphia police . . .' RLT, p.25.

p.38 'W. C.Fields, inimitable, eccentric . . .' NYPA, W. C. Fields clippings file.

p.40 'I have never forgotten the old days . . .' RFWC, p.450.

p.41 'He only carried one brand of cigar . . .' *Philadelphia Evening Bulletin*, FLP, 29 January 1980.

p.41 'I did everything possible . . .' Ibid.

Chapter 4

p.43 'Byrne Brothers,' etc. *NYDM*, 9 October 1893.

p.44 'I was fifteen years old . . .' LCMP.

p.44 'I still carry scars . . .' Ibid.

p.44 'I was born with a fatal facility . . .' BLNP, *The Sun*, Sydney, Australia, 12 April 1914.

p.44 'from then on . . .' RFWC, p.7.

p.45 'MISS MINNIE HALL . . .' FLP, Vaudeville scrapbooks.

p.46 'the one in which I balance . . .' *NYDM*, 26 January 1896.

p.46 'Ask any boy . . .' Quoted in *The Era*, 1 February 1902.

p.47 'Physically perfect . . .' FLP, Vaudeville scrapbooks.

p.48 'It's been a case of pure laziness . . .' *Motion Picture*, 1926.

p.48 'Those who knew him well . . .' etc. NYPA, W. C. Fields clippings file.

p.49 'I might still have that job . . .' Letter quoted by James Smart, in pamphlet, 'W. C. Fields in Philadelphia', Schakamoxon Society, 1972, p.13.

p.51 'THE GREAT CIGAR-BOX TRICK . . .' '*Selbit*': *The Magicians' Handbook* Dawborn & Ward, London, 1904, p.125.

p.53 'I thought I'd try to develop personality . . .' Bernard Sobel, *Burleycue: An Underground History of Burlesque*, NY, 1931, p.119.

p.54 'He always talked to his "properties" . . .' W. Buchanan-Taylor, *Shake the Bottle,* Heath Cranton, London, 1942, p.216 (with thanks to Michael Pointon).

Chapter 5

p.56 'Natatorium Hall . . .' etc. WCFA.

p.57 'He tramped to the booking offices . . .' RLT, pp.46–7.

p.58 'I got the five dollars . . .' *Theatre Magazine*, 1928.

p.58 'I worked on the stage . . .' Sobel, *Burleycue*, p.116.

p.59 'The things we did . . .' *Theatre Magazine*, 1928.

p.60 'When the show was set . . .' Sobel, *Burleycue*, p.117.

p.61 'THE MONTE CARLO GIRLS . . .' etc., WCFA.

p.61 'In those days . . .' Sobel, *Burleycue*, ibid., p.118.

p.62 'The audience was made up . . .' Fred Stone, *Rolling Stone*, McGraw Hill, NY, 1945, p.109.

p.63 'The Monte Carlo girls made their first . . .' NYDM, 4 February 1899.

p.63 'All that bothered Jim . . .' *Theatre Magazine*, 1928.

p.64 'it was a regular thing . . .' Sobel, *Burleycue*, p.98.

p.66 'I am at a loss to extend . . .' RFWC, letter, p.13.

p.67 'All I heard from Irwin . . .' *Theatre Magazine*, 1928.

p.67 'I tried to perfect my work . . .' Sobel, *Burleycue*, p.118.

p.68 'And did You pass anything . . .' RFWC, p.27.

p.70 '"It's a Tough Spot . . ."' MK.

Chapter 6

p.73 'Many of America's great fortunes . . .' Gilbert, *American Vaudeville*, p.197.

p.74 'We were in love with show business . . .' Burns, *All My Best Friends*, p.23.

p.74 'A vaudeville actor . . .' FA, p.238.

p.76 'Vaudeville families endured . . .' FA, p.241.

Chapter 7

p.82 'I thought I knew him . . .' BLNP.

p.84 'To understand comedy . . .' From 'Juggler of Laughs', Maude Cheatham, *Silver Screen*, April 1935.

p.84 'another woman . . .' AMPAS clipping file.

p.85 'I saw him long before . . .' Ibid.

p.87 'The building, which has . . .' *The Era*, 22 June 1901.

p.89 '"Anything particular . . ."' RLT, p.82.

p.90 'socking a bobby . . .' etc. RLT, pp.110, 112.

Chapter 8

p.91 Palace Theatre bill. TM, 23 February 1901.

p.93 'Another new turn at the Palace . . .' etc. *The Era*, 16 March 1901.

p.94 'Crowded auditoriums . . .' *The Era*, 13 April 1901.

p.94 'The King greeted the juggler . . .' RLT, p.81.

p.96 'To play one provincial town . . .' NYDM, 22 November 1902.

p.98 'No theatre, I thought . . .' Charles Chaplin, *My Autobiography*, Simon & Schuster, NY, 1964, p.110.

p.99 'The Dogman and his Son . . .' etc. Charles Castle, *The Folies Bergère*, Franklin Watts, NY, 1985.

p.99 'Weird and interesting Bohemian dances . . .' *The Era*, 11 May 1901.

Chapter 9

p.103 'I'll tell you of an experience . . .' *Standard*, 22 March 1913, WCFA.

p.104 'An officer among the audience . . .' *The Era*, 17 May 1902.

p.106 'The counters, fittings . . .' etc. TM, Hippodrome programmes, 1902.

p.106 'The management of the Hippodrome . . .' *The Era*, 8 November 1902.

p.107 'A great sensation . . .' Ibid.

p.108 'A HUMORIST JUGGLER . . .' TM, *Tatler*, 10 December 1902.

p.108 'a pussy-cat ditty . . .' *The Era*, 3 January 1903.

p.109 'his real clever work . . .' *The Era*, 24 January 1903.

Chapter 10

p.110 'One of the big laughing hits . . .' *NYDM*, 28 February 1903.

p.112 'Give me money, I get girl . . .' RFWC, p.197.

p.113 'The Australian people will have . . .' *The Era*, 29 May 1909.

p.113 'Mr. W. C. Fields makes his entry . . .' *Table Talk*, Australia, WCFA, 18 June 1903.

p.113 'He speaks not at all . . .' *Punch*, Australia, WFCA, 18 June 1903.

p.113 'a place where land and sea . . .' *Variety*, AMPAS, 23 December 1911 (Walter C. Kelly).

p.114 'W. C. Fields, an "eccentric juggler" . . .' *Sydney Daily Telegraph*, BLNP, 27 July 1903.

p.114 'Kinothol Pastilles . . .' etc., Sydney, WCFA, 26 July 1903.

p.115 'The send off given . . .' *Music Hall & Theatre Review*, Australia, WCFA, October 1903.

p.116 'The place is full of . . .' *Daily Sketch*, WCFA, 19 February 1914.

p.116 'When I played the Orpheum Circuit . . .' *Theatre Magazine*, October 1928.

p.117 'My appearance amused the natives . . .' Bill Yagoda, *Will Rogers*, Knopf, NY, 1994, p.59.

p.117 'Sir, – South Africa opens a new field . . .' *The Era*, 2 July 1904.

p.118 'There was the time . . .' 'Speaking of Benefits', NYPA, November 1923.

p.118 'after tea . . .' WCFA, 15 January 1904.

p.119 'on trains, in dressing rooms . . .' FA.

Chapter 11

p.121 'In his room at the hotel . . .' Eddie Cantor, *Take My Life*, Doubleday, NY, 1957, p.140.

p.121 'it was from his wife . . .' Museum of Modern Art, FLP, 1969.

p.122 'tongue was a magician's wand . . .' Quoted in Wes Gehring, *W. C. Fields, a Biobibliography*, Greenwood Press, p.22.

p.122 'Why, my dear innocent boy . . .' Mark Twain & Charles Dudely Warner, *The Gilded Age*, p.74.

p.122 'Never take an inferior liquor . . .' Ibid., p.108.

p.122 'The counting house clock . . .' Charles Dickens, *David Copperfield*.

p.123 'Two sheets of paper . . .' RFWC, p.29.

Chapter 12

p.124 'A youth with a black bag . . .' *London Morning Post*, WCFA, 5 April 1904.

p.125 'a perfect picture . . .' etc. *The Era*, 30 April 1904.

p.125 'Everything that comes to the Hippodrome . . .' *The Era*, 19 December 1903.

p.126 'Mr W. C.Fields . . . richly deserves . . .' *The Era*, 30 April 1904.

p.127 'But facts are chiels . . .' *The Era*, 9 April 1904.

p.127 'An exponent of the art of turtle-riding . . .' etc. *The Era*, 30 April 1904.

p.127 'The scientific alliance . . .' etc. *The Era*, 16 April 1904.

p.128 'On his European tour . . .' Blythe Foote Finke, *W. C. Fields, Renowned Comedian* . . . SamHar Press, NY, FLP, 1972.

p.128 'You're a very sick man . . .' RLT, p.86.

p.129 'After the Louis massacre . . .' Ed Sullivan Column, NYPA, W. C. Fields clippings file, 1938.

p.129 'My best friend died . . .' NYPA, Ibid.

p.130 'an American Underslung car . . .' RFWC, p.41.

p.130 'Kitty's cable I recd. yesterday . . .' RFWC, p.21.

p.131 '(Fields to Sato:) I met . . .' RFWC, p.26.

p.131 'Worst Case Fields . . .' etc. RFWC, p.27.

p.132 'gives a comicality to slackness . . .' *The Era*, 21 December 1907.

p.132 'The baby has just said . . .' RFWC, p.29.

p.133 'Not long after the marriage . . .' Finke, *W. C. Fields, Renowned Comedian* . . .

p.133 'the great earthquake and fire . . .' CM, p.11.

p.135 *'Enter attendant . . .'* etc. J.Hickory Wood, *Cinderella*, BLLC, 1904.

p.136 'FIELDS WILL NOT GO TO RUSSIA. . .' *NYDM*, 27 May 1905.

p.136 'everybody carrying books . . .' *NYDM*, 16 May 1903.

p.137 'I am going to do some neat foot work . . .' etc. RFWC, p.30.

Chapter 13

p.138 *'The curtain rises . . .'* etc. Hobart, *The Ham Tree*.

p.138 'tells us that he . . .' *The Era*, 28 June 1913.

p.139 'Weel about and turn about . . .' Robert C. Toll, *Blacking Up, The*

Minstrel Show in 19th Century America, Oxford University Press, 1974, p.28.

p.139 '*Enter Sherlock Baffles* . . .' Hobart, *The Ham Tree*.

p.140 'LAWRENCE: I love 'em . . .' Ibid.

p.140 'LORD SPOTCASH . . .' etc. Ibid.

p.142 'W. C. Fields surprised only . . .' *NYDM*, 9 September 1905.

p.142 'To their loved old . . .' *Metropolitan*, NYPA clippings file, 1905.

p.143 'As of old . . .' Ibid.

p.143 'HENRY: My boy . . .' Hobart, *The Ham Tree*.

p.144 'MCINTYRE: How far . . .' etc., Ibid.

p.146 'COMMODORE: My last encounter . . .' Script, *Mississippi*, AMPAS, 1935.

p.147 'When it comes to helping people . . .' Hobart, *The Ham Tree*.

Chapter 14

p.149 'Dear Wife, Your letter to hand . . .' RFWC, p.32.

p.150 'Glad to hear all at home . . .' RFWC, p.34.

p.151 'The biggest individual hit . . .' *NYDM*, 8 June 1907.

p.151 'Suffering sciatica . . .' RFWC, p.38.

p.151 'W. C. FIELDS TO TOUR THE ORIENT . . .' *NYDM*, 8 June 1907.

p.153 'That delightful humorist . . .' *The Era*, 29 August 1907.

p.153 'featuring a burlesque croquet shot . . .' *Variety*, NYPA, 23 April 1908.

p.153 'It may be a compliment to Fields . . .' *Sunday Chronicle*, WCFA, 11 June 1908.

p.154 'Furious driving . . .' etc. Harry Tate, 'Motoring', BLLC, 1912.

p.154 'Both are good enough . . .' *NYS*, NYPA, 28 November 1908.

p.155 ''THE MAN WHO JUGGLES . . .' *NYS*, NYPA, 19 December 1908.

p.155 'How a man of routine . . .' *Cleveland Plain Dealer*, NYPA, 11 February 1910.

p.157 Contract by Somers & Warner's Agency, courtesy of David Robinson.

p.158 'and needless to say, is "the" thing . . .' *The Era*, 16 September 1911.

p.159 'the beautiful Spanish singer . . .' *The Era*, 27 January 1912.

Chapter 15

p.161 'Mme Bernhardt to play . . .' Coliseum programme, TM, 16 June 1913.

p.163 'THE ROYAL PERFORMANCE . . .' *The Era*, 15 October 1913.

p.163 'As the Royal carriage approached . . .' *People*, WCFA, 12 October 1913.

p.163 'Immediately their Majesties . . .' etc. *The Era*, 15 October 1913.

p.164 'I am down here in Africa . . .' RFWC, p.51.

p.165 'Why W. C. Fields Hates Christmas . . .' Will Fowler, *Life*, 15 December 1972.

p.165 'W. C. Fields, de zwijgende humorist . . .' Pretoria, WCFA, 28 February 1914.

p.165 'After an absence . . .' *Sydney Daily Telegraph*, BNLP, 6 April 1914.

p.165 'Dear Hattie: – Enclosed . . .' RFWC, p.54.

p.166 'W. C. Fields At Home . . .' *Table Talk*, Australia, WCFA, 28 May 1914.

p.166 'He is out playing golf . . .' etc. *Mail*, Adelaide, WCFA, 15 June 1914.

p.166 'Dear Hattie: – On account of . . .' RFWC, p.54.

Chapter 16

p.171 'Do you have any idea . . .' Quoted in Norman Katkov, *The Fabulous Fanny*, Knopf, NY, 1953, p.59.

p.171 'Dear Santa . . .' Cantor, *Take My Life*, p.14.

p.173 'Obliged to terminate his Keith engagement . . .' NYPA, W. C. Fields clippings file, 14 January 1915.

p.173 'The Four Marx Brothers . . .' NYPA, 1915.

p.173 'They sang, danced . . .' RFWC, p.481.

p.173 'He said: "You see this hand . . ."' Groucho Marx and Richard J. Anobile, *The Marx Brothers' Scrapbook*, Darien House (Star Books), where 1976, p.34.

p.176 'His driving force . . .' Charles Higham, *Ziegfeld*, Henry Regnery, Chicago, 1972, p.233.

p.176 'not the movement and abandon . . .' Quoted in Yagoda, *Will Rogers*, p.147.

Chapter 17

p.179 'Probably at no time . . .' Eddie Cantor, *My Life in Your Hands*, Harper & Bros., NY, 1928, p.197.

p.180 'W. C. FIELDS SPEAKS! . . .' NYPA, W. C. Fields clippings file, 16 November 1915.

p.181 'Nearly all of my successful songs . . .' Quoted in AV, p.241–2.

p.181 'My good friend, Williams . . .' Quoted in Mabel Rowland, ed., *Bert Williams, Son of Laughter*, English Crafters, NY, 1923, pp.128.

p.184 'Dear Chickenchief . . .' Cantor, *My Life in Your Hands*, p.202.

p.185 'When we were on tour . . .' Cantor, *My Life in Your Hands*, p. 141–2.

Chapter 18

p.187 'John Bunny is dead . . .' Quoted in Kalton C. Lahue & Samuel Gill, *Clown Princes and Court Jesters*, A.S. Barnes, NY, 1970, p.68.

p.187 'Every newspaper carried . . .' David Robinson, *Chaplin, His Life & Art*, Paladin, London, p.152.

p.188 'My mustache denotes . . .' *Fools For Luck Press Book*, 1928, Paramount Pictures, LCMP.

p.191 'Your low cunning . . .' RFWC, p.58.

p.191 'For ten years . . .' RFWC, p.61.

Chapter 19

p.194 'I was going in the movies . . .' George Hobart, *Ziegfeld Follies of 1916*, LCMD.

p.195 'One night we were going . . .' FLP, W. C. Fields clippings file.

p.196 'Then suddenly from out of nowhere . . .' Script, *You Can't Cheat an Honest Man*, Universal Pictures.

p.197 'Mrs Faye Bunny . . .' *Sunday News*, NYPA, W. C. Fields clippings file, 26 June 1949.

p.198 'As time went on, I began to suspect . . .' *Los Angeles Times*, AMPAS, 5 May 1949.

p.199 'GIRL LEAVES RING TO W. C. FIELDS. . .' NYPA, W. C. Fields clippings file.

p.199 'Dear Bill: Mr K . . .' *Los Angeles Times* AMPAS, 5 May 1949.

p.199 'some years after I first helped her . . .' *Los Angeles Examiner*, AMPAS, 29 April 1949.

p.200 'The comedian's butler . . .' Will Fowler, *Reporters*, Roundtable, Calif., 1991, p.100n.

p.201 'Eighty-two per cent of all white . . .' RLT, p.68.

p.201 'Have you ever been exposed . . .' etc. CM, p.51.

p.202 'Bill adored beautiful girls . . .' Louise Brooks, *Lulu in Hollywood*, Limelight Editions, NY, 1982, p.78.

p.202 'Years of traveling . . .' Ibid., p.74.

p.202 'By now Bill's romance . . .' *Sunday News*, NYPA, W. C. Fields clippings file, 26 June 1949.

Chapter 20

p.204 '"Ziggy" was a great guy . . .' FLP, W. C. Fields clippings file.

p.205 'The funniest thing about comedy . . .' *The American*, NYPA, September 1934.

p.206 'Performers would take material . . .' Burns, *All My Best Friends*, p.62.

p.208 'Big and frightfully dopey looking dog . . .' Sketch: 'Fido, the Beautiful Dog', JTW.

p.209 'Ladies and gentlemen . . .' Sketch: 'Seerist Act', JTW.

p.210 "What has the lady on her head? . . ." Ibid.

p.210 'I want to say as Lincoln said . . .' Sketch: 'The Patriotic Politician', JTW.

p.210 'SCENCE: *Back drop* . . .' Sketch: 'An Episode of Lawn Tennis', LCMD.

p.211 'WOOLEY: Is anybody on the level . . .' George Hobart, *Zeigfeld Follies of 1917*, LCMD.

p.212 'FIELDS: Seeking sustenance . . .' Marc Connelly, *Voices Offstage*, p.67.

p.213 'AN EPISODE ON THE LINKS . . .' Sketch. LCMD.

Chapter 21

p.219 '(*Enter Reddan Green* . . .' George Hobart, *Ziegfeld Follies of 1916*, LCMD.

524

p.220 'ZAMINEM: (*to Loot* . . .' etc. Sketch: 'Just Before the Battle Mother', LCMD.

p.223 'KEANAN: Marry me and . . .' Sketch: 'The Mountain Sweep Stakes', LCMD.

p.224 'MRS FLIVERTON: My God . . .' etc. Sketch: 'The Family Ford', LCMD.

p.226 'You remember the rides in your car . . .' Herbert G. Goldman, *Fanny Brice, The Original Funny Girl*, Oxford University Press, NY, p.96.

p.228 'MRS FLIVERTON: You let her alone! . . .' Sketch: 'Off to the Country', LCMD.

p.229 'MRS FLIVERTON *screams, again* . . .' Ibid.

p.230 'By golly . . . I'd have more freedom . . .' The Smithsonian Collection of Newspaper Comics, Smithsonian/Abrams 1977, p.100, panel 3.

Chapter 22

p.234 Poppy was a . . .' AS oral histories.

p.234 'came together . . .' David Robinson, 'Dukenfield Meets McGargle', *Sight & Sound* 36, Summer 1967.

p.235 'PROF: This is evidently . . .' Dorothy Donnelly, *Poppy*, WCFA.

p.235 'PROF: I am Professor Eustace . . .' Ibid.

p.236 'PROF: Now, ladies and gentlemen . . .' Ibid.

p.236 'W. C. Fields makes "Poppy" . . .' *Evening World*, FLP, 'Poppy' clippings file.

p.236 'W. C. Fields . . . became a star . . .' FLP, ibid.

p.237 'At the moment, we can't remember anybody . . .' Quoted in RLT, p.155.

p.237 'His jaunty and shameless old mountebank . . .' FLP, ibid.

p.237 '"POPPY" STAR ALWAYS BEING CLAIMED . . .' FLP, ibid.

p.238 'You have been a lazy . . .' RFWC, p.65.

p.238 'You have so much character . . .' RFWC, pp.72-3.

p.238 'Enclosed please find cheque . . .' RFWC, p.73.

p.239 'PROF: I love stud poker . . .' Dorothy Donnelly, *Poppy*, WCFA.

Chapter 23

p.241 'A PLEA FOR CHICAGO HUSBANDS . . .' J. P. McEvoy, *Slams of Life, With Malice For All and Charity Towards None*, P.F. Volland, Chicago, 1919.

p.242 'No sweeter baby in the block . . .' Ibid.

p.242 'The most important factor . . .' typescript, article for *Philadelphia Inquirer*, FLP, undated.

p.243 'his luxurious custom . . .' Sinclair Lewis, *Babbitt*, 1921. (Quote from UK edition published by Vintage, 1994, p.98.)

p.244 'I am not making any efforts to adapt . . .' J. P. McEvoy clippings file, FLP.

p.244 'GERTIE: What's this one about . . .' J. P. McEvoy, *The Comic Supplement*, LCMD, 1924 version.

p.244 'Scene changes to "comic supplement interior" . . .' Ibid.

p.245 'the pathetic father . . .' Ibid.

p.245 'MANNISH WOMAN: Are you . . .' Ibid.

p.246 'What's that? A box of Smith Brothers . . .' Ibid.

p.248 'ICEMAN: ICE! ICE! . . .' J. P. McEvoy, *The Comic Supplement*, NYPA Microfilm, 1925 version.

p.248 'MA (*in a loud voice*): Myrtle! Myrtle! . . .' Ibid.

p.249 'MYRTLE: Does itsi-witsi . . .' Ibid.

p.249 'At rise of curtain . . .' Sketch: 'The Back Porch', LCMD.

p.251 'PA: I'm beginning to understand . . .' McEvoy, *The Comic Supplement*, NYPA microfilm, 1925.

p.251 '*In the entire scene* . . .' etc. Ibid.

p.252 'GERTIE: Cut his gizzard out . . .' Ibid.

p.252 'Florenz Ziegfeld waved his wand . . .' *The Star*, MK, 21 January 1925.

p.253 'Undoubtedly . . . the greatest extravaganza . . .' J. P. McEvoy clippings file, FLP.

p.253 'As far as Ziegfeld was concerned . . .' Norman Bel-Geddes, *Miracle in the Evening*, Doubleday, NY, 1960, p.307.

p.254 'J. P. MCEVOY NAILS HIS HOPES . . .' J. P. McEvoy clippings file, FLP.

p.254 'There are many little incidents . . .' *New Jersey Herald*, NYPA, 18 July 1920.

p.254 'He Knew What They Wanted'. *Saturday Evening Post*, 10 September 1932.

p.254 'W. C. Fields' Best Friend'. *This Week*, 26 July 1942.

p.255 'The outstanding feature . . .' *NY Sunday Times*, undated, MK.

Chapter 24

p.259 'The hardest thing to put into the movies . . .' LCMP.

p.260 'the most extraordinary man . . .' AS oral histories.

p.261 'a very high standard . . .' *Sally of the Sawdust* press releases, LCMP.

p.264 'He paid no attention . . .' Brooks, *Lulu in Hollywood*, p.79.

p.264 'Griffith would leave Bill alone . . .' AS, ibid.

p.265 'He gives actors credit . . . ' RFF, p.31.

p.267 'I prefer pantomime . . .' *Photoplay*, October 1925.

p.267 'I can be my own severest critic . . .' *Sally of the Sawdust* press release, LCMP.

p.268 'warmth and human sympathy . . .' RFF, p.30.

Chapter 25

p.270 'It is just a long-winded film . . .' *Variety*, 13 January 1926.

p.271 'Melodramatic, heart-throbbing . . .' *That Royle Girl*, press release, LCMP.

p.272 'In February, 1926, Paramount . . .' Brooks, *Lulu in*

Hollywood, p.80.

p.275 'an ex-chorus boy . . .' RFF, p.41.

p.275 'Eddie Sutherland said you had to argue . . .' AS oral histories.

p.275 'EXTRA WHITE-ROBED MEN . . .' *It's the Old Army Game*, press release, LCMP.

p.277 'Dear Nephew, In response to your query . . .' Undated letter, JTW.

p.278 'MRS MURCHISON: In short, the whole affair's . . .' etc. *You're Telling Me*, Paramount script, AMPAS.

p.280 'no great outstanding comedy wallop . . .' *Variety*, 3 November 1926.

p.281 'They sent me out to a golf course . . .' AS oral histories.

p.281 'In my first picture . . .' *The Potters*, press release, LCMP.

p.282 'If you should happen to be in New York . . .' Ibid.

p.284 'In 1927 most of Paramount's contract players . . .' RFF, p.59.

Chapter 26

p.287 All script entries from Paramount script file, *Two Flaming Youths*, AMPAS.

p.296 'Fields' native talents for juggling . . .' *Variety*, 11 January 1928.

p.296 'I was still married to Eddie . . .' Brooks, *Lulu in Hollywood*, p.82.

p.297 'This scintillating comedy . . .' *Fools For Luck*, press release, LCMP.

Chapter 27

p.298 'I have been badly handled . . .' RFWC, p.76.

p.298 'Dear Thompson, Your good letter read . . .' LCMD, Thomas Geraghty Collection.

p.299 'Goodbye, Bessie! . . .' Brooks, *Lulu in Hollywood*, p.84.

p.300 'I hope Chaplin's picture . . .' JTW.

p.300 'The rollicking tale of a dapper boarding house Romeo . . .' RFF, p.46.

p.300 'The Great McGillicuddy . . .' Typescript, JTW.

p.302 '*Scene showing interior of old country farmhouse* . . .' Sketch: 'Stolen Bonds', LCMD.

p.304 'he has used 175 pints of soup . . .' Typescript press release, FLP.

p.305 'CHARACTERS: DR O. HUGH HURT . . .' etc. Sketch: 'At the Dentist', LCMD.

p.306 'DENTIST: You didn't feel anything . . .' Ibid.

p.307 'FOLIAGE: Never mind . . .' Ibid.

p.307 'DENTIST: Now just where is the trouble . . .' Ibid.

p.308 'DENTIST: Would you like gas . . .' Ibid.

p.308 'I'll have the gas . . .' etc. *Dentistry*, BMLC.

p.308 'Q: Have you got the beard . . .' RFWC, pp.93–4.

p.309 'It's too small to call a car . . .' Sketch: 'The Midget Car', LCMD.

p.309 'BOGLE (*Getting out of car* . . .' Ibid.

Chapter 28

p.311 'Have just returned from Fla . . .' LCMD, Thomas Geraghty Collection.

p.315 'a genial and ingratiating rascal . . .' FLP, *Ballyhoo* file clippings, December 1930.

p.315 'A hundred and thirteen wild-cat banks . . .' Twain & Warner, *The Gilded Age*, p.73.

p.315 'From the moment that he rolls on the stage . . .' FLP *Ballyhoo* file clippings, December 1930.

p.316 'Exactly four persons were in orchestra seats . . .' Ibid.

p.316 'Scenes have been combined . . .' Ibid.

p.316 'W. C. had nothing to do now . . .' RFF, p.78.

Chapter 29

p.322 'I'll give the Talkies three years . . .' Robinson, *Chaplin, His Life & Art*, p.389.

p.322 'the idea . . . is not practical . . .' *NYT*, 21 May 1926.

p.323 'The potentialities of motion pictures . . .' Quoted in Kenneth Anger's *Hollywood Babylon*, Dell, NY, 1975, p.46.

p.323 'wilfull offence to any nation . . .' etc. Frank Miller, *Censored Hollywood*, Turner Publishing, 1994, p.40.

p.324 'no picture shall be produced . . .' Ibid., p.51.

p.325 'a regular guy . . .' Yagoda, *Will Rogers*, p.231.

p.325 'two fisted fighting egg . . .' Ibid., p.233.

p.325 '"The public loves torture . . ."' John Kobler, *Damned in Paradise*, Atheneum, 1977, p.264.

p.326 'corrupting the morals of youth . . .' Mae West, *Goodness Had Nothing To Do With It*, Prentice-Hall, Englefield, NJ, 1959, p.98.

p.326 'one of the few authentic stage pictures . . .' Ibid., p.113.

Chapter 30

p.327 'dressed in a pink frilly . . .' FLP, *Follies of 1918* clippings file.

p.329 'Dear Elise, Just received your letter . . .' JTW.

p.330 '"THE OUT HOUSE" INN . . .' JTW.

p.330 'a Promethean wit . . .' Joe Adamson, *Groucho, Harpo, Chico and Sometimes Zeppo*, Coronet, London, 1974, p.127.

p.333 'In re: "Million Dollar Legs . . ." Motion Picture Producers & Distributor's Association (MPPDA) files, AMPAS.

p.333 'Despite this title . . .' Ibid.

p.333 'Million Dollar Legs contest . . .' *Million Dollar Legs Press Book*, LCMP.

p.334 '1 The line . . .' etc. MPPDA files, AMPAS.

p.335 'Perhaps he doesn't exactly belong . . .' *New York Herald Tribune*, 31 July 1932.

p.336 'AGNES: When was it we played . . .' etc. Paramount script, *If I Had a*

Million, AMPAS.

p.338 'AGNES: If I was gonna pick a chaffeur . . .' Ibid.

p.338 'ROLLO: I find it very difficult . . .' Ibid.

Chapter 31

p.341 'I ran across him at Lakeside . . .' Mack Sennett with Cameron Shipp, *King of Comedy*, 1954; Mercury House San Francisco, 1990, p.265.

p.341 'wonderfully handsome and virile man . . .' Brooks, *Lulu in Hollywood*, p.75.

p.344 'Two reels of film and 20 minutes wasted . . .' From Donald Deschner, *The Films of W. C. Fields*, Citadel Press, p.77.

p.344 'When I have the stage all set for a Fields picture . . .' RFWC, p.269.

p.346 Script quotations from onscreen or LCMP dialogue-continuity-sheets (texts taken from on-screen prints).

Chapter 32

p.349 'was sending his brother . . .' etc. RLT, p.192.

p.350 'clutching fear of being discarded . . .' Brooks, *Lulu in Hollywood*, p.74.

p.351 'unjust concentration of wealth . . .' From *Harrap Encyclopedia of World History*, 1954, p.1056.

p.351 'March 15 is always a day of rare rejoicing . . .' W. C. Fields, *Fields for President*, Dodd, Mead & Co, 1940, p.47.

p.354 'You should not speak so disparagingly . . .' RFWC, p.74.

p.354 'Franklin Disraeli Rosefeld . . .' RFWC, p.195.

p.354 'I got an infected big toe . . .' Letter, JTW, 7 April 1942.

p.355 'Dear Hattie, I am in receipt of yours . . .' RFWC, p.143.

p.356 'This monograph has to do with . . .' Gene Fowler, *Show Business Illustrated*, Gene Fowler clippings file, AMPAS, 2 January 1962.

p.359 'a type of picture with which the censor boards . . .' MPPDA files, AMPAS.

p.359 '1 The line by Grace Allen . . .' Ibid.

p.359 'Fields' line . . .' etc. Ibid.

p.360 '. . . I happen to note today . . .' Ibid.

p.360 'If it is true . . .' Ibid.

p.360 'Delete the line . . .' etc. Ibid.

Chapter 33

p.363 'HUMPTY-DUMPTY: When I use a word . . .' Paramount script, AMPAS.

p.363 'W. C. FIELDS: Born of poor . . .' *Six of a Kind Press Book*, LCMP.

p.364 '"Mr Fields," the assistant director said . . .' CM, p.3.

p.366 'For one thing I am watering my orange trees . . .' *Hollywood Reporter*, 4th Anniversary Issue, AMPAS, December 1934.

p.366 'It – it just fits because you're cute . . .' CM, p.7.

p.367 'Police Called as Two are Hit in Row . . .' *New York World Telegram*, NYPA clippings file, 24 September 1937.

p.367 'Demoniacally intense . . .' Fowler, *The Second Handshake*, p.95.

p.368 'Either shit green . . .' Ibid., p.104.

p.368 'I'm not in love with Miss Bayes now . . .' Gene Fowler, *Good Night, Sweet Prince*, Viking Press, NY, 1944; Mercury House, San Francisco, 1989, p.138.

p.371 'SHERIFF: At the time of which I speak . . .' Paramount script, AMPAS.

p.372 'According to you . . .' etc. Ibid.

p.373 'CRAZY! W. C. Fields, Paramount's funny . . .' *Alice in Wonderland Press Book*, LCMP.

Chapter 34

p.376 'MCGONIGLE: On our last appearance . . .' Treatment in Paramount file, AMPAS; also in RFWC, p.272.

p.377 'they were hard to digest . . .' CM, p.71.

p.378 'MCGONIGLE: Come, let us have done . . .' etc. Paramount scripts, AMPAS.

p.378 'Quiet please! Quiet please . . .' Sketch: 'The Pullman Sleeper', LCMD.

p.378 'Do you mean to say . . .' Sketch: 'The Caledonian Express', LCMD.

p.379 '*Philanthroac* . . .' etc. Quoted in *Poppy Press Book*, LCMP.

p.380 'In the first act . . .' Quoted in *The Old Fashioned Way Press Book*, LCMD.

p.381 'MRS WENDLESCHAFFER: What's this? . . .' etc. Paramount scripts, AMPAS.

p.383 'MRS BISSONETTE: Don't smoke at the table . . .' etc. From *It's a Gift*, on-screen dialogue.

p.384 'W. C. FIELDS VIEWS SLEEP . . .' *Man on the Flying Trapeze Press Book*, LCMP.

p.384 'SALESMAN . . .' *It's a Gift*, ibid.

p.386 'there should be no objectionable exposure . . .' etc. MPPDA files, AMPAS.

p.386 '1 The reaction of the girl . . .' Ibid.

p.386 'There is no sea gull gag . . .' etc., Ibid.

p.387 'It's a moving picture theatre . . .' etc., Paramount scripts, AMPAS.

p.388 'There is something about a Martini . . .' AMPAS clipping file.

p.390 'I have thwarted the malevolent machinations . . .' etc. *David Copperfield*, on-screen dialogue.

p.390 'the fellow had four aces . . .' etc. Paramount scripts, AMPAS.

p.393 'MRS WOLFINGER: Ambrose . . .' etc. *Man on the Flying Trapeze*, on-screen dialogue.

p.393 'NEW BURGLAR: Legs . . .' etc. Ibid.

p.394 'MRS WOLFINGER: Wake up, Ambrose . . .' etc. Ibid. (To end of chapter.)

Chapter 35

p.399 'I was with him for years in the Follies . . .' RFWC, p.154.

p.399 'I came to the stage all of a sudden..' *Motion Picture*, NYPA, September 1935.

p.400 'Why Alcohol Has Taken the Place of the Dog . . .' RFWC, pp.145–51.

p.400 'FIELDS TO ENACT PRINCIPAL ROLE . . .' *American*, NYPA, 26 October 1935.

p.402 'POPPY: Pop, what do you think . . .' Paramount scripts, AMPAS.

p.403 'strolling figure costumed . . .' *Poppy Press Book*, LCMP.

p.403 'In the last two years . . .' *NYT*, 14 June 1936.

p.404 'Because they are the two outstanding clowns . . .' *New York Herald Tribune*, 15 March 1936.

p.404 'hosting his friends . . .' *New York World Telegram*, NYPA, 29 May 1936.

p.404 'W. C. Fields . . . the ex-vaudeville juggler . . .' *New York Sun*, 16 June 1936.

p.405 'She (the nurse) set it down by my bedside . . .' RFWC, p.202.

p.406 'FIELDS: Tell me, Charlie . . .' Quoted in Arthur Frank Wertheim, *Radio Comedy*, Oxford University Press, 1979, p.363.

p.407 'Say, by the way, what's that big sign . . .' Excerpt from *W. C. Fields On Radio*, Columbia Records CS9890.

p.408 'What's the score . . .' Excerpt from *The Great Radio Feuds*, Columbia Records KC33241.

p.408 'Throughout the Middle Ages . . .' Excerpt from *W. C. Fields On Radio*, Columbia Records CS9890.

p.408 'I haven't had a drop of water . . .' Quoted in RFWC, p.214.

p.408 'Quiet, you termite's flop-house . . .' Excerpt from *The Great Radio Feuds,* Columbia Records KC33241.

p.409 'an insolent caricature of religion . . .' Wertheim, *Radio Comedy*, p.364.

Chapter 36

p.410 'Bloom, you bastards! Bloom!', *MOLM*, p.49.

p.410 'Now I'm full of *joie la vie* . . .' *Liberty Magazine* clippings, FLP, 1937.

p.411 'FIELDS: How much? . . .' etc. W. C. Fields Comedy Sequences, *The Big Broadcast of 1938*, WCFA.

p.412 'NOTE: *Pardon me* . . .' Ibid.

p.412 'FIELDS: Be quick . . .' etc. Ibid.

p.413 '*Stewardesses crowd in* . . .' etc. Ibid.

p.414 'I trick trombone . . .' etc. Ibid.

Chapter 37

p.421 'Dear John [Barrymore] . . .' RFWC, pp.155–56.

p.422 'Universal Pictures. Production notes . . .' USC Doheny Library.

p.424 'From Mr W. C. Fields to Mr Cliff Work . . .' RFWC, p.321.

p.424 '. . . Care must be taken with the costume . . .' MPPDA files, AMPAS.

p.425 'Dec 20 – Pages 33 et seq . . .' Ibid.

p.425 'the lady with the most perfect figure . . .' RFWC, p.306.

p.426 'WHIPSNADE: I had quite an experience . . .' on-screen dialogue, *You Can't Cheat an Honest Man.*

p.426 'Hollywood (UP). W. C. Fields, who brought a keg . . .' Undated, NYPA, W. C. Fields clippings file.

p.426 'Claude Willie Dukenfield . . .' etc. RFWC, p.323.

p.426 'FATHER MEETS SOLDIER SON . . .' etc. Clippings, JTW.

p.426 'MOTHER ACCUSED . . .' Ibid.

p.426 '110 GLASSES WATER FATAL . . .' etc. Ibid.

p.427 'Baby Carl Yenson . . .' Ibid.

p.427 'I Licked My Constipation . . .' Ibid.

Chapter 38

p.428 'Sabotage! Decker has kicked history . . .' MOLM, p.25.

p.429 'He has been a peeping tom . . .' Fowler, *The Second Handshake.*

p.429 'the last of the Pharaohs . . .' MOLM, p.38.

p.429 'Bring it to me!' MOLM, p.129.

p.429 'Other people talk . . .' MOLM, p.39.

p.430 'I remember Shakespeare's words . . .' MOLM, pp.86–87.

p.430 'As I looked on . . .' MOLM, pp.103–04.

p.431 'An ambulatory case . . .' Will Fowler, personal interview.

p.431 'W. C. Fields held forth . . .' Errol Flynn, *My Wicked Wicked Ways*, Pan Books, London, 1961, pp.215–6.

p.431 'talk of a Presidential candidate . . .' *New York World Telegram*, NYPA, 6 July 1936.

p.432 'I am truly a candidate with both my feet . . .' Fields, *Fields for President*, p.10.

p.432 '*Never try to impress a woman* . . .' Ibid., p.31.

p.432 'Fields Formula For Fretting Females . . .' Ibid., pp.40–1.

p.433 'The reason Columbus discovered America . . .' Ibid., p.6.

p.433 'I was born in a humble log cabin . . .' etc. Ibid., p.13–14.

p.433 'Never show up for an interview in bare feet . . .' Ibid., p.152.

p.433 'Remember, folks . . .' Ibid., p.162.

Chapter 39

p.436 'a cross between The Drunkard . . .' RFWC, p.342.

p.436 'Corn With the Wind . . .' Ibid., p.343.

p.436 'Just dropped into town . . .' Ibid., p.353.

p.436 'I took the plot from Ferenc Molnar's . . .' George Eels & Stanley

Musgrove, *Mae West, a Biography*, William Morrow & Company, NY, 1982, p.195.

p.436 'While progress on this show . . .' Universal production notes, USC.

p.437 'I regret to be compelled to advise you . . .' MPPDA files, AMPAS.

p.437 'revealing white blouse . . .' etc. Ibid.

p.437 'Scene 158, page 55 . . .' Ibid.

p.438 'Dear Mr Breen . . .' Ibid.

p.438 'getting into bed with the goat . . .' etc. Ibid.

p.439 'Mr Joe Breen, c/o the Hays Office . . .' RFWC, pp.368–69.

p.439 'Suggestive of an unfavorable . . .' etc. MPPDA files, AMPAS.

p.440 'TWILLIE: Hey, what's this thing doing . . .' On-screen dialogue, *My Little Chickadee*, Universal Pictures.

p.441 'FLOWER BELLE: What a man!' etc. Ibid.

p.441 'TWILLIE: A tough paloma comes in there . . .' Ibid.

p.443 'FORMER W. C. FIELDS ESTATE . . .' Clippings files, AMPAS.

p.444 'All landlords should go to the electric chair . . .' etc. *MOLM*, pp.44–5.

p.444 'a Frans Hals burgomaster . . .' Ibid., p.46.

p.444 'It's capital versus labor all the time . . .' Ibid., p.48.

p.444 'well stocked with potables . . .' CM, p.156.

p.445 'You struck once at Las Encinas . . .' Letter, 20 April 1940, JTW.

p.445 'I am ready to take up arms . . .' RFWC, p.462.

p.445 'Remember how we talked over giving a benefit . . .' RFWC, p.466.

p.445 'Do you recall the "Monte Carlo Girls" . . .' RFWC, p.468.

p.446 'You speak English well for a Nazi! . . .' CM, p.191.

p.446 'All the play between Egbert . . .' MPPDA files, AMPAS.

Chapter 40

p.448 'MYRTLE (*to* GEORGE) . . .' J. P. McEvoy, *The Comic Supplement* 1925, NYPA.

p.450 'EGBERT (*to the bird*): Life, my ebony friend . . .' *The Bank Dick*, in *Three Films of W. C. Fields*, Faber & Faber, 1990, pp.127–8.

p.450 'I shall repair to the bosom of my family . . .' Ibid., p.129.

p.450 'used to drive in the chariot races . . .' etc. Ibid., p.136.

p.451 'Working with Bill . . .' RFF, p.228.

p.452 'SOUSE (*to* OG): Ten cents a share . . .' On-screen dialogue, *The Bank Dick*, Universal Pictures.

p.455 'Get your hot dogs! . . .' Universal script, USC.

p.455 'FIELDS: Would you like a glass of water . . .' etc. Ibid.

p.457 'SECRETARY: You big hoddy-doddy! . . .' On-screen dialogue, *Never Give a Sucker an Even Break*, Universal Pictures.

p.458 'PANGBORN: What's the title . . .' USC.

p.459 'Fields: There's this Irish character . . .' etc. Ibid.

p.459 'Cameraman: Pardon this intrusion . . .' etc. Ibid.

p.460 'Dear Mr Pivar . . .' etc. MPPDA files, AMPAS.

p.460 'Scene 168: In Fields' speech . . .' Ibid.

Chapter 41

p.462 '"If we hurry," Decker said . . .' *MOLM*, p.151.

p.462 'Mr Fields, this is my madam . . .' etc. Ibid., p.155.

p.462 '"I'm a portrait painter," said Decker . . .' Ibid., p.156.

p.463 'rehash of old business . . .' etc. RFWC, pp.413–14.

p.464 'I was just a kid at the time . . .' Quoted in *Arts & Entertainment TV Biography of W. C. Fields*, 1995.

p.464 'looked like the wrath of John Barleycorn . . .' *MOLM*, p.205.

p.465 'but I remained sober . . .' etc. NYPA clippings file, 13 November 1941.

p.465 'This is the oesophagus . . .' On-screen dialogue, Fields episode, *Tales of Manhattan*, 20th Century Fox.

p.466 'LIQUOR SHORTAGE GETS AROUND AT LAST . . .' NYPA clippings file, 4 December 1943.

p.467 'Holbein was left-handed . . .' *MOLM*, p.217.

p.467 'When a circus tent is struck in the night . . .' *MOLM*, p.220.

p.467 'The time to carry a pal . . .' etc. Ibid., p.221.

p.467 'We'll never go to . . .' etc. Ibid., p.223.

p.467 'I'm going to be cremated . . .' Ibid., p.223.

p.468 'We are sitting at the crossroads between art and nature . . .' Ibid., p.225.

p.468 'I always recall your Joke . . .' Letter, RFWC, 29 January 1943, p.474.

p.468 'caricature studies of a Washington woman . . .' *MOLM*, p.56.

p.468 'I was very happy to have you visit me . . .' Clippings files, AMPAS.

p.468 'You may rest assured . . .' Ibid.

p.469 'this terrible mess . . .' etc. RFWC, p.486.

p.469 'FIELDS: Sometimes I was in the Confederate Army . . .' RFWC, p.243.

p.470 'Just before the bottle, mother . . .' etc. Ibid., p.262.

p.470 *The San Quentin News*, etc. Clipping, JTW.

p.470 'Dear Uncle Willie . . .' 17 February 1944, JTW.

p.471 'Dear Uncle Claude . . .' 6 May 1944, JTW.

p.471 'would be more hilarious done . . .' Undated, United Artists production file on Sensations of 1945, USC.

p.471 'My great good friend, W. C. Fields . . .' United Artists script, USC.

p.471 'FIELDS: Aren't you cold, dear . . .' etc. Ibid.

p.472 'MATCH W. C. FIELDS' SCHNOZOLA . . .' *Sensations of 1945 Press Book*, LCMP.

p.473 'Miss Monti, who has been a paramour . . .' 27 July 1944, RFWC, p.494.

p.473 'cutting clippings . . .' 12 October 1944, RFWC, p.495.

p.473 'The little devils need help . . .' *MOLM*, p.102.

p.473 'Just for that . . .' Ibid., p.103.

p.474 'Mr Fields in his lifetime . . .' Fowler, *The Second Handshake*,

534

Ibid., p.131.

p.474 'Perhaps you were thinking of someone else . . .' 9 June 1946, RFWC, p.496.

p.475 'Dearest Nephew, Thanks for yours undated . . .' 17 May 1946, JTW.

p.475 'Dear Nephew, This Gideon J. Pillow . . .' 12 November 1946, JTW.

p.476 'Grab everything and run . . .' etc. CM, p.218.

p.476 'Turn it off! Cease . . .' Fowler, *The Second Handshake*, p.111.

p.476 'He brought his forefinger to his lips . . .' RFF, p.253.

Coda

p.479 'Where I'm livin' now . . .' Quoted in Gilbert, *American Vaudeville*, p.286.

Afterword

p.484 'Dr Dont worry about your heart . . .' etc. RFWC, pp.178, 181.

W. C. Fields – Select Bibliography

Allen, Fred, *Much Ado About Me*, Little, Brown, 1956.

Bel Geddes, Norman, *Miracle in the Evening: An Autobiography*, William Kelley, ed., Doubleday, New York, 1960.

Bergman, Andrew, *We're in the Money: Depression America and Its Films,* New York University Press, 1971; Haper & Row, New York, 1972.

Bordman, Gerald, *American Musical Theatre*, Oxford, 1978.

Brandon, Ruth, *The Life and Many Deaths of Harry Houdini,* Secker & Warburg, London, 1993.

Brooks, Louise, *Lulu in Hollywood*, Limelight Editions, New York, 1982.

Burns, George, *All My Best Friends*, G. P. Putnam's Sons, New York, 1989.

Cannell, J. C., *The Secrets of Houdini*, Hutchinson, London, 1932.

Cantor, Eddie, *My Life is in Your Hands*, Harper, New York, 1928.

— *Take My Life*, Doubleday & Co., New York, 1957.

— *As I Remember Them*, Duell, Sloan & Pierce, New York, 1963.

Castle, Charles, *'The Folies Bergere'*, Franklin Watts, New York, 1985.

Chaplin, Charles, *My Autobiography*, Simon & Schuster, New York, 1964.

Connelly, Marc, *Voices Offstage*, Holt Rinehart, New York, 1968.

Corio, Ann, with Joseph DiMona, *This Was Burlesque*, Grossett & Dunlap, New York, 1968.

Deschner, Donald, *The Films of W. C. Fields*, Citadel Press, 1966.

Dietz, Howard, *Dancing in the Dark*, New York, Bantam, New York, 1974.

Eels, George and Musgrove, Stanley, *Mae West, a Biography*, William Morrow & Company, New York, 1982.

Fields, Armond and L. Marc, *From the Bowery to Broadway*, Oxford University Press, 1993.

Fields, Ronald, *W. C. Fields by Himself*, Prentice-Hall, Englefield, NJ, 1973.

— *W. C. Fields, a Life on Film* (filmography), St. Martins Press, New York, 1984.

Fields, W. C., *Fields for President*, Dodd, Mead & Co, 1940.

Flynn, Errol, *My Wicked Wicked Ways*, Pan Books, London, 1961.

Fowler, Gene, *Good Night, Sweet Prince*, The Viking Press, New York, 1944, Mercury House, San Francisco, 1989.

— *Minutes of the Last Meeting*, The Viking Press, New York, 1984.

Fowler, Will, *The Second Handshake,* Lyle Stuart Inc., Secaucus, N. J. 1980.
– *Reporters,* Roundtable, Calif., 1991.
Gehring, Wes D., *W. C. Fields, a Biobibliography*, Greenwood Press, 1984.
– *Groucho and W. C. Fields, Huckster Comedians*, University Press of Mississippi, 1994.
Gilbert, Douglas, *American Vaudeville,* McGraw Hill, New York, 1940.
Goldman, Herbert G., *Fanny Brice, the Original Funny Girl,* Oxford University Press, New York, 1992.
Harding, James, *George Robey and the Music Hall,* Hodder & Stoughton, London, 1990.
Higham, Charles, *Ziegfeld,* Henry Regnery Co., 1972.
Hope, Bob, *The Road to Hollywood,* Doubleday & Co., New York, 1977.
Kahn, E. J., Jr, *The Merry Partners, the Age and Stage of Harrigan and Hart,* Random House, New York, 1955.
Katkov, Norman, *The Fabulous Fanny,* Knopf, New York, 1953.
Kobler, John, *Damned in Paradise: The Life of John Barrymore,* Atheneum, 1977.
Koszarski, Richard, *The Astoria Studio and Its Fabulous Films,* Dover, 1983.
Lahue, Kalton C. and Gill, Samuel, *Clown Princes and Court Jesters,* A. S. Barnes, New York, 1970.
Louvish, Simon, *It's a Gift,* BFI Publishing, London, 1994.
McEvoy, J. P., *Slams of Life: With Malice for All and Charity Towards None,* P. F. Volland, Chicago, 1919.
Miller, Frank, *Censored Hollywood,* Turner Publishing, 1994.
Monti, Carlotta, *W. C. Fields and Me,* Prentice-Hall, Englefield, NJ, 1971.
Robinson, David, *Chaplin, His Life & Art,* William Collins, 1985.
Rocks, David T., *W. C. Fields: An Annotated Guide,* McFarland, 1994.
Rogers, Will, *The Illiterate Digest,* Albert & Charles Boni, New York, 1924.
Rowland, Mabel, ed., *Bert Williams, Son of Laughter,* English Crafters, New York, 1923.
Saxon, A. H., *P. T. Barnum, the Legend and the Man,* Columbia University Press, New York, 1989.
'Selbit': The Magicians' Handbook, Dawborn & Ward, London, 1904.
Sennett, Mack, *King of Comedy,* as told to Cameron Shipp, Doubleday, New York, 1954.
Sklar, Robert, *Movie-Made America,* Vintage, New York, 1975, 1994.
Smart, James, *W. C. Fields in Philadelphia,* The Shackamaxon Society, Philadelphia, 1972.
Smith, H. Allen, *The Life and Legend of Gene Fowler,* William Morrow & Co., New York, 1977.
Sobel, Bernard, *Burleycue: An Underground History of Burlesque,* New York, Farrar & Reinhart, 1931.
– *A Pictorial History of Burlesque,* Bonanza Books, New York, 1956.

Stein Charles W. (ed.), *American Vaudeville As Seen by Its Contemporaries,* Knopf, New York, 1984.

Stone, Fred, *Rolling Stone,* McGraw Hill, New York, 1945.

Taylor, Robert Lewis, *W. C. Fields, His Follies and Fortunes,* New American Library, 1949, 1967.

Toll, Robert C., *Blacking Up: The Minstrel Show in 19th Century America,* Oxford University Press, 1974.

Wertheim, Arthur Frank, *Radio Comedy,* Oxford University Press, 1979.

West, Mae, *Goodness Had Nothing to Do With It,* 1959; MacFadden-Bartell, 1970.

Yagoda, Bill, *Will Rogers,* Knopf, New York, 1994.

Ziegfeld, Richard and Paulette, *The Ziegfeld Touch,* Harry N. Abrams, 1993.

Acknowledgements

This book could not have been written without the invaluable help of a host of persons who extended much more than a hearty handclasp. My greatest thanks go to the grandchildren of the Great Man, Bill, Ronald, Everett and Harriet Fields, with a bow to the fifth Fields, Allen, whom I was not able to meet. All have been generous in their support of this project, and I have been greatly encouraged by their obvious love and enthusiasm for their illustrious forebear. The pioneering scholarship of the family historian, Ronald Fields, provided vital clues to the accurate revision of old false trails, and I am particularly indebted to Bill, Ronald and Everett for providing access to the family archive. Joe Adamson provided initial contacts and his own invaluable insights into W. C. Fields' film career. Will Fowler, the Last Survivor of the 'last meetings' of his father Gene's Bundy Drive days, has been an acute observer and unrivalled raconteur of Bill Fields' inner circle. Tim Walker provided gems from his in-depth knowledge and peerless collection. A host of archivists have given of their time and efforts to help me root out clues, among then: Sam Gill of the Margaret Herrick Library of the Academy of Motion Picture Arts and Sciences, Geraldine Duclow and staff of the Theatre Collection at the Free Library of Philadelphia. Rod Bladel and staff of the Billy Rose Theatre Collection at the New York Public Library for the Performing Arts, Richard Koszarski of the Museum of the Moving Image at Astoria, New York, Miles Kreuger of the Institute of the American Musical in Los Angeles, Ned Comstock at the Doheny Library, University of Southern California, and staff at the Motion Picture and Manuscript Divisions of the Library of Congress in Washington. Special mention in dispatches to Walter Donohue, Victoria Buxton and staff at Faber and Faber for their diligent work on the manuscript. Warm thanks are also due to David Robinson, Anthony Slide, Herbert G. Goldman, Betty Lasky, Pat Silver-Lasky, Clyde Jeavons and staff at the British Film Institute, Joel Finler, Oren Moverman, Ted Wioncek, Isidore Haiblum, Stuart Schaar, Don and Maya Peretz, Jim Goldner, Rick Mitz, and of course to Mairi, who had to live with the Great McGonigle throughout. All are invited, at some future date, to imbibe a few noggins at the Black Pussy (Cat) Cafe.

Index